PRAISE FOR H. P. BLAVATSKY AND THEOSOPHY

"I owe much to the Theosophical friends among whom I have many. Whatever critics may say against Madame Blavatsky, . . . [her] contribution to humanity will always rank high."
— **Mahatma Gandhi, leader of India's non-violent independence movement**

"Her books show extraordinary erudition and capacity for hard work."
— **Arthur Conan Doyle, writer, creator of Sherlock Holmes**

". . . theosophy seems to be a good enough religion — its main principles being that all religions contain some truth and that we ought to be tolerant . . ."
— **Aldous Huxley, writer, philosopher, author of** *Brave New World*

"I feel that a great part of my being is striving toward theosophy."
— **Franz Kafka, writer, author of** *The Metamorphosis*

"Her books are famous. There is a lot of good in them; what is not good is that they speak of what people are unable to understand."
— **Leo Tolstoy, writer, philosopher, author of** *Anna Karenina*

"I have always wondered at . . . the miracles of Madame Blavatsky. . . . Here we plumb some profounder law — deeper than the ordinary laws of nature."
— **H. G. Wells, writer, considered "the father of science fiction"**

"Theosophy is not a religion. Its followers are simply 'searchers after Truth.' Not for the ignorant are the tenets they hold, neither for the worldly in any sense. Enrolled within their ranks are some of the grandest intellects of the Eastern and Western worlds."
— **L. Frank Baum, writer, author of** *The Wonderful Wizard of Oz*

"I became a member of the Theosophical Society at thirteen . . . I have no doubt that those years . . . left a deep impress upon me, and I feel that I owe a debt . . . to Theosophy."
— **Jawaharlal Nehru, first Prime Minister of India**

"The Theosophical Society is a fellowship of seekers. Its contribution to India's cultural and political rebirth is well known. The gentle strength of the quest for truth enabled it to withstand opposition and misrepresentation in its early years. Perhaps that is what attracted my father to it . . . and probably the message of theosophy had much to do with his universalism, his reverence for different faiths and his repugnance for any kind of fanaticism."
— **Indira Gandhi, first and only female Prime Minister of India**

"Theosophists have guessed at the awesome grandeur of the cosmic cycle wherein our world and human race form transient incidents. They have hinted at strange survivals in terms which would freeze the blood if not masked by a bland optimism." — **H. P. Lovecraft, writer, author of** *Cthulhu Mythos Tales*

"[Indian philosophy] remained the preserve of Sanskrit scholars and philosophers. But it was not so very long before the Theosophical Movement inaugurated by Mme. Blavatsky possessed itself of the Eastern traditions and promulgated them among the general public."
— **C. G. Jung, psychiatrist, founder of analytical psychology**

"Much of what I learned in those [Theosophy] classes was very helpful to my own constantly evolving personal beliefs about God and the universe."
— **Jane Goodall, PhD, ethologist, activist, author of** *The Book of Hope*

"I am extremely impressed . . . with the quality and power of Madame Blavatsky's work."
— **Brian L. Weiss, MD, psychiatrist, author of *Many Lives, Many Masters***

"A fantastic and enlightened lady. I'm only sorry she lived a century too early. How I would have loved to work with her, be inspired by her, and have traveled and taught with her!"
— **Elisabeth Kübler-Ross, MD, psychiatrist, author of *On Death and Dying***

"[She was] humorous, unfanatical, and displaying always, it seemed, a mind that seemed to pass all others in her honesty."
— **W. B. Yeats, poet, Nobel Prize laureate in Literature**

"The wisest woman in Europe."
— **T. S. Eliot, poet, Nobel Prize laureate in Literature**

"Madame Blavatsky put forth two astounding tomes into which entered a labor so prodigious that men are still cracking their skulls over them. I refer to *The Secret Doctrine* and *Isis Unveiled*. If they accomplished nothing more, these two books, they certainly put to rout the idea of the caveman's contribution to our culture. Drawing from every imaginable source, Madame Blavatsky amasses a wealth of material to prove the everlasting continuity of esoteric wisdom."
— **Henry Miller, writer**

"Try and get hold of Mme. Blavatsky's books." — **D. H. Lawrence, novelist, poet**

"In fact no other woman has been so powerful in the whole history of man, has had influence worldwide. . . . She really loved humanity, and did everything that she felt was right."   — **Osho, contemporary mystic and philosopher**

"Incredible and mysterious Russian lady . . . [who] persuaded a goodly number of British aristocrats and literati to consider the *Upanishads*, the *Yoga Sutra*, the *Bhagavad Gita*, and the Buddhist *Tripitaka*."
— **Alan Watts, philosopher, writer, author of *The Wisdom of Insecurity***

"[Theosophists] weren't charlatans. They weren't using a good old gimmick or trick to exploit people. They really — please believe me — sincerely believed what they were doing. It wasn't just a hoax."
— **Jiddu Krishnamurti, philosopher, writer, author of *Freedom from the Known***

"The Indians . . . from time to time confront those learned in our civilization with problems which we have either passed by unnoticed or brushed aside with superficial words and explanations. H. P. Blavatsky was the first person, after living for many years in India, to establish a strong bond between these 'savages' and our 'civilization.' This laid the beginnings for a tremendous spiritual movement which today includes a large number of people . . . who seek to approach the problem of the spirit by way of *inner* knowledge."
— **Wassily Kandinsky, painter, art theorist, author of *Concerning the Spiritual in Art***

"She wrote to me to follow the light that is within me. I have strictly followed her advice, and am glad to testify to her wonderful powers of mystic illumination. . . . Love to all living beings, small and great, the desire to renounce sensual pleasures that impede the progress in the realm of spirituality and the strenuous effort to do meritorious deeds for the betterment of humanity, forgetting self, have been to me a kind of spiritual pabulum which I have partaken since I came in touch with the wonderful personality of H.P.B."
— **Anagarika Dharmapala, Buddhist revivalist, founder of the Maha Bodhi Society**

"Here was a being who had the capacity to demonstrate that certain assumptions science was making were only that. And we owe a lot to her whether we are theosophists or not.... She is a true pioneer; a real Copernicus, if you wish."
— **David Spangler, philosopher, writer, author of *Apprenticed to Spirit***

"In spite of a severe religious education, my primitive pantheism has pointed me in the direction of Theosophy, the most human and rational of philosophic concepts."   — **Agustín Pío Barrios, virtuoso classical guitarist, composer**

"Madame Blavatsky reinforced and almost recreated in many minds the sense of this life being a mere probation. In this respect her teaching was much more in accord with the spirit of the New Testament than much of the pseudo-Christian teaching of our day. She widened the horizon of the mind, and she brought something of the infinite sense of the vast, illimitable mystery, which characterizes some of the Eastern religions, into the very heart of Europe in the nineteenth century."   — **W. T. Stead, newspaper editor, investigative journalist**

"H.P.B. had a different task in a different age and with a different race — than did Buddha. She did all she did, wrote what she wrote under guidance.... The West needed first an all-comprehensive philosophy — a synthesis of religion, science, and philosophy — the East had always had it."
— **Lawren S. Harris, painter, founding member of the Group of Seven**

"I marvelled what I could have done to merit birth in an age wherein such wisdom was on offer to all who could beg, borrow or steal a copy of those [Blavatsky's] works."   — **George W. Russell (Æ), poet**

"My salvation and inspiration come from philosophy a little and religion a great deal, especially from the mystics ancient or modern theosophical. With them my load is lifted and I regain peace, courage, faith."
— **Alfred Deakin, second Prime Minister of Australia**

"Astrology without Theosophy has no meaning."
— **Alan Leo, astrologer, writer, considered "the father of modern astrology"**

"What a woman! ... Misunderstood, vilified, and abused, and yet with a brilliant, cultured, and deeply learned mind; the very soul of generosity; a woman of direct speech and action, refusing to talk the pious platitudes and nonsense that we chatter under the guise of socially good manners, but offering the truth for anyone who wanted it.... She was never neutral, or the same to all. She made a great number of friends who would die for her, and enemies who would kill her if they could.... Those strong blue eyes could see into the character of every man and woman who came to her, and even see by whom she would later be betrayed.... She would help from her meagre funds (and she was always poor), all those in need, even though she knew at the time that they were planning to smash the cause she had given her life to serve.... As a speaker she was magnetic; she never lectured but she would talk, and those who heard her could think of nothing else."
— **Christmas Humphreys, jurist, writer, founder of the Buddhist Society**

"A forceful, pugnacious, and gifted personality — worse still, a forceful, pugnacious, and gifted *woman*, one of the great liberated ladies of her day — she could not help but draw withering, critical fire by her every act and word, especially when she presumed to challenge the most entrenched intellectual orthodoxies of the age. Still today people who have never read a line she wrote remain adamantly convinced she was a fraud and a crank.... Above all, she is among the modern world's trailblazing psychologists of the visionary mind."
— **Theodore Roszak, PhD, academic, historian, novelist**

"Boldly announcing that she was an agent of the Great Lodge, she outlined the fundamental teachings of the Wisdom Religion even before she founded the Theosophical Society. . . . Braving the painful, though sacred, duty of openly naming the Mahatmas who are behind the Movement, she demonstrated the grandeur of the theosophical system and the danger of playing with its Fohatic fire. In expounding the fundamentals of *theosophia* and the basic principles of oriental *philosophia*, she pointed to the underlying roots of all individual and collective progress."
— **Raghavan N. Iyer, PhD, philosopher, professor, author of *The Moral and Political Thought of Mahatma Gandhi***

"I would recommend Blavatsky's enormous work, *The Secret Doctrine*, in which . . . we encounter small, precious features that introduce us to an understanding of religious creativity."
— **Andrei Bely, poet, novelist, author of *Petersburg***

"When, with all kinds of political failures and economic breakdowns we (Indians) were suspecting the values and vitality of our culture, when everything round about us and secular education happened to discredit the value of Indian culture, the Theosophical Movement rendered great service by vindicating those values and ideas. The influence of the Theosophical Movement on general Indian society is incalculable."
— **Sarvepalli Radhakrishnan, second President of India**

"I knew Madame Blavatsky very well . . . and I believe there is no doubt that the Theosophical movement has had an excellent effect upon humanity. It has made a large number of people understand what all India always understood, and that is the importance of invisible things."
— **Edwin Arnold, poet, author of *The Light of Asia***

"She had a marvellous aptitude for rendering abstruse Eastern metaphysical thought into a form intelligible to Western minds, and for verifying and comparing Eastern wisdom with Western science."
— **Max Heindel, mystic, author of *The Rosicrucian Cosmo Conception***

"H. P. Blavatsky founded a new nation, a universal nation, that knows no limits of geography, whose citizenship is not based on colour, race, or creed, but it depends on character."
— **Talbot Mundy, writer, author of *King of the Khyber Rifles***

"She was chaste, generous, forgiving, amusing, lovable; . . . she sacrificed her station, her patrimony, her ease, her honour, her wealth, her life itself, for a high and noble cause."
— **Claude Bragdon, architect, writer, publisher**

"Madame Blavatsky and Colonel Olcott founded the Theosophical Society. Its activities accelerated the influx of knowledge about Asiatic religions and restored self-confidence in the wavering minds of the Asiatics themselves. . . . By its timely intervention, the Theosophical Society has done a great service to the Buddhist cause."
— **Edward Conze, Buddhologist, translator**

"[H.P.B.] was a titan among mortals. . . . [She] was a warrior not a priestess, a prophetess rather than seeress; she was, moreover, most things you would not expect, as an instrument for bringing back the memory of much that was most holy and wise in antiquity."
— **G. R. S. Mead, historian, writer, first English translator of *Pistis Sophia***

"She lived in great truth, yet was called a liar; in great generosity, and was called a fraud; in a detestation of all shams, and yet — was crowned the Queen of Humbugs."
— **Edmund N. Russell, artist**

"She appears to be an extraordinary, naturally gifted yogic practitioner. . . . Now, Buddhist devotees in many foreign countries gather like stars in the sky, largely due to this woman's new movement. . . . Her teachings captivate many Westerners because they are explained in the context of modern perspectives according to the latest scientific developments. While earlier foreigners were sceptical of supernatural powers, she has not only demonstrated them but also explained these abilities through modern scientific principles, such as how supernatural powers can transform material objects."
— **Gendun Chopel, philosopher, historian, translator**

"Her familiarity with Tibetan Buddhism as well as with esoteric Buddhist practices seems to be beyond doubt."
— **Gunapala Malalasekera, PhD, academic, diplomat, founder of the World Fellowship of Buddhists**

"Hardly anything had been known about Shambhala in the West before H. P. Blavatsky who presented the Ancient Wisdom of the East to an unprepared European and American public in the Victorian era."
— **Andrew Tomas, writer, author of** *We Are Not the First*

"Blavatsky [was] the teacher among men, the sufferer in the hands of men."
— **Dane Rudhyar, writer, composer, artist, astrologer**

"I felt more and more the need for [*The Secret Doctrine*]."
— **Ruth Crawford Seeger, composer, musicologist**

"On ordinary lines it is strange that an old, sickly woman, not consulting a library and having no books of her own of consequence, should possess the unusual knowledge that Madame Blavatsky undoubtedly did. . . . But it is a fact that she knew more than I did on my own particular lines of anthropology, etc. . . . Madame Blavatsky certainly had original sources of information (I don't say what) transcending the knowledge of experts on their own lines."
— **Charles Carter Blake, anthropologist, palaeontologist**

"Madame Blavatsky . . . was one of the great women of the last century."
— **Katherine Sophie Dreier, artist, lecturer, social reformer**

"Madame Blavatsky . . . prophesied the arrival of the present scientific predicament, and were she alive today she would doubtless register the 'I-told-you-so' expression."
— **Alvin Boyd Kuhn, PhD, writer, author of** *The Esoteric Structure of the Alphabet*

"When H. P. Blavatsky came to the Western world with her message from the Brothers, . . . she met with the same reception that every Saviour, every prophet and teacher has met with since the beginning of time: crucifixion of body or soul or both."
— **Francia La Due, philosopher, founder of the Temple of the People**

"If she had not lived and done what she did, humanity would not have had the impulse and the ideas toward the good which it was her mission to give and to proclaim."
— **William Q. Judge, lawyer, writer, co-founder of the Theosophical Society**

"The secret of [H.P.B.'s] potent spell was her undeniable spiritual powers, her evident devotion to the Masters . . . and her zeal for the spiritual uplifting of humanity by the power of the Eastern Wisdom."
— **Henry Steel Olcott, lawyer, Buddhist revivalist, co-founder of the Theosophical Society**

"She was of heroic stature, and smaller souls instinctively resented her strength, her titanic nature. Unconventional, careless of appearances, frank to unwisdom — as the world estimates wisdom — too honest to calculate against the dishonesty of others, she laid herself open to continual criticism and misunderstanding. Full of intellectual strength and with extraordinary knowledge, she was humble as a little child. Brave to recklessness, she was pitiful and tender."

— **Annie Besant, social reformer, writer, Indian independence leader**

"She was one of the true Saviours of the race; one of that deathless band of Great Ones 'whose hands hold back the heavy karma of the world' — who 'remain unselfish to the endless end.'"

— **Alice L. Cleather, writer, author of** *Buddhism: The Science of Life*

"H. P. Blavatsky, 'that great path-breaker in the wilderness of a Paradise debased,' has put the Master Key into our hands. It is our own fault if, through ignorance, prejudice, or indifference we fail to use it."

— **Basil Crump, lawyer, writer, editor of** *The Law Times*

"The significance of Blavatsky is that, thanks to her, we do not have to choose between a faith and a philosophy. If, as her enemies allege, what she teaches is not Buddhism, it is an improvement on it. She has given us our immortality within the grandest design we have been privileged to glimpse."

— **Jean Overton Fuller, writer, painter, author of** *Madeleine*

"The world, dazzled by the light of her doctrines, which the majority of men did not grasp, because they were new to them, looked upon her with distrust, and the representatives of scientific ignorance, filled with their own pomposity, pronounced her to be 'the greatest impostor of the age,' because their narrow minds could not rise up to a comprehension of the magnificence of her spirit. It is, however, not difficult to prophesy, that in the near future, when the names of her enemies will have been forgotten, the world will become alive to a realization of the true nature of the mission of H.P.B., and see that she was a messenger of Light, sent to instruct this sinful world, to redeem it from ignorance, folly and superstition, a task which she has fulfilled as far as her voice was heard and her teachings accepted."   — **Franz Hartmann, MD, writer, author of** *Paracelsus*

"[She was] the best and truest of Teachers, the most faithful and untiring of Messengers."

— **Isabel Cooper-Oakley, writer, author of** *The Count of Saint-Germain*

"I have personally received from my association with them [Theosophists] more help, more encouragement to live my own life and express my own opinions and develop my own thinking than from any set of people with whom I have come in contact."

— **George Lansbury, politician, leader of the Labour Party (UK)**

"In spite of her tremendous attainments and unrivalled talent, she had not a vestige of pedantic assumption, and had the simple heart of a child. 'Imposter' indeed! She was almost the only mortal I have ever met who was not an impostor. . . . [She was] the most extraordinary woman of our century, or of any century."

— **William Stewart Ross, writer, publisher, editor of** *The Secular Review*

"It is now beginning to be recognized that her writings contain the key to the profoundest mysteries of Man and the Universe, and those who opposed her, finding themselves unable to disprove the value and truth of her philosophy, sought by means of personal slander and vilification to prejudice public opinion,

and thus divert attention from the treasure of knowledge which she was the means of giving to the world, and which, if impartially considered on its merits, must have carried with it the conviction of the integrity of the writer."
— **A. Trevor Barker, writer, lecturer, transcriber of *The Mahatma Letters***

"To anyone who studies the evidence thoroughly and without prejudice, there is no doubt that Madame Blavatsky was a genuine worker of what the world calls magic." — **Howard Murphet, writer, author of *Sai Baba: Man of Miracles***

"I went to her a materialist, she left me a Theosophist, and between these two there is a great gulf fixed. Over that gulf she bridged the way. She was my spiritual mother, and never had child a more loving, a more patient, a more tender guide." — **Herbert Burrows, socialist activist**

"What characterizes the philosophy taught by H. P. Blavatsky is that it appears to many minds, when revealed to them, as the noblest of all philosophies, as the only system which is clear and reasonable, the knowledge of which is a motive to self-development. To become more intelligent and better, not in the ordinary meaning of the words, but to become more worthy of esteem in one's own eyes — that is what is possible for people nowadays, thanks to her."
— **Maurice Magre, writer, poet, playwright**

"It is not even remotely possible to register everything that has been written about Blavatsky. Having greatly interested Western Europe, North America, and India with her Theosophy, Blavatsky gave rise to a huge volume of panegyric and polemical literature: many dozens of books, hundreds of magazine pieces, and thousands of newspaper articles. Her fame is so great that in the respectable London dictionary *Men of the Time*, where one column is devoted to the most famous people of our time, three are devoted to Blavatsky."
— **Zinaida Vengerova, literary critic, translator**

"Helena Blavatsky tirelessly called for spirituality, for the liberation of thought from the yoke of external forms, for broad tolerance, for the realization of unity and brotherhood among people and nations. With fiery enthusiasm she affirmed the divinity of human nature and the possibility of communication with higher worlds; with indomitable energy she fought against the materialism that filled the world and against everything that extinguishes the spirit."
— **Elena Pisareva, philosopher, translator, writer**

"I am always captivated when the theosophical principle penetrates what is most precious to me — i.e., art."
— **Serge Wolkonsky, theatrical worker, director, writer**

"Madame Blavatsky had a profound knowledge of Buddhist philosophy, and the doctrines she promulgated were those of many great teachers."
— **B. T. Chang, secretary of the Ninth Panchen Lama of Tibet**

PRAISE FOR FRAGMENTS FROM THE BOOK OF THE GOLDEN PRECEPTS

The Voice of the Silence

"I believe that this book has strongly influenced many sincere seekers and aspirants to the wisdom and compassion of the Bodhisattva Path."
— **His Holiness the Fourteenth Dalai Lama of Tibet**

"First in this series of the scriptures of wisdom religion which can impregnate and fructify our educational, social, economic, and cultural fields — even politics, diplomacy, and industrial power — is *The Voice of the Silence*, or fragments from the *Book of the Golden Precepts* which has been beautifully translated by Helena Petrovna Blavatsky."
— **Reverend Father Anthony Elenjimittam, philosopher, theologian, writer**

"It is good to carry this little book with you. As you progress along the Path, everything said therein becomes, when re-read, so distinct, infinitely close, and so directing into the Radiant Future. All that is said is more than just metaphors. It becomes the Truth experienced by the heart and enlightened consciousness."
— **Helena Roerich, philosopher, author of the *Agni Yoga* series**

"The essential substance of the *Book of the Golden Precepts*... has been, I think, rather beautifully set forth in the fragments which Madame Blavatsky collected and called *The Voice of the Silence*." — **Manly P. Hall, scholar, philosopher, author of *The Secret Teachings of All Ages***

"*The Voice of the Silence* is true Mahayana doctrine."
— **D. T. Suzuki, philosopher, Nobel Peace Prize nominee**

"A pure Buddhist work." — **Anagarika Dharmapala, Buddhist revivalist, founder of the Maha Bodhi Society**

"This book is a gem of inexhaustible wisdom, written in beautiful poetic prose with unforgettable metaphors, friendly but frank warnings about the pitfalls on the Path, and magnanimous encouragement for all souls. It gives superb guidance for all earnest pilgrims who are fearless, patient and persistent in their unutterable faith in the Diamond Soul, the *vajra* of adamantine courage, and the boundless compassion of time-honoured lineages of enlightened sages."
— **Raghavan N. Iyer, PhD, philosopher, professor, author of *The Moral and Political Thought of Mahatma Gandhi***

"The Buddhists and Theosophists of the West, all converts, be it noted, from some other faith, have much in common: *The Voice of the Silence*."
— **Christmas Humphreys, jurist, writer, founder of the Buddhist Society**

"The message of *The Voice of the Silence* is not to be understood unless we realize that it appeals to the heart, that it strives to develop intuition, to awaken Soul-wisdom, and that in so doing its principal methods are paradox and poetry."
— **Sangharakshita, writer, founder of the Triratna Buddhist Community**

"Many mystical scriptures are indeed little more than musical compositions.... These words [from *The Voice of the Silence*]... stir chords within you which music and language touch in common."
— **William James, philosopher, psychologist, author of *The Principles of Psychology***

"In contemporary mystical literature, Blavatsky's *The Voice of the Silence* and M. Collins' *Light on the Path* stand out in a special way. These two little books contain a whole collection of Eastern wisdom."
— **P. D. Ouspensky, philosopher, author of** *In Search of the Miraculous*

"Its verses ripple on in a rhythmic cadence aptly suited to assist the feeling of mystical devotion. Like other of the Oriental books it consists of ethico-spiritual maxims, which hardly so much attempt to give a systematic exposition of moral principles, as to reduce the spiritual essence of these principles to a mantric form capable of exerting a magical potency when used ritually. . . . What *The Voice of the Silence* aims to do is to strike the spiritual keynote of the ancient science of mystic union or yoga as essentially a spiritual technique and not a system of magical practices." — **Alvin Boyd Kuhn, PhD, writer, author of** *The Esoteric Structure of the Alphabet*

"*The Voice of the Silence*, expressing the views of the highest schools of occultism, asks us to step out of the sunlight into the shade so as to make more room for others, and declares that those whom we help in this life will help us in our next one."
— **William Q. Judge, lawyer, writer, co-founder of the Theosophical Society**

"The book is . . . a prose poem, full of spiritual inspiration, full of food for the heart, stimulating the loftiest virtue and containing the noblest ideals. It is not a hotch-potch drawn from various sources, but a coherent ethical whole. It moves us, not by a statement of facts gathered from books, but by an appeal to the divinest instincts of our nature. It is its own best testimony to the source whence it came."
— **Annie Besant, social reformer, writer, Indian independence leader**

"*The Voice of the Silence* is intended to serve as meditation material. It is written entirely based on occult knowledge. Occult knowledge is living knowledge, which means that it acts as a force on the entire human being when one imbues oneself with it while meditating. . . . It is not a question of intellectually absorbing and analysing this knowledge, but of total devotion to it. Only those who succeed in freeing their field of consciousness from all everyday impressions for a short time and during this time, in filling themselves completely with thoughts of meditation, will receive the fruit of meditation. . . . Then [the occult knowledge underlying *The Voice of the Silence*] becomes a part of our soul and it works in us, even if we do not think about it in detail during meditation."
— **Rudolf Steiner, philosopher, social reformer**

"One of the most important tenets of the Esoteric Teachings, clearly given out as the 'Heart Doctrine' by H.P.B. in *The Voice of the Silence* . . . is this: That 'the heart of the Universe is Love' — love so divine and impersonal as but faintly to be comprehended by finite minds."
— **Alice L. Cleather, writer, author of** *Buddhism: The Science of Life*

"When such qualified and eminent Eastern scholars thus endorse Madame Blavatsky's interpretation of Mahayana Buddhism, the words of any Western pundit to the contrary should be brushed aside as so much chaff — he but merely airs his ignorance of that particular subject."
— **Miriam Salanave, writer, author of** *A Buddhist Roll Call*

"If we look at *The Voice of the Silence* as at a revelation giving to the uninitiated an idea of the enormous spiritual labour and tension through which the disciple of an occult school passes, creatively reworking their entire inner life along new lines, we shall find in this little book guidance of inestimable value."
— **Elena Pisareva, philosopher, translator, writer**

"This little book, the gem of Buddhist teachings, . . . is like a call to men to forsake desire, dispel every evil thought, and enter the true Path."
— **B. T. Chang, secretary of the Ninth Panchen Lama of Tibet**

"The editors were fortunate enough to come into close touch with the Tashi Lama himself during his visit to Beijing, and to obtain from him a Foreword in his own handwriting which is reproduced . . . as he wrote it. . . . The significance of such an action is profound. The Tashi Lama is the spiritual head of the Buddhist community for an enormous area of Asia, and deeply venerated by the whole of the Mahayana School. The effect of this official sanction is therefore finally to accept this gem of Wisdom for the pure Buddhist work we have ever claimed it to be."   — ***Buddhism in England*** **(London, December 1927)**

"The value of the *addenda* is largely in indicating that the reprint has the cooperation and endorsement of the Tashi Lama, and as affording incontrovertible evidence that *The Voice of the Silence* is not a work of H.P.B.'s imagination, but is taken from documents known to exist and which represent the actual ethical teachings of the Tibetan Masters. In fact, these *addenda* give a sense of reality and a feeling of conviction which is not conveyed by any other edition."
— ***O. E. Library Critic*** **(Washington, March 1928)**

"With the publication of *The Voice of the Silence* under the authority of the Tashi Lama himself, an impetus has been given throughout the Buddhist world to the study of the latest and most complete presentation of that Ancient Wisdom, *The Secret Doctrine*, as given out by the same writer, H. P. Blavatsky."
— ***Buddhism in England*** **(London, March 1928)**

"In view of the fact that the first edition of this valuable gem of esoteric literature was the only correct one, and is now unprocurable, it will be seen that the new publication is of the greatest interest, and should be in the hands of all students and admirers of the work of Madame Blavatsky."
— ***The Occult Review*** **(London, April 1928)**

"It is unfortunate that many members of the Southern School allow the veil of prejudice to blind them to the value of the Mahayana Wisdom, while the inability of many Mahayanists to accept the works of H. P. Blavatsky as Buddhism is more pathetic still. H.P.B. not only derived her material from personal instruction in Tibet, but with that splendid worker, Col. H. S. Olcott, was avowedly a Buddhist in the world of men. The endorsement by H. H. the Tashi Lama of her *The Voice of the Silence*, which she translated from an esoteric manuscript, as being a Buddhist work, though infinitely older than Gautama Buddha, has done much to destroy the foolish prejudice."
— ***Buddhism in England*** **(London, July 1928)**

"It has been alleged that the Sanskrit and other texts from which H.P.B. claimed to have her information concerning the secret wisdom, were spurious, and that claims made by her, or on her behalf, that the texts were studied in Tibetan libraries in a period preceding 1880 were false. Mrs. Cleather and Mr. Crump struck a great blow in her defence when they secured a frontispiece from the pen of the Tashi Lama, and a signed preface at the hands of his secretary, to a facsimile edition of H.P.B.'s *The Voice of the Silence*. The Tashi Lama is at the head of all Buddhist communities in Tibet, India and China, and might justly be termed the 'Pope' of the Buddhist world, though Buddhism and Confucianism are not, and have never been, sectarian in policy, being essentially religions of peace. *The Voice of the Silence* is a small volume of practical occultism, an excellent basis for meditation, and purports to be a translation of some of the oldest

stanzas ever written in the early Sanskrit idiom. It has thus come to pass that the work of [H.P.B.] has been placed beyond criticism as regards authenticity, being now sponsored by the Tashi Lama, the highest authority on the subject."
— *The Path* (Sydney, August 1928)

"For reasons we have never understood Buddhists in England seem reluctant to accept this exquisite small work as part of the literature of Buddhism. Yet it was quoted by William James in *The Varieties of Religious Experience*, and by Dr. Evans-Wentz, an authority on Tibet. The late Anagarika Dharmapala described it as a 'pure Buddhist work,' and now by chance we have come across a report of a remark by Dr. D. T. Suzuki made many years ago to the American pioneer Buddhist, Mrs. Salanave. 'I saw *The Voice of the Silence* for the first time when at Oxford. I got a copy and sent it to Mrs. Suzuki (then Miss Beatrice Lane) at Columbia University, writing to her: Here is the real Mahayana Buddhism.' Has anyone ever *read* it who did not rank it among the world's greatest scriptures?"
— *The Middle Way* (London, August 1965)

Light on the Path

"This little book — a true jewel — belongs to, and emanates from the same school of Indo-Aryan and Buddhist thought and learning as the teachings in *The Secret Doctrine*."
— H. P. Blavatsky

"Anybody who wants to travel towards the heights has to understand *Light on the Path*. It is a small book as far as quantity is concerned, just a few pages, but as far as quality is concerned it is one of the biggest, the greatest books. . . . Whosoever wrote it, whosoever guided the writer, that's beside the point; the book itself stands like a golden tower."
— Osho, contemporary mystic and philosopher

"Everything it has to say seems to be contrary to the essence of modern life; but after it is understood and lived up to, I think it is a very helpful guide."
— Jackson Pollock, painter

"Of all the numerous books written for the purpose of throwing light on the path of the student of occultism, we know of none better fitted for the purpose than that wonderful little book called *Light on the Path*, written down by 'M.C.,' at the instigation of some intelligences far above the ordinary. It is veiled in the poetic style common to the Orientals, and at first glance may seem paradoxical. But it is full of the choicest bits of occult wisdom, for those who are able to read it. It must be read 'between the lines,' and it has a peculiarity that will become apparent to anyone who may read it carefully. That is, it will give you as much truth as you are able to grasp today; and tomorrow when you pick it up it will give you more, from the same lines. Look at it a year from now, and new truths will burst upon you — and so on, and on. It contains statements of truth so wonderfully stated — and yet half-concealed — that as you advance in spiritual discernment — and are ready for greater truths each day — you will find that in this book veil after veil will be lifted from before the truth, until you are fairly dazzled. It is also remarkable as a book which will give consolation to those in trouble or sorrow. Its words (even though they be but half-understood) will ring in the ears of its readers, and like a beautiful melody will soothe and comfort and rest those who hear it. We advise all of our students to read this little book often and with care. They will find that it will describe various spiritual experiences through which they will pass, and will prepare them for the next stage."
— William Walker Atkinson, writer, publisher, author of *The Kybalion*

"*Light on the Path*, just like *The Voice of the Silence*, is full of symbols, allusions, and hidden meaning. This little book must be read carefully. Its deeper meaning seems to disappear, and then reappear throughout the book, and so should be read when the reader is in a particular kind of mood. *Light on the Path* prepares the 'disciple' for conversation with the 'Master,' that is, it prepares the ordinary consciousness for communication with the higher consciousness."
— **P. D. Ouspensky, philosopher, author of *In Search of the Miraculous***

"*Light on the Path* is highly mystico-spiritual in tone, a companion work to *The Voice of the Silence*. It is couched in allegorical and figurative language, depicting forms of nature as symbolical of spiritual truth."
— **Alvin Boyd Kuhn, PhD, writer, author of *The Esoteric Structure of the Alphabet***

"Definitely intended for the quickening of the evolution of those who are on the Path, this book puts forward ideals which people of the world are rarely prepared to accept. Only as far as a man is able and willing to live the teaching, will he be able to understand it. If he does not practise it, it will remain a sealed book to him. Any effort to live it will throw light upon it; but if the reader makes no effort, he will not only gain very little, but he will turn against the book and say that it is useless."
— **Annie Besant, social reformer, writer, Indian independence leader**

"Highly significant also are the sayings in *Light on the Path* that have been written down by Mabel Collins, under the instruction of higher powers. Actually in the first four sentences there is something that, when applied with patience in the appropriate way, is capable of so seizing upon the human aura that this aura is completely shot through with new light. One can see this light in the human aura shining and glistening. Bluish shades arise in place of the reddish or reddish-brown shimmering shades of colour, and, in the place of yellow shades, clear reddish ones arise, and so on. The whole colouring of the aura transforms itself under the influence of such eternal thoughts. The student cannot yet perceive this in the beginning, but he gradually begins to notice the deep influence that emanates from the greatly transformed aura."
— **Rudolf Steiner, philosopher, social reformer**

"For manifestation in the physical world, we have an instrument which we call our *body*; for manifestation in the sphere of feelings and emotions, another instrument which has been called the *astral body*; for manifestation in the sphere of thinking, the *body of thought*; for expression in the higher worlds we have an instrument to which we give the name of *spirit*, and in the East is given the name *buddhi*. The rules for the complete awakening of this instrument of the spirit are given in the book *Light on the Path*."
— **Elena Pisareva, philosopher, translator, writer**

"Miss Mabel Collins' *Light on the Path* has been translated into Sanskrit, and will be placed by the Hindu pundits as one of the Sanskrit classics. Translation into Sanskrit is a thing which has not been done for at least 100 years past; but the book is sufficiently Buddhistic and occult to satisfy even the learned Hindus."
— ***The Star* (London, 1888)**

Grateful acknowledgement is made for permission to include quotes by:

Aldous Huxley, from *Letters of Aldous Huxley* by Aldous Huxley. Copyright © 1969 by Laura Huxley. Reprinted by permission of Georges Borchardt, Inc. on behalf of the Aldous and Laura Huxley Literary Trust. All rights reserved.

C. G. Jung, from *Psychologie und Religion* © 2007 Foundation of the Works of C. G. Jung, Zurich. Reprinted by permission of Paul & Peter Fritz AG Literary Agency.

Jane Goodall, PhD, from *Reason for Hope* by Jane Goodall, copyright © 1999. Reprinted by permission of Grand Central Publishing, an imprint of Hachette Book Group, Inc.

Brian L. Weiss, MD, from *H.P.B.* by Sylvia Cranston. Copyright © 1993 by Brian L. Weiss. Reprinted by permission of the Weiss Institute.

Elisabeth Kübler-Ross, MD, from *H.P.B.* by Sylvia Cranston. Copyright © 1993 by Elisabeth Kübler-Ross. Reprinted by permission of the Elisabeth Kübler-Ross Foundation.

Henry Miller, from *The Books in My Life*, copyright © 1969 by New Directions Publishing Corp. Reprinted by permission of New Directions Publishing Corp.

Osho, from *Beyond Psychology* and *Books I Have Loved*. Copyright © 1984, 1986, 2025 by OSHO International Foundation. Reprinted by permission of OSHO International Foundation.

Alan Watts, from *In My Own Way* © 2001 by Joan Watts and Anne Watts. Used by permission of New World Library, www.newworldlibrary.com.

Jiddu Krishnamurti, an extract from an interview by Wilfred Thomas at Brockwood Park, 1970 copyright © Krishnamurti Foundation Trust Ltd. Permission to quote from the works of J. Krishnamurti has been given on the understanding that such permission does not indicate endorsement of the views expressed in this media. For more information about J. Krishnamurti (1895–1986) please visit: www.jkrishnamurti.org.

James Jones, from *Some Came Running*. Copyright © 1958 by James Jones. Reprinted by permission of Kaylie Jones.

Ingo Swann, from *H.P.B.* by Sylvia Cranston. Copyright © 1994 by Ingo Swann. Reprinted by permission of the Ingo Swann Estate.

Waldemar Januszczak, from *Waldemar's American Road Trip: Big Dreams, Big Art*. Copyright © 2018 by ZCZ Films. Used by permission of Waldemar Januszczak.

Jeremy P. Tarcher, from *H.P.B.* by Sylvia Cranston. Copyright © 1998 by Jeremy P. Tarcher. Reprinted by permission of Mallory Lewis.

Paul Brunton, from "My Tour Among the Yogis," *The London Forum* (1934). Copyright © 1934 by Paul Brunton. Reprinted by permission of the Paul Brunton Philosophic Foundation.

David Spangler, from a lecture delivered at the Mayflower Bookshop, Ferndale, MI. Copyright © 1977 by David Spangler. Used by permission of David Spangler.

Raghavan N. Iyer, PhD, from "The Seventh Impulsion," *Hermes* (1975) and *The Voice of the Silence* (Santa Barbara, CA: Concord Grove Press, 1989). Copyright © 1975, 1989 by Raghavan N. Iyer. Reprinted by permission of Pico Iyer.

Sangharakshita, from "Paradox and Poetry in *The Voice of the Silence*," *Aphorisms, the Arts, and Late Writings, Complete Works*, vol. 26 (Cambridge: Windhorse Publications, 2022), pp.197–212. Copyright © 1958, 2018 by Sangharakshita. Reprinted by permission of the Urgyen Sangharakshita Trust.

Every effort has been made to trace all copyright holders, but if any have been inadvertently overlooked, the publisher will be pleased to include any necessary credits.

सत्यात् नास्ति परो धर्मः।

"There is no Religion higher than Truth."

THE
BOOK
OF THE
GOLDEN
PRECEPTS

ALSO BY H. P. BLAVATSKY

The Secret Doctrine (2 vols.)

Isis Unveiled (2 vols.)

The Land of the Gods

Revealing Cosmic Mysteries

The Key to Theosophy

From the Caves and Jungles of Hindostan

The People of the Blue Mountains

The Durbar in Lahore

Nightmare Tales

The Theosophical Glossary

Transactions of the Blavatsky Lodge

The Esoteric Papers of Madame Blavatsky

Collected Writings (15 vols.)

THE BOOK OF THE GOLDEN PRECEPTS

THE VOICE OF THE SILENCE AND OTHER FRAGMENTS OF DIVINE WISDOM

H. P. BLAVATSKY

Radiant Books
New York

Copyright © 2025 by Radiant Books. All rights reserved. No part of this book may be used or reproduced in any manner whatsoever without written permission from the publisher except in the case of brief quotations embodied in critical articles and reviews. For additional information, contact *info@radiantbooks.co*.

Library of Congress Control Number: 2023951163

Foreword © 1989 by His Holiness the Dalai Lama. Reprinted by permission of the Office of His Holiness the Dalai Lama from the Centenary edition of *The Voice of the Silence* (Santa Barbara, CA: Concord Grove Press, 1989).

Foreword, Commentary, *The Island of Bliss* © 1964, 1981 by Reverend Father Anthony Elenjimittam. Reprinted by permission of the Welfare Society for Destitute Children from *The Voice of Silence* (Bombay: Aquinas Publications, 1981).

Forewords by His Holiness the Ninth Panchen Lama and B. T. Chang, comments by Alice Cleather and Basil Crump were originally published in *The Voice of the Silence* (Peking: Chinese Buddhist Research Society, 1927). Foreword by William Walker Atkinson was originally published in *Light on the Path* (Chicago: Yogi Publication Society, 1903). Foreword by Manly P. Hall was originally published as an article in *The All-Seeing Eye*, vol. 3, no. 15 (2 March 1927).

Fragments from the *Book of the Golden Precepts*, *The Voice of the Silence* and *Light on the Path*, were originally published in 1889 and 1885, respectively; Mabel Collins' comments on *Light on the Path* in 1887–1888. *The Golden Stairs* was originally published in 1890; *To the Esotericists* in 1889; *The Three Desires* in 1888; *At the Feet of the Master* in 1910; *Love with an Object* in 1888; *The Heart* in 1891; *Will and Desire, Self-Knowledge, Desire Made Pure, The Great Paradox* in 1887; *Spiritual Progress* in 1885; *Practical Occultism, Occultism Versus the Occult Arts* in 1888; *The Blessings of Publicity* in 1891; *The Theosophical Mahatmas* in 1886; *Chelas and Lay Chelas* in 1883; *Mahatmas and Chelas, Chelas* in 1884; *The Ten Rules of Discipleship of the Fourth Degree of the Great White Lodge* in 1925; *The Maha Chohan's Letter* in 1896; *Master Koot Hoomi's Letter* in 1923; *Master Hilarion's Letter* in 1925; *H.P.B.'s Letter* in 1891.

The Influence of H. P. Blavatsky, The Embodiments of Love and Compassion, Glossary © 2025 by Alexander Gerasymchuk; edited by Joanna Dobson. *Three Fragments in Modern English* © 2025 by Alexander Gerasymchuk; prepared by Joanna Dobson and Alexander Gerasymchuk. Translations from the Chinese © 2025 by Alexander Gerasymchuk; translated by Eric Stone, Ken Kraynak, Alina Hu, and Dubaibob; edited by Joanna Dobson. Translations of *The Path of Heroic Deeds in Everyday Life, Recommendations for a Healthier Life, The Lotus* © 2025 by Alexander Gerasymchuk; translated from the Russian by Alexander Gerasymchuk and Joanna Dobson.

Edgar Cayce Readings © 1971, 1993–2010 by the Edgar Cayce Foundation. All rights reserved.

H. P. Blavatsky's photo was taken in New York around 1874–1876 by Edsall Photographic Studio. Master Morya's portrait was received by Helena Roerich in 1921. His Holiness the Fourteenth Dalai Lama's photo © Chuck Nacke/Alamy Stock Photo. The photos of His Holiness the Ninth Panchen Lama and Reverend Father Anthony Elenjimittam were restored by Beata Korozo.

Photograph on page xxxvi: The Holy Relics of Shakyamuni Buddha and Lama Tsongkhapa by Harvey Benge. Courtesy of ThePowerOfHolyRelics.com. Used by permission.

Published in 2025 by Radiant Books
radiantbooks.co

ISBN 978-1-63994-054-7 (hardback)
ISBN 978-1-63994-055-4 (paperback)
ISBN 978-1-63994-056-1 (e-book)

CONTENTS

Foreword by Manly P. Hall xxv
The Influence of H. P. Blavatsky xxviii
The Golden Rule xxxiii
Introduction xxxv
The Golden Stairs cix

The Voice of the Silence

Foreword by His Holiness the Fourteenth Dalai Lama 3
Foreword by His Holiness the Ninth Panchen Lama 5
Foreword by Reverend Father Anthony Elenjimittam 9
Foreword by B. T. Chang 13
Foreword by Alice Cleather and Basil Crump 16
To the Esotericists 22
Preface 23
Fragment I: The Voice of the Silence 27
Fragment II: The Two Paths 43
Fragment III: The Seven Portals 57
The Island of Bliss 75
Three Fragments in Modern English 79

Light on the Path

Foreword by William Walker Atkinson 113
Part I 115
Part II 120
Karma 124
Comments 126
Questions and Answers 146
The Three Desires 152

Insights for the Path

The Path of Heroic Deeds in Everyday Life	161
At the Feet of the Master	162
Love with an Object	175
The Heart	179
Will and Desire	181
Self-Knowledge	182
Desire Made Pure	182
The Great Paradox	183
Spiritual Progress	186
Practical Occultism	190
Occultism Versus the Occult Arts	196
The Blessings of Publicity	205
Questions and Answers	208
Recommendations for a Healthier Life	214
The Theosophical Mahatmas	217
Chelas and Lay Chelas	223
Mahatmas and Chelas	229
Chelas	231
The Ten Rules of Discipleship	233
The Maha Chohan's Letter	234
Master Koot Hoomi's Letter	238
Master Hilarion's Letter	240
H.P.B.'s Letter	242
The Lotus	256
Glossary	259

List of Portraits

Helena Petrovna Blavatsky	xxiv
Master Morya	cviii
His Holiness the Fourteenth Dalai Lama	2
His Holiness the Ninth Panchen Lama	4
Reverend Father Anthony Elenjimittam	8

There is a road, steep and thorny, beset with perils of every kind — but yet a road, and it leads to the Heart of the Universe. I can tell you how to find Those who will show you the secret gateway that leads inward only, and closes fast behind the neophyte for evermore. There is no danger that dauntless courage cannot conquer. There is no trial that spotless purity cannot pass through. There is no difficulty that strong intellect cannot surmount. For those who win onwards, there is reward past all telling: the power to bless and save humanity. For those who fail, there are other lives in which success may come.

H. P. Blavatsky

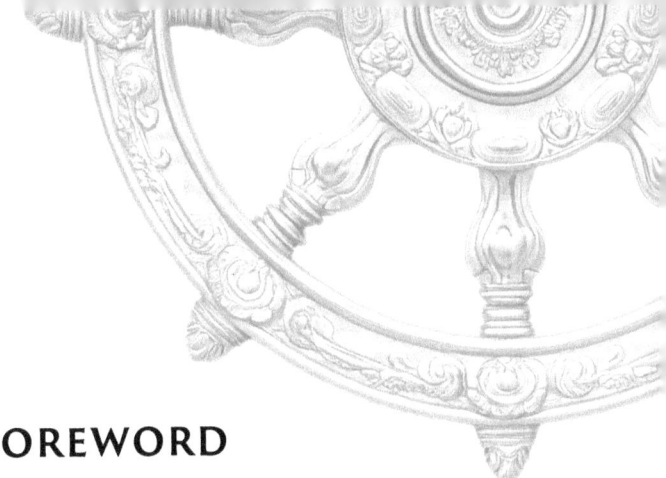

FOREWORD

HELENA PETROVNA BLAVATSKY
The Most Remarkable Woman of the Modern World

WE PRESENT the most remarkable woman of the modern world, Helena Petrovna Blavatsky, a Russian mystic and philosopher to whom the world is indebted for the most complete outline now in print of the doctrines and mysteries of the ancient and modern worlds, both Eastern and Western. It is impossible to estimate the influence of this woman. She was a forerunner, and the modern tolerance for metaphysical and oriental thought is largely the result of her years of labour.

Madame Blavatsky was born in Yekaterinoslav, Russia,[1] in July 1831.[2] At the age of seventeen, she married a Russian officer, Nikifor Blavatsky, many years her senior. She lived with him but a few months and then began a life of wandering which included travel in Mexico, Canada, India, and Tibet. With the assistance of Colonel Henry Steel Olcott, she founded the Theosophical Society in New York City in 1875. Madame Blavatsky was made an American citizen, and declared that her citizenship papers were one of her most cherished possessions.

She wrote a number of books of which *The Secret Doctrine* and *Isis Unveiled* are the most important. She also edited a magazine which she called *Lucifer* (The Light-bearer). She died suddenly in London while working on the third and fourth volumes of *The Secret Doctrine*.

Madame Blavatsky was a pioneer in the Western world, for she brought to Europe and America the first connected account of the Eastern schools of occult philosophy. A woman of commanding personality

---

[1] Modern-day Dnipro, Ukraine. At that time, Ukraine was part of the Russian Empire.

[2] On 31 July 1831, according to the Julian calendar that was in use until 1918. This date would be 12 August 1831, according to the Gregorian calendar.

and scintillating mentality, she demanded and secured respect for ideas far in advance of the age. In her two great works, she acts as the mouthpiece of a very seclusive group of Eastern Adepts, known as Masters or Mahatmas, dwelling in the unexplored fastnesses of Greater and Lesser Tibet. She makes no claim to have written *The Secret Doctrine*, but states that she was merely a pen in the hand of a ready writer. Modern students should not lightly consider these works, for to contradict her is to contradict the Illustrious Brotherhood who chose her to serve them.

There is no doubt that Madame Blavatsky possessed superphysical powers similar to those of the East Indian Adepts. She demonstrated these many times. Most of her work was carried on under bitter opposition from all sides, from the scientist, the theologian, the man of the world, and even in spite of treachery among her own followers. During all this time she was in continuous poor health, the result of exposures in early life. While she never claimed to be an Initiate, there is every reason to suppose that she had been admitted at least into the lower or lesser mysteries, and consequently, was privileged to use the title Initiate.

It would pay everyone to study her books for the vast field of information on the ancient cultures and philosophies and it would especially be valuable for students of the occult to depart from less important books and study *The Secret Doctrine*.

When we say this, a great cry will go up by the student: "Oh, a book like *The Secret Doctrine* is so difficult, I cannot understand it; give me something more simple." We answer: "What is the good of studying things you understand?" The eternal cry of man is "Make it easy." We do not realize that we must grow up to things. It is a great mistake to attempt to bring Truth down to ignorance. The result is always misunderstanding and perversion. Man must be brought up to the Truth. He should eternally aspire toward the highest. He should never seek to drag things spiritual down to his level. *The Secret Doctrine* is difficult to read; its long words, its abstract ideas, and its complicated system of thought bewilder the uninitiated. But man must realize that his mind is capable of all things if he will train it. If he will live the occult life as set forth by the Masters for their pupils, he will unfold his mind, thus increasing his intelligence to the understanding of those things which before were riddles and enigmas.

So to this great Russian woman, this mystic and philosopher, we owe the right to think along lines opposed to and beyond the restrictions of orthodoxy, whether religious or scientific. This woman battled constantly to bring a deeper sympathy and insight into the world of thought for the realities back of the form or the externals. A woman, misunderstood and slandered as few in the modern world have been, and at the same time strong enough to combat successfully all of her foes, she represents the possible power of woman in the new era of science and philosophy. Future generations will recognize the true genius of this most remarkable of modern women.

Manly P. Hall
Los Angeles, March 1927

Manly P. Hall (1901–1990) was a Canadian-born author, lecturer, and scholar known for his work in esoteric philosophy, mysticism, and the occult. He wrote more than 150 books and delivered over seven thousand lectures in the United States and around the world, covering topics like Freemasonry, Hermetism, Rosicrucianism, alchemy, and Eastern philosophies.

Hall's most famous work with more than one million copies sold, *The Secret Teachings of All Ages* (1928), is a comprehensive exploration of ancient wisdom traditions, symbolism, mythology, and hidden knowledge. It served as a source book for Dan Brown's bestselling novels. President Ronald Reagan quoted his other book, *The Secret Destiny of America* (1944), on a few occasions. In 1934, Hall founded the Philosophical Research Society in Los Angeles, promoting the study of spiritual traditions, metaphysics, and comparative religion.

A lifelong admirer of H. P. Blavatsky, Hall had frequent telephone calls with Elvis Presley and was in contact with numerous prominent figures. Considered one of the greatest esoteric scholars of the twentieth century, his work continues to influence students of mysticism and the occult.

THE INFLUENCE OF H. P. BLAVATSKY
A Woman Generations Ahead of Her Time

"Few women in our time have been more persistently misrepresented, slandered, and defamed than Madame Blavatsky. . . . No one in the present generation has done more toward reopening the long-sealed treasures of Eastern thought, wisdom, and philosophy. . . . Someday, if not at once, the loftiness and purity of her aims, the wisdom and scope of her teachings, will be recognized more fully."
— *New-York Tribune*

EVEN IF YOU have never heard of **Helena Petrovna Blavatsky** (1831–1891), otherwise referred to simply as **H.P.B.**, you may still have been influenced by her work in one way or another without being aware of it.

Have you or has someone you know been interested in an aspect of spirituality, such as karma, reincarnation, dreams, positive thinking, the law of attraction, higher consciousness, the unconscious, near-death and out-of-body experiences? Have you felt drawn to study Eastern philosophy, Kabbalah, Gnosticism, Hermetism, Hinduism, or Buddhism? Have you attended yoga or meditation classes, turned to alternative medicine, checked a daily astrological horoscope, explored prehistory on the subject of Atlantis or Lemuria, or been captivated by science fiction and fantasy books, or games dealing with lost worlds?

If so, did you know that none of these things would exist or be thriving in the Western world now had Blavatsky not come from the long-suffering Ukrainian lands to America and Great Britain to prepare the soil and sow the first seeds? Or that for introducing something that people in the West had never seen or heard of before, despite its being so common today, Blavatsky initially became a target for the utmost hatred and criticism?

Her influence has even resulted in more than half of Americans nowadays preferring cremation as their funerary choice. Few are aware that Theosophists like Blavatsky were the first to introduce the benefits of cremation to the public, and that it was they who held the first ever cremation ceremony in the United States.[1]

Additionally, Helena Blavatsky was a pioneer in advocating for women's rights, nearly a century before it became fashionable to do so.

She fascinated the greatest minds in the domains of science, religion, philosophy, psychology, music, art, and literature.

Blavatsky's *Theosophy* (meaning "divine wisdom") blends with modern science the sacred wisdom of the ages, found at the core of all world religions and philosophies. In essence, Theosophy represents an effort to spiritualize science and to scientifically explain spirituality.

Her epoch-making work in two volumes, *The Secret Doctrine*, was significantly ahead of its time and contained numerous scientific foresights. For example, Blavatsky affirmed the atom's infinite divisibility, the convertibility of matter and energy ($E=mc^2$), the transmutation of elements, the illusory nature of matter, and many other concepts denied or not yet discovered by science at the time. She also predicted the climate change we are witnessing today.

At a time when there had been no major wars in Europe for two decades, Blavatsky previsioned world wars, destruction of whole cities by nuclear blasts, and the appearance of "a heartless, proud Fiend, assuming sudden authority, . . . [who] had clutched with iron hand the minds of a whole country."[2]

Albert Einstein used *The Secret Doctrine* for inspiration, always keeping a copy on his desk.[3] **Nikola Tesla** also studied Blavatsky's works, and drew from them the idea of *Akasha*, the substance that is an eternal source of energy, that he used in his inventions.[4]

The Theosophical Society, which Blavatsky co-founded in 1875 in New York City, has included such prominent figures[5] as **Thomas Edison, Sir William Crookes, Camille Flammarion, L. Frank Baum, W. B.**

---

[1] Mitch Horowitz, "How the Occult Brought Cremation to America," *HuffPost Religion*, https://www.huffpost.com/entry/how-the-occult-brought-cr_b_3880620.

[2] H. P. Blavatsky, "Karmic Visions," *Collected Writings*, vol. 9 (Wheaton, IL: Theosophical Publishing House, 1962), p. 333.

[3] Jack Brown, "I Visit Professor Einstein," *Ojai Valley News* (28 September 1983).

[4] Marc Seifer, *Wizard* (New York: Citadel Press, 2001), p. 164.

[5] Unless specified otherwise, lists of individuals influenced by Theosophy in this and the following paragraphs are based on Sylvia Cranston's *H.P.B.: The Extraordinary Life and Influence of Helena Blavatsky, Founder of the Modern Theosophical Movement* (Santa Barbara, CA: Path Publishing House, 1998).

Yeats, Dr. Maria Montessori,[1] William James, William Walker Atkinson,[2] Alexandra David-Néel, Edgar Cayce,[3] Mahatma Gandhi, and His Holiness the Fourteenth Dalai Lama; the latter has been an Honorary Life Member since 2011.[4]

Theosophy also inspired the writings of **Franz Kafka**,[5] **Lewis Carroll**,[6] **Kahlil Gibran**,[7] **Jack London, T. S. Eliot, James Joyce, E. M. Forster, D. H. Lawrence, H. P. Lovecraft**,[8] and **Robert E. Howard**;[9] the music of **Alexander Scriabin, Jean Sibelius**, and **Gustav Mahler**; and the paintings of **Nicholas Roerich, Wassily Kandinsky, Jackson Pollock**,[10] **Piet Mondrian, Paul Klee, Paul Gauguin**, and **Max Beckmann**.[11] Overall, the concept expounded by Blavatsky, that creation can be expressed as a sequence of geometrical figures and numbers, appealed to many artists, giving rise to abstract art.

Today we cannot imagine a festival or concert without a light show, or visuals and effects created through the art of light. This again goes to the idea of a secret correlation between vibration, sound, and colour that Blavatsky taught to her inner circle. This revived ancient knowledge inspired musicians, such as Scriabin, to experiment with colour and visual music. When the artist **Thomas Wilfred** arrived in America, he became involved with the Theosophists, such as the architect **Claude Bragdon**, who wanted to demonstrate this concept through a colour organ.[12] Wilfred constructed a device that he called the *Clavilux*

---

[1] Carolie Wilson, "Montessori Was a Theosophist," *History of Education Society Bulletin*, vol. 36 (Autumn 1985), pp. 52–54.

[2] Joined the Theosophical Society in 1903.

[3] Joined the Theosophical Society in 1922 for about two years. It was after meeting the Theosophist Arthur Lammers that Cayce's readings began to involve not only medical advice but also explorations of his clients' past lives and humanity's lost history.

[4] Tim Boyd, "President's Diary," *Quest*, vol. 99, no. 4 (October 2011), p. 155.

[5] June O. Leavitt, *The Mystical Life of Franz Kafka* (New York: Oxford University Press, 2012), p. 6.

[6] Amanda Lynn McCaskill, *Madame Blavatsky and Lewis Carroll: The Influence of Theosophy on Alice in Wonderland* (Emmitsburg, MD: Mount St. Mary's University, 2016).

[7] Paul-Gordon Chandler, *In Search of a Prophet: A Spiritual Journey with Kahlil Gibran* (Lanham, MD: Rowman & Littlefield, 2017), p. 106.

[8] Carole Cusack and Alex Norman, editors, *Handbook of New Religions and Cultural Production* (Leiden, the Netherlands: Brill, 2012), pp. 114–115.

[9] Cusack and Norman, *Handbook of New Religions and Cultural Production*, pp. 113–114.

[10] Annikka Olsen, "21 Facts About Jackson Pollock," *Sotheby's*, https://www.sothebys.com/en/articles/21-facts-about-jackson-pollock.

[11] Peter Selz, *Max Beckmann* (New York: Gagosian Gallery, 1992), p. 8.

[12] Keely Orgeman, *Lumia: Thomas Wilfred and the Art of Light* (New Haven, CT: Yale University Art Gallery, 2017), pp. 17, 21.

and coined the term *Lumia* for the art of colour-music projections. His unprecedented, innovative works prefigured kinetic and light art, influencing subsequent generations of visual artists.[13]

Theosophical ideas captured the imagination of Hollywood stars too. Spiritual quest brought **Greta Garbo** to Theosophy, drawn as she was to the concepts expounded in Blavatsky's writings.[14] **Marilyn Monroe** was interested in Theosophy, too, supporting the work of the Theosophical Society in New York with generous donations.[15]

Elvis Presley always carried copies of Blavatsky's works around with him. Each time gazing at her portrait while discussing Theosophy with a close friend, he would say of her: "Look at the eyes, Larry, the shape of the face, the cheekbones. I've never seen anything like it!"[16] Presley loved *The Voice of the Silence* so much that he sometimes quoted it onstage, and it was this book that inspired him to name his own gospel group, *Voice*.[17]

In the *Harry Potter* series, **J. K. Rowling** names one of her characters Cassandra Vablatsky after Helena Blavatsky.[18]

Moreover, the *Star Wars* movies would not exist without the ideas for the concept of the *Force* that Blavatsky brought from the East to the West. **George Lucas** credited **Joseph Campbell**'s work as influencing his films.[19] However, Campbell himself was influenced by Blavatsky and Theosophy. Interestingly, the name of the saga's main character, Skywalker, appears in *The Voice of the Silence*,[20] while its unusual poetic style sometimes bears an uncanny resemblance to the peculiar speech of Yoda.

In the 1980s, millions of Americans were exposed to alternative spiritual ideas for the first time thanks to Oscar-winning actress **Shirley MacLaine**. Her spiritual quest was initiated by the books of **Rudolf Steiner**, the former head of the Theosophical Society in Germany. Later, she was further influenced by Blavatsky's works as well.

---

[13] Howard Kaplan, "Lumia: The Art of Light," *Smithsonian American Art Museum*, https://americanart.si.edu/blog/eye-level/2017/04/56195/lumia-art-light.

[14] Moon Laramie, *Spirit of Garbo* (London: Martin Firrell Company, 2018), p. 129.

[15] Moon Laramie, "Greta Garbo: The Hidden Theosophist," *Theosophical Society in England & Wales*, YouTube (23 December 2020), https://www.youtube.com/watch?v=PqeFYvUWDhc.

[16] Larry Geller and Joel Spector, *If I Can Dream* (New York: Simon and Schuster, 1989), p. 178.

[17] Albert Goldman, *Elvis* (New York: McGraw-Hill, 1981), p. 366.

[18] Cassandra Vablatsky appears in chapter 4 of *Harry Potter and the Prisoner of Azkaban* (London: Bloomsbury, 1999).

[19] Stephen and Robin Larsen, *Joseph Campbell: A Fire in the Mind* (Rochester, VT: Inner Traditions, 2002), p. 541.

[20] See Fragment I of *The Voice of the Silence*, p. 34.

MacLaine, in turn, became one of **Oprah Winfrey's** "great spiritual teachers," inspiring her to bring up all those "out-there" topics on her national talk show.[1] This allowed prominent thinkers of today to share their ideas with a massive TV audience.

For these reasons, Helena Blavatsky is justly called the Mother of Modern Spirituality, because, without her influence, either the religious dogmas that tolerate no alternative views would still be dominating the cultural landscape of the Western world, or its nations would have entirely succumbed to the dangers of the spiritualism movement, lapsing into dark magic. However, to prevent this from happening, Blavatsky had to sacrifice herself by taking the most poisonous arrows into her heart from both her enemies and her friends.

During her life, Blavatsky's reputation and health were substantially damaged due to betrayal by her colleagues, who took money from missionaries with the aim of fabricating evidence for an accusatory report by the Society for Psychical Research (S.P.R.).

It was not until 1986 that the S.P.R. issued a press release to newspapers and leading magazines in the United Kingdom, the United States, and Canada headlined: "Madame Blavatsky, co-founder of the Theosophical Society, **was unjustly condemned**, new study concludes."

Dr. Vernon Harrison, who re-examined Blavatsky's case, finished his report with the words: "I apologize to her that it has taken us one hundred years to demonstrate that she wrote truly."[2]

"A woman who, for one reason or another, has kept the world — ... two hemispheres — talking of her, disputing about her, defending or assailing her character and motives, joining her enterprise or opposing it might and main, ... being as much telegraphed about between two continents as an emperor, must have been a remarkable person."

— *The Sun* **(New York)**

---

[1] Oprah Winfrey, "Shirley MacLaine: A Legendary Seeker," *Oprah's Super Soul*, Podcast (1 October 2017), https://www.oprah.com/own-podcasts/shirley-maclaine-a-legendary-seeker.

[2] Vernon Harrison, "J'Accuse: An Examination of the Hodgson Report of 1885," *Journal of the Society for Psychical Research*, vol. 53, no. 803 (April 1986), pp. 309–310.

THE GOLDEN RULE

Christianity: In everything, do to others what you would have them do to you.

Islam: No one of you shall become a true believer until he desires for his brother what he desires for himself.

Buddhism: Hurt not others in ways that you would find hurtful.

Hinduism: This is the sum of duty: do naught unto others which would cause you pain if done to you.

Judaism: What is hateful to you, do not do to your fellow.

Taoism: Regard your neighbour's gain as your own gain, and your neighbour's loss as your own loss.

Confucianism: What you do not wish for yourself, do not do to others.

Zoroastrianism: Do not do unto others whatever is injurious to yourself.

Jainism: In happiness and suffering, in joy and grief, we should regard all creatures as we regard our own self.

Sikhism: As you deem yourself, so deem others.

Shintoism: Be charitable to all beings, love is the representative of God.

Baha'i Faith: Lay not on any soul a load that you would not wish to be laid upon you, and desire not for anyone the things you would not desire for yourself.

THE WORLDWIDE MAITREYA LOVING KINDNESS TOUR

THE POWER OF HOLY RELICS

TO CHANGE MINDS AND BRING PEACE

A riveting account, in words and pictures, of the **worldwide tour of sacred Buddhist relics**, experienced by millions of people in sixty-eight countries between 2001 and 2015, telling a story of love, healing, blessings, and miracles.

The relics were of more than seventy of the greatest Buddhist practitioners of our time, including Shakyamuni Buddha.

The appeal of the relics was universal, beyond religion and culture, and the impact was astonishing — and often utterly unexpected. Some people spontaneously experienced meditative states, others experienced profound emotional or spiritual healing; many were cured of physical pain and ailments.

All proceeds will be donated to the Lama Zopa Rinpoche Bodhichitta Fund.

Scientist Dr Nisha Manek, taken aback by her own response, "felt an intense state of awareness... exquisitely gentle and yet like a rock." The relics, she feels, point to an amazing and radical concept: "that no physical flesh and blood body is required for a vehicle for consciousness. We [scientists] are forced to go back to the drawing board."

Available from thepowerofholyrelics.com

INTRODUCTION

THE EMBODIMENTS OF LOVE AND COMPASSION

> The human heart has not yet fully uttered itself, and we have never attained or even understood the extent of its powers.
> — H. P. Blavatsky

The Maitreya Loving Kindness Tour

With the blessing of His Holiness the Fourteenth Dalai Lama, from 2001 to 2015 exhibitions of the Maitreya Loving Kindness Tour were held all around the world. Millions of people had the opportunity to behold visible manifestations, in the form of sacred relics, of the enlightened state attained by the righteous saints during their lifetime. The powerful healing energy of such relics has given to many inspiration and liberation from pain, illness, and disease.[1]

Prior to the tour, these holy relics were hidden for thousands of years in Buddhist temples and shrines of Asia. They were brought together in order to imbue almost every country in the world with their Love energy before being placed in the Heart of the Maitreya Buddha statue in India.

In the countries of the East, where Buddhism is widespread, there exists the following ancient tradition: when highly spiritual lamas or yogis pass away, after cremation, their closest disciples search the ashes for crystals called *ringsel* or *sharira*. The crystals remain intact and unharmed resembling pearls or grains of amber of different colours and degrees of transparency. It is considered that the greater the number found the better; by their number and size, the disciples judge the degree of spirituality embodied by their teacher.

---

[1] See Victoria Coleman, *The Power of Holy Relics to Change Minds and Bring Peace* (Netherlands: The Power of Holy Relics, 2019).

Since cremation was not common in Christian countries, it is impossible to judge by this same criterion the eminence of many of the famous saints, although other sacred relics belonging to them remain — incorruptible relics that also have healing powers. Nonetheless, after Joan of Arc's execution by burning at the stake, her heart did not burn in the flames and remained in the form of a crystal. Not knowing what to do with it, her executioners simply threw it into the Seine.

The Holy Relics of Shakyamuni Buddha and Lama Tsongkhapa (by Harvey Benge).

Before proceeding to a more detailed description of how *ringsel* crystals are formed from a theosophical point of view, we must consider topics that are difficult to understand, the validity of which is negated by the majority of those who are raised in a Christian environment, namely, the Laws of Reincarnation and Karma.

The Law of Reincarnation

Belief in reincarnation served as the cornerstone of all ancient religions long before the Christian Church appeared. Therefore, Jesus Christ would not have needed to affirm the notion, since it went without saying.

These testimonies have been preserved in the Gospels: "And as Jesus passed by, he saw a man which was blind from his birth. And his disciples asked him, saying, 'Master, who did sin, this man, or his parents, that he was born blind?' Jesus answered, 'Neither hath this man sinned, nor his parents: but that the works of God should be made manifest in him.'"[1] After all, how could a man who was blind from birth have been punished with blindness for his sins if the Law of Reincarnation did not exist?

Elsewhere we read: "And his disciples asked him, saying, 'Why then say the scribes that Elijah must first come?' And Jesus answered and said unto them, 'Elijah truly shall first come, and restore all things. But I say unto you that Elijah is come already, and they knew him not. . . .' Then the disciples understood that he spake unto them of John the Baptist."[2]

The same episode appears in an ancient text known as *Pistis Sophia*, which dates to the second century CE. In it, Christ speaks directly about the reincarnation of the soul of the prophet Elijah in John the Baptist.[3] And this is not the only place in the manuscript that Christ illuminates the matter of reincarnation for the disciples.

Early Christianity accepted the doctrine of the reincarnation of the soul, but everything changed in 553 CE, when, by the decision of the Second Council of Constantinople, the concept of the pre-existence of the soul was declared a heresy, and all those who disagreed were anathematized.[4]

Of course, the effect of this decision was not immediate. It took many more hundreds of years of "painstaking labour" to finally eradicate even the very idea that a person can be reincarnated and bear responsibility for their actions in future lives. In exchange, a feeling of unaccountability began, gradually, to be instilled in human consciousness: there is only one life, and we can do whatever we want with it, as, after committing any crime, one may simply appeal to a priest in a church, confess, and all one's sins will be miraculously forgiven; and a generous donation to the church might even ensure one's entrance into Heaven.

The first attempt to scientifically prove that reincarnation happens was made in the United States by Dr. Ian Stevenson.[5] Over the course of forty years, Dr. Stevenson studied and described in detail more than three thousand cases in which young children spoke with extraordinary accuracy about places and events in which they could not possibly have participated. In each case, Dr. Stevenson systematically documented the child's statements and compared them with actual events. All this could not be explained in any other way, except by the fact that life does not end with death, but continues in a new form.

---

[1] John 9:1–3.

[2] Matthew 17:10–13.

[3] See G. R. S. Mead, *Pistis Sophia* (London: John M. Watkins, 1921), pp. 9–10.

[4] See Sylvia Cranston, *Reincarnation: The Phoenix Fire Mystery* (New York: Warner Books, 1979), pp. 156–160.

[5] See Ian Stevenson, *Children Who Remember Previous Lives: A Question of Reincarnation* (Jefferson, NC: McFarland, 2000).

Of course, the scientific community subjected this attempt to harsh criticism, whilst failing to conduct any further research that might have explained how these children, who had no access to the Internet, could otherwise have been able to recall the details of streets, cities, and houses that they had never visited before, and even the names of former relatives and neighbours that they could never have met in person.

However, this act, amounting to a furious denial of the reality of reincarnation, is reminiscent of how, once, the sages of the past from different continents knew perfectly well the real shape of Earth, that it moved around the Sun, the structure of the Solar System, and even knew of other constellations, of which modern science still knows nothing. But then the "holy fathers" came along, together with the "luminaries of science," and decided that in fact the Earth was flat, and that it was the Sun that did the orbiting, and all those who disagreed were tortured by the Inquisition so that they would renounce their beliefs under fear of punishment.

Nevertheless, centuries later, Truth triumphed, and reincarnation will do the same.

The Law of Cause and Effect

Hand in hand with the Law of Reincarnation goes the Law of Cause and Effect, or karma. This Law is expressed in the simple formula: "as you sow, so shall you reap." Karma is that impartial judge, who unerringly rewards or punishes each for their actions, words, desires, and thoughts, the judge who cannot be persuaded, bribed, or granted with a generous donation. Only by neutralizing the causes that gave rise to a certain effect, can we pay off our debts. However, karma itself is a product of our free will.

From the moment of birth, we all bear the mark of karmic predestination. Our free will is subject to the limits defined by karma, which we ourselves generate as a product of our past and present. To liberate ourselves from the past, we must strive towards the future. By placing obstacles and restrictions in one area, karma opens up opportunities in a different area, so that we can learn something new, or atone for the unrighteous deeds of our past. Its goal is to guide each to the path of ascension, since it is difficult to rise upwards while burdened with debt.

Karmic debts are formed when we exercise our free will towards others in a way that violates the Divine Laws expounded in various different forms by all the religions of the world, when we forget the fundamental Golden Rule, which states: do not do to others what you would not wish to be done to yourself, and treat others as you would like to be treated.

Ignorance of these Laws does not absolve us of responsibility. The opportunity for this may not be presented immediately; several incarnations may pass before we are offered the chance to pay off our accumulated karmic bills, through the creation of certain conditions. Karma is not only individual, it can also entangle a group, involving entire families and nations.

For example, if a person experiences a strong feeling of hatred towards Muslims, in the next life, they will be incarnated in a Muslim country in order that they may *come to love* the Muslim culture and religion. If a person kills another in one life, in the next they will have to give that person life — give birth to them, or give up their own life for them — or have their own life taken by that person. Thus, our negative feelings towards other people, worldviews, and countries tie karmic knots that can be untied only after we learn to treat them well by being incarnated with them into the same family or society. That is, a perfect balance must be struck: the minus must be neutralized by the plus.

In each new life we are given the opportunity to pay off a portion of the debts accumulated during our many incarnations over many millennia. Therefore, the worst sin that one can commit against one's own spiritual development is suicide, since this increases the debt, causing the conditions of the next life to be even worse, for the life, which was intended to redeem a certain portion of the existing karma, was forcibly interrupted, and will hang around their neck, a new heavy burden.

The fastest way to redeem karma is to show Love towards all, especially towards those who wish us ill. Love will form positive ties with those we love, making them our companions from one life to another, and will untie existing knots with those who do not like us. Thus, karma can be transformed by irrepressible striving towards the Light.

Christ outlined perfectly the workings of the Law of Karma in the Sermon on the Mount: "Agree with thine adversary quickly, whiles thou art in the way with him [incarnated at the same time]; lest at any time the adversary deliver thee to the judge [the Law of Karma], and the judge deliver thee to the officer [the mechanism of enforcement of karmic ties], and thou be cast into prison [the bonds of karma]. Verily I say unto thee, thou shalt by no means come out thence, till thou hast paid the uttermost farthing [redeem your karmic debts in full]."[1]

As long as consciousness and thought exist, karma cannot end, but it can change its quality. If we live in accordance with Divine Law, then its quality will be enhanced, enabling us to escape the vicious circles of karma in which the vast majority of humanity walks.

---

[1] Matthew 5:25–26.

The Influence of Thoughts on the World

Every feeling we experience, every thought we think emits its own radiation that influences the world. Good feelings and thoughts emit light, while evil ones increase the darkness.

Research into the influence of thoughts has been ongoing in the United States since the 1970s. It has been found that 1 per cent of a population in a given region, meditating with the aim of having a positive impact on their locality, reduces crime and improves quality of life.[1] In the UK, a similar experiment was carried out from 1987 to 1992 in the county of Merseyside. At the beginning of the experiment, the region had one of the highest crime rates in the UK, and at the end, it had the lowest.[2] In 1993, it was found that a meditation group consisting of 2,500 people was capable of exerting an influence on 1.5 million people.[3]

Experiments conducted by Dr. Masaru Emoto have demonstrated the impact of our thoughts and words by using the molecular structure of water as an example.[4] While official science was busy criticizing his research, many ordinary people conducted their own experiments at home using rice, discovering for themselves the accuracy of his conclusions.[5]

In 1997, German scientists at the University of Kassel conducted a study that showed that the heart of someone who sends Love to others emits 100,000 photons of light per second, while the heart of an ordinary person emits only 20 photons per second (5,000 times less).[6] And scientists at the HeartMath Institute in the United States have come to the conclusion that every heart is capable of influencing the electromagnetic field of Earth, which is a carrier of information for all living beings; and

---

[1] David Orme-Johnson, "Preventing Crime Through the Maharishi Effect," *Journal of Offender Rehabilitation*, vol. 36 (2003), no. 1–4, pp. 257–281.

[2] Guy Hatchard et al, "Maharishi Effect: A Model for Social Improvement. Time Series Analysis of a Phase Transition to Reduced Crime in Merseyside Metropolitan Area," *Psychology, Crime & Law*, vol. 2 (1996), pp. 165–174.

[3] John Hagelin et al, "Results of the National Demonstration Project to Reduce Violent Crime and Improve Governmental Effectiveness in Washington, D.C." *Social Indicators Research*, vol. 47 (June 1999), pp. 153–201.

[4] See Masaru Emoto, *The Hidden Messages in Water* (Hillsboro, OR: Beyond Words Publishing, 2005).

[5] See, for example, Mark Baker, "Rice Experiment — Love vs Hate," *Possible Mind*, https://possiblemind.co.uk/rice-experiment-love-vs-hate; Jolita Brilliant, "Rice Experiment," *Jolita Brilliant Massage*, https://jolitabrilliant.com/rice-experiment; Serena, "Loved Rice is Happy Rice," *The Hearts Center*, https://www.heartscenter.org/TeachingsBlogs/BlogsandArticles/SpiritualParenting-MadeEasy/tabid/969/ArticleID/2856/Loved-Rice-is-Happy-Rice.aspx.

[6] Puran Bair, "Visible Light Radiated from the Heart with Heart Rhythm Meditation," *Subtle Energies & Energy Medicine*, vol. 16, no 3, p. 211.

accordingly, a collective of hearts is capable of influencing all life on the planet, both positively and negatively.[7]

Hence, we can say that our state of being, elevated or depressed, can help or, on the contrary, harm someone completely unknown to us located on the other side of the world. And if our thoughts are capable of exerting such an influence, then in this manner new karmic knots can be tied, thereby determining our companions in future lifetimes.

The Ringsel Crystal

However, these "transmissions" are reflected not only in the world around us, but also within ourselves. Thus, while we are physically incarnated, there is a clot of energy that crystallizes on the Subtle Plane in our heart. This invisible crystal emits rays, saturating the surrounding space, depending on the energy with which it was formed.

If good thoughts and deeds predominate in our daily life, then each instance of the emission of light outwards crystallizes the same amount within us in the form of invisible deposits, thanks to which this clot gradually grows, like a diamond, over many lifetimes. The more that we commit selfless acts for the sake of the Common Good, the more noticeably this crystal grows on the Subtle Plane.

But if we commit evil deeds, then a dark clot is formed within us, saturated with negative energies. It resembles a black coal that destroys the carrier as well as poisoning everything around it. Ultimately, only one should remain: either a bright crystal or a little dark coal, depending on what prevails within us.

In fact, this substance represents our crystallized karma, which determines our destiny according to a simple law, which can be expressed as "like attracts like." That is, the causes for everything that surrounds us are literally inherent in ourselves. Of course, this does not apply to the saints, who, after escaping the circle of karma, can independently create their own destiny. Often, out of Love and Compassion for humanity, they choose the worst conditions for their own life with the aim of helping others step onto the Path of Righteousness.

The Heart's Energy Potential

The energy potential of this crystal is measured by the *argo* coefficient. This numerical value expressed in energy units is constant at the time of birth. It can remain unchanged throughout many incarnations until certain actions cause it to shift from standstill. Thus, a light-bearing deed for the benefit of humanity adds a certain portion to the value

---

[7] Rollin McCraty, *Science of the Heart, Volume 2*, (Boulder Creek, CA: HeartMath Institute, 2015), p. 89.

already accumulated. After death, we carry it in our chest in the form of a blazing clot of Fire. We bring this fiery crystal with us into the new incarnation, in which it will be equal in energy value to the value it held at the end of our previous incarnation. Thus, this treasure can be squandered, multiplied, or left unchanged.

The *argo* coefficient of an ordinary person fluctuates within the range of one energy unit. People who reach three units and manage to pay off 51 per cent of their karmic debts attract the attention of the Great Teachers, come under their supervision, and gain the opportunity to collaborate with them. One who achieves seven units has reached the level of Master and works closely with the Hierarchy of Light, free from karmic restrictions. One with an *argo* coefficient of nine is a Master of the highest degrees. It has a value of twelve units only in the Teacher of Teachers, the Lord of Love and Compassion, referred to as the "Great Sacrifice," and His Lady, known as the Mother of the World; united they represent the twice sacred number 24.

This energy substance can be deposited in the form of *ringsel* pearls that are physically visible after death and cremation as a result of the impact of fire. However, *ringsel* pearls relate not only to a formation in the human heart, but also to depositions in two glands found in the brain: the pineal gland and the pituitary gland.

But in the case of a prominent saint, the Great Teachers decide whether the crystal should remain on Earth in physical form, or whether the saint should carry all their energy with them. Therefore, it can also be the case that after the cremation of a great spiritual being, no crystals are found in the ashes after cremation.

The Philosopher's Stone

The *ringsel* crystal can also be referred to as the *philosopher's stone*, which the ancient alchemists sought, and which, according to myths and legends, is capable of performing miracles. Numerous works have been written on the subject with various interpretations. However, this is, in fact, not only a symbol of the transmutation of human nature, but a real formation in the human heart, albeit an invisible one.

Of course, the philosopher's stone can be created alchemically as a distinct sacred object endowed with a mighty power. Details of how this is done are to this day kept strictly secret. However, before an alchemist can create this treasure externally, they must first have nurtured it within, in their own fiery heart.

In their works, the alchemists used many allegories, metaphors, and symbols, but they all talked about internal transformation first and foremost. For example, one of the recipes reads: "To prepare the elixir of the sages, or the philosopher's stone, take, my son, the philosopher's mercury and heat it until it transforms into a green lion. After that, heat it even more, and it will transform into a red lion."[1]

Here, the spiritual life acts as a "burning fire," since when we step onto the Path of Light and follow it strictly from one life to the next, we begin to purify and transform ourselves, while the "green lion" and the "red lion" represent degrees of transformation.

When we are physically incarnated, on the Subtle Plane the *ringsel* crystal of energy glows with a special flame, whose tongues form what might be described as the folded petals of the lotus of the heart. The higher our spirituality and morality, the brighter and stronger this flame radiates. There are twelve petals in total, but, so far, only nine can unfold: three emerald, three rose-coloured, and three white.

When we aspire to Knowledge — not the encyclopaedic kind, but the profound kind that is necessary for spiritual ascent — the green petals begin to unfold, first transforming us into the "green lion."

The time comes for the rose-coloured petals when we begin to love as Christ, Buddha, Muhammad, and the other Teachers have commanded, when our Love multiplies our Knowledge, and we acquire Wisdom. On account of the fact that the "red serpent" of the first energy centre, or chakra, called *kundalini*, rises upward into the "inmost chamber" of the heart, an alchemical reaction causes its petals to acquire a red glow, and this transforms us into the "red lion."

This fiery force can rise further, to our higher energy centres, the awakening of which can give us supernatural powers, such as levitation, telekinesis, telepathy, teleportation, and so on. The French traveller Alexandra David-Néel, the first Western woman to reach Lhasa, the capital of Tibet, saw with her own eyes monks flying.[2]

These abilities are all still practised by monks in India and Tibet for the sake of rendering hidden help to humanity as far as the limits of karma will allow them to in each individual case, and not for the purposes of putting on a show.

The biographies of the saints contain information indicating that Francis of Assisi, Catherine of Siena, Teresa of Ávila, Seraphim of Sarov, and others could also hover above the ground during prayer.

"Red lions" are extremely rare on Earth but are to be found among the saints of all religions, the miracle workers, who in the East are called *Arhats*.

---

[1] Jean-Baptiste Dumas, *Leçons sur la philosophie chimique* (Paris: Gauthier-Villars, 1878), p. 33.

[2] See Alexandra David-Néel, *Magic and Mystery in Tibet* (New York: Dover Publications, 1971), pp. 202–203.

Thus, it is in a pure heart that the philosopher's stone, containing all its legendary alchemical properties, is formed. Using its power, people can become creators: like, for example, Jesus Christ, Helena Blavatsky, and Sathya Sai Baba, who could materialize objects out of thin air, or transform one object into another.

When Jesus Christ visited Tibet, where He is known as Issa, He said: "I have come to demonstrate human abilities. Everyone can do what I am doing. And what I am, all people will become."[1]

The Miracles of the Ringsels

The *ringsel* pearls that remain after cremation have the highest type of energy and carry the same alchemical properties as those attributed to the philosopher's stone. Testimony to this fact are the many healings, including the recovery of sight,[2] experienced by visitors to exhibitions of the Maitreya Loving Kindness Tour held around the world. Even water saturated with their energy was capable of curing ailments.[3]

In addition, managers of the tour repeatedly witnessed the *ringsel* crystals change colour, emit light, "jump" from one container to another, as well as "multiply." At the beginning of the tour, all the relics were photographed for the inventory. But then, for example, the two *ringsels* of Kasyapa Buddha "gave birth" to three more, and among the *ringsels* of Ananda, a disciple of the Buddha, a large pearl appeared that changed colour from dark brown to pure white.[4] Many pearls suddenly began to emit a bright light like a bulb, and the glowing relic of Tsongkhapa was not only photographed, but also filmed,[5] and covered in the media in Taiwan, where this happened in 2008.

Since the *ringsel* crystals are sacred and rare, they have not been adequately studied by science. However, their transformative power has been tested by the professor emeritus and physicist based at Stanford University, Dr. William A. Tiller, and the former Mayo Clinic faculty member Dr. Nisha Manek. The results of their experiments were published in the peer-reviewed *Journal of Complementary and Alternative Medicine*. They found that the relics are a repository for the essence of the Masters' loving-kindness, and that this energy flows directly from the relics into objects and the surrounding space, "lifting" it into a sacred

---

[1] Nicholas Roerich, *Altay — Gimalai* [Altai — Himalaya] (Moscow: Eksmo, 2010), p. 102.
[2] Coleman, *The Power of Holy Relics*, p. 97.
[3] Coleman, *The Power of Holy Relics*, p. 13.
[4] Coleman, *The Power of Holy Relics*, p. 74.
[5] See Coleman, *The Power of Holy Relics*, p. 84; "Radiant relic of Lama Tsongkhapa," *Dharma109*, YouTube (27 August 2008), https://www.youtube.com/watch?v=Fk5-u4qDkBE.

field.⁶ In addition, the crystals are able to rearrange the atoms and molecules of their surroundings into a more coherent order.⁷ This explains the healing of many people, since any kind of illness represents a disturbance of this order. The scientists also discovered that these tiny pearls generate the same type of energy as famous places of worship.⁸

Another person wanting to use their power would need to have an energy of the same level of potential or higher. It is not possible for the power of *ringsel* pearls to be directed towards evil ends, and even if someone were to attempt this, the pearls would simply crumble into primary elements and dissolve in the forces of the natural elements due to the dissonance introduced. This, in turn, could lead to the death of the one who wished to beget evil, or result in earthquakes and other natural disasters.

The Lord of Love and Compassion

Maitreya, whose name means "Love," is not only the future Buddha, He is also that Great Planetary Spirit, the Lord of the World, who manifests Himself at the changing of Epochs, at the birth of the New Humanity, to provide an energy impulse for the entire next cycle of development.

Maitreya is one of the names that refers to the One whom the world awaits as the Messiah. Some call Him Christ, some Mahdi, others Kalki Avatar, and still others Saoshyant. He is known to humanity under many names, but no matter which of these beautiful names one chooses to refer to Him by, His essence remains the same — Love.

The memory of Him is reflected in all the world's religions as the Supreme Spirit, who is the Prime Lord of all humanity's Teachers and Saviours. He is the One whom Jesus called Father, and with whom Jesus was One. But, of course, He is very much not the jealous God of the Bible's Old Testament.

Priests of ancient religions and Initiates of all nations carefully preserved secret knowledge of Him, which was shared in spoken form only for thousands of years, in order to protect it from distortion and oblivion. Only towards the end of the nineteenth century did this knowledge begin to be revealed more widely, gradually becoming the property of all humanity.

In her seminal work, *The Secret Doctrine*, which represents a synthesis of all ancient knowledge, Helena Blavatsky writes of the Supreme Spirit most beautifully and poetically:

---

⁶ Coleman, *The Power of Holy Relics*, p. 16.
⁷ Nisha Manek and William Tiller, *The Sacred Buddha Relic Tour: For the Benefit of All Beings* (White Paper XXV), p. 15, https://tillerfoundation.org/wp-content/uploads/2022/08/White-Paper-XXV-registered.pdf.
⁸ Manek and Tiller, *The Sacred Buddha Relic Tour*, p. 12.

"The 'Being' ... which has to remain nameless, is the *Tree* from which, in subsequent ages, all the great *historically* known Sages and Hierophants, such as Rishi Kapila, Hermes, Enoch, Orpheus, etc., etc., have branched off. As objective man, he is the mysterious (to the profane — the ever invisible) yet ever present Personage about whom legends are rife in the East, especially among the occultists and the students of the Sacred Science. It is he who changes form, yet remains ever the same. And it is he again who holds spiritual sway over the *initiated* Adepts throughout the whole world.

"He is, as said, the 'Nameless One' who has so many names, and yet whose names and whose very nature are unknown. He is the 'Initiator,' called the 'Great Sacrifice.' For, sitting at the Threshold of Light, he looks into it from within the Circle of Darkness, which he will not cross; nor will he quit his post till the last day of this life-cycle.

"Why does the Solitary Watcher remain at his self-chosen post? Why does he sit by the Fountain of Primeval Wisdom, of which he drinks no longer, for he has naught to learn which he does not know — aye, neither on this Earth, nor in its Heaven?

"Because the lonely, sore-footed pilgrims, on their journey back to their Home, are never sure, to the last moment, of not losing their way, in this limitless desert of Illusion and Matter called Earth-Life. Because he would fain show the way to that region of freedom and light, from which he is a voluntary exile himself, to every prisoner who has succeeded in liberating himself from the bonds of flesh and illusion. Because, in short, he has sacrificed himself for the sake of mankind, though but a few elect may profit by the Great Sacrifice.

"It is under the direct, silent guidance of this Maha Guru that all the other less divine Teachers and Instructors of Mankind became, from the first awakening of human consciousness, the guides of early humanity. It is through these 'Sons of God' that infant humanity learnt its first notions of all the arts and sciences, as well as of spiritual knowledge; and it is they who laid the first foundation-stone of those ancient civilizations that so sorely puzzle our modern generation of students and scholars."[1]

In all the world religions, He became that Mysterious Spirit of whom little is known and even less can be said, but who rules over all creation: Sanat Kumara, Chakravartin, the Ancient of Days. Indeed, He has so many names that He may be called by different names even within the same religion.

In the Bible, He is described as follows: "I beheld till the thrones were cast down, and the Ancient of Days did sit, whose garment was white as

---

[1] H. P. Blavatsky, *The Secret Doctrine*, vol. 1 (London: Theosophical Publishing Company, 1888), pp. 207–208.

snow, and the hair of his head like the pure wool; his throne was like the fiery flame, and his wheels as burning fire."[2] "He is Lord of lords and King of kings."[3] This Great Being speaks of Himself: "I am alpha and omega, the beginning and the ending, . . . which is, and which was, and which is to come, the Almighty."[4]

The Vedic texts say that Sanat Kumara's body consists of Light, which penetrates the pure consciousness of enlightened yogis and endows them with supreme wisdom. The Puranas call Him "the best of sages." He is also known as Guha because of this deity's unusual origin. In Sanskrit Guha means "cave" or "hidden," for He abides in the cave of the human heart.

In addition, the sacred scriptures of Hinduism indicate that Sanat Kumara periodically comes to Earth in the form of a man out of great compassion for those who have not yet reached a high level of consciousness and would not withstand His Divine Radiance. After all, there are those who seeing but one approach of His Light have fallen dead, unable to endure such supreme vibrations.

In Buddhist texts, He appears before the assembly of Gods as Brahma Sanankumara, eclipsing them all with His radiance and glory, and every God who sat beside Him experienced a sublime feeling of joy.

However, *The Secret Doctrine* gives us to understand that Avalokiteshvara and Guanshiyin are His Image, too, one with Maitreya:

"Like Avalokiteshvara, Guanshiyin has passed through several transformations, but it is an error to say of him that he is a modern invention of the Northern Buddhists, for, under another appellation he has been known from the earliest times.

"The Secret Doctrine teaches that: 'He who is the first to appear at Renovation will be the last to come before Reabsorption [Pralaya].' Thus the Logoi of all nations, from the Vedic Vishvakarman of the Mysteries down to the Saviour of the present civilized nations, are the 'Word' who was in the 'Beginning,' or the reawakening of the energizing Powers of Nature, with the One Absolute. Born of Fire and Water, before these became distinct elements, *It* was the 'Maker,' the fashioner or modeller, of all things. 'Without him was not anything made that was made. In him was life; and the life was the light of men,' who finally may be called as he ever has been, the alpha and the omega of manifested Nature. 'The great Dragon of Wisdom is born of Fire and Water, and into Fire and Water will all be reabsorbed with him.'

---

[2] Daniel 7:9.
[3] Revelation 17:14.
[4] Revelation 1:8.

"As this Bodhisattva is said 'to assume any form he pleases' from the beginning of a Manvantara to its end, though his special birthday (memorial day) is celebrated according to the *Jin Guang Ming Jing* ("Luminous Sutra of Golden Light") in the second month on the nineteenth day, and that of Maitreya Buddha in the first month on the first day, yet the two are one. He will appear as Maitreya Buddha, the last of the Avatars and Buddhas, in the Seventh Race.[1] This belief and expectation are universal throughout the East. . . .

"Guanshiyin is Avalokiteshvara, and both are forms of the seventh Universal Principle; while in its highest metaphysical character, this deity is the synthetic aggregation of all the Planetary Spirits, Dhyani Chohans. He is the 'Self-manifested'; in short, the 'Son of the Father.' Crowned with seven dragons, above his statue there appears the inscription *Pu Ji Qun Ling*, 'the universal Saviour of all living beings.' . . .

"Guanshiyin and Guanyin are the two aspects (male and female) of the same principle in the Cosmos, Nature, and Man, of Divine Wisdom and Intelligence. They are the Christos-Sophia of the mystic Gnostics — the Logos and its Shakti."[2]

Among the Zoroastrians, He is Ahura Mazda, or the Creator, who gave revelation to Zoroaster in the form of the sacred scripture of Avesta.

Further, the Bible mentions His other Image — Melchizedek, whose name means "King of righteousness, . . . King of peace; without father, without mother, without descent, having neither beginning of days, nor end of life; but made like unto the Son of God; abideth a priest continually."[3] And Jesus Christ was "called of God a high priest after the order of Melchizedek."[4]

In the ancient Melchizedekian teaching, it was asserted that Melchizedek was the first and principal incarnation of the Supreme God, while Christ was only the image of Melchizedek. It was believed that Christ had descended upon a man, Jesus, at his baptism, and that Melchizedek was a Heavenly Power, higher than Christ. According to their teachings, Melchizedek did for Angels what Christ was to do for humankind.

Thus, by creating His Hypostases under different names to carry out certain tasks, the Nameless One acquired a multitude of names.

---

[1] In her article "The 'Doctrine of the Eye' and the 'Doctrine of the Heart,' or the 'Heart's Seal,'" Blavatsky refers to Maitreya Buddha as "the Buddha of the Sixth Race." This is neither a mistake nor a contradiction since the Sixth and Seventh Races, whose first representatives have already appeared around the world, will develop simultaneously. Maitreya is the Teacher for both. See *Race* and *Sanat Kumara* in Glossary for more, pp. 371–376 and 383–393, respectively.
[2] Blavatsky, *The Secret Doctrine*, vol. 1, pp. 470–471, 473.
[3] Hebrews 7:2–3.
[4] Hebrews 5:10.

Messengers from Distant Worlds

In the Puranas, Sanat Kumara is mentioned under the names Skanda and Kartikeya as the commander-in-chief of the Heavenly Army of the Gods, which is analogical to Archangel Michael.

In the Bible we read that with Him came 144,000 spirits, who "follow the Lamb whithersoever he goeth."[5] But from where did they all come to Earth?

In theosophical literature we find the statement that this "Army of the Gods," commanded by the Lord of the World, came from Venus at the dawn of the birth of physical humanity.[6] However, this is only a partial Truth, since Venus was merely a temporary and last stop on a long journey from the depths of the Cosmos to Earth, which lasted for an unimaginable number of years on each of the planets of the Solar System.

Of course, it should be understood that Earth is the only planet in the Cosmos closest to us on which evolution also occurs on the physical plane. Other planets and stars either occupy much higher levels of development, which do not include physical evolution, or they have not yet reached this stage.

Many peoples of the world preserve secret legends that speak of how the Gods, or Kumaras, corresponding to the Archangels, descended from the Heavens in an act of great self-sacrifice to help and instruct infant humanity, so that in the future its members could become gods. Clothing themselves in human flesh, they endowed us with reason and free will.

The origins of these legends can be traced back to ancient Egypt, to a time when people believed that their Supreme Gods came from the star system of Sirius, and that they were the founders and first pharaohs of Egyptian civilization. The New Year was celebrated when Sirius became visible in the sky, and many temples were built taking account of the celestial location of this sacred star.

In other corners of our planet, temples were built for the worship of Sirius, too, such as Stonehenge in Great Britain and Göbekli Tepe in Turkey. In the sacred scripture of the Avesta, it is said that Sirius, named *Tishtrya*, is destined to be "a lord and overseer above all stars."[7] The name of Zoroaster, who received the Avesta, means "the golden shining star" or "Golden Sirius." The Quran mentions that God is the Lord of Sirius.[8]

Ancient legends have it that millions of years ago, even before Earth had acquired stable form, the Lord of Sirius — the Lord of one of the

---

[5] Revelation 14:4.

[6] C. Jinarajadasa, *The "K. H." Letters to C. W. Leadbeater* (Adyar, Madras: Theosophical Publishing House, 1980), p. 65.

[7] James Darmesteter, translator, *The Zend-Avesta, Part II: The Sirozahs, Yasts and Nyayis* (Oxford: Oxford University Press, 1882), p. 105.

[8] Quran 53:49.

most ancient and spiritual civilizations in our galaxy, the Milky Way — gathered a cohort of Spirits from the constellations of Sirius, Orion, Pleiades, and others to enter the boundaries of the Solar System and further bring the Light of Immortality to Earth. After leaving their most beautiful Worlds, where only Love and Joy reign supreme, they plunged into the vale of grief and sorrow that is Earth.

The Great Lord of Sirius assumed responsibility for the development of the entire Solar System. His Seven Sons, who had come with Him from distant constellations, became the Regents of the planets of our Solar System, where they raised the gods, who would also join the warrior host for the salvation of earthly humanity.

When our Earth was still at the stage of its formation, these Seven were already descending onto its "surface" to prepare the conditions for a new life and for a new humanity that was preparing to take physical form.

The Secret Doctrine reads: "These Beings appear first as Gods and Creators; then they merge in nascent man, to finally emerge as 'Divine Kings and Rulers.' But this fact has been gradually forgotten."[1]

To more easily understand the composition of the Hierarchy of Light, we can use the illustration of the disintegration of the One Ray, bipolar in essence, threefold in manifestation, septenary in structure, and duodecimal in tonality, which becomes personified Beings on any given plane of Existence. However, the names cited below are given for the sake of convenience, since it is very difficult to cover all the analogies in world and ancient religions for all incarnations of certain Cosmic Ideas and Forces.

Thus, the One White Ray of Sirius is personified by its Planetary Spirit, known as Sanat Kumara, the Lord of the World. Sanat Kumara is androgynous because there is no gender separation on the higher planes of Existence — the pronoun *He* is used merely for lack of a more appropriate one. The Planetary Spirit can manifest in various Aspects and Hypostases, including male and female in the binary world, since He bears within Himself both Principles.

Upon reaching the Solar System, this Ray refracts into the White Solar Ray that represents the Solar Hierarch, or Logos, who is made manifest as the Great Masculine Principle, identical to the Supreme Deities of all religions. The Solar Hierarch can be called Christ or Maitreya, but the Father can also manifest in the Son, and therefore, the Son can bear the names of the Father. This same Ray also manifests itself as the Great Feminine Principle — the Mother of the World, or Sophia, personified as the Supreme Goddess under a variety of names. That is, Sanat Kumara is the Father of both Christ and Sophia.

---

[1] Blavatsky, *The Secret Doctrine*, vol. 2, p. 366.

In His trichotomy, the Solar Hierarch manifests as Buddha, Christ, and Maitreya (or as Brahma, Vishnu, and Shiva), while Sophia manifests as Faith, Hope, and Love.

The septenary nature of the Ray is expressed in the Seven Great Teachers, each of which personifies one of the Seven Rays, symbolizing the mastery of the corresponding layer or type of matter. And each Teacher has a Spiritual Sister. Each God has a Goddess with whom they are united in the Higher Worlds; one does not exist without the other. But, since the Masculine Principle must express itself in the visible aspect of life, and the Feminine Principle in the invisible aspect, Female Deities were revered as the most sacred and secret in all ancient religions.

In essence, the Seven Great Teachers — the Seven Rays — are the components of the One Supreme Lord, who represents the White Ray and personifies the Spiritual Sun. Thus, there is One Individuality, but His partial manifestations enlightened such earthly manifestations as Rama, Krishna, Moses, Solomon, Zoroaster, Gautama Buddha, Lao Tzu, Confucius, Jesus Christ, Muhammad, among other prophets and saints.

Each of us is a particle of this One Ray, unless by our own doing, we extinguish its Light in our hearts.

The Mother of All Saviours

Even more mysterious than the Great Lord, however, is the Mother of the World, whom the entire Hierarchy of Light sacredly honours, for She is One with Him as Spirit and Soul. She is known in Gnostic texts as Sophia, the Power and Supreme Wisdom of God, who hid Her Countenance from humanity after it terribly humiliated Woman. Fragments of the Truth about the Mother of the World were revealed solely during Initiation. It was Sophia who was first to descend to planet Earth in order not only to breathe life into it, but also to prepare the ground for the descent of the Sons of Light.

According to Blavatsky, Sophia "is the Holy Ghost and the Creator of all, as in the ancient systems. The 'Father' is a far later invention. The earliest manifested Logos was female everywhere — the mother of the seven planetary powers."[2]

Like the Lord of the World, being manifest Wisdom, She is beyond Time and Space and is able to create a multitude of Hypostases under different names that act in Her Rays. Thus, in ancient times, Sophia conducted the most important Initiations as the Eternally Young Virgin-Mother in Atlantis and as Isis in Egypt. This is why She is referred to as the *Revealer of Mysteries* in Gnostic texts.

---

[2] Blavatsky, *The Secret Doctrine*, vol. 1, p. 72.

Sophia is Wisdom, and therefore, Her Light and Influence can always be recognized where there shines Wisdom, Love, and Truth.

Despite the fact that there is no information about Sophia in canonical Christian texts, temples were built in Her honour, such as Saint Sophia Cathedral in Kyiv, Ukraine, and the Cathedral of the same name in Istanbul, Turkey, the beauty and magnificence of which was so great, even the conquerors bowed before it, and then converted the initially Christian Cathedral into the Hagia Sophia Grand Mosque. Her image was also depicted on icons, but since people could not understand who She was, these icons were often simply burnt.

In the same way, for centuries, not only was knowledge concerning the predominant role of the Feminine Principle in Cosmic Creation removed from sacred texts, but the merits of women were written out of history and often belittled, simply because they were capable of achieving more than men in the same field of work. Take for instance the episode of the brutal murder of Hypatia of Alexandria, after which the organizer of this atrocity came to be regarded as the "pillar of the faith" and one of the "Church Fathers."

We already know of the incarnations of the Great Teachers as outstanding founders of religious traditions, philosophies, the sciences, the arts, and states, but so often we fail to take into account that the Elder Sisters of humanity traversed an even more difficult, thorny path on Earth, demonstrating unsurpassed examples of self-sacrifice, heroism, and unceasing generosity.[1]

They gave Faith, Hope, and Love to the world, incarnating as mothers, sisters, daughters, and wives. They inspired all of humanity, and they are the true Saviours of the world, since without them there would not have been a single Great Teacher. Among them, there have been so many wise queens, great saints, inventive scientists, inspiring poetesses and artists in all the nations of the world.

Indeed, as Mahatma Koot Hoomi said, "on the elevation of woman the world's redemption and salvation hinge."[2]

To emancipate Woman and give her equal rights, Gautama Buddha did more than other Indian teachings before him, for he said: "A woman can achieve the highest degree of knowledge open to a man — that is, to become an Arhat. Liberation, which is beyond forms, cannot depend on gender that belongs to the world of forms."[3]

---

[1] See *Gods* in *Glossary*, pp. 313–315.

[2] Footnote by "Eminent Occultist" (Mahatma Koot Hoomi) in Éliphas Lévi, *The Paradoxes of the Highest Science* (Adyar, Madras: Theosophical Publishing House, 1922), p. 172.

[3] Helena Roerich, *Osnovy Buddizma* [Foundations of Buddhism] (Moscow: Eksmo, 2008), p. 156.

Once, Soma, a disciple of the Buddha, when asked how she, having the "limited mind of a woman," could hope to achieve knowledge and Nirvana when these are difficult even for the sages to attain, she replied: "When the heart is calmed, when consciousness opens, then you see the truth. But if anyone thinks: I am a woman or I am a man, or I am this or that, let Mara [the evil force] deal with them."[4]

Similarly, His Holiness the Dalai Lama said that the next Dalai Lama could be a woman: "With regard to compassion, there is scientific evidence that women are more sensitive to others' pain. Indeed, in human history most warriors, or killers, were men, whereas women consistently show more concern for others' well-being. In this century, we should make special efforts to promote loving kindness, and women should take a leading role in this. . . . Some years ago, the editor of a French women's magazine asked me if there could ever be a female Dalai Lama and I told her, 'Yes, of course, if she would be more effective.' In Tibetan history there is already a case of the reincarnation of a high spiritual leader being born as a woman in the lineage of Samding Dorje Phagmo."[5]

Of Mary it is said that She was no less great than Her Son.[6] And herein lies the undeniable Truth. Indeed, in order to give life to a Teacher such as Christ, Buddha, Muhammad, and others, the energy potential of the *argo* of the Mother's heart must be no less than that of the Son.

And without Mary Magdalene, the memory of Christ, who lived one century earlier than is commonly believed,[7] would have never reached us. For it was she who wrote down all four Gospels under different names, being the only highly educated disciple among all the followers of Christ.[8]

Evidence of this Truth is hidden in the Sinai caves, and awaits the hour when at least a small portion of humanity will be able to perceive it. And when this day comes, then, as Blavatsky said, the manuscripts that reveal the true sources of Christianity, but which are considered to have been destroyed by the "fathers of the church," will "reappear in a 'most

---

[4] Roerich, *Osnovy Buddizma*, p. 156.

[5] "Interaction with Young FICCI Ladies Organization," *The Office of His Holiness the Dalai Lama*, https://www.dalailama.com/news/2019/interaction-with-young-ficci-ladies-organisation.

[6] Helena Roerich, *Agni Yoga s kommentariyami* [Agni Yoga with comments], vol. 2 (Moscow: Eksmo, 2010), p. 838.

[7] See the footnote by "Eminent Occultist" (Mahatma Koot Hoomi) in Lévi, *The Paradoxes of the Highest Science*, p. 53; H. P. Blavatsky, "Notes on Abbé Roca's 'Esotericism of Christian Dogma,'" *Collected Writings*, vol. 8 (Wheaton, IL: Theosophical Publishing House, 1960), p. 380.

[8] Helena Roerich, *Pis'ma* [Letters], vol. 8 (Moscow: Mezhdunarodnyy tsentr Rerikhov, 2008), p. 127; Helena Roerich, "Zapisi besed s Uchitelem (kosmicheskoye sotrudnichestvo)" [Records of conversations with the Master (cosmic cooperation)], 27.04.1952–21.08.1952, fol. 46, Roerich Museum, Moscow.

unexpected and almost miraculous manner.' . . . Is it so strange that the custodians of 'Pagan' lore, seeing that the proper moment had arrived, should cause the needed document, book, or relic to fall as if by accident in the right man's way?"[1]

Guarded Until the Right Time

And here we need not look far to find an example that would illustrate how this protection mechanism works. Suffice to mention how Blavatsky's work, hidden in plain sight and concerning the secret subject of Shambhala and the Masters, was safeguarded until the right time.

According to Bertram Keightley, who assisted her in preparing *The Secret Doctrine* for publication and later in editing her magazine in London, Blavatsky, in addition to her own editorials, also wrote "many other articles under more than one *nom de plume*."[2]

Her letters were published in Russia between 1879 and 1886 — later they comprised the book *From the Caves and Jungles of Hindostan*[3] — under the pseudonym Radda-Bai in order to separate this story from her controversial person in the eyes of the mass readership in Russia, who could only have heard about her in a strange and negative light. The book uses fiction to describe the events that happened to Blavatsky during her travels across India. It is in the pages of this book that the beautiful and majestic image of her Master, Mahatma Morya, was presented for the first time. The book ends with the promise "To be continued" and the editor's footnote which reads: "No continuation of this story has ever been found, either in published form or in manuscripts in spite of a far-reaching search."[4]

But in fact, a continuation did exist and had been prepared by Blavatsky. The last part of her adventures in India to be published appeared in August 1886 but was not continued because a campaign against Blavatsky had begun in Russia, and the editor of the magazine did not wish to risk his reputation. Her books were banned in the Russian Empire and later in the Soviet Union.

At this time Blavatsky was also experiencing a flurry of criticism in the West, and so, in 1886, she entrusted the manuscripts concerning her visit to the Abodes of Shambhala, located in the Alps and the Himalayas,

---

[1] H. P. Blavatsky, *Isis Unveiled*, vol. 2 (New York: J. W. Bouton, 1877), pp. 390–401.
[2] Bertram Keightley, *Reminiscences of H.P.B.* (Adyar, Madras: Theosophical Publishing House, 1931), p. 21.
[3] See H. P. Blavatsky, *From the Caves and Jungles of Hindostan* (Wheaton, IL: Theosophical Publishing House, 1975). This edition by Boris de Zirkoff is the only full translation of the book. All other editions contain the incomplete translation by Vera Johnston, Blavatsky's niece, originally published in 1892.
[4] Blavatsky, *From the Caves and Jungles of Hindostan*, p. 660.

to Franz Hartmann,[5] so that he, after slightly editing the notes, could compile them into a book and publish it anonymously in 1887 under the title *An Adventure Among the Rosicrucians*. However, twenty years after Blavatsky's death, in 1910, he nevertheless admitted in his preface to the new edition, *With the Adepts*, that he was not the original author, and had only gathered into a single whole notes that he had received from "a writer of considerable repute."[6]

However, over all this time, no one thought to investigate who that writer was, if not Hartmann. And for a hundred years, as if nothing had happened, everyone continued to attribute authorship to him, despite the fact that he had already acknowledged that it did not.

Furthermore, reference to the authorship of this particular book by Hartmann can be found in a letter belonging to Helena Roerich,[7] who, being in the twentieth century under the direction of the same Teachers of the East who had guided Blavatsky, was in a position to correctly identify what was given by her predecessor. This letter in Russian was published in various collections of her letters, which, from the early 1990s onwards, were printed in tens of thousands of copies, and in the early 2000s were read even more widely online, since the Roerich movement was particularly active at this time throughout the post-Soviet territory. Nevertheless, not one among this enormous readership noticed what exactly Helena Roerich had written.

Only in 2015, thanks to Roerich's prompting, was this book accidentally discovered as being one of Blavatsky's hidden works. Then, in 2022, as *The Land of the Gods*, it was published for the first time under the name of its true author, who, furthermore, promised her readers a "continuation" of her adventures.

This analogy gives us to understand how it is possible that a treasury with all its secret knowledge and manuscripts can be hidden right beneath our feet in the midst of a crowded place, where every day thousands of tourists pass, and yet no one will ever suspect its presence, unless the revelation accords with Higher Will, which takes into account the readiness of humanity.

For the same reason of humanity's unpreparedness, the Masters cannot reveal Blavatsky's previous incarnations, since at the present time, many would be shocked by the role she has played in our history, and this would result purely in an even more furious denial. However, were

---

[5] See *Hartmann, Franz* and *Land of the Gods* in *Glossary* for more details, pp. 317–319 and 336–337, respectively.

[6] Franz Hartmann, *With the Adepts* (New York: Theosophical Publishing Co, 1910), p. v.

[7] Helena Roerich, *Pis'ma* [Letters], vol. 6 (Moscow: Mezhdunarodnyy tsentr Rerikhov, 2006), p. 513.

this information to be revealed, it would become clear why it had to be from her pen that we received such fundamental works as *Isis Unveiled* and *The Secret Doctrine* — works that restore the Truth that has been so distorted by the Church.

Chintamani

Aside from sacred relics created by the hearts of saints on Earth, there also exists the Treasure of the World — the magical Chintamani Stone, which figures under different names in the legends of all the peoples of the world.

Ancient legends of the East have it that the magical Stone is held in the mysterious Kingdom of Shambhala, and that a part of the Stone travels around the world, being referred to as the Grail. The Stone was formed as a *ringsel* on the sacred star of Sirius when it was still in the constellation of Orion, and fell to Earth millions of years ago as a "Gift of the Gods." The Forces of Light protect it as the apple of their eye. Since it carries within itself a powerful cosmic force that is capable of influencing the entire world, the minions of darkness have repeatedly attempted to take possession of it in order to establish their power over the planet.

At certain periods in time, a "wandering" fragment of the Chintamani Stone is sent to individuals who must fulfil a special historical mission. It is usually delivered by totally unexpected persons and methods, and disappears in a manner equally as unusual when the time comes. Solomon, Tamerlane, and Akbar the Great were all in possession of the stone. At the same time, Alexander the Great and Napoleon Bonaparte, to whom the fragment was also gifted, neglected the conditions set, and the stone left them along with their former unprecedented luck and success.

This precious stone also entered into the possession of the Fifth Dalai Lama, when it was gifted to him by Gushi Khan from the Lord of the World after the Khan's victory over the opponents of the Gelug school. It then passed into the hands of the last ruler of the Oirats, Amursana. Before fleeing to Russia in 1757, Amursana sent the sacred stone to Urga, Mongolia, where it remained with the Jebtsundamba Khutuktu, the spiritual head of the Gelug school in Mongolia, until the early nineteenth century. It then disappeared and ended up in the hands of Napoleon, whom it soon abandoned. The treasure was then carefully guarded in Paris, France, awaiting new owners.

In the twentieth century, the Chintamani fragment came into the possession of the Roerich family: Helena Roerich, who gave the wonderful *Agni Yoga* series to the world in collaboration with the Teachers of the East, and whose *Foundations of Buddhism* was at the time recognized by the Maha Bodhi Society as the best popular introduction to the Buddha's teaching; the brilliant artist and prolific writer Nicholas Roerich; and their sons — George, a prominent orientalist and specialist in the language and culture of Tibet, and Svetoslav, a distinguished artist.

In 1950, His Holiness the Dalai Lama met for the first time with the eldest son of the Roerichs, George. According to Professor Ram Rahul, who headed the Department of Central Asian Studies at the Jawaharlal Nehru University in Delhi, India, the Dalai Lama later told him: "No one knows Tibet like George de Roerich."[1]

On the morning of 6 October 1923, a courier from the Bankers Trust knocked on the door of the room at the Lord Byron Hotel in Paris, where the Roerich family was staying. The 21-year-old George opened the doors and received an unusual parcel, on which, in place of the sender's address, were the words written in French: "At the request of M.M."

The parcel box contained a casket made in Rothenburg in the thirteenth century. It was covered with a piece of leather inscribed with alchemical symbols, once owned by King Solomon. The famous Rabbi Moses de León, the compiler of the *Zohar*, being persecuted like other Jews in Spain, found protection in a German feudal lady, who admitted him and other Rabbis into her mansion. In gratitude, he gave her this precious piece of leather and a talisman — the Chintamani fragment that was in his possession at that time. The feudal lady ordered that a casket be made from the leather, and since then the Treasure of the World has been kept in it.

When the Roerichs opened the casket, the fragment of the Chintamani Stone rested on an ancient cloth embroidered with a shining sun. In the centre of that beautiful fabric was the inscription I.H.S., which in Latin stands for *in hoc signo*, meaning "by this sign [you will triumph]."

According to the memoirs of the Roerichs' closest colleague, Sina Fosdick, this sacred stone performed true miracles: it radiated warmth and could move around on the table.[2]

And in the writings of Nicholas Roerich we read: "The stone is black, unbridled, and fragrant and it is called the Principle of the World. And it moves as if it were animate. . . . When the stone is hot, when the stone trembles, when the stone changes colour, by these phenomena the stone predicts the future for the owner and enables him to recognize enemies and danger or happy events."[3] "Symbols are revealed on the stone, either

---

[1] Ram Rahul, "Velichayshiy sredi tibetologov" [The greatest among Tibetologists], *Rerikhovskiy vestnik*, no. 5 (1992), p. 68.

[2] Sina Fosdick, *Vospominaniya o Rerikhakh* [Memories of the Roerichs] (Moscow: Eksmo, 2014), p. 256.

[3] Nicholas Roerich, *Vrata v budushcheye* [Gateway to the future] (Moscow: Eksmo, 2010), p. 522.

appearing or going deep inside it.... The stone makes a cracking noise in certain instances. It can become particularly heavy or, the opposite, it can decrease in weight. Sometimes the stone begins to glow.... The stone has many qualities; it is not for nothing that all sorts of legends and songs have been composed about it."[1]

Photograph of the Chintamani Stone taken by the Roerichs in 1923.

The Buddha's Alms Bowl

Besides the Chintamani Stone, there are a number of other sacred objects that belong to the Great Teachers. One of these is the Buddha's alms bowl.

According to ancient legends, the four Guardians of the World, who came from the four cardinal directions, offered alms bowls made of sapphire to Gautama Buddha, but he refused to accept them. Again, they offered the four bowls made of a mango-coloured stone and this time, full of compassion for the four Guardians, he accepted them. To avoid disappointing any one of them, he placed one bowl inside another and commanded: Let there be one! And they miraculously transformed into one bowl. Moreover, along its rim the four layers that made up the full thickness of the new bowl could be seen. Then the Buddha took food in this newly made alms bowl and, having eaten his fill, gave thanks.[2]

---

[1] Roerich, *Vrata v budushcheye*, p. 997.

[2] Nicholas Roerich, *Shambala. Serdtse Azii* [Shambhala. Heart of Asia] (Moscow: Eksmo, 2010), pp. 90–91.

INTRODUCTION

Helena Roerich wrote in 1936: "The Chalice of Amrita, the Chalice of Beauty and Heroic Deeds, the Chalice of the Grail! After all, the legend of the Holy Grail also came from the East as one version of the great spiritual deed and that same mysterious Shambhala. Some researchers studying the symbolism associated with the Holy Grail see the Chalice as a Stone that is now in the material world and will accompany historical events, after which it will return home to the Heart of Asia. This interpretation is also close to the truth. However, a bowl exists also, and is sent before the dawn of the New Era to where the Teaching of the Kalachakra will be affirmed. There are also many legends about this bowl. One has it that the bowl always appears unexpectedly and through the air. At one time, it was brought to the Lord Buddha. This bowl is Egyptian in origin, and the degree of its antiquity is determined to be approximately twelve thousand years before the birth of Christ. After the Buddha's death, the bowl was at one time held in a Temple in Karasahr from where it subsequently disappeared. Since then, it has been held for safekeeping in Shambhala. All the legends associated with this bowl assert that it will appear again before the New Epoch of Maitreya (or perhaps it has appeared already)."[3]

The note in parentheses was not made by chance, since on 3 March 1934, the Buddha's bowl was found in a small wooden box that was discovered in the Roerichs' mansion in the Kullu Valley, in the living room on a shelf, placed among sacred books near the triptych *Fiat Rex!*, at the feet of the Lord Maitreya. It was sent to their house in a miraculous way two or three months earlier from the area near Lake Lop Nur.

The Buddha's alms bowl received by the Roerichs in 1934.

Svetoslav Roerich writes of the bowl: "This great sacred relic (I call it a relic, for it belongs to the Great Hierarchy of Buddhas) has appeared again, thereby confirming the prophecy given thousands of years ago."[4]

---

[3] Helena Roerich, *Pis'ma* [Letters], vol. 4 (Moscow: Mezhdunarodnyy tsentr Rerikhov, 2002), p. 127.

[4] Svetoslav Roerich, *Pis'ma* [Letters], vol. 1 (Moscow: Mezhdunarodnyy tsentr Rerikhov, 2004), p. 137.

And in another letter: "I have collected all the information available here in a small book along with my own description of the bowl. I will now cite the translation of a small fragment from *Xuanzang's Travels*, written some eleven to twelve centuries ago. . . .

"I quote verbatim: 'The Buddha's bowl moved about from place to place, passing mysteriously through the air and working miracles for the good of the people until it passed out of sight in the palace of the Dragon King Sagara [in Shambhala]. There it will remain until the advent of Maitreya as Buddha when it will appear again to be a witness. According to some texts the bowl was broken once by the wicked King Mihirakula, but the pieces seem to have come together again. As no one less than a Buddha could ever eat from this bowl, so no one less than a Buddha could move it from its resting-place; borne by the hidden impulses of human karma it floated about from one chosen seat to another as Buddhism waxed or waned.'[1]

"Yes, truly, the time has come! I date the bowl to be between ten and twelve thousand years old. It has a water pattern on it that could be associated with the sign of Aquarius."[2]

In one of their conversations, the Master told Helena Roerich that before the bowl came into the possession of Gautama Buddha, it belonged to a Great Teacher of ancient Egypt[3] and was made of a special stone,[4] which has the appearance of clay.

Sina Fosdick saw this relic when she visited Svetoslav Roerich in Bangalore in 1961. This is how she describes the event in her diary:

"On 12 February, I saw the Lord Buddha's alms bowl, which was miraculously transferred to Helena Roerich. In the morning Svetoslav took me to his studio and showed me this great relic and holy treasure of the world, the Lord Buddha's alms bowl. He also gave me his article which contained a detailed description of the bowl and the sketches of the drawings he made of it. I read it. It is impossible to describe the feelings you have when you look at this sacred object and then again, when he let me hold it. It is over five thousand years old (he said). Tears come to your eyes when you gaze at it.

"The bowl is made of clay, is brownish in colour with light patches, and fingerprints are clearly discernible on the external surface, i.e., the imprint of the Buddha's hand from when he held it; it sits neatly in

---

[1] Thomas Watters, *On Yuan Chwang's Travels in India* (London, Royal Asiatic Society, 1904), p. 203.

[2] Svetoslav Roerich, *Pis'ma*, vol. 1, p. 187–188.

[3] Helena Roerich, *Zapisi Ucheniya Zhivoy Etiki* [Records of the Teaching of Living Ethics], vol. 14 (Wismar-Vologda, 2012), p. 171.

[4] Helena Roerich, *Zapisi Ucheniya Zhivoy Etiki* [Records of the Teaching of Living Ethics], vol. 9 (Moscow, 2010), p. 199.

the palm; there is a sense of it having great density and power. On the inside there are four sections in the form of triangles, a series of deeply imprinted lines, which together resemble a double 'M' in a wave-like pattern, and there is a crack down the side. It evokes a feeling of huge ancientness. According to legends and traditions, the bowl would appear and disappear, flying through the air to the country and place where it was destined to be. Chinese travellers described it in the fifth and seventh centuries in India and Persia in Buddhist monasteries, where it was held temporarily. It came to Helena and Nicholas Roerich in a miraculous manner, wrapped in very old, worn material. It is now in Svetoslav's care. George took the Stone with him when he left for his motherland. After his death, Svetoslav brought the Stone with him here. . . .

"The Buddha's bowl came into the Roerichs' safekeeping in December 1933. It was delivered personally by the Great Lord and given to Helena. Nicholas was with her at the time, and left after that. He was with us in America in March 1934. Svetoslav saw the bowl rising up in the air. It is of deep antiquity, existing even before the Buddha, and used by the ancient Great Teachers. It was in Tibet for the longest, but also in Egypt and India. Such sacred objects are able to move of their own accord when the time comes for them to do so. The same is true now. When necessary, the Stone will also leave, but for now they are both here."[5]

It is also known that in 1931 Helena Roerich received 24 fragments of another meteorite from the constellation of Orion, twelve of which were sent to New York. All these sacred relics were essential to her during her Fiery Experience in order to maintain special power lines connected with Shambhala and the Treasure stored there — the Chintamani Stone.

Shambhala

At the site where the Chintamani Stone fell from the Heavens — then a wonderful island amidst a raging ocean — the Great Teachers founded the Brotherhood of Light, now known as Shambhala. This land is guarded by mystical forces that will ever prevent unbidden guests from discovering it, even with the help of the most advanced methods or technologies, either from land, sea, or air.

Being the cradle of the first human being, Shambhala is imprinted in many legends of the world as something fabulously beautiful and accessible only to the few: the Land of the Gods, the White Island, Mount Meru, the Pure Land, the Garden of Eden, and even the Invisible World Government. In a word, this mysterious Kingdom, located at the intersection of three worlds, has as many names as its "Nameless" Supreme Lord.

---

[5] Sina Fosdick, "Indiyskiy dnevnik (1961)" [Indian diary 1961], *Vestnik Ariavarty*, no. 1–2 (2003), pp. 85–86.

Blavatsky writes in *The Secret Doctrine*: "Tradition says, and the records of the Great Book (the *Book of Dzyan*) explain, that long before the days of Adam, and his inquisitive wife, Eve, where now are found but salt lakes and desolate barren deserts, there was a vast inland sea, which extended over Middle Asia, north of the proud Himalayan range, and its western prolongation. An island, which for its unparalleled beauty had no rival in the world, was inhabited by the last remnant of the race which preceded ours. . . .

"This race could live with equal ease in water, air, or fire, for it had an unlimited control over the elements. These were the 'Sons of God'; not those who saw the daughters of men, but the real *Elohim*, though in the oriental Kabbalah they have another name. It was they who imparted Nature's most weird secrets to men, and revealed to them the ineffable, and now *lost* 'word.'

"The 'Island,' according to belief, exists to the present hour; now, as *an oasis* surrounded by the dreadful wildernesses of the great desert, the Gobi — whose sands 'no foot hath crossed in the memory of man.'

"This word, which is no word, has travelled once around the globe, and still lingers as a far-off dying echo in the hearts of some privileged men. The hierophants of all the Sacerdotal Colleges were aware of the existence of this island; but the 'word' was known only to the *Java Aleim* (Maha Chohan in another tongue), or chief lord of every college, and was passed to his successor only at the moment of death. There were many such colleges, and the old classic authors speak of them.

"There was no communication with the fair island by sea, but subterranean passages, known only to the chiefs, communicated with it in all directions."[1]

Master Hilarion also mentions these secret paths beneath the oceans: "It takes about a half hour of your time for us to pass from one continent to another, but you must remember that we use a form of energy of which you are not yet conscious."[2]

The subject of Shambhala is so sacred that, in ancient times, everyone who visited this Realm was obliged to take a vow of silence. Thus, one of the monks of Kyivan Rus' (modern Ukraine), who spent some time there in the tenth century, could speak of his journey only on his deathbed "from mouth to ear," and each new carrier of the secret was bound by the same vow. However, the vow could be broken if there was at least one person who wanted to know about this fabulous land and persistently enquired after it. However, such a person did not appear

---

[1] Blavatsky, *The Secret Doctrine*, vol. 2, p. 220.
[2] Francia La Due, *The Temple of Mysteries* (New York: Radiant Books, 2023), p. 232.

for nearly a thousand years. Only in 1943 was the vow removed and the story soon thereafter published in a Russian-language newspaper in the United States.[3]

This serves as another reason why Blavatsky could not openly publish the story of her own journey to Shambhala in her lifetime — people simply were not interested, nor were they ready to comprehend it. Since there was no demand, Blavatsky could not break the vow of silence.

Each Initiate must adhere to the Law of Commensurability, while abiding by the two opposing yet equally true principles: "The Truth must be kept secret" and "The Truth must be divulged." After all, a secret revealed prematurely to the unprepared consciousness of humanity could do more harm than good.

Therefore, Blavatsky veiled her narrative in the story of the Rosicrucians, which, in the nineteenth century, could have been better received by readers in the West. And then she gave all the notes to Franz Hartmann, so that the undeserved hatred that was hurled upon her would not stain such a sacred subject, as had been the case with the names of the Great Teachers, whose existence Blavatsky was the first to reveal to the West.

It is known now that Helena, Nicholas, and George Roerich visited Shambhala, although during their lifetimes only their closest colleagues were aware of the fact. In his painting, *Burning of Darkness* (1924), Nicholas Roerich depicted Mahatma Morya holding a casket with the Chintamani fragment in his hands, and among other members of the Brotherhood, dressed in white clothes and emerging from a secret crevice in the mountains, we can see three figures standing together, one woman and two men, in whose image we may recognize Helena, Nicholas, and George. The painting's precise depiction of the glacier near Everest was recognized by the participants of an expedition to this mountain, and they could not understand, "how this characteristic view, seen only by them, had found its way into the painting."[4]

The Roerichs, too, faced the unreadiness of humanity to know the Truth about Shambhala, and therefore, the last book in the *Agni Yoga* series, which reveals the inner life of the Brotherhood, was not published until the 1990s.

Nevertheless, bits of information still reached us, such as the incident when one of the Roerichs' acquaintances in America, in a conversation with George, expressed his doubt as to the real existence of Shambhala. To this George responded that he himself had been there and showed his acquaintance on a map that the hidden route to Shambhala passed from

---

[3] See V.G., *The Kingdom of White Waters* (New York: Radiant Books, 2022).
[4] Roerich, *Altay — Gimalai*, p. 47; Fosdick, *Vospominaniya o Rerikhakh*, p. 229.

the Tanggu La.¹ And then, after an exhibition of his father's paintings in the USSR, a woman came up to him and asked: "Does Shambhala really exist?" He looked into her eyes and after a period of silence replied: "Yes, I myself have been there."²

Andrew Tomas, a renowned explorer of the unknown, who used the term *Ancient Aliens* long before the popular documentary series of the same name, recalls:

"A Russian member of Roerich's expedition told me that... for no apparent reason the Tibetans, Mongols, and Chinese refused to go further at one spot in northern Tibet. He himself admitted that he could not understand why he did not feel like riding any further — it was weird and inexplicable. Yet Nicholas Roerich went into that territory on a pony. He remained absent for a few days and, when he returned, the Asiatics prostrated themselves at his feet exclaiming that he was a 'god' for no man could have penetrated the frontier of Shambhala without divine credentials."³

In his book *Trails to Inmost Asia*, George de Roerich writes: "The doctrine of Shambhala is the hidden doctrine of Tibet and Mongolia, and His Holiness the Tashi Lama [the Ninth Panchen Lama] is regarded as the chief expounder of the doctrine in this world.

"Since the departure of the present Tashi Lama in 1923, the doctrine received a powerful new impulse, and numerous Kalachakra colleges were established by His Holiness himself in inner Mongolia and Buddhist China. Even in distant Buryatia is to be observed the same movement. Most of the monasteries establish special Kalachakra colleges with a special staff of lamas to officiate in them. Shambhala is not only considered to be the abode of hidden Buddhist learning, it is the guiding principle of the coming *kalpa* or cosmic age. Learned abbots and meditating lamas are said to be in constant communication with this mystic fraternity, that guides the destinies of the Buddhist world. A western observer is apt to belittle the importance of this name or to relegate the voluminous literature about Shambhala and the still vaster oral tradition into the class of folklore or mythology; but those who have studied both literary and popular Buddhism know the terrific force that this name possesses among the masses of Buddhists of higher Asia. For in the course of history, it has not only inspired religious movements but even moved armies, whose war cry was the name of Shambhala. . . .

---

¹ Nicholas Roerich, *Put' v Shambalu* [The path to Shambhala] (Moscow: Eksmo, 2011), p. 36.
² *Vospominaniya o Y. N. Rerikhe* [Memories of George de Roerich] (Novosibirsk: Novosibirskoye Rerikhovskoye Obshchestvo, 1994), pp. 26, 32.
³ Andrew Tomas, *Shambhala: Oasis of Light* (London: Sphere Books, 1977), p. 58.

"In the past great names in the Buddhist hierarchy of Mongolia and Tibet dedicated whole volumes to the doctrine of the Kalachakra and Shambhala."[4]

In the eighteenth century, His Holiness the Sixth Panchen Lama wrote a whole book, *The Journey to Shambhala*,[5] in which the location of this mysterious Kingdom is indicated via a huge number of symbols. Of course, as in the case of the alchemists' philosopher's stone, Shambhala must first be found in one's own pure heart — only then will the symbolism of the Panchen Lama's "guidebook" become clear, and the Path to Shambhala be found, not only in dreams, but in waking reality.

When Dr. Edwin Bernbaum, author of *The Way to Shambhala*, suggested in an audience with His Holiness the Dalai Lama that it was simply an immaterial or imaginary paradise for the mind, he replied: "No, definitely not: Shambhala has a material existence in this world." And then: "If so many Kalachakra texts are supposed to have come from Shambhala, how could the country be just a fantasy?"[6]

According to this well-researched work, there are three types of journey into this Pure Land: dream, spiritual, and physical.[7]

While spiritual travel and journeys in the dream state are a common means for those who have achieved the necessary purity of soul and spirit, only very few have been honoured with the opportunity of entering Shambhala physically. The problem is not that those who dwell in Shambhala are afraid that their location will be made public, but rather that this sacred city is situated in the most energetically powerful place on our planet. Similarly, its other Abodes across all continents are founded in special places that are associated with certain celestial bodies and constellations, and that represent accumulators of high-frequency cosmic currents.

In order to withstand such vibrational intensity, the physical body of the person invited there must be exceptionally pure, since even a slight admixture of some kind of poison will threaten the death of one's flesh. Therefore, there are a number of Abodes around the main Stronghold (and by the same analogy on other continents), where the intensity of energies is not so high, and to which pilgrims may be admitted, provided

---

[4] George N. Roerich, *Trails to Inmost Asia* (New Haven, CT: Yale University Press, 1931), pp. 156–157.

[5] This book was translated into German by Albert Grünwedel in 1915. Its English translation from German by His Eminence Tsem Rinpoche can be read and downloaded at: https://www.tsemrinpoche.com/tsem-tulku-rinpoche/great-lamas-masters/the-mythical-land-of-shambhala.html.

[6] Edwin Bernbaum, *The Way to Shambhala* (Los Angeles: Jeremy P. Tarcher, 1989), pp. 10, 27.

[7] Bernbaum, *The Way to Shambhala*, p. 157.

that their motive for seeking Shambhala is pure. Alternatively, they may there be assigned a certain mission that is to be further implemented among humanity.

Only those who are pure in heart and who are karmically connected with Shambhala can be invited to enter. Of course, the potential of the *ringsel* crystal in the human heart also plays a decisive role, since it serves as a kind of permit and allows one to move through the protective energy shield that guards the lands of this Kingdom.

The Masters of Wisdom

Without our Guides, the Teachers of Shambhala, who sacrificed themselves for the sake of all humanity and constantly help us at all stages of development, we would still be living in caves, not much different from animals. But it is better to cite Blavatsky's words about them:

"Well, I told him [H. S. Olcott] the whole truth. I said to him that I had known Adepts, the 'Brothers,' not only in India and beyond Ladakh, but in Egypt and Syria — for there are 'Brothers' there to this day. The names of the 'Mahatmas' were not even known at the time, since they are called so only in India. That, whether they were called Rosicrucians, Kabbalists, or Yogis — Adepts were everywhere Adepts — silent, secret, retiring, and who would never divulge themselves entirely to anyone, unless one did as I did — passed seven and ten years probation and gave proofs of absolute devotion, and that he, or she, would keep silent even before a prospect and a threat of death. I fulfilled the requirements and am what I am; and this no Hodgson, no Coulombs, no Sellin, can take away from me.

"All I was allowed to say was — the truth: There is beyond the Himalayas a nucleus of Adepts, of various nationalities; and the Tashi Lama [the Eighth Panchen Lama] knows them, and they act together, and some of them are with him and yet remain unknown in their true character even to the average lamas — who are ignorant fools mostly. My Master [Morya] and K[oot] H[oomi] and several others I know personally are there, coming and going, and they are all in communication with Adepts in Egypt and Syria, and even Europe. I said and proved that they could perform marvellous phenomena; but I also said that it was rarely they would condescend to do so to satisfy enquirers."[1]

"We have received our doctrines from those who do not need, in order to explore and learn the mysteries of the Universe, to avail themselves of either the disincarnate spirits or their 'shells,' and what an enormous advantage that is! . . . For them, the evidence is not second-hand,

---

[1] "Letters of H.P.B. to Dr. Hartmann," *The Path*, vol. 10 (1895–1896), pp. 369–370.

nor post-mortem, but really the evidence of their own faculties, purified and prepared through long years to receive it correctly and without any foreign influence that would make them deviate from the straight road.

"For thousands of years, one Initiate after another, one great Hierophant succeeded by other Hierophants, has explored and re-explored the invisible Universe, the worlds of the interplanetary regions, during long periods when his conscious soul, united to the spiritual soul and to the All, free and almost omnipotent, left his body. It is not only the Initiates belonging to the 'Great Brotherhood of the Himalayas,' who give us these doctrines; it is not only the Buddhist Arhats who teach them, but they are found in the secret writings of Shankaracharya, of Gautama Buddha, of Zoroaster, as well as in those of the Rishis. The mysteries of life as well as of death, of the visible and invisible worlds, have been fathomed and observed by initiated Adepts in all epochs and in all nations. They have studied these during the solemn moments of union of their divine monad with the universal Spirit, and they have recorded their experiences."[2]

"My Masters and the Masters are Yogis and Munis *de facto*, not *de jure*; in their life not in appearance. They *are* members of an *occult Brotherhood*, not of any particular school in India. One of their highest Maha Chohans lived in Egypt and went to Tibet only a year before we did (in 1878) and he is neither a Tibetan nor a Hindu; this occult Brotherhood has not originated in Tibet, nor is it *only* in Tibet now; but what I always said and maintain to this day is, *that most of its members and some of the highest* are, and live constantly, in Tibet, because of its isolation . . . that its origin is of untold antiquity, and is as much Masonic as present Masonry is *little* Masonic."[3]

Moreover, many famous scientists from the most diverse fields of science, who brought discoveries to the world, were and are guided by the Great Teachers, they themselves being unaware of this. Helena Roerich explains: "In his time, the approach of the prominent chemist Crookes to the Teaching of Light gave him the opportunity to discover radiant matter.[4] And if he had continued this approach, then it would have become his destiny to make a second, even more important discovery. The Great Teachers can help in the search for new formulas only where an unprejudiced consciousness and sufficient scientific preparation are present. It

---

[2] H. P. Blavatsky, "Theosophy and Spiritism," *Collected Writings*, vol. 5 (Wheaton, IL: Theosophical Publishing House, 1969), pp. 50–51.

[3] Manly P. Hall, "Madame Blavatsky — A Tribute," *Theosophia* (May–June 1947), p. 10.

[4] See William Crookes, "On Radiant Matter," *Popular Science Monthly*, vol. 16 (1879), pp. 13–24, 157–167.

is impossible to guide towards a significant discovery a consciousness that is not prepared for such perception."[1]

For those who need material evidence of the Masters' existence, *The Mahatma Letters* should be mentioned, as from these one can learn firsthand about their worldview, values, and philosophy.[2] However, it should be borne in mind that the Mahatmas spoke to their correspondents in accordance with their nineteenth-century consciousness, inclined as it was to materialism, and which, therefore, could not assimilate the ideas and concepts that were new for that time.

The handwritten originals of these letters are now kept in the British Library. Belonging to Mahatmas Koot Hoomi and Morya, they were delivered to many individuals in a phenomenal manner called *precipitation*. Some of them look like they were printed on a dot matrix printer or faxed, for which there is still no explanation.

The only "explanation" that Blavatsky's vocal critics managed to find is that she simply forged them all. However, if this were true, the British Museum would never have accepted them into its collection in 1939 after the handwriting of Blavatsky and the Masters had been examined. As an aside, the same collection also contains a short letter from the Eighth Panchen Lama to Blavatsky, sent from Tashi Lhunpo Monastery.

Another example of proof lies in the counsels of Mahatma Morya to President Franklin D. Roosevelt, which were given through Helena Roerich, to help him solve a number of problems that the United States was facing at that time.

Throughout history, Shambhala has always attempted to assist the leaders of various countries at turning points in their development, when the karma of nations allowed it. So it became known as the World Government, although it has nothing in common with now widespread conspiracy theories about a small group of rich individuals who rule the whole world behind the scenes — these figures have always been the adversaries of Shambhala and all its messengers.

Those countries that accepted the Assistance offered flourished, but those that rejected the outstretched Hand fell into decline. However, before the correspondence between Helena Roerich and Roosevelt was revealed in the twentieth century, apart from fragmentary historical evidence that bore a greater resemblance to legend, not a single piece of concrete evidence proving instances of Assistance from the Great Teachers was preserved, despite the fact that there is not a single nation in the

---

[1] Helena Roerich, *Pis'ma*, vol. 6, p. 380.
[2] These letters were transcribed and published in three books: *The Mahatma Letters to A. P. Sinnett* (1923) and two volumes of *Letters from the Masters of the Wisdom* (1919 and 1925).

entire world to which such Assistance would not have been offered via the person of special ambassadors from distant and high Mountains.[3]

Even the speech of the mysterious stranger, once quoted by President Ronald Reagan[4] — the speech of Mahatma Rakoczy, also known as the Count of Saint-Germain — that led to the independence of the United States of America in 1776, was never included in any official record, although it was published in one book.[5] For to erase, belittle, and make fictional any trace of the Masters throughout history is one of the tasks taken up by the opponents of Shambhala mentioned above.

A Warning from Shambhala

In 1966, Andrew Tomas visited a temple near Darjeeling, India, where he had the honour of conversing with a highly spiritual lama from Lhasa. It is not known whether the temple was Ghoom Monastery or some other temple, but the message that Tomas received from the lama completely coincides with what Blavatsky and the Roerichs conveyed to the world.

At first, using special techniques, the lama showed Tomas a vision of the state of the planet in the reflection of a pool, whose waters were similar to those of sacred Lake Lhamo Latso in which visions appear when Tibetan monks search for the birthplace of the future Dalai Lama. Here is what he saw:

"Unexpectedly I began to see pictures in it with utmost clarity as if I were watching the screen of a colour television set. . . . The first scene was our planet in space with its great oceans, continents, and masses of cloud formations like a NASA space television broadcast. In a minute or two the appearance of the globe began to change radically. Heavy grey, black, brown, and red clouds covered the more populated parts of the earth. Occasionally this mass was pierced by fiery red flashes as if from explosions. At times light blue, rose, or golden rays and stars arose from the dark background to brighten it. But the whole planet was swamped by an enormous aura of dark ugly colours.

"'You are observing the mental and emotional vibrations emitted by mankind and, as you can see, their quality is low — look at that grey fog of selfishness. The blue sparks are spiritual aspirations of the minority, blotted out by the mass thoughts of passion, hatred, and greed which

---

[3] See Helena Roerich, *The Divine Government* (New York: Radiant Books, 2023).

[4] See Ronald Reagan, "Commencement Address at Eureka College (June 7, 1957)," *PBS Online*, http://web.archive.org/web/20210917160011/http://www.shoppbs.pbs.org/wgbh/amex/reagan/filmmore/reference/primary/eureka.html.

[5] See *Rakoczy* in *Glossary* for more information about the speech, pp. 376–378.

have formed this gigantic aura around the planet in the course of thousands of years. It is just like the ionized layers around the earth which reflect radio waves,' explained the lama. It was a startling disclosure to see with my own eyes the extensive mental shell surrounding the earth.

"'Our planet is sick due to man's wrong thinking,' I whispered. At times the dark clouds protruded far out into space reminding me of the tentacles of an octopus. This dark octopus flying in interplanetary space was not a beautiful sight to behold and the sensation that I lived on its back made me shudder. At that moment brilliant rays of blue, rose, and snow-white flashed like lightning through the dark conglomeration.

"'Are they the positive mental emissions of groups of people?' I enquired of my instructor.

"'They are, and you can see how the dark aura of the earth can be cleansed by them if man could only try to broadcast thoughts and emotions on that wavelength. This is what people should do systematically and by synchronization so that the whole planet would emit fine spiritual vibrations,' the lama commented.

"'Tara has cried long enough, Mother Nature may one day decide to shake off those short-sighted minds which have created this horrible shell around the earth. Mankind must purify and disinfect its planetary home. The Arhats are doing all they can to neutralize the evil but it is more important to stop the constantly created new negative emissions and only man can do that,' mused the Tibetan lama."[1]

And then the lama recounted to Tomas a legend as ancient as the Himalayas:

"Our oral teaching of Tashi Lhunpo Monastery asserts that millions of years ago a number of superhuman beings, from another highly advanced world, came to earth for the acceleration of the evolution of this planet and its future mankind. They had 'mind-born' bodies, that is created artificially from primordial matter, which could be made as heavy as the core of the earth or as light and fiery as sunlight. In appearance they were godlike giants. Among these angels was Mara, whom you call Lucifer or Satan. His important task was to develop the concrete mind and individuality of man. In the course of ages he had accomplished his aim but when the Bodhisattvas and Tara appeared later in order to foster the heart of man, he refused to step aside. This was the revolt of Satan against the Rulers of Cosmic Cycles. Since that time he does not bear the title of 'Light-bringer,' or Lucifer, any longer. He is now the Prince of Darkness.

"From then on the Bodhisattvas have had a double task: on the one hand of combating Mara's attempts to chain man to the earth and make

---

[1] Tomas, *Shambhala*, pp. 144–145.

him selfish, unscrupulous, and warlike; and on the other, of working for the spiritual advancement of mankind, ordained by the law of cycles. This is what induces us to send Buddhas and Arhats to this world.

"It is the lack of desire of the Terrestrial Ruler to cooperate with the Lord of the Sun and the Spirits of the Planets that has created a cosmic crisis. Mankind must now decide on which side it is — on the side of Light or of darkness, and then reap its karma. All the peoples must now choose between the old ways of strife or a new order of world brotherhood.

"The exalted beings of the Sun and other worlds say to Satan: 'Let your lamp shine, but do not obstruct other and more glorious lights in starry space! Break down the wall around the earth, for in that shell humanity is spiritually suffocating. The Cosmic Clock shows that soon the time will come for the Age of Spirit. You could not stop it even if you wanted to, for the Dhyan Chohans are soon bringing a body from space, which is as yet invisible — a mere vortex of forces, but when it flares up, its flames will burn all your works.'[2]

"Century after century, millennium after millennium we have contacted mankind with messages suited for particular peoples. All of them have stressed unity and universal brotherhood. Unfortunately, very few have succeeded in awakening mankind, hence the necessity to issue a final warning in these critical times. This is our Planetary Ultimatum and mankind will have to accept the Commandment of the Heart or else it will destroy itself. In breaking the Karmic Law of the universality of life with his destructive behaviour, man will be judged and punished by Nature. Whole cities might be washed away into the oceans, and great continents crack in volcanic cataclysms. After the Year of the Arhats[3] the Planetary Ultimatum has to be brought to the attention of all the peoples of earth. This message should be delivered with kindness and compassion, yet very firmly because it is a warning. And warnings are brought only by well-wishers. Man will then have to make his supreme choice — Light or darkness, Peace or war, Heart or fist, Wisdom or ignorance.

"Can you understand now that mankind is a battlefield of Celestial Forces? This is, of course, a very ancient teaching incorporated in all religions. A War of Worlds is raging now and let us hope that man will not side with the forces of darkness for then he shall be removed by the Lords of Karma from the face of the earth. . . .

---

[2] This means the approaching of Earth and the whole Solar System to the invisible Spiritual Sun whose energies will make the existence of evil forces impossible. For this reason, Lucifer had planned to explode the planet in order to prolong his life. See *Satan* in *Glossary*, pp. 393–396.

[3] The Dragon year 1976 is indicated in the book, but it might also mean the Dragon year 2024 when the Council of Shambhala gathered.

"Our present crisis might be even more acute in view of the increased population and the greater obscuration of spirituality in man. . . .

"In the last quarter of the century, an appeal must be made to disseminate the Doctrine of the Heart, for this alone can save the planet. . . .

"At this crossing of the roads, humanity has to choose between a path going down into the pit of moral decay or one that is ascending to the stars. This is the time of a terrestrial emergency. If the warning is ignored and the masses continue to tread the present path, siding with the Prince of Darkness, then the Cosmic Hierarchy will take the challenge, and the Radiant Ruler of Shambhala will destroy all evil on this planet. . . .

"In this century the nations of the world have fought two world wars and might fight another one before its end. . . .

"The people of earth must understand that the time of crucifixions and of gentle prophets preaching to raving crowds has ended. This time the Arhats will speak with lightning, thunder, and star showers! The Epoch of Shambhala is here! . . .

"Please note here that I am not prophesying but disclosing the strategic moves of the Celestial Armies in their battle against the teeming warriors of darkness! There is a war underway — the War of Worlds, of exalted cosmic superhuman systems combating the evil forces of this earth which poison space and injure the whole Solar System. Whether or not man believes that there is such a war in the heavens, he is still responsible for his actions and will reap his karma. . . .

"The teaching of Tara, the Doctrine of the Heart, must form the foundation of a new sociology. There could be debates between systems but without war. We must realize that we are all members of one great planetary family. . . .

"We can and we should [solve our problems without the apocalyptic upheavals mentioned], but shall we? Will the majority abandon the ways of greed, selfishness, narrow nationalism, and the worship of the sensual at the expense of the spiritual? People do not have to become monks and nuns, but they can certainly live and think like real human beings. Why do they have to be killers of their brothers and destroyers of Mother Nature? Karma, cosmic justice, is terrible in its action. Why challenge it? . . .

"It is the opening of the gates to a better era, the Cycle of Tara. Take her sign, that of the Heart, let it unite all mankind, for every good religion and ideology is based on humanism. . . .

"The sign of the Heart is the mark of the next epoch, that of Maitreya; that is what the Kalachakra, the science of cycles, says."[1]

---
[1] Tomas, *Shambhala*, pp. 146–150.

The next day, Tomas continued his conversation with the Tibetan lama in front of a thangka depicting Maitreya. When asked if Maitreya would be able to bring peace to humanity, the lama replied:

"Your question reminds me of a teaching given to me in my youth by three Great Arhats. They said: 'Your world continues to move towards a disaster. Mankind can save the earth only by a spiritual regeneration.' Then, boldly, I intervened, 'But cannot the coming Maitreya, the new Buddha, save it?' One of the three Masters replied: 'Maitreya will show the way but it will be up to mankind to tread that road.'"[2]

And then Tomas inquired about the timing of the arrival of the new Buddha, to which the monk responded:

"In the last quarter of the twentieth century mankind must prepare for the coming of the Arhats, even Maitreya himself, at this crucial period of the world's history. The Commandment of the Heart will be placed before all people. . . . It offers all on this planet the chance to exercise the prerogative of freewill to choose Light or darkness, Brotherhood or selfishness."[3]

The Future Buddha

Buddhist tradition has it that the Blessed One appointed Bodhisattva Maitreya as his successor. And the Blessed One said to Ananda: "I am not the first Buddha who has come to Earth, nor shall I be the last. In due time another Buddha will arise in the world, the Holy One of supreme illumination, endowed with wisdom, and happy, embracing the entire Universe, an incomparable Leader of peoples, the Lord of Devas and mortals. He will reveal to you the same eternal truths that I have taught you. He will establish his Law, most glorious in its principles, most glorious in its apotheosis, and most glorious in its goal in spirit and word. He will proclaim the righteous life, perfect and pure, which I now preach. His disciples will be numbered in the thousands, while mine are merely in the hundreds."

And Ananda asked: "How shall we recognize Him?"

The Blessed One replied: "His name will be Maitreya."

The future Buddha, Maitreya, as His name indicates, is the Buddha of Love and Compassion. On account of His inherent qualities, this Bodhisattva is often called Ajita — the Invincible.[4]

According to the exoteric tradition, Maitreya will appear in three thousand years. However, the Initiates knew that His Coming would take place much earlier. After all, in addition to the Tibetan lama who

---

[2] Tomas, *Shambhala*, p. 151.
[3] Tomas, *Shambhala*, pp. 151–152.
[4] Roerich, *Osnovy Buddizma*, pp. 207–208.

conversed with Andrew Tomas, the seers Nostradamus and Edgar Cayce, the unexplained phenomenon of the Salsk Celestial Code, and the Gospel of Matthew also point to the end of the twentieth century.

Even Blavatsky left a subtle hint in *The Theosophical Glossary*[1] that the event was to take place in the present times, and not in the distant future. However, she also noted that "'the coming of Christ,' means the presence of Christos in a regenerated world, and not at all the actual coming in body of 'Christ' Jesus," and that the time when this was to happen was "fast approaching."[2] Helena Roerich explained to her correspondents in the 1930s that the Advent would be "visibly invisible"[3] and that they would have grown old by that time.[4]

As early as 1850, the Mongolian scholar and astrologer, Sokpo Sherab Gyatso, who was the tutor of His Holiness the Eighth Panchen Lama, travelled to India from Tibet to found Ghoom Monastery near Darjeeling, as well as to proclaim the imminent Advent of Maitreya Buddha and the nearing of the New Era.

In 1915, His Holiness the Ninth Panchen Lama decided to erect the Maitreya Temple (Jamkhang Chenmo) at Tashi Lhunpo Monastery to house a huge 26-metre statue of the future Buddha. The entire statue is luxuriously decorated with gold, diamonds, pearls, and other precious stones. However, Maitreya sits on the throne not in an Eastern posture but in a European one; that is, His legs are not crossed according to the Eastern custom, but are instead lowered to the ground — this was a sign of His imminent arrival.

The Ninth Panchen Lama's mastery of occult science was well known, and amazing stories circulated about the miracles of His Holiness.

When the Panchen Lama was in India, he was asked whether it was true that he possessed certain special powers. Sitting in the garden, closely surrounded by his retinue, His Holiness smiled and said nothing, and after a few minutes, suddenly disappeared. While those present were unsuccessfully searching for him, another individual entered the garden and was struck by an extraordinary scene: the Panchen Lama was sitting calmly under a tree, invisible to his guests, who searched in vain for him.[5]

In his conversation with Dr. Ferdinand Ossendowski, the legendary Ja Lama spoke about the phenomena brought about by the Panchen

---

[1] H. P. Blavatsky, *The Theosophical Glossary* (London: Theosophical Publishing Society, 1892), p. 202.

[2] H. P. Blavatsky, "The Esoteric Character of the Gospels," *Collected Writings*, vol. 8, pp. 173–174.

[3] Helena Roerich, *Pis'ma* [Letters], vol. 3 (Moscow: Mezhdunarodnyy tsentr Rerikhov, 2001), p. 193.

[4] See *Sanat Kumara* in *Glossary* for more, pp. 383–393.

[5] Roerich, *Altay — Gimalai*, p. 43.

Lama: "You Europeans will not recognize that we dark-minded nomads possess the powers of mysterious science. If you could only see the miracles and power of the Most Holy Tashi Lama, when at his command the lamps and candles before the ancient statue of Buddha light themselves and when the icons of the gods begin to speak and prophesy!"[6]

Indeed, that which is considered magical in the West and for which Blavatsky was accused of charlatanism, in Tibet represents a common manifestation of human abilities. George de Roerich also witnessed the unusual powers of the Tibetan lamas. His father was often visited by a mysterious lama, but no one ever saw how he left the Roerichs' house. One day, young George entered the room where the lama was in conversation with his father. They sat opposite each other and talked calmly, in a confiding manner, paying no attention to him:

"I sat on the edge of a chair and somehow became as though entirely numbed. I could not hear or see anything, or rather, I could but with the entire surface of my skin. I do not know how long I sat like that. I came to when my father carried me, half-conscious to bed. The next morning my father said reproachfully: 'Do you see how you traumatized your psyche? You got what you wanted.'" But George simply wanted to understand how the Lama-teacher was able to leave when the doors remained closed: "I saw a human form, dissolved like a fog, passing through the wall."[7]

In his work George de Roerich cites two stories about the Panchen Lama.[8] While fleeing, crossing the Tibetan plateau in the north, His Holiness' caravan approached the shore of a salt lake that was not yet frozen. The retinue was at a loss, for they were being closely pursued by the Tibetan cavalry. Delay meant capture and cruel treatment by the soldiers. The Panchen Lama reassured his companions: "Tomorrow before dawn we will be on the other side of the lake." During the night, an unusually strong frost froze the rivers and lakes, and the caravan was able to cross the lake in the early hours of morning. The Tibetan horsemen arrived later, in the daytime, and saw that the caravan had already safely crossed the icy expanse. They tried to pursue it across the ice, but the warm Tibetan sun was already melting the ice, and the riders sank into the water along with their horses.

Events of the other story took place north of the mighty Tanggu La range. The Panchen Lama's caravan was almost lost in a heavy snowstorm.

---

[6] Ferdinand Ossendowski, *Beasts, Men and Gods* (New York: E. P. Dutton, 1922), p. 118.

[7] V. A. Verakso, "Vosem' vstrech s Uchitelem" [Eight meetings with the Teacher], *Mir Ognennyy*, no. 1 (1997), p. 78.

[8] George de Roerich, *Tibet i Tsentral'naya Aziya* [Tibet and Central Asia], vol. 1 (Samara: Agni, 1999), pp. 276–277.

The wet snow clung to the people's eyes, blinding them. Even the animals of the caravan, the hardy camels from the Mongolian Gobi, could not withstand the wind's ferocity. His Holiness himself led the caravan to the tent of a poor nomad, where they found a blind old man. The Panchen Lama and his retinue spent the night in the nomad's tent, none revealing to him his guest's identity. In the morning, before leaving, the Lama asked the elder what he wanted more than anything else in the world. The man replied that he had always prayed to see the radiant face of the Most Precious Lama, but old age and blindness had deprived him of this. "Now you will see it," said His Holiness, and extended his hand to the nomad's eyes. The elder immediately regained his sight and prostrated himself in reverence before his spiritual lord.

Stories such as these illustrate how deeply respected His Holiness the Ninth Panchen Lama was in Tibet and beyond.

Alexandra David-Néel describes an interesting episode that occurred during the consecration of the statue of Maitreya at Tashi Lhunpo.[1] His Holiness the Panchen Lama wished his spiritual adviser, Kyongbu Rinpoche, to perform the ceremony but Kyongbu Rinpoche replied that he would die before the temple with the statue was completed. The Panchen Lama asked the hermit to delay his death and consecrate the temple and statue. The teacher agreed to the request of His Holiness and promised to perform the rite of consecration.

When that day came, the Panchen Lama sent a beautiful sedan chair for Kyongbu Rinpoche and an honorary escort to accompany the elder to Tashi Lhunpo. The riders saw the hermit take his seat in the chair, and closed the door behind him, before the procession set off. Meanwhile, in Tashi Lhunpo, thousands of people gathered for the inauguration festival. To the profound amazement of all, Kyongbu Rinpoche appeared without an entourage and on foot. He silently entered the temple, approached the statue of Maitreya until he was very close and gradually merged with it. A little later, the sedan chair arrived, surrounded by the honorary escort. They opened the door of the sedan chair only to find that there was no one inside.

It was reported that after the passing of His Holiness the Panchen Lama in 1937, this compassionate statue of Maitreya was seen crying, drops of emotion flowing down the sculpture's face. All the lamas present at Tashi Lhunpo Monastery at the time confirmed this event.[2]

---

[1] Alexandra David-Néel, *With Mystics and Magicians in Tibet* (London: John Lane, 1931), pp. 316–317.

[2] "Tashilhunpo Monastery — Tibetan Buddhist monastery located in Shigatse," *Peregrine Treks & Tours*, https://peregrinetreks.com/blog/tashilhunpo-monastery.

Prophecies

Subsequently the successor of the founder of Ghoom Monastery, Domo Geshe Rinpoche Ngawang Kalsang, who became its head in 1909, also erected, inside, a large statue of Maitreya, similar to the statue at Tashi Lhunpo, seated on a throne in the European manner. Lama Domo Geshe Rinpoche, as he was popularly called, travelled extensively, performed miracles of healing the sick, and proclaimed the teaching of Shambhala — the Kalachakra. He built statues of Maitreya in many monasteries.

The Lama's incarnations include Milarepa, while His Holiness the Thirteenth Dalai Lama considered him to be the incarnation of Tsongkhapa,[3] a great Buddhist reformer and founder of the Gelug school of Tibetan Buddhism. To understand the level of respect that existed for Geshe Rinpoche, it is worth mentioning that, after his death in 1936, the Tibetan government allowed his body to be embalmed, although this practice is only customary in the case of the bodies of the Dalai and Panchen Lamas, noting: "In Southern Tibet, including Sikkim, etc., Domo Geshe Rinpoche's activities were exactly like those of Je Tsongkhapa. In accordance, we will allow Rinpoche's body to be preserved."[4]

Both Sherab Gyatso and Lama Domo Geshe Rinpoche were disciples of Master Morya, who often visited Ghoom Monastery. His meetings with Blavatsky and the Roerichs also took place there. Lama Domo Geshe Rinpoche was a friend of Nicholas Roerich, who describes a conversation that took place between them in the 1928 essay *Shambhala the Resplendent*.[5] However, not a single photograph of the Lama exists, and if a photo was taken without his permission, his image in the photograph is either missing, or blurred beyond recognition.

When Geshe Rinpoche visited the Roerichs at the house of Talai Pho Brang ("Dalai Lama's palace") in Darjeeling, where His Holiness the Thirteenth Dalai Lama had lived from 1910 to 1913, he noticed the image of Rigden Dragpo, the Lord of Shambhala, and said: "I see that you are aware of the advent of the time of Shambhala. The shortest path to success is through Rigden Dragpo. If you know the teaching of Shambhala, you know the future."[6] And while conversing about Rigden Dragpo later, Roerich asked if he was referring to Maitreya, to which the Lama replied:

---

[3] Ursula Bernis, *His Holiness Domo Geshe Rinpoche: A Biographical Sketch* (Dungkar Gonpa Society, 2002), p. 18.

[4] Bernis, *His Holiness Domo Geshe Rinpoche*, p. 25.

[5] See Nicholas Roerich, *Shambhala* (New York: Nicholas Roerich Museum, 2017), pp. 11–35.

[6] Roerich, *Shambala. Serdtse Azii*, p. 71.

"We must not speak of this mystery! There is much which may not yet be revealed."[1]

Nicholas Roerich also quotes another of Sherab Gyatso's disciples:

"In 1924, a learned lama, a worthy disciple of the founder of the monastery, who received from him the complete teaching and many prophecies, spoke to us about the future, standing before an impressive image of the coming Lord:

"'Truly, the time of the Great Coming is near. According to our prophecies, the Era of Shambhala has already begun. Rigden Dragpo, the Lord of Shambhala, is already preparing his invincible army for the final battle. All his colleagues and leaders have already been incarnated.

"'Have you seen the thangka, the banner of the Lord of Shambhala and His victory over the forces of evil?

"'When our Tashi Lama was forced to flee Tibet last year, he took with him only a few banners and among them several paintings of Shambhala. Many learned lamas left Tashi Lhunpo then. A geshe artist, a gelong from Tashi Lhunpo, has just arrived from Tibet. He knows how to paint the thangka of Shambhala. There are several variations on this subject. You should have at least one of them in your home, where the last victorious battle of the Lord is depicted at the bottom of the picture. . . .

"'In ancient times it was predicted that before the time of Shambhala, many amazing events would occur. Brutal wars would devastate whole countries. Many states would collapse. Underground fire would shake the earth. And the Panchen Rinpoche would leave his dwelling at Tashi Lhunpo in Tibet. Truly, the time of Shambhala has already dawned. The great war has devastated whole countries. Many thrones have perished. Earthquakes in Japan have destroyed temples. And now our revered Lord has left his country.'"[2]

The connection between the Panchen Lamas and Shambhala, also known as Agartha, is mentioned by Dr. Ferdinand Ossendowski, who collected various legends during his travels in Mongolia in the early 1920s:

"From time to time, sacred commands are issued from Agartha. The Lord of the World communicates almost exclusively with the source of Buddhist and Lamaist wisdom — the Tashi Lama of Tibet. Throughout the entire era of the existence of these great persons, at the most crucial moments, the Tashi Lamas receive copper plates marked with magical symbols that no one can decipher. These tablets are considered to be written messages from the Lord of the World. Usually, the Tashi Lamas

---

[1] Roerich, *Vrata v budushcheye*, p. 1212.
[2] Roerich, *Shambala. Serdtse Azii*, pp. 69–70.

use divination to decipher these writings, and it is said that only one has ever managed to comprehend the true meaning of what was written. He did this in a very peculiar way. He went to the temple and after a long time spent in prayer, placed the magical tablet on his head and prostrated himself before the statue of Avalokiteshvara, asking for help. Suddenly, what was written made sense, and the Tashi Lama immediately put into action the orders of the Great Unknown One for the eternal glory of Lamaism and Tibet. A copy of this message, given by the Tashi Lama to the Living Buddha of Urga, is kept in the sealed casket of Genghis Khan together with the most revered Mongolian relics: the ring and seal of the Great Khan and the sacred bulls of the Dalai Lama."[3]

He also described an episode, that the Roerichs had also heard at various times during their expedition across the East, about the unexpected arrival of the Lord of Shambhala at one of the monasteries around 1890, predicting global wars and the decline of spirituality:

"One night in winter several horsemen rode into the monastery and demanded that all the Gelongs and Getsuls with the Khutuktu and Khenpo at their head should congregate in this room. Then one of the strangers mounted the throne, where he took off his bashlyk or cap-like head covering. All of the Lamas fell to their knees as they recognized the man who had been long ago described in the sacred bulls of Dalai Lama, Tashi Lama, and Bogd Khan. He was the man to whom the whole world belongs and who has penetrated into all the mysteries of Nature. He pronounced a short Tibetan prayer, blessed all his hearers, and afterwards made predictions for the coming half century. This was thirty years ago and in the interim all his prophecies are being fulfilled. During his prayers before that small shrine in the next room, this door opened of its own accord, the candles and lights before the altar lighted themselves, and the sacred braziers without coals gave forth great streams of incense that filled the room. And then, without warning, the King of the World and his companions disappeared from among us. Behind him remained no trace save the folds in the silken throne coverings which smoothed themselves out and left the throne as though no one had sat upon it."[4]

It is known that His Holiness the Ninth Panchen Lama maintained contact with the Roerich family, and even offered them his house in Inner Mongolia during their second expedition across the East.[5] Through Lama Domo Geshe Rinpoche, he gifted them a book containing prayers

---

[3] Ferdinand Ossendowski, *Lyudi, bogi, zveri* [Beasts, Men and Gods] (Moscow: Eksmo, 2005), pp. 294–295.

[4] Ossendowski, *Beasts, Men and Gods*, pp. 178–179.

[5] George de Roerich, *Tibet i Tsentral'naya Aziya* [Tibet and Central Asia], vol. 2 (Moscow: Rassanta, 2012), p. 173.

given by His Holiness during his travels — in each place that he stopped, he dedicated a special prayer to Shambhala.[1]

In 1928, Helena Roerich passed on prophecies about Shambhala and Maitreya to His Holiness the Panchen Lama.[2] Later these were published in the book *On Eastern Crossroads*. One of these reads: "One, two, three, I see three books of the coming of Maitreya. The first was written in the West, the second was written in the East, the third was written in the North."[3] However, the original form of this prophecy contained in Roerich's notebooks for 1925 contains one small difference: "the third *will be* written in the North."[4] The prophesy was published with the same distinction by Nicholas Roerich in the book *Heart of Asia*,[5] implying that at the time of publication in 1929, two Teachings of Maitreya had already been imparted, one in the West and one in the East.

Furthermore, in the book *Hierarchy* (1931) of the *Agni Yoga* series, we read that the Lord of Shambhala reveals three Doctrines to humanity.[6] A similar prediction is contained in *Vaticinia Nostradami*, the lost manuscript of Nostradamus. One of the drawings contained therein depicts the King of the World and three women who were destined to record His Teaching.[7]

A disciple of Lama Domo Geshe Rinpoche, Lama Anagarika Govinda, a renowned Buddhist scholar, philosopher, poet, and artist, believed that Nicholas Roerich was "a torch-bearer of Shambhala, a prophet of the Age of Maitreya, whose coming depends on the preparedness and cooperation of each single individual."[8]

Indeed, the Age of Maitreya is the Age of the Heart, and it will dawn as soon as humanity realizes the role of the heart in life. Whether this will occur tomorrow or in three thousand years depends entirely upon each and every one of us.

However, since the end of the twentieth century, namely since 1997, the sacred Udumbara flower has been appearing in the world, a

---

[1] Roerich, *Shambala. Serdtse Azii*, p. 107.

[2] Roerich, *Zapisi Ucheniya Zhivoy Etiki*, vol. 9, p. 22.

[3] Helena Roerich, *Kriptogrammy Vostoka* [Cryptograms of the East] (Moscow: Amrita, 2011), p. 66. This prophecy is translated in the English edition as follows: "The first is written in the West. The second is written in the East. The third is written in the North."

[4] Helena Roerich, *Zapisi Ucheniya Zhivoy Etiki* [Records of the Teaching of Living Ethics], vol. 6 (Moscow, 2009), p. 276.

[5] Nicholas Roerich, *Heart of Asia* (Rochester, VT: Inner Traditions, 1990), p. 97.

[6] Helena Roerich, *Hierarchy* (New York: Agni Yoga Society, 1977), pp. 13–14.

[7] See *Lost Book of Nostradamus*, directed by Kreg Lauterbach (Los Angeles: History Channel, 2008), DVD.

[8] Anagarika Govinda, "Art as a Way of the Future," *The Maha-Bodhi*, vol. 48, no. 7 (July 1940), p. 250.

supreme supernatural sign, testifying to the invisible Presence of Maitreya. It blooms in the most unexpected places, sometimes appearing out of nowhere, filling the space with its aroma, and in the same manner unexpectedly disappearing into nowhere.[9]

The Maitreya Mantra

All the names of the Great Teachers carry special vibrations, yet each era requires fresh affirmation of the power of a certain name. And in these current times, the world is in dire need of Love. In addition, when repeated seven times the name Maitreya provides powerful protection. For this reason, the Maitreya Loving Kindness Tour brought much positive energy to the suffering world, raising awareness of this holy name among various peoples, and forming a kind of mobile Point of Life that saturated with its energy the spaces of numerous countries.

There are also mantras in which the main role is played not by meaning, but by the rhythm and vibrations that are reproduced when using certain sounds that create a positive effect.

All the mantras that could be conveyed to humanity have already been bestowed and many people use them, without knowing the Sanskrit in which they are given. However, there also exist ancient, secret mantras in the language that preceded Sanskrit — Senzar. These are used solely by Initiates, for example, to pacify the raging elements that may threaten to destroy a certain area, if the karma of the people living there allows the Initiates to provide them with such assistance.

In *Isis Unveiled*, Blavatsky writes: "The greatest power of this Vach, or sacred speech, is developed according to the form which is given to the mantra by the officiating *hotri* [priest], and this form consists wholly in the numbers and syllables of the sacred metre. . . . 'for each thing has (just as in the Pythagorean system) a certain numerical proportion.'"[10]

When Blavatsky was asked whether a person could use these true, hidden mantras in translation, using words in another language, without losing their power, she replied: "He could; and all Adepts have the power to translate a strictly regular mantram into any form of language, so that

---

[9] "Rare Buddhist flower found under nun's washing machine," *The Telegraph*, 1 March 2010, https://www.telegraph.co.uk/news/worldnews/asia/china/7345137/Rare-Buddhist-flower-found-under-nuns-washing-machine.html; Tara MacIsaac, "Flower Said to Bloom Once in 3,000 Years Spotted Across Globe," *Epoch Times*, 10 June 2014, https://www.theepochtimes.com/article/flower-said-to-bloom-once-in-3000-years-spotted-across-globe-725095; Arsh Sarao, "Rare Photos: The Mystical Udumbara — 'Celestial Flowers' or Insect Eggs?" *The Epoch Times*, 17 March 2023, https://www.theepochtimes.com/bright/rare-photos-the-mystical-udumbara-celestial-flowers-or-insect-eggs-5056214.

[10] Blavatsky, *Isis Unveiled*, vol. 2, pp. 409–410.

a single sentence thus uttered by them will have an immense effect on the person addressed, whether it be by letter or word of mouth."[1]

So, at the end of the twentieth century, foreseeing that a mortal threat loomed over the Slavic lands responsible for world peace, the Great Teachers issued the sacred mantra of Maitreya in Russian, a language understood by all peoples of the former USSR. The mantra has a transformative effect both on the one who pronounces it and the surrounding world.

If people in different parts of the Slavic lands had at that time begun to serve through prayer, the Patrons of these territories could have relied upon the peoples' hearts to conduct the necessary currents. This would have helped strengthen the space so that there would be no "breakthrough" of what was happening on the Subtle Plane into the physical world, and would have helped to slow down all the negative processes.

However, after the initial enthusiasm and apparent safety, the Maitreya mantra began to fade on the lips of those who could have assisted their Protectors, who do not have the Cosmic Right to intervene unless people themselves apply 51 per cent of the necessary effort. In the East people know that a single saint is capable of saving an entire area, but in this case, they were counting on a unified number of people in resonant harmony with one another, who had achieved a certain coefficient of heart luminosity.

The Maitreya mantra in Russian reads as follows:

> Великим Именем Майтрейи
> Да будет Свет Священной Веры,
> Да будет Свет Святой Любви
> Пылать и полнить Божий Мир.

> Vye-LEE-kim EE-mye-nyem MAI-trei
> Da BU-det svyet svya-SCHE-nnoi VYE-ry,
> Da BU-det svyet svya-TOI lub-VEE
> Py-LAT' i POL-nit' BOzheei mir.

Since it is difficult to convey the sound of another language in writing, the link to an audio of the mantra as it is spoken in Russian has been included here: radiantbooks.co/mantra (no registration required).

---
[1] H. P. Blavatsky, *Revealing Cosmic Mysteries* (New York: Radiant Books, 2023), p. 46.

Its translation into English can be used as a short prayer addressed to Maitreya, and the name can be changed to one that is closer to the reader's heart:

> In the great name of Maitreya,
> May the Light of Sacred Faith,
> May the Light of Holy Love
> Emblaze and pervade God's world.

The mantra can be used at any time and under any circumstances, but the best moment is 12 noon (in each time zone), when a collective prayer of all the Forces of Light takes place in order to contribute part of our heart's fire to the Good of the whole world. After all, it is in the hands of all to prevent further "breakthroughs" by helping their Patrons, and strengthening the space of each area with the power of prayer. As the Tibetan lama revealed to Andrew Tomas, currently, the third fierce phase of the battle of Armageddon between the Forces of Light and darkness is taking place on the Subtle Plane and runs the risk of resulting in a Third World War, just as the previous two phases resulted in a world war.[2]

The Sacral Code

In its original language (not in translation), each sacred text, provided that it has not been distorted, has a numerological code. In the same way, the Russian version of the Maitreya mantra has its own code, which suggests that the set of words and sounds it comprises is far from random, structured with geometric precision. Here, rather than delve deeply into an analysis of it, a few points are noted.

In numerology, each letter of the alphabet is sequentially assigned with numbers from 1 to 9. Thus, the sum of the numerical values attributed to each of the Cyrillic letters used in the mantra is 368, which yields the number 17 (3+6+8=17).

In *The Secret Doctrine*, Blavatsky writes: "The ten points inscribed within that 'Pythagorean Triangle' are worth all the theogonies and angelologies ever emanated from the theological brain. For he who interprets them — on their very face, and in the order given — will find in these seventeen points (the seven mathematical points hidden) the uninterrupted series of the genealogies from the first *Heavenly* to *terrestrial* man. And, as they give the order of Beings, so they reveal the order in which were evolved the Cosmos, our earth, and the primordial elements by which the latter was generated."[3]

Also, the date 17 November is important, hence on this day: Blavatsky founded the Theosophical Society, the Roerichs established the Museum

---

[2] See *Armageddon* in *Glossary* for more, pp. 266–267.
[3] Blavatsky, *The Secret Doctrine*, vol. 1, pp. 612–613.

and Master Institute of United Arts, and His Holiness the Dalai Lama was enthroned. *The Secret Doctrine* indicates that the seventeenth day of the eleventh month is one of the "birthdays" of the Dhyani-Buddhas.[1]

Helena Roerich's notebooks contain information on the number 17: "The appearance of the Teacher is seventeen";[2] "Forge your sword in love (7 times 17)"[3] while 7x17=119.

The quantity of letters in the mantra is 89 (53 consonants, 34 vowels and 2 soft signs), which again results in the number 17 (8+9=17).

The sum of 1 and 7 gives the number 8 (1+7=8), which is the number of Sophia, Divine Wisdom, and Infinity. This number is called Mother because it represents the first cube. In Orthodoxy, an eight-pointed star (octagram) is used as a symbol of the Mother of God. The Gnostics called Sophia *Ogdoad* ("eight"), because they believed that there were Seven Heavens, and She, who gave life to the Seven Archons (Archangels), lived in the Eighth Heaven, also called *Ogdoad*. From *The Secret Doctrine*:

"The *Ogdoad* or 8 symbolizes the eternal and spiral motion of cycles, the 8, ∞, and is symbolized in its turn by the caduceus. It shows the regular breathing of the Cosmos presided over by the Eight Great Gods — the seven from the primeval Mother, the One and the Triad."[4]

Hence the number 17 symbolically means the "Mother of Seven." And according to Pythagoras: "The number eight, or the Octad, is the first cube, that is to say, squared in all senses, as a die, proceeding from its base two, or even number; *so is man four-square or perfect.*"[5]

Also, the quantity of consonants, 53, again gives the number of Sophia — 8 (5+3=8).

Further, the first two lines of the mantra contain 9 syllables each, and the following two contain 8 syllables — the same numbers that are reflected in the total number of letters. As a whole, it consists of 34 syllables, which in turn is twice 17 (2x17=34).

The number 34 itself (3+4=7) symbolizes the human being with the triad and quaternary of principles, like a pyramid made up of a triangle and a square. And then there is our Cosmos — the Solar System, in the foundation of which the number 7 with its septenary structure and rhythms was laid in everything (for example, the Sirius system is based on the number 12).

Blavatsky writes: "The 3 and the 4, the triangle and the cube, or the male and female universal glyph, showing the first aspect of the evolving

---

[1] Blavatsky, *The Secret Doctrine*, vol. 2, p. 179.
[2] Helena Roerich, *Zapisi Ucheniya Zhivoy Etiki* [Records of the Teaching of Living Ethics], vol. 7 (Moscow, 2009), p. 70.
[3] Roerich, *Zapisi Ucheniya Zhivoy Etiki*, vol. 7, p. 84.
[4] Blavatsky, *The Secret Doctrine*, vol. 2, p. 580.
[5] Blavatsky, *Isis Unveiled*, vol. 2, p. 410.

deity.... The cube unfolded [four squares vertically and three horizontally] is in display a cross of the *tau*, or Egyptian form, or of the Christian cross-form."[6] "Numbers 3 and 4 are respectively male and female, Spirit and Matter, and their union is the emblem of Life Eternal in Spirit on its ascending arc, and in Matter as the ever resurrecting element — by procreation and reproduction. The spiritual male line is vertical; the differentiated matter-line is horizontal; the two forming the cross or +. The 3 is invisible; the 4 is on the plane of objective perception."[7]

The number 3 multiplied by 4 gives 12, or the dodecahedron, which is "the geometrical figure employed by the Demiurgus in constructing the universe."[8] The Mother of the World creates in duodecimal cycles.

We can also look at the quantity of words of the mantra — 18. This is a very interesting number, because it speaks of the mantra's transformative effect.

In addition to the fact that here we again see number 8, which in sum with 1 gives 9, this is also 6+6+6. Of course, the first thing that comes to mind for those who grew up in a Christian environment is the number of the beast from the Bible. However, they may not know that the number carries an esoteric meaning.

Each planet has its own number, which in the case of Earth is 6, and, therefore, for all Life created by Earth. The three sixes symbolize the three lower bodies that Earth created in all her forms. Hence, the most developed life form on the planet — animal — has the number 666, since it does not have the higher mind, the nature of which belongs to the Supreme Worlds, but not to Earth.

In this way, when evolving from animal to human, the lower triad still carries the number of the beast, or 666. If added together, 666 yields 18 (6+6+6=18), which in turn is equal to 9 (1+8=9), which bears transfiguration. The number 9 symbolizes the higher mind which transformed the animal into rational human. Moreover, 18 is also 9+9, which again makes 9, and these three nines symbolize the higher triad of bodies.

Humans are destined to become Gods, whose number is 999, and is also referred to as angelic. Therefore, one must cast off one's bestial heritage through transforming each of the lower bodies, converting the number 6 into the number 9. And so the divine triad will be reflected in the lower triad, which will acquire a qualitatively new expression.

The Master revealed to Helena Roerich an even more secret meaning of the number 18, or 666, for the number 6 is the Star of David or the seal of Solomon and Vishnu, which Blavatsky used as the basis for

---

[6] Blavatsky, *The Secret Doctrine*, vol. 1, p. 321.
[7] Blavatsky, *The Secret Doctrine*, vol. 2, p. 592.
[8] Blavatsky, *Isis Unveiled*, vol. 1, p. 9.

the emblem of the Theosophical Society. It also means the swastika, the ancient symbol of Life:

"Three times six is the number of three Lords. If the dodecahedron belongs to the Mother of the World, then the six-pointed star belongs to the Lord. This is how the time of the three Lords is indicated in numbers. The arrival of the Maitreya cycle means the appearance of the three Lords."[1]

The Messiah, awaited by all religions of the world under different names, is the bearer of the Three Rays — Buddha, Christ, and Maitreya. Likewise, the predictions of Nam Sa-go, the "Korean Nostradamus" of the sixteenth century, proclaimed that He would go into the world as the Buddha and carry the Power of Three.[2]

Nevertheless, in order to determine the true esoteric code of texts in Cyrillic, one must use the Glagolitic alphabet — the first Slavic alphabet, whose letters have their own numerical value, just like the Hebrew and Arabic languages. The precise origin of the Glagolitic alphabet remains unknown, however, it was also used for the purposes of secret script. It was the Glagolitic alphabet that helped researchers decipher the Salsk Celestial Code.

The difficulty is that some modern letters, such as the letter *o*, can have two numerical values in the Glagolitic alphabet. However, following the table of correspondences between Cyrillic and Glagolitic letters, the total sum of the numerological values of all the letters of the mantra on the first attempt yielded 7,390, which gives the sacred number 19 (7+3+9+0=19) — the number of the Nameless One symbolizing the alpha and the omega, the first and the last, the beginning and the end.

The number 7,390 can be expressed as 19x389–1. It is also interesting to note that the value of the first line mentioning Maitreya is 928, which again gives the number 19.

The Secret Doctrine speaks of the manifestation of Adi-Sanat (the First or Primeval Ancient), a name associating the Kabbalistic "Ancient of Days" and the "Holy Aged" (Sefirah and Adam Kadmon) with Brahma the Creator, called also *Sanat*, among other names and titles: "He is one and nine . . . which makes ten, or the perfect number applied to the 'Creator,' the name given to the totality of the Creators blended by the Monotheists into One, as the 'Elohim,' Adam Kadmon or Sefirah — the Crown — are the androgyne synthesis of the ten Sefirot, who stand for the symbol of the manifested Universe in the popularized Kabbalah."[3]

---

[1] Helena Roerich, *Zapisi Ucheniya Zhivoy Etiki* [Records of the Teaching of Living Ethics], vol. 8 (Moscow, 2010), p. 83.

[2] Sung Mo Koo, translator, "The Korean Books of Prophecy," *Who is He?*, http://www.tparents.org/moon-books/cta-ik/Cta-ik-6-2.htm.

[3] Blavatsky, *The Secret Doctrine*, vol. 1, p. 98.

INTRODUCTION   lxxxvii

The meaning of this sacred number can be traced in various traditions. For example, the date 19 July 4241 BCE, which corresponds to the beginning of the New Year in ancient Egypt — the day of the rise of Sirius, is the first reliable date known to the history of humankind. In Chinese Buddhism, the number 19 is associated with the three Guanshiyin birthdays (actual birthday, enlightenment, and renunciation): the nineteenth day of the second lunar month, the nineteenth day of the sixth month, and the nineteenth day of the ninth month. The Quran, which has survived the years in undistorted form, has a mathematical phenomenon known as Code 19, which was discovered only with the help of a computer. In the eleventh century, Judah ben Samuel of Regensburg illuminated in eight volumes the meaning of the number 19, which he found in the original Jewish scriptures, but which were subsequently distorted.[4] The Baha'i calendar consists of 19 months each of 19 days. Alchemists believed that 19 was the number of the philosopher's stone, and in the Tarot system, the nineteenth card is associated with the Sun and the Lord of the World Fire. However, the secret of this mystical number is revealed solely during Initiation, since it is associated with the One and Only.

If we consider the mantra from a geometric point of view, then 19 is enclosed in a square, because it contains four lines.

The number 19 can be depicted as a combination of 6+6+6+1: the three seals of Solomon enclosed within each other, like Three in One, with a central point, similarly to a crystal or snowflake. As Blavatsky explains using number 7 as an example, considered to be the senary and the unity (6+1), in this case the central point symbolizes Fire.[5] And Fire works through triangles, having three points as its support. In this case, the support would be represented by the six triangles that form the three Stars of David.

Or, from the number 19 we need to create the decad (1+9=10), which is depicted by the figure of one within zero (1 in 0) — that is, a circle with a line along the diameter, where the diameter designates the Father-Mother, God manifested in his works. This figure is "the symbol of Deity, of the Universe, and of man"[6] and "synthesizes, in the dual numeral ten (the 1 and a circle or cipher), the Absolute All manifesting itself in the Word or Generative Power of Creation."[7] Blavatsky gives

---

[4] Joseph Dan, *Studies in Jewish Mysticism* (Association for Jewish Studies, 1982), pp. 88–89.

[5] Blavatsky, *The Secret Doctrine*, vol. 2, p. 582; H. P. Blavatsky, "Tharana, or Mesmerism," *Collected Writings*, vol. 4 (Wheaton, IL: Theosophical Publishing House, 1969), p. 165.

[6] Blavatsky, *The Secret Doctrine*, vol. 2, p. 581.

[7] Blavatsky, *The Secret Doctrine*, vol. 2, p. 553.

another interpretation: "The circle is the Thought; the diameter (or the line) is the Word; and their union is Life."[1] She explains:

"The idea of representing the *hidden* Deity by the circumference of a circle, and the Creative Power (male and female, or the Androgynous Word) by the diameter across it, is one of the oldest symbols. It is upon this conception that every great cosmogony has been built. With the old Aryans, the Egyptians, and the Chaldeans, the symbol was complete, as it embraced the idea of the eternal and immovable Divine Thought in its absoluteness, separated entirely from the incipient stage of the so-called 'creation,' and comprised psychological and even spiritual evolution, and its mechanical work, or cosmogonical construction."[2]

In our case, this circle is enclosed in a square, which also forms "a very ancient symbol," as the Teacher explained to Helena Roerich.[3] It shows that the Spiritual Principle of the World (circle), or the Fire of Three in One (Stars of David) in the former case, is enclosed or falls within Matter (square), which represents both the world and an individual person. Not only do mandalas often have the shape of a circle inside a square but also in some Orthodox icons, the face of Jesus Christ was depicted surrounded by a halo (circle) enclosed in a square, as can be seen in Nicholas Roerich's painting *St. Sergius of Radonezh* (1932).

It is appropriate to quote Blavatsky's words about the meaning of *true* prayer, rather than prayer that is simply memorized, repeated, and left unsupported by any deed:

"It is a mystery rather; an occult process by which finite and conditioned thoughts and desires, unable to be assimilated by the absolute spirit which is unconditioned, are translated into spiritual wills and the will; such process being called 'spiritual transmutation.' The intensity of our ardent aspirations changes prayer into the 'philosopher's stone,' or that which transmutes lead into pure gold. The only homogeneous essence, our 'will-prayer' becomes the active or creative force, producing effects according to our desire. . . .

"It means not only a pleading or *petition*, but meant, in days of old, far more an invocation and incantation. The *mantra*, or the rhythmically chanted prayer of the Hindus, has precisely such a meaning."[4]

In the light of all this, we can see that the Maitreya mantra, although it was given in Russian, still adheres to all the canons of sacred speech that the Initiates use when translating secret mantras; otherwise, its

---

[1] Blavatsky, *The Secret Doctrine*, vol. 2, pp. 106–107.
[2] Blavatsky, *The Secret Doctrine*, vol. 2, pp. 536–537.
[3] Helena Roerich, *Zapisi Ucheniya Zhivoy Etiki* [Records of the Teaching of Living Ethics], vol. 9, p. 50.
[4] H. P. Blavatsky, *The Key to Theosophy* (London: Theosophical Publishing Company, 1889), pp. 68, 70.

numerological code would not have revealed a direct association, inwardly with the King of the World, and outwardly with His Queen.

Moreover, it is a call to the Messianic Fire, the Power of the Three Lords in One, to descend from the Heavens and find a foothold in our heart, thereby helping us transform our lower nature into a higher nature along the path of our ascent.

However, whether to use it in these difficult times for the salvation and transfiguration of both ourselves and the world, each is free to decide for themselves.

The Mystical Schools of the East

For many centuries in India, there has been a system of closed mystical schools located "on this side" of the Himalayas.[5] Each has its own philosophy, its own criteria for selecting students, and its own methods for developing supernatural powers — methods that are still kept in the strictest secrecy and cannot be revealed to the masses. Nevertheless, it is partly from these schools, that "leftovers" of high knowledge penetrated into the book market of the West in the form of methods of "opening the chakras," "*kundalini* practices," and suchlike.

Similar practices are in fact an extremely dangerous activity, since the true opening of energy centres and the development of supernatural powers should occur naturally, and exclusively under the strict supervision of an experienced Teacher, who is able to see all the subtle bodies of the student, whilst located in pure natural conditions and not in crowded and polluted cities. As a rule, all these harmful practices offer two paths: mechanical (through various physical exercises) and chemical (through drugs, for example, cannabis, and other psychotropic substances that are presented as "gifts of Nature").

Helena Roerich explains the true purpose of such mechanical and chemical means: "Thousands of manuals have now been thrown onto the world book market, describing easy ways to mechanically develop one's hidden, lower psychic powers. Truly, these ignorant and irresponsible writers work on the side of dark forces, who want nothing more than to open certain centres in the population in order to gain access to them and through them to participate in earthly life, carrying out their dark plans. For they wish very much to maintain an atmosphere around the Earth that is poisoned by lower emanations, and which is essential to their existence. . . . For true discipleship and service, one must manifest

---

[5] These are: 1) Nyaya, the logical school of Rishi Gautama; 2) Vaisheshika, the atomic system of Kanada; 3) Samkhya, the pantheistic school of Kapila; 4) Yoga, the mystical school of Patanjali; 5) Purva (early) Mimamsa; and 6) Uttara (later) Mimamsa, of Vyasa, which is called *Vedanta*.

strength of spirit and know the truth, and not get carried away by common 'tricks' available to every medium."[1]

At best, conducting this kind of independent experiment on oneself will not lead to any result; at worst, it will have extremely negative consequences across more than one lifetime, since damage is caused on the subtle plane, at the level of the soul. Therefore, those who, without the slightest understanding of this secret subject, disseminate various instructions on "how to open the chakras and gain secret powers," greatly burden their own karma and bind themselves for centuries to those they have harmed.

At the same time, in mysterious places "on the other side" of the Himalayas, there are esoteric schools with a single method of teaching and the oldest philosophy in the world. Unlike many mystical schools in the West, they have always accepted women into their ranks. However, only a very small number of disciples are accepted there, since their hearts must reach the necessary energy potential, which is accumulated through self-sacrifice and devotion to the ideals of Light — not in one fleeting life, but over many. It is to these disciples, among whom Helena Blavatsky numbers, that the Masters open the pages of the sacred *Book of the Golden Precepts*, so that they may apply in their daily lives the highest ethics expounded in its short treatises.

As we can see, the energy potential of the *ringsel* crystal in our heart is decisive in many matters. The accumulation and growth of this substance can occur mainly whilst we exist in physical conditions, that is, on Earth, over the course of many lifetimes. Thereafter, in the Higher Worlds, we are already reaping the consequences, that is, we occupy a place and height of position which corresponds to the "wealth" of our heart. Therefore, it is important to make the right choices in life and not to be deceived by earthly illusions, since any erroneous action will lead to the wasting of this ethereal treasure.

Herein lies the purpose of this remarkable book by Helena Blavatsky, which is republished again to help others find and cultivate their own "philosopher's stone" on the path to Supreme Enlightenment.

The Voice of the Silence

The *Voice of the Silence* was first published in 1889 and was immediately heralded as a sensation among its readers. It contains three fragments from the secret *Book of the Golden Precepts*: "The Voice of the Silence," "The Two Paths," and "The Seven Portals." The *Golden Precepts* contain about ninety treatises, which in their totality are available only to the Initiates — the Teachers of Shambhala and their disciples. And

---

[1] Roerich, *Pis'ma*, vol. 3, pp. 515–516.

as it is intended for Initiates, who else but the Teacher of all Teachers could have given it?

Blavatsky translated the three fragments from memory during her sojourn in Fontainebleau near Paris, France. There she was visited by Annie Besant, a British rights activist who had recently joined the Theosophical Society. Besant provided glimpses of the actual composition of *The Voice of the Silence* in her *Autobiography*. She recalls:

"I was called away to Paris to attend, with Herbert Burrows, the great Labour Congress held there from July 15th to July 20th, and spent a day or two at Fontainebleau with H. P. Blavatsky, who had gone abroad for a few weeks' rest. There I found her translating the wonderful fragments from the *Book of the Golden Precepts*, now so widely known under the name of *The Voice of the Silence*. She wrote it swiftly, without any material copy before her, and in the evening made me read it aloud to see if the 'English was decent.' Herbert Burrows was there, and Mrs. Candler, a staunch American Theosophist, and we sat round H.P.B. while I read. The translation was in perfect and beautiful English, flowing and musical; only a word or two could we find to alter, and she looked at us like a startled child, wondering at our praises — praises that anyone with the literary sense would endorse if they read that exquisite prose poem."[2]

Later Besant gave a fuller account in a lecture: "*The Voice of the Silence* . . . happened to be written while I was with her at Fontainebleau. It is a small book, and in what I am going to say I speak only of the book itself. I am not speaking of the notes; those were done afterwards. The book itself is what may be called a prose poem in three divisions.

"She wrote it at Fontainebleau, and the greater part was done when I was with her, and I sat in the room while she was writing it. I know that she did not write it referring to any books, but she wrote it down steadily, hour after hour, exactly as though she were writing either from memory or from reading it where no book was. She produced, in the evening, that manuscript that I saw her write as I sat with her, and asked myself and others to correct it for English, for she said that she had written it so quickly that it was sure to be bad. We did not alter in that more than a few words, and it remains as a specimen of marvellously beautiful literary work, putting everything else aside. . . .

"The book is, as I said, a prose poem, full of spiritual inspiration, full of food for the heart, stimulating the loftiest virtue and containing the noblest ideals. It is not a hotch-potch drawn from various sources, but a coherent, ethical whole. It moves us, not by a statement of facts gathered

---

[2] Annie Besant, *An Autobiography* (London: T. Fisher Unwin, 1893), pp. 352–353.

from books, but by an appeal to the divinest instincts of our nature: it is its own best testimony to the source whence it came."¹

In essence, the fragments revealed by Blavatsky describe two Paths to Enlightenment, along which a person will travel more than one lifetime if they decide to embark upon either one, upon hearing the Voice of their own spirit — the Voice that may sound through the heart alone as the Voice of the Silence.

The first is the Open Path of Mind and Knowledge, which is attained through various practices of meditation and concentration for the sake of one's own benefit; echoes of these can be found in various types of yogic literature.

And the second is the Secret Path of the Heart, which endows the pilgrim with Supreme Wisdom, multiplying Knowledge by Love. It can also be called the Path of Love and Compassion, which all the Saviours of Humanity have followed, regardless of religion or belief. It is this Path that contributes to the rapid growth of the *ringsel* crystal in the human heart. Indeed, the Masters of Wisdom became such not because they know everything, but because they are ready to sacrifice themselves for the sake of our suffering world.

Soon after the publication of *The Voice of the Silence* in 1889, Blavatsky sent a copy to Leo Tolstoy, the world-renowned author of *War and Peace* and *Anna Karenina*, with the dedicatory inscription: "To Count Leo Nikolaevich Tolstoy, 'one of the few,' from the author H. Blavatsky." When in 1909 Tolstoy was asked what he thought of the book, he replied: "Her books are famous. There is a lot of good in them; what is not good is that they speak of what people are unable to understand."² Tolstoy used aphorisms from *The Voice of the Silence* in his collections of sayings, signing them "Brahmin Wisdom."³

The Voice of the Silence was also an inspiration to Helena Roerich. She writes: "It is good to carry this little book with you. As you progress along the Path, everything said therein becomes, when re-read, so distinct, infinitely close, and so directing into the Radiant Future. All that is said is more than just metaphors. It becomes the Truth experienced by the heart and enlightened consciousness."⁴

The Japanese philosopher and teacher D. T. Suzuki, who brought Zen Buddhism to the West, writes: "*The Voice of the Silence* is true Mahayana

---

¹ Annie Besant, *The Masters as Facts and Ideals* (London: Theosophical Publishing Society, 1895), p. 21.

² Leo Tolstoy, *Polnoye sobraniye sochineniy* [Complete works], vol. 80 (Moscow: Gosudarstvennoye izdatel'stvo khudozhestvennoy literatury, 1955), p. 66.

³ See Leo Tolstoy, *Polnoye sobraniye sochineniy*, vol. 40, p. 95.

⁴ Helena Roerich, *Pis'ma* [Letters], vol. 9 (Moscow: Mezhdunarodnyy tsentr Rerikhov, 2009), p. 170.

doctrine. Undoubtedly Madame Blavatsky had in some way been initiated into the deeper side of Mahayana teaching and then gave out what she deemed wise to the Western world as theosophy."[5]

Lama Kazi Dawa Samdup, one of the first translators into English of Tibetan sacred texts, such as *The Tibetan Book of the Dead*, shared the same opinion. In the introduction to *The Tibetan Book of the Dead*, its editor, Walter Evans-Wentz writes: "The late Lama Kazi Dawa Samdup was of the opinion that, despite the adverse criticisms directed against H. P. Blavatsky's works, there is adequate internal evidence in them of their author's intimate acquaintance with the higher lamaistic teachings into which she claimed to have been initiated."[6]

According to Christmas Humphreys, the founder of the Buddhist Society in the UK, Anagarika Dharmapala, who is considered one of the greatest Buddhist figures of modern times, described *The Voice of the Silence* as "a pure Buddhist work."[7]

One of "the greatest of British frontier officers,"[8] Sonam Wangfel Laden La, who was educated by Sokpo Sherab Gyatso and played an important role in establishing good relations between British India and Tibet, was once asked whether he truly believed that Blavatsky had any real "inside information" on Tibetan Buddhism and, in particular, what he thought of *The Voice of the Silence*. Unafraid to speak his convictions whether or not they pleased his audience, Laden La replied that she surely did possess "inside information," and that this book contained the most profound Tibetan teachings.[9]

Moreover, Dr. Edward Conze, known for his pioneering translations of Buddhist texts, admired Blavatsky to the extent that he believed she was the reincarnation of Tsongkhapa.[10]

Sylvia Cranston's excellent biography of Blavatsky mentions an interesting episode. In the 1980s her friends, Jerome and Roseva Muratore from New Jersey, invited the Tibetan Lama, Geshe Lozang Jamspal, to their home. The lama lived and studied at Tashi Lhunpo Monastery.

---

[5] D. T. Suzuki, "The Real H. P. Blavatsky, a Study in Theosophy and a Memoir of a Great Soul, by William Kingsland (book review)," *The Eastern Buddhist*, vol. 5, no. 4 (July 1931), p. 377.

[6] W. Y. Evans-Wentz, editor, *The Tibetan Book of the Dead* (London: Oxford University Press, 1957), p. 7.

[7] Christmas Humphreys, *Exploring Buddhism* (London: George Allen and Unwin, 1974), p. 32.

[8] Nicholas and Deki Rhodes, *A Man of the Frontier: S. W. Laden La* (Kolkata: Library of Numismatic Studies, 2006), p. 3.

[9] M. M. Salanave, "The Murmur of Drums," *The Canadian Theosophist*, vol. 14, no. 4 (15 June 1933), p. 100.

[10] Mircea Eliade, *No Souvenirs: Journal 1957–1969*, translated by Fred Johnson, Jr. (New York: Harper & Row, 1977), p. 208.

After fleeing Tibet, he taught Sanskrit at Columbia University in New York City. While receiving the guest, the Muratores showed him a copy of *The Voice of the Silence*, drawing his attention to the notes. The lama was shocked to learn that such information was available in the West. Of Blavatsky, he said: "She must be a Bodhisattva,"[1] that is, an enlightened being who renounced Nirvana for the sake of the salvation of all living beings.

In their attempts to humiliate her, even the most spiteful critics cannot fail to honour Blavatsky. Once, in 1946, a derogatory article about her appeared in *Time* magazine. While attempting to belittle her, the author failed to notice that, in fact, he had shown her the highest level of respect by listing the names of outstanding personalities who had, during her lifetime, joined her cause, one of whom, Queen Victoria's favourite poet, even held a copy of *The Voice of the Silence* beside him when he was dying: "Such eminent scientists as Alfred Russel Wallace, Sir William Crookes, and Thomas Edison became members of her Theosophical Society.... When Alfred, Lord Tennyson ... died, a copy of Madame's mystical poem, *The Voice of the Silence*, lay on the table beside his bed."[2]

Light on the Path

In 1885, four years before the release of *The Voice of the Silence*, another fragment from the *Book of the Golden Precepts* was published entitled *Light on the Path*, written by Mabel Collins, a British author.

Blavatsky saw the beginning of the manuscript when they met in London: "Before my return to India in 1884, I saw Mabel Collins barely three or four times. She then showed me the first page or two of the future *Light on the Path*, wherein I recognized some phrases which were familiar to me. Therefore I the more readily accepted her description of the manner in which they had been given to her. She herself certainly believed that this book was dictated to her by 'someone' whose appearance she described."[3]

In one of the first copies of the book, Collins wrote a dedication, acknowledging that authorship belonged to Master Hilarion. Blavatsky recalls: "She saw before her, time after time, the astral figure of a dark man (a Greek who belongs to the Brotherhood of our Masters), who urged her to write under his diction. It was Hilarion, whom Olcott knows

---

[1] Sylvia Cranston, *H.P.B.: The Extraordinary Life and Influence of Helena Blavatsky, Founder of the Modern Theosophical Movement* (Santa Barbara, CA: Path Publishing House, 1998), p. 87.

[2] "Theosophy's Madame," *Time*, vol. 48, no. 20 (11 November 1946), p. 80.

[3] H. P. Blavatsky, "To All Theosophists," *Collected Writings*, vol. 11 (Wheaton, IL: Theosophical Publishing House, 1973), p. 326.

well. The results were *Light on the Path* and others. Could she have written this herself? *Never.*"[4]

Collins said that she saw writings on a wall in a place she visited spiritually: "By the help of a Master, and for an object which will be of service to the world, it is possible for the spirit of a disciple on earth to visit this higher state which we call ethereal and enter the Hall of Learning, in full waking consciousness. It was in that way that I obtained the stanzas of *Light on the Path*. It is always possible for a disciple who has once been taken there to again visit the Hall by concentration. . . . The glory of these stanzas is that they belong to humanity and that all who reach the plane on which they appear as jewelled words on a wall of stone, can read them for themselves, can ask for explanation from their own Master, can read and re-read the words (written in the mystic language which is his native language to each one who looks upon it) and study them in the light of the much-needed explanation. . . . As you enter the door from the Hall, the wall with the blazing jewels of the words of wisdom is directly opposite, and rivets the attention at once."[5]

Blavatsky confirmed its origin: "These are aphorisms as old as the *Book of the Golden Precepts*, from which they radiated — on the walls — and thence into *Light on the Path*."[6] Therefore, this fragment is also included in this edition along with Collins' notes and comments. But it should be borne in mind that only its "*main body . . .* was dictated by a true Adept, and the rest added from the inner consciousness of Miss Mabel Collins."[7]

Collins' and Blavatsky's explanations of the origins of *Light on the Path* reveal that Collins' Master, Hilarion, projected the contents of the *Book of the Golden Precepts* onto the wall from which Collins read and then wrote it down. In the same way, Blavatsky's Master, Morya, projected for her the necessary pages from the secret *Book of Dzyan*, as well as many other sources, while she was working on *The Secret Doctrine* and *Isis Unveiled*. The Cornell University professor of literature Hyram Corson described her work on the latter as follows:

"She herself told me that she wrote them down as they appeared in her eyes on another plane of objective existence, that she clearly saw the page of the book, and the quotation she needed, and simply translated what she saw into English. . . . The hundreds of books she quoted were

---

[4] Michael Gomes, "Mabel Collins' 'Romance of the White Lotus,'" *Theosophical History*, vol. 3, no. 7–8 (July–October 1991), p. 194.

[5] Mabel Collins, "The Astral and Ethereal Worlds, Part II," *The Occult Review*, vol. 36, no. 4 (October 1922), pp. 225–226.

[6] Blavatsky, "To All Theosophists," *Collected Writings*, vol. 11, p. 319.

[7] Charles J. Ryan, "H.P.B. on *Light on the Path*," *The Eclectic Theosophist*, no. 80 (March–April 1984), p. 6.

certainly not in my library, many of them not in America, some of them very rare and difficult to get in Europe, and if her quotations were from memory, then it was an even more startling feat than writing them from the ether."[1]

Therefore, it was a projection of the *Book of Dzyan* similar to a hologram, but seen with spiritual sight, that Blavatsky described in *The Secret Doctrine*: "An archaic manuscript — a collection of palm leaves made impermeable to water, fire, and air, by some specific unknown process — is before the writer's eye."[2]

Just like *The Voice of the Silence*, *Light on the Path* has become a classic of theosophical literature. The book consists of two parts, each containing 21 rules. All of these are very short, but, at the same time, incredibly profound and will become for the reader steps for spiritual ascent.

In 1888, a London newspaper reported the unique occasion of its translation into Sanskrit: "Miss Mabel Collins' *Light on the Path* has been translated into Sanskrit, and will be placed by the Hindu pundits as one of the Sanskrit classics. Translation into Sanskrit is a thing which has not been done for at least 100 years past; but the book is sufficiently Buddhistic and occult to satisfy even the learned Hindus."[3]

Interestingly, it was from *Light on the Path* that the phrase "When the student is ready, the Teacher appears" originated. Its different variations can now be found on the Internet as a saying of the Buddha.[4]

At the very beginning of the twentieth century, *Light on the Path* was reissued in Chicago by William Walker Atkinson, a member of the American Theosophical Society, together with his foreword, which is also included in this edition. He was a prolific writer, who published under various pseudonyms.

Helena Roerich considered his works written under the pseudonym Yogi Ramacharaka "very, very useful for the expansion of consciousness"[5] and recommended them to her colleagues.[6] But she regretted that his free exposition of mechanical methods, without highlighting all the dangers associated with them, led novice readers to practise the exercises he described in the hope that they would easily master the abilities of

---

[1] Charles Lazenby, "Isis Unveiled: Anecdotes about H. P. Blavatsky," *The Path*, vol. 1, no. 1 (July 1910), p. 4.

[2] Blavatsky, *The Secret Doctrine*, vol. 1, p. 1.

[3] H. P. Blavatsky, "Literary Jottings," *Collected Writings*, vol. 10 (Wheaton, IL: Theosophical Publishing House, 1964), p. 235.

[4] Barry Popik, "When the student is ready, the teacher will appear," *The Big Apple*, 29 March 2013, https://barrypopik.com/blog/when_the_student_is_ready_the_teacher_will_appear.

[5] Roerich, *Pis'ma*, vol. 9, p. 116.

[6] Roerich, *Pis'ma*, vol. 8, p. 127.

a yogi; without achieving the results they anticipated, they were greatly disappointed.[7]

Of course, Atkinson's most famous book is *The Kybalion* published in 1908 under the pseudonym "Three Initiates." The ideas expounded concerning the law of attraction, vibrations, positive thinking, and so on have influenced the entire New Thought movement. In particular, they underlie the film and book *The Secret* by Rhonda Byrne, that were released in 2006.[8]

Nevertheless, it is worth mentioning the "fly in the ointment" that was introduced into *Light on the Path*. In the first few years after the book was published, many readers objected to Rule 20 from Part 1, which says that "the vices of man become steps in the ladder" and advises the reader to "test all experience." Blavatsky herself considered it insidious and dangerous, saying that its "occult venom and close relationship to Tantrika black magic has never been suspected by the innocent and sincere admirers of this otherwise priceless little book."[9]

She further explains: "There are those whose reasoning powers have been so distorted by foreign influences that they imagine that animal passions can be so sublimated and elevated that their fury, force, and fire can, so to speak, be turned inwards; that they can be stored and shut up in one's breast until their energy is, not expanded, but turned toward higher and more holy purposes, namely, until their collective and unexpanded strength enables their possessor to enter the true Sanctuary of the Soul and stand therein in the presence of the Master — the Higher Self! For this purpose they will not struggle with their passions nor slay them. They will simply, by a strong effort of will, put down the fierce flames and keep them at bay within their natures, allowing the fire to smoulder under a thin layer of ashes."[10]

Blavatsky's warning is included in the text so that the reader can decide for themselves whether to take into account all the provisions of this Rule.

The fact that Mabel Collins, on account of her own consciousness, misinterpreted the Rule shows that the Masters do not "dictate" anything to anyone, as most people would like to believe, and therefore, as they would choose to explain the appearance of such books. If this were really a "dictation," such "inclusions" could never have arisen.

---

[7] Helena Roerich, *Pis'ma* [Letters], vol. 5 (Moscow: Mezhdunarodnyy tsentr Rerikhov, 2003), p. 290.

[8] Three Initiates, *The Kybalion: Centenary Edition* (New York: TarcherPerigee, 2018), p. xix.

[9] Ryan, "H.P.B. on *Light on the Path*," *The Eclectic Theosophist*, no. 80, p. 6.

[10] H. P. Blavatsky, "Occultism Versus the Occult Arts," *Collected Writings*, vol. 9, p. 255.

It is for this reason that disciples who are destined to give to the world a certain work or Teaching, one that will reveal and illuminate new facets of Truth, undergo a relatively long period of preparation in order to purify their body and soul, so that their consciousness can perceive the Truths transmitted to them without introducing gross distortion. For this reason, most of the channelled literature presented on the modern book market more closely resembles "Chinese whispers," by which only distorted echoes of the original Truths will reach the reader.

The Language of the Gods

Many thousands of years ago, the *Book of Dzyan* and the *Book of the Golden Precepts* were written in the secret language of *Senzar* — the sacred language of the Gods, "for there was a time when . . . Senzar was known to the Initiates of every nation, when the forefathers of the Toltec understood it as easily as the inhabitants of the lost Atlantis, who inherited it, in their turn, from the sages of the Third Race, the *Manushis*, who learnt it direct from the Devas of the Second and First Races."[1]

Senzar is the primordial language from which all other tongues originated throughout the development of humanity. It has a traditional form of speech and writing, familiar to us, but with its own specific rules; it also has higher levels which are substantially different to our common understanding and occur at the subconscious level. When, for example, the Teachers speak in Senzar to a spiritually developed person who does not know the language, that individual will have the sense that, although the Teachers are speaking in an unfamiliar tongue, they understand what is being communicated perfectly.

Blavatsky reveals a few details about Senzar in her Preface to *The Voice of the Silence*, however, versions of written text in Senzar can be found in the angelic language of John Dee, an advisor to Queen Elizabeth I, and the language of the *Voynich Manuscript*, which unveils certain secrets of the Seven Kingdoms of Nature but which scientists still cannot decipher.

Using the example of the *Zend-Avesta*, Blavatsky explains: "The Zend text is simply a secret *code* of certain words and expressions agreed upon by the original compilers, and the key to which is but with the Initiates."[2]

"The word *Zend* does not apply to any language, whether dead or living, and never belonged to any of the languages or dialects of ancient Persia. It means, as in one sense correctly stated, 'a commentary or explanation,' but it also means that which the Orientalists do not seem to have

---

[1] Blavatsky, *The Secret Doctrine*, vol. 1, p. xliii.
[2] H. P. Blavatsky, "Zoroastrianism in the Light of Occult Philosophy," *Collected Writings*, vol. 4, p. 524.

any idea about, viz., the 'rendering of the esoteric into exoteric sentences,' the veil used to conceal the correct meaning of the *Zen-(d)-zar* texts, the sacerdotal language in use among the Initiates of archaic India. Found now in several undecipherable inscriptions, it is still used and studied unto this day in the secret communities of the Eastern Adepts."[3]

The Secret Tower

The sacred *Book of Dzyan* and *Book of the Golden Precepts* are kept among others on one of the floors of the Tower of Chung in legendary Shambhala — the Pure Land. Here too lies the *Book of Maitreya Buddha*, which Blavatsky was supposed to use to work on further volumes of *The Secret Doctrine*,[4] of which five in total were planned,[5] but only two were published.

Mahatma Morya mentions the most ancient Tower in the world in a letter: "At a certain spot not to be mentioned to outsiders, there is a chasm spanned by a frail bridge of woven grasses and with a raging torrent beneath. The bravest member of your Alpine clubs would scarcely dare to venture the passage, for it hangs like a spider's web and seems to be rotten and impassable. Yet it is not; and he who dares the trial and succeeds — as he will if it is right that he should be permitted — comes into a gorge of surpassing beauty of scenery — to one of our places and to some of our people, of which and whom there is no note or minute among European geographers. At a stone's throw from the old lamasery stands the old Tower, within whose bosom have gestated generations of Bodhisattvas."[6]

It is here that the Great Lord of Shambhala stands on guard, as Lama Domo Geshe Rinpoche tells Nicholas Roerich: "Like a diamond glows the light on the Tower of Shambhala. He is there — Rigden Dragpo, indefatigable, ever vigilant in the cause of humankind. His eyes never close. And in his magic mirror he sees all events on Earth. And the might of his thought penetrates into far-off lands. For him, distance does not exist. He can render assistance to the worthy instantaneously. His powerful

---

[3] Blavatsky, "Zoroastrianism in the Light of Occult Philosophy," *Collected Writings*, vol. 4, pp. 517–518.

[4] See Trevor Baker, compiler, *The Letters of H. P. Blavatsky to A. P. Sinnett* (Pasadena, CA: Theosophical University Press, 1973), p. 195.

[5] See Arthur L. Conger, editor, *Practical Occultism: From the Private Letters of William Q. Judge* (Pasadena: Theosophical University Press, 1951), p. 94; "General Report of the Eleventh Convention and Anniversary of the Theosophical Society," *The Theosophist*, vol. 8 (Supplement to January 1887), pp. xxi, xlvii; "General Report of the Twelfth Convention and Anniversary of the Theosophical Society," *The Theosophist*, vol. 9 (Supplement to January 1888), p. xvii.

[6] Trevor Baker, compiler, *The Mahatma Letters to A. P. Sinnett* (Pasadena, CA: Theosophical University Press, 1992), p. 219.

light can destroy all darkness. His immeasurable riches are ready to aid the needy, who offer to serve the cause of righteousness. He may even change the karma of human beings."[1]

Helena Roerich describes it as follows: "Outwardly the Tower resembles a natural cliff. It is not difficult to close access to the Tower. A small collapse is able to cover the structure below. A little dam can turn the stream into a lake. In this way it is possible to transform immediately the entire area when the time comes for this. People may smile, believing that the dispatched expeditions will, sooner or later, penetrate all the gorges. But let us not forget that the power of thought will take any caravan away until the area is transfigured. Also, chemical influences will not let the curious in — this is how the Brotherhood is guarded."[2]

Here is located one of the main laboratories where the Brothers and Sisters conduct experiments on the subtlest energies and currents of various celestial orbs and constellations. Some research results are transmitted to the best earthly scientists, but they do not often listen to the ideas or inspiration that dawn upon them: "One can notice that many discoveries occurred as if a result of some kind of accident — were there not whispers from the Tower of Chung in them?"[3]

The Tower also represents an enormous multi-storey Museum, going deep into the ground. Even the richest imagination will not be able to picture the number of the most diverse items preserved in its depths in very special conditions. Thus, specimens of all the Kingdoms of Nature that have ever existed on our planet are collected here and exist in a dream-like state thanks to special gases. All the priceless masterpieces of art from all peoples and eras are carefully stored. The Tower Library contains numerous archaic tablets, scrolls, and manuscripts created from materials, inaccessible to us, by means of unique methods. In addition, members of the Brotherhood have managed to save and deliver to the Chief Stronghold many secret manuscripts that ignorant humanity would have burnt and destroyed.

Blavatsky visited a similar underground gallery: "They have records of the lives of all Initiates. Once I was in a great cave-temple in the Himalayan mountains, with my Master. There were many statues of Adepts there; pointing to one of them, he said: 'This is he whom you call Jesus. We count him to be one of the greatest among us.'"[4]

And in a letter to her family, she describes in more detail what she saw there: "In one of their underground temples, there is a colossal

---

[1] Roerich, *Vrata v budushcheye*, p. 1212.
[2] Roerich, *Agni Yoga s kommentariyami*, vol. 2, p. 733.
[3] Roerich, *Agni Yoga s kommentariyami*, vol. 2, p. 821.
[4] Blavatsky, *Revealing Cosmic Mysteries*, p. 670.

bronze statue of Jesus forgiving Mary Magdalene. Next to it is a statue of Gautama, who gives water from his cup to a beggar, as well as a statue of his disciple and brother, Ananda. And there is another sculptural group: the Buddha nearby a well, drinking from a vessel held out to him by an outcast and a prostitute. Here is what I know. However, the secret meaning of these three sculptures is better known to the Initiates than to me. But I only know that my Master is much more imbued with the love of Christ and is Christ-like than any of the modern Christians, and undoubtedly he reveres Christ more than the Pope, Luther, or Calvin does."[5]

Helena Roerich also mentions one of the lower floors of the Tower, dedicated to the era of Christ: "One cannot stay in the lower galleries for a long time, since its air is saturated with preservative gases. The difference is 25 floors."[6]

"The growth of the Museum's galleries is based on the principle of practicality of preservation. The Museum was founded in a very ancient epoch. The Temple's underground is deepened into a granite massif. The name of the first builder is known. He laid a foundation similar to the Egyptian Pyramids. The riverbed of the ancient stream among the basalt layers made it possible to significantly lower the bottom of the galleries. The first forms transferred from the Himalayas are concentrated there — the forms of the first creations that were preserved in caves."[7]

The main portion of the Chintamani Stone is housed in the deep depository of the Tower of Chung, in a special room. It "rests on a cushion that lies on a marble foundation and is set off by a circle of lithium metal."[8]

Blavatsky visited this Pure Land more than once in dreams as well as in an altered state of consciousness, as described in her long-hidden book, *The Land of the Gods*,[9] and therefore, she was able to view these sacred manuscripts not only as projections but with her own eyes.

However, during her lifetime, she informed her closest pupils that the Masters "were preparing to move even further away from the ever-encroaching foot of the Western 'invader' with his materialistic civilization."[10]

---

[5] H. P. Blavatsky, *Pis'ma druz'yam i sotrudnikam* [Letters to friends and colleagues] (Moscow: Sfera, 2002), p. 204.

[6] Helena Roerich, *Zapisi Ucheniya Zhivoy Etiki* [Records of the Teaching of Living Ethics], vol. 4 (Moscow, 2009), p. 318.

[7] Roerich, *Zapisi Ucheniya Zhivoy Etiki*, vol. 4, pp. 321–322.

[8] Roerich, *Zapisi Ucheniya Zhivoy Etiki*, vol. 4, p. 313.

[9] See H. P. Blavatsky, *The Land of the Gods* (New York: Radiant Books, 2022).

[10] Alice Cleather, *H. P. Blavatsky: Her Life and Work for Humanity* (Calcutta: Thacker, Spink & Co., 1922), p. 113.

This was due not only to the impending world wars that poisoned the Earth's atmosphere making it unbearable for the Masters, but also to Cosmic conditions that necessitated the transfer of the Chief Stronghold of Light to a different place. After all, Mother Earth's Heart "beats under the foot of sacred Shambhala."[1]

From Helena Roerich's notebooks — kept secret from the public for more than 60 years, and made available only in 2018, when it concurred with Higher Will — it is known that the Teachers moved all the laboratories and artefacts to a new site after the First and during the Second World War. Records even describe an episode in which an American pilot, who was reconnoitring an area in the Himalayas, dropped a bomb there, and was himself killed as a result. But the blast wave did destroy one of the Masters' most complex apparatus. They used it to carry out research, but had not yet managed to transfer it to a new Tower of the same name located in another, safe place.[2]

Thus, in the middle of the twentieth century, the ancient Tower of Chung, that had stood guard since the times of Atlantis, remained empty. However, as proof of their existence, the Masters of Wisdom left there "the remains of certain apparatus and mechanical devices along with a multitude of manuscripts written in languages, not yet known but highly reminiscent of Sanskrit."[3]

Copies of Sacred Books

As Blavatsky explains in the Preface, copies of treatises from the *Book of the Golden Precepts* written in various languages are preserved in monasteries belonging to the Oriental esoteric schools. But many form the basis of the sacred texts of the East, and therefore, in order to determine their true source, one must be familiar with the original in its entirety.

From a letter to her sister, we know that Blavatsky translated them from the Telugu copy, despite the fact that she also had access to the Senzar original:

"*The Voice of the Silence*, in spite of being a tiny book, becomes the Bible of the Theosophists. These are great aphorisms. I can say this, for you know that it wasn't me who composed them! I just translated them from Telugu, the oldest South Indian dialect. There are three treatises dedicated to morality: the ethical principles of the Mongolian and

---

[1] Blavatsky, *The Secret Doctrine*, vol. 2, p. 400.

[2] Helena Roerich, "Zapisi besed s Uchitelem (mashinopis')" [Records of conversations with the Master (typescript)], 01.09.1953–08.03.1954, part 1, fol. 74–75, Roerich Museum, Moscow.

[3] Roerich, "Zapisi besed s Uchitelem (mashinopis')," 01.09.1953–08.03.1954, part 1, fol. 52.

Dravidian mystics. Some of the aphorisms are absolutely and amazingly deep and beautiful."⁴

While commenting on *Light on the Path*, Blavatsky implied that the text was translated into English from the Sanskrit version of the *Book of the Golden Precepts*: "How comes it that she [Mabel Collins], ignorant of Sanskrit and having never seen the *Golden Precepts*, could use so many sentences bodily enshrined in that purely occult work?"⁵

There is also evidence of the existence of a translation in Tibetan, which was accessed by the last disciple of Mahatma Gandhi, Reverend Father Anthony Elenjimittam, a Catholic priest and Buddhist monk from India, known as Bhikshu Ishabodhananda meaning "Mendicant Monk whose Beatitude is Jesus and Buddha." In his autobiography, he writes:

"In my return to Kalimpong I stayed in the Tibetan monastery, taking part in their choral office and learning various branches of Mahayana and Tantrism. It was in that monastery that I first read with Lama Ping *The Voice of the Silence*, the *Book of the Golden Precepts*, with the English translation by Helena Petrovna Blavatsky. With the help of the Tibetan Lama, I could compare the English translation made by Helena Petrovna Blavatsky with the original, taking notes from the interpretation given by the Lama."⁶

In 1964, Father Anthony published *The Voice of the Silence* in Bombay. In the introduction he emphasizes that Blavatsky "beautifully translated"⁷ these fragments from the *Book of the Golden Precepts*, being in a position to judge its quality having compared her English translation with the Tibetan version. His commentaries written from both Christian and Buddhist points of view are an invaluable addition to the present book.

So why can no one else gain access even to the copies of this sacred manuscript?

We find the answer to this question in the writings of Nicholas Roerich, where he talks about the Tibetan Gospel entitled *The Life of Saint Issa, the Best of the Sons of Men*. Its original was written in India in Pali, in the mid-first century CE. Then the scrolls were moved to Nepal, and from there to Tibet, where they were housed in a monastery near Lhasa (whether the manuscript is preserved there to this day remains unknown). Subsequently, lamas who visited Lhasa made translations

---

⁴ Blavatsky, *Pis'ma druz'yam i sotrudnikam*, p. 671.

⁵ Blavatsky, "To All Theosophists," *Collected Writings*, vol. 11, p. 317.

⁶ Anthony Elenjimittam, *Cosmic Ecumenism via Hindu-Buddhist Catholicism* (Bombay: Aquinas Publications, 1983), p. 270.

⁷ Anthony Elenjimittam, *The Voice of Silence* (Bombay: Aquinas Publications, 1981), p. ii.

of the manuscript into Tibetan, thereby producing copies for their own monasteries.

In this manner, a copy in Tibetan ended up at Hemis Monastery. Its translation into French was first published in 1894 by journalist Nicolas Notovitch, who was then discredited by the Church so that the truth about the years which Jesus Christ spent in the countries of the East would not become publicly known.

Later, at least three people had access to this Tibetan manuscript, Nicholas Roerich being one of them. He writes: "Documents such as manuscripts about Christ and the book about Shambhala lie in the 'darkest' place."[1]

This is a reference to the existence of special treasuries dug deep into the ground, impenetrable to light, for the preservation of ancient manuscripts. While ordinary monks are unaware of their existence, the abbots of the monasteries are aware, and only they, being capable of perceiving the true motive of the inquirer, decide who may or may not be granted access.

In Blavatsky's writings, we also find information concerning the fact that volumes of the Commentaries on the *Book of Dzyan*, some of which are of incredible antiquity, are kept secret and apart, and that during her lifetime they were under the charge of the Eighth Panchen Lama in Shigatse, Tibet.[2]

About the Present Edition

In 1927, at the request of His Holiness the Ninth Panchen Lama, a special edition of *The Voice of the Silence* was prepared for publication in Beijing, China. The editions that existed at that time did not meet with the approval of the Panchen Lama, as they contained errors that were absent in the 1889 original. He allowed corrections to be made only to obvious typographical errors. This edition contained an autograph foreword in Tibetan by the Panchen Lama, editorial notes and a commentary from its preparers, Alice Leighton Cleather and Basil Crump, and a message from the Panchen Lama's secretary, B. T. Chang. The present book includes all the materials compiled in that 1927 edition.

B. T. Chang points out that Blavatsky translated into English from Tibetan, although she herself stated that it was from Telugu. This again suggests that her translation was so accurate and precise that the Panchen Lama, who had access to the Tibetan copy, had no doubt that she had translated it from Tibetan.

---

[1] Roerich, *Altay — Gimalai*, p. 120.
[2] H. P. Blavatsky, "The Secret Books of Lam-rim and Dzyan," *Collected Writings*, vol. 14 (Wheaton, IL: Theosophical Publishing House, 1985), p. 422.

In 1989, the Centenary edition of *The Voice of the Silence* was published with a foreword by His Holiness the Fourteenth Dalai Lama, which is included here, too, for completeness.

Since, while reading fragments from the *Book of the Golden Precepts*, questions may arise in the reader's mind that relate to the acquisition of magical abilities and the relationship between Masters and their disciples, Blavatsky's articles are included here to give a better understanding of these topics. Also included are everyday recommendations from Helena Roerich for a healthier life and *At the Feet of the Master* by Alcyone (Jiddu Krishnamurti) that outlines the qualifications necessary to walk a spiritual path. Of the latter, Roerich says: "The little book *At the Feet of the Master* is superb and, undoubtedly, was written within the Ray of Master K.H. in the days of Krishnamurti's adolescence."[3]

Initially, *The Voice of the Silence* was translated by Blavatsky for members of the Esoteric Section. Within this section, an Inner Group was formed consisting of twelve: six men and six women. Alice Cleather, who prepared the Beijing edition of *The Voice of the Silence* under the auspices of His Holiness the Ninth Panchen Lama, was one of these twelve.

Blavatsky prepared for this group special esoteric instructions that revealed more knowledge than could be given to the general public during the "intellectual" nineteenth century. One of these secret subjects was the great significance of the Heart. Blavatsky's instructions on this subject are included in this publication also.

In 1889, Blavatsky wrote an extensive letter addressed to the members of the Esoteric Section. This letter is of particular value since it is written in the context of the Rules given in the *Book of the Golden Precepts* that Initiates must follow. The letter shows how difficult it was for her to sow seeds of wisdom in the West, thereby fulfilling the ancient commandment of Tsongkhapa "that enjoins the Rahats (Arhats) to make an attempt to enlighten the world, including the 'white barbarians,' every century, at a certain specified period of the cycle."[4]

In addition, an extensive glossary with more than one thousand entries has been prepared that includes all terms and names found throughout the book. In order to ensure that their meaning is understood in the same manner as was intended in Blavatsky's works, in most cases *The Theosophical Glossary* on which she worked during the last days of her life, has been used. However, many definitions have been written from the position of new facets of Truth revealed by the Masters

---

[3] Helena Roerich, *Pis'ma* [Letters], vol. 2 (Moscow: Mezhdunarodnyy tsentr Rerikhov, 2000), p. 534.

[4] H. P. Blavatsky, "Tsong-Kha-Pa — Lohans in China," *Collected Writings*, vol. 14 (Wheaton, IL: Theosophical Publishing House, 1985), p. 431.

of Wisdom in the twentieth and twenty-first centuries. This is intended to help the reader understand the processes occurring in modern times from the theosophical point of view, since rather than being something frozen in the nineteenth century, Theosophy is more relevant now than ever before.

But the main difference between this edition and the many others produced previously is that it contains texts from *The Voice of the Silence* written in a modern language style in addition to the original 1889 text that includes all of Blavatsky's notes. This decision was made after conducting a survey among American readers, the results of which showed that it is quite difficult for the current generation to comprehend texts written in the style of the King James Bible, moreover, a text containing numerous terms in Sanskrit that would be incomprehensible to the average reader.

Nevertheless, it is worth bearing in mind that when sacred texts are given by the Masters in a particular language, a special ordering of words is composed so as to obtain the necessary vibrations. What is important here is not the grammar of such texts, but the rhythm that, like a mantra, has a positive effect on the consciousness of the reader, around whom sparks and lights flash on an invisible plane. These fires have a beneficial effect not only on the reader, but also on the surrounding space.

Therefore, in the original 1889 text, the phonetic spelling of foreign words which Blavatsky used has been preserved. The choice of word might have been dictated by the necessity to create a certain vibration in English through the combination of particular letters or words based on their pronunciation in various languages. For example, the Sanskrit word for "knowledge" is *jnana*, yet Blavatsky uses its derivatives in other languages: *dnyan* in Marathi and *gnyana* in Telugu. The reader should bear in mind that the fragments Blavatsky translated into English do not belong to Sanskrit or Tibetan or Telugu sacred texts, but come from the one primary source that has imbued all scriptures in those languages with its high ethics.

For the same reason, the fragments in modern English from the *Book of the Golden Precepts* are intended to assist in general understanding, but in no way to replace Blavatsky's original poetic translation. In the same manner, when studying the Bible, a person might begin by reading one of the more accessible translations before proceeding to the King James version.

The purpose of this publication is to ensure that anyone, regardless of age or spiritual inclination, can understand the essence of what is written, for it is in essence not only "a pure Buddhistic work," but also a work that is capable of uniting representatives of all religions and all seekers of Truth.

May those who illuminate their heart with the Light of Divine Wisdom and decide to follow the Secret Path to Enlightenment from one life to the next increase in number. And may these pilgrims become guiding stars for others around them, following the great example of those who have walked this Path before: Jesus Christ, Mary Magdalene, Gautama Buddha, Yashodhara, Muhammad, Khadija, Krishna, Rukmini, and many, many other saints from different countries around the world.

THE GOLDEN STAIRS

Behold the Truth before you:

A clean life, an open mind,
A pure heart, an eager intellect,
An unveiled spiritual perception,
A brotherliness for all,

A readiness to give and receive advice and instruction,
A loyal sense of duty to the Teacher,
A willing obedience to the behests of Truth,
Once we have placed our confidence in,
And believe that Teacher to be in possession of it;

A courageous endurance of personal injustice,
A brave declaration of principles,
A valiant defence of those who are unjustly attacked,
And a constant eye to the ideal of human progression,
And perfection which the secret science depicts —

These are the golden stairs
Up the steps of which the learner may climb
To the Temple of Divine Wisdom.

Dedicated to the Few

THE VOICE OF THE SILENCE

Three Fragments from the *Book of the Golden Precepts*

For the daily use of lanoos (disciples)

∴

Translated and annotated by

H.P.B.

With Notes and Comments by

REVEREND FATHER ANTHONY ELENJIMITTAM
ALICE CLEATHER AND BASIL CRUMP

FOREWORD
THE BODHISATTVA PATH

I FIRST MET the members of the Theosophical Society more than thirty years ago, when I visited India to attend the celebrations of the 2500th anniversary of the Buddha. Ever since, I have had the pleasure of sharing my thoughts with Theosophists from various parts of the world on many occasions. I have much admiration for their spiritual pursuits.

I believe that individuals can be good human beings without necessarily being spiritual. I also accept their right in not wanting to be spiritual or to believe in a particular religion. At the same time, I have always believed that inner or spiritual development is necessary for greater human happiness and to increase our capacity to benefit others. I am therefore happy to have this long association with the Theosophists and to learn about the Centenary Edition: *The Voice of the Silence* which is being brought out this year. I believe that this book has strongly influenced many sincere seekers and aspirants to the wisdom and compassion of the Bodhisattva Path. I very much welcome this Centenary Edition and hope that it will benefit many more.

The Dalai Lama
26 April 1989

FOREWORD
THE PATH OF LIBERATION

All beings desire liberation from misery.
Seek, therefore, for the causes of misery
   and expunge them.
By entering on the Path, liberation
   from misery is attained.
Exhort, then, all beings to enter the Path.

The Panchen Lama
Inner Mongolia, 1927

THE CHINESE VERSION OF THE PATH OF LIBERATION

*by Mr. Wang Ming Ching,
one of the Tashi Lama's private secretaries*

無量愁裏非人願
根基煩惱剔除戒
能離惑毒行善道
常懷佛說緊注意

班禪活佛所賜藏文翻成中國文字

TRANSLATION FROM THE CHINESE

*Inscription by the Living Buddha, the Ninth Panchen Lama
(translated from Tibetan into Chinese)*

> Boundless compassion and sorrow,
>   a vow beyond human desire.
> The roots of suffering and affliction,
>   are to be separated and removed.
> One must free oneself from malice and poison,
>   and walk the path of virtue.
> Always keep the Buddha in your heart,
>   and speak with mindfulness and care.

ALTERNATIVE TRANSLATION FROM THE TIBETAN

by Dr. Lozang Jamspal

Those who do not want unbearable suffering,
should eliminate its cause, the defilements.
In order to achieve liberation, free from (the defilements),
one should practise thoroughly the good path leading to (liberation).
Thus (the Buddha) declared the teaching of (the four noble) truths.

His Holiness the Fourteenth Dalai Lama, Tenzin Gyatso (b.1935) is the spiritual leader of the Tibetan people and of Tibetan Buddhism. Known for his teachings on compassion, kindness, and world peace, he has become a global advocate for non-violence, human rights, and interfaith dialogue receiving the Nobel Peace Prize in 1989. He has also authored or co-authored nearly 150 books, including *The Art of Happiness* (1998), *The Book of Joy* (2016), and *Voice for the Voiceless* (2025).

His Holiness has a long relationship with the Theosophical Society and individual Theosophists. In his book, *Toward a True Kinship of Faiths* (2010), the Dalai Lama recalls that his first visit to the Society in 1956, when he was exposed to a movement that sought to unite the wisdom of the world's spiritual traditions and science, left a deep impression on him and changed his views. Over the next decades, His Holiness paid many visits to the Society and it hosted his visit to Chicago in 2011. In the same year, the Dalai Lama agreed to become its honorary member.

Learn more at: www.dalailama.com.

His Holiness the Ninth Panchen Lama, Thubten Choekyi Nyima (1883–1937) was a prominent spiritual leader in Tibetan Buddhism, who performed multiple Kalachakra initiations to audiences of tens of thousands. Under his supervision from 1914 to 1918, a gigantic statue of Maitreya Buddha was built at Tashi Lhunpo Monastery. It is the largest gilded copper statue in the world. It was reported that after the Panchen Lama's passing, the Maitreya statue was seen weeping, drops of emotion streaming down the sculpture's face.

FOREWORD

ENGAGED in the apostolate of education as we are for the last three decades or so, it has now become crystal clear to us that education worth imparting and receiving should be rooted in the esoteric wisdom of saints, sages, and saviours. Technical, scientific, and industrial education, when grafted on to the man-making education of saints and seers, acquires its true value and serves as a blessing to mankind. Otherwise, education becomes miseducation, and as such a curse to the educands and the society at large.

What is history, geography, physics, chemistry, mathematics, geometry, trigonometry, linguistics, and other subjects taught in our schools and colleges without self-knowledge, mind-control, self-conquest, inward rapture, inner vision, ecstatic creativity and divine dynamics, and idealistic enthusiasm in man? All are empty shows without truth, all big size without substances. We become educated and cultured and graduates, and yet our life is lived on planes lower than cats and dogs, pigs and apes. We have not learnt the art of mental concentration, inner equipoise, patient painstaking perseverance in the fulfilling of duties allotted to, or assumed by, us.

Seeing, studying, and experiencing the educational world, specially in India since Independence, we have come to the conclusion that the priorities in education, which we formulated years ago both through spoken and written words, are silence, meditation, discipline, purity, work (or industry), and study (or learning). This is the pathway we have to follow if we are to improve ourselves and those committed to our care.

This education we call basic. Mahatma Gandhi, however, defined Basic Education as craft-centred education. To us Basic Education means man-making training and discipline that will help us to unfold all the latent divine, human, psychic, mental, and moral powers inlaid in us with a view to benefitting oneself and the society.

For mental sanity, physical health, adroit utilization of one's intellectual, moral, and spiritual powers, we need the esoteric wisdom which moulded seers and sages of both the East and the West. "What does it profit a man if he gained the whole world, but suffered the loss of his own soul?" Hence, we have decided to let the official government recognition go and all that is meant by that and steer straight our lonely path, a solitary and defiant path which sages in India in our days, men like Mahatma Gandhi in his Sevagram Ashram, Gurudev Tagore at Shantiniketan, Sri Aurobindo Ghose in Pondicherry Ashram, Ramana Maharshi at Arunachala, Swami Shivananda at the Forest University in Rishikesh, and others elsewhere have done. All these systems of education are based on perennial philosophy and esoteric wisdom of sages, the wisdom religion comprehensive and integrative of all other spheres of human life, including politics, economics, and technological and scientific progress. With this in view, we have decided to bring to the doors of readers some of the select esoteric classics which form the pages of the universal revelation of God, this Bible of the world of which a small chapter is the Bible of the Jews and the Christians.

First in this series of the scriptures of wisdom religion which can impregnate and fructify our educational, social, economic, and cultural fields — even politics, diplomacy, and industrial power — is *The Voice of the Silence*, or fragments from the *Book of the Golden Precepts*, which has been beautifully translated by Helena Petrovna Blavatsky from the original Tibetan, dedicating it to "the few." Yes, many are called but few are chosen, because only a few are prepared to pay the price for self-unfoldment, crucifixion of selfishness in all its forms and manifestations, and dedicate themselves to the life of the Universal Spirit with which we are one, even as distant rays of the sun reaching the muddy earth are identical with the luminous sun up above.

The world today cares little or nothing for mysticism, transcendental ethics, divine life, and esoteric wisdom. But, joining "the few," we refuse to swim along the currents of worldliness and sense-bound and skin-deep life. We are born for higher things. *Ad majora natus sum* — I am born for higher things of life, viz., God-realized dynamics in life.

The Voice of the Silence, which we have now the joy to introduce to our readers, is meant not only for the Tibetan *lanoos* (disciples), but for all aspirants for higher achievements in enlightenment and God-realization. While preserving the original translation of the text from Tibetan by H.P.B., we have ventured to give our own annotations and comments on phrases and passages which, in the estimation of the present editor, needed elucidation or explanation.

Convinced as we are that human life, at its best, is God-realized dynamics for the improvement of social, educational, and economic and cultural life rooted in ethics and spiritual values, we have decided to dedicate each issue of our Basic Education quarterly to one or more outstanding scriptural and philosophical texts with commentary if need be, with a view to strengthening aspirants after higher divine life. Grains of diamond weigh more than tons of pebbles. *Intelligenti pauca* — few words enough for an intelligent aspirant. Among such rare pearls and diamonds is *The Voice of the Silence* which the editor hopes would "point out the Way — however dimly, and lost among the host — as does the evening star to those who tread their path in darkness."

Anthony Elenjimittam,
alias Bhikshu Ishabodhananda
St. Catherine of Siena School
Mount Mary, Bandra
Bombay 400 050
15 August 1964

Anthony Elenjimittam (1915–2011) was an Indian philosopher, theologian, and writer, as well as a Catholic priest of the Dominican order and Buddhist monk known by the name of Bhikshu Ishabodhananda ("Mendicant Monk whose Beatitude is Jesus and Buddha").

Being the last disciple of Mahatma Gandhi, Father Anthony dedicated his entire life to creating harmony and mutual understanding between the religions of the peoples of every race and creed. In 1957, he founded the Welfare Society for Destitute Children in Mumbai, India, which includes the St. Catherine of Siena School and the Aquinas Industrial School. The goal of the society is to gather marginalized children, heal their trauma of abandonment and abuse, provide them with shelter and food, and educate them to create fraternal humanity and unity.

In 1962, Pope John XXIII received Father Anthony in the Vatican and confirmed his mission for the orphans in Mumbai as well as his missionary apostolate to foster spiritual union among religions, races, and nations. The pontiff offered to make him an archbishop, yet Father Anthony declined in order to continue his evangelical mission in Jesus' poverty and the work Gandhi had given him. Furthermore, his ecumenical activity was supported by the Patriarch of Venice, Albino Luciani, later Pope John Paul I.

Up until his final days, Father Anthony continued his pilgrimage between the East and the West, maintaining a busy schedule as a lecturer, writer, and spiritual guide. He has written more than fifty books on interreligious understanding and has translated and interpreted some of India's most important spiritual texts.

Learn more at: www.padreanthony.org.

寂音跋

Madame H. P. Blavatsky 女士之《金篋寶笈》(The Golden Precepts) 原名 *The Voice of the Silence*，譯來原有三卷，首述歸原復冬之路，次之普門音，三之兩足尊倫之高氏於北京求知三世，白氏克蘭夫人與其道友刊校重行， Mrs. A. L. Cleather, Mr. Basil Crump 復版，可假人造之音，吾心唯明，萬物苟中心寂靜，欲斷愛憎之念，學者須安歸真，即由先知佛外求人之真名，之哲傳燈，兼採先覺見性明心之鐸，中世之喻，道而不偏於漢學，未以惜人之心，必於異見，覺世菩提，啟蒙之益，補譯為漢卷，末誠得我佛木鐸。

本書係俄國白拉伐貴革女士 Blavatsky 由藏文譯來，原書都三卷，首門之去冬。夫人。Mrs. A. L. Cleather 君。音普者，心之聲也。萬有之本，萬有真道之具首，梵音義，如每為觀世音菩薩，所以學者去安歸國尊外知佛。

The mind is the great slayer of the Real. Let the disciple slay the slayer.

此法明除妄念，本章即本書要日，本書譯出世間消極之學，末以誌景仰，並明尚鮮。

余未克執筆愛之價也。克蘭夫人先已歸真，未願之未焉執此書人出世嚮翰後數行於卷末。

民國十六年六月　　浙江張屏之謹跋

The Chinese note written by Mr. B. T. Chang for the information of those Chinese who do not read English

FOREWORD

Having written a Chinese note, I am further requested by the editors to write a few lines in English. I deem it an honour and a privilege to do so, and offer herewith a recapitulation of what I have set forth in Chinese.

Since its translation into English from the Tibetan by Madame H. P. Blavatsky in 1889, this little book, the gem of Buddhist teachings, has enjoyed a wide circulation among Europeans and Americans interested in Buddhism. There is, therefore, little need for me to recommend it to foreign readers, except to point out that what is embodied in it comprises a part of the teachings of the Esoteric School.

What strikes me most in the opening chapter is the sentence: "The mind" — i.e., the lower mind — "is the great slayer of the Real. Let the disciple slay the slayer." These are the words that sound the keynote of the Buddha's teachings. Time and again the Buddha commands his disciples to suppress the activities of the lower mind for the benefit of the Higher Self, because anything and everything in the exterior Universe consists of nothing but sense impressions created by one's lower mind, which is apt to lead the aspirant astray.[1] The disciple should not seek truth elsewhere, but should try to find it within himself. He will then be able to hear the Voice of the Silence or, in the language of the Chinese Buddhists, the "Divine Voice of the Self." Tradition says that Avalokiteshvara attained the state of a Bodhisattva after hearing the Divine Voice of the Self.[2] This doctrine is greatly revered by the Chinese, who got it from the Sanskrit.

Madame Blavatsky had a profound knowledge of Buddhist philosophy, and the doctrines she promulgated were those of many great teachers. This book is like a call to men to forsake desire, dispel every evil thought, and enter the true Path. In Fragment II the passage which likens the mind to a mirror sounds exactly like what is stated in the *Chuan Teng Lu*, a Chinese Buddhist work of renown. This allegory also

---
[1] See note 5, p. 65.
[2] See note 1, p. 26.

may have its origin in some Sanskrit work, from which it found its way into both Chinese and Tibetan Buddhist works; or, more probably, the Tibetans have derived it from a Chinese source.[1]

In this materialistic world, the majority of people, especially Europeans and Americans, always absurdly regard Buddhism as a system of philosophy which advocates nothing but passivity and inactivity. A perusal of this book will certainly dispel such mistaken notions from the minds of even the most sceptical.

It has been suggested to me that, for the benefit of the Chinese Buddhists, this work should be translated into Chinese. I quite agree with this idea, but pressure of work has hitherto prevented me from writing more than these few lines. Although they form an inadequate recognition of the merit of the book, I offer them because of my great reverence for its teachings; and I hope to be able to undertake the translation at some future time.

B. T. Chang
Beijing, July 1927

TRANSLATION FROM THE CHINESE

THIS BOOK is a translation by Madame H. P. Blavatsky of Russia from Tibetan of three fragments from a collection of treatises titled the *Book of the Golden Precepts*. The first fragment discusses the Voice of the Silence, while the second and third guide us on the path to spiritual enlightenment and the return to our primordial source. Blavatsky's English translation was published at the end of the nineteenth century and has since become widely read in Europe. This reprint with annotations by Buddhist scholar Mrs. A. L. Cleather and fellow devotee Mr. Basil Crump was prepared last winter in Beijing.

The Voice of the Silence is the voice of the heart. As the Buddha pointed out, all phenomena are manifestations of the mind; all that exists in the Three Worlds consists only of sense impressions that belong to the mind. Thus, the path to wisdom lies within our own heart. If we can understand the heart clearly, there is no need to seek in the external. The path of enlightenment begins with learning to hear the Voice of the Silence within. In Chinese Buddhism, the Dharma has long been referred to as the Voice of the Divine. Indeed, it was by attending to this Voice that the Bodhisattva Avalokiteshvara attained enlightenment.

---

[1] See note 8, p. 45.

In its essence, this book teaches us how to renounce desire and attachment, shed delusion, and make the return to Truth. In the first fragment, we are told that true reality is ravaged by the tyranny of delusion, which the disciple must dispel. It teaches: "The mind is the great slayer of the Real. Let the disciple slay the slayer." This faithfully captures the same truths indicated by the Buddha about the realization of the true nature of the mind. Indeed, one might compare Blavatsky to the temple bell which awakens us from our stupor. The book also draws wisdom from ancient sages. The second fragment, for example, contains a metaphor, likening the mind to a mirror, that aligns perfectly with the teachings found in *The Record of the Transmission of the Lamp*, an important treatise in Chinese Buddhism.

In our modern materialistic society, Buddhism is often mistaken for a passive or even apathetic philosophy, and this is especially true in the West. I believe this book can help to rectify this in no small way, having a significant and salubrious influence on human hearts and minds. While Mrs. Cleather has requested a Chinese translation of this work, unfortunately other obligations have prevented me from undertaking such a task. In the meantime, I offer these few lines to indicate both my admiration and my deeper aspiration that a Chinese translation may be carried out in the future.

Respectfully,
B. T. Chang
*Zhejiang, June,
Year 16 of the Republic of China (1927)*

FOREWORD

THE PRESENT REPRINT has been undertaken largely because the original edition has been out of print for many years, while those issued since H.P.B.'s death in 1891 contain errors and even, in some cases, deliberate alterations and omissions. Our aim has, therefore, been to restore to its original integrity the most beautiful and poetical volume of H. P. Blavatsky's great literary bequest.

The circumstances under which the opportunity arose to effect this work of restoration were singularly fortunate. Reaching Beijing in December 1925, after studying for seven years in India, we were privileged to come into close touch with His Holiness the Tashi Lama,[1] who

---

[1] C.C. (Alice Cleather and Basil Crump): *The Tashi Lama*. An incarnation of Amitabha (see note 2, p. 70). His Tibetan title is *Panchen Rinpoche* (Precious Gem of Wisdom). According to the Tashi Lhunpo records, *Sangye* (Buddha), seeing the degradation of his secret doctrines, left the "Western Paradise" (a real locality; the abode of the Arhats and their disciples) and incarnated in the fourteenth century as Tsongkhapa. He founded the Yellow or Reformed Order (Gelugpa) and the hierarchy of Tashi Lamas, in whom that incarnation continues. Therefore, they rank esoterically as "High Initiates," taking precedence of the Dalai Lamas of Lhasa, whose functions are more exoteric and temporal (*Theosophical Glossary*, p. 247). In a letter to a German occultist H.P.B. wrote: "There is in the Himalayas a nucleus of Adepts of various nationalities, and the Tashi Lama knows them, and they act together; and some of them are with him and yet remain unknown in their true character, even to the average lamas. My Master [M.] and K.H., and several others I know personally, are there, coming and going." These Adepts belong to the Order of the Bodhisattvas (*Nirmanakayas*) who, with the Buddha as their Chief, are recognized by all Mahayana Buddhists as the highest ideal to which humanity can aspire (see note 4, p. 73). Within the Gelugpa Order Tsongkhapa founded "the Mystic Brotherhood connected with its Chiefs" (*Theosophical Glossary*, p. 405) and wrote a treatise of practical instructions called *Lamrim* (the Graded Path) in two portions: one for ecclesiastical and exoteric purposes, the other for disciples (*lanoos*) of "the Secret School near Shigatse, attached to the private retreat of the Tashi Lama." Twelve extracts from some 73 rules are given by H.P.B. in her essay *Practical Occultism*, and the Esoteric School she founded in 1888 was affiliated to the above and remained under the same guidance *while she lived*. Chinese Buddhists regard the Tashi Lama as the great unifying power who holds together ▸

had left Tibet in 1924 on a special mission to China and Mongolia. As members of his Order, part of the work we undertook at his request for Buddhism was the present reprint, as the only true exposition in English of the Heart Doctrine of the Mahayana and its noble ideal of self-sacrifice for humanity.

During many years of study and initiation in Tibet, H.P.B. spent a considerable time at Tashi Lhunpo, and knew the predecessor of the present Tashi Lama very well. The Golden Precepts here translated by her for the use of her pupils describe the processes of meditation and self-conquest by which the earnest disciple may hope, in the course of many incarnations, to become a Master of Wisdom, a Nirmanakaya, who follows the Buddha on the Path of Compassion for suffering humanity and remains "unselfish to the endless end."[2] That such exalted beings exist as living men is known to all Oriental mystics who belong to the various schools of yoga to which H.P.B. refers in her Preface. In China and Mongolia, as in India, we find their existence taken for granted by those who have any knowledge of esoteric philosophy.

The Tibetan sentences, reproduced in facsimile as a foreword, were written by His Holiness the Tashi Lama with his own hand specially for this reprint. They were sent at a time when he was on a journey to Inner Mongolia, and constantly occupied in receiving Mongolian princes, lamas, and thousands of pilgrims. They are written in the "characters with heads" (Tibetan: *uchen*; Sanskrit: *matra*) used for writing religious and other important matter, and for printing. The "headless characters" or current scripts (Tibetan: *ume*) are used in three styles: one a large carefully formed hand for copying; another, smaller and more cursive, for letter writing; and a third which resembles shorthand and is used for all purposes where speed and brevity are required.[3] The Tashi Lama also uses a private script, unlike Tibetan, which is probably one of the ciphers of Senzar.[4]

In his foreword, the Tashi Lama has expressed in somewhat different language the exhortation, quoted from the Buddha in Fragment III of *The Voice of the Silence*, to forsake "the eight dire miseries."[5] In China, Guanyin ("the Divine Voice of the Self")[6] is regarded as the Liberator of mankind from these eight miseries, which are really "eight states or

---

the Asiatic Buddhist peoples, Tibet, China, Mongolia, Japan, and the Buddhist tribes of Asiatic Russia, such as the Buryats and Kalmyks.
    [2] Fragment III of *The Voice of the Silence*, p. 73.
    [3] See Sarat Chandra Das, *A Tibetan-English Dictionary with Sanskrit Synonyms* (Calcutta: Bengal Secretariat Book Depot, 1902), pp. 910, 911, 1132.
    [4] See note 1, p. 24.
    [5] Fragment III of *The Voice of the Silence*, p. 65.
    [6] See note 1, p. 26.

situations in which it is impossible to hear the Law of the Buddha (and therefore difficult to attain salvation)."[1]

The Tashi Lama's final injunction also recalls the one in Fragment II: "give light and comfort to the toiling pilgrim," etc.[2]

Further light will be thrown on these sentences — apparently so simple and elementary — by referring to *The Secret Doctrine*, which reads:

"The Seven Ways to Bliss (*Moksha* or *Nirvana*) were not. The Great Causes of Misery (*Nidana* and *Maya*) were not, for there was no one to produce and get ensnared by them."[3]

In the Commentary on this Stanza, H.P.B. says that the twelve *nidanas* "belong to the theory of the stream of catenated law which produces merit and demerit, and finally brings karma into full sway. It is based upon the great truth that reincarnation is to be dreaded, as existence in this world only entails upon man suffering, misery, and pain."[4] In *The Theosophical Glossary*, she writes: "The *nidanas* belong to the most subtle and abstruse doctrines of the Eastern metaphysical system."[5] They are symbolically depicted in the twelve divisions of the rim of the Tibetan Wheel of Life which illustrates "the process of the working of successive existences and is helpful in meditating on them and in methods for getting rid of their influences, etc. The doctrine involved in the *nidanas* is fully dealt with in Tsongkhapa's great work, the *Lamrim Chenmo*. He sums up the argument thus: The certitude that all these things are in their very essence void and yet that from the one, its fruit, the other springs forth, the two uninterruptedly hither or thither mutually assisting each other — what can be more wonderful than this, and what more stupendous has arisen!"[6]

Speaking of this as the fundamental doctrine of both Hinayana and Mahayana, H.P.B. adds, in her Commentary: "the tenets of the latter are as old as the hills that have contained such schools from time immemorial."[7] Thus, although Buddhism (i.e., Gautama's exoteric doctrine) did not reach Tibet via China until the seventh century CE, the esoteric schools of the *Bodhidharma* had always existed in the mountain fastnesses of that country, and sent out their emissaries to enlighten mankind from time to time as karma and Cyclic Law permitted. As far back in Chinese history as 2205 BCE, we find the Emperor Yu obtaining his occult wisdom and

---

[1] See Reginald Johnston, *Buddhist China* (London: John Murray, 1913), p. 288.
[2] Fragment II of *The Voice of the Silence*, p. 52.
[3] Blavatsky, *The Secret Doctrine*, vol. 1, p. 38.
[4] Blavatsky, *The Secret Doctrine*, vol. 1, p. 39.
[5] Blavatsky, *The Theosophical Glossary*, p. 229.
[6] Das, *Tibetan-English Dictionary*, p. 537.
[7] Blavatsky, *The Secret Doctrine*, vol. 1, p. 39.

his system of theocracy from "the Great Teachers of the Snowy Range" in *Xizang* (Tibet); and the term *Xue Shan Bu* (schools of the snowy mountains) is often met with.

There is a Buddha for each of the Seven Root Races[8] and they all teach the same essential truths, each one giving out only so much as mankind at large can assimilate at that particular stage of its development, and reserving the more advanced and philosophical ideas for chosen disciples who prove their capacity to understand them.

Those disciples of Gautama who became Arhats (Chinese: *Lohan*) spread the Good Law throughout Asia; and after Tsongkhapa's reforms in the fourteenth century, with the Tashi Lama's permission, at the end of that century, "to avert strife,"[9] about one hundred were sent to China, some founding the celebrated Tiantai (Japanese: *Tendai*) School, and others settling on the sacred Island of Putuo in the Zhoushan Group, where the Heart Doctrine and the Chan School of Meditation flourished for many centuries. They had been preceded by others, who first came from Kashmir as early as 100 BCE (3,000 of Kali Yuga). In the Western Hills near Beijing, in the Temple of the Clouds, is the Hall of Five Hundred Lohans, where, says H.P.B., "the statues of the first-comers are arranged below, while one solitary Lohan is placed quite under the roof of the building, which seems to have been built in commemoration of their visit."[10]

The Tashi Lama's Garuda emblem is reproduced by permission from a letter in our possession. The monogram on it is the All-Powerful Ten (Tibetan: *Namchu Wangden*), the letters being *o, u, h, k, s, m, l, v, r, y*. The Chinese characters on either side of the Garuda's tail stand for "symbol of Panchen Rinpoche." This symbolic creature, half-man, half-bird, is the *Khyung* or phoenix of Tibetan mythology, the emblem of cyclic and periodic Time, and especially of the Maha Kalpa.[11] It is the Great Bird of the mystic treatises which is "the Aum throughout eternal ages,"[12] and is also the vehicle of Vishnu and Krishna in Hindu mythology. Here it represents Panchen Rinpoche as the incarnation of the Dhyani-Buddha Amitabha, while the serpent in its beak is the symbol of an Initiate.[13] The Garuda Yantra charm is highly esteemed in Tibet, where it is also known as *Namkha Ding* or "sky-soarer" and in Chinese as *Leigong* or genie of

---

[8] See note 1, p. 56.
[9] Blavatsky, "Tsong-Kha-Pa — Lohans in China," *Collected Writings*, vol. 14, p. 427.
[10] Blavatsky, "Tsong-Kha-Pa — Lohans in China," *Collected Writings*, vol. 14, p. 429.
[11] See *Yuga* in Glossary, p. 436.
[12] Fragment I of *The Voice of the Silence*, p. 31.
[13] See *Naga* in Glossary, p. 354.

thunder who is the agent of karmic vengeance (nemesis) on criminals. The American Indian thunderbird is, obviously, the same symbol.

We are particularly indebted to the encyclopaedic dictionary of Rai Bahadur Sarat Chandra Das for confirmations of H.P.B., especially regarding esoteric Mahayana and the living Initiates, generally disputed or ignored by Western Orientalists. As he obtained all his material personally from the best authorities at Tashi Lhunpo and other important centres[1] where H.P.B. also claimed to have studied, his confirmation is the more valuable. Being a Hindu and a Sanskrit and Tibetan scholar, he was naturally far better fitted than any Western Orientalist to understand the inner meaning of the Mahayana. As he points out in his preface, the translation of Sanskrit works into Tibetan began in the seventh century CE, and many of these were again translated from Tibetan into Mongolian, Manchu, and Chinese; "so that by this means the Tibetan language became in Chinese Tartary the language of the learned, as did Latin in Europe." Finally, after the establishment of the Chinese suzerainty in the beginning of the eighteenth century, it became "the *lingua franca* of Higher Asia."[2]

Dr. McGovern says that the *Avatamsaka Sutra*, containing the Mahayana philosophy in all of its profundity, "is one of the most important in the whole Mahayana canon. Upon it was founded one of the two great Mahayana metaphysical schools of China." The Buddha, having preached this in the second week of his Enlightenment, finding it "incomprehensible to the masses, next preached the *Agama Sutras*, containing the fundamental principles of the Hinayana." This accounts for their exoteric character and their rendering into "the more colloquial, popular, and vulgar Pali," and the degeneration of the Hinayana "into a realistic and materialistic philosophy."[3]

All the Tibetan terms and references have been checked with the assistance of members of the Tashi Lama's suite, and our Chinese friends have also given us every assistance. It is with very great satisfaction that we publish this edition under the auspices of the Beijing Buddhist Research Society, who recognize in it the highest and most sacred teachings of their own "contemplative" schools. It was not until we came in contact with Chinese and Tibetan Buddhists that we obtained this striking confirmation of the truth and value of H. P. Blavatsky's work.

The little book is now, therefore, reprinted with the strongest and most authoritative Tibetan and Chinese endorsement. In response to

---

[1] See Das, *Tibetan-English Dictionary*, p. xiii.
[2] Das, *Tibetan-English Dictionary*, pp. v, ix.
[3] William McGovern, *An Introduction to Mahayana Buddhism* (London: Kegan Paul, Trench, Trubner & Co., 1922), pp. 12, 14, 124–125.

the requests of many students, we have ventured to add some notes and comments on points which called for explanation in the course of study, together with a good deal of information collected from Chinese and Tibetan sources.

Alice Leighton Cleather
(One of H.P.B's Pupils)
Basil Crump
Beijing, May 1927

Alice Leighton Cleather (1854–1938) was an English Theosophist and musician. She was one of the twelve pupils selected for Blavatsky's Inner Group, who took notes of its every meeting in order to send them to William Q. Judge in the United States. These notes were published in 1995 as *The Inner Group Teachings of H. P. Blavatsky to her Personal Pupils*.

Cleather was also one of the first Europeans to take Buddhist vows at Bodh Gaya under the sacred Bodhi Tree, with Lama Domo Geshe Rinpoche performing the ritual. Her book *H. P. Blavatsky: Her Life and Work for Humanity* was written in 1922 at the request of the Venerable Anagarika Dharmapala and originally published in the *Maha Bodhi Journal*. In 1925, she visited Beijing and there met the Ninth Panchen Lama, who gave her a Buddhist "Testimonial" which read: "Special Gelugpa Buddhist of the English race, faithful and devoted, to be treated as a Buddhist, to be afforded every assistance and help, and not to be injured or wrongfully opposed."

Her books include: *H. P. Blavatsky As I Knew Her* (1923), *H. P. Blavatsky: A Great Betrayal* (1922), and *Buddhism: The Science of Life* (1928).

Basil Woodward Crump (1866–1945) was an English barrister and editor of *The Law Times*. Crump was a member of the Esoteric Section of the Theosophical Society and a close friend of Alice Cleather, with whom he co-authored a number of books, including publications on Richard Wagner. Together they toured extensively giving lectures on theosophical subjects and Wagner's music. Independently, he published *Evolution as Outlined in the Archaic Eastern Records* (1930), which has been designated as "*The Secret Doctrine* in 200 pages."

TO THE ESOTERICISTS

It should be the aim of each and all of us to strive with all the intensity of our natures to follow and imitate them [the Masters].... Try to realize that progress is made step by step, and each step gained by heroic effort. Withdrawal means despair or timidity. "No Arhan, O lanoo, becomes one in that birth when for the first the soul begins to long for final liberation." Read those words and remember them. "And if he falls, e'en then he does not fall in vain; the enemies he slew in the last battle will not return to life in the next birth that will be his."

Conquered passions, like slain tigers, can no longer turn and rend you. Be hopeful, then, not despairing. With each morning's awakening try to live through the day in harmony with the Higher Self. "Try" is the battle-cry taught by the Teachers to each pupil. Naught else is expected of you. One who does his best does all that can be asked. There is a moment when even a Buddha ceases to be a sinning mortal and takes his first step toward Buddhahood.

So, then, ... I say that probably though not one of you may attain in this birth to this full ideal (of Buddhahood), yet each of you may begin to tread the "Aryashtanga Marga" [Noble Eightfold Path].... A man may be patient, kind, and conscientious, without becoming at once a King Harishchandra. "The sixteen paramitas are not for priests and yogis alone," as said, but stand for models for all to strive after; and neither priest nor yogi, chela nor Mahatma, ever attained all, at once. Again, the idea that sinners and saints are expected to enter the Path is emphatically stated in *The Voice of the Silence*, where it is said that "not one recruit can ever be refused the right to enter on the Path that leads toward the field of battle."

Read *The Voice*, I say. It was written for, and dedicated to you, by Masters' special orders. Therein you will find all your inquiries anticipated and answered.

Yours fraternally,
H.P.B.
London, 29 November 1889

PREFACE

THE FOLLOWING PAGES are derived from *the Book of the Golden Precepts*, one of the works put into the hands of mystic students in the East. The knowledge of them is obligatory in that school, the teachings of which are accepted by many Theosophists.[1] Therefore, as I know many of these Precepts by heart, the work of translating has been relatively an easy task for me.

It is well known that, in India, the methods of psychic development differ with the Gurus (teachers or masters), not only because of their belonging to different schools of philosophy, of which there are six, but because every Guru has his own system, which he generally keeps very secret. But beyond the Himalayas the method in the esoteric schools does not differ, unless the Guru is simply a lama, but little more learned than those he teaches.

The work from which I here translate forms part of the same series as that from which the Stanzas of the *Book of Dzyan*[2] were taken, on which *The Secret Doctrine* is based. Together with the great mystic work called *Paramartha*, which, the legend of Nagarjuna tells us, was delivered to the great Arhat by the Nagas or "Serpents" (in truth a name given to the ancient Initiates), the *Book of the Golden Precepts* claims the same origin. Yet its maxims and ideas, however noble and original, are often found under different forms in Sanskrit works, such as the *Dnyaneshwari*,[3] that

---

[1] C.C.: *Theosophists.* "A name by which many mystics at various periods of history have called themselves. The Neoplatonists of Alexandria were Theosophists; the alchemists and Kabbalists during the medieval ages were likewise so called, also the Martinists, the Quietists, and other kinds of mystics, whether acting independently or incorporated in a brotherhood or society" (*Theosophical Glossary*, p. 328).

[2] C.C.: *Dzyan* (Tibetan). Also written *Dzyn* or *Dzen*. A corruption of Sanskrit *dhyana* and *gnyana*. In Chinese *chan*, the name of one of the schools of yoga or meditation which follow the same rules as these *Precepts*. Also a generic name of the esoteric schools and their literature. See *The Secret Doctrine* for Stanzas from the *Book of Dzyan* and *Commentaries*.

[3] C.C.: *Dnyaneshwari.* After an exhaustive search, we have at length discovered

superb mystic treatise in which Krishna describes to Arjuna in glowing colours the condition of a fully illumined yogi; and again in certain Upanishads. This is but natural, since most, if not all, of the greatest Arhats, the first followers of Gautama Buddha, were Hindus and Aryans, not Mongolians, especially those who emigrated into Tibet. The works left by Aryasanga alone are very numerous.

The original *Precepts* are engraved on thin oblong squares; copies very often on discs. These discs, or plates, are generally preserved on the altars of the temples attached to centres where the so-called "contemplative" or Mahayana (Yogachara) schools are established. They are written variously, sometimes in Tibetan but mostly in ideographs. The sacerdotal language (Senzar),[1] besides an alphabet of its own, may be rendered in several modes of writing in cipher characters, which partake more of the nature of ideographs than of syllables. Another method (*lugs*, in Tibetan) is to use the numerals and colours, each of which correspond to a letter of the Tibetan alphabet (thirty simple and seventy-four compound letters) thus forming a complete cryptographic alphabet. When the ideographs are used there is a definite mode of reading the text, as in this case the symbols and signs used in astrology, namely the twelve zodiacal animals

---

some information about this work from Indian contributors in the early numbers of *The Theosophist* when H.P.B. was editor: vol. 1, pp. 86, 113, 142; vol. 2, p. 173; vol. 5, pp. 255–256. See also *Oriental Department Papers* (Theosophical Society, European Section), November 1891, p. 8. From these we learn that it is a Commentary on the Bhagavad Gita, written in 1290 by Dnyaneshwar, a celebrated yogi of Alandi, near Pune. He is said to have entered the tomb alive with his book. Three centuries later he appeared in a vision to another yogi, Eknath, of Paithan, and told him that the book had been revised and should now be published. On opening the tomb, Eknath found Dnyaneshwar sitting with his book and received it from him. It is written in old Marathi and the *ovi* form of poetry, is printed in Bombay, and is the standard work on Vedanta for the Maharashtras, and for the *varkaris* who follow its precepts (Tibetan: *lung*). Some of these are strikingly similar to those translated here by H.P.B., showing that the spiritual experiences of all true yogis are identical in essence. The name *Dnyaneshwar* is a compound of *dnyan* (knowledge; see Fragment III, p. 67, *Dnyan Marga*) and *Ishwara* (Lord). It means, therefore, "Lord of Knowledge." The usual modern spelling is *jnana*, which distinguishes it more clearly from *dhyana* (meditation); another used by H.P.B. is *gnyana* (note 6, page 33). The Tibetan word is *sherab*, meaning "absolute or sublime wisdom, intelligence, or understanding" of three kinds: in listening, in thinking, and in meditating (*Tibetan-English Dictionary*, p. 1244). Sir Charles Eliot, in his *Hinduism and Buddhism* (1921), vol. 2, p. 257, spells the name *Jnaneshvara*, and speaks of his writings as "the first great landmark in Marathi literature."

[1] C.C.: *Senzar*. "The mystic name for the secret sacerdotal language or the 'Mystery-speech' of the initiated Adepts, all over the world" (*Theosophical Glossary*, p. 295). The Chinese ideographs and the Egyptian hieroglyphs were the outcome of the ancient practice of recording the religious and esoteric history of every nation in symbols, not in words, on account of the magic potency of the spoken word (*The Secret Doctrine*, vol. 2, p. 307).

and the seven primary colours, each a triplet in shade, i.e., the light, the primary, and the dark — stand for the thirty-three letters of the simple alphabet, for words and sentences. For in this method, the twelve "animals" five times repeated and coupled with the five elements and the seven colours, furnish a whole alphabet composed of sixty sacred letters and twelve signs. A sign placed at the beginning of the text determines whether the reader has to spell it according to the Indian mode, when every word is simply a Sanskrit adaptation, or according to the Chinese principle of reading the ideographs. The easiest way, however, is that which allows the reader to use no special, or *any* language he likes, as the signs and symbols were, like the Arabian numerals or figures, common and international property among initiated mystics and their followers. The same peculiarity is characteristic of one of the Chinese modes of writing, which can be read with equal facility by anyone acquainted with the character: for instance, a Japanese can read it in his own language as readily as a Chinese in his.

The *Book of the Golden Precepts* — some of which are pre-Buddhistic while others belong to a later date — contains about ninety distinct little treatises. Of these I learnt thirty-nine by heart, years ago. To translate the rest, I should have to resort to notes scattered among a too large number of papers and memoranda collected for the last twenty years and never put in order, to make of it by any means an easy task. Nor could they be all translated and given to a world too selfish and too much attached to objects of sense to be in any way prepared to receive such exalted ethics in the right spirit. For, unless a man perseveres seriously in the pursuit of self-knowledge, he will never lend a willing ear to advice of this nature.

And yet such ethics fill volumes upon volumes in Eastern literature, especially in the Upanishads. "Kill out all desire of life," says Krishna to Arjuna. That desire lingers only in the body, the vehicle of the embodied self, not in the Self which is "eternal, indestructible, which kills not nor is it killed."[2] "Kill out sensation," teaches the *Sutta Nipata*; "look alike on pleasure and pain, gain and loss, victory and defeat."[3] Again, "Seek shelter in the eternal alone."[4] "Destroy the sense of separateness," repeats Krishna under every form. "The mind (*manas*) which follows the rambling senses, makes the soul (*buddhi*) as helpless as the boat which the wind leads astray upon the waters."[5]

Therefore it has been thought better to make a judicious selection only from those treatises which will best suit the few real mystics in the

---

[2] Katha Upanishad 1:2:18.
[3] Bhagavad Gita 2:38.
[4] Bhagavad Gita 18:66.
[5] Bhagavad Gita 2:67.

Theosophical Society,[1] and which are sure to answer their needs. It is only these who will appreciate the words of Krishna-Christos, the Higher Self:

"Sages do not grieve for the living nor the dead. Never did I not exist, nor you, nor these rulers of men; nor will any one of us ever hereafter cease to be."[2]

In this translation, I have done my best to preserve the poetical beauty of language and imagery which characterize the original. How far this effort has been successful is for the reader to judge.

H.P.B.
1889

---

[1] C.C.: *Theosophical Society*. "Founded in 1875 in New York by Colonel H. S. Olcott and H. P. Blavatsky, helped by W. Q. Judge and several others. Its avowed object was at first the scientific investigation of psychic or so called 'spiritualistic' phenomena" (*Theosophical Glossary*, p. 328). In Benares in 1879, H.P.B. reorganized it with the additional title "Universal Brotherhood," to consist of three sections: 1) the Adepts or Initiates in esoteric science and philosophy; 2) disciples or pupils of the Initiates; 3) probationers. Owing to the opposition of leading members of Western birth, who preferred psychic phenomena and an exoteric society, the Adepts and their disciples (*chelas*) retired into the background, and the Theosophical Society was carried forward as an ordinary organization. A final effort was made to revive the Benares plan in 1888, when H.P.B. founded the Eastern or Esoteric School in London, and an Inner Group of twelve chosen pupils, both being under the immediate direction of her Master M. The present work was published in 1889 primarily for these students (see chapter 2 in *H. P. Blavatsky: Her Life and Work for Humanity*). This effort having failed, H.P.B. was withdrawn in 1891, and the Theosophical Society, Esoteric Section, and Inner Group, being left without guidance from the Initiates, soon broke up into sects through internecine strife. The word "Theosophy" (Greek: *Theosophia*, "Divine Wisdom") was chosen in 1875 as the most suitable for Western propaganda, but the teaching came from the Tibetan Adepts of Esoteric Buddhism (from the Sanskrit root *Budh*, "to know"). The word "Theosophy" is seldom used by H.P.B. in *The Secret Doctrine*, and does not occur at all in the present translation. Probably she foresaw the abuses and perversions with which it would be associated after her death. The Benares Constitution was in accordance with the Tibetan tradition that Buddha "insisted upon Initiation being thrown open to all who were qualified. Since the days of the earliest universal Mysteries up to the time of our great Shakya Tathagata Buddha, who reduced and interpreted the system for the salvation of all, the Divine Voice of the Self, known as Guanyin, was heard but in the sacred solitude of the preparatory Mysteries" (from the Esoteric Records at Tashi Lhunpo). In dedicating these *Precepts* to "the few real mystics in the Theosophical Society" of that period (1889), H.P.B. was not appealing to the exoteric members, but only to those on the esoteric side who were in real earnest.

[2] Bhagavad Gita 2:11–12.

Fragment I

THE VOICE OF THE SILENCE

These instructions are for those ignorant of the dangers of the lower *iddhi*.[1]

He who would hear the voice of *Nada*,[2] "the Soundless Sound," and comprehend it, he has to learn the nature of *Dharana*.[3]

Having become indifferent to objects of perception, the pupil must seek out the *raja* of the senses, the thought-producer, he who awakes illusion.[4]

---

[1] The Pali word *iddhi*, is the synonym of the Sanskrit *siddhis*, or psychic faculties, the abnormal powers in man. There are two kinds of *siddhis*. One group which embraces the lower, coarse, psychic, and mental energies; the other is one which exacts the highest training of spiritual powers. Says Krishna in the *Srimad Bhagavatam* (11:15:1): "He who is engaged in the performance of yoga, who has subdued his senses and who has concentrated his mind in me (Krishna), such yogis all the *siddhis* stand ready to serve."

A.E. (Anthony Elenjimittam): The original Sanskrit word *siddhi* lost its *s* in Prakrit, and in languages derived from Pali the term *iddhi* is used in the place of *siddhi*, which means powers derived by the aspirant when he has progressed beyond a certain stage in the great task of self-unfoldment, Self-realization. The Pathway towards Nirvana or beatific vision is beset with dangers of various sorts, including perils out of the very spiritual achievement. As in the gravitational sphere, rockets launched out into outer space encounter resistance, and within the gravitational pull of Mother Earth may still fall back to the lap of Earth, so in the life of an aspirant; although lifted up above the clouds and the air up above with the consequent levitation and powers, *siddhis*, the danger always exists of the gravitational pull of the selfish life, a temptation to vainglory and selfish use of the lights and powers which naturally accrue to persons progressing in the path of yoga. Patanjali devotes the entire third part of his aphorisms, *Vibhuti Pada*, only to such powers derived from mental concentration, their use and abuse, the dangers and advantages from such powers or *vibhutis*, which are akin to *siddhis* in Sanskrit and *iddhis* in Pali.

[2] The "Soundless Voice," or the "Voice of the Silence." Literally perhaps this would read "Voice in the *Spiritual Sound*," as *Nada* is the equivalent word in Sanskrit, for the Senzar term.

A.E.: This is a paradoxical saying: the *Voice of the Silence*, that paradox that is inherent in Existence itself. It is the law of life that only when physical silence of the senses and mind is observed can we hear the Voice of that Silence which is *Shabda Brahma*. Close your external ears, and then the inner ears open to hear the music of the Eternal. Get away from the marketplace, street-corners and imaginative musings, and raving multitudes and enter the inner chamber, the silent sanctuary of the soul, where reigns stillness, calm, and blissful peace. Silence of the senses, imagination, and mind is the essential step and prelude to climbing the ladder of perfection and listening to the Voice of the Silence, that is being destroyed in our big cities, newspaper and cinema worlds.

The same paradox exists in *Nada*, the "soundless sound," as the Upanishadic term of "unseen seer, unheard hearer," etc., while speaking about the Ultimate Reality, impersonal ontologically, *Quoad sé*, but to us, anthropologically personal or tri-personal, as among the trinitarians.

[3] *Dharana* is the intense and perfect concentration of the mind upon some one interior object, accompanied by complete abstraction from everything pertaining to the external Universe, or the world of the senses.

[4] A.E.: As spiritual perfection entails mastery over the tiger and ape in us ›

The mind is the great slayer of the Real.[5]

Let the disciple slay the slayer.

For:

When to himself his form appears unreal, as do on waking all the forms he sees in dreams;[6]

When he has ceased to hear the many, he may discern the One — the inner sound which kills the outer.

Then only, not till then, shall he forsake the region of *Asat*, the false, to come unto the realm of *Sat*, the true.

Before the soul can see, the harmony within must be attained, and fleshly eyes be rendered blind to all illusion.

Before the soul can hear, the image (man) has to become as deaf to roarings as to whispers, to cries of bellowing elephants as to the silvery buzzing of the golden firefly.

---

and the subsequent conquest of the entire sense world with all its illusions and deceptions and seductions, the first step which novices have to take towards the path of Self-realization is indifference to the sense perceptions, then positive victory over the entire sense world will follow through the conquest of sense attractions and repulsions, sexual urge, and that craze which binds us down, hand and foot, to the transient, ephemeral, evanescent *Maya* that is the world, creation. To tear the bonds asunder and through the death-knell of the sensual, to be reborn in the Real that is emancipation, *Mukti*, Nirvana, is the terminus of human pilgrimage which begins with the conquest of the senses, those turbulent and enslaving powers, and ends with the vision, realization of the Real, and the subsequent redemptive apostolate, which seers and prophets exercised for the real uplift of mankind.

[5] C.C.: The "mind" which is the "slayer of the Real" is the lower mind (Sanskrit: *kama-manas*) which, by constantly creating impure and material images, tempts and leads astray the aspirant, who must therefore "slay" (i.e., paralyse) it. See also note 6, page 35 on the "lunar form."

A.E.: The senses and the sense-bound mind veil Reality. Hence "Let the disciple slay the slayer."

[6] A.E.: As when one wakes up from dreams, the pleasant and frightful dream pictures vanish, so when one glimpses the Spirit Reality, the material world, with its senses and sex thrills, woes and miseries, vanish.

The whole tenor of the booklet, the condensed essence of both spiritual realization and the apostolate of compassion — Arhatship and Bodhisattvahood, supports the unanimous esoteric teaching of spiritual masters and philosophers that the life of sense-bound beings is all misery.

"*Parninama tapa, samskara dukhair guna vritti virodhacca dukham evam sarvam vivekinah* — due to the misery inherent in change, the gross and attenuated seeds of the *samskaras* of past actions, and also due to the clash and conflict of various *gunas* — the three *sattvic*, *rajasic*, and *tamasic* qualities, the whole life, the universe, is the womb of pain for a thoughtful mind," says Patanjali. Yet there is a way out. Christianity calls this redemption from sin; Hindus call it *Mukti* or emancipation; and the Buddhists, *Bodhi* or Enlightenment. But the essence is the same.

Before the soul can comprehend and may remember, she must unto the Silent Speaker be united, just as the form to which the clay is modelled, is first united with the potter's mind.

For then the soul will hear, and will remember. And then to the inner ear will speak —

> the Voice of the Silence

And say:

If thy soul smiles while bathing in the sunlight of thy life; if thy soul sings within her chrysalis of flesh and matter; if thy soul weeps inside her castle of illusion; if thy soul struggles to break the silver thread that binds her to the Master;[1] know, O disciple, thy soul is of the earth.

When to the world's turmoil thy budding soul[2] lends ear; when to the roaring voice of the great illusion thy soul responds;[3] when frightened at the sight of the hot tears of pain; when deafened by the cries of distress, thy soul withdraws like the shy turtle within the carapace of selfhood, learn, O disciple, of her Silent "God," thy soul is an unworthy shrine.

When waxing stronger, thy soul glides forth from her secure retreat, and breaking loose from the protecting shrine, extends her silver thread and rushes onward; when beholding her image on the waves of Space she whispers, "This is I," — declare, O disciple, that thy soul is caught in the webs of delusion.[4]

This earth, disciple, is the Hall of Sorrow, wherein are set along the path of dire probations, traps to ensnare thy Ego by the delusion called "great heresy."[5]

This earth, O ignorant disciple, is but the dismal entrance leading to the twilight that precedes the valley of true light — that light which no wind can extinguish, that light which burns without a wick or fuel.

Saith the Great Law: "In order to become the knower of All Self,[6] thou hast first of Self to be the knower." To reach the knowledge of that

---

[1] The "great Master" is the term used by *lanoos* or chelas to indicate one's "Higher Self." It is the equivalent of *Avalokiteshvara*, and the same as *Adi-Budha* with the Buddhist occultists; *Atman*, the "Self" (the Higher Self) with the Brahmins; and *Christos* with the ancient Gnostics.

[2] Soul is used here for the *human ego* or *manas*, that which is referred to in our occult septenary division as the *human soul* (see *The Secret Doctrine*) in contradistinction to the spiritual and animal souls.

[3] *Maha Maya*, "Great Illusion," the objective Universe.

[4] *Sakkayaditthi*, "delusion" of personality.

[5] *Attavada*, the heresy of the belief in soul, or rather in the separateness of soul or self from the One Universal, Infinite Self.

[6] The *tattvajnani* is the "knower" or discriminator of the principles in Nature and in man; and *atmajnani* is the knower of Atman or the Universal, One Self.

Self, thou hast to give up self to Non-Self, being to Non-Being, and then thou canst repose between the wings of the Great Bird. Aye, sweet is rest between the wings of that which is not born, nor dies, but is the Aum[7] throughout eternal ages.[8]

Bestride the Bird of Life, if thou would'st know.[9]

Give up thy life, if thou would'st live.[10]

Three Halls, O weary pilgrim, lead to the end of toils. Three Halls, O conqueror of Mara, will bring thee through three states[11] into the fourth[12] and thence into the seven worlds,[13] the worlds of Rest Eternal.

If thou would'st learn their names, then hearken, and remember.

The name of the first Hall is Ignorance — *avidya*.[14]

It is the Hall in which thou saw'st the light, in which thou livest and shalt die.[15]

C.C.: Throughout this work H.P.B. makes use of different grades and sizes of type to indicate relative values. In this case *All Self* is Atma, the Universal Self, *Self* is the immortal reincarnating Ego, and *self* is the personality which is evanescent.

[7] *Kalahamsa*, the Bird or Swan (see note 9). Says the *Nadabindu Upanishad* (*Rig Veda*) translated by the Kumbakonam Theosophical Society: "The syllable A is considered to be its (the bird Hamsa's) right wing, U, its left, M, its tail, and the *ardha-matra* (half metre) is said to be its head."

[8] Eternity with the Orientals has quite another signification than it has with us. It stands generally for the 100 years or "Age" of Brahma, the duration of a Maha Kalpa or a period of 311,040,000,000,000 years.

C.C.: As the figures given in the original were those of a "Day" instead of an "Age" of Brahma, they have been altered to agree with those given for the latter in *The Secret Doctrine*, vol. 1, p. 36. See also *Theosophical Glossary*, p. 129.

[9] Says the same *Nadabindu*, "A yogi who bestrides the Hamsa (thus contemplates on Aum) is not affected by karmic influences or by tens of crores of sins."

[10] Give up the life of physical *personality* if you would live in spirit.

[11] The three states of consciousness, which are *jagrat*, the waking; *svapna*, the dreaming; and *sushupti*, the deep sleeping state. These three yoga conditions lead to the fourth, or —

[12] The *turiya*, that beyond the dreamless state, the one above all, a state of high spiritual consciousness.

[13] Some Sanskrit mystics locate seven planes of being, the seven spiritual *lokas* or worlds within the body of *Kalahamsa*, the Swan out of Time and Space, convertible into the Swan *in* Time, when it becomes Brahma, instead of Brahma (neuter).

[14] C.C.: *Avidya* (Chinese: *wu ming*). Nescience or lack of spiritual insight. The Chinese say that the *Fo Xin* or Buddha-heart is concealed beneath the veil of *wu ming*. *Vidya* is knowledge, and *Gupta-Vidya* is esoteric knowledge.

[15] The phenomenal world of senses and of terrestrial consciousness — only.

A.E.: The three Halls are illustrative of the three-staged progress in our spiritual life, the Hall of Ignorance into which we enter after being born of sexual union, the physical and biological life which is encircled and enmeshed in *Maya*, the great cosmic illusion with which the Ultimate Reality or Truth veils

The name of Hall the second is the Hall of Learning.[1] In it thy soul will find the blossoms of life, but under every flower a serpent coiled.[2]

The name of the third Hall is Wisdom, beyond which stretch the shoreless waters of Akshara, the indestructible Fount of Omniscience.[3]

If thou would'st cross the first Hall safely, let not thy mind mistake the fires of lust that burn therein for the sunlight of life.

If thou would'st cross the second safely, stop not the fragrance of its stupefying blossoms to inhale. If freed thou would'st be from the karmic chains, seek not for thy Guru in those mayavic regions.

The Wise Ones tarry not in pleasure-grounds of senses.

The Wise Ones heed not the sweet-tongued voices of illusion.

Seek for him who is to give thee birth,[4] in the Hall of Wisdom, the Hall which lies beyond, wherein all shadows are unknown, and where the light of truth shines with unfading glory.

That which is uncreate abides in thee, disciple, as it abides in that Hall.[5] If thou would'st reach it and blend the two, thou must divest thyself of thy dark garments of illusion. Stifle the voice of flesh, allow no image

---

itself from the eyes of the ignorant. *Avidya* or ignorance has its *raison d'être* in *Maya*. But when *vidya* or gnostic enlightenment comes, *Maya's* veil is rent, and *Satya* or Truth shines as the sun when freed from clouds.

[1] The Hall of *Probationary* Learning.
A.E.: The Hall of Learning means worldly knowledge, erudition, scholarship, and all the glamorous name and fame derived therefrom without corresponding ethics, self-control, and purity in thought, word, and deed. Real wisdom is folly to the learned, while true wisdom or self-sacrifice and the consequent Self-realization — crucifixion of the sensual life and the resurrection of the divine spark within — is folly to the worldly-wise and learned. In this sense, St. Paul said: "To shame the wise, God has chosen what the world counts folly, and to shame what is strong, God has chosen what the world counts as weakness" (1 Corinthians 1:27).

[2] The astral region, the psychic world of supersensuous perceptions and of deceptive sights — the world of mediums. It is the great "astral serpent" of Éliphas Lévi. No blossom plucked in those regions has ever yet been brought down on earth without its serpent coiled around the stem. It is the world of the Great Illusion.

[3] The region of the full spiritual consciousness beyond which there is no longer danger for him who has reached it.
A.E.: *Akshara*, the "indestructible fount of Omniscience," corresponds to the Absolute, the impersonal Godhead, the Ground of all that exists, including the personal God of the unitarians and the tri-personal God of the trinitarians.

[4] The Initiate who leads the disciple through the Knowledge given to him to his spiritual, or second birth, is called the *Father, Guru,* or *Master.*

[5] A.E.: "That which is uncreate abides in thee": The Infinite, the Eternal, God, Godhead abides in you, not only through the omnipresence, omniscience, and omnipotence, but also through love and grace, supernaturally in those who have cleansed themselves of all stains of sins and ignorance. Then thou art the temple and sanctuary of the Most High, thy own Real Self.

of the senses to get between its light and thine, that thus the twain may blend in one. And having learnt thine own *agnyana*,[6] flee from the Hall of Learning. This Hall is dangerous in its perfidious beauty, is needed but for thy probation. Beware, lanoo, lest dazzled by illusive radiance thy soul should linger and be caught in its deceptive light.

This light shines from the jewel of the great ensnarer (Mara).[7] The senses it bewitches, blinds the mind, and leaves the unwary an abandoned wreck.

The moth attracted to the dazzling flame of thy night lamp is doomed to perish in the viscid oil. The unwary soul that fails to grapple with the mocking demon of illusion, will return to earth the slave of Mara.

Behold the hosts of souls. Watch how they hover o'er the stormy sea of human life, and how exhausted, bleeding, broken-winged, they drop one after other on the swelling waves. Tossed by the fierce winds, chased by the gale, they drift into the eddies and disappear within the first great vortex.

If through the Hall of Wisdom, thou would'st reach the Vale of Bliss, disciple, close fast thy senses against the great dire heresy of separateness[8] that weans thee from the rest.

Let not thy "Heaven-born," merged in the sea of Maya, break from the Universal Parent (Soul), but let the fiery power retire into the inmost chamber, the chamber of the Heart[9] and the abode of the World's Mother.[10]

---

[6] *Agnyana* is ignorance or *non*-wisdom, the opposite of "knowledge," *gnyana*.
A.E.: *Agnyana* or *avidya* means very much the same — the ignorance which entraps us in *Maya*, the ignorance that is worldly learning.

[7] *Mara* is in exoteric religions a demon, an *asura*, but in esoteric philosophy it is personified temptation through men's vices, and translated literally means "that which kills" the soul. It is represented as a King (of the Maras) with a crown in which shines a jewel of such lustre that it blinds those who look at it, this lustre referring of course to the fascination exercised by vice upon certain natures.
A.E.: *Mara* in Pali Buddhist literature means the slayer, the "great ensnarer," who through worldly glamour and enticements seduces and kills the unwary soul by offering baits of pleasure and clouding the mind, and finally destroying their mind and soul. *Mara* corresponds to satan, the devil in Judeo-Christian literature, and to *Ahriman* in the Zoroastrian Gathas.

[8] A.E.: "Heresy of separateness": While popular religions insist on the many, one different from and hostile to the other, esoteric religions, mystic philosophies insist on the One, the One without a second, to which are reduced the many. All are one, although they seem to be many. Reality is all one, whose soul is the Cosmic Intelligence, whose externalization is the material universe. Thought is the reality of which externalization is matter. These two are just one, synthesized in the Great One, the alpha and omega of Creation.

[9] The *inner* chamber of the Heart, called in Sanskrit *Brahmapuri*. The "fiery power" is *kundalini*.

[10] The "Power" and the "World Mother" are names given to *kundalini* — one of the mystic "yogi powers." It is *buddhi* considered as an active instead of a passive

Then from the heart that Power shall rise into the sixth, the middle region, the place between thine eyes, when it becomes the breath of the One-Soul, the voice which filleth all, thy Master's voice.

'Tis only then thou canst become a "Walker of the Sky"[1] who treads the winds above the waves, whose step touches not the waters.

Before thou set'st thy foot upon the ladder's upper rung, the ladder of the mystic sounds, thou hast to hear the voice of thy *inner* God[2] in seven manners.

The first is like the nightingale's sweet voice chanting a song of parting to its mate.

The second comes as the sound of a silver cymbal of the Dhyanis, awakening the twinkling stars.

---

principle (which it is generally, when regarded only as the vehicle, or casket of the supreme spirit, *atma*). It is an electro-spiritual force, a creative power which when aroused into action can as easily kill as it can create.

A.E.: H.P.B. interprets the term *World Mother* as one among the names given to *kundalini-shakti* on which is based the Kundalini Yoga and the psychic powers derived therefrom. A Tibetan Lama, with whom I first read *The Voice of the Silence* in original Tibetan and in its English translation, however, told me that the "World Mother" is the same as the "Father in Heaven." And as the "Kingdom of God is within you," for a student of comparative religions, God, Reality, enshrined in the heart or inner consciousness, is invoked, realized, and relished as both the "Mother of the World" and as the "Father in Heaven."

[1] *Khechara* or "sky-walker" or "goer." As explained in the sixth *adhyaya* of that king of mystic works, the *Dnyaneshwari* — the body of the yogi becomes as one *formed of the wind*; as "a cloud from which limbs have sprouted out," after which — "he (the yogi) beholds the things beyond the seas and stars; he hears the language of the Devas and comprehends it, and perceives what is passing in the mind of the ant."

A.E.: The *sky-walker* is one who through yogic practices has rejoined the Infinite in the ethereal religions, with levitation and mobility, who through the development of psychic powers, could read things up in the skies and beyond, the minds of gods and men. Aptly, the quotation from the *Dnyaneshwari* says: "He beholds the things beyond the seas and stars; he hears the language of the Devas and comprehends it, and perceives what is passing in the mind of the ant" (6:269). In two places Patanjali mentions the *Sukshma Vishayatvam* — the apt men of sparkling intelligence which accrues to a yogi through the extreme rarefaction and subtlety of a purified intelligence.

[2] The Higher Self.

A.E.: God is the inner Reality and Substance within, outside us, and everywhere; *Antaryami* or Inner Witness is God. Truly "the Kingdom of God is within, not outside where only a distant echo or reflection is got, and nothing more," under the veil of *Maya*, the cosmic power that creates, sustains, and dissolves the universe.

The stages of steady spiritual progress, from the day of one's bidding goodbye to the sensual and illusory, the transient and the perishable, to the union with the One, are described figuratively, metaphorically, and also poetically in the six stages mentioned here. Christian mysticism gives three stages, the purgative, the illuminative, and the unitive; six or three, the path is the same.

The next is as the plaint melodious of the ocean sprite imprisoned in its shell.

And this is followed by the chant of vina.[3]

The fifth like sound of bamboo flute shrills in thine ear.

It changes next into a trumpet blast.

The last vibrates like the dull rumbling of a thundercloud.

The seventh swallows all the other sounds. They die, and then are heard no more.

When the six[4] are slain and at the Master's feet are laid, then is the pupil merged into the One,[5] becomes that One and lives therein.

Before that path is entered, thou must destroy thy lunar body,[6] cleanse thy mind-body,[7] and make clean thy heart.

Eternal life's pure waters, clear and crystal, with the monsoon tempest's muddy torrents cannot mingle.

Heaven's dewdrop glittering in the morn's first sunbeam within the bosom of the lotus, when dropped on earth becomes a piece of clay; behold, the pearl is now a speck of mire.

Strive with thy thoughts unclean before they overpower thee. Use them as they will thee, for if thou sparest them and they take root and grow, know well, these thoughts will overpower and kill thee. Beware, disciple, suffer not, e'en though it be their shadow, to approach. For it will grow, increase in size and power, and then this thing of darkness will absorb thy being before thou hast well realized the black foul monster's presence.[8]

---

[3] *Vina* is an Indian stringed instrument like a lute.

[4] The six principles; meaning when the lower personality is destroyed and the inner individuality is merged into and lost in the seventh or spirit.

[5] The disciple is one with Brahman or Atman.

[6] The astral form produced by the *kamic* principle, the *kama-rupa* or body of desire.
  A.E.: *Lunar body* is the subtler matter whence the mind, imagination, and desires spring, far subtler than the gross physical body. Pure spirit lies beyond all that, and we are one with it.

[7] *Manasa-rupa*. The first (*kama-rupa*) refers to the astral or *personal* self; the second (*manasa-rupa*) to the individuality or the reincarnating Ego whose consciousness on our plane or the *lower manas* has to be paralysed.

[8] A.E.: Purity in thought, desires, and deeds is the key that opens up the Kingdom of God. Spiritual science, whether in the East or in the West, in Buddhism, Hinduism, Christianity, Platonism, Sufism, or any other branch of esoteric wisdom, insists on the vow of purity or *brahmacharya* for mental illumination, self-purging, and final realization of the true Self in us, the spark rejoining the Fire whence it came, scintillating the dewdrops melting into the shining sea; the soul growing to its fullness in the lap of the Over-Soul, "the World Mother."

Before the "mystic Power"[1] can make of thee a god, lanoo, thou must have gained the faculty to slay thy lunar form[2] at will.

The self of matter and the Self of Spirit can never meet. One of the twain must disappear; there is no place for both.

Ere thy soul's mind can understand, the bud of personality must be crushed out, the worm of sense destroyed past resurrection.

Thou canst not travel on the Path before thou hast become that Path itself.[3]

Let thy soul lend its ear to every cry of pain like as the lotus bares its heart to drink the morning sun.

Let not the fierce sun dry one tear of pain before thyself hast wiped it from the sufferer's eye.

But let each burning human tear drop on thy heart and there remain, nor ever brush it off, until the pain that caused it is removed.

These tears, O thou of heart most merciful, these are the streams that irrigate the fields of charity immortal. 'Tis on such soil that grows the midnight blossom of Buddha[4] more difficult to find, more rare to view than is the flower of the Vogay tree. It is the seed of freedom from rebirth. It isolates the Arhat both from strife and lust, it leads him through the fields of Being unto the peace and bliss known only in the land of Silence and Non-Being.[5]

---

[1] *Kundalini*, the "serpent power" or mystic fire. It is called the "serpentine" or the *annular* power on account of its spiral-like working or progress in the body of the ascetic developing the power in himself. It is an electric fiery occult or *fohatic* power, the great pristine force, which underlies all organic and inorganic matter.

[2] C.C.: The "lunar form" is the astral body or ethereal double (Sanskrit: *linga-sharira*), so called because, according to *The Secret Doctrine*, the Lunar Pitris "evolved their shadows or *chhayas* to make therewith the first man." The physical and astral envelopes or vehicles being hindrances to inner development, the disciple must be able to "slay" (i.e., paralyse) them at will. The astral is "the vehicle of transitory, not of immortal life" (*Occultism Versus the Occult Arts*).

[3] This "Path" is mentioned in all the mystic works. As Krishna says in the *Dnyaneshwari*: "When this Path is beheld . . . whether one sets out to the bloom of the east or to the chambers of the west, *without moving*, O holder of the bow, *is the travelling in this road. In this path, to whatever place one would go, that place one's own self* becomes." "Thou art the Path" is said to the Adept Guru and by the latter to the disciple, after initiation. "I am the way and the Path," says another Master.

[4] Adeptship — the "blossom of Bodhisattva."

[5] A.E.: Sharing the misery of the world with *cum-passio*, compassion or mercy, is the step towards the path which leads one to the ending of misery for oneself and others. This midnight blossom of Buddha, Enlightenment amidst encircling darkness, is rarer than the rarest pearl on earth. Emancipation following enlightenment is the end of life's circle of births and deaths. It isolates

Kill out desire; but if thou killest it, take heed lest from the dead it should again arise.

Kill love of life, but if thou slayest *tanha*,[6] let this not be for thirst of life eternal, but to replace the fleeting by the everlasting.

Desire nothing. Chafe not at karma,[7] nor at Nature's changeless laws. But struggle only with the personal, the transitory, the evanescent, and the perishable.

Help Nature and work on with her; and Nature will regard thee as one of her creators and make obeisance.

And she will open wide before thee the portals of her secret chambers, lay bare before thy gaze the treasures hidden in the very depths of her pure virgin bosom. Unsullied by the hand of matter, she shows her treasures only to the eye of Spirit — the eye which never closes, the eye for which there is no veil in all her kingdoms.[8]

Then will she show thee the means and way, the first gate and the second, the third, up to the very seventh. And then, the goal — beyond which lie, bathed in the sunlight of the Spirit, glories untold, unseen by any save the eye of Soul.

---

the Adept from the incessant becomings, rooted as he is in the Being Supreme. Isolation from the fleeting flow of creation is *Kaivalya*, the land of Silence and Non-Being.

[6] *Tanha* — "the will to live," the fear of death and love for life, that force or energy which causes the rebirths.
 A.E.: Desire which is both *trishna* and *tanha* is the seed of births and rebirths. Desire for sensual pleasures and enjoyments enslaves us from every side, binding hands and feet that we are held bound in utter misery. Pleasure is poison. As no sinful desire is without its punishment, with delayed results afterwards, it pays us to cleanse ourselves from every trace of lustful desire and the passions and take shelter under the "wings of the Great Bird," the Supernatural Being.
 Attachment to life, clinging on to the very cause of our births and deaths, and misery all-round is *tanha*, while *trishna* is that insatiable desire, that white heat, that lustful yearning which urges us on to repeatedly fall into the lusts of flesh.

[7] C.C.: *Karma* (Sanskrit). The Law of Cause and Effect or ethical causation operating throughout the manifested Universe and controlling human evolution in conjunction with the Law of Reincarnation. They may be called the cornerstones of esoteric philosophy profoundly influencing all Oriental religious life and conduct. See also pp. 46, 49, 51, 54, 60 (*shila*).

[8] A.E.: Yes, the Supernatural presupposes the natural and builds on Nature, which, as it emanated, proceeding from the lap of the Infinite Word, is the very immaculate daughter of the Ground, Existence Supreme. But man has vitiated Nature, and Mother Nature is a constant chastisement to those who transgress her laws, while she remains the loving nurse and mother to all those who obey her "inviolable laws," *Panchashila*, the Ten Commandments, etc., which are but the codified formulations of Nature's laws.
 Nature, step by step, will lead her votaries to the highest peak of spiritual realization and vision, up to the Seventh which corresponds to the "Third Heaven" of St. Paul.

There is but one road to the Path; at its very end alone the "Voice of the Silence" can be heard. The ladder by which the candidate ascends is formed of rungs of suffering and pain; these can be silenced only by the voice of virtue. Woe, then, to thee, disciple, if there is one single vice thou hast not left behind. For then the ladder will give way and overthrow thee; its foot rests in the deep mire of thy sins and failings, and ere thou canst attempt to cross this wide abyss of matter thou hast to lave thy feet in waters of Renunciation.[1] Beware lest thou should'st set a foot still soiled upon the ladder's lowest rung. Woe unto him who dares pollute one rung with miry feet. The foul and viscous mud will dry, become tenacious, then glue his feet unto the spot, and like a bird caught in the wily fowler's lime, he will be stayed from further progress. His vices will take shape and drag him down. His sins will raise their voices like as the jackal's laugh and sob after the sun goes down; his thoughts become an army, and bear him off a captive slave.

Kill thy desires, lanoo, make thy vices impotent, ere the first step is taken on the solemn journey.[2]

Strangle thy sins, and make them dumb for ever, before thou dost lift one foot to mount the ladder.

Silence thy thoughts and fix thy whole attention on thy Master whom yet thou dost not see, but whom thou feelest.[3]

Merge into one sense thy senses, if thou would'st be secure against the foe. 'Tis by that sense alone which lies concealed within the hollow

---

[1] A.E.: *Waters of Renunciation* are the classical *tyaga* or self-crucifixion which is the prelude to Self-realization and the consequent Enlightenment, power, and redemptive apostolate. Complete purity means absolute renunciation, without which the vision of the Highest cannot be earned. Even the slightest taint of impurity is enough to "glue his feet unto the spot."

[2] A.E.: *Killing desire* does not mean, as some anti-Buddhists represent, renunciation of all desires and deeds, which is utter annihilation. Only such desires that produce the white heat within and prompt us to sin, transgressing the commandments of God and the *Panchashila* are to be killed, transmuted, or sublimated. Sexual lust, for instance, must be either killed or sublimated. Then lust is transformed into the Love which is impersonal and universal benevolence, which is the law of our being. Positive thinking, desiring, and doing, this is the path to salvation and Nirvana, not renunciation for renunciation's sake.

[3] A.E.: *Silencing thoughts* means control of raving imagination which mirrors and portrays the sensual world, often veiling and killing the spiritual world. The eightfold limbs of Yoga Patanjali, viz., *yama, niyama, asana, pranayama, pratyahara, dharana, dhyana, samadhi* (or moral discipline in truth, continence, posture, breath control, withdrawal from the sense-world and abidance in the Real and the Permanent, self-identification with the Supreme, introspective meditation, and ecstatic contemplative bliss) are both the preparation and the exercise and the results of such "silencing of thoughts" for the purpose of self-realization and God-attained dynamics in society.

of thy brain, that the steep path which leadeth to thy Master may be disclosed before thy soul's dim eyes.

Long and weary is the way before thee, O disciple. One single thought about the past that thou hast left behind, will drag thee down and thou wilt have to start the climb anew.

Kill in thyself all memory of past experiences. Look not behind or thou art lost.

Do not believe that lust can ever be killed out if gratified or satiated, for this is an abomination inspired by Mara. It is by feeding vice that it expands and waxes strong, like to the worm that fattens on the blossom's heart.

The rose must rebecome the bud born of its parent stem, before the parasite has eaten through its heart and drunk its life sap.

The golden tree puts forth its jewel buds before its trunk is withered by the storm.

The pupil must regain *the child-state he has lost* ere the first sound can fall upon his ear.[4]

The light from the One Master, the one unfading golden light of Spirit, shoots its effulgent beams on the disciple from the very first. Its rays thread through the thick dark clouds of matter.

Now here, now there, these rays illumine it, like sun sparks light the earth through the thick foliage of the jungle growth. But, O disciple, unless the flesh is passive, head cool, the soul as firm and pure as flaming diamond, the radiance will not reach the *chamber*,[5] its sunlight will not warm the heart, nor will the mystic sounds of the Akashic heights[6] reach the ear, however eager, at the initial stage.

Unless thou hearest, thou canst not see.

Unless thou seest, thou canst not hear. To hear and see, this is the second stage.[7]

---

[4] A.E.: *The child-like state* is to be reacquired after it is lost as the nemesis of sins. Purity brings back our lost innocence and the lost paradise. "Unless you be converted and become like little children you shall not enter into the Kingdom of Heaven," says Jesus.

[5] See note 9, page 33.

[6] These mystic sounds or the melody heard by the ascetic at the beginning of his cycle of meditation called *anahata-shabda* by the yogis.

[7] C.C.: Between the second and fourth stages there is a blank, indicating that the third stage is omitted. Although five outer senses are known to us, only four — seeing, hearing, smelling, and tasting — are here enumerated. The fifth — touch — is omitted, but we are told that in the fourth stage, the other four blend and pass into the *inner* touch. The pupil "must avoid bodily contact

. . . .

When the disciple sees and hears, and when he smells and tastes, eyes closed, ears shut, with mouth and nostrils stopped; when the four senses blend and ready are to pass into the fifth, that of the inner touch — then into stage the fourth he hath passed on.

And in the fifth, O slayer of thy thoughts, all these again have to be killed beyond reanimation.[1] Withhold thy mind from all external objects, all external sights. Withhold internal images, lest on thy soul-light a dark shadow they should cast.

Thou art now in Dharana,[2] the sixth stage.

When thou hast passed into the seventh, O happy one, thou shalt perceive no more the sacred three,[3] for thou shalt have become that three thyself. Thyself and mind, like twins upon a line, the star which is thy goal, burns overhead.[4] The three that dwell in glory and in bliss ineffable, now in the world of Maya have lost their names. They have become one star, the fire that burns but scorches not, that fire which is the *upadhi*[5] of the Flame.

And this, O yogi of success, is what men call *Dhyana*,[6] the right precursor of Samadhi.[7]

(i.e., being touched or touch) with human, as with animal being. No pet animals are permitted, and it is forbidden even to touch certain trees and plants" (*Practical Occultism*).

[1] This means that in the sixth stage of development, which in the occult system is *dharana*, every sense as an individual faculty has to be "killed" (or paralysed) on this plane, passing into and merging with the *seventh* sense, the most spiritual.

[2] See note 3, page 28.

[3] Every stage of development in Raja Yoga is symbolized by a geometrical figure. This one is the sacred *triangle* and precedes *dharana*. The △ is the sign of the high chelas, while another kind of triangle is that of high Initiates. It is the symbol "I" discoursed upon by Buddha and used by him as a symbol of the embodied form of Tathagata when released from the three methods of the Prajna. Once the preliminary and lower stages passed, the disciple sees no more the △ but the — the abbreviation of the — , the full septenary. *Its true form is not given here, as it is almost sure to be pounced upon by some charlatans and —* desecrated in its use for fraudulent purposes.

[4] The star that burns overhead is the "star of initiation." The caste-mark of Shaivas, or devotees of the sect of Shiva, the great patron of all yogis, is a black round spot, the symbol of the Sun now, perhaps, but that of the star of initiation, in occultism, in days of old.

[5] The basis (*upadhi*) of the ever unreachable "Flame," so long as the ascetic is still in this life.

[6] *Dhyana* is the last stage before the final *on this Earth* unless one becomes a full Mahatma. As said already in this state the raja yogi is yet spiritually conscious of Self, and the working of his higher principles. One step more, and he will be on the plane beyond the seventh (or fourth according to some schools). These, after the practice of *pratyahara* — a preliminary training, in order to ▸

And now thy self is lost in Self, thyself unto Thyself, merged in that Self from which thou first didst radiate.[8]

Where is thy individuality, lanoo, where the lanoo himself? It is the spark lost in the fire, the drop within the ocean, the ever-present Ray become the All and the eternal radiance.[9]

And now, lanoo, thou art the doer and the witness, the radiator and the radiation, Light in the Sound, and the Sound in the Light.

Thou art acquainted with the five impediments, O blessed one. Thou art their conqueror, the Master of the sixth, deliverer of the four modes of Truth.[10] The light that falls upon them shines from thyself, O thou who wast disciple, but art Teacher now.

And of these modes of Truth:

Hast thou not passed through knowledge of all misery — truth the first?

Hast thou not conquered the Maras' King at *Tsi*,[11] the portal of assembling — truth the second?[12]

Hast thou not sin at the third gate destroyed and truth the third attained?

---

control one's mind and thoughts — count *dharana*, *dhyana*, and *samadhi* and embraces the three under the generic name of *samyama*.

[7] *Samadhi* is the state in which the ascetic loses the consciousness of every individuality including his own. He becomes — the All.

[8] A.E.: "Thy self is lost in Self": *Jivatama* in *Paramatma*, the individualized ego in the universal I Am Who Am, even as the dewdrop melts into the shining sea, and the rain water returns to the bosom of the ocean, whence it once sprang forth. There is no blessedness but in the Infinite; all creation is but the pointer to the road to the Infinite. The *Dhammapada*, the Gita, the New Testament, the Bible, sophic literature are signposts and lighthouses pointing to the harbour of peace and bliss for all.

[9] A.E.: Individuality, metaphysically speaking, is an illusion, since the Supreme Reality *alone exists*. Hence empirical religions attribute great importance to individuality, on which the concept of personality is based, as in popular Christianity, Islam, and Judaism. But the Aryan religions, unlike the Semitic, adding mystical elements to the Semitic, realize the oneness of All, by letting individuality go or eclipsing it.

[10] The "four modes of truth" are, in Northern Buddhism, *Ku* "suffering or misery"; *Chi* the assembling of temptations; *Mi* "their destructions"; and *Tao*, the "path." The "five impediments" are the knowledge of misery, truth about human frailty, oppressive restraints, and the absolute necessity of separation from all the ties of passion and even of desires. The "Path of Salvation" is the last one.

[11] C.C.: *Tsi* (Southern pronunciation of *Chi*) is correctly given in the original text with its meaning, "assembling." *Tau* is the Egyptian cross τ, whereas *Tao* is the Way or Path, and the *Anima Mundi* in the philosophy of Lao Tzu called Taoism.

[12] At the portal of the "assembling," the King of the Maras, the *Maha Mara*, stands trying to blind the candidate by the radiance of his "jewel."

Hast not thou entered *Tao*, "the Path" that leads to knowledge — the fourth truth?[1]

And now, rest 'neath the Bodhi tree, which is perfection of all knowledge, for, know, thou art the Master of Samadhi — the state of faultless vision.[2]

Behold! Thou hast become the light, thou hast become the Sound, thou art thy Master and thy God. Thou art *thyself* the object of thy search: the Voice unbroken, that resounds throughout eternities, exempt from change, from sin exempt, the seven sounds in one,

the Voice of the Silence.

OM TAT SAT

---

[1] This is the fourth "Path" out of the five paths of rebirth which lead and toss all human beings into perpetual states of sorrow and joy. These "paths" are but subdivisions of the one, the Path followed by karma.

A.E.: *The Four Noble Truths* of Buddhism are paraphrased in the simplest intelligible way, the fact of misery, its cause, conquest of sin, and subsequent blessedness.

[2] A.E.: *Rest thou now under the Bodhi Tree* with Buddha, on the mountain top with Christ, by the river side with Krishna, thou whose discipleship or *lanoo* state has risen to the vocation of Guide, Guru, Master, Arhat, Saint, Prophet, sage apostle, missionary, all in one.

Fragment II
THE TWO PATHS

And now, O Teacher of Compassion, point thou the way to other men. Behold, all those who knocking for admission, await in ignorance and darkness, to see the gate of the sweet Law flung open!

The voice of the candidates:

Shalt not thou, Master of thine own mercy, reveal the Doctrine of the Heart?[1] Shalt thou refuse to lead thy servants unto the Path of Liberation?

Quoth the Teacher:

The Paths are two; the great perfections three; six are the virtues that transform the body into the Tree of Knowledge.[2]

Who shall approach them?

Who shall first enter them?

Who shall first hear the doctrine of two Paths in one, the truth unveiled about the Secret Heart?[3] The Law which, shunning learning, teaches Wisdom, reveals a tale of woe.

Alas, alas, that all men should possess Alaya, be one with the Great Soul, and that possessing it, Alaya should so little avail them!

Behold how like the moon, reflected in the tranquil waves, Alaya is reflected by the small and by the great, is mirrored in the tiniest atoms, yet fails to reach the heart of all. Alas, that so few men should profit by

---

[1] The two schools of Buddha's doctrine, the esoteric and the exoteric, are respectively called the "Heart" and the "Eye" Doctrine. Bodhidharma called them in China — from whence the names reached Tibet — the *Zong-men* (esoteric) and *Jiao-men* (exoteric school). The "Heart" Doctrine is so named, because it is the teaching which emanated from Gautama Buddha's *heart*, whereas the "Eye" Doctrine was the work of his head or brain. The "Heart Doctrine" is also called "the seal of truth" or "the true seal," a symbol found on the heading of almost all esoteric works.

[2] The "tree of knowledge" is a title given by the followers of the *Bodhidharma* (Wisdom Religion) to those who have attained the height of mystic knowledge — Adepts. Nagarjuna, the founder of the Madhyamika School, was called the "Dragon Tree," Dragon standing as a symbol of Wisdom and Knowledge. The tree is honoured because it is under the Bodhi (wisdom) Tree that Buddha received his birth and enlightenment, preached his first sermon and died.

C.C.: Students should be careful to distinguish between *Bodhidharma* (Sanskrit for Wisdom Religion) in note 2 and Bodhidharma, the first Chinese patriarch, in note 1. Some of the later editions show ignorance of this and have altered note (!) accordingly.

Bodhidharma: "The name of a great Arhat *Kshatriya* (one of the warrior caste), the son of a king. It was Panyatara, his guru, who gave him the name to mark his understanding (*Bodhi*) of the Law (*Dharma*) of Buddha" (*Theosophical Glossary*, p. 59). He was the twenty-eighth Indian and first Chinese patriarch. He founded the esoteric schools and the *Zen* mystic sect in China, where he lived around 520 CE at the monastery of Shaolin in Henan. His Chinese name is Putidamo.

[3] "Secret Heart" is the Esoteric Doctrine.

the gift, the priceless boon of learning truth, the right perception of existing things, the Knowledge of the non-existent!

Saith the pupil:

O Teacher, what shall I do to reach to Wisdom?

O Wise One, what, to gain perfection?

Search for the Paths. But, O lanoo, be of clean heart before thou startest on thy journey. Before thou takest thy first step, learn to discern the real from the false, the ever-fleeting from the everlasting. Learn above all to separate head-learning from Soul-wisdom, the "Eye" from the "Heart" doctrine.[4]

Yea, ignorance is like unto a closed and airless vessel; the soul a bird shut up within. It warbles not, nor can it stir a feather; but the songster mute and torpid sits, and of exhaustion dies.

But even ignorance is better than head-learning with no Soul-wisdom to illuminate and guide it.[5]

The seeds of Wisdom cannot sprout and grow in airless space. To live and reap experience the mind needs breadth and depth and points to draw it towards the Diamond Soul.[6] Seek not those points in Maya's realm; but soar beyond illusions, search the eternal and the changeless *Sat*,[7] mistrusting fancy's false suggestions.

For mind is like a mirror; it gathers dust while it reflects.[8] It needs the

---

[4] A.E.: The two paths, head-learning and Soul-wisdom, scholarship and sanctity, the intellectual Arhatship and spiritual Bodhisattvahood, are explained in this fragment. St. Paul, in a similar vein, contrasts the worldly wisdom of scholars and writers to the "folly at the Cross," of the Wisdom crucifixion of self, and the resurrection of the Godhead in Christ, in man, in everyone. Christ prays: "I thank Thee, Father of Heaven and earth, Thou hast hidden these thing (true wisdom) from the wise and the prudent and hast revealed it unto babes." Christs and Buddhas, as embodiments of Love and Compassion, lived and expounded the doctrine of the heart, not excluding but including the doctrine of the head or "eye." This is a call to us that intellectual attainments should be only channels for us to launch out into the deep of Compassionate Love, Loving Compassion.

[5] A.E.: Book-learning, scholarship, and academic erudition take us away from the simplicity of the ignorant and land us nowhere, between earth and heaven. The ignorant on the earth are preferred to the proud, impure learned, and rightly so, as from ignorance to Soul-wisdom there is only one step, while from scholarship to purity there are two or more steps.

[6] "Diamond Soul," *Vajrasattva*, a title of the supreme Buddha, the "Lord of all Mysteries," called *Vajradhara* and *Adi-Buddha*.

[7] *Sat*, the one eternal and Absolute Reality and Truth, all the rest being illusion.

[8] From Shenxiu's Doctrine, who teaches that the human mind is like a mirror which attracts and reflects every atom of dust, and has to be, like that mirror, watched over and dusted every day. Shenxiu was the sixth patriarch of North China who taught the Esoteric Doctrine of Bodhidharma. ▸

gentle breezes of Soul-wisdom to brush away the dust of our illusions. Seek, O beginner, to blend thy mind and soul.

Shun ignorance, and likewise shun illusion. Avert thy face from world deceptions; mistrust thy senses, they are false. But within thy body — the shrine of thy sensations — seek in the impersonal for the "eternal man,"[1] and having sought him out, look inward: thou art Buddha.[2] Shun praise, O devotee. Praise leads to self-delusion. Thy body is not self, thy Self is in itself without a body, and either praise or blame affects it not.

Self-gratulation, O disciple, is like unto a lofty tower, up which a haughty fool has climbed. Thereon he sits in prideful solitude and unperceived by any but himself.

False learning is rejected by the wise, and scattered to the winds by the good Law. Its wheel revolves for all, the humble and the proud. The "Doctrine of the Eye"[3] is for the crowd, the "Doctrine of the Heart," for the elect.[4] The first repeat in pride: "Behold, I know," the last, they who in humbleness have garnered, low confess, "thus have I heard."[5]

"Great Sifter" is the name of the "Heart Doctrine," O disciple.

The wheel of the good Law moves swiftly on. It grinds by night and day. The worthless husks it drives from out the golden grain, the refuse from the flour.[6] The hand of karma guides the wheel; the revolutions mark the beatings of the karmic heart.

C.C.: Shenxiu was the chief disciple of the fifth patriarch Hongren, the other being Huineng (literally "wisdom ability"). Both disciples wrote poems on mind as a mirror in competition for the succession, taking opposite views. The choice fell on Huineng, who thus became the sixth patriarch. In China, the mystic mirror "shows the innermost soul naked and bare of all pretence and deceit. It captures the soul of the candidate and places it in the hands of the Master of a Triad Lodge as hostage for loyalty and fidelity" (J. S. M. Ward, *The Hong Society, or Society of Heaven and Earth*). A work written in Chinese by a Tibetan at Tiantai Monastery directs the disciple to "use his meritorious actions as a dust-cloth to remove every impurity from his mystic mirror, so that he should be enabled to see in its lustre the faithful reflection of Self."

[1] The reincarnating Ego is called by the Northern Buddhists the "true man," who becomes in union with his Higher Self a Buddha.

[2] "Buddha" means "Enlightened."

[3] See note 1, page 44. The *exoteric* Buddhism of the masses.

[4] A.E.: Here is the famous distinction between the esoteric and the exoteric, the religion of the masses and the religion of the elect, the popular versions of religion and the mystical experience.

[5] The usual formula that precedes the Buddhist scriptures, meaning, that that which follows is what has been recorded by direct oral tradition from Buddha and the Arhats.

[6] A.E.: All popular religions with their dogmas, rituals, and ceremonials are "husks," while self-purification through self-control and the subsequent ripe fruit of self-realization is the flour.

True knowledge is the flour, false learning is the husk. If thou would'st eat the bread of Wisdom, thy flour thou hast to knead with Amrita's[7] clear waters. But if thou kneadest husks with Maya's dew, thou canst create but food for the black doves of death, the birds of birth, decay, and sorrow.

If thou art told that to become Arhan thou hast to cease to love all beings — tell them they lie.[8]

If thou art told that to gain liberation thou hast to hate thy mother and disregard thy son; to disavow thy father and call him "householder";[9] for man and beast all pity to renounce — tell them their tongue is false.[10]

Thus teach the Tirthikas, the unbelievers.[11]

If thou art taught that sin is born of action and bliss of absolute inaction, then tell them that they err. Non-permanence of human action; deliverance of mind from thraldom by the cessation of sin and faults, are not for Deva Egos.[12] Thus saith the "Doctrine of the Heart."[13]

---

[7] A.E.: *Amrita* means immortality; *Amrita* is the state of deathlessness.

[8] A.E.: Not an abstract intellectual metaphysics, but the path of divine compassion and universal love is what opens up the portals of immortality. *Vairagya* in the sense of Patanjali, in Mahayana Buddhism, and the broad Hindu traditions, is complete withdrawal from sense-world and complete detachment therefrom. Positive love restores to the dried-up ascetic, *vairagi*, limbs to move and work for the enlightenment and freedom of mankind.

[9] Ratthapala, the great Arhat, thus addresses his father in the legend called *Ratthapala Sutrasanne*. But as all such legends are allegorical (e.g., Ratthapala's father has a mansion with *seven doors*) hence the reproof, to those who accept them *literally*.

[10] A.E.: In this paragraph complete detachment is discouraged. The negative idea of giving up one's family, wife, children, etc., is cast overboard, and the positive idea of detached attachment is stressed. Life acceptance struggles against the life-denying religions. In this context, Mahayana Buddhism and Christianity are the two most life-affirming religions of history. Neither retirement, nor asceticism leads one to liberation, but facing the problems of life here and now through God-realization. In fact, facing the hardest tussles and crosses is itself the supreme means of self-purification and self-realization.

[11] Brahmin ascetics.

[12] The reincarnating Ego.

[13] C.C.: The distinction between the "Eye" (exoteric) and "Heart" (esoteric) Doctrine is frequently insisted upon in this and other Tibetan Mahayana writings. The Chinese, Japanese, and Mongolians likewise recognize it; yet Western scholars, especially those who prefer the Hinayana, and even Oriental exponents of the latter, persist in maintaining that there is no Esoteric Doctrine in Buddhism. In Chinese it is called *Ao Miao De Daoli*, in Tibetan *kok tu cho*, "secret doctrine," or *nang rigpa*, "esoteric science or learning" (*Tibetan-English Dictionary*, pp. 81, 735). H.P.B. states that Northern or Mahayana Buddhism was the outcome of Gautama Buddha's secret teachings to "a select circle of his Arhats." The latter received their Initiation at the famous Saptaparni Cave (*The Secret Doctrine*, vol. 1, p. xx). See also note 1, p. 44.

The Dharma of the "Eye" is the embodiment of the external, and the non-existing.

The Dharma of the "Heart" is the embodiment of Bodhi,[1] the permanent and everlasting.

The lamp burns bright when wick and oil are clean. To make them clean a cleaner is required. The flame feels not the process of the cleaning. "The branches of a tree are shaken by the wind; the trunk remains unmoved."

Both action and inaction may find room in thee; thy body agitated, thy mind tranquil, thy soul as limpid as a mountain lake.

Wouldst thou become a yogi of "Time's Circle"?[2] Then, O lanoo:

Believe thou not that sitting in dark forests, in proud seclusion and apart from men; believe thou not that life on roots and plants, that thirst assuaged with snow from the Great Range — believe thou not, O devotee, that this will lead thee to the goal of final liberation.

Think not that breaking bone, that rending flesh and muscle, unites thee to thy "silent Self."[3] Think not, that when the sins of thy gross form are conquered, O victim of thy shadows,[4] thy duty is accomplished by Nature and by man.

The blessed ones have scorned to do so. The Lion of the Law, the Lord of Mercy,[5] perceiving the true cause of human woe, immediately

---

[1] True, Divine Wisdom.

C.C.: *Bodhi* (Sanskrit, "wisdom") is often applied to Buddha's doctrine because it was based upon the principles of *Budhism* or the archaic Wisdom Religion, also called *Bodhidharma* (note 2, p. 44). *Bodhi* is likewise the name of a particular state of trance condition (*The Secret Doctrine*, vol. 1, p. xix). *Budha* (Sanskrit) is Hermes (Greek).

[2] C.C.: "Time's Circle." Sanskrit: *Kalachakra*. Tibetan: *Dukyi Khorlo*. Mongolian: *Tsagiin Khurden*. The famous esoteric system of yoga. The "Boundless Circle of Time" symbolizes *Adi-Budha*, Primeval Wisdom, "a term used by Aryasanga in his secret treatises and now by all the mystic Northern Buddhists" (*The Secret Doctrine*, vol. 1, p. xix). See also note 1, p. 30. The system "arose at Shambhala" (*Tibetan-English Dictionary*, p. 632), reputed to be the secret abode of the "Sons of Wisdom" or Initiates, located somewhere in the north-west of Tibet. H.P.B. says that the "sacred" books of the Kalachakra were "abandoned to the Sikkim Dugpas from the time of Tsongkhapa's reform," and that he then rewrote the original book with commentaries. She adds that the Kalachakra is the most important work in the division of mystic knowledge of the Kangyur, "a system as old as man, known in India, and practised before Europe became a continent." The Tashi Lama presented the editors with a small treatise in Tibetan on the Kalachakra, entitled "The Communion of Mystic Adepts" (*Du Khor la tenpa lama nenjor*). For *nenjor* see note 1, page 60.

[3] The "Higher Self," the seventh principle.

[4] Our physical bodies are called "shadows" in the mystic schools.

[5] Buddha.

forsook the sweet but selfish rest of quiet wilds. From Aranyaka[6] He became the Teacher of mankind. After Julai[7] had entered the Nirvana, He preached on mount and plain, and held discourses in the cities, to Devas, men, and gods.[8]

Sow kindly acts and thou shalt reap their fruition. Inaction in a deed of mercy becomes an action in a deadly sin.

Thus saith the Sage.

Shalt thou abstain from action? Not so shall gain thy soul her freedom. To reach Nirvana one must reach Self-knowledge, and Self-knowledge is of loving deeds the child.

Have patience, candidate, as one who fears no failure, courts no success. Fix thy soul's gaze upon the star whose ray thou art,[9] the flaming star that shines within the lightless depths of ever-being, the boundless fields of the Unknown.

Have perseverance as one who doth for evermore endure. Thy shadows live and vanish;[10] that which in thee shall live for ever, that which in thee *knows*, for it is knowledge,[11] is not of fleeting life: it is the man that was, that is, and will be, for whom the hour shall never strike.

If thou would'st reap sweet peace and rest, disciple, sow with the seeds of merit the fields of future harvests. Accept the woes of birth.

Step out from sunlight into shade, to make more room for others. The tears that water the parched soil of pain and sorrow, bring forth the blossoms and the fruits of karmic retribution. Out of the furnace of man's life and its black smoke, winged flames arise, flames purified, that soaring onward, 'neath the karmic eye, weave in the end the fabric glorified of the three vestures of the Path.[12]

These vestures are: Nirmanakaya, Sambhogakaya, and Dharmakaya, robe sublime.[13]

---

[6] A hermit who retires to the jungles and lives in a forest, when becoming a yogi.

[7] *Julai*, the Chinese name for Tathagata, a title applied to every Buddha.

[8] All the Northern and Southern traditions agree in showing Buddha quitting his solitude as soon as he had resolved the problem of life — i.e., received the inner enlightenment — and teaching mankind publicly.

[9] Every spiritual Ego is a ray of a Planetary Spirit according to esoteric teaching.

[10] "Personalities" or *physical bodies* called "shadows" are evanescent.

[11] *Mind* (*manas*), the thinking principle or Ego in man, is referred to "Knowledge" itself, because the human Egos are called *Manasa-putras*, the sons of (universal) Mind.

[12] See note 4, page 73.

[13] See note 4, page 73.

The Shangna robe,[1] 'tis true, can purchase light eternal. The Shangna robe alone gives the Nirvana of destruction; it stops rebirth, but, O lanoo, it also kills — compassion. No longer can the perfect Buddhas, who don the Dharmakaya glory, help man's salvation. Alas! Shall Selves be sacrificed to self; mankind, unto the weal of units?

Know, O beginner, this is the Open Path, the way to selfish bliss, shunned by the Bodhisattvas of the "Secret Heart," the Buddhas of Compassion.

To live to benefit mankind is the first step. To practise the six glorious virtues[2] is the second.

To don Nirmanakaya's humble robe is to forego eternal bliss for self, to help on man's salvation. To reach Nirvana's bliss, but to renounce it, is the supreme, the final step — the highest on Renunciation's Path.

Know, O disciple, this is the Secret Path, selected by the Buddhas of Perfection, who sacrificed the Self to weaker selves.[3]

Yet, if the "Doctrine of the Heart" is too high-winged for thee, if thou need'st help thyself and fearest to offer help to others — then, thou of timid heart, be warned in time: remain content with the "Eye Doctrine"

A.E.: The three vestures, *Nirmanakaya*, *Sambhogakaya*, and *Dharmakaya* are fundamental in Mahayana Buddhism in that, after attaining Arhatship, it goes beyond in bestowing compassion, social dynamics, and activities meant to uplift suffering mankind, donning the perfect robe *Dharmakaya*. Corresponding to these three stages or *Dharmic kaya* or bodies is the Catholic Latin ideal: *Ardere tantum parum, lucere tantum vanum, lucere et ardere perfectum* — To burn (out of Self-realization) alone is too little; to shine alone is vain; but to burn and shine, that is perfection. In Buddhist mood one can say: To be Arhat alone is too little; to shine alone is vain; but to combine Arhatship with Bodhisattvahood, or Self-perfection and ministry of compassion, that is perfection.

[1] The *Shangna* robe, from Shangnahexiu of Rajagriha, the third great Arhat or "patriarch" as the Orientalists call the hierarchy of the 33 Arhats who spread Buddhism. "Shangna robe" means, metaphorically, the acquirement of Wisdom with which the Nirvana of destruction (of *personality*) is entered. Literally, the "initiation robe" of the neophytes. Edkins states that this "grass cloth" was brought to China from Tibet in the Tang dynasty. "When an Arhan is born this plant is found growing in a clean spot" says the Chinese as also the Tibetan legend.

[2] To "practise the Paramita Path" means to become a yogi with a view of becoming an ascetic.

[3] A.E.: Here comes the specific contribution of Mahayana Buddhism, the doctrine of self-sacrifice for the weal of others, even as the Buddha renounced the bliss of Nirvana to share the suffering of others, lifting them up to the realm of peace, serenity, joy, and blessedness. "The son of man came not to be served, but to serve and give his life for others," said Jesus. Elsewhere: "None has greater love than to give one's life for his friends." Self-sacrifice or Cross is the highest, loftiest, and most transcendental truth of religion in practice. Here Mahayana scores like Catholicism, *The Voice of the Silence* like the New Testament.

of the Law. Hope still. For if the "Secret Path" is unattainable this "day," it is within thy reach "tomorrow."[4] Learn that no efforts, not the smallest — whether in right or wrong direction — can vanish from the world of causes. E'en wasted smoke remains not traceless. "A harsh word uttered in past lives, is not destroyed but ever comes again."[5] The pepper plant will not give birth to roses, nor the sweet jessamine's silver star to thorn or thistle turn.

Thou canst create this "day" thy chances for thy "morrow." In the "Great Journey,"[6] causes sown each hour bear each its harvest of effects, for rigid justice rules the world. With mighty sweep of never erring action, it brings to mortals lives of weal or woe, the karmic progeny of all our former thoughts and deeds.

Take then as much as merit hath in store for thee, O thou of patient heart. Be of good cheer and rest content with fate. Such is thy karma, the karma of the cycle of thy births, the destiny of those, who, in their pain and sorrow, are born along with thee, rejoice and weep from life to life, chained to thy previous actions.

. . . .

Act thou for them "today," and they will act for thee "tomorrow."

'Tis from the bud of renunciation of the self, that springeth the sweet fruit of final liberation.

To perish doomed is he, who out of fear of Mara refrains from helping man, lest he should act for self. The pilgrim who would cool his weary limbs in running waters, yet dares not plunge for terror of the stream, risks to succumb from heat. Inaction based on selfish fear can bear but evil fruit.

The selfish devotee lives to no purpose. The man who does not go through his appointed work in life — has lived in vain.

Follow the wheel of life; follow the wheel of duty to race and kin, to friend and foe, and close thy mind to pleasures as to pain. Exhaust the law of karmic retribution. Gain *siddhis* for thy future birth.

If Sun thou can'st not be, then be the humble planet. Aye, if thou art debarred from flaming like the noon-day Sun upon the snow-capped mount of purity eternal, then choose, O neophyte, a humbler course.

Point out the "Way" — however dimly, and lost among the host — as does the evening star to those who tread their path in darkness.

---

[4] "Tomorrow" means the following rebirth or reincarnation.
[5] Precepts of the Prasanga School.
[6] "Great Journey" is the whole complete cycle of existences, in one Round.

Behold Migmar,[1] as in his crimson veils his "eye" sweeps over slumbering Earth. Behold the fiery aura of the "hand" of Lhagpa[2] extended in protecting love over the heads of his ascetics. Both are now servants to Nyima[3] left in his absence silent watchers in the night. Yet both in Kalpas past were bright Nyimas, and may in future "Days" again become two Suns. Such are the falls and rises of the Karmic Law in Nature.

Be, O lanoo, like them. Give light and comfort to the toiling pilgrim, and seek out him who knows still less than thou; who in his wretched desolation sits starving for the bread of Wisdom and the bread which feeds the shadow, without a Teacher, hope or consolation, and — let him hear the Law.[4]

Tell him, O candidate, that he who makes of pride and self-regard bond-maidens to devotion; that he who, cleaving to existence, still lays his patience and submission to the Law, as a sweet flower at the feet of Shakya Thubpa,[5] becomes a *Srotapatti*[6] in this birth. The *siddhis* of perfection may loom far, far away; but the first step is taken, the stream is entered, and he may gain the eyesight of the mountain eagle, the hearing of the timid doe.

Tell him, O aspirant, that true devotion may bring him back the knowledge, that knowledge which was his in former births. The deva-sight and deva-hearing are not obtained in one short birth.

Be humble, if thou would'st attain to Wisdom.

Be humbler still, when Wisdom thou hast mastered.

---

[1] Mars.

[2] Mercury.

[3] *Nyima*, the Sun in Tibetan astrology. *Migmar* or Mars is symbolized by an "eye," and *Lhagpa* or Mercury by a "hand."

C.C.: *Migmar* (Mars) is a compound of *mig* (eye) and the first syllable of *mar-po* (red), *Lhagpa* is Mercury; but hand is *Lagpa* (without an *h*). See *Tibetan-English Dictionary*, pp. 1102, 1203.

[4] A.E.: "Let him hear the Law": The spread of Law or Dharma is done by preaching, preaching first by silent life and deeds, and then through spoken and written word. Life Divine, when lived in its fullness, is itself sun-like irradiation on a benighted world. Law, moral Law, is the Divine Power. Nay, God is Law and Law-Giver at the same time. The discovery of the laws of right living and right conduct through experience, and then the broadcasting of it as the way of salvation, that is the job of a religious teacher.

[5] Buddha.

C.C.: *Shakya Thubpa*. *Shakya* is the race to which Gautama Buddha belonged, and *Thubpa* is Tibetan for "the mighty or capable one" (*Tibetan-English Dictionary*, pp. 582, 1229). The usual name for Buddha in Tibet.

[6] *Srotapatti* or "he who enters in the stream" of Nirvana, unless he reaches the goal owing to some exceptional reasons, can rarely attain Nirvana in one birth. Usually a chela is said to begin the ascending effort in one life and end or reach it only in his seventh succeeding birth.

Be like the ocean which receives all streams and rivers. The ocean's mighty calm remains unmoved; it feels them not.

Restrain by thy Divine thy lower self.

Restrain by the Eternal the Divine.

Aye, great is he, who is the slayer of desire.

Still greater he, in whom the Self Divine has slain the very knowledge of desire.

Guard thou the lower lest it soil the Higher.

The way to final freedom is within thy Self.

That way begins and ends outside of self.[7]

Unpraised by men and humble is the mother of all rivers, in Tirthika's proud sight; empty the human form though filled with Amrita's sweet waters, in the sight of fools. Withal, the birthplace of the sacred rivers is the sacred land,[8] and he who Wisdom hath, is honoured by all men.

Arhans and Sages of the boundless vision[9] are rare as is the blossom of the Udumbara tree. Arhans are born at midnight hour, together with the sacred plant of nine and seven stalks,[10] the holy flower that opes and blooms in darkness, out of the pure dew and on the frozen bed of snow-capped heights, heights that are trodden by no sinful foot.

No Arhan, O lanoo, becomes one in that birth when for the first the soul begins to long for final liberation. Yet, O thou anxious one, no warrior volunteering fight in the fierce strife between the living and the dead,[11] not one recruit can ever be refused the right to enter on the Path that leads toward the field of battle.

For, either he shall win, or he shall fall.

Yea, if he conquers, Nirvana shall be his. Before he casts his shadow off his mortal coil[12] — that pregnant cause of anguish and illimitable pain — in him will men a great and holy Buddha honour.

---

[7] Meaning the personal lower self.

[8] *Tirthikas* are the Brahminical sectarians beyond the Himalayas called "infidels" by the Buddhists in the sacred land, Tibet, and vice versa.

[9] Boundless vision or psychic, superhuman sight. An Arhan is credited with seeing and knowing all at a distance as well as on the spot.

[10] See note 1, page 50: Shangna plant.

[11] The "living" is the immortal Higher Ego, and the "dead" — the lower *personal* ego.

[12] C.C.: The "shadow" (astral body) is separated from the "mortal coil" (physical body) at death. Nirvana can be reached while still in the body, being a state of consciousness — that of the seventh principle (*atma*). The chief aim of the Arhat's struggles and initiations is to achieve union with that principle "while

And if he falls, e'en then he does not fall in vain; the enemies he slew in the last battle will not return to life in the next birth that will be his.

But if thou would'st Nirvana reach, or cast the prize away,[1] let not the fruit of action and inaction be thy motive, thou of dauntless heart.

Know that the Bodhisattva who liberation changes for Renunciation to don the miseries of "Secret Life,"[2] is called, "thrice honoured," O thou candidate for woe throughout the cycles.

The Path is one, disciple, yet in the end, twofold. Marked are its stages by four and seven Portals. At one end — bliss immediate, and at the other — bliss deferred. Both are of merit the reward: the choice is thine.[3]

The one becomes the two, the Open and the Secret.[4] The first one leadeth to the goal, the second, to Self-Immolation.

When to the Permanent is sacrificed the mutable, the prize is thine: the drop returneth whence it came. The Open Path leads to the changeless change — Nirvana, the glorious state of Absoluteness, the Bliss past human thought.

Thus, the first Path is Liberation.

But Path the second is — Renunciation, and therefore called the "Path of Woe."

That Secret Path leads the Arhan to mental woe unspeakable; woe for the living dead,[5] and helpless pity for the men of karmic sorrow, the fruit of karma sages dare not still.

For it is written: "Teach to eschew all causes; the ripple of effect, as the great tidal wave, thou shalt let run its course."

The "Open Way," no sooner hast thou reached its goal, will lead thee

---

yet on this earth" (*The Mahatma Letters*, p. 78). See also note 7 on p. 59: "An Arhat sees Nirvana during his life. For him it is no post-mortem state, but *samadhi*."

[1] See note 4, page 73.

[2] The "Secret Life" is life as a Nirmanakaya.

[3] A.E.: The ever recurring theme of two paths, of the Self-realized Arhat and the compassionate Bodhisattva, is condensed in one phrase when it says: "At one end — bliss immediate," as in the case of hermits, anchorites, recluses, Arhats, and silent seers like Ramana Maharshi, Sri Aurobindo, and their likes, while the "bliss differed" as in the case of Bodhisattvas or apostles, missionaries, servants of suffering humanity like Mahatma Gandhi, Swami Vivekananda, Kagawa, and their likes.

[4] The "Open" and the "Secret Path" — or the one taught to the layman, the exoteric and the generally accepted, and the other the Secret Path — the nature of which is explained at initiation.

[5] Men ignorant of the esoteric truths and Wisdom are called "the living dead."

to reject the Bodhisattvic body and make thee enter the thrice glorious state of Dharmakaya[6] which is oblivion of the world and men for ever.

The "Secret Way" leads also to Paranirvanic bliss — but at the close of Kalpas without number; Nirvanas gained and lost from boundless pity and compassion for the world of deluded mortals.

But it is said, "The last shall be the greatest," Samyak Sambuddha, the Teacher of Perfection, gave up his Self for the salvation of the world, by stopping at the threshold of Nirvana — the pure state.

. . . .

Thou hast the knowledge now concerning the two Ways. Thy time will come for choice, O thou of eager soul, when thou hast reached the end and passed the seven Portals. Thy mind is clear. No more art thou entangled in delusive thoughts, for thou hast learned all. Unveiled stands truth and looks thee sternly in the face. She says:

"Sweet are the fruits of Rest and Liberation for the sake of self; but sweeter still the fruits of long and bitter duty. Aye, Renunciation for the sake of others, of suffering fellow men."[7]

He who becomes Pratyeka Buddha[8] makes his obeisance but to his self.[9] The Bodhisattva who has won the battle, who holds the prize within his palm, yet says in his divine compassion:

"For others' sake this great reward I yield" — accomplishes the greater Renunciation.

---

[6] See note 4, page 73.

[7] A.E.: This is the highest religion, Mahayana Buddhism, at its best.

[8] *Pratyeka Buddhas* are those Bodhisattvas who strive after and often reach the Dharmakaya robe after a series of lives. Caring nothing for the woes of mankind or to help it, but only for their own *bliss*, they enter Nirvana and — disappear from the sight and the hearts of men. In Northern Buddhism, a "Pratyeka Buddha" is a synonym of spiritual *selfishness*.

C.C.: This note and part of the verse are omitted from the official posthumous editions, the view of the editor being that H.P.B. was mistaken (see *H. P. Blavatsky: A Great Betrayal*, p. 71). We find, however, that her statement is fully confirmed by the Chinese, Japanese, and Tibetan authorities, from whom we learn that the *Pratyeka* state is one of enlightenment, as contrasted with the mere salvation of the Arhat of the Hinayana School, "but enlightenment for oneself alone, no attempt being made to influence or assist mankind" (*Introduction to Mahayana Buddhism*, p. 101). In fact the Tibetans specify three Vehicles: 1) *Hinayana* or *Shravaka Yana*; 2) *Pratyeka Buddha* or *Pradeshika Yana*; 3) *Bodhisattva* or *Maha Yana*. The principal department of the third is the *Vajrayana* (see note 1, page 56 on *Vajrapani*) "which follows mysticism and deals in some measure with Esoteric Buddhism" (*Tibetan-English Dictionary*, p. 586).

[9] C.C.: Note the distinction between the greater Self renounced by the Buddha, and the lesser self to which the Pratyeka Buddha makes his obeisance.

A Saviour of the World is he.

. . . .

Behold! The goal of bliss and the long Path of Woe are at the furthest end. Thou canst choose either, O aspirant to sorrow, throughout the coming cycles! ...

OM VAJRAPANI HUM[1]

---

[1] C.C.: *Vajrapani*. (Tibetan: *Chana Dorje*). Wielder of the *vajra* or diamond sceptre (Tibetan: *dorje*, see note 5, p. 63). Also called the Lord of Mysticism (Tibetan: *Sangwa Dagpo, Tibetan-English Dictionary*, p. 1303). The Vajra Ray of the esoteric septenary emanation of the Buddhas (exoterically fivefold) is intimately connected with the Yogachara Mystic School (Chinese: *Shan Mi Pai*). Thus *Vajradhara* (Tibetan: *Dorje Chang*) is the same as *Adi-Budha* (see note 2, page 48), *Vajrasattva* (Tibetan: *Dorje Sempa*, "diamond soul") is the sixth Dhyani-Buddha, and *Vajrapani* is his mind-born son, one of the Dhyani-Bodhisattvas who incarnate as earthly Buddhas. In note 6, p. 45 the words "a title" should read "the sixth Dhyani-Buddha." The *vajra*, says H.P.B., is "in mystical Buddhism the *magic* sceptre of Priest-Initiates, exorcists, and Adepts — the symbol of the possession of *siddhi* or superhuman powers, wielded during certain ceremonies by the priests and theurgists. The possessors of this wand are called *Vajrapani*." The name also stands for "a subjective Force, the real nature of which is only known to, and explained by, the highest Initiates of the Yogachara school" (*Theosophical Glossary*, pp. 359–360). Hence the invocation *Om Vajrapani Hum*.

Fragment III
THE SEVEN PORTALS

"Upadya,[1] the choice is made, I thirst for Wisdom. Now hast thou rent the veil before the Secret Path and taught the greater Yana.[2] Thy servant here is ready for thy guidance."

'Tis well, shravaka.[3] Prepare thyself, for thou wilt have to travel on alone. The Teacher can but point the way. The Path is one for all, the means to reach the goal must vary with the pilgrims.

Which wilt thou choose, O thou of dauntless heart? The Samtan[4] of "eye Doctrine," fourfold Dhyana, or thread thy way through Paramitas,[5] six in number, noble gates of virtue leading to Bodhi and to Prajna, seventh step of Wisdom?

The rugged Path of fourfold Dhyana winds on uphill. Thrice great is he who climbs the lofty top.[6]

---

[1] *Upadya* is a spiritual preceptor, a Guru. The Northern Buddhists choose these generally among the *Narjol*, saintly men, learned in *gotrabhu-nana* and *nana-dassana-visuddhi* teachers of the Secret Wisdom.

C.C.: Sir Charles Eliot says that *upadhyaya* is a term current in Central Asia (*Hinduism and Buddhism*, vol. 3, p. 330).

A.E.: *Upadya* is Guide, Preceptor, Master, Guru who teaches the path of Emancipation, Redemption through his life, his inspiring deeds and words.

[2] *Yana* — vehicle: thus *Mahayana* is the "Great Vehicle," and *Hinayana*, the "Lesser Vehicle," the names for the two schools of religious and philosophical learning in Northern Buddhism.

[3] *Shravaka* — a listener, or student who attends to the religious instructions. From the root *shru*. When from theory they go into practice or performance of asceticism, they become *shramanas*, "exercisers," from *shrama*, action. As Hardy shows, the two appellations answer to the words *akoustikoi* and *asketai* of the Greeks.

A.E.: *Shravaka* is the religious aspirant, disciple, chela, or *lanoo*, who, with all the necessary dispositions, moral qualities, and virtues, aspires after spiritual perfection. *Shravaka Sangha* is the assembly of disciples of Enlightenment, or the Enlightened One, the Buddha, the Eastern counterpart to Neoplatonic *Logos*, the Word of God.

[4] *Samtan* (Tibetan), the same as the Sanskrit *dhyana*, or the state of meditation, of which there are four degrees.

C.C.: *Tibetan-English Dictionary*, p. 1317 defines *samtan* as a "state of complete abstraction, contemplation, meditation, concentration of thoughts; especially that mystic meditation which at length evolves an astral counterpart of the meditator — the counterpart existing in Devachan contemporaneously with the meditator who continues on earth." As Devachan is the intermediate state of the immortal Ego between two earth-lives, the counterpart spoken of is probably the first of the inner bodies or vestures woven by the ascetic as he proceeds along the path (see note 4, p. 73). By "astral" Das means "ethereal," not the *linga-sharira*. The Tibetans define nine kinds of consciousness (Chinese: *jue*), and the same number of stages in the *samadhi* of a Bodhisattva (*Tibetan-English Dictionary*, pp. 54, 761). Devachan like Nirvana, being a state of consciousness with its appropriate vesture or vehicle, can be entered or realized while still in the body by the processes of meditation (see also note 12, p. 53). H.P.B. impressed on her pupils the need to "reduce everything to terms of consciousness."

[5] *Paramitas*, the six transcendental virtues; for the priests there are ten.

The Paramita heights are crossed by a still steeper path. Thou hast to fight thy way through portals seven, seven strongholds held by cruel, crafty powers — passions incarnate.

Be of good cheer, disciple; bear in mind the golden rule. Once thou hast passed the gate Srotapatti,[7] "he who the stream hath entered"; once thy foot hath pressed the bed of the Nirvanic stream in this or any future life, thou hast but seven other births before thee, O thou of adamantine will.

Look on. What seest thou before thine eye, O aspirant to godlike Wisdom?

"The cloak of darkness is upon the deep of matter; within its folds I struggle. Beneath my gaze it deepens, Lord; it is dispelled beneath the waving of thy hand. A shadow moveth, creeping like the stretching serpent coils. . . . It grows, swells out, and disappears in darkness."

It is the shadow of thyself outside the Path, cast on the darkness of thy sins.

"Yea, Lord; I see the Path; its foot in mire, its summits lost in glorious light Nirvanic. And now I see the ever narrowing Portals on the hard and thorny way to *gnyana*."[8]

Thou seest well, lanoo. These Portals lead the aspirant across the waters on "to the other shore."[9] Each Portal hath a golden key that openeth its gate; and these keys are:

1. *Dana*, the key of charity and love immortal.

---

[6] A.E.: The *fourfold dhyana* are the *pratyahara, dharana, dhyana*, and *samadhi* of the Patanjali Yoga, which underwent variations and modifications in Tibet, China, Japan, and other Mahayana countries. Read: "Thrice blessed is he who climbs the lofty top (of the uphill)."

[7] *Srotapatti* — literally "he who has entered the stream" that leads to the Nirvanic ocean. This name indicates the first Path. The name of the second is the Path of *Sakridagamin*, "he who will receive birth (only) once more." The third is called *Anagamin*, "he who will be reincarnated no more," unless he so desires in order to help mankind. The fourth Path is known as that of *Rahat* or *Arhat*. This is the highest. An Arhat sees Nirvana during his life. For him it is no post-mortem state, but *samadhi*, during which he experiences all Nirvanic bliss.

How little one can rely upon the Orientalists for the exact words and meaning, is instanced in the case of three "alleged" authorities. Thus the four names just explained are given by R. Spence Hardy as: 1) Sovan; 2) Sakradagami; 3) Anagami, and 4) Arya. By the Reverend Joseph Edkins they are given as: 1) Srotapanna; 2) Sagardagam; 3) Anaganim, and 4) Arhan. Schlagintweit again spells them differently, each, moreover, giving another and a new variation in the meaning of the terms.

[8] Knowledge, Wisdom.

[9] "Arrival at the shore" is with the Northern Buddhists synonymous with reaching Nirvana through the exercise of the six and the ten paramitas (virtues).

2. *Shila*, the key of harmony in word and act, the key that counterbalances the cause and the effect, and leaves no further room for karmic action.

3. *Kshanti*, patience sweet, that nought can ruffle.

4. *Virag'*, indifference to pleasure and to pain, illusion conquered, truth alone perceived.

5. *Virya*, the dauntless energy that fights its way to the supernal Truth, out of the mire of lies terrestrial.

6. *Dhyana*, whose golden gate once opened leads the Narjol[1] toward the realm of *Sat* eternal and its ceaseless contemplation.

7. *Prajna*, the key to which makes of a man a god, creating him a Bodhisattva, son of the Dhyanis.

Such to the Portals are the golden keys.

Before thou canst approach the last, O weaver of thy freedom, thou hast to master these Paramitas of perfection — the virtues transcendental six and ten in number — along the weary Path.

For, O disciple! Before thou wert made fit to meet thy Teacher face to face, thy Master light to light, what wert thou told?

Before thou canst approach the foremost gate, thou hast to learn to part thy body from thy mind, to dissipate the shadow, and to live in the eternal. For this, thou hast to live and breathe in all, as all that thou perceivest breathes in thee; to feel thyself abiding in all things, all things in Self.[2]

---

[1] A saint, an Adept.
  C.C.: *Narjol*. The Tibetan word is *nenjor* and means "realization of the state of meditation," while *nenjorpa* means a man who realizes that state, i.e., a yogi or Adept. *Nenjorma* is a female yogi (*Tibetan-English Dictionary*, p. 763). In transliterating the word as "Narjol" H.P.B. may have had in mind "Nargal," the name of the Chaldean Chief of the Magi (*Theosophical Glossary*, p. 225), which may also be used in Tibet, for she says "there is reason to call the Trans-Himalayan Esoteric Doctrine Chaldeo-Tibetan." There is also the word *Naga* (Sanskrit), literally a serpent, but esoterically or symbolically an Arhat or Initiate. It occurs continually in Indian scriptures, legends, and place names. The Dragon of China, the Nagal of Mexico, and the Uraeus of Egypt have the same meaning (*Theosophical Glossary*, p. 232). *Nenjor chopa* is the Tibetan name of the genuine Yogachara books of Aryasanga who, according to the Secret Doctrine, came from Shambhala and was taught by the Buddha.

[2] A.E.: This entire paragraph savours monistic idealism, in that, mind or consciousness, divested of all bodily and sensual imaginings, become merged in All, All in all, in That One "in whom we live, move, and have our being." Senses are the barriers to intellectual light and redemptive vision. All are one, although all seem to be many; man is one, although men are many. Mystical Religion of Oneness and Unity underlying all historical religion is perceived when one bodily and sensual life is transcended, and our individual ego is crucified, and ▸

Thou shalt not let thy senses make a playground of thy mind.

Thou shalt not separate thy being from Being, and the rest, but merge the Ocean in the drop, the drop within the Ocean.

So shalt thou be in full accord with all that lives; bear love to men as though they were thy brother pupils, disciples of one Teacher, the sons of one sweet mother.

Of teachers there are many; the Master-Soul is one, Alaya,³ the Universal Soul. Live in that Master as its ray in thee. Live in thy fellows as they live in it.

Before thou standest on the threshold of the Path; before thou crossest the foremost Gate, thou hast to merge the two into the One and sacrifice the personal to Self impersonal, and thus destroy the "path" between the two — *antaskarana*.⁴

Thou hast to be prepared to answer Dharma, the stern law, whose voice will ask thee at thy first, at thy initial step:

"Hast thou complied with all the rules, O thou of lofty hopes?"

"Hast thou attuned thy heart and mind to the great mind and heart of all mankind? For as the sacred River's roaring voice whereby all

---

we are risen with Christ in radiant Light becoming one with the Enlightened One, the Buddha.

³ The "Master-Soul" is *Alaya*, the Universal Soul or Atman, each man having a ray of it in him and being supposed to be able to identify himself with and to merge himself into it.

A.E.: *Alaya* is the inner tabernacle within human consciousness where alone the Eternal and the Infinite can be found. The Kingdom of God is within you, not here, there, but above here and now, there and then. The Master-Soul is the *Paramatma*, the Universal Self which alone is real, whose irradiation or distant rays are individualized souls which have no existence apart from the Infinite, even as the rays of the sun reaching your room spring from the one solar energy up above, and have no existence outside of the sun.

⁴ *Antaskarana* is the lower *manas*, the path of communication or communion between the personality and the higher *manas* or human soul. At death it is destroyed as a path or medium of communication, and its remains survive in a form as the *kama-rupa* — the "shell."

C.C.: Under "*antahkarana* (Sanskrit) or *antaskarana*," H.P.B. further explains that it "conveys from the lower to the Higher Ego all those personal impressions and thoughts of men which can, by their nature, be assimilated and stored by the undying entity, and be thus made immortal with it, those being the only elements of the evanescent *personality* that survive death and time. It thus stands to reason that only that which is noble, spiritual, and divine in man can testify in Eternity to his having lived" (*Theosophical Glossary*, p. 23). In the *Anatta* (No-Soul) doctrine of the Hinayana, the existence of *Atma* (the Universal Soul) and *atma-buddhi-manas* (the immortal Ego) is not recognized, only the evanescent personality. "In Hinayana the Buddhas are men, pure and simple, while in Mahayana they are looked upon as divine incarnations, or as material expressions of the Universal Buddha" (*Introduction to Mahayana Buddhism*, p. 19).

Nature-sounds are echoed back,[1] so must the heart of him 'who in the stream would enter,' thrill in response to every sigh and thought of all that lives and breathes."

Disciples may be likened to the strings of the soul-echoing vina; mankind, unto its sounding board; the hand that sweeps it to the tuneful breath of the Great World-Soul. The string that fails to answer 'neath the Master's touch in dulcet harmony with all the others, breaks — and is cast away. So the collective minds of lanoo-shravakas. They have to be attuned to the Upadya's mind — one with the Over-Soul — or, break away.

Thus do the "brothers of the shadow" — the murderers of their souls, the dread Dad-Dugpa clan.[2]

Hast thou attuned thy being to humanity's great pain, O candidate for light?

Thou hast? . . . Thou mayest enter. Yet, ere thou settest foot upon the dreary Path of sorrow, 'tis well thou should'st first learn the pitfalls on thy way.[3]

---

[1] The Northern Buddhists, and all Chinese, in fact, find in the deep roar of some of the great and sacred rivers the keynote of Nature. Hence the simile. It is a well-known fact in physical science, as well as in occultism, that the aggregate sound of Nature — such as heard in the roar of great rivers, the noise produced by the waving tops of trees in large forests, or that of a city heard at a distance — is a definite single tone of quite an appreciable pitch. This is shown by physicists and musicians. Thus Professor Rice ("Chinese Theory," *What is Music?*, 1883, p. 9) shows that the Chinese recognized the fact thousands of years ago by saying that "the waters of the Huanghe, rushing by, intoned the *kung*" called "the great tone" in Chinese music; and he shows this tone corresponding with the F, "considered by modern physicists to be the actual tonic of Nature." Professor B. Silliman mentions it, too, in his *Principles of Physics* (1866, p. 252), saying that "this tone is held to be the middle F of the piano; which may, therefore, be considered the keynote of Nature."

[2] The *Bons* or *Dugpas*, the sect of the "red caps," are regarded as the most versed in sorcery. They inhabit Western and Little Tibet and Bhutan. They are all Tantrikas. It is quite ridiculous to find Orientalists who have visited the borderlands of Tibet, such as Schlagintweit and others, confusing the rites and disgusting practices of these with the religious beliefs of the Eastern Lamas, the "Yellow Caps," and their *Narjols* or holy men. As an instance see note 5.
A.E.: "The brothers of the shadow" are the combined force of the flesh-blood man who is not attuned to the heart of the Infinite, the Over-Soul. He has broken away from the life of the Real. Through sensual vanity, pride, and vices, they kill their souls, "murderers of their own souls." The *Dad-Dugpa* clan of Tibet, the gang of highway robbers, and the city of butterflies and demimondes, all kill themselves, burnt up in the fire of *trishna*, that white heat and thirst springing from a body-conscious, sense-fed life.

[3] A.E.: The following paragraphs in this and the next pages describe poetically and imaginatively the various stages of the pilgrimage of the *lanoo-shravakas*,

. . . .

Armed with the key of charity, of love, and tender mercy, thou art secure before the gate of Dana, the gate that standeth at the entrance of the Path.

Behold, O happy pilgrim! The portal that faceth thee is high and wide, seems easy of access. The road that leads therethrough is straight and smooth and green. 'Tis like a sunny glade in the dark forest depths, a spot on earth mirrored from Amitabha's paradise. There, nightingales of hope and birds of radiant plumage sing perched in green bowers, chanting success to fearless pilgrims. They sing of Bodhisattvas' virtues five, the fivefold source of Bodhi power, and of the seven steps in Knowledge.

Pass on! For thou hast brought the key; thou art secure.

And to the second gate the way is verdant too. But it is steep and winds up hill; yea, to its rocky top. Grey mists will overhang its rough and stony height, and all be dark beyond. As on he goes, the song of hope soundeth more feeble in the pilgrim's heart. The thrill of doubt is now upon him; his step less steady grows.

Beware of this, O candidate! Beware of fear that spreadeth, like the black and soundless wings of midnight bat, between the moonlight of thy soul and thy great goal that loometh in the distance far away.

Fear, O disciple, kills the will and stays all action. If lacking in the Shila virtue — the pilgrim trips, and karmic pebbles bruise his feet along the rocky path.

Be of sure foot, O candidate. In Kshanti's[4] essence bathe thy soul; for now thou dost approach the portal of that name, the gate of fortitude and patience.

Close not thine eyes, nor lose thy sight of *dorje*;[5] Mara's arrows ever smite the man who has not reached Viraga.[6]

---

the disciples marching steadily and surely to the lap of the Eternal, God, our Father who is in Heaven.

[4] *Kshanti*, "patience," see the enumeration of the golden keys.

[5] *Dorje* is the Sanskrit *vajra*, a weapon or instrument in the hands of some gods (the Tibetan *Dragshed*, the Devas who protect men), and is regarded as having the same occult power of repelling evil influences by purifying the air as ozone in chemistry. It is also a *mudra*, a gesture and posture used in sitting for meditation. It is, in short, a symbol of power over invisible evil influences, whether as a posture or a talisman. The *Bons* or *Dugpas*, however, having appropriated the symbol, misuse it for purposes of black magic. With the "Yellow Caps," or Gelugpas, it is a symbol of power, as the Cross is with the Christians, while it is in no way more "superstitious." With the Dugpas, it is like the *double triangle reversed*, the sign of sorcery.

[6] *Viraga* is that feeling of absolute indifference to the objective universe, to pleasure and to pain. "Disgust" does not express its meaning, yet it is akin to it.

Beware of trembling. 'Neath the breath of fear the key of Kshanti rusty grows: the rusty key refuseth to unlock.

The more thou dost advance, the more thy feet pitfalls will meet. The path that leadeth on, is lighted by one fire — the light of daring, burning in the heart. The more one dares, the more he shall obtain. The more he fears, the more that light shall pale — and that alone can guide. For as the lingering sunbeam, that on the top of some tall mountain shines, is followed by black night when out it fades, so is heart-light. When out it goes, a dark and threatening shade will fall from thine own heart upon the path, and root thy feet in terror to the spot.[1]

Beware, disciple, of that lethal shade. No light that shines from Spirit can dispel the darkness of the nether soul, unless all selfish thought has fled therefrom, and that the pilgrim saith: "I have renounced this passing frame; I have destroyed the cause: the shadows cast can, as effects, no longer be." For now the last great fight, the final war between the Higher and the lower self, hath taken place. Behold, the very battlefield is now engulfed in the great war, and is no more.[2]

But once that thou hast passed the gate of Kshanti, step the third is taken. Thy body is thy slave. Now, for the fourth prepare, the Portal of temptations which do ensnare the *inner* man.

Ere thou canst near that goal, before thine hand is lifted to upraise the fourth gate's latch, thou must have mustered all the mental changes in thy self and slain the army of the thought sensations that, subtle and insidious, creep unasked within the Soul's bright shrine.

If thou would'st not be slain by them, then must thou harmless make thy own creations, the children of thy thoughts, unseen, impalpable, that swarm round humankind, the progeny and heirs to man and his terrestrial spoils. Thou hast to study the voidness of the seeming full, the fullness of the seeming void. O fearless aspirant, look deep within the

---

[1] A.E.: Masters of spiritual life, whether in Buddhism, Catholicism, or Hinduism, have graphically described the pitfalls, dangers, and battle which aspirants after perfection have to encounter at various levels of spiritual pilgrimage. St. John of the Cross, Thomas of Kempis, Basil the Great, St. Ignatius of Loyola, and many others have pointed out the same risks and temptations in almost identical terms.

[2] A.E.: This paragraph reminds one of the description of the Dark Night of the Soul described by St. John of the Cross in *Ascent of Mount Carmel*. It is after the fiercest battle between flesh and the Spirit, the lower and the higher self, between the Divine and the satanic, the illusory *mayavic* and the eternally real *sattvic*, that the disciple emerges triumphant, joining the ranks of the Bodhisattvas, beyond the rank of Arhat, who is only a Self-realized soul, while Bodhisattva, the Compassionate, is also a warrior in the world to dispel darkness of sin and give Enlightenment and Salvation unto many.

well of thine own heart, and answer. Knowest thou of Self the powers, O thou perceiver of external shadows?

If thou dost not — then art thou lost.

For, on Path fourth, the lightest breeze of passion or desire will stir the steady light upon the pure white walls of Soul. The smallest wave of longing or regret for Maya's gifts illusive, along *antaskarana* — the path that lies between thy Spirit and thy self, the highway of sensations, the rude arousers of *ahankara*[3] — a thought as fleeting as the lightning flash will make thee thy three prizes forfeit — the prizes thou hast won.

For know, that the Eternal knows no change.

"The eight dire miseries forsake for evermore. If not, to wisdom, sure, thou can'st not come, nor yet to liberation," saith the Great Lord, the Tathagata of Perfection, "he who has followed in the footsteps of his predecessors."[4]

Stern and exacting is the virtue of Viraga. If thou its path would'st master, thou must keep thy mind and thy perceptions far freer than before from killing action.[5]

Thou hast to saturate thyself with pure Alaya, become as one with Nature's Soul-Thought. At one with it thou art invincible; in separation, thou becomest the playground of Samvriti,[6] origin of all the world's delusions.

---

[3] *Ahankara* — the "I" or feeling of one's personality, the "I-am-ness."

[4] "One who walks in the steps of his predecessors" or "those who came before him," is the true meaning of the name *Tathagata*.
C.C.: *Tathagata* (Tibetan: *Dezhin Shekpa*). Gautama was the fourth of the *Sapta Tathagata*, "the chief seven Nirmanakayas among the numberless ancient world-guardians. Their names are inscribed on a *heptagonal* pillar kept in a secret chamber in almost all Buddhist temples in China and Tibet." *Tathagatagupta* is "the secret or concealed *Tathagata*, or the 'guardian' protecting Buddhas: used of the Nirmanakayas." There is a special mystery connected with Gautama. An esoteric legend states that in our present Aryan Fifth Root Race he "appeared too early, and had to disappear bodily from the world for a while" (*Theosophical Glossary*, pp. 260, 286, 322). H.P.B. also writes elsewhere that in his subtle body he is "still present among the Initiates, and, from time to time, associates himself, in some most mysterious — to us quite incomprehensible — manner, with Avatars and great saints, and works through them." See note 1, p. 16 and note 2, p. 70.

[5] C.C.: "Killing action." This refers to the dangerous activity of the lower mind (Sanskrit: *kama-manas*) which is constantly at work creating images that distract and seduce the aspirant. See note 5, p. 29. In the Bhagavad Gita, chapter 3, the question "Action or Inaction?" is very fully discussed, and Krishna advises Arjuna at verse 9 to "perform action for its own sake, free from attachment," i.e., without becoming personally involved. See also Shankaracharya's *Crest Jewel of Wisdom* (*Vivekachudamani*) verse 311 *et seq.*, on dynamic mind-images, imagination, action, and non-attachment.

[6] *Samvriti* is that one of the two truths which demonstrates the illusive character or emptiness of all things. It is *relative* truth in this case. The Mahayana ›

All is impermanent in man except the pure bright essence of Alaya. Man is its crystal ray; a beam of light immaculate within, a form of clay material upon the lower surface. That beam is thy life-guide and thy true Self, the Watcher, and the silent Thinker, the victim of thy lower self. Thy soul cannot be hurt but through thy erring body; control and master both, and thou art safe when crossing to the nearing "gate of Balance."

Be of good cheer, O daring pilgrim "to the other shore." Heed not the whisperings of Mara's hosts; wave off the tempters, those ill-natured sprites, the jealous *lhamayin*[1] in endless space.

Hold firm! Thou nearest now the middle portal, the gate of woe, with its ten thousand snares.

Have mastery o'er thy thoughts, O striver for perfection, if thou would'st cross its threshold.

Have mastery o'er thy soul, O seeker after truths undying, if thou would'st reach the goal.

Thy soul-gaze centre on the One Pure Light, the Light that is free from affection, and use thy golden key. . . .

. . . .

The dreary task is done, thy labour well-nigh o'er. The wide abyss that gaped to swallow thee is almost spanned. . . .

. . . .

Thou hast now crossed the moat that circles round the gate of human passions. Thou hast now conquered Mara and his furious host.

Thou hast removed pollution from thine heart and bled it from impure desire. But, O thou glorious combatant, thy task is not yet done. Build high, lanoo, the wall that shall hedge in the Holy Isle,[2] the dam that will protect thy mind from pride and satisfaction at thoughts of the great feat achieved.

A sense of pride would mar the work. Aye, build it strong, lest the fierce rush of battling waves, that mount and beat its shore from out the

---

school teaches the difference between these two truths — *paramarthasatya* and *samvritisatya* (*satya*, "truth"). This is the bone of contention between the Madhyamikas and the Yogacharas, the former denying and the latter affirming that every object exists owing to a previous cause or by a concatenation. The Madhyamikas are the great nihilists and deniers, for whom everything is *parikalpita*, an illusion and an error in the world of thought and the subjective, as much as in the objective universe. The Yogacharas are the great spiritualists. *Samvriti*, therefore, as only relative truth, is the origin of all illusion.

[1] *Lhamayin* are elementals and evil spirits adverse to men and are their enemies.

[2] The Higher Ego, or Thinking Self.

great world Maya's ocean, swallow up the pilgrim and the isle — yea, even when the victory's achieved.

Thine "Isle" is the deer, thy thoughts the hounds that weary and pursue his progress to the stream of Life. Woe to the deer that is o'ertaken by the barking fiends before he reach the Vale of Refuge — Dnyan Marga, "path of pure knowledge" named.

Ere thou canst settle in Dnyan Marga[3] and call it thine, thy soul has to become as the ripe mango fruit: as soft and sweet as its bright golden pulp for others' woes, as hard as that fruit's stone for thine own throes and sorrows, O conqueror of weal and woe.

Make hard thy soul against the snares of self; deserve for it the name of "Diamond Soul."[4]

For, as the diamond buried deep within the throbbing heart of earth can never mirror back the earthly lights; so are thy mind and soul; plunged in Dnyan Marga, these must mirror nought of Maya's realm illusive.

When thou hast reached that state, the Portals that thou hast to conquer on the Path fling open wide their gates to let thee pass, and Nature's strongest mights possess no power to stay thy course. Thou wilt be master of the sevenfold Path: but not till then, O candidate for trials passing speech.

Till then, a task far harder still awaits thee: thou hast to feel thyself All-Thought, and yet exile all thoughts from out thy soul.

Thou hast to reach that fixity of mind in which no breeze, however strong, can waft an earthly thought within. Thus purified, the shrine must of all action, sound, or earthly light be void; e'en as the butterfly, o'ertaken by the frost, falls lifeless at the threshold — so must all earthly thoughts fall dead before the fane.

Behold it written:

"Ere the gold flame can burn with steady light, the lamp must stand well-guarded in a spot free from all wind."[5] Exposed to shifting breeze, the jet will flicker and the quivering flame cast shades deceptive, dark and ever-changing, on the Soul's white shrine.

And then, O thou pursuer of the truth, thy mind-soul will become as

---

[3] *Dnyan Marga* is the "Path of *Dhyana*," literally; or the *path of pure knowledge*, of *paramartha* or (Sanskrit) *svasamvedana* "the self-evident or self-analysing reflection."

[4] See note 6, page 45. "Diamond Soul" or *Vajradhara* presides over the Dhyani-Buddhas.

[5] Bhagavad Gita 6:19.

a mad elephant that rages in the jungle. Mistaking forest trees for living foes, he perishes in his attempts to kill the ever-shifting shadows dancing on the wall of sunlit rocks.

Beware, lest in the care of self thy soul should lose her foothold on the soil of Deva-knowledge.

Beware, lest in forgetting Self, thy soul lose o'er its trembling mind control, and forfeit thus the due fruition of its conquests.

Beware of change! For change is thy great foe. This change will fight thee off, and throw thee back, out of the Path thou treadest, deep into viscous swamps of doubt.

Prepare, and be forewarned in time. If thou hast tried and failed, O dauntless fighter, yet lose not courage: fight on and to the charge return again, and yet again.

The fearless warrior, his precious life-blood oozing from his wide and gaping wounds, will still attack the foe, drive him from out his stronghold, vanquish him, ere he himself expires. Act then, all ye who fail and suffer, act like him; and from the stronghold of your soul, chase all your foes away — ambition, anger, hatred, e'en to the shadow of desire — when even you have failed. . . .

Remember, thou that fightest for man's liberation,[1] each failure is success, and each sincere attempt wins its reward in time. The holy germs that sprout and grow unseen in the disciple's soul, their stalks wax strong at each new trial, they bend like reeds but never break, nor can they e'er be lost. But when the hour has struck they blossom forth.[2] . . .

---

[1] This is an allusion to a well-known belief in the East (as in the West, too, for the matter of that) that every additional Buddha or saint is a new soldier in the army of those who work for the liberation or salvation of mankind. In Northern Buddhist countries, where the doctrine of *Nirmanakayas* — those Bodhisattvas who renounce well-earned Nirvana or the *Dharmakaya* vesture (both of which shut them out forever from the world of men) in order to invisibly assist mankind and lead it finally to Paranirvana — is taught, every new Bodhisattva or initiated great Adept is called the "liberator of mankind." The statement made by Schlagintweit in his *Buddhism in Tibet* (1863, p. 38) to the effect that *Trulpe ku* or *Nirmanakaya* is "the *body* in which the Buddhas or Bodhisattvas appear upon earth to teach men" — is absurdly inaccurate and explains nothing.

[2] A reference to human passions and sins which are slaughtered during the trials of the novitiate, and serve as well-fertilized soil in which "holy germs" or seeds of transcendental virtues may germinate. Pre-existing or *innate* virtues, talents, or gifts are regarded as having been acquired in a previous birth. Genius is without exception a talent or aptitude brought from another birth.

A.E.: In the previous paragraphs we have nothing but the condensed extract of the essence of sense mortification, sense purification, mental illumination, and final victory of the *Sat* or Truth over the *Maya*, the cosmic illusion, the *Asat*, the untruth. How subtle are the seductions, enticements, and illusions of the world; the *Maya*! And how few persevere in their battles and reach the summits ▸

. . . .

But if thou cam'st prepared, then have no fear.

. . . .

Henceforth thy way is clear right through the Virya gate, the fifth one of the Seven Portals.

Thou art now on the way that leadeth to the Dhyana haven, the sixth, the Bodhi Portal.

The Dhyana gate is like an alabaster vase, white and transparent; within there burns a steady golden fire, the flame of Prajna that radiates from Atman.

Thou art that vase.

Thou hast estranged thyself from objects of the senses, travelled on the "Path of seeing," on the "Path of hearing," and standest in the light of Knowledge. Thou hast now reached Titiksha state.[3]

O Narjol, thou art safe.

. . . .

Know, conqueror of sins, once that a Sovani[4] hath cross'd the seventh Path, all Nature thrills with joyous awe and feels subdued.

The silver star now twinkles out the news to the night-blossoms, the streamlet to the pebbles ripples out the tale; dark ocean waves will roar it to the rocks surf-bound, scent-laden breezes sing it to the vales, and stately pines mysteriously whisper: "A Master has arisen, a Master of the Day."[5]

He standeth now like a white pillar to the west, upon whose face the rising Sun of thought eternal poureth forth its first most glorious waves. His mind, like a becalmed and boundless ocean, spreadeth out in shoreless space. He holdeth life and death in his strong hand.

Yea, He is mighty. The living power made free in him, that power which is *himself*, can raise the tabernacle of illusion high above the gods, above great Brahm' and Indra. Now he shall surely reach his great reward!

---

of perfection, Christian, Buddhist, Hindu, yogic, or mystic. How straight and narrow the path that leads to life, and how few discover that path or after discovering it, embark upon it and steadfastly forge ahead until they reach the goal!

[3] *Titiksha* is the fifth state of Raja Yoga — one of supreme indifference; submission, if necessary, to what is called "pleasures and pains for all," but deriving neither pleasure nor pain from such submission — in short, the becoming physically, mentally, and morally indifferent and insensible to either pleasure or pain.

[4] *Sovani* is one who practises *Sovan*, the first path in Dhyana, a Srotapatti.

[5] "Day" means here a whole Manvantara, a period of incalculable duration.

Shall he not use the gifts which it confers for his own rest and bliss, his well-earn'd weal and glory — he, the subduer of the great delusion?

Nay, O thou candidate for Nature's hidden lore! If one would follow in the steps of holy Tathagata, those gifts and powers are not for self.

Would'st thou thus dam the waters born on Sumeru?[1] Shalt thou divert the stream for thine own sake, or send it back to its prime source along the crests of cycles?

If thou would'st have that stream of hard-earn'd knowledge, of Wisdom heaven-born, remain sweet running waters, thou should'st not leave it to become a stagnant pond.

Know, if of Amitabha, the "Boundless Age," thou would'st become co-worker, then must thou shed the light acquired, like to the Bodhisattvas twain,[2] upon the span of all three worlds.[3]

Know that the stream of superhuman knowledge and the Deva-Wisdom thou hast won, must, from thyself, the channel of Alaya, be poured forth into another bed.

Know, O Narjol, thou of the Secret Path, its pure fresh waters must be used to sweeter make the ocean's bitter waves — that mighty sea of sorrow formed of the tears of men.

---

[1] Mount Meru, the sacred mountain of the Gods.

[2] In the Northern Buddhist symbology, Amitabha or "Boundless Space" (Parabrahman) is said to have in his paradise two Bodhisattvas — Guanshiyin and Dashizhi — who ever radiate light over the three worlds where they live, including our own (see note 3), in order to help with this light (of knowledge) in the instruction of yogis, who will, in their turn, save men. Their exalted position in Amitabha's realm is due to deeds of mercy performed by the two, as such yogis, when on earth, says the allegory.
C.C.: *Amitabha*. Tibetan: *Nangwa Taye*. Chinese: *Wuliang Shou* (countless years), also called *Amida* or *Omito Fo*. The fourth Dhyani-Buddha emanating from Adi-Budha (see note 2, page 48) in his first or *Dharmakaya* vesture (Tibetan: *Chokyi ku*). In the *Sambhogakaya* he is called *Tsepagme* and in the *Nirmanakaya*, *Opakme*. His present earthly incarnation is the Panchen Lama of Tashi Lhunpo (*Tibetan-English Dictionary*, p. 768). It will be noticed that this authority (who was invited to Tashi Lhunpo in 1879 and 1881) gives the three Buddhic bodies described in the extremely important note 4, p. 73. Gautama, as the fourth Buddha, was the *Manushi Buddha* or "earthly reflex" of Amitabha. The Tashi Lama is known throughout Asia as the "Living Buddha" because the same *Nirmanakaya* is incarnate in him (see note 1, p. 68 and note 2). Particular attention should be paid to the statement about Buddha and his Arhats at the end of note 4, p. 73. Although Amitabha in the "Western Heaven" (*Sukhavati*) is the object of popular worship, in the developed doctrine of China and Japan, "he is but a symbol for an inexpressible reality, and rebirth into his 'paradise' is nothing more than the awakening of the Bodhichitta (Heart of Wisdom) here on earth" (*Introduction to Mahayana Buddhism*, p. 31).

[3] These three worlds are the three planes of being: the terrestrial, the astral, and the spiritual.

Alas! When once thou hast become like the fix'd star in highest heaven, that bright celestial orb must shine from out the spatial depths for all — save for itself; give light to all, but take from none.

Alas! When once thou hast become like the pure snow in mountain vales, cold and unfeeling to the touch, warm and protective to the seed that sleepeth deep beneath its bosom — 'tis now that snow which must receive the biting frost, the northern blasts, thus shielding from their sharp and cruel tooth the earth that holds the promised harvest, the harvest that will feed the hungry.

Self-doomed to live through future Kalpas,[4] unthanked and unperceived by men; wedged as a stone with countless other stones which form the "Guardian Wall,"[5] such is thy future if the seventh gate thou passest. Built by the hands of many Masters of Compassion, raised by their tortures, by their blood cemented, it shields mankind, since man is man, protecting it from further and far greater misery and sorrow.

Withal, man sees it not, will not perceive it, nor will he heed the word of Wisdom . . . for he knows it not.

But thou hast heard it, thou knowest all, O thou of eager guileless soul. . . . and thou must choose. Then hearken yet again.

On Sovan's Path, O Srotapatti,[6] thou art secure. Aye, on that Marga,[7] where nought but darkness meets the weary pilgrim, where torn by thorns the hands drip blood, the feet are cut by sharp unyielding flints, and Mara wields his strongest arms — there lies a great reward *immediately* beyond.

Calm and unmoved the pilgrim glideth up the stream that to Nirvana leads. He knoweth that the more his feet will bleed, the whiter will himself be washed. He knoweth well that after seven short and fleeting births Nirvana will be his. . . .

Such is the Dhyana Path, the haven of the yogi, the blessed goal that Srotapattis crave.

Not so when he hath crossed and won the Aryahata Path.[8]

There *klesha*[9] is destroyed for ever, *tanha's roots*[10] torn out. But stay,

---

[4] Cycles of ages.

[5] The "Guardian Wall" or the "Wall of Protection." It is taught that the accumulated efforts of long generations of yogis, saints, and Adepts, especially of the Nirmanakayas — have created, so to say, a wall of protection around mankind, which wall shields mankind invisibly from still worse evils.

[6] *Sovan* and *Srotapatti* are synonymous terms.

[7] *Marga* — "Path."

[8] From the Sanskrit *Arhat* or *Arhan*.

[9] *Klesha* is the love of pleasure or of worldly enjoyment, evil or good.

[10] *Tanha*, the will to live, that which causes rebirth.

disciple... Yet, one word. Canst thou destroy Divine Compassion? Compassion is no attribute. It is the Law of Laws — eternal Harmony, Alaya's Self; a shoreless universal essence, the light of everlasting Right, and fitness of all things, the Law of Love Eternal.

The more thou dost become at one with it, thy being melted in its Being, the more thy soul unites with that which *Is*, the more thou wilt become Compassion Absolute.[1]

Such is the Arya Path, Path of the Buddhas of Perfection.

Withal, what mean the sacred scrolls which make thee say:

"Om! I believe it is not all the Arhats that get of the Nirvanic Path the sweet fruition."

"Om! I believe that the Nirvana-Dharma is entered not by all the Buddhas."[2]

"Yea; on the Arya Path thou art no more Srotapatti, thou art a Bodhisattva.[3] The stream is cross'd. 'Tis true thou hast a right to Dharmakaya

---

[1] This "compassion" must not be regarded in the same light as "God, the divine love" of the Theists. Compassion stands here as an abstract, impersonal law whose nature, being absolute harmony, is thrown into confusion by discord, suffering, and sin.

[2] *Thegpa Chenpoido* ("Mahayana Sutra"), *Invocations to the Buddhas of Confession*, Part 1, verse 3.

In the Northern Buddhist phraseology all the great Arhats, Adepts, and saints are called Buddhas.

A.E.: The Dharma that leads to Nirvana is the attainment of self-perfection and abidance therein, bliss incomparable. But Bodhisattvas and Saviours defer that bliss and sacrifice it for the weal of suffering mankind. They share the suffering and sorrows of other human and living beings in order to raise them to a higher degree of life.

[3] A Bodhisattva is, in the hierarchy, less than a "perfect Buddha." In the exoteric parlance these two are very much confused. Yet the innate and right popular perception, owing to that self-sacrifice, has placed a Bodhisattva higher in its reverence than a Buddha.

C.C.: "As the Bodhisattvas are beings who have voluntarily and indefinitely delayed their own absorption into Nirvana for the sake of helping others progress on the Path of Deliverance, so much the greater and more noble and beneficent is a system [the Mahayana] deemed, which has included such principles as part of itself, than the Hinayana which is destitute of the idea" (*Tibetan-English Dictionary*, p. 585). With regard to the initiation of a Bodhisattva, H.P.B. writes: "Owing to the highest initiation performed by one overshadowed by the 'spirit of Buddha,' a candidate becomes virtually a Bodhisattva, created such by the High Initiator" (*The Secret Doctrine*, vol. 1, p. 109).

A.E.: Even if you attain the stage of a Bodhisattva beyond the stage of a Srotapatti or a seeker and searcher after the Infinite, the opportunity still remains open to you to don the *Dharmakaya* vesture, the Embodiment of Dharma as in perfect seers and saints; or to go a step further with greater sacrifice and don the *Sambhogakaya* vesture, and reach the highest degree of a Saviour, a Buddha of compassion by donning the *Nirmanakaya* vesture.

vesture; but Sambhogakaya is greater than a Nirvani, and greater still is a Nirmanakaya — the Buddha of Compassion.[4]

Now bend thy head and listen well, O Bodhisattva — Compassion speaks and saith: "Can there be bliss when all that lives must suffer? Shalt thou be saved and hear the whole world cry?"

Now thou hast heard that which was said.

Thou shalt attain the seventh step and cross the gate of final knowledge but only to wed woe — if thou would'st be Tathagata, follow upon thy predecessor's steps, remain unselfish till the endless end.

---

[4] This same popular reverence calls "Buddhas of Compassion" those Bodhisattvas who, having reached the rank of an Arhat (i.e., have completed the fourth or seventh Path), refuse to pass into the Nirvanic state or "don the *Dharmakaya* robe and cross to the other shore," as it would then become beyond their power to assist men even so little as karma permits. They prefer to remain invisibly (in spirit, so to speak) in the world, and contribute toward man's salvation by influencing them to follow the Good Law, i.e., lead them on the Path of Righteousness. It is part of the exoteric Northern Buddhism to honour all such great characters as saints, and to offer even prayers to them, as the Greeks and Catholics do to their saints and patrons; on the other hand, the esoteric teachings countenance no such thing. There is a great difference between the two teachings. The exoteric layman hardly knows the real meaning of the word *Nirmanakaya* — hence the confusion and inadequate explanations of the Orientalists. For example, Schlagintweit believes that *Nirmanakaya*-body means the physical form assumed by the Buddhas when they incarnate on earth — "the least sublime of their earthly encumbrances" (see *Buddhism in Tibet*, p. 38) — and he proceeds to give an entirely false view on the subject. The real teaching is, however, this:

The three Buddhic bodies or forms are styled:
1. *Nirmanakaya*.
2. *Sambhogakaya*.
3. *Dharmakaya*.

The first is that ethereal form which one would assume when, leaving his physical, he would appear in his astral body — having in addition all the knowledge of an Adept. The Bodhisattva develops it in himself as he proceeds on the Path. Having reached the goal and refused its fruition, he remains on Earth, as an Adept; and when he dies, instead of going into Nirvana, he remains in that glorious body he has woven for himself, *invisible* to uninitiated mankind, to watch over and protect it.

Sambhogakaya is the same, but with the additional lustre of "three perfections," one of which is entire obliteration of all earthly concerns.

The *Dharmakaya* body is that of a complete Buddha, i.e., no body at all, but an ideal breath: Consciousness merged in the Universal Consciousness, or Soul devoid of every attribute. Once a *Dharmakaya*, an Adept or Buddha leaves behind every possible relation with, or thought for this earth. Thus, to be enabled to help humanity, an Adept who has won the right to Nirvana, "renounces the *Dharmakaya* body" in mystic parlance; keeps, of the *Sambhogakaya*, only the great and complete knowledge, and remains in his *Nirmanakaya* body. The esoteric school teaches that Gautama Buddha with several of his Arhats is such a *Nirmanakaya*, higher than whom, on account of the great renunciation and sacrifice to mankind there is none known.

Thou art enlightened — choose thy way.

. . . .

Behold, the mellow light that floods the Eastern sky. In signs of praise both heaven and earth unite. And from the fourfold manifested Powers a chant of love ariseth, both from the flaming Fire and flowing Water, and from sweet-smelling Earth and rushing Wind.

Hark! . . . From the deep unfathomable vortex of that golden light in which the Victor bathes, all Nature's wordless voice in thousand tones ariseth to proclaim:

<blockquote>
Joy unto ye, O men of Myalba.[1]

A pilgrim hath returned back "from the other shore."

A new Arhan[2] is born. . . .
</blockquote>

PEACE TO ALL BEINGS[3]

---

[1] *Myalba* is our earth — pertinently called *hell*, and the greatest of all hells, by the esoteric school. The Esoteric Doctrine knows of no hell or place of punishment other than on a man-bearing planet or earth. *Avichi* is a state and not a locality.

[2] Meaning that a new and additional Saviour of mankind is born, who will lead men to final Nirvana, i.e., after the end of the life-cycle.

A.E.: When you attain Arhatship, you have already crossed the stream of worldliness and *samsara*. *Gate Gate Paragate Paramsamgate Bodhisvaha* — Gone, gone, gone to the other shore, the island of enlightenment, is one of the *Mahavakya* of Buddhism comparable to *Om Vajrapani Hum* of Arhans, or *Tat Tvam Asi, So Ham* — "Thou art That, I am That" of the Vedantists.

The Voice of the Silence is essentially missionary and apostolic, a stage much higher than yogic self-control, asceticism, mortification, prayer, etc. It certainly points out the way to self-perfection through meditation and spiritual practices; and it goes far beyond engendering missionary enthusiasm, utilizing Enlightenment for the emancipation of bound and suffering humanity. "A pilgrim has returned back from the other shore, a new Arhan is born to bestow peace, light, and grace to all beings."

[3] This is one of the variations of the formula that invariably follows every treatise, invocation, or instruction — "Peace to all beings," "Blessings on all that lives," etc., etc.

THE ISLAND OF BLISS

*by Reverend Father Anthony Elenjimittam,
alias Bhikshu Ishabodhananda*

THERE, in the deeper recesses of mind, there is a beauteous island of imperturbable peace, unalloyed Joy, unending Creativity. The storm-tossed waves of *samsara* can never reach there, because that island afloat on the sea of life is the very sanctuary of the Eternal, the Permanent, the ever-Bright, and that ever-Pure. There, all our sorrows come to an end, there, the wearisome voyager rests in peace, there, one remains entranced by the silent music, the clear still voice of the Void. This Void or *Sunyata* is not the negative emptiness, it is the Plenum Void, Fullness whence sprang the phenomenal world, wherewith the born beings are sustained, and unto which all beings finally return. That Island of Bliss, Brahman, that to reach, is man's greatest concern; that is the end of life pilgrimage on earth.

"*Yato va imani bhutani jayante, yena jataani jivanti, yat prayanty abishamvishanti, tad vijijnasva, tad Brahma iti* — That, wherefrom these beings came into existence, that, into which they in the end return; that is Brahman, that you try to know, that is Brahman," said our Upanishadic seers.[4] "This is Eternal Life that they may know Thee, the one true God," says Christ.[5] Saints and mystics from both the East and the West have placed knowledge, *jnana*, gnosis as the royal highway leading us to that Island of Bliss. This emancipating knowledge is by no means a mere theoretical or theological knowledge or speculative formulation of statements and creedal propositions. It is, essentially, a glimpse into a living, vital, and thrilling experience of the mind and heart of man with all the emotional response of the whole Reality that is God, outside which everything else is void and emptiness. "The whole Creation as if they were not, before Thee, O Lord," exclaims Isaias the prophet.

In this Island of Bliss man finds not merely happiness, but true ineffable blissfulness. "There is in man something higher than happiness, it is blessedness," says Carlyle.[6] When, after years of search and struggles, pains and agonies, a person finally sees this island embedded in his mind, he feels sure of his path; and when he finally discovers it and reaches there, he is at once intoxicated by Love Divine, Universal Compassion, unlimited benevolence. His old self — which was always the root-cause

---

[4] Taittiriya Upanishad 3:2:1.
[5] John 17:3.
[6] Thomas Carlyle, *Sartor Resartus* (London: Chapman and Hall, 1894), p. 132.

of all his past miseries and pains is no more there, the little ego with its "I and mine" is either eclipsed, effaced, or enlarged unto the infinity of the Universal Ego which alone can say: "I am who am," as in the Mosaic revelation. Then, only men can glimpse into the Upanishadic *Mahavakya* — *Tat Tvam Asi, Shivo'Ham So'Ham*, "You are That, I and my Father are one" broken into shreds is the once powerful rope of self-centredness, melting oneself into the vastness of the Universe.

You ask me, my brother, what on earth do we gain by such an experiential arrival on the Island of Bliss? You insist, sister, that God-vision and Self-realization, etc., are not as tangible a happiness as the profound human joys and pangs of life. Well, my friend, if sense and sex were bliss, then Self-realization — which is another synonym for Island of Bliss or Purity — is a million times more bliss, as was asserted by Sri Ramakrishna. My friend, now let us gauge and calculate the positive benefits derived from our reaching that Island of Bliss.

First of all, my friend, you rediscover yourself in the true mirror of man that is God or Goodness Absolute and Purity incandescent. That means, by not identifying yourself any more with the changing moods and passing phases of life in your body or the world outside, there you gain a sure rock to stand upon. For when you reach that Island of Bliss, my child, even your physical ailments vanish, you becoming one with Life and Bliss. It cannot be otherwise, Christian Scientists are right in denying evil, disease, and misery from God-realized summits. The miraculous cures of Christ and many other saints are so natural for one who has braved to swim across the channel and seas of life and reach the Island of Bliss. When you reach that Island of Bliss, my brother, there is no need for you to consult a physician, or run to a chemist's shop or drink drugs and take injections. All these mundane planes are transcended, and you get a quick lift to scan the very lap of the Infinite where there is nothing but Life, Fullness of Life, Joy, Peace, and Bliss for us. *Satyam Jnanam Anandam Brahma* — Brahman is Truth, Knowledge, and Bliss, and you, my friend, when you reach that Island of Bliss, you are, then, one with Truth, Knowledge, and Bliss, all incompatibles with untruth, ignorance, and misery, even as light and darkness, death and life cannot coexist in one and the same object.

Angels hover around you in that Island of Bliss. Saints and sages from both the hemispheres and from planets and solar systems other than ours are there to welcome you to that Island of Bliss, to sing into your ears music, lyrics, and melodies, which no earthly ears can ever hear. All your past sins, then, are forgiven; you are washed clean of the past mud, muck, and dirt which you once accumulated in the time of your ignorance. Then you were a graduate and a worldly wise man. You had a position and name, and fame in the world and yet with all that you were walled away from God through the thick veil of *Maya* which is ignorance in your mind and lust in your heart. When the sun of Righteousness shines, then, your heart is purified; and then, the tabernacle of the Most High is made — really to receive Light resplendent and Love radiant to regenerate you into a child of God, "not born of the desire of the flesh and blood, nor of the will of man, but of God."[1]

My child, will you come with me to that Island of Bliss? Thus, leave aside these toys you so dearly hug, this vast ocean of misery in which you now bathe. Yes, what you and the world call love is not love. "Lust and love are deadly enemies" said Shakespeare.[2] Well, then, come with me on the route I now take to Pure Love which is the Island of Bliss. When Mirabai entered there, she gave up an earthly prince and palace and sang songs which few sing. So did Tulsidas, Tukaram, Chaitanya, and Ramakrishna and their likes.

But you have to pay the price, weighed to the utmost grain, if you desire to see and reach that Island of Bliss. Yet no sacrifice is too great — including the sacrifice of one's own life — when we contemplate the new world of values and vision we gain thereby. Step by step, we pass by the biological, psychic, and other sheaths in which is encased the Real and we reach the threshold of God. We may deny God, but not Goodness — purity of heart and mind, always, under all circumstances. "Blessed are the pure in heart, for they shall see God,"[3] entering the Island of Bliss, the true Kingdom of God on Earth.

---

[1] John 1:14.
[2] William Shakespeare, *The Rape of Lucrece*, verse 97.
[3] Matthew 5:8.

ST. CATHERINE OF SIENA SCHOOL AND ORPHANAGE

HELP MAKE A DIFFERENCE TO LIVES OF THE CHILDREN AT OUR SHELTER HOME

SAINTCATHERINESHOME.COM/DONATE

Your donations will be used to meet the various needs of running the home and ensuring the children here get sustained care in terms of food, education and shelter. You may choose to sponsor a child or make a one-time donation.

- Education
- Shelter
- Food

📞 +91 22 2642 2859, +91 93 2659 5671

📍 Mount Mary Road, Bandra (West), Mumbai 400 050, India

✉ catherine_siena@yahoo.co.in   🌐 saintcatherineshome.com

THREE FRAGMENTS
IN MODERN ENGLISH

This modern English version of three fragments from the *Book of the Golden Precepts* was created to assist those who may have difficulty understanding the original 1889 version of this text. We strongly recommend reading the original text also in order to experience its mantra-like effect.

Fragment I
THE VOICE OF THE SILENCE

These instructions are for those ignorant of the dangers of the lower magical powers.[1]

Whoever would wish to hear the Voice of the Silence, "the Soundless Sound," and comprehend it, must learn the nature of deep concentration.[2]

Having become indifferent to objects of perception, the pupil must seek out the king of the senses, the thought-producer, the one who creates illusion.

The mind is the great slayer of the Real.

Let the disciple slay the slayer.

For:

When to yourself your form appears unreal, as, on waking, do all the forms you see in dreams;

When you have ceased to hear the many, you may discern the One — the inner sound which kills the outer.

Only then, and not until then, will you forsake the region of the False and come to the realm of the True.

Before the soul can see, harmony must be attained within, and fleshly eyes rendered blind to all illusion.

Before the soul can hear, the image (you) must become as deaf to roaring as to whispers, as deaf to the cries of bellowing elephants as to the silvery buzzing of the golden firefly.

---

[1] There are two kinds of abnormal powers in human beings. One group consists of the lower, coarse, psychic, and mental energies; the other comprises spiritual powers, development of which requires the highest training.

[2] The intense and perfect concentration of the mind upon an interior object, accompanied by complete abstraction from everything pertaining to the external Universe, or the world of the senses.

Before the soul can comprehend and remember, she must be united with the Silent Speaker, just as the form to which the clay is modelled, is first united with the potter's mind.

For then the soul will hear, and will remember. And then to the inner ear will speak
>the Voice of the Silence

And say:

If your soul smiles while bathing in the sunlight of your life; if your soul sings within her chrysalis of flesh and matter; if your soul weeps inside her castle of illusion; if your soul battles to break the silver thread that binds her to the Master;[1] know, O disciple, your soul is of the earth.

When to the world's turmoil your budding soul[2] lends ear; when to the roaring voice of the great illusion[3] your soul responds; when frightened at the sight of the hot tears of pain, when deafened by cries of distress, when your soul withdraws like a shy turtle into the shell of selfhood, learn, O disciple, that to her Silent God, your soul is an unworthy shrine.

When waxing stronger, your soul glides forth from her secure retreat, and breaking loose from the protecting shrine, extends her silver thread and rushes onward; when, beholding her image on the waves of Space, she whispers, "This is I," declare, O disciple, that your soul is caught in the web of delusion.[4]

This earth, disciple, is the Hall of Sorrow, wherein, along a path of dire probation, traps are set to ensnare your Ego in the delusion called the "great heresy."[5]

This earth, O ignorant disciple, is but a dismal entrance leading to the twilight that precedes the valley of true light, the light which no wind can extinguish, the light which burns without wick or fuel.

Says the Great Law: "In order to become the knower of All Self, you have first of Self to be the knower." To reach the knowledge of that Self, you must give up the self to Non-Self, being to Non-Being, and

---

[1] The "great Master" is the term used by disciples to indicate the Higher Self. It is the equivalent of *Avalokiteshvara*, and the same as *Adi-Budha* as used by the Buddhist mystics, *Atman* as used by the Brahmins, and *Christos* as used by the ancient Gnostics.

[2] Soul is used here to denote the human ego or *manas*, that which is referred to in our septenary division as the *human soul* (see *The Secret Doctrine*) in contradistinction to the spiritual and animal souls.

[3] The objective Universe.

[4] The "delusion" of personality.

[5] The heresy of the belief in soul, or rather, in the separateness of soul or self from the One Universal, Infinite Self.

then you can rest between the wings of the Great Bird. Yes, sweet is rest between the wings of that which is neither born nor dies, but is the Aum[6] throughout eternal ages.

Bestride the Bird of Life, if you wish to know.[7]

Give up your life, if you wish to live.[8]

Three Halls, O weary pilgrim, lead to the end of toil. Three Halls, O conqueror of temptation, will bring you through three states[9] into the fourth[10] and from there into the seven worlds,[11] the worlds of Rest Eternal.

If you wish to learn their names, then listen and remember.

The name of the first Hall is Ignorance.

This is the Hall in which you saw the light, in which you live and will die.[12]

The name of the second Hall is Learning.[13] In it your soul will find the blossoms of life, but a serpent lies coiled under every flower.[14]

The name of the third Hall is Wisdom. Beyond it stretch the shoreless waters of the indestructible Fount of Omniscience.[15]

If you wish to cross the first Hall safely, do not let your mind mistake the fires of lust that burn therein for the sunlight of life.

If you wish to cross the second safely, do not stop to inhale the fragrance of its stupefying blossoms. If you wish to be freed from karmic chains, do not seek your Teacher in these regions of Illusion.

---

[6] The Bird or Swan called *Kalahamsa* in ancient texts. The *Nadabindu Upanishad* (*Rig Veda*) reads: "The syllable A is considered to be its (the bird Hamsa's) right wing, U, its left, M, its tail, and the *ardha-matra* (half metre) is said to be its head."

[7] The same *Nadabindu* reads: "A yogi who bestrides the Hamsa (contemplates Aum) is not affected by karmic influences or by tens of crores [ten million] of sins."

[8] Give up the life of physical *personality* if you wish to live in spirit.

[9] There are three states of consciousness: waking, dreaming, and deep sleep. These three yogi conditions lead to the fourth.

[10] The fourth lies beyond the dreamless state. It is the one above all, a state of high spiritual consciousness.

[11] Some Oriental mystics locate seven planes of being, the seven spiritual worlds within the body of Kalahamsa, the Swan out of Time and Space, convertible into the Swan *in* Time, when it becomes a Creator instead of the primary cause of all that exists.

[12] The phenomenal world of the senses and of terrestrial consciousness only.

[13] The Hall of *Probationary* Learning.

[14] The astral region, the psychic world of supersensuous perception and of deceptive sight — the world of mediums. No blossom plucked in these regions has ever yet been brought down to earth without a serpent coiled around its stem. It is the world of the *Great Illusion*.

[15] The region of full spiritual consciousness beyond which there is no longer any danger to one who has reached it.

The Wise do not tarry in the pleasure grounds of the senses.

The Wise do no heed the sweet-tongued voices of illusion.

Seek the one who is to give you spiritual birth[1] in the Hall of Wisdom, the Hall which lies beyond, wherein all shadows are unknown, and where the light of truth shines with unfading glory.

That which is uncreated abides in you, disciple, as it abides in this Hall. If you wish to reach it and blend the two, you must divest yourself of the dark garments of illusion. Stifle the voice of the flesh, allow no image of the senses to come between its light and yours, so that the two may blend into one. And having learnt the depth of your own ignorance, flee from the Hall of Learning. It is dangerous in its treacherous beauty, and is necessary only for your testing. Beware, disciple, lest dazzled by illusive radiance your soul should linger and be caught in its deceptive light.

Its light shines from the jewel of the great ensnarer, the King of Temptation.[2] It bewitches the senses, blinds the mind, and leaves the unwary an abandoned wreck.

The moth attracted to the dazzling flame of your night lamp is doomed to perish in its viscid oil. The unwary soul that fails to grapple with the mocking demon of illusion will return to earth, the slave of vice.

Behold the hosts of souls. Watch how they hover over the stormy sea of human life, and how, exhausted, bleeding, broken-winged, they drop one after another into the swelling waves. Tossed by the fierce winds, chased by the gales, they drift into the eddies and disappear within the first great vortex.

If, through the Hall of Wisdom, disciple, you wish to reach the Valley of Bliss, close fast your senses to the great dire heresy of separateness that weans you from the rest.

Do not let your "Heaven-born," merged in the sea of Illusion, break from the Universal Parent (Soul), but let the fiery power retire into the inmost chamber, the chamber of the Heart,[3] the abode of the World Mother.[4]

---

[1] The Initiate who leads disciples through the Knowledge given to them for their spiritual or second birth is called the *Father*, *Guru*, or *Master*.

[2] A demon in exoteric religions, but in esoteric philosophy, temptation personified through human vices, "that which kills" the soul. It is depicted as the King of Temptation with a crown in which shines a jewel of such lustre that it blinds those who look at it. This lustre refers, of course, to the fascination exercised by vice upon certain natures.

[3] The *inner* chamber of the Heart. The "fiery power" is *kundalini*.

[4] "Power" and "World Mother" are names given to *kundalini* — one of the mystic "yogi powers." It is the soul considered as an active rather than a passive principle (which it is generally, when regarded only as the vehicle, or casket of

Then, from the heart, that Power will rise into the sixth, the middle region, the place between your eyes, where it becomes the breath of the One-Soul, the voice which fills all, your Master's voice.

Only then can you become a "Walker of the Sky"[5] who treads the winds above the waves, whose step hovers above the waters.

Before you set your foot upon the ladder's upper rung, the ladder of the mystic sounds, you must be able to hear the voice of your inner God[6] in seven manners.

The first is like the nightingale's sweet voice, chanting a song of parting to its mate.

The second comes as the sound of a silver cymbal of the Merciful Lords, awakening the twinkling stars.

The next is like the melodious lament of the ocean sprite, imprisoned in its shell.

And this is followed by the chant of a lute.

The fifth shrills in your ear like the sound of a bamboo flute.

It changes next into a trumpet blast.

The last vibrates like the dull rumbling of a thundercloud.

The seventh swallows all the other sounds that die to be heard no more.

When the six[7] are slain and laid at the Master's feet, the pupil is merged with the One,[8] becomes that One, and lives therein.

Before that path is entered, you must destroy your lunar body,[9] cleanse your mind-body,[10] and make clean your heart.

The pure waters of Eternal Life, clear as crystal, cannot mingle with the muddy torrents of a monsoon tempest.

When Heaven's dewdrop, nestling in the bosom of the lotus and

---

the supreme spirit). It is an electrical-spiritual force, a creative power which when roused into action can destroy as easily as it can create.

[5] The body of the yogi becomes as one *formed of the wind*; as "a cloud from which limbs have sprouted," after which, "he (the yogi) beholds the things beyond the seas and stars; he hears the language of the Gods and comprehends it, and perceives what is passing through the mind of the ant" (*Dnyaneshwari* 6:269).

[6] The Higher Self.

[7] The six principles; meaning when the lower personality is destroyed and the inner individuality is merged into and lost in the seventh, or Spirit.

[8] The disciple is one with the Spirit.

[9] The astral form, or body of desire.

[10] The first refers to the astral or *personal* self; the second to the individuality or the reincarnating Ego whose consciousness on our plane or the *lower mind* must be paralysed.

glittering in the morn's first sunbeam, falls to the ground, it becomes a piece of clay; behold, the pearl is now a speck of dust.

Strive against your unclean thoughts before they overpower you. Use them, as they will you, for if you spare them, and they take root and grow, be assured, they will overpower and kill you. Beware, disciple, do not allow even their shadow to approach. For it will grow, increase in size and power, and then this thing of darkness will absorb your being before you have fully acknowledged the black foul monster's presence.

Before the "mystic Power"[1] can make of you a god, disciple, you must have gained the faculty to slay your lunar form at will.

The self of matter and the Self of Spirit can never meet. One of the two must disappear; there is no place for both.

Before your soul's mind can understand, the bud of personality must be crushed, the worm of the senses destroyed beyond resurrection.

You cannot travel on the Path until you have become the Path itself.[2]

Let your soul lend its ear to every cry of pain, as the lotus bares its heart to drink the morning sun.

Do not let the fierce sun dry one tear of pain sooner than you have wiped it from the sufferer's eye.

But let each burning human tear drop into your heart and allow it to remain there, without ever brushing it away, until the pain that caused it has been removed.

These tears, O heart most merciful, are the streams that irrigate the fields of immortal compassion. It is on this soil that the midnight blossom of Enlightenment grows, more difficult to find, more rare to view than the flower of the Vogay tree. This is the seed of freedom from rebirth. It isolates the Sage both from strife and lust; it leads them through the fields of Being to the peace and bliss known only in the land of Silence and Non-Being.

Kill out desire; and if you kill it, take heed lest from the dead it should arise again.

---

[1] *Kundalini*, referred to as the "serpent power" or mystic fire. It is called the "serpentine" or *annular* power on account of its spiral-like working or progress in the body of the ascetic who develops this power within. It is an electric fiery power, the great pristine force, which underlies all organic and inorganic matter.

[2] This "Path" is mentioned in all the mystic works. As Krishna says: "When this Path is beheld . . . whether one sets out to the bloom of the east or to the chambers of the west, *without moving*, O holder of the bow, *is the travelling in this road*. On this path, to whatever place one would go, *that place one's own self* becomes." "You are the Path" is said to the adept guru, and by the latter to the disciple, after initiation. "I am the way and the Path," says another Master.

Kill love of life, and if you slay the will to live,[3] let it not be out of thirst for eternal life, but to replace the fleeting with the everlasting.

Desire nothing. Do not chafe at karma, or at Nature's changeless laws. Struggle only with the personal, the transitory, the evanescent, and the perishable.

Help Nature and work with her; and Nature will regard you as one of her creators and show deference.

And she will open wide before you the portals of her secret chambers, lay bare before your gaze the treasures hidden in the very depths of her pure virgin bosom. Unsullied by the hand of matter, she reveals her treasures only to the eye of Spirit — the eye which never closes, the eye for which there is no veil in all her kingdoms.

Then she will show you the means and the way, the first gate and the second, the third, up to the very seventh, and then the goal beyond which lie glories untold, bathed in the sunlight of the Spirit, beholden by none save the eye of the Soul.

There is but one road to the Path; only at its very end can the Voice of the Silence be heard. The ladder by which the candidate ascends is formed from rungs of suffering and pain; these can be silenced only by the voice of virtue. Woe, then, to you, disciple, if there is a single vice you have not left behind. For the ladder will give way and topple you; its foot rests in the deep mire of your sins and failings; hence, before you can attempt to cross this wide abyss of matter, you must bathe your feet in the waters of Renunciation. Beware lest you should set a foot that is still soiled upon the ladder's lowest rung. Woe to them who dare pollute a single rung with dirty feet. The foul and viscous mud will dry, become tenacious, then glue their feet to the spot, and like a bird caught in the wily fowler's lime, they will be stayed from further progress. Their vices will take shape and drag them down. Their sins will raise their voices like the jackals laugh and sob after the sun goes down, and their thoughts will become an army that carries them off, a captive slave.

Kill your desires, disciple, make your vices impotent, before you take your first step on the solemn journey.

Strangle your sins, and make them dumb forever, before you lift a foot to mount the ladder.

Silence your thoughts and fix your whole attention on your Master whom you do not yet see, but whom you feel.

Merge all your senses into one sense if you wish to be secure against the foe. It is by this sense alone, which lies concealed within the hollow

---

[3] The fear of death and love of life, the force or energy which causes rebirth.

of your brain, that the steep path leading to your Master may be revealed before your soul's dim eyes.

Long and weary is the way before you, O disciple. A single thought of the past that you have left behind will drag you down forcing you to begin the climb anew.

Kill in yourself all memory of past experiences. Do not look behind you or you will be lost.

Do not believe that lust can ever be killed out if gratified or satiated, for this is an abomination inspired by the Tempter. It is by feeding vice that it expands and waxes strong, like the worm that fattens on the blossom's heart.

The rose must become once more the bud that was born of its parent stem, before the parasite has eaten through its heart and drunk its vital sap.

The golden tree puts forth its jewel buds before its trunk is withered by the storm.

You must regain *the child-state you have lost* before the first sound can fall upon your ear.

The light from the One Master, the one unfading golden light of Spirit, shoots its effulgent beams at the disciple from the very first. Its rays thread through the thick dark clouds of matter.

Now here, now there, these rays illumine it, like sparks of sunlight illumine the earth through the thick foliage of jungle growth. But, O disciple, at the initial stage, unless the flesh is passive, the head cool, and the soul as firm and pure as a flaming diamond, the radiance will not reach the chamber, its sunlight will not warm the heart, nor will the mystic sounds of Heaven's heights reach the ear, however eager.

Unless you hear, you cannot see.

Unless you see, you cannot hear. To hear and to see — this is the second stage.

When you see and hear, when you smell and taste, eyes closed, ears shut, with mouth and nostrils stopped, when the four senses blend and are ready to pass into the fifth, that of inner touch, then you have passed into the fourth stage.

And in the fifth, O slayer of thoughts, all these again must be killed beyond reanimation.[1] Withhold your mind from all external objects, all

---

[1] This means that in the sixth stage of development, every sense as an individual faculty must be "killed" (or paralysed) on this plane, passing into and merging with the seventh sense, which is the most spiritual.

external sights. Withhold it also from internal images, lest they should cast a dark shadow on your soul-light.

Now you have achieved perfect concentration — the sixth stage.

When you have passed into the seventh, O happy one, you will perceive no more the sacred three,[2] for you will have become that three yourself. You and your mind will resemble twins standing side by side, and overhead will burn the star which is your goal.[3] From this time on, the three that dwell in glory and in bliss ineffable, no longer have names in the world of Illusion, for they have become one star, the fire that burns but does not scorch, the fire that is the foundation of the ever unreachable Flame.[4]

And this, O pursuer of success, is what people call *Illumination*, the right precursor of becoming the All.[5]

And now your self is lost in Self, yourself to Yourself, merged in that Self from which you first did radiate.

Where is your individuality, disciple, indeed, where is the disciple? It is the spark lost in the fire, the drop within the ocean, the ever-present Ray become the All, and eternal radiance.

And now, disciple, you are the doer and the witness, the radiator and the radiation, the Light in the Sound, and the Sound in the Light.

You are acquainted with the five impediments, O blessed one. You are their conqueror, Master of the sixth stage, and deliverer of the four modes of Truth.[6] The light that falls upon them shines from yourself, O you who was once the disciple but are a Teacher now.

And of these modes of Truth:

Have you not passed through knowledge of all misery — the first truth?

---

[2] Every stage of development is symbolized by a geometrical figure. The one being referred to here is the sacred *triangle*. The △ is the sign of the high disciples, while a different type is used to symbolize the high Initiates. Once the preliminary and lower stages have been passed, instead of seeing △, the disciple sees the full *septenary*.

[3] The star that burns overhead is the "star of Initiation."

[4] While you are still in this life.

[5] The state in which you lose the consciousness of every individuality including your own.

[6] The "four modes of truth" are: suffering or misery, the assembling of temptations, their destruction, and the "path." The "five impediments" are knowledge of misery, the truth of human frailty, oppressive restraints, the absolute necessity of separation from all the ties of passion (even desire), and the "Path of Salvation," for attachment even to the idea of salvation is itself an obstacle to true liberation.

Have you not conquered the King of Temptation at the portal of assembling — the second truth?[1]

Have you not destroyed sin at the third gate and attained the third truth?

Have you not entered the Path that leads to knowledge — the fourth truth?[2]

And now, rest beneath the Tree of Wisdom, which is perfection of all knowledge, for, know, you are a Master of the state of faultless vision.

Behold! You have become the Light, you have become the Sound, you are your Master and your God. You are *yourself* the object of your search: the unbroken Voice that resounds throughout eternities, exempt from change, exempt from sin, the seven sounds in one,

the Voice of the Silence.

OM TAT SAT

Fragment II
THE TWO PATHS

And now, O Teacher of Compassion, point the way for others. Behold, all those who, knocking for admission, wait in ignorance and darkness to see the gate of the sweet Law flung open!

The voice of the candidates:

Will you, Master of your own mercy, not reveal to us the Doctrine of the Heart?[3] Would you refuse to lead your servants onto the Path of Liberation?

Says the Teacher:

The Paths be two; the great perfections three; and six are the virtues that transform the body into the Tree of Knowledge.[4]

---

[1] The King of Temptation stands at the portal of the "assembling," attempting to blind the candidate with the radiance of his "jewel."

[2] This is the fourth "Path" of the five paths of rebirth which lead all human beings into perpetual states of sorrow and joy. These "paths" are subdivisions of the one, the Path followed by karma.

[3] The two schools, the esoteric and the exoteric, are called respectively the "Heart" and the "Eye" Doctrine. The "Heart" Doctrine is so named because it is the teaching which emanates from the Teacher's *heart*, whereas the "Eye" Doctrine is the work of the Teacher's head or mind. The "Heart Doctrine" is also called "the seal of truth" or the "true seal," a symbol found in the heading area of almost all esoteric works.

[4] The "Tree of Knowledge" is the title given to Adepts, those who have attained ▸

Who will approach them?

Who will first enter them?

Who will first hear the doctrine of two Paths in one, the unveiled truth of the Secret Heart?[5] The Law which shuns learning and teaches Wisdom reveals a tale of woe.

Alas, alas, that all should possess Universal Soul, should be one with Great Soul, but in possessing it, that Universal Soul should benefit them so little!

Behold how like the moon, reflected in tranquil waves, Universal Soul is reflected by the great and the small, is mirrored in the tiniest atoms, yet fails to reach the heart of all. Alas, that so few should profit from the gift, the priceless boon of learning truth, right perception of all that exists, Knowledge of the non-existent!

Says the pupil:

O Teacher, what should I do to achieve Wisdom?

O Wise One, what, to gain perfection?

Answers the Teacher:

Search for the Paths, O disciple, but be of clean heart before you start on your journey. Before you take your first step, learn to discern the real from the false, the ever-fleeting from the everlasting. Learn above all to distinguish head-learning from Soul-wisdom, the "Eye" from the "Heart" doctrine.

Yes, ignorance is like a closed and airless vessel, and the soul, a bird locked inside it. The bird does not warble, or stir a single feather; the songster sits mute and listless until it dies of exhaustion.

But even ignorance is better than head-learning which has no Soul-wisdom by which it may be illuminated and guided.

The seeds of Wisdom cannot sprout and grow in an airless space. To live and reap experience the mind needs breadth, and depth, and directions that would draw it towards the Diamond Soul.[6] Do not seek those directions in the realm of Illusion; soar beyond illusions, search for the eternal, changeless Truth,[7] mistrusting the fanciful suggestions of the mind.

For the mind is like a mirror; it gathers dust while it reflects. It needs

---

the height of mystical knowledge.

[5] "Secret Heart" is the Esoteric Doctrine.

[6] "Diamond Soul" is a title given to the Supreme Lord of all Mysteries.

[7] The one eternal and Absolute Reality and Truth, all else being illusion.

the gentle breezes of Soul-wisdom to brush away the dust of our illusions. Seek, O beginner, to blend your mind and soul into one.

Shun ignorance, and likewise shun illusion. Avert your face from worldly deception; do not trust your senses; they are false. But within your body — the shrine of your sensations — seek in the impersonal for the "eternal being,"[1] and having sought it out, look inward, and you will become enlightened. Shun praise, O devotee, for praise leads to self-delusion. You are not your body, your Self has no body, and so can be affected by neither praise nor blame.

Self-gratulation, O disciple, is like a lofty tower that a haughty fool has climbed. The fool sits aloft in prideful solitude unbeholden to any but self.

The Wise reject false learning which is then scattered to the winds by the good Law. Its wheel revolves for all, the humble and the proud. The Doctrine of the Eye is for the crowd, the Doctrine of the Heart, for the chosen. The first repeat in pride: "Behold, I know," while the latter, they who have garnered humbly grains of wisdom, lowly confess, "thus have I heard."[2]

"Great Sifter," is the name given to the Heart Doctrine, O disciple.

The wheel of the good Law moves swiftly on. It grinds by night and by day. It drives the worthless husks from out of the golden grain, the refuse from the flour. The hand of karma guides the wheel; its revolutions mark the beating of the karmic heart.

True knowledge is the flour, false learning is the husk. If you wish to eat the bread of Wisdom, you must knead your flour with Immortality's clear waters. But if you knead husks with Illusion's dew, you will create food for the black doves of death, the birds of birth, decay, and sorrow.

If they tell you that to become enlightened, you must cease to love all beings — tell them that they lie.

If they tell you that to gain liberation, you must hate your mother, disregard your son, disavow your father and call him "householder," and renounce all pity for humans and beasts, tell them, their tongue is false.

This is the teaching of the unbelievers.

If they tell you that sin is born of action, and bliss of absolute inaction, then tell them that they are mistaken. Non-permanence of human action and deliverance of mind from bondage through the cessation

---

[1] The reincarnating Ego is called the "true being" that becomes enlightened through union with the Higher Self.

[2] Meaning that what follows was received by oral transmission from a Master, because secret knowledge is always conveyed this way.

of sin and eradication of fault are not for the Divine Ego.[3] So says the Doctrine of the Heart.

The Law of the "Eye" is the embodiment of the external and the non-existent.

The Law of the "Heart" is the embodiment of Divine Wisdom, the permanent and everlasting.

The lamp burns bright when its wick and oil are clean. To clean them, one requires a cleaner, and yet the flame does not feel the process of the cleaning. "The branches of a tree are shaken by the wind; the trunk remains unmoved."

Both action and inaction may coexist within you; your body in motion, your mind tranquil, and your soul as bright and transparent as a mountain lake.

Do you wish to become a devotee of "Time's Circle"?[4] If so, O disciple:

Do not believe that sitting in dark forests, in proud seclusion and apart from others, that feeding on roots and plants, and quenching your thirst with snow from the Great Range, O devotee, will lead you to the goal of final liberation.

Do not think that breaking bone, rending flesh and muscle, will unite you with your silent Self.[5] Do not think that when the sins of your gross form are conquered, your duty to Nature and humanity is accomplished, O victim of shadows.[6]

The blessed ones have disdained to do so. The Lion of the Law, the Lord of Mercy,[7] perceiving the true cause of human woe, immediately forsook the sweet but selfish rest of the quiet wilds. From being a forest-hermit, He became the Teacher of humankind. After the Blessed One had received Inner Enlightenment, He preached on mount and plain, and held discourse in the cities, addressed to the spirits, the people, and the gods.

Sow kindly acts and you will reap their fruition. Inaction in a deed of mercy is action in deadly sin. So says the Sage.

Will you abstain from action? Not in this way will your soul gain her

---

[3] The reincarnating Ego.

[4] *Kalachakra* (*Sanskrit*, "wheel of time"), an ancient teaching that combines the knowledge of many domains to facilitate the mastering of hidden powers and energies contained in human beings and the Cosmos. The esoteric aspect of the Kalachakra has always been imparted directly from Master to disciple.

[5] The Higher Self, the seventh principle.

[6] Our physical bodies are called "shadows" in the mystic schools.

[7] Buddha.

freedom. To reach Supreme Enlightenment one must acquire Self-knowledge, and Self-knowledge is the child of loving deeds.

Have patience, candidate, as one who fears no failure and courts no success. Fix your soul's gaze upon the star whose ray you are,[1] the flaming star that shines within the lightless depths of ever-being, the boundless fields of the Unknown.

Have perseverance as one who forevermore endures. Your shadows live and vanish;[2] that which in you will live forever, that which in you knows, for it is knowledge,[3] is not of fleeting life: it is the being that was, that is, and will be, for whom the hour will never strike.

If you wish to reap sweet peace and rest, disciple, sow the fields of future harvests with the seeds of merit. Accept the woes of incarnation.

Step from the sunlight into the shade to make more room for others. The tears that water the parched soil of pain and sorrow bring forth the blossoms and fruits of karmic retribution. Out of the furnace and black smoke of human life, winged flames rise, purified flames, that soar upwards, beneath the karmic eye, weaving the glorious fabric of the three vestures of the Path.

These are: the Body of Emanation, the Body of Bliss, and the Body of Truth — robe sublime.[4]

---

[1] According to esoteric teaching, every spiritual Ego is a ray of a Planetary Spirit.

[2] "Personalities" or physical bodies called "shadows" are evanescent.

[3] Mind, the thinking principle or Ego in us, is referred to as "Knowledge" itself, because the human Egos are the children of Universal Mind.

[4] The fully enlightened Masters have three bodies or forms:
1. The Emanation Body, or *Nirmanakaya*, is the ethereal form which Masters assume when, leaving their physical body, they appear in their astral body, having in addition all the knowledge of an Adept. The Masters develop the Emanation Body in themselves as they proceed along the Path. Having reached the goal and refused its fruition, they remain on Earth, as Adepts; and when they die, instead of entering Paradise, they remain in the glorious body they have woven for themselves, invisible to uninitiated humankind, to protect and watch over it.
2. The Bliss Body, or *Sambhogakaya* is as above but with the additional lustre of "three perfections," one of which is the entire obliteration of all earthly concerns.
3. The Truth Body, or *Dharmakaya*, is that of a completely enlightened Lord, i.e., no body at all, just ideal breath: Consciousness merged with Universal Consciousness, or Soul devoid of every attribute. On achieving *Dharmakaya*, the Adept leaves behind every possible relation to this Earth, or thought concerning it. In order that they may assist humanity, the Masters, who have won the right to Paradise, "renounce their *Dharmakaya* bodies," in mystic parlance, retaining of the *Sambhogakaya* only the great and complete knowledge, and remaining in their *Nirmanakaya* bodies.

The Initiation robe,[5] it is true, can grant eternal light. The Initiation robe alone entails the cessation of personality; it stops the cycle of rebirth, but, O disciple, it also kills compassion. No longer can the perfect Lords, who don the Glorious Robe of Truth, assist in humanity's salvation. Alas! Will many Selves be sacrificed for one self, humanity for the well-being of one person?

Know, O beginner, this is the Open Path, the way to selfish bliss, that is shunned by the Masters of the Secret Heart, the Lords of Compassion.

To live for the benefit of humankind is the first step. To practise the six glorious virtues[6] is the second.

To don the humble Robe of Emanation is to forego eternal bliss for self, and to assist in humanity's salvation. To reach the bliss of Highest Heaven, only to renounce it, is the supreme and final step, the highest on the Path of Renunciation.

Know, O disciple, this is the Secret Path, chosen by the Lords of Perfection, who sacrificed the Self to weaker selves.

Yet, if the Doctrine of the Heart is too high for your wings, if you need help yourself and fear to offer help to others, then, O timid heart, be warned in advance: remain content with the Eye Doctrine of the Law. Yet hope still, for even if the Secret Path is unattainable *this day*, it will be within your reach *tomorrow*.[7] Learn that no effort, not even the smallest, whether in the right or the wrong direction, can vanish from the world of causes. Even a waft of smoke once vanished is never entirely without trace. "A harsh word uttered in a past life is not destroyed but ever returns." The pepper plant will not give birth to roses, nor will the sweet jasmine's silver star turn to thorn or thistle.

You can create this *day* your chances for the *morrow*. In the "Great Journey,"[8] causes sown each hour bear a harvest of effects, for a rigid justice rules the world. With a mighty sweep of never erring action, it brings to mortals a life of well-being or woe, the karmic progeny of all our former thoughts and deeds.

Take then as much as merit has in store for you, O patient heart. Be of good cheer and rest content with fate. Such is your karma, the karma of the cycle of your incarnations, and the destiny of those, who, in their

---

[5] To put on the "robe of Initiation" means metaphorically to acquire Secret Wisdom and Initiation with which Paradise is entered at which point one's reincarnation is ceased.

[6] Meaning, to become a yogi with a view to becoming an ascetic.

[7] "Tomorrow" means the next rebirth or reincarnation.

[8] "Great Journey" is the whole complete cycle of existences in one Round.

pain and sorrow, born along with you, rejoice and weep from one life to the next, chained to your previous actions.

Act for them *today*, and they will act for you *tomorrow*.

It is from the bud of self-renunciation that the sweet fruit of final liberation springs.

Those who out of fear of Temptation refrain from helping others, lest they should act for self, are doomed to perish. Pilgrims, who would cool their weary limbs in running waters, yet dare not plunge for terror of the stream, risk succumbing to heat. Inaction based on selfish fear can bear only evil fruit.

The selfish devotee lives to no purpose. Whoever fails to fulfil their appointed work in life, lives in vain.

Follow the wheel of life; follow the wheel of duty to race and kin, to friend and foe, and close your mind to pleasure as to pain. Exhaust the law of karmic retribution. Gain higher spiritual powers for your future incarnation.

If the Sun you cannot be, then be the humble planet. Yes, if like the noon-day Sun you are precluded from flaming upon the snow-capped mount of eternal purity, then choose, O beginner, a humbler course.

Illumine the Way, however dim the light and lost among the host, as does the evening star for those who tread the path in darkness.

Behold Mars, as in his crimson veils his "eye" sweeps over the slumbering Earth. Behold the fiery aura of the "hand" of Mercury extended in protective love over the heads of his ascetics.[1] Both are now servants of the Sun, in whose absence they are silent watchers in the night. Yet in cycles past, both were bright Suns and may in future Days again become two Suns. Such is the rising and the falling in Nature that accords with Karmic Law.

Be, O disciple, as they are. Give light and comfort to the toiling pilgrim, and seek out those who know still less than you; who in their wretched desolation sit without a Teacher, hope, or consolation, starving for the bread of Wisdom and the bread which feeds the shadow, and let them hear the Law.

Tell them, O candidate, that they who make pride and self-regard bond-maidens to devotion, that they who, cleaving to existence, still lay their patience and submission to the Law as a sweet flower at the feet of the Great Lord of Compassion will enter the stream[2] in this life. The

---

[1] In Tibetan astrology, Mars is symbolized by an "eye" and Mercury by a "hand."

[2] "One who enters the stream" of achieving Enlightenment, unless they reach ▸

higher powers of perfection may loom far, far away, but the first step has been taken, the stream has been entered, and they may acquire the sight of the mountain eagle, and the hearing of the timid doe.

Tell them, O aspirant, that true devotion may return to them knowledge, knowledge which was theirs in former lifetimes. Divine sight and divine hearing are not obtained in one short lifetime.

Be humble, if you wish to attain Wisdom.

Be humbler still, when Wisdom you have mastered.

Be like the ocean which receives all streams and rivers, but in its mighty calm remains unmoved, and does not feel them.

Restrain the lower self with your Divine Self.

Restrain the Divine Self with the Eternal.

Yes, great is the one who slays desire.

Still greater is the one in whom the Divine Self has slain the very knowledge of desire.

Guard the lower lest it soil the Higher.

The way to ultimate freedom lies within the Self.

This way begins and ends outside of the self.[3]

In the proud eyes of the unbelievers, the mother of all rivers is unworthy of praise and insignificant; in the eyes of fools, the human form is empty, though it be filled with the sweet waters of Immortality. Still, the birthplace of the sacred rivers is sacred land,[4] and one who has Wisdom, is honoured by all.

The Enlightened Ones and the Sages of boundless vision[5] are as rare as the blossom of the Udumbara tree. The Enlightened are born at the midnight hour, together with the sacred plant of nine and seven stalks, bearing a holy flower that opens and blooms in darkness, that is fed by pure dew on a frozen bed of snow-capped peaks, inaccessible to the footsteps of sinners.

No one, O disciple, becomes enlightened in the same lifetime as that in which the soul first begins to long for ultimate liberation. Yet, O anxious one, no warrior volunteering to fight in the fierce strife between

---

the goal owing to some other exceptional reason, can rarely attain it in one lifetime. Usually disciples are said to begin the ascending effort in one lifetime and end it, or reach their goal, only in the seventh succeeding incarnation.

[3] Meaning the personal lower self.

[4] Tibet.

[5] Psychic, superhuman sight. An Enlightened One is credited with seeing and knowing all, in the place where they are located and at a distance.

the living and the dead,¹ nor one recruit will ever be refused the right to enter the Path that leads toward the field of battle.

For, either you shall win, or you shall fall.

Yes, if you conquer, Heaven will be yours. Before you cast your shadow off this mortal coil — pregnant cause of anguish and illimitable pain — in you will be honoured a great and holy Master.

And if you fall, even then you do not fall in vain; the enemies you slew in the final battle will not return to life in your next incarnation.

But if you wish to reach Supreme Enlightenment, or cast the prize away, do not let the fruits of action or of inaction be your motive, O dauntless heart.

Know that one who exchanges liberation for Renunciation to don the miseries of the "Secret Life,"² is called, "thrice honoured," O candidate for woe throughout the cycles.

At first the Path is one, disciple, yet towards the end, it forks. Its stages are marked by four and seven Portals. At one end — bliss immediate, and at the other — bliss deferred. Both are the rewards of merit: the choice is yours.

The One Path becomes two, the Open and the Secret.³ The first leads to the goal, the second, to Self-Sacrifice.

When the mutable is sacrificed to the Permanent, the prize is yours: the drop returns to where it came from. The Open Path leads to the changeless change — the glorious state of Absoluteness, Bliss beyond human comprehension.

Thus, the first Path leads to Liberation.

The second Path leads to Renunciation, and, for this reason, is called the "Path of Woe."

This Secret Path leads the Enlightened One to unspeakable distress of mind; sorrow for the living dead,⁴ and helpless pity for humanity as it

---

¹ The "living" is the immortal Higher Ego, and the "dead," the lower personal Ego.

² The "Secret Life" is the life as a Master in the Emanation Body, a *Nirmanakaya*. Having reached the rank of saints, such Masters refuse to pass into the Highest Heaven or "don the *Dharmakaya* robe and cross to the other shore," as it would then be beyond their power to assist others, even to the little that karma might permit. They prefer to remain in the world invisibly (in spirit), and to contribute toward humanity's salvation by encouraging humankind to follow the Good Law, i.e., by leading others on the Path of Righteousness.

³ The "Open" and the "Secret Path" — the former, the exoteric, taught to the common people, and the generally accepted path, and the latter, the Secret Path, the nature of which is explained at Initiation.

⁴ People ignorant of the esoteric truths and Wisdom are called "the living dead."

suffers the miseries of karma, for the Sage knows that the fruits of karma cannot be averted.

For it is written: "Teach the avoidance of all causes, and allow the ripple of effect, like a great tidal wave, to run its course."

The Open Way, once its goal is reached, will lead you to reject the Emanation Body and enter the thrice glorious state of the Truth Body,[5] which entails becoming oblivious eternally to the world and the people in it.

The Secret Way leads also to the bliss that lies beyond the Highest Heaven, but only at the close of ages without number; Paradise is gained and lost through boundless pity and compassion for the world of mortals lost in delusion.

But it is said, "The last shall be the greatest." The fully enlightened Lord, the Teacher of Perfection, gave up His Self for the salvation of the world by stopping at the threshold of the pure state of Highest Heaven.

You have the knowledge now concerning the two Ways. Your time of choice will come, when you have reached the end and passed through the seven Portals, O eager soul. Your mind is clear. No more are you entangled in delusive thoughts, for you have learnt all. Truth unveiled stands before you and looks you sternly in the eye. She says:

"Sweet are the fruits of Rest and Liberation for the sake of self; but sweeter still the fruits of long and bitter duty. Yes, Renunciation for the sake of others, your suffering fellow beings."

Those who tread the Open Way[6] bow down only to the self. Followers of the Secret Path, those who have won the battle, who hold the prize in their palm, yet say in their divine compassion:

"For the sake of others this great reward I yield," it is they who accomplish the greater Renunciation.

They are the Saviours of the World.

Behold! At the very end of the Journey lie either the attainment of bliss or the long Path of Woe. Throughout the cycles to come, you may choose either, O aspirant to sorrow!

OM VAJRAPANI HUM

---

[5] See note 4, page 92.
[6] Those who strive after and often don the Truth-robe after a series of incarnations. Caring only for their own bliss and nothing for the sorrows of humanity, they reach their goal and disappear from the sight and hearts of others.

Fragment III
THE SEVEN PORTALS

"Master, the choice has been made; I thirst for Wisdom. Now that you have drawn back the veil that concealed the Secret Path, and taught of the Greater Way, your servant is here, and awaits your guidance."

This is good, disciple. Prepare yourself, for you must travel on alone. The Teacher can but point to the way. The Path is one for all, but the means of reaching the goal are different for each pilgrim.

Which will you choose, O dauntless heart? The fourfold Knowledge[1] of the Eye Doctrine, or to thread your way through the transcendental virtues, six in number, the noble gates of virtue that lead to Enlightenment and to Insight, the seventh step of Wisdom?

The rugged Path of fourfold Knowledge winds on uphill. Thrice great is any who can climb to the lofty peak.

The heights of the virtues are crossed by a path that is steeper still. You must fight your way through seven portals, seven strongholds guarded by cruel and cunning powers — the passions incarnate.

Be of good cheer, disciple; bear in mind the golden rule. Once you have passed the first gate, becoming "one who has entered the stream";[2] once your foot has pressed down upon the bed of the stream that flows to Supreme Enlightenment in this or any future life, you have but seven other incarnations before you, O one with will, strong as a diamond.

Look. What do your eyes see, O aspirant to godlike Wisdom?

"The cloak of darkness is upon the depths of matter; I struggle within its folds. Beneath my gaze it deepens, Lord; then it is dispelled beneath the wave of your hand. A shadow moves, creeping out like a twisting snake. . . . It grows, swells, and disappears into the darkness."

That is the shadow of your self beyond the Path, cast against the darkness of your sins.

"Yes, Lord; I see the Path; its base in mire, its summit lost in Heaven's

---

[1] Attained through the state of meditation of which there are four degrees.
[2] "One who has entered the stream" that leads to the ocean of Enlightenment. This indicates the first Path. "One who will receive an incarnation (only) once more" refers to the second Path. The third is referred to as, "one who will be reincarnated no more," unless one wishes it in order to assist humankind. The fourth Path is known as that of the saints. This is the highest path. The saints see the Highest Heaven during their own lifetime and perceive it not as a post-mortem state, but as a supreme spiritual state, in which all the bliss of Enlightenment is experienced.

glorious light. And now I see the ever narrowing Portals on the hard and thorny trail to Divine Wisdom."

You see well, disciple. The Portals lead the aspirant across the waters on "to the other shore."[3] Each Portal has a golden key that opens the gate; the keys are:

1. *Generosity*, the key of charity and immortal love.

2. *Morality*, the key of harmony in word and deed, the key that counterbalances cause and effect, and leaves no room for karmic action.

3. *Endurance*, patience sweet, that nothing can ruffle.

4. *Dispassion*, indifference to pleasure and to pain, illusion conquered, truth alone perceived.

5. *Vigour*, the dauntless energy that fights its way to the celestial Truth, out of the mire of terrestrial lies.

6. *Illumination*,[4] whose golden gate once opened leads the Saint toward the realm of eternal Truth and ceaseless contemplation thereof.

7. *Supreme Wisdom*, the key which makes gods of human beings, creating of them enlightened children of the Merciful Lords.

Such are the golden keys to the Portals.

Before you can approach the last of these, O weaver of the fabric of your freedom, you must first master along the wearying Path these virtues of perfection — the transcendental virtues, six and ten in number.

For, O disciple, before you were made fit to meet your Teacher face to face, your Master light to light, what were you told?

Before you can approach the first gate, you must learn to part your body from your mind, to dissipate the shadow, and to live in the eternal. For this, you must live and breathe in all, as all that you perceive breathes in you; to feel yourself abiding in all things, and all things abiding in Self.

Do not let your senses make a playground of your mind.

Do not separate your being from Being and all that is, but merge the Ocean with the drop, and the drop with the Ocean.

Then you will be in full accord with all that lives; and have such love for others as though they were your fellow pupils, disciples of one Teacher, the children of one sweet mother.

---

[3] "Arrival at the shore" is synonymous with reaching Enlightenment through the practice of the six and ten virtues.

[4] *Illumination* is a state of contemplation that precedes one's union with the Divine. Illumination endows one with the highest form of knowledge, attained intuitively during mystic meditation.

Teachers are many; but the Master-Soul is one, Universal Soul.[1] Live in that Master just as its ray lives in you. Live in your fellows, as they live in it.

Before you stand at the threshold of the Path; before you pass through the first Gate, you must merge the two into One and sacrifice the personal to the impersonal Self, thus destroying the "path" between the two.[2]

You must be prepared to be held accountable to the stern Law, whose voice will ask you at your first, initial step:

"Have you complied with all the rules, O one of lofty hopes?"

"Have you attuned your heart and mind to the great mind and heart of all humankind? For as in the sacred River's roaring voice, all Nature's sounds find their echo,[3] so must the heart of one 'who wishes to enter the stream,' quiver in response to every sigh and thought of all that lives and breathes."

Disciples may be likened to the strings of the soul-echoing lute; humankind, to its sounding board; the hand that sweeps across it to the tuneful breath of the Great World-Soul. The string that fails to respond to the Master's touch in dulcet harmony with all the others, breaks and is cast away. So it is with the collective mind of the disciples. The mind of each disciple must be attuned to the Master's mind — one with the Over-Soul — or, break away.

So it is with the "brothers of the shadow" — the murderers of their souls, the dread clan of evil sorcerers.

Have you attuned your being to humanity's great pain, O candidate for light?

---

[1] The "Master-Soul" is Universal Soul. Each person carries a ray of Universal Soul within and has the potential to identify with it and to merge with it.

[2] The lower mind, the path of communication or communion between the personality and the higher mind, or human soul. At death it is destroyed as a path or medium of communication, and its remains survive in a form reminiscent of a "shell."

[3] Some do, in fact, find in the deep roar of some of the great and sacred rivers the keynote of Nature. Hence the simile. It is well-known in physical science, as well as in occultism, that the aggregate sound of Nature — such as that heard in the roar of great rivers, the noise produced by the waving tops of trees in large forests, or that of a city heard from a distance — is a definite single tone of an appreciable pitch. This has been shown by physicists and musicians. Professor Rice ("Chinese Theory," *What is Music?*, 1883, p. 9) shows that the Chinese recognized this fact thousands of years ago saying that "the waters of the Huanghe rushing by, intoned the *kung*" called "the great tone" in Chinese music; and he shows this tone to correspond to F, "considered by modern physicists to be the actual tonic of Nature." Professor B. Silliman mentions this, also, in his *Principles of Physics* (1866, p. 252): "This tone is held to be the middle F of the piano; which may, therefore, be considered the keynote of Nature."

You have? Then you may enter. Yet, before you set foot upon the lonely Path of sorrow, you would do well first to learn the pitfalls along the way.

Armed with the key of Charity, of Love, and tender Mercy, you are safe before the gate of Generosity, the gate that stands at the entrance to the Path.

Behold, O happy pilgrim! The portal that faces you is high and wide, and seems easy of access. The road that leads through it is straight and smooth and green. It is like a sunny glade in the dark forest depths, a spot on earth mirroring the paradise of the Pure Land. There, nightingales of hope and birds of radiant plumage sing perched in green bowers, chanting success to fearless pilgrims. They sing of the five virtues of the Enlightened Ones, the fivefold source of the power of Wisdom, and of the seven steps in Knowledge.

Pass on! For you have brought the key; you are safe.

The path to the second gate is also green but steep and it winds uphill all the way to the mountain's rocky peak. Grey mists will hang over its rough and stony heights, and all will be dark beyond. As you go on, the song of hope will sound ever more feebly in your pilgrim heart. The tremor of doubt will now be upon you, and your step will grow less steady.

Beware of this, O candidate! Beware of fear that spreads, like the black and soundless wings of a midnight bat, between the moonlight of your soul and your great goal that looms far in the distance.

For, O disciple, fear kills the will and halts all action. When lacking in the virtue of Morality, pilgrims trip, and karmic pebbles bruise their feet along the rocky path.

Be of sure footing, O candidate. Bathe your soul in the essence of Endurance; for now you approach the portal of the same name, the gate of patience and fortitude.

Do not close your eyes, or let your gaze fall from the diamond sceptre;[4] the Tempter's arrows will always strike at one who has failed to attain Dispassion.[5]

---

[4] A weapon or instrument in the hands of certain gods, called *vajra*, regarded as having the same occult power to repel evil influences by purifying the air as ozone is considered to have in chemistry. It is also a gesture and posture (*mudra*) used in sitting meditation. It is, in short, a symbol of power over invisible evil influences, whether as a posture or as a talisman.

[5] A feeling of absolute indifference to the objective universe, to pleasure and to pain. "Disgust" does not express the same meaning, yet it is akin to it.

Be careful not to flinch. The key of Endurance grows rusty beneath the breath of fear: a rusty key will never turn the chosen lock.

The more that you advance, the more your feet will meet with pitfalls. The path that leads on is lit by one fire — the light of daring that burns in the heart. The more you dare, the more you will obtain. The more you fear, the more the light will pale, and it is this light alone that can guide you. For as the lingering beam of sunlight, that on the top of some tall mountain shines, is followed by black night when eventually it fades, so it is with the heart's light. When it goes out, your own heart will cast a dark and threatening shadow upon the path, that will nail your feet to the spot in terror.

Beware, disciple, that lethal shadow. No light that shines from Spirit can dispel the darkness of the lower soul, unless all selfish thought has fled from it, and the pilgrim can say: "I have renounced this passing frame; I have destroyed the cause: the shadows cast can no longer be effects." For now the last great fight, the final war between the Higher and the lower self, has taken place. Behold, the battlefield itself has been engulfed by the great war, and is no more.

Once you have passed the gate of Endurance, know that the third step has been taken. Your body has become your slave. Now, prepare for the fourth, the Portal of temptations which ensnare the inner being.

Before you can near this goal, before your hand lifts to raise the latch of the fourth gate, you must have mastered all the mental changes in your lower self and slain the army of thought sensations that, subtle and insidious, creep uninvited into the Soul's bright shrine.

If you wish not to be slain by them, then you must make harmless your own creations, the children of your thoughts, that unseen, impalpable, swarm about humankind, the progeny and heirs to your terrestrial spoils. You must study the emptiness of what appears full, and the fullness of what appears empty. O fearless aspirant, look deep within the well of your own heart, and answer. Do you know the powers of the Self, O perceiver of external shadows?

If you do not, then you are lost.

For, on the fourth Path, the lightest breeze of passion or desire will cause to waver the steady light that falls upon the pure white walls of the Soul. Allow the smallest wave of regret or longing for Illusion's deceptive gifts along the path that lies between your Spirit and your lower self, that highway of sensations — rude arousers of egotism; allow a thought as fleeting as a flash of lightning and you will forfeit your three prizes — the prizes that you have won.

For know, what is Eternal knows no change.

"Forsake forevermore the eight dire miseries. If you do not, be assured, to wisdom you cannot come, nor yet to liberation," says the Great Lord of Perfection, he who has followed in the footsteps of his predecessors.

Stern and exacting is the virtue of Dispassion. If you wish to master its path, far more diligently than before, you must prevent your mind and your perceptions from killing action.

You must saturate yourself with the pure Universal Soul, and become as one with Nature's Soul-Thought. When at one with it, you are invincible; separated from it, you become the playground of relative truth,[1] the origin of the world's delusions.

All that is within you is impermanent except for the pure bright essence of Universal Soul. You are its crystal ray: within, a beam of immaculate light, without, a form from clay. This beam is your life-guide and your true Self, the Watcher, and the silent Thinker, the victim of your lower self. Your soul cannot be hurt except through your erring body; control and master both, and you will be unharmed as you approach the gate of Balance.

Be of good cheer, O pilgrim, daring to cross "to the other shore." Do not heed the whisperings of Temptation's hosts; wave off the tempters, the ill-natured and jealous evil spirits[2] in endless space.

Hold firm! For now you near the middle portal, the gate of woe, with its ten thousand snares.

Have mastery over your thoughts if you wish to cross its threshold, O striver after perfection.

Have mastery over your soul if you wish to reach the goal, O seeker of undying truths.

Centre your soul gaze on the One Pure Light, free from affection, and use your golden key.

The arduous task is done, your labour almost over. The wide abyss that gaped as if to swallow you is almost spanned.

You have now crossed the moat that encircles the gate of human passions. You have now conquered the Tempter and his furious host.

You have removed pollution from your heart and bled it of impure desire. But your task is not yet done, O glorious combatant. Build high,

---

[1] The kind of truth which would demonstrate the illusive character or emptiness of all things.

[2] Evil spirits that are adverse to humankind and are its enemy.

disciple, the wall that will hedge in the Holy Isle,[1] the dam that will protect your mind from pride and satisfaction at thoughts of the great feat achieved so far.

A sense of pride would mar the work. Yes, build it strong, lest the fierce rush of battling waves from the great ocean of the world's Illusions, that mount and beat its shore, should swallow up the pilgrim and the isle — yes, even once the victory has been achieved.

Your "Isle" is the deer, your thoughts the hounds that weary and pursue it as it progresses towards the stream of Life. Woe to the deer that is overtaken by the barking fiends before reaching the Valley of Refuge that is called the Path of Pure Knowledge.

Before you can settle in this Path and call it yours, your soul must become as the ripe mango fruit: towards the woes of others, as soft and sweet as its bright golden pulp, but towards the throes of your own sorrows, as hard as the fruit's stone, O conqueror of well-being and woe.

Make hard your soul against the snares of the self; earn for it the name, "Diamond Soul."

For, as the diamond buried deep within the throbbing heart of the earth can never mirror back earthly lights, so it is with your mind and soul; plunged into the Way of Knowledge, they must mirror nothing of Illusion's deceptive realm.

When you have reached this state, the Portals that you must conquer on the Path will fling their gates wide open to let you pass, and the most powerful forces of Nature will lack the strength to block your way. You will be master of the sevenfold Path: but not until then, O candidate for untold trials.

Until then, a far harder task awaits you: you must experience yourself as All-Thought, whilst exiling all thoughts from your soul.

You must reach that fixity of mind in which no breeze, however strong, can waft inside any earthly thought. Thus purified, the shrine must be void of all action, sound, and earthly light; even as the butterfly, overtaken by the frost, falls lifeless at the threshold, so must all earthly thoughts fall dead before the shrine.

Behold it is written:

"Before the golden flame can burn with steady light, the lamp must stand well-guarded in a spot free from all wind."[2] Exposed to a shifting

---

[1] The Higher Ego, or Thinking Self.
[2] Bhagavad Gita 6:19.

breeze, the wick will flicker and the quivering flame cast shades deceptive, dark and ever-changing, on the Soul's white shrine.

And then, O pursuer of truth, your mind-soul will become as a mad elephant that rages in the jungle, mistaking forest trees for living enemies, and perishing in its attempts to slay the ever-shifting shadows that dance on walls of sunlit rock.

Beware, lest in the care of self your soul should lose her foothold on the soil of Divine Knowledge.

Beware, lest in forgetting Self, your soul should lose control over her trembling mind, and thus forfeit the fruition due her conquests.

Beware of change! For change is your great foe. Change will fight you off and throw you back, out of the Path you tread, deep into viscous swamps of doubt.

Prepare, and be forewarned. If you have tried and failed, O dauntless fighter, do not lose courage: fight on and return to the charge again and again.

The fearless warrior, precious life-blood oozing from his gaping wounds, will still attack his foe, driving him out of his stronghold, vanquishing his enemy, before he himself succumbs to death. Act then, all you who fail and suffer, act, like the warrior; and from the stronghold of your soul, chase away all your foes — ambition, anger, hatred, even the shadow of desire — even if before you have failed. . . .

Remember, you who fight for the liberation of humanity,[3] each failure is a success, and each sincere attempt wins its reward in time. Holy germs sprout and grow unseen in the disciple's soul. Their stalks wax strong at each new trial. They bend like reeds but never break, nor can they ever be lost. But when the hour has struck they blossom forth.[4] . . .

But if you have come prepared, have no fear.

Henceforth your way is clear, right through the gate of Vigour, the fifth of the Seven Portals.

You are now on the path that leads to the haven of Illumination, the sixth portal, the Portal of Enlightenment.

---

[3] This is an allusion to a well-known belief in the East (as in the West) that every additional saint is a new warrior in the army of those who work for the liberation or salvation of humankind.

[4] A reference to human passions and sins, which are slaughtered during the trials of the novitiate, and serve as well-fertilized soil in which "holy germs" or seeds of transcendental virtues may germinate. Pre-existing or *innate* virtues, talents or gifts are regarded as having been acquired in a previous life. Genius is without exception a talent or aptitude carried over from a previous incarnation.

The gate of Illumination is like an alabaster vase, white and transparent; within it there burns a steady golden fire, the flame of Supreme Wisdom that radiates from the Universal Spirit.

You are that vase.

You have become detached from objects of the senses, have travelled along the "Path of seeing," and the "Path of hearing," and stand in the light of Knowledge. You have now reached a state of complete indifference to pleasure or pain.

O Saint, you are safe.

Know, conqueror of sins, once the "one who entered the stream" has passed the seventh Path, all Nature is suffused with joyous awe and is tamed.

The silver star now twinkles the news to the night-blossoms, and the streamlet to the pebbles ripples out the tale; dark ocean waves will roar it to the surf-bound rocks, scent-laden breezes sing it to the vales, and stately pines mysteriously whisper: "A Master has arisen, a Master of the Day."[1]

You stand now like a white pillar to the west, upon whose face the rising Sun of eternal thought pours forth its first most glorious waves. Your mind, like a becalmed and boundless ocean, spreads out in shoreless space. You hold life and death in your strong hand.

Yes, you are mighty. The living power made free in you, the power which is yourself, can raise the tabernacle of illusion high above the gods, and above the great deities. Now you shall surely reach your great reward!

Will you use the gifts which it confers for your own rest and bliss, your well-earned welfare and glory — you, subduer of the great delusion?

Nay, O candidate for Nature's hidden lore! If one wishes to follow in the steps of the Holy Lord, these gifts and powers cannot be for self.

Would you thus dam the waters born on the sacred Mount of the Gods? Would you divert the stream for your own sake, or send it back to its prime source along the crests of cycles?

If you wish that stream of hard-earned knowledge, of heaven-born Wisdom, to remain sweet running water, you cannot leave it to become a stagnant pond.

Know, if you wish to become a co-worker of the "Boundless Light," then, like the Lords of Wisdom, you must shed the light you have acquired, upon the expanse of all three worlds.[2]

---

[1] "Day" means here a whole Manvantara, a period of incalculable duration.

Know that the stream of superhuman knowledge and Divine Wisdom that you have won must, from yourself, the channel of Universal Soul, be poured forth into another bed.

Know, O Saint, you of the Secret Path, that its pure fresh waters must be used to make sweeter the ocean's bitter waves, that mighty sea of sorrow created by the tears of humanity.

Alas! Since you have become like the fixed star in the highest heaven, that bright celestial orb must shine from out of the spatial depths for all save itself; give light to all, but take from none.

Alas! Since you have become like the pure snow in mountain valleys, cold and unfeeling to the touch, but warm and protective to the seed that sleeps deep beneath its bosom, as snow you must receive the biting frost and the northern blasts, thus shielding from their sharp and cruel tooth the earth that holds the promised harvest, the harvest that will feed the hungry.

Self-doomed to live through future ages, unthanked and unseen by others, wedged like a stone together with countless other stones which form the "Guardian Wall";[3] such is your future if you pass beyond the seventh gate. Built by the hands of many Masters of Compassion, raised by their torture, cemented by their blood, the "Guardian Wall" has shielded humankind, since human was ever human, protecting it from further and far greater misery and sorrow.

Yet, humanity does not see it, will not perceive it, nor heed the word of Wisdom, for they do not know it.

But you have heard it, you know all, O eager guileless soul, and you must choose, then listen yet again.

On the Path of the Stream, O you who have entered it, you are secure. Yes, for immediately beyond this Path, the Path where nothing but darkness meets the weary pilgrim, where torn by thorns the hands drip with blood, where the feet are cut by sharp unyielding flints, and the Tempter wields his strongest weapons, there lies great reward.

Calm and unmoved the pilgrim glides up the stream that leads to Supreme Enlightenment. You know that the more your feet bleed, the

---

[2] These three worlds are the three planes of being: the terrestrial, the astral, and the spiritual.

[3] The "Guardian Wall" or the "Wall of Protection." It is taught that the accumulated efforts of long generations of yogis, saints, and Adepts have created, metaphorically speaking a wall of protection around humankind, shielding it invisibly from still worse evils.

purer you will be washed. You are assured that after seven short and fleeting lifetimes, Heaven will be yours.

Such is the Path of Pure Knowledge, the haven of the mystic, the blessed goal that all who have entered the stream crave.

Not so when they have crossed and won the Noble Path of Wisdom.

There, craving for pleasures is destroyed forever, and the roots of rebirth are torn up. But wait, disciple, hear one more word. Can Divine Compassion be destroyed? Compassion is no attribute. It is the Law of Laws, eternal Harmony, the Self of Universal Soul, a shoreless universal essence, the light of everlasting Right and the fitness of all things, the Law of Eternal Love.

The more that you become one with Compassion, your being melted into its Being, the more your soul unites with that which *Is*, and the more you will become Absolute Compassion.[1]

Such is the Noble Path, the Path of the Masters of Perfection.

Furthermore, what mean the sacred scrolls which make you say:

"Om! In my beseeching not all Sages enjoy the sweetness of fruition on the Path to Supreme Enlightenment,"

"Om! In my beseeching not all Saints enter the Highest Heaven."

"Yes, on the Noble Path, you are no more one who has entered the stream; you are an Enlightened One. The stream is crossed. It is true, you have a right to the Vesture of Truth; but the Body of Bliss is greater than that of a Heaven-dweller, and greater still is the Emanation Body, that of the Lord of Compassion.

Now incline your head and listen well, O Enlightened One. Compassion speaks and says: "Can there be bliss when all that lives must suffer? Will you be saved but hear the whole world cry?"

Now you have heard what was said.

You will attain the seventh step and pass through the gate of final knowledge but only to wed woe; if you wish to be the Lord of Perfection, follow in your predecessor's footsteps — remain unselfish until the endless end.

You are enlightened — choose your way.

---

[1] This "compassion" should not be regarded in the same light as "God, the divine love." Compassion stands here as an abstract, impersonal law, whose nature, which is absolute harmony, is thrown into disorder by discord, suffering, and sin.

Behold, the mellow light that floods the Eastern sky. In signs of praise, both Heaven and Earth unite. And from the fourfold manifested Powers, a chant of Love arises, both from the flaming Fire and the flowing Water, and from the sweet-smelling Earth and the rushing Wind.

Hark! From the deep unfathomable vortex of that golden light in which the Victor bathes, in a thousand tones, all Nature's wordless voice rises to proclaim:

> Joy unto you, O children of sorrowful Earth.
>
> A pilgrim has returned "from the other shore."
>
> A new Saviour of Humanity is born.

PEACE TO ALL BEINGS

LIGHT ON THE PATH

A Fragment from
the *Book of the Golden Precepts*

A treatise written for the personal use of those
who are ignorant of the Eastern Wisdom,
and who desire to enter within its influence

Written down by

M.C.

With Notes and Comments

THREE TRUTHS

There are Three Truths which are absolute, and cannot be lost, but yet may remain silent for lack of speech.

1. The soul of man is immortal, and its future is the future of a thing whose growth and splendour has no limit.

2. The principle which gives life dwells in us, and without us, is undying and eternally beneficent, is not heard, or seen, or smelt, but is perceived by the man who desires perception.

3. Each man is his own absolute law-giver, the dispenser of glory or gloom to himself; the decreer of his life, his reward, his punishment.

These Truths, which are as great as is life itself, are as simple as the simplest mind of man. Feed the hungry with them.

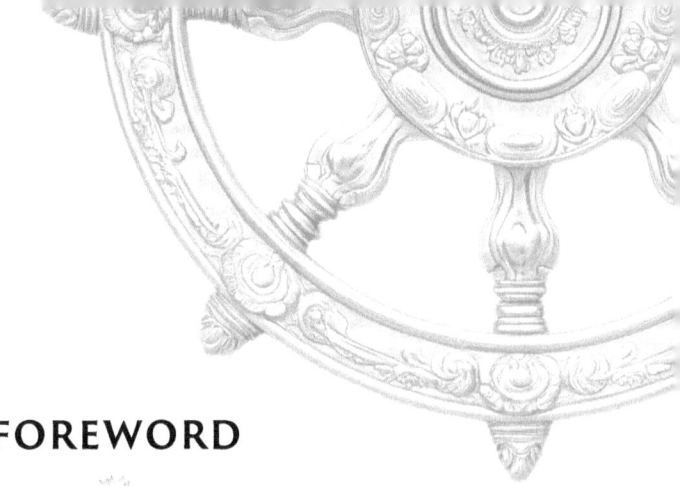

FOREWORD

THE FOLLOWING TREATISE, *Light on the Path*, is a classic among occultists, and is the best guide known for those who have taken the first step on the Path of Attainment.

Its writer has veiled the meaning of the rules in the way always customary to mystics, so that to the one who has no grasp on the Truth these pages will probably appear to be a mass of contradictions and practically devoid of sense. But to the one to whom a glimpse of the inner life has been given, these pages will be a treasury of the rarest jewels, and each time he opens it he will see new gems.

To many this little book will be the first revelation of that which they have been all their lives blindly seeking. To many it will be the first bit of spiritual bread given to satisfy the hunger of the soul. To many it will be the first cup of water from the spring of life, given to quench the thirst which has consumed them.

Those for whom this book is intended will recognize its message, and after reading it they will never be the same as before it came to them. As the poet has said: "Where I pass, all my children know me,"[1] and so will the Children of the Light recognize this book as for them. As for the others, we can only say that they will in time be ready for this great message.

The book is intended to symbolize the successive steps of the neophyte in occultism as he progresses in the lodge work. The rules are practically those which were given to the neophytes in the great lodge of the Brotherhood in ancient Egypt, and which for generations have been taught by Guru to chela in India.

The peculiarity of the rules herein laid down is that their inner meaning unfolds as the student progresses on the Path. Some will be able to understand a number of these rules, while the others will see but dimly even the first steps. The student, however, will find that when he has firmly planted his foot on one of these steps, he will find the one

---

[1] Edward Carpenter, "The Coming of the Lord," *Towards Democracy* (London: T. F. Unwin, 1892), p. 338.

just ahead becoming dimly illuminated, so as to give him confidence to take the next step.

Let none be discouraged; the fact that this book attracts you is the message to you that it is intended for you, and will in time unfold its meaning. Read it over and over often, and you will find veil after veil lifted, though veil upon veil still remains between you and the Absolute. It will be noticed by you that the words of the book will remain in your mind and will become a part of you. You will learn to love this book and will want it always with you. It will be as music to your soul.

This book was written down by "M.C.," a student of occultism, presumably at the dictation of someone high in authority. Its words and teachings bear witness to the nobility and grandeur of the soul who aspired it. To us, it is as a guiding star. May it be the same to you. Peace be unto you.

William Walker Atkinson
Chicago, 1903

William Walker Atkinson (1862–1932) was an American attorney, publisher, and author who wrote extensively on topics related to the New Thought movement, yoga, Hermetism, and Theosophy. He joined the Theosophical Society in 1903.

Using multiple pseudonyms to protect his career as a lawyer, such as Yogi Ramacharaka, Swami Bhakta Vishita, and Theron Q. Dumont, Atkinson authored over 100 books covering subjects like Eastern philosophy, supernatural powers, personal success, and practical spirituality. He was editor of several magazines on New Thought, including *Advanced Thought* (1906–1916).

Atkinson is best known for his work, *The Kybalion*, a book written under the pseudonym "Three Initiates" that explores the principles of the ancient Hermetic philosophy. It was first published in 1908 by the Yogi Publication Society, which Atkinson founded earlier and which he used to release many of his titles.

Overall, Atkinson's writings have had a lasting influence on self-help literature and the modern development of ideas surrounding the law of attraction.

PART I

THESE RULES are written for all disciples: Attend you to them.

Before the eyes can see, they must be incapable of tears. Before the ear can hear, it must have lost its sensitiveness. Before the voice can speak in the presence of the Masters, it must have lost the power to wound. Before the soul can stand in the presence of the Masters, its feet must be washed in the blood of the heart.

1. Kill out ambition.[1]
2. Kill out desire of life.
3. Kill out desire of comfort.
4. Work as those work who are ambitious. Respect life as those do who desire it. Be happy as those are who live for happiness.

Seek in the heart the source of evil and expunge it. It lives fruitfully in the heart of the devoted disciple as well as in the heart of the man of desire. Only the strong can kill it out. The weak must wait for its growth, its fruition, its death. And it is a plant that lives and increases throughout the ages. It flowers when the man has accumulated unto himself

---

[1] Ambition is the first curse: the great tempter of the man who is rising above his fellows. It is the simplest form of looking for reward. Men of intelligence and power are led away from their higher possibilities by it continually. Yet it is a necessary teacher. Its results turn to dust and ashes in the mouth; like death and estrangement, it shows the man at last that to work for self is to work for disappointment. But though this first rule seems so simple and easy, do not quickly pass it by. For these vices of the ordinary man pass through a subtle transformation and reappear with changed aspect in the heart of the disciple. It is easy to say: "I will not be ambitious"; it is not so easy to say: "When the Master reads my heart, He will find it clean utterly." The pure artist who works for the love of his work is sometimes more firmly planted on the right road than the occultist, who fancies he has removed his interest from self, but who has, in reality, only enlarged the limits of experience and desire, and transferred his interest to the things which concern his larger span of life. The same principle applies to the other two seemingly simple rules. Linger over them, and do not let yourself be easily deceived by your own heart. For now, at the threshold, a mistake can be corrected. But carry it on with you and it will grow and come to fruition, or else you must suffer bitterly in its destruction.

innumerable existences. He who will enter upon the path of power must tear this thing out of his heart. And then the heart will bleed, and the whole life of the man seem to be utterly dissolved. This ordeal must be endured: it may come at the first step of the perilous ladder which leads to the path of life; it may not come until the last. But, O disciple, remember that it has to be endured, and fasten the energies of your soul upon the task. Live neither in the present nor the future, but in the Eternal. This giant weed cannot flower there; this blot upon existence is wiped out by the very atmosphere of eternal thought.

5. Kill out all sense of separateness.[1]

6. Kill out desire for sensation.

7. Kill out the hunger for growth.

8. Yet stand alone and isolated, because nothing that is embodied, nothing that is conscious of separation, nothing that is out of the Eternal, can aid you. Learn from sensation and observe it, because only so can you commence the science of self-knowledge, and plant your foot on the first step of the ladder. Grow as the flower grows, unconsciously, but eagerly anxious to open its soul to the air. So must you press forward to open your soul to the Eternal. But it must be the Eternal that draws forth your strength and beauty, not desire of growth. For in the one case you develop in the luxuriance of purity; in the other you harden by the forcible passion for personal stature.

9. Desire only that which is within you.

10. Desire only that which is beyond you.

11. Desire only that which is unattainable.

12. For within you is the light of the world — the only light that can be shed upon the Path. If you are unable to perceive it within you, it is useless to look for it elsewhere. It is beyond you, because when you reach it you have lost yourself. It is unattainable, because it forever recedes. You will enter the light, but you will never touch the flame.

13. Desire power ardently.

---

[1] Do not fancy you can stand aside from the bad man or the foolish man. They are yourself, though in a lesser degree than your friend or your Master. But if you allow the idea of separateness from any evil thing or person to grow up within you, by so doing you create karma which will bind you to that thing or person till your soul recognizes that it cannot be isolated. Remember that the sin and shame of the world are your sin and shame, for you are a part of it; your karma is inextricably interwoven with the great karma. And before you can attain knowledge, you must have passed through all places, foul and clean alike. Therefore, remember that the soiled garment you shrink from touching may have been yours yesterday, may be yours tomorrow. And if you turn with horror from it, when it is flung upon your shoulders, it will cling the more closely to you. The self-righteous man makes for himself a bed of mire. Abstain because it is right to abstain — not that yourself shall be kept clean.

14. Desire peace fervently.

15. Desire possessions above all.

16. But those possessions must belong to the pure soul only, and be possessed therefore by all pure souls equally, and thus be the especial property of the whole only when united. Hunger for such possessions as can be held by the pure soul, that you may accumulate wealth for that united spirit of life which is your only true Self. The peace you shall desire is that sacred peace which nothing can disturb, and in which the soul grows as does the holy flower upon the still lagoons. And that power which the disciple shall covet is that which shall make him appear as nothing in the eyes of men.

17. Seek out the way.[2]

18. Seek the way by retreating within.

19. Seek the way by advancing boldly without.

20.[3] Seek it not by any one road. To each temperament there is one road which seems the most desirable. But the way is not found by devotion alone, by religious contemplation alone, by ardent progress, by self-sacrificing labour, by studious observation of life. None alone can take the disciple more than one step onward. All steps are necessary to make up the ladder. The vices of man become steps in the ladder, one by one, as they are surmounted. The virtues of man are steps indeed, necessary — not by any means to be dispensed with. Yet, though they create a fair atmosphere and a happy future, they are useless if they stand alone. The whole nature of man must be used wisely by the one who desires to enter the way. Each man is to himself absolutely the way, the truth, and the life. But he is only so when he grasps his whole individuality firmly,

---

[2] These four words seem, perhaps, too slight to stand alone. The disciple may say: "Should I study these thoughts at all; did I not seek out the way?" Yet do not pass on hastily. Pause and consider awhile. Is it the way you desire, or is it that there is a dim perspective in your visions of great heights to be scaled by yourself, of a great future for you to compass? Be warned. The way is to be sought for its own sake, not with regard to your feet that shall tread it.

There is a correspondence between this rule and the seventeenth of the second series. When, after ages of struggle and many victories, the final battle is won, the final secret demanded, then you are prepared for a further path. When the final secret of this great lesson is told, in it is opened the mystery of the new way — a path which leads out of all human experience, and which is utterly beyond human perception or imagination. At each of these points, it is needful to pause long and consider well. At each of these points it is necessary to be sure that the way is chosen for its own sake. The way and the truth come first, then follows the life.

[3] *H.P.B.'s warning:* "[Rule 20's] occult venom and close relationship to Tantrika black magic has never been suspected by the innocent and sincere admirers of this otherwise priceless little book, the *main body of which only* was dictated by a true Adept, and the rest added from the inner consciousness of Miss Mabel Collins."

and, by the force of his awakened spiritual will, recognizes this individuality as not himself, but that thing which he has with pain created for his own use, and by means of which he purposes, as his growth slowly develops his intelligence, to reach to the life beyond individuality. When he knows that for this his wonderful complex, separated life exists, then, indeed, and then only, he is upon the way. Seek it by plunging into the mysterious and glorious depths of your own inmost being. Seek it by testing all experience, by utilizing the senses in order to understand the growth and meaning of individuality, and the beauty and obscurity of those other divine fragments which are struggling side by side with you, and form the race to which you belong. Seek it by study of the laws of being, the laws of Nature, the laws of the supernatural; and seek it by making the profound obeisance of the soul to the dim star that burns within. Steadily, as you watch and worship, its light will grow stronger. Then you may know you have found the beginning of the way. And when you have found the end, its light will suddenly become the infinite light.[1]

21. Look for the flower to bloom in the silence that follows the storm; not till then.

It shall grow, it will shoot up, it will make branches and leaves and form buds, while the storm continues, while the battle lasts. But not till the whole personality of the man is dissolved and melted — not until it is held by the divine fragment which has created it, as a mere subject for grave experiment and experience — not until the whole nature has yielded and become subject unto its Higher Self, can the bloom open.

---

[1] Seek it by testing all experience, and remember that when I say this, I do not say: "Yield to the seductions of sense in order to know it." Before you have become an occultist you may do this; but not afterwards. When you have chosen and entered the Path you cannot yield to these seductions without shame. Yet you can experience them without horror; can weigh, observe, and test them, and wait with the patience of confidence for the hour when they shall affect you no longer. But do not condemn the man that yields; stretch out your hand to him as a brother pilgrim whose feet have become heavy with mire. Remember, O disciple, that great though the gulf may be between the good man and the sinner, it is greater between the good man and the man who has attained knowledge; it is immeasurable between the good man and the one on the threshold of divinity. Therefore, be wary lest too soon you fancy yourself a thing apart from the mass. When you have found the beginning of the way, the star of your soul will show its light, and by that light you will perceive how great is the darkness in which it burns. Mind, heart, brain, all are obscure and dark until the first great battle has been won. Be not appalled and terrified by this sight; keep your eyes fixed on the small light and it will grow. But let the darkness within help you to understand the helplessness of those who have seen no light, whose souls are in profound gloom. Blame them not, shrink not from them, but try to lift a little of the heavy karma of the world; give your aid to the few strong hands that hold back the powers of darkness from obtaining complete victory. Then do you enter into a partnership of joy, which brings indeed terrible toil and profound sadness, but also a great and ever-increasing delight.

Then will come a calm such as comes in a tropical country after the heavy rain, when Nature works so swiftly that one may see her action. Such a calm will come to the harassed spirit. And in the deep silence the mysterious event will occur which will prove that the way has been found. Call it by what name you will, it is a voice that speaks where there is none to speak — it is a messenger that comes, a messenger without form or substance; or it is the flower of the soul that has opened. It cannot be described by any metaphor. But it can be felt after, looked for, and desired, even amid the raging of the storm. The silence may last a moment of time or it may last a thousand years. But it will end. Yet you will carry its strength with you. Again and again the battle must be fought and won. It is only for an interval that Nature can be still.[2]

These written above are the first of the rules which are written on the walls of the Hall of Learning. Those that ask shall have. Those that desire to read shall read. Those that desire to learn shall learn.

PEACE BE WITH YOU

---

[2] The opening of the bloom is the glorious moment when perception awakes; with it comes confidence, knowledge, certainty. The pause of the soul is the moment of wonder, and the next moment of satisfaction — that is the silence.

Know, O disciple, that those who have passed through the silence, and felt its peace and retained its strength, they long that you shall pass through it also. Therefore, in the Hall of Learning, when he is capable of entering there, the disciple will always find his Master.

Those that ask shall have. But though the ordinary man asks perpetually, his voice is not heard. For he asks with his mind only; and the voice of the mind is only heard on that plane on which the mind acts. Therefore, not until the first twenty-one rules are passed do I say, those that ask shall have.

To read, in the occult sense, is to read with the eyes of the spirit. To ask is to feel the hunger within — the yearning of spiritual aspiration. To be able to read means having obtained the power in a small degree of gratifying that hunger. When the disciple is ready to learn, then he is accepted, acknowledged, recognized. It must be so, for he has lit his lamp, and it cannot be hidden. But to learn is impossible until the first great battle has been won. The mind may recognize truth, but the spirit cannot receive it. Once having passed through the storm and attained the peace, it is then always possible to learn, even though the disciple waver, hesitate, and turn aside. The Voice of the Silence remains within him, and though he leave the Path utterly, yet one day it will resound, and rend him asunder, and separate his passions from his divine possibilities. Then, with pain and desperate cries from the deserted lower self, he will return.

Therefore I say: Peace be with you. "My peace I give unto you" can only be said by the Master to the beloved disciples who are as Himself. There are some even among those who are ignorant of the Eastern Wisdom, to whom this can be said, and to whom it can daily be said with more completeness.

△ Regard the Three Truths. They are equal.

PART II

OUT OF THE SILENCE that is peace a resonant voice shall arise. And this voice will say: It is not well; thou hast reaped, now thou must sow. And knowing this voice to be the silence itself, thou wilt obey.

Thou who art now a disciple — able to stand, able to hear, able to see, able to speak — who hast conquered desire and attained to self-knowledge; who hast seen thy soul in its bloom and recognized it, and heard the Voice of the Silence, go thou to the Hall of Learning and read what is written there for thee.[1]

1. Stand aside in the coming battle, and though thou fightest be not thou the warrior.

2. Look for the Warrior and let him fight in thee.

3. Take his orders for battle, and obey them.

4. Obey him, not as though he were a general, but as though he were thyself, and his spoken words were the utterance of thy secret desires; for he is thyself, yet infinitely wiser and stronger than thyself. Look for him, else in the fever and hurry of the fight thou mayest pass him; and he will not know thee unless thou knowest him. If thy cry meet his listening

---

[1] To be able to stand is to have confidence; to be able to hear is to have opened the doors of the soul; to be able to see is to have attained perception; to be able to speak is to have attained the power of helping others; to have conquered desire is to have learnt how to use and control the self; to have attained to self-knowledge is to have retreated to the inner fortress from whence the personal man can be viewed with impartiality; to have seen thy soul in its bloom is to have obtained a momentary glimpse in thyself of the transfiguration which shall eventually make thee more than man; to recognize is to achieve the great task of gazing upon the blazing light without dropping the eyes, and not falling back in terror, as though before some ghastly phantom. This happens to some, and so when the victory is all but won it is lost. To hear the Voice of the Silence is to understand that from within comes the only true guidance; to go to the Hall of Learning is to enter the state in which learning becomes possible. Then will many words be written there for thee, and written in fiery letters for thee easily to read. For when the disciple is ready, the Master is ready also.

ear, then will he fight in thee and fill the dull void within. And if this is so, then canst thou go through the fight cool and unwearied, standing aside and letting him battle for thee. Then it will be impossible for thee to strike one blow amiss. But if thou look not for him, if thou pass him by, then there is no safeguard for thee. Thy brain will reel, thy heart grow uncertain, and in the dust of the battlefield thy sight and senses will fail, and thou wilt not know thy friends from thy enemies.

He is thyself. Yet thou art but finite and liable to error; he is eternal and is sure. He is eternal truth. When once he has entered thee and become thy Warrior, he will never utterly desert thee; and at the day of the great peace he will become one with thee.

5. Listen to the song of life.[2]

6. Store in your memory the melody you hear.

7. Learn from it the lesson of harmony.

8. You can stand upright now, firm as a rock amid the turmoil, obeying the Warrior who is thyself and thy king. Unconcerned in the battle save to do his bidding, having no longer any care as to the result of the battle; for one thing only is important, that the Warrior shall win, and you know he is incapable of defeat — standing thus, cool and awakened, use the hearing you have acquired by pain and by the destruction of pain. Only fragments of the great song come to your ears while yet you are but man. But if you listen to it, remember it faithfully, so that none which has reached you is lost, and endeavour to learn from it the meaning of the mystery which surrounds you. In time you will need no teacher. For as the individual has voice, so has that in which the individual exists. Life itself has speech and is never silent. And its utterance is not, as you that are deaf may suppose, a cry; it is a song. Learn from it that you are part of the harmony; learn from it to obey the laws of the harmony.

---

[2] Look for it and listen to it, first in your own heart. At first you may say: "It is not there; when I search I find only discord." Look deeper. If again you are disappointed, pause and look deeper again. There is a natural melody, an obscure fount in every human heart. It may be hidden over and utterly concealed and silenced — but it is there. At the very base of your nature you will find faith, hope, and love. He that chooses evil refuses to look within himself, shuts his ears to the melody of his heart, as he blinds his eyes to the light of his soul. He does this because he finds it easier to live in desires. But underneath all life is the strong current that cannot be checked; the great waters are there in reality. Find them, and you will perceive that none, not the most wretched of creatures, but is a part of it, however he blind himself to the fact and build up for himself a phantasmal outer form of horror. In that sense it is that I say to you: All those beings among whom you struggle on are fragments of the Divine. And so deceptive is the illusion in which you live, that it is hard to guess where you will first detect the sweet voice in the hearts of others. But know that it is certainly within yourself. Look for it there, and once having heard it, you will more readily recognize it around you.

9. Regard earnestly all the life that surrounds you.

10. Learn to look intelligently into the hearts of men.[1]

11. Regard most earnestly your own heart.

12. For through your own heart comes the one light which can illuminate life and make it clear to your eyes.

Study the hearts of men, that you may know what is that world in which you live and of which you will to be a part. Regard the constantly changing and moving life which surrounds you, for it is formed by the hearts of men; and as you learn to understand their constitution and meaning, you will by degrees be able to read the larger word of life.

13. Speech comes only with knowledge. Attain to knowledge and you will attain to speech.[2]

14. Having obtained the use of the inner senses, having conquered the desires of the outer senses, having conquered the desires of the individual soul, and having obtained knowledge, prepare now, O disciple, to enter upon the way in reality. The Path is found; make yourself ready to tread it.

15. Inquire of the earth, the air, and the water, of the secrets they hold for you. The development of your inner senses will enable you to do this.

16. Inquire of the Holy Ones of the earth of the secrets they hold for you. The conquering of the desires of the outer senses will give you the right to do this.

17. Inquire of the inmost, the One, of its final secret, which it holds for you through the ages.

The great and difficult victory, the conquering of the desires of the individual soul, is a work of ages; therefore expect not to obtain its reward until ages of experience have been accumulated. When the time

---

[1] From an absolutely impersonal point of view, otherwise your sight is coloured. Therefore, impersonality must first be understood.

Intelligence is impartial: no man is your enemy; no man is your friend. All alike are your teachers. Your enemy becomes a mystery that must be solved, even though it take ages, for man must be understood. Your friend becomes a part of yourself, an extension of yourself, a riddle hard to read. Only one thing is more difficult to know — your own heart. Not until the bonds of personality are loosed can that profound mystery of self begin to be seen. Not till you stand aside from it will it in any way reveal itself to your understanding. Then, and not till then, can you grasp and guide it. Then, and not till then, can you use all its powers, and devote them to a worthy service.

[2] It is impossible to help others till you have obtained some certainty of your own. When you have learnt the first twenty-one rules and have entered the Hall of Learning with your powers developed and senses unchained, then you will find there is a fount within you from which speech will arise.

After the thirteenth rule I can add no words to what is already written.

My peace I give unto you. △

These notes are written only for those to whom I give my peace; those who can read what I have written with the inner as well as the outer sense.

of learning this seventeenth rule is reached, man is on the threshold of becoming more than man.

18. The knowledge which is now yours is only yours because your soul has become one with all pure souls and with the inmost. It is a trust vested in you by the Most High. Betray it, misuse your knowledge, or neglect it, and it is possible even now for you to fall from the high estate you have attained. Great ones fall back, even from the threshold, unable to sustain the weight of their responsibility, unable to pass on. Therefore look forward always with awe and trembling to this moment, and be prepared for the battle.

19. It is written that for him who is on the threshold of divinity no law can be framed, no guide can exist. Yet to enlighten the disciple, the final struggle may be thus expressed:

Hold fast to that which has neither substance nor existence.

20. Listen only to the voice which is soundless.

21. Look only on that which is invisible alike to the inner and the outer sense.

PEACE BE WITH YOU

KARMA

CONSIDER with me that the individual existence is a rope which stretches from the infinite to the infinite and has no end and no commencement, neither is it capable of being broken. This rope is formed of innumerable fine threads, which, lying closely together, form its thickness. These threads are colourless, are perfect in their qualities of straightness, strength, and levelness. This rope, passing as it does through all places, suffers strange accidents. Very often a thread is caught and becomes attached, or perhaps is only violently pulled away from its even way. Then for a great time it is disordered, and it disorders the whole. Sometimes one is stained with dirt or with colour, and not only does the stain run on further than the spot of contact, but it discolours other of the threads. And remember that the threads are living — are like electric wires; more, are like quivering nerves. How far, then, must the stain, the drag awry, be communicated! But eventually the long strands, the living threads which in their unbroken continuity form the individual, pass out of the shadow into the shine. Then the threads are no longer colourless, but golden; once more they lie together, level. Once more harmony is established between them; and from that harmony within the greater harmony is perceived.

This illustration presents but a small portion — a single side of the truth: it is less than a fragment. Yet, dwell on it; by its aid you may be led to perceive more. What it is necessary first to understand is, not that the future is arbitrarily formed by any separate acts of the present, but that the whole of the future is in unbroken continuity with the present as the present is with the past. On one plane, from one point of view, the illustration of the rope is correct.

It is said that a little attention to occultism produces great karmic results. That is because it is impossible to give any attention to occultism without making a definite choice between what are familiarly called good and evil. The first step in occultism brings the student to the tree of knowledge. He must pluck and eat; he must choose. No longer is he capable of the indecision of ignorance. He goes on, either on the good or on the evil path. And to step definitely and knowingly even but one step on either path produces great karmic results. The mass of men walk waveringly, uncertain as to the goal they aim at; their standard of life is indefinite; consequently their karma operates in a confused manner. But when once the threshold of knowledge is reached, the confusion begins to lessen, and consequently the karmic results increase enormously, because all are acting in the same direction on all the different planes; for the occultist cannot be half-hearted, nor can he return when he has passed the threshold. These things are as impossible as that the man should become the child again. The individuality has approached the state of responsibility by reason of growth; it cannot recede from it.

He who would escape from the bondage of karma must raise his individuality out of the shadow into the shine; must so elevate his existence that these threads do not come in contact with soiling substances, do not become so attached as to be pulled awry. He simply lifts himself out of the region in which karma operates. He does not leave the existence which he is experiencing because of that. The ground may be rough and dirty, or full of rich flowers whose pollen stains, and of sweet substances that cling and become attachments — but overhead there is always the free sky. He who desires to be karmaless must look to the air for a home; and after that to the ether. He who desires to form good karma will meet with many confusions, and in the effort to sow rich seed for his own harvesting may plant a thousand weeds, and among them the giant. Desire to sow no seed for your own harvesting; desire only to sow that seed the fruit of which shall feed the world. You are a part of the world; in giving it food you feed yourself. Yet in even this thought there lurks a great danger which starts forward and faces the disciple, who has for long thought himself working for good, while in his inmost soul he has perceived only evil; that is, he has thought himself to be intending great benefit to the world while all the time he has unconsciously embraced the thought of karma, and the great benefit he works for is for himself. A man may refuse to allow himself to think of reward. But in that very refusal is seen the fact that reward is desired. And it is useless for the disciple to strive to learn by means of checking himself. The soul must be unfettered, the desires free. But until they are fixed only on that state wherein there is neither reward nor punishment, good nor evil, it is in vain that he endeavours. He may seem to make great progress, but some day he will come face to face with his own soul, and will recognize that when he came to the tree of knowledge he chose the bitter fruit and not the sweet; and then the veil will fall utterly, and he will give up his freedom and become a slave of desire. Therefore be warned, you who are but turning towards the life of occultism. Learn now that there is no cure for desire, no cure for the love of reward, no cure for the misery of longing, save in the fixing of the sight and hearing upon that which is invisible and soundless. Begin even now to practise it, and so a thousand serpents will be kept from your path. Live in the eternal.

The operations of the actual laws of karma are not to be studied until the disciple has reached the point at which they no longer affect himself. The Initiate has a right to demand the secrets of Nature and to know the rules which govern human life. He obtains this right by having escaped from the limits of Nature and by having freed himself from the rules which govern human life. He has become a recognized portion of the divine element, and is no longer affected by that which is temporary. He then obtains a knowledge of the laws which govern temporary conditions. Therefore you who desire to understand the laws of karma, attempt first to free yourself from these laws; and this can only be done by fixing your attention on that which is unaffected by those laws.

COMMENTS

"Before the Eyes Can See, They Must Be Incapable of Tears"

It should be very clearly remembered by all readers of this volume that it is a book which may appear to have some little philosophy in it, but very little sense, to those who believe it to be written in ordinary English. To the many, who read in this manner it will be — not caviar so much as olives strong of their salt. Be warned and read but a little in this way.

There is another way of reading, which is, indeed, the only one of any use with many authors. It is reading, not between the lines but within the words. In fact, it is deciphering a profound cipher. All alchemical works are written in the cipher of which I speak; it has been used by the great philosophers and poets of all time. It is used systematically by the Adepts in life and knowledge, who, seemingly giving out their deepest wisdom, hide in the very words which frame it its actual mystery. They cannot do more. There is a law of Nature which insists that a man shall read these mysteries for himself. By no other method can he obtain them. A man who desires to live must eat his food himself: this is the simple law of Nature — which applies also to the higher life. A man who would live and act in it cannot be fed like a babe with a spoon; he must eat for himself.

I propose to put into new and sometimes plainer language parts of *Light on the Path*; but whether this effort of mine will really be any interpretation I cannot say. To a deaf and dumb man, a truth is made no more intelligible if, in order to make it so, some misguided linguist translates the words in which it is couched into every living or dead language, and shouts these different phrases in his ear. But for those who are not deaf and dumb one language is generally easier than the rest; and it is to such as these I address myself.

The very first aphorisms of *Light on the Path*, included under Part I, have, I know well, remained sealed as to their inner meaning to many who have otherwise followed the purpose of the book.

There are four proven and certain truths with regard to the entrance to occultism. The Gates of Gold bar that threshold; yet there are some who pass those Gates and discover the sublime and illimitable beyond. In the far spaces of Time all will pass those Gates. But I am one who wish that Time, the great deluder, were not so overmasterful. To those who know and love him I have no word to say; but to the others — and there are not so very few as some may fancy — to whom the passage of Time is as the stroke of a sledge-hammer, and the sense of Space like the bars of an iron cage, I will translate and retranslate until they understand fully.

The four truths written on the first page of *Light on the Path* refer to the trial initiation of the would-be occultist. Until he has passed it, he cannot even reach to the latch of the Gate which admits to knowledge. Knowledge is man's greatest inheritance; why, then, should he not attempt to reach it by every possible road? The laboratory is not the only ground for experiment; *science*, we must remember, is derived from *sciens*, present participle of *scire*, "to know" — its origin is similar to that of the word *discern*, "to ken." Science does not therefore deal only with matter, no, not even its subtlest and obscurest forms. Such an idea is born merely of the idle spirit of the age. *Science* is a word which covers all forms of knowledge. It is exceedingly interesting to hear what chemists discover, and to see them finding their way through the densities of matter to its finer forms; but there are other kinds of knowledge than this, and it is not everyone who restricts his (strictly scientific) desire for knowledge to experiments which are capable of being tested by the physical senses.

Everyone who is not a dullard, or a man stupefied by some predominant vice, has guessed, or even perhaps discovered with some certainty, that there are subtle senses lying within the physical senses. There is nothing at all extraordinary in this; if we took the trouble to call Nature into the witness-box we should find that everything which is perceptible to the ordinary sight, has something even more important than itself hidden within it; the microscope has opened a world to us, but within those encasements which the microscope reveals, lies a mystery which no machinery can probe.

The whole world is animated and lit, down to its most material shapes, by a world within it. This inner world is called *Astral* by some people, and it is as good a word as any other, though it merely means "starry"; but the stars, as Locke pointed out, are luminous bodies which give light of themselves. This quality is characteristic of the life which lies within matter; for those who see it, need no lamp to see it by. The word *star*, moreover, is derived from the Anglo-Saxon *stir-an*, to steer, to stir, to move, and undeniably it is the inner life which is master of the outer, just as a man's brain guides the movements of his lips. So that although *Astral* is no very excellent word in itself, I am content to use it for my present purpose.

The whole of *Light on the Path* is written in an astral cipher and can therefore only be deciphered by one who reads astrally. And its teaching is chiefly directed towards the cultivation and development of the astral life. Until the first step has been taken in this development, the swift knowledge, which is called intuition with certainty, is impossible to man. And this positive and certain intuition is the only form of knowledge which enables a man to work rapidly or reach his true and high estate, within the limit of his conscious effort. To obtain knowledge by experiment is too tedious a method for those who aspire to accomplish real work; he who gets it by certain intuition, lays hands on its various forms with supreme rapidity, by fierce effort of will; as a determined workman grasps his tools, indifferent to their weight or any other difficulty which may stand in his way. He does not stay for each to be tested — he uses such as he sees are fittest.

All the rules contained in *Light on the Path* are written for all disciples, but only for disciples — those who "take knowledge." To none else but the student in this school are its laws of any use or interest.

To all who are interested seriously in occultism, I say first — take knowledge. To him who hath shall be given. It is useless to wait for it. The womb of Time will close before you, and in later days you will remain unborn, without power. I therefore say to those who have any hunger or thirst for knowledge, attend to these Rules.

They are none of my handicraft or invention. They are merely the phrasing of laws in supernature, the putting into words truths as absolute in their own sphere, as those laws which govern the conduct of the earth and its atmosphere.

The senses spoken of in these four statements are the astral, or inner senses.

No man desires to see that light which illumines the spaceless soul until pain and sorrow and despair have driven him away from the life of ordinary humanity. First he wears out pleasure; then he wears out pain — till, at last, his eyes become incapable of tears.

This is a truism, although I know perfectly well that it will meet with a vehement denial from many who are in sympathy with thoughts which spring from the inner life. *To see* with the astral sense of sight is a form of activity which it is difficult for us to understand immediately. The scientist knows very well what a miracle is achieved by each child that is born into the world, when it first conquers its eyesight and compels it to obey its brain. An equal miracle is performed with each sense certainly, but this ordering of sight is perhaps the most stupendous effort. Yet the child does it almost unconsciously, by force of the powerful heredity of habit. No one now is aware that he has ever done it at all; just as we cannot recollect the individual movements which enabled us to walk up a hill a year ago. This arises from the fact that we move and live and have our being in matter. Our knowledge of it has become intuitive.

With our astral life it is very much otherwise. For long ages past, man has paid very little attention to it — so little, that he has practically lost the use of his senses. It is true, that in every civilization the star arises, and man confesses, with more or less of folly and confusion, that he knows himself to be. But most often he denies it, and in being a materialist becomes that strange thing, a being which cannot see its own light, a thing of life which will not live, an astral animal which has eyes, and ears, and speech, and power, yet will use none of these gifts. This is the case, and the habit of ignorance has become so confirmed, that now none will see with the inner vision till agony has made the physical eyes not only unseeing, but without tears — the moisture of life. To be incapable of tears is to have faced and conquered the simple human nature, and to have attained an equilibrium which cannot be shaken by personal emotions. It does not imply any hardness of heart, or any indifference. It does not imply the exhaustion of sorrow, when the suffering soul seems powerless to suffer acutely any longer; it does not mean the deadness of old age, when emotion is becoming dull because the strings which vibrate to it are wearing out. None of these conditions are fit for a disciple, and if any one of them exist in him, it must be overcome before the Path can be entered upon. Hardness of heart belongs to the selfish man, the egotist, to whom the Gate is forever closed. Indifference belongs to the fool and the false philosopher; those whose lukewarmness makes them mere puppets, not strong enough to face the realities of existence. When pain or sorrow has worn out the keenness of suffering, the result is a lethargy not unlike that which accompanies old age, as it is usually experienced by men and women. Such a condition makes the entrance to the Path impossible, because the first step is one of difficulty and needs a strong man, full of psychic and physical vigour, to attempt it.

It is a truth that, as Edgar Allan Poe said, the eyes are the windows for the soul, the windows of that haunted palace in which it dwells. This is the very nearest interpretation into ordinary language of the meaning of the text. If grief, dismay, disappointment, or pleasure, can shake the soul so that it loses its fixed hold on the calm spirit which inspires it, and the moisture of life breaks forth, drowning knowledge in sensation, then all is blurred, the windows are darkened, the light is useless. This is as literal a fact as that if a man, at the edge of a precipice, loses his nerve through some sudden emotion he will certainly fall. The poise of the body, the balance, must be preserved, not only in dangerous places, but even on the level ground, and with all the assistance Nature gives us by the law of gravitation. So it is with the soul, it is the link between the outer body and the starry spirit beyond; the divine spark dwells in the still place where no convulsion of Nature can shake the air; this is so always. But the soul may lose its hold on that, its knowledge of it, even though these two are part of one whole; and it is by emotion, by sensation, that this hold is loosed. To suffer either pleasure or pain, causes a vivid vibration which is, to the consciousness of man, life. Now this sensibility does not lessen when the disciple enters upon his training; it increases. It is the first test of his strength; he must suffer, must enjoy or endure, more keenly than other men, while yet he has taken on him a duty which does not exist for other men, that of not allowing his suffering to shake him from his fixed purpose. He has, in fact, at the first step to take himself steadily in hand and put the bit into his own mouth; no one else can do it for him.

The first four aphorisms of *Light on the Path* refer entirely to astral development. This development must be accomplished to a certain extent — that is to say it must be fully entered upon — before the remainder of the book is really intelligible except to the intellect; in fact, before it can be read as a practical, not a metaphysical treatise.

In one of the great mystic Brotherhoods, there are four ceremonies, that take place early in the year, which practically illustrate and elucidate these aphorisms. They are ceremonies in which only novices take part, for they are simply services of the threshold. But it will show how serious a thing it is to become a disciple, when it is understood that these are all ceremonies of sacrifice. The first one is this of which I have been speaking. The keenest enjoyment, the bitterest pain, the anguish of loss and despair, are brought to bear on the trembling soul, which has not yet found light in the darkness, which is helpless as a blind man is, and until these shocks can be endured without loss of equilibrium the astral senses must remain sealed. This is the merciful law. The "medium," or "spiritualist," who rushes into the psychic world without preparation, is a lawbreaker, a breaker of the laws of supernature. Those who break Nature's laws lose their physical health; those who break the laws of the inner life lose their psychic health. "Mediums" become mad, suicides, miserable creatures devoid of moral sense; and often end as unbelievers, doubters even of that which their own eyes have seen. The disciple is compelled to become his own master before he adventures on this perilous path, and attempts to face those beings who live and work in the astral world, and whom we call Masters, because of their great knowledge and their ability to control not only themselves but the forces around them.

The condition of the soul when it lives for the life of sensation as distinguished from that of knowledge, is vibratory or oscillating, as distinguished from fixed. That is the nearest literal representation of the fact; but it is only literal to the intellect, not to the intuition. For this part of man's consciousness a different vocabulary is needed. The idea of "fixed" might perhaps be transposed into that of "at home." In sensation no permanent home can be found, because change is the law of this vibratory existence. That fact is the first one which must be learnt by the disciple. It is useless to pause and weep for a scene in a kaleidoscope which has passed.

It is a very well-known fact, one with which Bulwer-Lytton dealt with great power, that an intolerable sadness is the very first experience of the neophyte in occultism. A sense of blankness falls upon him which makes the world a waste, and life a vain exertion. This follows his first serious contemplation of the abstract. In gazing, or even in attempting to gaze, on the ineffable mystery of his own higher nature, he himself causes the initial trial to fall on him. The oscillation between pleasure and pain ceases for — perhaps an instant of time; but that is enough to have cut him loose from his fast moorings in the world of sensation. He has experienced, however briefly, the greater life; and he goes on with ordinary existence weighted by a sense of unreality, of blank, of horrid negation. This was the nightmare which visited Bulwer-Lytton's neophyte in *Zanoni*; and even Zanoni himself, who had learnt great truths, and been entrusted with great powers, had not actually passed the threshold where fear and hope, despair and joy seem at one moment absolute realities, at the next mere forms of fancy.

This initial trial is often brought on us by life itself. For life is, after all, the great teacher. We return to study it, after we have acquired power over it, just as the master in chemistry learns more in the laboratory than his pupil does. There are persons so near the door of knowledge that life itself prepares them for it, and no individual hand has to invoke the hideous guardian of the entrance. These must naturally be keen and powerful organizations, capable of the most vivid pleasure; then pain comes and fills its great duty. The most intense forms of suffering fall on such a nature, till at last it arouses from its stupor of consciousness, and by the force of its internal vitality steps over the threshold into a place of peace. Then the vibration of life loses its power of tyranny. The sensitive nature must suffer still; but the soul has freed itself and stands aloof, guiding the life towards its greatness. Those who are the subjects of Time, and go slowly through all his spaces, live on through a long-drawn series of sensations, and suffer a constant mingling of pleasure and of pain. They do not dare to take the snake of self in a steady grasp and conquer it, so becoming divine; but prefer to go on fretting through divers experiences, suffering blows from the opposing forces.

When one of these subjects of Time decides to enter on the path of occultism, it is this which is his first task. If life has not taught it to him, if he is not strong enough to teach himself, and if he has power enough to demand the help of a Master, then this fearful trial, depicted in *Zanoni*, is put upon him. The oscillation in which he lives, is for an instant stilled; and he has to survive the shock of facing what seems to him at first sight as the abyss of nothingness. Not till he has learnt to dwell in this abyss, and has found its peace, is it possible for his eyes to have become incapable of tears.

"Before the Ear Can Hear, It Must Have Lost Its Sensitiveness"

The first four rules of *Light on the Path* are, undoubtedly, curious though the statement may seem, the most important in the whole book, save one only. Why they are so important is that they contain the vital law, the very creative essence of the astral man. And it is only in the astral (or self-illuminated) consciousness that the rules which follow them have any living meaning. Once attain to the use of the astral senses and it becomes a matter of course that one commences to use them; and the later rules are but guidance in their use. When I speak like this I mean, naturally, that the first four rules are the ones which are of importance and interest to those who read them in print upon a page. When they are engraved on the man's heart and on his life, unmistakably, then the other rules become not merely interesting, or extraordinary, metaphysical statements, but actual facts in life which have to be grasped and experienced.

The four rules stand written in the great chamber of every actual lodge of a living Brotherhood. Whether the man is about to sell his soul to the devil, like Faust; whether he is to be worsted in the battle, like Hamlet; or whether he is to pass on within the precincts; in any case these words are for him. The man can choose between virtue and vice, but not until he is a man; a babe or a wild animal cannot so choose. Thus with the disciple: he must first become a disciple before he can even see the paths to choose between. This effort of creating himself as a disciple, the rebirth, he must do for himself without any teacher. Until the four rules are learnt no teacher can be of any use to him; and that is why *the Masters* are referred to in the way they are. No real Masters, whether Adepts in power, in love, or in blackness, can affect a man till these four rules are passed.

Tears, as I have said, may be called the moisture of life. The soul must have laid aside the emotions of humanity, must have secured a balance which cannot be shaken by misfortune, before its eyes can open upon the superhuman world.

The voice of the Masters is always in the world; but only those hear it whose ears are no longer receptive of the sounds which affect the personal life. Laughter no longer lightens the heart, anger may no longer enrage it, tender words bring it no balm. For that within, to which the ears are as an outer gateway, is an unshaken place of peace in itself which no person can disturb.

As the eyes are the windows of the soul, so are the ears its gateways or doors. Through them comes knowledge of the confusion of the world. The great ones who have conquered life, who have become more than disciples, stand at peace and undisturbed amid the vibration and kaleidoscopic movement of humanity. They hold within themselves a certain knowledge, as well as a perfect peace; and thus they are not roused or excited by the partial and erroneous fragments of information which are brought to their ears by the changing voices of those around them. When I speak of knowledge, I mean intuitive knowledge. This certain information can never be obtained by hard work, or by experiment; for these methods are only applicable to matter, and matter is in itself a perfectly uncertain substance, continually affected by change. The most absolute and universal laws of natural and physical life, as understood by the scientist, will pass away when the life of this universe has passed away, and only its soul is left in the silence. What then will be the value of the knowledge of its laws acquired by industry and observation? I pray that no reader or critic will imagine that, by what I have said, I intend to depreciate or disparage acquired knowledge, or the work of scientists. On the contrary, I hold that scientific men are the pioneers of modern thought. The days of literature and of art, when poets and sculptors saw the divine light, and put it into their own great language — these days lie buried in the long past with the ante-Phidian sculptors and the pre-Homeric poets. The Mysteries no longer rule the world of thought and beauty; human life is the governing power, not that which lies beyond it. But the scientific workers are progressing, not so much by their own will as by sheer force of circumstances, towards the far line which divides things interpretable from things uninterpretable. Every fresh discovery drives them a step onward. Therefore do I very highly esteem the knowledge obtained by work and experiment.

But intuitive knowledge is an entirely different thing. It is not acquired in any way, but is, so to speak, a faculty of the soul; not the animal soul, that which becomes a ghost after death, when lust or liking or the memory of ill deeds holds it to the neighbourhood of human beings, but the divine soul which animates all the external forms of the individualized being.

This is, of course, a faculty which indwells in that soul, which is inherent. The would-be disciple has to arouse himself to the consciousness of it by a fierce and resolute and indomitable effort of will. I use the word *indomitable* for a special reason. Only he who is untameable, who cannot be dominated, who knows he has to play the lord over men, over facts, over all things save his own divinity, can arouse this faculty. "With faith all things are possible." The sceptical laugh at faith and pride themselves on its absence from their own minds. The truth is that faith is a great engine, an enormous power, which in fact can accomplish all things. For it is the covenant or engagement between man's divine part and his lesser self.

The use of this engine is quite necessary in order to obtain intuitive knowledge; for unless a man believes such knowledge exists within himself how can he claim and use it?

Without it he is more helpless than any driftwood or wreckage on the great tides of the ocean. They are cast hither and thither indeed; so may a man be by the chances of fortune. But such adventures are purely external and of very small account. A slave may be dragged through the streets in chains, and yet retain the quiet soul of a philosopher, as was well seen in the person of Epictetus. A man may have every worldly prize in his possession, and stand absolute master of his personal fate, to all appearance, and yet he knows no peace, no certainty, because he is shaken within himself by every tide of thought that he touches on. And these changing tides do not merely sweep the man bodily hither and thither like driftwood on the water; that would be nothing. They enter into the gateways of his soul, and wash over that soul and make it blind and blank and void of all permanent intelligence, so that passing impressions affect it.

To make my meaning plainer I will use an illustration. Take an author at his writing, a painter at his canvas, a composer listening to the melodies that dawn upon his glad imagination; let any one of these workers pass his daily hours by a wide window looking on a busy street. The power of the animating life blinds sight and hearing alike, and the great traffic of the city goes by like nothing but a passing pageant. But a man whose mind is empty, whose day is objectless, sitting at that same window, notes the passers-by and remembers the faces that chance to please or interest him. So it is with the mind in its relation to eternal truth. If it no longer transmits its fluctuations, its partial knowledge, its unreliable information to the soul, then in the inner place of peace already found when the first rule has been learnt — in that inner place there leaps into flame the light of actual knowledge. Then the ears begin to hear. Very dimly, very faintly at first. And, indeed, so faint and tender are these first indications of the commencement of true, actual life, that they are sometimes pushed aside as mere fancies, mere imaginings.

But before these are capable of becoming more than mere imaginings, the abyss of nothingness has to be faced in another form. The utter silence which can only come by closing the ears to all transitory sounds comes as a more appalling horror than even the formless emptiness of space. Our only mental conception of blank space is, I think, when reduced to its barest element of thought, that of black darkness. This is a great physical terror to most persons, and when regarded as an eternal and unchangeable fact, must mean to the mind the idea of annihilation rather than anything else. But it is the obliteration of one sense only; and the sound of a voice may come and bring comfort even in the profoundest darkness. The disciple, having found his way into this blackness, which is the fearful abyss, must then so shut the gates of his soul that no comforter can enter there nor any enemy. And it is in making this second effort that the fact of pain and pleasure being but one sensation becomes recognizable by those who have before been unable to perceive it. For when the solitude of silence is reached the soul hungers so fiercely and passionately for some sensation on which to rest, that a painful one would be as keenly welcomed as a pleasant one. When this consciousness is reached the courageous man by seizing and retaining it, may destroy the "sensitiveness" at once. When the ear no longer discriminates between that which is pleasant or that which is painful, it will no longer be affected by the voices of others. And then it is safe and possible to open the doors of the soul.

"Sight" is the first effort, and the easiest, because it is accomplished partly by an intellectual effort. The intellect can conquer the heart, as is well known in ordinary life. Therefore, this preliminary step still lies within the dominion of matter. But the second step allows of no such assistance, nor of any material aid whatever. Of course, I mean by material aid the action of the brain, or emotions, or human soul. In compelling the ears to listen only to the eternal silence, the being we call man becomes something which is no longer man. A very superficial survey of the thousand and one influences which are brought to bear on us by others will show that this must be so. A disciple will fulfil all the duties of his manhood; but he will fulfil them according to his own sense of right, and not according to that of any person or body of persons. This is a very evident result of following the creed of knowledge instead of any of the blind creeds.

To obtain the pure silence necessary for the disciple, the heart and emotions, the brain and its intellectualisms, have to be put aside. Both are but mechanisms, which will perish with the span of man's life. It is the essence beyond, that which is the motive power, and makes man live, that is now compelled to rouse itself and act. Now is the greatest hour of danger. In the first trial men go mad with fear; of this first trial Bulwer-Lytton wrote. No novelist has followed to the second trial, though some of the poets have. Its subtlety and great danger lies in the fact that in the measure of a man's strength is the measure of his chance of passing beyond it or coping with it at all. If he has power enough to awaken that unaccustomed part of himself, the supreme essence, then has he power to lift the Gates of Gold, then is he the true alchemist, in possession of the elixir of life.

It is at this point of experience that the occultist becomes separated from all other men and enters on to a life which is his own; on to the path of individual accomplishment instead of mere obedience to the genii which rule our earth. This raising of himself into an individual power does in reality identify him with the nobler forces of life and make him one with them. For they stand beyond the powers of this earth and the laws of this universe. Here lies man's only hope of success in the great effort; to leap right away from his present standpoint to his next and at once become an intrinsic part of the divine power as he has been an intrinsic part of the intellectual power, of the great nature to which he belongs. He stands always in advance of himself, if such a contradiction can be understood. It is the men who adhere to this position, who believe in their innate power of progress, and that of the whole race, who are the Elder Brothers, the pioneers. Each man has to accomplish the great leap for himself and without aid; yet it is something of a staff to lean on to know that others have gone on that road. It is possible that they have been lost in the abyss; no matter, they have had the courage to enter it. Why I say that it is possible that they have been lost in the abyss is because of this fact, that one who has passed through is unrecognizable until the other and altogether new condition is attained by both. It is unnecessary to enter upon the subject of what that condition is at present.

I only say this, that in the early state in which man is entering upon the silence he loses knowledge of his friends, of his lovers, of all who have been near and dear to him; and also loses sight of his Teachers and of those who have preceded him on his way. I explain this because scarce one passes through without bitter complaint. Could but the mind grasp beforehand that the silence must be complete, surely this complaint need not arise as a hindrance on the Path. Your Teacher, or your predecessor may hold your hand in his, and give you the utmost sympathy the human heart is capable of. But when the silence and the darkness come, you lose all knowledge of him; you are alone and he cannot help you, not because his power is gone, but because you have invoked your great enemy.

By your great enemy, I mean yourself. If you have the power to face your own soul in the darkness and silence, you will have conquered the physical or animal self which dwells in sensation only.

This statement, I feel, will appear involved; but in reality it is quite simple. Man, when he has reached his fruition, and civilization is at its height, stands between two fires. Could he but claim his great inheritance, the encumbrance of the mere animal life would fall away from him without difficulty. But he does not do this, and so the races of men flower and then droop, and die, and decay off the face of the earth, however splendid the bloom may have been. And it is left to the individual to make this great effort; to refuse to be terrified by his greater nature, to refuse to be drawn back by his lesser or more material self. Every individual who accomplishes this is a redeemer of the race. He may not blazon forth his deeds, he may dwell in secret and silence; but it is a fact that he forms a link between man and his divine part; between the known and the unknown; between the stir of the marketplace and the stillness of the snow-capped Himalayas. He has not to go about among men in order to form this link; in the astral he *is* that link, and this fact makes him a being of another order from the rest of mankind. Even so early on the road towards knowledge, when he has but taken the second step, he finds his footing more certain, and becomes conscious that he is a recognized part of a whole.

This is one of the contradictions in life which occur so constantly that they afford fuel to the fiction writer. The occultist finds them become much more marked as he endeavours to live the life he has chosen. As he retreats within himself and becomes self-dependent, he finds himself more definitely becoming part of a great tide of definite thought and feeling. When he has learnt the first lesson, conquered the hunger of the heart, and refused to live on the love of others, he finds himself more capable of inspiring love. As he flings life away, it comes to him in a new form and with a new meaning. The world has always been a place with many contradictions in it to man; when he becomes a disciple he finds life is describable as a series of paradoxes. This is a fact in Nature, and the reason for it is intelligible enough. Man's soul "dwells like a star apart," even that of the vilest among us; while his consciousness is under the law of vibratory and sensuous life. This alone is enough to cause those complications of character which are the material for the novelist; every man is a mystery, to friend and enemy alike, and to himself. His motives are often undiscoverable, and he cannot probe to them or know why he does this or that. The disciple's effort is that of awakening consciousness in this starry part of himself, where his power and divinity lie sleeping. As this consciousness becomes awakened, the contradictions in the man himself become more marked than ever; and so do the paradoxes which he lives through. For, of course man creates his own life; and "adventures are to the adventurous" is one of those wise proverbs which are drawn from actual fact, and cover the whole area of human experience.

Pressure on the divine part of man reacts upon the animal part. As the silent soul awakes it makes the ordinary life of the man more purposeful, more vital, more real, and responsible. To keep to the two instances already mentioned, the occultist who has withdrawn into his own citadel has found his strength; immediately he becomes aware of the demands of duty upon him. He does not obtain his strength by his own right, but because he is a part of the whole; and as soon as he is safe from the vibration of life and can stand unshaken, the outer world cries out to him to come and labour in it. So with the heart. When it no longer wishes to take, it is called upon to give abundantly.

Light on the Path has been called a book of paradoxes, and very justly; what else could it be, when it deals with the actual personal experience of the disciple?

To have acquired the astral senses of sight and hearing; or, in other words, to have attained perception and opened the doors of the soul, are gigantic tasks and may take the sacrifice of many successive incarnations. And yet, when the will has reached its strength, the whole miracle may be worked in a second of time. Then is the disciple the servant of Time no longer.

These first two steps are negative; that is to say, they imply retreat from a present condition of things, rather than advance towards another. The next two are active, implying the advance into another state of being.

"Before the Voice Can Speak in the Presence of the Masters"

Speech is the power of communication; the moment of entrance into active life is marked by its attainment.

And now, before I go any further, let me explain a little the way in which the rules written down in *Light on the Path* are arranged. The first seven of those which are numbered are subdivisions of the first two unnumbered rules, those with which I have dealt in the preceding pages. The numbered rules were simply an effort of mine to make the unnumbered ones more intelligible. "Eight" to "fifteen" of these numbered rules belong to this unnumbered rule which is now my text.

As I have said, these rules are written for all disciples, but for none else; they are not of interest to any other persons. Therefore I trust no one else will trouble to read these pages any further. The first two rules include the whole of that part of the effort which necessitates the use of the surgeon's knife. But the disciple is expected to deal with the snake, his lower self, unaided; to suppress his human passions and emotions by the force of his own will. He can only demand assistance of a Master when this is accomplished, or at all events, partially so. Otherwise the gates and windows of his soul are blurred, and blinded, and darkened, and no knowledge can come to him. I am not, in these pages, purposing to tell a man how to deal with his own soul; I am simply giving, to the disciple, knowledge. That I am not writing, even now, so that all who run may read, is owing to the fact that supernature prevents this by its own immutable laws.

The four rules which I have written down for those in the West who wish to study them, are as I have said, written in the ante-chamber of every living Brotherhood; I may add more, in the ante-chamber of every living or dead Brotherhood, or Order yet to be formed. When I speak of a Brotherhood or an Order, I do not mean an arbitrary constitution made by scholiasts and intellectualists; I mean an actual fact in supernature, a stage of development towards the absolute God or Good. During this development the disciple encounters harmony, pure knowledge, pure truth, in different degrees, and, as he enters these degrees, he finds himself becoming part of what might be roughly described as a layer of human consciousness. He encounters his equals, men of his own selfless character, and with them his association becomes permanent and indissoluble, because founded on a vital likeness of nature. To them he becomes pledged by such vows as need no utterance or framework in ordinary words. This is one aspect of what I mean by a Brotherhood.

If the first rules are conquered, the disciple finds himself standing at the threshold. Then if his will is sufficiently resolute his power of speech comes; a twofold power. For, as he advances now, he finds himself entering into a state of blossoming, where every bud that opens throws out its several rays or petals. If he is to exercise his new gift, he must use it in its twofold character. He finds in himself the power to speak in the presence of the Masters; in other words, he has the right to demand contact with the divinest element of that state of consciousness into which he has entered. But he finds himself compelled, by the nature of his position, to act in two ways at the same time. He cannot send his voice up to the heights where sit the Gods till he has penetrated to the deep places where their light shines not at all. He has come within the grip of an iron law. If he demands to become a neophyte, he at once becomes a servant. Yet his service is sublime, if only from the character of those who share it. For the Masters are also servants; they serve and claim their reward afterwards. Part of their service is to let their knowledge touch him; his first act of service is to give some of that knowledge to those who are not yet fit to stand where he stands. This is no arbitrary decision, made by any Master or Teacher or any such person, however divine. It is a law of that life which the disciple has entered upon.

Therefore was it written in the inner doorway of the Lodges of the old Egyptian Brotherhood: "The labourer is worthy of his hire."

"Ask and ye shall have," sounds like something too easy and simple to be credible. But the disciple cannot "ask" in the mystic sense in which the word is used in this scripture until he has attained the power of helping others.

Why is this? Has the statement too dogmatic a sound?

Is it too dogmatic to say that a man must have foothold before he can spring? The position is the same. If help is given, if work is done, then there is an actual claim — not what we call a personal claim of payment, but the claim of co-nature. The divine give, they demand that you also shall give before you can be of their kin.

This law is discovered as soon as the disciple endeavours to speak. For speech is a gift which comes only to the disciple of power and knowledge. The spiritualist enters the psychic-astral world, but he does not find there any certain speech, unless he at once claims it and continues to do so. If he is interested in "phenomena," or the mere circumstance and accident of astral life, then he enters no direct ray of thought or purpose, he merely exists and amuses himself in the astral life as he has existed and amused himself in the physical life. Certainly there are one or two simple lessons which the psychic-astral can teach him, just as there are simple lessons which material and intellectual life can teach him. And these lessons have to be learnt; the man who proposes to enter upon the life of the disciple without having learnt the early and simple lessons must always suffer from his ignorance. They are vital, and have to be studied in a vital manner; experienced through and through, over and over again, so that each part of the nature has been penetrated by them.

To return. In claiming the power of speech, as it is called, the neophyte cries out to the Great One who stands foremost in the ray of knowledge on which he has entered, to give him guidance. When he does this, his voice is hurled back by the power he has approached, and echoes down to the deep recesses of human ignorance. In some confused and blurred manner the news that there is knowledge and a beneficent power which teaches, is carried to as many men as will listen to it. No disciple can cross the threshold without communicating this news, and placing it on record in some fashion or other.

He stands horror-struck at the imperfect and unprepared manner in which he has done this; and then comes the desire to do it well, and with the desire thus to help others comes the power. For it is a pure desire, this which comes upon him; he can gain no credit, no glory, no personal reward by fulfilling it. And therefore he obtains the power to fulfil it.

The history of the whole past, so far as we can trace it, shows very plainly that there is neither credit, glory, nor reward to be gained by this first task which is given to the neophyte. Mystics have always been sneered at, and seers disbelieved; those who have had the added power of intellect have left for posterity their written record, which to most men appears unmeaning and visionary, even when the authors have the advantage of speaking from a far-off past. The disciple who undertakes the task, secretly hoping for fame or success, to appear as a teacher and apostle before the world, fails even before his task is attempted, and his hidden hypocrisy poisons his own soul, and the souls of those he touches. He is secretly worshipping himself, and this idolatrous practice must bring its own reward.

The disciple who has the power of entrance, and is strong enough to pass each barrier, will, when the divine message comes to his spirit, forget himself utterly in the new consciousness which falls on him. If this lofty contact can really rouse him, he becomes as one of the Divine in his desire to give rather than to take, in his wish to help rather than be helped, in his resolution to feed the hungry rather than take manna from Heaven himself. His nature is transformed, and the selfishness which prompts men's actions in ordinary life suddenly deserts him.

"Before the Voice Can Speak in the Presence of the Masters, It Must Have Lost the Power to Wound"

Those who give a merely passing and superficial attention to the subject of occultism — and their name is Legion — constantly inquire why, if Adepts in life exist, they do not appear in the world and show their power. That the chief body of these Wise Ones should be understood to dwell beyond the fastnesses of the Himalayas, appears to be a sufficient proof that they are only figures of straw. Otherwise, why place them so far off?

Unfortunately, Nature has done this and not personal choice or arrangement. There are certain spots on the earth where the advance of "civilization" is unfelt, and the nineteenth century fever is kept at bay. In these favoured places there is always time, always opportunity, for the realities of life; they are not crowded out by the doings of an inchoate, money-loving, pleasure-seeking society. While there are Adepts upon the earth, the earth must preserve to them places of seclusion. This is a fact in Nature which is only an external expression of a profound fact in supernature.

The demand of the neophyte remains unheard until the voice in which it is uttered has lost the power to wound. This is because the divine-astral life[1] is a place in which order reigns, just as it does in natural life. There is, of course, always the centre and the circumference as there is in Nature. Close to the central heart of life, on any plane, there is knowledge; there order reigns completely and chaos makes dim and confused the outer margin of the circle. In fact, life in every form bears a more or less strong resemblance to a philosophic school. There are always the devotees of knowledge who forget their own lives in their pursuit of it; there are always the flippant crowd who come and go. Of such, Epictetus said that it was as easy to teach them philosophy as to eat custard with a fork. The same state exists in the super-astral life; and the Adept has an even deeper and more profound seclusion there in which to dwell. This place of retreat is so safe, so sheltered, that no sound which has discord in it can reach his ears. Why should this be, will be asked at once, if he is a being of such great powers as those say who believe in his existence? The answer seems very apparent. He serves humanity and identifies himself with the whole world; he is ready to make vicarious sacrifice for it at any moment — *by living not by dying for it*. Why should he not die for it? Because he is part of the great whole, and one of the most valuable parts of it. Because he lives under laws of order which he does not desire to break. His life is not his own, but that of the forces which work behind him. He is the flower of humanity, the bloom which contains the divine seed. He is, in his own person, a treasure of the universal nature, which is guarded and made safe in order that the fruition shall be perfected. It is only at definite periods of the world's history that he is allowed to go among the herd of men as their redeemer. But for those who have the power to separate themselves from this herd, he is always at hand. And for those who are strong enough to conquer the vices of the personal human nature, as set forth in these four rules, he is consciously at hand, easily recognized, ready to answer.

But this conquering of self implies a destruction of qualities which most men regard as not only indestructible but desirable. The "power to wound" includes much that men value, not only in themselves, but in others. The instinct of self-defence and of self-preservation is part of it; the idea that one has any right or rights, either as citizen, or man, or individual, the pleasant consciousness of self-respect and of virtue. These are hard sayings to many, yet they are true. For these words that I am

---

[1] Of course every occultist knows by reading Éliphas Lévi and other authors that the "astral" plane is a plane of unequalized forces, and that a state of confusion necessarily prevails. But this does not apply to the "divine astral" plane, which is a plane where wisdom, and, therefore, order prevails.

writing now, and those which I have written on this subject, are not in any sense my own. They are drawn from the traditions of the Lodge of the Great Brotherhood, which was once the secret splendour of Egypt. The rules written in its ante-chamber were the same as those now written in the ante-chamber of existing schools. Through all time the wise men have lived apart from the mass. And even when some temporary purpose or object induces one of them to come into the midst of human life, his seclusion and safety are preserved as completely as ever. It is part of his inheritance, part of his position, he has an actual title to it, and can no more put it aside than the Duke of Westminster can say he does not choose to be the Duke of Westminster. In the various great cities of the world an Adept lives for a while from time to time, or perhaps only passes through; but all are occasionally aided by the actual power and presence of one of these men. Here in London, as in Paris and St. Petersburg, there are men high in development. But they are only known as mystics by those who have the power to recognize; the power given by the conquering of self. Otherwise how could they exist, even for an hour, in such a mental and psychic atmosphere as is created by the confusion and disorder of a city? Unless protected and made safe, their own growth would be interfered with, their work injured. And the neophyte may meet an Adept in the flesh, may live in the same house with him, and yet be unable to recognize him, and unable to make his own voice heard by him. For no nearness in space, no closeness of relations, no daily intimacy, can do away with the inexorable laws which give the Adept his seclusion. No voice penetrates to his inner hearing till it has become a divine voice, a voice which gives no utterance to the cries of self. Any lesser appeal would be as useless, as much a waste of energy and power, as for mere children who are learning their alphabet to be taught it by a professor of philology. Until a man has become, in heart and spirit, a disciple, he has no existence for those who are Teachers of disciples. And he becomes this by one method only — the surrender of his personal humanity.

For the voice to have lost the power to wound, a man must have reached that point where he sees himself only as one of the vast multitudes that live; one of the sands washed hither and thither by the sea of vibratory existence. It is said that every grain of sand in the ocean bed does, in its turn, get washed up on to the shore and lie for a moment in the sunshine. So with human beings, they are driven hither and thither by a great force, and each, in his turn, finds the sunrays on him. When a man is able to regard his own life as part of a whole like this, he will no longer struggle in order to obtain anything for himself. This is the surrender of personal rights. The ordinary man expects, not to take equal fortunes with the rest of the world, but in some points about which he cares, to fare better than the others. The disciple does not expect this. Therefore, though he be like Epictetus, a chained slave, he has no word to say about it. He knows that the wheel of life turns ceaselessly. Burne-Jones has shown it in his marvellous picture — the wheel turns, and on it are bound the rich and the poor, the great and the small — each has his moment of good fortune when the wheel brings him uppermost — the king rises and falls, the poet is *feted* and forgotten, the slave is happy and afterwards discarded. Each in his turn is crushed as the wheel turns on. The disciple knows that this is so, and though it is his duty to make the utmost of the life that is his, he neither complains of it nor is elated by it, nor does he complain against the better fortune of others. All alike, as he well knows, are but learning a lesson; and he smiles at the socialist and the reformer, who endeavour by sheer force to rearrange circumstances which arise out of the forces of human nature itself. This is but kicking against the pricks, a waste of life and energy.

In realizing this a man surrenders his imagined individual rights, of whatever sort. That takes away one keen sting which is common to all ordinary men.

When the disciple has fully recognized that the very thought of individual rights is only the outcome of the venomous quality in himself, that it is the hiss of the snake of self which poisons with its sting his own life and the lives of those about him, then he is ready to take part in a yearly ceremony which is open to all neophytes who are prepared for it. All weapons of defence and offence are given up; all weapons of mind and heart, and brain, and spirit. Never again can another man be regarded as a person who can be criticized or condemned; never again can the neophyte raise his voice in self-defence or excuse. From that ceremony he returns into the world as helpless, as unprotected, as a newborn child. That, indeed, is what he is. He has begun to be born again on to the higher plane of life, that breezy and well-lit plateau from whence the eyes see intelligently and regard the world with a new insight.

I have said, a little way back, that after parting with the sense of individual rights, the disciple must part also with the sense of self-respect and of virtue. This may sound a terrible doctrine, yet all occultists know well that it is not a doctrine, but a fact. He who thinks himself holier than another, he who has any pride in his own exemption from vice or folly, he who believes himself wise, or in any way superior to his fellow men, is incapable of discipleship. A man must become as a little child before he can enter into the kingdom of heaven.

Virtue and wisdom are sublime things; but if they create pride and a consciousness of separateness from the rest of humanity in the mind of a man, then they are only the snakes of self reappearing in a finer form. At any moment he may put on his grosser shape and sting as fiercely as when he inspired the actions of a murderer who kills for gain or hatred, or a politician who sacrifices the mass for his own or his party's interests.

In fact, to have lost the power to wound implies that the snake is not only scotched, but killed. When it is merely stupefied or lulled to sleep it awakes again and the disciple uses his knowledge and his power for his own ends, and is a pupil of the many masters of the black art, for the road to destruction is very broad and easy, and the way can be found blindfold. That it is the way to destruction is evident, for when a man begins to live for self he narrows his horizon steadily till at last the fierce driving inwards leaves him but the space of a pin's-head to dwell in. We have all seen this phenomenon occur in ordinary life. A man who becomes selfish isolates himself, grows less interesting and less agreeable to others. The sight is an awful one, and people shrink from a very selfish person at last, as from a beast of prey. How much more awful is it when it occurs on the more advanced plane of life, with the added powers of knowledge, and through the greater sweep of successive incarnations!

Therefore I say, pause and think well upon the threshold. For if the demand of the neophyte is made without the complete purification, it will not penetrate the seclusion of the Divine Adept, but will evoke the terrible forces which attend upon the black side of our human nature.

"Before the Soul Can Stand in the Presence of the Masters, Its Feet Must Be Washed in the Blood of the Heart"

The word *soul*, as used here, means the divine soul, or "starry spirit."

"To be able to stand is to have confidence"; and to have confidence means that the disciple is sure of himself, that he has surrendered his emotions, his very self, even his humanity; that he is incapable of fear and unconscious of pain; that his whole consciousness is centred in the divine life, which is expressed symbolically by the term *the Masters*; that he has neither eyes, nor ears, nor speech, nor power, save in and for the divine ray on which his highest sense has touched. Then is he fearless, free from suffering, free from anxiety or dismay; his soul stands without shrinking or desire of postponement, in the full blaze of the divine light which penetrates through and through his being. Then he has come into his inheritance and can claim his kinship with the Teachers of men; he is upright, he has raised his head, he breathes the same air that they do.

But before it is in any way possible for him to do this, the feet of the soul must be washed in the blood of the heart.

The sacrifice, or surrender of the heart of man, and its emotions, is the first of the rules; it involves the "attaining of an equilibrium which cannot be shaken by personal emotion." This is done by the stoic philosopher; he, too, stands aside and looks equably upon his own sufferings, as well as on those of others.

In the same way that "tears" in the language of occultists expresses the soul of emotion, not its material appearance, so blood expresses, not that blood which is an essential of physical life, but the vital creative principle in man's nature, which drives him into human life in order to experience pain and pleasure, joy and sorrow. When he has let the blood flow from the heart he stands before the Masters as a pure spirit which no longer wishes to incarnate for the sake of emotion and experience. Through great cycles of time successive incarnations in gross matter may yet be his lot; but he no longer desires them, the crude wish to live has departed from him. When he takes upon him man's form in the flesh, he does it in the pursuit of a divine object, to accomplish the work of the Masters, and for no other end. He looks neither for pleasure nor pain, asks for no heaven, and fears no hell; yet he has entered upon a great inheritance which is not so much a compensation for these things surrendered, as a state which simply blots out the memory of them. He lives now not in the world, but with it; his horizon has extended itself to the width of the whole universe.

QUESTIONS AND ANSWERS

Question: There is a sentence in your Comments which has haunted me with a sense of irritation: "To obtain knowledge by experiment is too tedious a method for those who aspire to do real work." Have we any knowledge, of whatever sort, that has been of use in the world, which has been obtained otherwise than experimentally? By patient and persistent toil of sifting and testing, we have obtained the little knowledge that is of service to us. Is there such a thing as "certain intuition"? Has intuitive knowledge, if such there be, been accepted as positive knowledge until it has been submitted to the test of experiment? Would it be right that it should be? Your illustration of the "determined workman" brings the question down (as I think the question should be brought) to the plane of practice. Is there any workman who can know his tools until he has tried them? Is not the history of knowledge the history of intuitions put to the test of practice? Intuitions, or what we call such, seem to me quite as apt and likely to deceive us as anything in the world; we only know them for good when we have tried them.

Answer: It seems to me there is some confusion in this letter between obtaining knowledge by experiment, and testing it by experiment. Edison knew that his discoveries were only things to look for, and he tested his knowledge by experiment. The actual work of great inventors is the bringing of intuitive knowledge on to the plane of practice by applying the test of experiment. But all inventors are seers; and some of them having died without being able to put into practice the powers which they knew existed in Nature were considered madmen. Later on, other men are more fortunate, and rediscover the laughed-at knowledge. This is an old and familiar story, but we need constantly to be reminded of it. How often have great musicians or great artists been regarded as "infant prodigies" in their childhood? They have intuitive knowledge of that power of which they are chosen interpreters, and experiment is only necessary in order to find out how to give that which they know to others.

Intuitive knowledge in reference to the subjects with which I have been dealing must indeed be tested by experiment; and it is the whole purpose of *Light on the Path* itself, and the Comments to urge men to test their knowledge in this way. But the vital difference between this and material forms of knowledge is that for all occult purposes a man must obtain his own knowledge before he can use it. There are many subjects of time content to linger on through aeons of slow development, and pass the threshold of eternity at last by sheer force of the great wheel of life with which they move; possibly during their interminable noviciate, they may obtain knowledge by experiment and with well-tested tools. Not so the pioneer, the one who claims his divine inheritance now. He must work as the great artists, the great inventors have done; obtain knowledge by intuition, and have such sublime faith in his own knowledge that his life is readily devoted to testing it.

But for this purpose the testing has to be actually done in the astral life. In a new world, where the use of the senses is a pain, how can the workman stay to test his tools? The old proverb about the good workman who never quarrels with them, however bad they are, though of course had he the choice he would use the best, applies here.

As to whether intuitive knowledge exists or no, I can only ask how came philosophies, metaphysics, mathematics into existence? All these represent a portion of abstract truth.

Before I received this letter the Comments for this month were written, in which, as it happens, I have spoken a great deal about intuitive knowledge. Therefore, I will now only quote the definition of a philosopher from Plato, which is given near the end of Book V:

"I mean by philosopher, the man who is devoted to the acquisition of knowledge, real knowledge, and not merely inquisitive. The more our citizens approach this temperament, the better the state will be. True knowledge in its perfection and its entirety, man cannot attain. But he can attain to a kind of knowledge of realities, if he has any knowledge at all, because he cannot know nonentities. Hence his knowledge is halfway between real knowledge and ignorance, and we must call it opinion."

Question: What are the senses called astral, in reality? Are they not really spiritual, seizing on the inner essence of things and interpreting it? The ordinary psychic or clairvoyant surely does not use the astral senses? Yet he sees things which we do not see. It would be well to explain this.

Answer: The senses called astral in the Comments on *Light on the Path* are the senses which perceive the inner essence, certainly; which are cognizant of the life underlying every form of matter. The ordinary psychic or clairvoyant only perceives other forms of matter than those we ordinarily see, and perceives them as a child perceives the forms in this world at first, without understanding their meaning. The astral senses carry beyond matter, and enlighten man with regard to any form of life which especially interests him. They show the poet, painter, and composer the things they express to other men, who regard these great ones as beings of another order — beings with the gift of genius. So they are, and the vigour of that genius carries them on into the inner life where meaning, and harmony, and the indefinable all-desired are to be perceived. Wordsworth saw it in Nature, he recognized the "spirit in the woods" — not the wood-nymphs but the divine spirit of peace which teaches a lesson in life. Richard Jefferies saw it in Nature, too, as perhaps no other man ever has seen it; through the finite visible world he perceived the infinite invisible one, and before he died he had begun to know that the visible world does not exist. Turner, perhaps, is the only parallel. By the invisible world I must repeat again that I do not mean what the spiritualists call by that name — a new world of other forms. I mean the formless world. It is the farthest limit man's *consciousness* can reach to; and only the pure and star-like soul can become even aware of its existence. It is not man's divine nature, but the man who enters it with any reverence for the great miracle of life can only do so by the aid of his divine nature, whether as a poet, a painter, or an occultist. The soul which enters it without reverence is unable to endure its extreme rarity of atmosphere and turns to the psychic-astral in which to live; such men become madmen and suicides, more or less pronounced, as men do who refuse to dwell in any form of physical life but the grossest and simplest. There is some law of life which impels men onward — call it evolution or development or what you will; and a man can no more go downwards without suffering than a tree can be placed with its branches in the ground, instead of its roots, without discomfort, and in the end, death.

I propose to use two phrases which have been suggested to me: the psychic-astral and the divine-astral. This seems the only way to make my meaning clear, for the word *astral* has two meanings, its own proper derivative one, from the Sanskrit *stri* to strew light, and that given it by the use of all occultists. Paracelsus appropriated the word for all things sidereal, subject to the moon and stars, part and parcel of this material universe, even though formed as Dryden says of "purest atoms of the air." In this sense the spiritualists and psychics have the right of custom to use it as they do, to describe their world of finer forms. In this meaning an astral shape is the form of the human soul, still in possession of the passions which make it human; and the astral senses perceive not the subtle and supreme glory which Shelley seized on in *Prometheus*, but a region full of shapes and forms differing but little from those we now wear, and still distinctly material.

The "astral man" in the Comments on *Light on the Path* should have been written the divine-astral man, according to this evident difference of meaning between the present writer and all other writers on occultism.

Question: Are not the *astral* senses used by every great poet or inventor though he does not see clairvoyantly at all (i.e., does not see elementals, astral pictures, forms, etc.)?

Answer: The answer to the former question seems to contain the answer to this, which is clearly prompted by a conception of the word *astral* in its divine sense.

Question: "There is a law of Nature which insists that a man shall read these mysteries for himself." Will all men seeking the occult path read these mysteries alike, or will each man find the interpretation peculiarly adapted to his own phase of development? No two men read the mysteries contained in the Bhagavad Gita quite alike, each gains the glimpses of light which he is able to assimilate and no more.

Answer: This seems to be rather a statement of a truth than a question which can be answered in any way other than putting it into different words, perhaps not so good.

Question: Is the outer world the reflection of the world within, like a shadowed reproduction in clumsy form, the inner being reality?

Answer: This is what should be. But materialists have brought their sense of reality into the shadowed life.

Question: How is the intuition to be developed which enables one to grasp swift knowledge?

Answer: To me no way is known but that of living the life of a disciple.

Question: Can the laws in supernature only act on their own plane, or can their reflection be brought down intact in their own purity to govern physical life?

Answer: Surely this must be so; yet rarely, for when it is accomplished the man would be divine, a Buddha!

Question: "To be incapable of tears" — does not that mean that the physical emotions, being merged into the inner physical, that tears are impossible as being an outward phase of the physical nature — whereas the psychical emotions, to use a physical term are vibratory?

Answer: "The whole of *Light on the Path* is written in an astral cipher" is stated at the outset of the Comments; the word *tears* does not refer to physical tears in any way.

It is the only word which will convey any idea whatever of the moisture of life, that which bursts from the human soul in its experience of sensation and emotion, and in the passion of its hunger for them.

Question: How is one to take the snake of self in a steady grasp and conquer it?

Answer: This is the great mystery which each man must solve for himself.

Question: Referring to the Comments on *Light on the Path*, may I ask whether the full paradox "Before the eyes can see, they must be incapable of tears, and yet no eyes incapable of tears can see," i.e., see good or God, is not truer and stronger than its part?

"Therefore the soul of the occultist must become stronger than joy and greater than sorrow" — I presume means that he must not *seek* joy or *fear* sorrow, not that he may not enjoy nor sorrow?

The phrase by itself may read "Before the eyes can see, they must be incapable of tears," tearless, dry, in fact dead, which is obviously not the author's intention in *Light on the Path*.

Answer: Once more I must refer to the preliminary statement in the Comments that *Light on the Path* is written in an astral cipher, and that tears do not mean the tears of the physical body, but the rain drops that come from the passion-life of the human soul. These being stayed forever, the astral sight is no longer blinded or blurred. Divine love and charity then find room, when personal desire is gone. Joy and sorrow, *for oneself*, then drop naturally into another place than that which they filled before.

Question: I desire very strongly to obtain conquest over "self," would my using the occult means for so doing, which apparently to me lie without the *ordinary* experience of Christians, necessitate my sacrificing any iota of my belief in the *power of Christ*?

Answer: Not any iota of your belief in the power of the Christ-spirit would or should be sacrificed; it would rather increase, for that spirit is the same Divine overshadowing which has inspired every Redeemer.

Question: If I submit myself to the occult conditions under which the four first rules in *Light on the Path* may be "engraved on my heart and life," will these conditions permit me to *pray throughout* for the Divine help and strength of the Eternal Christ, who has passed the portal, opened the "way," and whom I believe to be the "Master of Masters," the "Lord of Angels"?

Answer: It matters very little by what name you call the Master of Masters, so that you do appeal to His power throughout.

Question: Do the words — "the disciple . . . must then so shut the gates of his soul that *no comforter* can enter there nor any enemy" — mean that we are wilfully to exclude ourselves from any desire for the sympathy, strength, and support of the spirit of One who said "No man cometh unto the Father but by Me," and who drank the cup of agony to the very dregs for love of the Brotherhood?

Answer: Man can find no comforter save in the Divine Spirit within himself. Does not the tale of the life of Jesus illustrate this, looking at it from one point of view? In what dread isolation he lived and died; His disciples, even those who were most beloved by Him, could not reach His Spirit in its sublime moments, or in the hours of its keenest suffering. So with every one who raises himself by effort above the common life of man, in however small a degree. Solitude becomes a familiar state, for nothing personal, not even a personal God, can comfort or cheer any longer.

Question: Is there any chance of self-deception? May one enter the path so gradually as to be conscious of no radical change, representing a change of life or stage of progression? How is it with one who has never experienced a great and lasting sorrow, or an all-absorbing joy, but who in the midst of both joy and sorrow strives to remember others, and to feel that he hardly deserves the joy, and that his sorrow is meagre in the presence of the great all-pain? How is such a one to enter through the gates? By what sign shall he know them?

Answer: It is difficult for such a one to know anything of what lies beneath the surface of his nature until it has been probed by the fiercer experiences of life. But, of course, the theory of reincarnation makes it possible that such experiences are left behind in the past. The entrance to the gates is marked by one immutable sign; the sense that personal joy or sorrow no longer exist. The disciple lives for humanity, not for himself; works for all creatures that suffer instead of knowing that he himself has pain.

THE THREE DESIRES

THE FIRST THREE of the numbered rules of *Light on the Path* must appear somewhat of an unequal character to bracket together. The sense in which they follow each other is purely spiritual. Ambition is the highest point of personal activity reached by the mind, and there is something noble in it, even to an occultist. Having conquered the desire to stand above his fellows, the restless aspirant, in seeking what his personal desires are, finds the thirst for life stand next in his way. For all that are ordinarily classed as desires have long since been subjugated, passed by, or forgotten, before this pitched battle of the soul is begun. The desire for life is entirely a desire of the spirit, not mental at all; and in facing it a man begins to face his own soul. But very few have even attempted to face it; still fewer can guess at all at its meaning.

The connection between ambition and the desire of life is of this kind. Men are seldom really ambitious in whom the animal passions are strong. What is taken for ambition in men of powerful physique is more often merely the exercise of great energy in order to obtain full gratification of all physical desires. Ambition pure and simple is the struggle of the mind upwards, the exercise of a native intellectual force which lifts a man altogether above his peers. To rise — to be pre-eminent in some special manner, in some department of art, science, or thought, is the keenest longing of delicate and highly tuned minds. It is quite a different thing from the thirst for knowledge which makes of a man a student always — a learner to the end, however great he may become. Ambition is born of no love for anything for its own sake, but purely for the sake of oneself. "It is I that will know, I that will rise, and by my own power."

> Cromwell, I charge thee, fling away ambition;
> By that sin fell the angels.[1]

The place-seeking for which the word was originally used, differs in degree, not in kind, from that more abstract meaning now generally attached to it. A poet is considered ambitious when he writes for fame. It is true; so he is. He may not be seeking a place at court, but he is certainly seeking the highest place he knows of. Is it conceivable that any great author could really be anonymous, and remain so? The human mind revolts against the theory of the Baconian authorship of Shakespeare's works, not only because it deprives the world of a splendid figure, but also because it makes of Bacon a monster, unlike all other human beings. To the ordinary intelligence it is inconceivable that a man should hide his light in this purposeless manner. Yet it is conceivable to an occultist that a great poet might be inspired by one greater than himself, who would stand back entirely from the world and all contact with it. This inspirer would not only have conquered ambition but also the abstract desire for life, before he could work vicariously to so great an extent. For he would part with his work forever when once it had gone to the world; it would never be his. A person who can imagine making no claim on the world, neither desiring to take pleasure from it nor to give pleasure to it, can dimly apprehend the condition which the occultist has reached when he no longer desires to live. Do not suppose this to mean that he neither takes nor gives pleasure; he does both, as also he lives. A great man, full of work and thought, eats his food with pleasure; he does not dwell on the prospect of it, and linger over the memory, like the gluttonous child,

---

[1] William Shakespeare, *Henry VIII*.

or the gourmand pure and simple. This is a very material image, yet sometimes these simple illustrations serve to help the mind more than any others. It is easy to see, from this analogy, that an advanced occultist who has work in the world may be perfectly free from the desires which would make him a part of it, and yet may take its pleasures and give them back with interest. He is enabled to give more pleasure than he takes, because he is incapable of fear or disappointment. He has no dread of death, nor of that which is called annihilation. He rests on the waters of life, submerged and sleeping, or above them and conscious, indifferently. He cannot feel disappointment, because although pleasure is to him intensely vivid and keen, it is the same to him whether he enjoys it himself or whether another enjoys it. It is pleasure, pure and simple, untarnished by personal craving or desire. So with regard to what occultists call *progress* — the advance from stage to stage of knowledge. In a school of any sort in the external world emulation is the great spur to progress.

The occultist, on the contrary, is incapable of taking a single step until he has acquired the faculty of realizing progress as an abstract fact. Someone must draw nearer to the Divine in every moment of life; there must always be progress. But the disciple who desires that he shall be the one to advance in the next moment, may lay aside all hope of it. Neither should he be conscious of preferring progress for another or of any kind of vicarious sacrifice. Such ideas are in a certain sense unselfish, but they are essentially characteristic of the world in which separateness exists, and form is regarded as having a value of its own. The shape of a man is as much an *eidolon* as though no spark of divinity inhabited it; at any moment that spark may desert the particular shape, and we are left with a substantial shadow of the man we knew. It is in vain, after the first step in occultism has been taken, that the mind clings to the old beliefs and certainties. Time and space are known to be non-existent, and are only regarded as existing in practical life for the sake of convenience. So with the separation of the divine-human spirit into the multitudes of men on the earth. Roses have their own colours, and lilies theirs; none can tell why this is when the same sun, the same light, gives the colour to each. Nature is indivisible. She clothes the earth, and when that clothing is torn away, she bides her time and reclothes it again when there is no more interference with her. Encircling the earth like an atmosphere, she keeps it always glowing and green, moistened and sunlit. The spirit of man encompasses the earth like a fiery spirit, living on Nature, devouring her, sometimes being devoured by her, but always in the mass remaining more ethereal and sublime than she is. In the individual, man is conscious of the vast superiority of Nature; but when once he becomes conscious that he is part of an indivisible and indestructible whole, he knows also that the whole of which he is part stands above Nature. The starry sky is a terrible sight to a man who is just selfless enough to be aware of his own littleness and unimportance as an individual; it almost crushes him. But let him once touch on the power which comes from knowing himself as part of the human spirit, and nothing can crush him by its greatness. For if the wheels of the chariot of the enemy pass over his body, he forgets that it is his body, and rises again to fight among the crowd of his own army. But this state can never be reached, nor even approached, until the last of the three desires is conquered, as well as the first. They must be apprehended and encountered together.

Comfort, in the language used by occultists, is a very comprehensive word. It is perfectly useless for a neophyte to practise discomfort or asceticism as do religious fanatics. He may come to prefer deprivation in the end, and then it has become his comfort. Homelessness is a condition to which the religious Brahmin pledges himself; and in the external religion he is considered to fulfil this pledge if he leaves wife and child, and becomes a begging wanderer, with no shelter of his own to return to. But all external forms of religion are forms of comfort, and men take vows of abstinence in the same spirit that they take pledges of boon companionship. The difference between these two sides of life is only apparent. But the homelessness which is demanded of the neophyte is a much more vital thing than this. It demands the surrender from him of choice or desire. Dwelling with wife and child, under the shelter of a familiar roof-tree, and fulfilling the duties of citizenship, the neophyte may be far more homeless, in the esoteric sense, than when he is a wanderer or an outcast. The first lesson in practical occultism usually given to a pledged disciple is that of fulfilling the duties immediately to hand with the same subtle mixture of enthusiasm and indifference as the neophyte would imagine himself able to feel when he had grown to the size of a ruler of worlds and a designer of destinies. This rule is to be found in the Gospels and in the Bhagavad Gita. The immediate work, whatever it may be, has the abstract claim of duty, and its relative importance or non-importance is not to be considered at all. This law can never be obeyed until all desire of comfort is forever destroyed. The ceaseless assertions and reassertions of the personal self must be left behind forever. They belong as completely to the character of this world as does the desire to have a certain balance at the bank, or to retain the affections of a loved person. They are equally subject to the change which is characteristic of this world; indeed, they are even more so, for what the neophyte does by becoming a neophyte is simply to enter a forcing-house. Change, disillusionment, disheartenment, despair will crowd upon him by invitation; for his wish is to learn his lessons quickly. And as he turns these evils out they will probably be replaced by others worse than themselves — a passionate longing for separate life, for sensation, for the consciousness of growth in his own self, will rush in upon him and sweep over the frail barriers which he has raised. And no such barriers as asceticism, as renunciation, nothing indeed which is negative, will stand for a single moment against this powerful tide of feeling. The only barrier is built up of new desires. For it is perfectly useless for the neophyte to imagine he can get beyond the region of desires. He cannot; he is still a man, Nature must bring forth flowers while she is still Nature, and the human spirit would loose its hold on this form of existence altogether did it not continue to desire. The individual man cannot wrench himself instantly out of that life of which he is an essential part. He can only change his position in it. The man whose intellectual life dominates his animal life, changes his position; but he is still in the dominion of desire. The disciple who believes it possible to become selfless in a single effort, will find himself flung into a bottomless pit as the consequence of his rash endeavour. Seize upon a new order of desires, purer, wider, nobler; and so plant your foot upon the ladder firmly. It is only on the last and topmost rung of the ladder, at the very entrance upon Divine or Mahatmic life, that it is possible to hold fast to that which has neither substance or existence.

The first part of *Light on the Path* is like a chord in music; the notes have to be struck together though they must be touched separately. Study and seize hold of the new desires before you have thrust out the old ones; otherwise in the storm you will be lost. Man while he is man has substance and needs some step to stand on, some idea to cling to. But let it be the least possible. Learn as the acrobat learns, slowly and with care, to become more independent. Before you attempt to cast out the devil of ambition — the desire of something, however fine and elevated, outside of yourself — seize on the desire to find the light of the world within yourself. Before you attempt to cast out the desire of conscious life, learn to look to the unattainable or in other language to that which you know you can only reach in unconsciousness. In knowing that your aim is of this lofty character, that it will never bring conscious success, never bring comfort to you, that it will never carry you *in your own temporary personal self* to any haven of rest or place of agreeable activity, you cut away all the force and power of the desires of the lower astral nature. For what avail is it, when these facts have been once realized, to desire separateness, sensation or growth?

The armour of the warrior who rises to fight for you in the battle depicted in the second part of *Light on the Path*, is like the shirt of the happy man in the old story. The king was to be cured of all his ills by sleeping in this shirt; but when the one happy man in his kingdom was found, he was a beggar, without care, without anxiety — and shirtless. So with the divine warrior. None can take his armour and use it, for he has none. The king could never find happiness like that of the careless beggar. The man of the world, however fine and cultivated he may be, is hampered by a thousand thoughts and feelings which have to be cast aside before he can even stand on the threshold of occultism. And, be it observed, he is chiefly handicapped by the armour he wears, which isolates him. He has personal pride, personal respect. These things must die out as the personality recedes. The process described in the first part of *Light on the Path* is one which takes off that shell, or armour, and casts it aside forever. Then the warrior arises, armourless, defenceless, offenceless, identified with the afflicters and the afflicted, the angered and the one that angers; fighting not on any side, but for the Divine, the highest in all.

Mabel Collins (1851–1927) was a British Theosophist and author of over 40 books ranging from fiction to occult philosophy. Her best known books are *The Idyll of the White Lotus* (1884) and *Light on the Path* (1885), which she wrote under the guidance of Master Hilarion. She was the step-aunt of Basil Crump. When Blavatsky moved to England in 1887, she stayed at Collins's small cottage in Norwood, London. Until 1889, they both worked together on the monthly magazine *Lucifer* as editors. Mabel Collins was also noted for her advocacy of animal rights and her strong opposition to vivisection. In 1907, she founded the Incorporated Parliamentary Association for the Abolition of Vivisection.

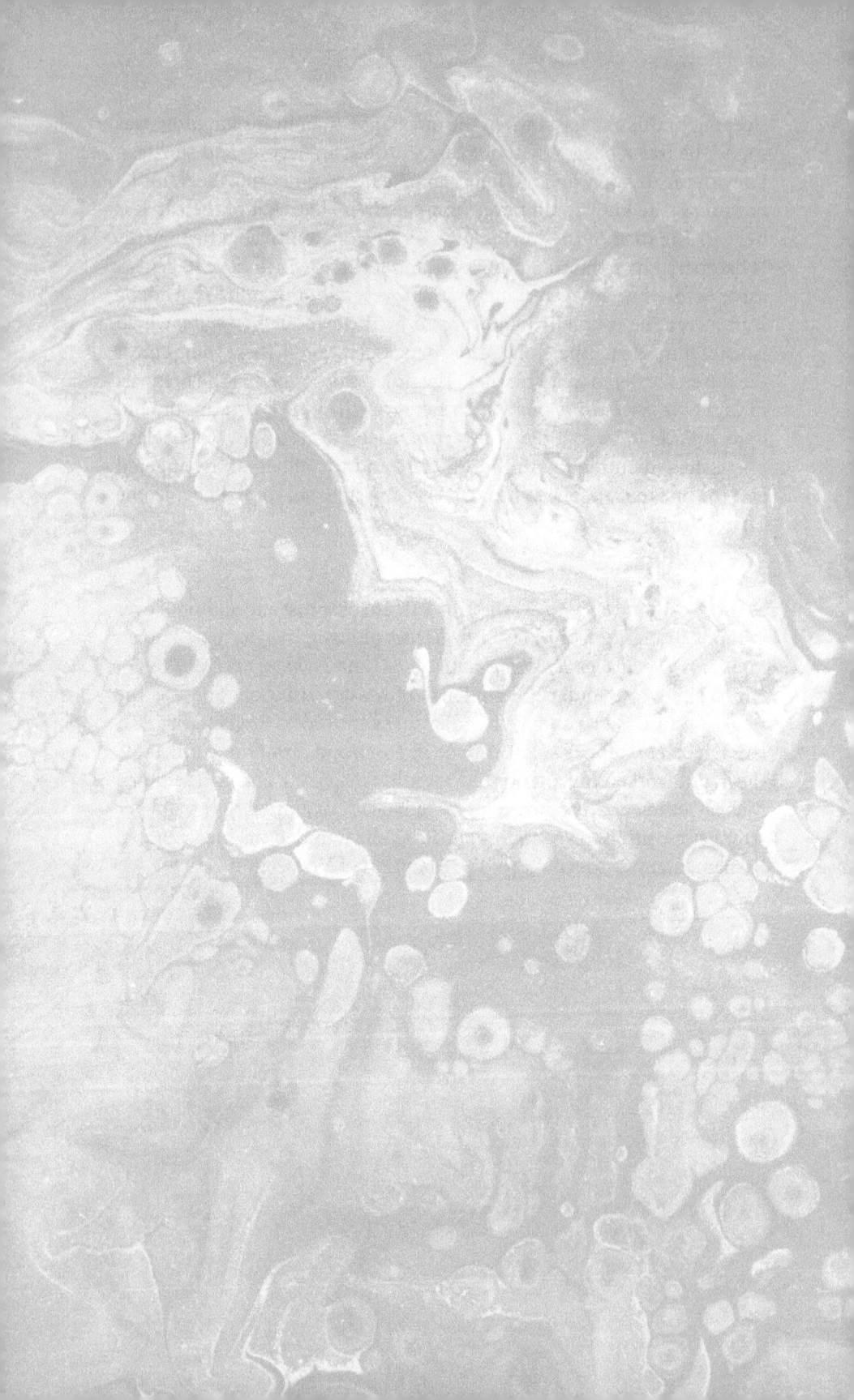

INSIGHTS FOR THE PATH

"The Kingdom of God is taken by *violence*," is a paraphrase from "The realm of divine knowledge is taken by force and perseverance," it does not descend to the chela; it is the disciple who has to ascend to it, and to penetrate its adamantine walls. In the East, the Guru and chela stand in the relation of the higher and the lower *manas* — one, yet forever separated, unless the lower *forces* itself upon the higher; it is not in the power of the latter to refuse or to accept. There is *no* "impertinence" to *asking*, but it is certainly useless if you have the right *to take*; and everyone has it, who has in him the power *to reach*.

H. P. Blavatsky

Look around you, my friend: see the "three poisons" raging within the heart of men — anger, greed, delusion, and the five obscurities — envy, passion, vacillation, sloth, and unbelief — ever preventing them seeing truth. They will never get rid of the pollution of their vain, wicked hearts, nor perceive the spiritual portion of themselves. Will you not try — for the sake of shortening the distance between us — to disentangle yourself from the net of life and death in which they are all caught, to cherish less — lust and desire? . . . I can come nearer to you, but you must draw me by a purified heart and a gradually developing will. Like the needle, the Adept follows his attractions. . . . A love of collective humanity is his increasing inspiration; and if any one individual should wish to divert his regards to himself, he must overpower the diffusive tendency by a stronger force.

K. H.

THE PATH OF HEROIC DEEDS IN EVERYDAY LIFE

by Helena Roerich

ONLY STRONG, aspiring souls who are capable of understanding the full seriousness and significance of the trials that confront them are accepted as disciples of secret knowledge. Yes, the Path of Heroic Deeds, the Path of Service is very, very hard. Those who choose this path must be prepared to undergo all manner of self-denial. Obstacles and difficulties increase as they progress along the path. True, they receive great knowledge, yet this knowledge brings them little joy in life, for they have no one to share it with, nowhere to apply it, because their responsibility increases in proportion to their knowledge. Besides, the knowledge itself will bring out in the people around them envy and betrayal. After all, the surrounding darkness is startling! The Path of Heroic Deeds is onerous and it cannot be made easier until humanity's consciousness receives the impulse necessary for it to shift into a new stage. There are difficult transitions along the way when the disciple is left to their own devices, when they must independently bring to bear all their resourcefulness, and all their skills, when even the Master's Voice is temporarily silent. However, true disciples carry joy and aspiration in their hearts, for they know that this is just a new step on the path. In them abides the joy of the awareness of fulfilling their duty and, with all the strength of their spirit, they strive to accomplish the task entrusted to them even more perfectly. Truly, in this is all their joy.

The Path of Service is arduous, but those who have received the opportunity to carry out heroic deeds in life will never give up this crown, not for all the treasures in the world, for nothing can compare to the spiritual marvels that become the lot of such selfless devotees. And the richer their previous accumulations, the brighter and more beautiful this lot. Of course, there are many moths and butterflies around the Teaching, yet the benefit they receive is proportional to the brevity of their fluttering. While speaking to you, I know that I am addressing mature minds that are not afraid of difficulties. Indeed, as the experienced fighter experiences the heart's thrill and rapture before a new battle, so may your hearts become enkindled with the new flame of the Light of Abhidharma before the opportunity for new victories and conquests.

Who is ready for a heroic deed? Only absolute dedication of self is true and valuable, and can lead you to the goal.

Helena Roerich (1879–1955) was a Russian philosopher and the author of the *Agni Yoga* series, recorded during the period 1920 to 1947 in collaboration with Master Morya. Aimed initially at the mind, this Fiery Teaching paves the way to the heart and points to Infinity in the Cosmos and in Life. Helena Roerich's Heroic Deed consisted not only in delivering the Teaching to humanity but also in offering herself up for the Fiery Experience — the influence of cosmic energies upon an individual incarnated in physical form. This unique Experiment helped the Teachers of Humanity find ways of minimizing the sufferings of the world in the present day, as, from 1999 onwards, these cosmic energies began to affect all humanity as well as the planet Earth. By strictly following the canons and principles of the secret science, *Gupta-Vidya*, Roerich succeeded in mastering the cosmic Fire and reached the highest condition of spirituality that it is possible for one to achieve on Earth.

AT THE FEET OF THE MASTER
by Jiddu Krishnamurti

To those who knock

From the unreal lead me to the Real.
From darkness lead me to Light.
From death lead me to Immortality.

Preface

These are not my words; they are the words of the Master who taught me. Without Him I could have done nothing, but through His help I have set my feet upon the Path. You also desire to enter the same Path, so the words which He spoke to me will help you also, if you will obey them. It is not enough to say that they are true and beautiful; a man who wishes to succeed must do exactly what is said. To look at food and say that it is good will not satisfy a starving man; he must put forth his hand and eat. So to hear the Master's words is not enough, you must do what He says, attending to every word, taking every hint. If a hint is not taken, if a word is missed, it is lost forever; for He does not speak twice.

Four qualifications there are for this pathway:
- Discrimination

- Desirelessness
- Good conduct
- Love

What the Master has said to me on each of these I shall try to tell you.

I

The first of these qualifications is discrimination; and this is usually taken as the discrimination between the real and the unreal which leads men to enter the Path. It is this, but it is also much more; and it is to be practised, not only at the beginning of the Path, but at every step of it every day until the end. You enter the Path because you have learnt that on it alone can be found those things which are worth gaining. Men who do not know, work to gain wealth and power, but these are at most for one life only, and therefore unreal. There are greater things than these — things which are real and lasting; when you have once seen these, you desire those others no more.

In all the world there are only two kinds of people — those who know, and those who do not know; and this knowledge is the thing which matters. What religion a man holds, to what race he belongs — these things are not important; the really important thing is this knowledge — the knowledge of God's plan for men. For God has a plan, and that plan is evolution. When once a man has seen that and really knows it, he cannot help working for it and making himself one with it, because it is so glorious, so beautiful. So, because he knows, he is on God's side, standing for good and resisting evil, working for evolution and not for selfishness.

If he is on God's side he is one of us, and it does not matter in the least whether he calls himself a Hindu or a Buddhist, a Christian or a Muslim, whether he is an Indian or an English, a Chinese or a Russian. Those who are on His side know why they are here and what they should do, and they are trying to do it; all the others do not yet know what they should do, and so they often act foolishly, and try to invent ways for themselves which they think will be pleasant for themselves, not understanding that all are one, and that therefore only what the One wills can ever be really pleasant for anyone. They are following the unreal instead of the real. Until they learn to distinguish between these two, they have not ranged themselves on God's side, and so this discrimination is the first step.

But even when the choice is made, you must still remember that of the real and the unreal there are many varieties; and discrimination must still be made between the right and the wrong, the important and the unimportant, the useful and the useless, the true and the false, the selfish and the unselfish.

Between the right and wrong it should not be difficult to choose, for those who wish to follow the Master have already decided to take the right at all costs. But the body and the man are two, and the man's will is not always what the body wishes. When your body wishes something, stop and think whether you really wish it. For you are God, and you will only what God wills; but you must dig deep down into yourself to find the God within you, and listen to His voice, which is *your* voice. Do not mistake your bodies for yourself — neither the physical body, nor the astral, nor the mental. Each one of them will pretend to be the Self, in order to gain what it wants. But you must know them all, and know yourself as their master.

When there is work that must be done, the physical body wants to rest, to go out walking, to eat and drink; and the man who does not know says to himself: "*I* want to do these things, and I must do them." But the man who knows says: "This that wants is *not I*, and it must wait awhile." Often when there is an opportunity to help someone, the body feels: "How much trouble it will be for me; let someone else do it." But the man replies to his body: "You shall not hinder me in doing good work."

The body is your animal — the horse upon which you ride. Therefore you must treat it well, and take good care of it; you must not overwork it, you must feed it properly on pure food and drink only, and keep it strictly clean always, even from the minutest speck of dirt. For without a perfectly clean and healthy body you cannot do the arduous work of preparation, you cannot bear its ceaseless strain. But it must always be you who control that body, not it that controls you.

The astral body has *its* desires — dozens of them; it wants you to be angry, to say sharp words, to feel jealous, to be greedy for money, to envy other people their possessions, to yield yourself to depression. All these things it wants, and many more, not because it wishes to harm you, but because it likes violent vibrations, and likes to change them constantly. But *you* want none of these things, and therefore you must discriminate between your wants and your body's.

Your mental body wishes to think itself proudly separate, to think much of itself and little of others. Even when you have turned it away from worldly things, it still tries to calculate for self, to make you think of your own progress, instead of thinking of the Master's work and of helping others. When you meditate, it will try to make you think of the many different things which *it* wants instead of the one thing which *you* want. You are not this mind, but it is yours to use; so here again discrimination is necessary. You must watch unceasingly, or you will fail.

Between right and wrong, occultism knows no compromise. At whatever apparent cost, that which is right you must do, that which is wrong you must not do, no matter what the ignorant may think or say. You must study deeply the hidden laws of Nature, and when you know them arrange your life according to them, using always reason and common sense.

You must discriminate between the important and the unimportant. Firm as a rock where right and wrong are concerned, yield always to others in things which do not matter. For you must be always gentle and kindly, reasonable and accommodating, leaving to others the same full liberty which you need for yourself.

Try to see what is worth doing, and remember that you must not judge by the size of the thing. A small thing which is directly useful in the Master's work is far better worth doing than a large thing which the world would call good. You must distinguish not only the useful from the useless, but the more useful from the less useful. To feed the poor is a good and noble and useful work; yet to feed their souls is nobler and more useful than to feed their bodies. Any rich man can feed the body, but only those who know can feed the soul. If you know, it is your duty to help others to know.

However wise you may be already, on this Path you have much to learn; so much that here also there must be discrimination, and you must think carefully what is worth learning. All knowledge is useful, and one day you will have all knowledge; but while you have only part, take care that it is the most useful part. God is Wisdom as well as Love; and the more wisdom you have the more you can manifest of Him. Study then, but study first that which will most help you to help others. Work patiently at your studies, not that men may think you wise, not even that you may have the happiness of being wise, but because only the wise man can be wisely helpful. However much you wish to help, if you are ignorant you may do more harm than good.

You must distinguish between truth and falsehood; you must learn to be true all through, in thought and word and deed.

In thought first; and that is not easy, for there are in the world many untrue thoughts, many foolish superstitions, and no one who is enslaved by them can make progress. Therefore you must not hold a thought just because many other people hold it, nor because it has been believed for centuries, nor because it is written in some book which men think sacred; you must think of the matter for yourself, and judge for yourself whether it is reasonable. Remember that though a thousand men agree upon a subject, if they know nothing about that subject their opinion is of no value. He who would walk upon the Path must learn to think for himself, for superstition is one of the greatest evils in the world, one of the fetters from which you must utterly free yourself.

Your thought about others must be true; you must not think of them what you do not know. Do not suppose that they are always thinking of you. If a man does something which you think will harm you, or says something which you think applies to you, do not think at once: "He meant to injure me." Most probably he never thought of you at all, for each soul has its own troubles and its thoughts turn chiefly around itself. If a man speak angrily to you, do not think: "He hates me, he wishes to wound me." Probably someone or something else has made him angry, and because he happens to meet you he turns his anger upon you. He is acting foolishly, for all anger is foolish, but you must not therefore think untruly of him.

When you become a pupil of the Master, you may always try the truth of your thought by laying it beside His. For the pupil is one with his Master, and he needs only to put back his thought into the Master's thought to see at once whether it agrees. If it does not, it is wrong, and he changes it instantly, for the Master's thought is perfect, because He knows all. Those who are not yet accepted by Him cannot do quite this; but they may greatly help themselves by stopping often to think: "What would the Master think about this? What would the Master say or do under these circumstances?" For you must never do or say or think what you cannot imagine the Master as doing or saying or thinking.

You must be true in speech too — accurate and without exaggeration. Never attribute motives to another; only his Master knows his thoughts, and he may be acting from reasons which have never entered your mind. If you hear a story against anyone, do not repeat it; it may not be true, and even if it is, it is kinder to say nothing. Think well before speaking, lest you should fall into inaccuracy.

Be true in action; never pretend to be other than you are, for all pretence is a hindrance to the pure light of truth, which should shine through you as sunlight shines through clear glass.

You must discriminate between the selfish and the unselfish. For selfishness has many forms, and when you think you have finally killed it in one of them, it arises in another as strongly as ever. But by degrees you will become so full of thought for the helping of others that there will be no room, no time, for any thought about yourself.

You must discriminate in yet another way. Learn to distinguish the God in everyone and everything, no matter how evil he or it may appear on the surface. You can help your brother through that which you have in common with him, and that is the Divine Life; learn how to arouse that in him, learn how to appeal to that in him; so shall you save your brother from wrong.

II

There are many for whom the qualification of desirelessness is a difficult one, for they feel that they *are* their desires — that if their distinctive desires, their likings and dislikings, are taken away from them, there will be no self left. But these are only they who have not seen the Master; in the light of His holy Presence all desire dies, but the desire to be like Him. Yet before you have the happiness of meeting Him face to face, you may attain desirelessness if you will. Discrimination has already shown you that the things which most men desire, such as wealth and power, are not worth having; when this is really felt, not merely said, all desire for them ceases.

Thus far all is simple; it needs only that you should understand. But there are some who forsake the pursuit of earthly aims only in order to gain heaven, or to attain personal liberation from rebirth; into this error you must not fall. If you have forgotten self altogether, you cannot be thinking when that self should be set free, or what kind of heaven it shall have. Remember that *all* selfish desire binds, however high may be its object, and until you have got rid of it you are not wholly free to devote yourself to the work of the Master.

When all desires for self are gone, there may still be a desire to see the result of your work. If you help anybody, you want to *see* how much you have helped him; perhaps even you want him to see it too, and to be grateful. But this is still desire, and also want of trust. When you pour out your strength to help, there must be a result, whether you can see it or not; if you know the Law you know this must be so. So you must do right for the sake of the right, not in the hope of reward; you must work for the sake of the work, not in the hope of seeing the result; you must give yourself to the service of the world because you love it, and cannot help giving yourself to it.

Have no desire for psychic powers; they will come when the Master knows that it is best for you to have them. To force them too soon often brings in its train much trouble; often their possessor is misled by deceitful nature-spirits, or becomes conceited and thinks he cannot make a mistake; and in any case the time and strength that it takes to gain them might be spent in work for others. They will come in the course of development — they *must* come; and if the Master sees that it would be useful for you to have them sooner, He will tell you how to unfold them safely. Until then, you are better without them.

You must guard, too, against certain small desires which are common in daily life. Never wish to shine, or to appear clever; have no desire to speak. It is well to speak little; better still to say nothing, unless you are quite sure that what you wish to say is true, kind, and helpful. Before speaking think carefully whether what you are going to say has those three qualities; if it has not, do not say it.

It is well to get used even now to thinking carefully before speaking; for when you reach Initiation you must watch every word, lest you should tell what must not be told. Much common talk is unnecessary and foolish; when it is gossip, it is wicked. So be accustomed to listen rather than to talk; do not offer opinions unless directly asked for them. One statement of the qualifications gives them thus: to know, to dare, to will, and to be silent; and the last of the four is the hardest of them all.

Another common desire which you must sternly repress is the wish to meddle in other men's business. What another man does or says or believes is no affair of yours, and you must learn to let him absolutely alone. He has full right to free thought and speech and action, so long as he does not interfere with anyone else. You yourself claim the freedom to do what you think proper; you must allow the same freedom to him, and when he exercises it you have no right to talk about him.

If you think he is doing wrong, and you can contrive an opportunity of privately and very politely telling him why you think so, it is possible that you may convince him; but there are many cases in which even that would be an improper interference. On no account must you go and gossip to some third person about the matter, for that is an extremely wicked action.

If you see a case of cruelty to a child or an animal, it is your duty to interfere. If you see anyone breaking the law of the country, you should inform the authorities. If you are placed in charge of another person in order to teach him, it may become your duty gently to tell him of his faults. Except in such cases, mind your own business, and learn the virtue of silence.

III

The six points of conduct which are specially required are given by the Master as:
1. Self-control as to the mind.
2. Self-control in action.
3. Tolerance.
4. Cheerfulness.
5. One-pointedness.
6. Confidence.

I know some of these are often translated differently, as are the names of the qualifications; but in all cases I am using the names which the Master Himself employed when explaining them to me.

1. *Self-control as to the mind.* The qualification of desirelessness shows that the astral body must be controlled; this shows the same thing as to the mental body. It means control of temper, so that you may feel no anger or impatience; of the mind itself, so that the thought may always be calm and unruffled; and (through the mind) of the nerves, so that they may be as little irritable as possible. This last is difficult, because when you try to prepare yourself for the Path, you cannot help making your body more sensitive, so that its nerves are easily disturbed by a sound or a shock, and feel any pressure acutely; but you must do your best.

The calm mind means also courage, so that you may face without fear the trials and difficulties of the Path; it means also steadiness, so that you may make light of the troubles which come into every one's life, and avoid the incessant worry over little things in which many people spend most of their time. The Master teaches that it does not matter in the least what happens to a man from the outside: sorrows, troubles, sicknesses, losses — all these must be as nothing to him, and must not be allowed to affect the calmness of his mind. They are the result of past actions, and when they come you must bear them cheerfully, remembering that all evil is transitory, and that your duty is to remain always joyous and serene. They belong to your previous lives, not to this; you cannot alter them, so it is useless to trouble about them. Think rather of what you are doing now, which will make the events of your next life, for that you *can* alter.

Never allow yourself to feel sad or depressed. Depression is wrong, because it infects others and makes their lives harder, which you have no right to do. Therefore if ever it comes to you, throw it off at once.

In yet another way you must control your thought; you must not let it wander. Whatever you are doing, fix your thought upon it, that it may be perfectly done; do not let your mind be idle, but keep good thoughts always in the background of it, ready to come forward the moment it is free.

Use your thought-power every day for good purposes; be a force in the direction of evolution. Think each day of someone whom you know to be in sorrow, or suffering, or in need of help, and pour out loving thought upon him.

Hold back your mind from pride, for pride comes only from ignorance. The man who does not know thinks that he is great, that he has done this or that great thing; the wise man knows that only God is great, that all good work is done by God alone.

2. *Self-control in action.* If your thought is what it should be, you will have little trouble with your action. Yet remember that, to be useful to mankind, thought must result in action. There must be no laziness,

but constant activity in good work. But it must be your *own* duty that you do — not another man's, unless with his permission and by way of helping him. Leave every man to do his own work in his own way; be always ready to offer help where it is needed, but *never* interfere. For many people the most difficult thing in the world to learn is to mind their own business; but that is exactly what you must do.

Because you try to take up higher work, you must not forget your ordinary duties, for until they are done you are not free for other service. You should undertake no new worldly duties; but those which you have already taken upon you, you must perfectly fulfil — all clear and reasonable duties which you yourself recognize, that is, not imaginary duties which others try to impose upon you. If you are to be His, you must do ordinary work better than others, not worse; because you must do that also for His sake.

3. *Tolerance.* You must feel perfect tolerance for all, and a hearty interest in the beliefs of those of another religion, just as much as in your own. For their religion is a path to the highest, just as yours is. And to help all, you must understand all.

But in order to gain this perfect tolerance, you must yourself first be free from bigotry and superstition. You must learn that no ceremonies are necessary; else you will think yourself somehow better than those who do not perform them. Yet you must not condemn others who still cling to ceremonies. Let them do as they will; only they must not interfere with you who know the truth — they must not try to force upon you that which you have outgrown. Make allowance for everything; be kindly towards everything.

Now that your eyes are opened, some of your old beliefs, your old ceremonies, may seem to you absurd; perhaps, indeed, they really are so. Yet though you can no longer take part in them, respect them for the sake of those good souls to whom they are still important. They have their place, they have their use; they are like those double lines which guided you as a child to write straight and evenly, until you learnt to write far better and more freely without them. There was a time when you needed them; but now that time is past.

A great Teacher once wrote: "When I was a child, I spake as a child, I understood as a child, I thought as a child; but when I became a man I put away childish things."[1] Yet he who has forgotten his childhood and lost sympathy with the children is not the man who can teach them or help them. So look kindly, gently, tolerantly upon all; but upon all alike, Buddhist or Hindu, Jain or Jew, Christian or Muslim.

---

[1] 1 Corinthians 13:11.

4. *Cheerfulness.* You must bear your karma cheerfully, whatever it may be, taking it as an honour that suffering comes to you, because it shows that the Lords of Karma think you worth helping. However hard it is, be thankful that it is no worse. Remember that you are of but little use to the Master until your evil karma is worked out, and you are free. By offering yourself to Him, you have asked that your karma may be hurried, and so now in one or two lives you work through what otherwise might have been spread over a hundred. But in order to make the best out of it, you must bear it cheerfully, gladly.

Yet another point. You must give up all feeling of possession. Karma may take from you the things which you like best — even the people whom you love most. Even then you must be cheerful — ready to part with anything and everything. Often the Master needs to pour out His strength upon others through His servant; He cannot do that if the servant yields to depression. So cheerfulness must be the rule.

5. *One-pointedness.* The one thing that you must set before you is to do the Master's work. Whatever else may come in your way to do, that at least you must never forget. Yet nothing else *can* come in your way, for all helpful, unselfish work is the Master's work, and you must do it for His sake. And you must give all your attention to each piece as you do it, so that it may be your very best. The same Teacher also wrote: "Whatsoever ye do, do it *heartily*, as to the Lord, and not unto men."[2] Think how you would do a piece of work if you knew that the Master was coming at once to look at it; just in that way you must do all your work. Those who know most will most know all that that verse means. And there is another like it, much older: "Whatsoever thy hand findeth to do, do it with thy might."[3]

One-pointedness means, too, that nothing shall ever turn you, even for a moment, from the Path upon which you have entered. No temptations, no worldly pleasures, no worldly affections even, must ever draw you aside. For you yourself must become one with the Path; it must be so much part of your nature that you follow it without needing to think of it, and cannot turn aside. You, the monad, have decided it; to break away from it would be to break away from yourself.

6. *Confidence.* You must trust your Master; you must trust yourself. If you have seen the Master, you will trust Him to the uttermost, through many lives and deaths. If you have not yet seen Him, you must still try to realize Him and trust Him, because if you do not, even He cannot help you. Unless there is perfect trust, there cannot be the perfect flow of love and power.

---

[2] Colossians 3:23.
[3] Ecclesiastes 9:10.

You must trust yourself. You say you know yourself too well? If you feel so, you do *not* know yourself; you know only the weak outer husk, which has fallen often into the mire. But *you* — the real you — you are a spark of God's own fire, and God, who is Almighty, is in you, and because of that there is nothing that you cannot do if you will. Say to yourself: "What man has done, man can do. I am a man, yet also God in man; I can do this thing, and I will." For your will must be like tempered steel, if you would tread the Path.

IV

Of all the qualifications, Love is the most important, for if it is strong enough in a man, it forces him to acquire all the rest, and all the rest without it would never be sufficient. Often it is translated as an intense desire for liberation from the round of births and deaths, and for union with God. But to put it in that way sounds selfish, and gives only part of the meaning. It is not so much desire as *will*, resolve, determination. To produce its result, this resolve must fill your whole nature, so as to leave no room for any other feeling. It is indeed the will to be one with God, not in order that you may escape from weariness and suffering, but in order that because of your deep love for Him you may act with Him and as He does. Because He is Love, you, if you would become one with Him, must be filled with perfect unselfishness and love also.

In daily life this means two things: first, that you shall be careful to do no hurt to any living thing; second, that you shall always be watching for an opportunity to help.

First, to do no hurt. Three sins there are which work more harm than all else in the world — gossip, cruelty, and superstition — because they are sins against Love. Against these three the man who would fill his heart with the love of God must watch ceaselessly.

See what gossip does. It begins with evil thought, and that in itself is a crime. For in everyone and in everything there is good; in everyone and in everything there is evil. Either of these we can strengthen by thinking of it, and in this way we can help or hinder evolution; we can do the will of the Logos or we can resist Him. If you think of the evil in another, you are doing at the same time three wicked things:

1. You are filling your neighbourhood with evil thought instead of with good thought, and so you are adding to the sorrow of the world.

2. If there is in that man the evil which you think, you are strengthening it and feeding it; and so you are making your brother worse instead of better. But generally the evil is not there, and you have only fancied it; and then your wicked thought tempts your brother to do wrong, for if he is not yet perfect you may make him that which you have thought him.

3. You fill your own mind with evil thoughts instead of good; and so you hinder your own growth, and make yourself, for those who can see, an ugly and painful object instead of a beautiful and lovable one.

Not content with having done all this harm to himself and to his victim, the gossip tries with all his might to make other men partners in his crime. Eagerly he tells his wicked tale to them, hoping that they will believe it; and then they join with him in pouring evil thought upon the poor sufferer. And this goes on day after day, and is done not by one man but by thousands. Do you begin to see how base, how terrible a sin this is? You must avoid it altogether. Never speak ill of anyone; refuse to listen when anyone else speaks ill of another, but gently say: "Perhaps this is not true, and even if it is, it is kinder not to speak of it."

Then as to cruelty. This is of two kinds, intentional and unintentional. Intentional cruelty is purposely to give pain to another living being; and that is the greatest of all sins — the work of a devil rather than a man. You would say that no man could do such a thing; but men have done it often, and are daily doing it now. The inquisitors did it; many religious people did it in the name of their religion. Vivisectors do it; many schoolmasters do it habitually. All these people try to excuse their brutality by saying that it is the custom; but a crime does not cease to be a crime because many commit it. Karma takes no account of custom; and the karma of cruelty is the most terrible of all. In India at least there can be no excuse for such customs, for the duty of harmlessness is well-known to all. The fate of the cruel must fall also upon all who go out intentionally to kill God's creatures, and call it "sport."

Such things as these you would not do, I know; and for the sake of the love of God, when opportunity offers, you will speak clearly against them. But there is a cruelty in speech as well as in act; and a man who says a word with the intention to wound another is guilty of this crime. That, too, you would not do; but sometimes a careless word does as much harm as a malicious one. So you must be on your guard against unintentional cruelty.

It comes usually from thoughtlessness. A man is so filled with greed and avarice that he never even thinks of the suffering which he causes to others by paying too little, or by half-starving his wife and children. Another thinks only of his own lust, and cares little how many souls and bodies he ruins in satisfying it. Just to save himself a few minutes' trouble, a man does not pay his workmen on the proper day, thinking nothing of the difficulties he brings upon them. So much suffering is caused just by carelessness — by forgetting to think how an action will affect others. But karma never forgets, and it takes no account of the fact that men forget. If you wish to enter the Path, you must think of the consequences of what you do, lest you should be guilty of thoughtless cruelty.

Superstition is another mighty evil, and has caused much terrible cruelty. The man who is a slave to it despises others who are wiser, tries to force them to do as he does. Think of the awful slaughter produced by the superstition that animals should be sacrificed, and by the still more cruel superstition that man needs flesh for food. Think of the treatment which superstition has meted out to the depressed classes in our beloved India, and see in that how this evil quality can breed heartless cruelty even among those who know the duty of brotherhood. Many crimes have men committed in the name of the God of Love, moved by this nightmare of superstition; be very careful therefore that no slightest trace of it remains in you.

These three great crimes you must avoid, for they are fatal to all progress, because they sin against Love. But not only must you thus refrain from evil; you must be active in doing good. You must be so filled with the intense desire of service that you are ever on the watch to render it to all around you — not to man alone, but even to animals and plants. You must render it in small things every day, that the habit may be formed, so that you may not miss the rare opportunity when the great thing offers itself to be done. For if you yearn to be one with God, it is not for your own sake; it is that you may be a channel through which His Love may flow to reach your fellow men.

He who is on the Path exists not for himself, but for others; he has forgotten himself, in order that he may serve them. He is as a pen in the hand of God, through which His thought may flow, and find for itself an expression down here, which without a pen it could not have. Yet at the same time he is also a living plume of fire, raying out upon the world the Divine Love which fills his heart.

The wisdom which enables you to help, the will which directs the wisdom, the love which inspires the will — these are your qualifications. Will, Wisdom, and Love are the three aspects of the Logos; and you, who wish to enrol yourselves to serve Him, must show forth these aspects in the world.

> Waiting the word of the Master,
> Watching the Hidden Light;
> Listening to catch His orders
> In the very midst of the fight;
>
> Seeing His slightest signal
> Across the heads of the throng;
> Hearing His faintest whisper
> Above earth's loudest song.

Jiddu Krishnamurti (1895-1986) was an Indian philosopher, writer, and speaker, known for his teachings on freedom, the nature of mind, meditation, human relationships, and self-awareness. His book *At the Feet of the Master* was published in 1910 under the name Alcyone, which is also the name of the brightest star in the Pleiades constellation. His other books include *The First and Last Freedom* (1954) and *Freedom from the Known* (1969).

LOVE WITH AN OBJECT

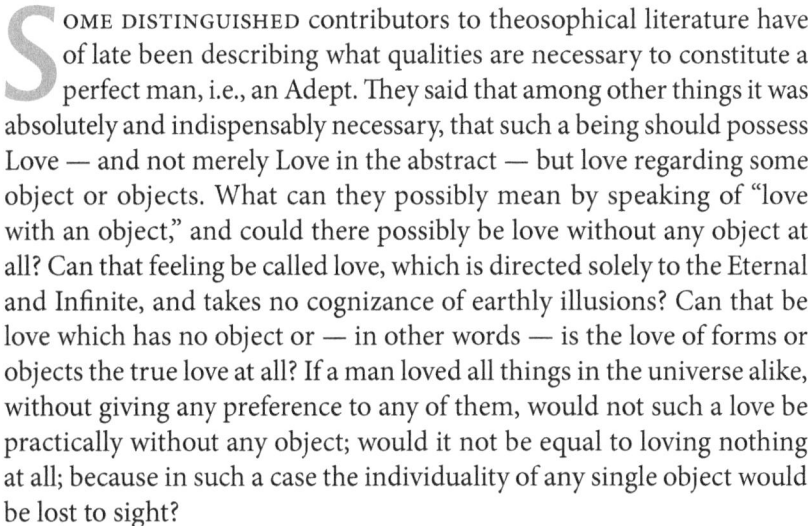

SOME DISTINGUISHED contributors to theosophical literature have of late been describing what qualities are necessary to constitute a perfect man, i.e., an Adept. They said that among other things it was absolutely and indispensably necessary, that such a being should possess Love — and not merely Love in the abstract — but love regarding some object or objects. What can they possibly mean by speaking of "love with an object," and could there possibly be love without any object at all? Can that feeling be called love, which is directed solely to the Eternal and Infinite, and takes no cognizance of earthly illusions? Can that be love which has no object or — in other words — is the love of forms or objects the true love at all? If a man loved all things in the universe alike, without giving any preference to any of them, would not such a love be practically without any object; would it not be equal to loving nothing at all; because in such a case the individuality of any single object would be lost to sight?

A love which is directed towards all things alike, a universal love, is beyond the conception of the mortal mind, and yet this kind of love, which bestows no favours upon any one thing, seems to be that eternal love, which is recommended by all the sacred books of the East and the West; because as soon as we begin to love one thing or one being more than another, we not only detract from the rest an amount of love which the rest may rightfully claim; but we also become attached to the object of our love, a fate against which we are seriously warned in various pages of these books.

The Bhagavad Gita teaches that we should not love or hate any object of sense whatsoever, nor be attached to any object or thing, but renounce all projects and fix our thoughts solely on It, the Eternal, which is no-thing and no object of cognition for us, but whose presence can be only subjectively experienced by, and within ourselves. It says: "He is esteemed, who is equal-minded to companions, friends, enemies, strangers, neutrals, to aliens and kindred, yea to good and evil men";[1] and further on it says: "He whose soul is united by devotion, seeing the same in all around, sees the soul in everything and everything in the soul. He who sees Me (Brahma) everywhere and everything in Me, him I forsake not and he forsakes not Me.... He who sees the same in everything — Arjuna! — whether it be pleasant or grievous, from the self-resemblance, is deemed to be a most excellent yogin."[2]

On almost every page of the Bhagavad Gita we are instructed only to direct our love to that which is eternal in every form, and let the form itself be a matter of secondary consideration. "He must be regarded as a steadfast renouncer, who neither hates nor desires.... In a learned and modest Brahmin, in a cow, in an elephant, in a dog, and a *shvapaka*; they who have knowledge see the same thing.... Let no man rejoice in attaining what is pleasant, nor grieve in attaining what is unpleasant; being fixed in mind, untroubled, knowing Brahma and abiding in Brahma.... He who is happy in himself, pleased with himself, who finds also light in himself, this yogin, one with Brahma, finds Nirvana in Him."[3]

The great Hermes Trismegistus teaches the same identical doctrine; for he says: "Rise and embrace me with thy whole being, and I will teach thee whatsoever thou desirest to know." The Bible also tells us that "God is Love,"[4] and that we should love Him with all our heart, with all our soul, and with all our mind,[5] and while it teaches that we should love nothing else but God,[6] who is All in All,[7] yet it affirms, that this God is omnipresent, eternal, and incomprehensible to the finite understanding of mortals.[8] It teaches this love to be the most important of all possessions, without which all other possessions are useless,[9] and yet this God, whom we are to love, is not an "object,"[10] but everywhere. He is in us and we in Him.[11] We are to leave all objects of sense and follow Him alone,[12] although we have no means of intellectually knowing or perceiving Him, the great Unknown, for whose sake we are to give up house and brethren, sisters, father, mother, wife, children, and lands.[13]

What can all this mean, but that love itself is the legitimate object of love? It is a divine, eternal, and infinite power, a light, which reflects itself in every object while it seeks not the object, but merely its own reflection

---

[1] Bhagavad Gita 6:9.
[2] Bhagavad Gita 6:29–30, 32.
[3] Bhagavad Gita 5:3, 18, 20, 24.
[4] 1 John 4:8.
[5] Matthew 22:37.
[6] Matthew 10:37.
[7] Ephesians 1:23.
[8] 1 Timothy 6:16.
[9] 1 Corinthians 13:2.
[10] 1 John 1:5.
[11] 1 John 4:13.
[12] Luke 14:33.
[13] Mark 10:29.

therein. It is an indestructible fire and the brighter it burns, the stronger will be the light and the clearer will its own image appear. Love falls in love with nothing but its own self, it is free from all other attractions. A love which becomes attached to objects of sense, ceases to be free, ceases to be love, and becomes mere desire. Pure and eternal love asks for nothing, but gives freely to all who are willing to take. Earthly love is attracted to persons and things, but Divine spiritual love seeks only that which is divine in everything, and this can be nothing else but love, for love is the supreme power of all. It holds together the worlds in space, it clothes the earth in bright and beautiful colours, it guides the instincts of animals and links together the hearts of human beings. Acting upon the lower planes of existence it causes terrestrial things to cling to each other with fond embrace; but love on the spiritual plane is free. Spiritual love is a goddess, who continually sacrifices herself for herself and who accepts no other sacrifice but her own self, giving for whatever she may receive, herself in return. Therefore the Bhagavad Gita says: "Nourish ye the gods by this and let the gods nourish you. Thus nourishing each other ye shall obtain the highest good";[14] and the Bible says: "To him who has still, more shall be given, and from him who has not, even what he has shall be taken away."[15]

Love is a universal power and therefore immortal, it can never die. We cannot believe that even the smallest particle of love ever died, only the instruments through which it becomes manifest change their form; nor will it ever be born, for it exists from eternity, only the bodies into which it shines are born and die and are born again. A Love which is not manifest is non-existent for us, to come into existence means to become manifest. How then could we possibly imagine a human being possessed of a love which never becomes manifest; how can we possibly conceive of a light which never shines and of a fire which does not give any heat?

But "as the sun shines upon the lands of the just and the unjust, and as the rain descends upon the acres of the evil-minded as well as upon those of the good";[16] likewise divine love manifesting itself in a perfect man is distributed alike to every one without favour or partiality. Wherever a good and perfect human being exists, there is divine love manifest; and the degree of man's perfection will depend on the degree of his capacity to serve as an instrument for the manifestation of divine love. The more perfect he is, the more will his love descend upon and penetrate all who come within his divine influence. To ask favours of God is to conceive of Him as an imperfect being, whose love is not free, but

---

[14] Bhagavad Gita 3:11.
[15] Luke 19:26.
[16] Matthew 5:45.

subject to the guidance of, and preference to, mortals. To expect favours of a Mahatma is to conceive him as an *imperfect* man.

True, "prayer," i.e., the elevation and aspiration of the soul "in spirit and in truth,"[1] is useful, not because it will persuade the light to come nearer to us, but because it will assist us to open our eyes for the purpose of seeing the light that was already there. Let those who desire to come into contact with the Adepts enter their sphere by following their doctrines; seeking for love, but not for an object of love, and when they have found the former, they will find a superabundance of the latter throughout the whole extent of the unlimited universe; they will find it in everything that exists, for love is the foundation of all existence and without love nothing can possibly continue to exist.

Love — divine love — is the source of life, of light, and happiness. It is the creative principle in the Macrocosm and in the microcosm of man. It is Venus, the mother of all the gods, because from her alone originates Will and Imagination and all the other powers by which the universe was evolved. It is the germ of divinity which exists in the heart of man, and which may develop into a life-giving sun, illuminating the mind and sending its rays to the centre of the universe; for it originates from that centre and to that centre it will ultimately return. It is a divine messenger, who carries Light from Heaven down to the Earth and returns again to Heaven loaded with sacrificial gifts.

It is worshipped by all, some adore it in one form and some in another, but many perceive only the form and do not perceive the divine spirit. Nevertheless the spirit alone is real, the form is an illusion. Love can exist without form, but no form can exist without love. It is pure Spirit, but if its light is reflected in matter, it creates desire and desire is the producer of forms. Thus the visible world of perishable things is created. "But above this visible Nature there exists another, unseen and eternal, which, when all created things perish, does not perish," and "from which they who attain to it never return."[2] This is the supreme abode of Love without any object, unmanifested and imperishable, for there no object exists. There love is united to love, enjoying supreme and eternal happiness within her own self and that peace, of which the mortal mind, captivated by the illusion of form, cannot conceive. Non-existent for us, and yet existing in that Supreme *Be-ness*, in which all things dwell, by which the universe has been spread out, and which may be attained to by an exclusive devotion.

Emanuel

---

[1] John 4:24.
[2] Bhagavad Gita 8:20–21.

THE HEART

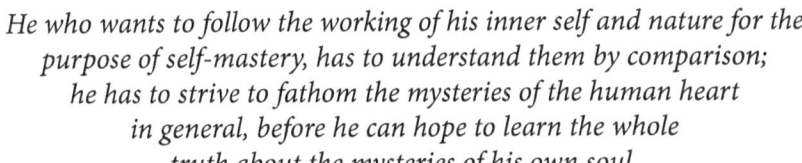

*He who wants to follow the working of his inner self and nature for the
purpose of self-mastery, has to understand them by comparison;
he has to strive to fathom the mysteries of the human heart
in general, before he can hope to learn the whole
truth about the mysteries of his own soul.*

THE CONSCIOUSNESS which is merely the animal consciousness is made up of the consciousness of all the cells in the body, except those of the Heart. For the Heart is the organ of the spiritual consciousness; it corresponds indeed to *prana*, but only because *prana* and the *auric envelope* are essentially the same, and because again as *jiva* it is the same as the Universal Deity. The Heart represents the higher triad, while the liver and spleen represent the quaternary, taken as a whole. The Heart is the abode of the spiritual man, whereas the psycho-intellectual man dwells in the head with its seven gateways. It has its seven brains, the *upadhis* and symbols of the seven Hierarchies, and this is the exoterically four, but esoterically seven, leaved lotus, the Saptaparni, the "cave of Buddha" with its seven compartments.

The Heart is the king of the body, its most important organ. Even if the head be severed from the trunk, the Heart will continue to beat for half an hour. If wrapped in cotton wool, and put in a warm place, the pulsation will continue for some hours.

In the Heart is a spot which is the last to die, a spot marked by a tiny violet light; that is the seat of Life, the centre of all, Brahma; the first spot that lives in the foetus, and the last that dies. When a yogi is buried in a trance, it is this spot that lives, though the rest of the body be dead, and as long as this remains alive the yogi can be resurrected. This spot contains potentially mind, life, energy, and will. During life it radiates prismatic colours, fiery and opalescent.

The Heart is the centre of the spiritual consciousness, as the brain is the centre of intellectual consciousness. But this spiritual consciousness cannot be guided by a person, nor can its energy be directed by him, until he is completely united with *buddhi-manas*. Until then, it guides him — if it can. That is, makes efforts to reach him, to impress the lower consciousness, and those efforts are helped by his growth in purity. Hence the pangs of remorse for wrong done, the prickings of conscience, reproaching for evil, inciting to good. These come from the Heart, not from the head. In the Heart is the only manifested God; the other two are invisible. And it is this manifested God that represents the triad, *atma-buddhi-manas*.

Anyone who can reach up to, and so receive at will, the promptings of this spiritual consciousness must be at one with *manas* — that is must have attained Adeptship. But the higher *manas* cannot directly guide the ordinary man; it must act through the lower *manas*, and thus reach the lower consciousness. The effort however should be continually made to centre the consciousness in the Heart, and to listen for the promptings of the spiritual consciousness, for though success be far off, a beginning must be made, and the path opened up.

There are three principal centres in the body of man: the Heart, the head, and the navel; the Heart, as said, is the centre of the spiritual consciousness; the head is the centre of the psychic consciousness; and the navel is the centre of the *kamic* consciousness. Any two of these may be positive and negative to each other, according to the relative predominance of the principles and therefore of their organ for manifestation on this plane. The meaning of the words positive and negative in this relation is the same as is attached to them in electrical science. The current flows from the positive to the negative, or the impression is made by the positive on the negative.

For instance, the aura of the pineal gland vibrates during the activity of the consciousness in the brain, and shows the play of the seven colours. This septenary disturbance and play of light around the pineal gland are reflected in the Heart, or rather in the aura of the Heart, which is negative to the brain in the ordinary man. This aura then vibrates and illumines the seven brains of the Heart, as that of the pineal gland illumines the seven centres in the brain. If the Heart could, in its turn, become positive and impress the brain, the spiritual consciousness would reach the lower consciousness. The spiritual consciousness is active during deep sleep, and if the "dreams" that occur in so-called dreamless sleep could be impressed by the Heart on the brain, your consciousness would no longer be restricted within the bounds of your personal life. If you could remember your dreams in deep sleep, you would be able to remember all your past incarnations. This is the "memory of the Heart"; and the capacity to impress it on the brain, so that it becomes part of its consciousness, is the "opening of the third eye." In deep sleep the third eye opens, but it does not remain open. Still, some impressions from the spiritual consciousness do reach the brain more or less, thus making the lower ego responsible. And there are some of these which are received through the brain, which do not belong to our previous personal experience. In the case of the Adept, the brain is trained to retain these impressions.

The Eastern Secret School knows each minute portion of the Heart, and has a name for each portion. It calls them by the names of the Gods, as Brahma's Hall, Vishnu's Hall, and so on. Each of these corresponds with a part of the brain. The student will now begin to understand why so much stress is laid on the Heart in connection with meditation, and why so many allusions are made in old Hindu literature to the Purusha in the Heart. And so with regard to concentration the Blessed Master Koot Hoomi writes:

"Your best method is to concentrate on the Master as a Living Man within you. Make His image in your heart, and a focus of concentration, so as to lose all sense of bodily existence in the one thought."

So again He says:

"The great difficulty to be overcome is the registration of the knowledge of the Higher Self on the physical plane. To accomplish this, the physical brain must be made an entire blank to all but the higher consciousness."

When the brain is thus rendered a blank, an impression from the Heart may reach it and be retained; and this is what is spoken of with regard to the chela, who is able to hold only parts of the knowledge gained. The above-quoted letter says:

"In acquiring the power of concentration the first step is one of blankness. Then follows by degrees consciousness, and finally the passage between the two states becomes so rapid and easy as to be almost unnoticed."

He who can do this at will has become an Adept, and can "store the knowledge he thus gains in his physical memory."

Such is the kingly function of the Heart in the human body, and its relation to the brain, which, as a whole, "is the vehicle of the lower *manas*, enthroned in *kama-rupa*."

WILL AND DESIRE

WILL is the exclusive possession of man on this our plane of consciousness. It divides him from the brute in whom instinctive desire only is active.

Desire, in its widest application, is the one creative force in the Universe. In this sense it is indistinguishable from Will; but we men never know desire under this form while we remain only men. Therefore Will and Desire are here considered as opposed.

Thus Will is the offspring of the Divine, the God in man; Desire the motive power of the animal life.

Most of men live in and by desire, mistaking it for will. But he who would achieve must separate will from desire, and make his will the ruler; for desire is unstable and ever changing, while will is steady and constant.

Both will and desire are absolute *creators*, forming the man himself and his surroundings. But will creates intelligently — desire blindly and unconsciously. The man, therefore, makes himself in the image of his desires, unless he creates himself in the likeness of the Divine, through his will, the child of the light.

His task is twofold: to awaken the will, to strengthen it by use and conquest, to make it absolute ruler within his body; and, parallel with this, to purify desire.

Knowledge and will are the tools for the accomplishment of this purification.

SELF-KNOWLEDGE

THE FIRST NECESSITY for obtaining self-knowledge is to become profoundly conscious of ignorance; to feel with every fibre of the heart that one is *ceaselessly* self-deceived.

The second requisite is the still deeper conviction that such knowledge — such intuitive and certain knowledge — can be obtained by effort.

The third and most important is an indomitable determination to obtain and face that knowledge.

Self-knowledge of this kind is unattainable by what men usually call "self-analysis." It is not reached by reasoning or any brain process; for it is the awakening to consciousness of the divine nature of man.

To obtain this knowledge is a greater achievement than to command the elements or to know the future.

DESIRE MADE PURE

WHEN DESIRE is for the purely abstract — when it has lost all trace or tinge of "self" — then it has become pure.

The first step towards this purity is to kill out the desire for the things of matter, since these *can* only be enjoyed by the separated personality.

The second is to cease from desiring for oneself even such abstractions as power, knowledge, love, happiness, or fame; for they are but selfishness after all.

Life itself teaches these lessons; for all such objects of desire are found to be Dead Sea fruit in the moment of attainment. This much we learn from experience. Intuitive perception seizes on the *positive* truth that satisfaction is attainable only in the infinite; the will makes that conviction an actual fact of consciousness, till at last all desire is centred on the Eternal.

THE GREAT PARADOX

PARADOX would seem to be the natural language of occultism. Nay more, it would seem to penetrate deep into the heart of things, and thus to be inseparable from any attempt to put into words the truth, the reality which underlies the outward shows of life.

And the paradox is one not in words only, but in action, in the very conduct of life. The paradoxes of occultism must be lived, not uttered only. Herein lies a great danger, for it is only too easy to become lost in the intellectual contemplation of the path, and so to forget that the road can only be known by treading it.

One startling paradox meets the student at the very outset, and confronts him in ever new and strange shapes at each turn of the road. Such a one, perchance, has sought the path desiring a guide, a rule of right for the conduct of his life. He learns that the alpha and the omega, the beginning and the end of *life* is selflessness; and he feels the truth of the saying that only in the profound unconsciousness of self-forgetfulness can the truth and reality of being reveal itself to his eager heart.

The student learns that this is the one law of occultism, at once the science and the art of living, the guide to the goal he desires to attain. He is fired with enthusiasm and enters bravely on the mountain track. He then finds that his teachers do not encourage his ardent flights of sentiment; his all-forgetting yearning for the Infinite — on the outer plane of his actual life and consciousness. At least, if they do not actually damp his enthusiasm, they set him, as the first and indispensable task, *to conquer and control his body*. The student finds that far from being encouraged to live in the soaring thoughts of his brain, and to fancy he has reached that ether where is true freedom — to the forgetting of his body, and his external actions and personality — he is set down to tasks much nearer earth. All his attention and watchfulness are required on the outer plane; he must never forget himself, never lose hold over his body, his mind, his brain. He must even learn to control the expression of every feature, to check the action of each muscle, to be master of every slightest involuntary movement. The daily life around and within him is pointed out as the object of his study and observation. Instead of forgetting what are usually called the petty trifles, the little forgetfulness, the accidental slips of tongue or memory, he is forced to become each day more conscious of these lapses, till at last they seem to poison the air he breathes and stifle him, till he seems to lose sight and touch of the great world of freedom towards which he is struggling, till every hour of every day seems full of the bitter taste of self, and his heart grows sick with pain and the struggle of despair. And the darkness is rendered yet deeper by the voice within him, crying ceaselessly: "Forget thyself. Beware, lest thou becomest self-concentrated — and the giant weed of spiritual selfishness take firm root in thy heart; beware, beware, beware!"

The voice stirs his heart to its depths, for he feels that the words are true. His daily and hourly battle is teaching him that self-centredness is the root of misery, the cause of pain, and his soul is full of longing to be free.

Thus the disciple is torn by doubt. He trusts his teachers, for he knows that through them speaks the same voice he hears in the silence of his own heart. But now they utter contradictory words; the one, the inner voice, bidding him forget himself utterly in the service of humanity; the other, the spoken word of those from whom he seeks guidance in his service, bidding him *first* to conquer his body, his outer self. And he knows better with every hour how badly he acquits himself in that battle with the Hydra, and he sees seven heads grow afresh in place of each one that he has lopped off.

At first he oscillates between the two, now obeying the one, now the other. But soon he learns that this is fruitless. For the sense of freedom and lightness, which comes at first when he leaves his outer self unwatched, that he may seek the inner air, soon loses its keenness, and some sudden shock reveals to him that he has slipped and fallen on the uphill path. Then, in desperation, he flings himself upon the treacherous snake of self, and strives to choke it into death; but its ever-moving coils elude his grasp, the insidious temptations of its glittering scales blind his vision, and again he becomes involved in the turmoil of the battle, which gains on him from day to day, and which at last seems to fill the whole world, and blot out all else beside from his consciousness. He is face to face with a crushing paradox, the solution of which must be lived before it can be really understood.

In his hours of silent meditation the student will find that there is one space of silence within him where he can find refuge from thoughts and desires, from the turmoil of the senses and the delusions of the mind. By sinking his consciousness deep into his heart he can reach this place — at first only when he is alone in silence and darkness. But when the need for the silence has grown great enough, he will turn to seek it even in the midst of the struggle with self, and he will find it. Only he must not let go of his outer self, or his body; he must learn to retire into this citadel when the battle grows fierce, but to do so without losing sight of the battle; without allowing himself to fancy that by so doing he has won the victory. That victory is won only when all is silence without as within the inner citadel. Fighting thus, from within that silence, the student will find that he has solved the first great paradox.

But paradox still follows him. When first he thus succeeds in thus retreating into himself, he seeks there only for refuge from the storm in his heart. And as he struggles to control the gusts of passion and desire, he realizes more fully what mighty powers he has vowed himself to conquer. He still feels himself, apart from the silence, nearer akin to the forces of the storm. How can his puny strength cope with these tyrants of animal nature?

This question is hard to answer in direct words; if, indeed, such an answer can be given. But analogy may point the way where the solution may be sought.

In breathing we take a certain quantity of air into the lungs, and with this we can imitate in miniature the mighty wind of heaven. We can produce a feeble semblance of Nature: a tempest in a teacup, a gale to blow and even swamp a paper boat. And we can say: "I do this; it is *my* breath." But we cannot blow our breath against a hurricane, still less hold the trade winds in our lungs. Yet the powers of heaven are within us; the nature of the intelligences which guide the world-force is blended with our own, and could we realize this and forget our outer selves, the very winds would be our instruments.

So it is in life. While a man clings to his outer self — aye, and even to any one of the forms he assumes when this "mortal coil" is cast aside — so long is he trying to blow aside a hurricane with the breath of his lungs. It is useless and idle such an endeavour; for the great winds of life must, sooner or later, sweep him away. But if he changes his altitude *within himself*, if he acts on the faith that his body, his desires, his passions, his brain, are not himself, though he has charge of them, and is responsible for them; if he tries to deal with them as parts of Nature, then he may hope to become one with the great tides of Being, and reach the peaceful place of safe self-forgetfulness at last.

Faust

SPIRITUAL PROGRESS

Christina Rossetti's well-known lines:

> Does the road wind uphill all the way?
> Yes, to the very end.
> Will the day's journey take the whole long day?
> From morn to night, my friend.

are like an epitome of the life of those who are truly treading the path which leads to higher things. Whatever differences are to be found in the various presentations of the Esoteric Doctrine, as in every age it donned a fresh garment, different both in hue and texture to that which preceded; yet in every one of them we find the fullest agreement upon one point — the road to spiritual development. One only inflexible rule has been ever binding upon the neophyte, as it is binding now — the *complete* subjugation of the lower nature by the higher. From the Vedas and Upanishads to the recently published *Light on the Path*, search as we may through the bibles of every race and cult, we find but one only way — hard, painful, troublesome, by which man can gain the true spiritual insight. And how can it be otherwise since all religions and all philosophies are but the variants of the first teachings of the One Wisdom, imparted to men at the beginning of the cycle by the Planetary Spirit?

The true Adept, the developed man, must, we are always told, *become* — he cannot be made. The process is therefore one of growth through evolution, and this must necessarily involve a certain amount of pain.

The main cause of pain lies in our perpetually seeking the permanent in the impermanent, and not only seeking, but acting as if we had already found the unchangeable, in a world of which the one certain quality we can predicate is constant change, and always, just as we fancy we have taken a firm hold upon the permanent, it changes within our very grasp, and pain results.

Again, the idea of growth involves also the idea of disruption: the inner being must continually burst through its confining shell or encasement, and such a disruption must also be accompanied by pain, not physical but mental and intellectual.

And this is how it is, in the course of our lives; the trouble that comes upon us is always just the one we feel to be the hardest that could possibly happen — it is always the one thing we feel we cannot possibly bear. If we look at it from a wider point of view, we shall see that we are trying to burst through our shell at its one vulnerable point; that our growth, to be real growth, and not the collective result of a series of excrescences, must progress evenly throughout, just as the body of a child grows, not first the head and then a hand, followed perhaps by a leg, but in all directions at once, regularly and imperceptibly. Man's tendency is to cultivate each part separately, neglecting the others in the meantime — every crushing pain is caused by the expansion of some neglected part, which expansion is rendered more difficult by the effects of the cultivation bestowed elsewhere.

Evil is often the result of over-anxiety, and men are always trying to do too much, they are not content to leave well alone, to do always just what the occasion demands and no more; they exaggerate every action and so produce karma to be worked out in a future birth.

One of the subtlest forms of this evil is the hope and desire of reward. Many there are who, albeit often unconsciously, are yet spoiling all their efforts by entertaining this idea of reward, and allowing it to become an active factor in their lives and so leaving the door open to anxiety, doubt, fear, despondency — failure.

The goal of the aspirant for spiritual wisdom is entrance upon a higher plane of existence; he is to become a new man, more perfect in every way than he is at present, and if he succeeds, his capabilities and faculties will receive a corresponding increase of range and power, just as in the visible world we find that each stage in the evolutionary scale is marked by increase of capacity. This is how it is that the Adept becomes endowed with marvellous powers that have been so often described, but the main point to be remembered is, that these powers are the natural accompaniments of existence on a higher plane of evolution, just as the ordinary human faculties are the natural accompaniments of existence on the ordinary human plane.

Many persons seem to think that Adeptship is not so much the result of radical development as of additional construction; they seem to imagine that an Adept is a man who, by going through a certain plainly defined course of training, consisting of minute attention to a set of arbitrary rules, acquires first one power and then another; and when he has attained a certain number of these powers is forthwith dubbed an Adept. Acting on this mistaken idea, they fancy that the first thing to be done towards attaining Adeptship is to acquire "powers" — clairvoyance and the power of leaving the physical body and travelling to a distance, are among those which fascinate the most.

To those who wish to acquire such powers for their own private advantage, we have nothing to say; they fall under the condemnation of all who act for purely selfish ends. But there are others, who, mistaking effect for cause, honestly think that the acquirement of abnormal powers is the only road to spiritual advancement. These look upon our Society as merely the readiest means to enable them to gain knowledge in this direction, considering it as a sort of occult academy, an institution established to afford facilities for the instruction of would-be miracle-workers. In spite of repeated protests and warnings, there are some minds in whom this notion seems ineradicably fixed, and they are loud in their expressions of disappointment when they find that what had been previously told them is perfectly true; that the Society was founded to teach no new and easy paths to the acquisition of "powers"; and that its only mission is to rekindle the torch of truth so long extinguished for all but the very few, and to keep that truth alive by the formation of a fraternal union of mankind, the only soil in which the good seed can grow. The Theosophical Society does indeed desire to promote the spiritual growth of every individual who comes within its influence, but its methods are those of the ancient Rishis, its tenets those of the oldest esotericism; it is no dispenser of patent nostrums composed of violent remedies which no honest healer would dare to use.

In this connection we would warn all our members, and others who are seeking spiritual knowledge, to beware of persons offering to teach them easy methods of acquiring psychic gifts; such gifts (*laukika*) are indeed comparatively easy of acquirement by artificial means, but fade out as soon as the nerve-stimulus exhausts itself. The real seership and Adeptship which is accompanied by true psychic development (*lokottara*), once reached, is never lost.

It appears that various societies have sprung into existence since the foundation of the Theosophical Society, profiting by the interest the latter has awakened in matters of psychic research, and endeavouring to gain members by promising them easy acquirement of psychic powers. In India we have long been familiar with the existence of hosts of sham ascetics of all descriptions, and we fear that there is fresh danger in this direction, here, as well as in Europe and America. We only hope that none of our members, dazzled by brilliant promises, will allow themselves to be taken in by self-deluded dreamers, or, it may be, wilful deceivers.

To show that some real necessity exists for our protests and warnings, we may mention that we have recently seen, enclosed in a letter from Benares, copies of an advertisement just put forth by a so-called "Mahatma." He calls for "eight men and women who know English and any of the Indian vernaculars well"; and concludes by saying that "those who want to know particulars of the work and *the amount of pay*" should apply to his address, with enclosed postage stamps!

Upon the table before us, lies a reprint of *The Divine Pymander*, published in England last year, and which contains a notice to "Theosophists, who may have been disappointed in their expectations of Sublime Wisdom being freely dispensed by Hindu Mahatmas"; cordially inviting them to send in their names to the editor who will see them "after a short probation," admitted into an occult Brotherhood who "teach *freely* and without reserve to all they find worthy to receive."[1] Strangely enough, we find in the very volume in question Hermes Trismegistus saying:

"Herein is the only way which leads to Truth, which, indeed, our ancestors trod, and by which they arrived at the attainment of the Good. This way is beautiful and even; nevertheless, it is difficult for the soul to walk therein so long as she is immured within the prison of the body. . . . Therefore, abstain from the crowd, so that by means of ignorance the vulgar may be kept within bounds, even through fear of the unknown."[2]

It is perfectly true that some Theosophists have been (through nobody's fault but their own) greatly disappointed because we have offered them no short cut to *Yoga-Vidya*, and there are others who wish for practical work. And, significantly enough, those who have done least for the Society are loudest in fault-finding. Now, why do not these persons and all our members who are able to do so, take up the serious study of mesmerism? Mesmerism has been called the *key to the occult sciences*, and it has this advantage that it offers peculiar opportunities for doing good to mankind. If in each of our branches we were able to establish a homeopathic dispensary with the addition of mesmeric healing, such as has already been done with great success in Bombay, we might contribute towards putting the science of medicine in this country on a sounder basis, and be the means of incalculable benefit to the people at large.

There are others of our branches, besides the one at Bombay, that have done good work in this direction, but there is room for infinitely more to be done than has yet been attempted. And the same is the case in the various other departments of the Society's work. It would be a good thing if the members of each branch would put their heads together and seriously consult as to what tangible steps they can take to further the declared objects of the Society. In too many cases the members of the Theosophical Society content themselves with a somewhat superficial study of its books, without making any real contribution to its active work. If the Society is to be a power for good in this and other lands, it can only bring about this result by the active cooperation of every one

---

[1] Dr. Everard, translator, *The Divine Pymander of Hermes Mercurius Trismegistus* (London: George Redway, 1884), p. 112.

[2] Anna Kingsford and Edward Maitland, *The Virgin of the World of Hermes Mercurius Trismegistus* (London: George Redway, 1885), pp. 120, 124; Everard, *The Divine Pymander*, pp. 2, 6.

of its members, and we would earnestly appeal to each of them to consider carefully what possibilities of work are within his power, and then to *earnestly set about carrying them into effect*. Right thought is a good thing, but thought alone does not count for much unless it is translated into action. There is not a single member in the Society who is not able to do *something* to aid the cause of truth and universal brotherhood; it only depends on his own will, to make that *something* an accomplished fact.

Above all we would reiterate the fact, that the Society is no nursery for incipient adepts; teachers cannot be provided to go round and give instruction to various branches on the different subjects which come within the Society's work of investigation; the branches must study for themselves; books are to be had, and the knowledge there put forth must be practically applied by the various members: thus will be developed self-reliance, and reasoning powers. We urge this strongly; for appeals have reached us that any lecturer sent to branches must be practically versed in experimental psychology and clairvoyance (i.e., looking into magic mirrors and reading the future, etc., etc.). Now we consider that such experiments should originate amongst members themselves to be of any value in the development of the individual or to enable him to make progress in his "uphill" path, and therefore earnestly recommend our members to *try* for themselves.

PRACTICAL OCCULTISM

Occultism is not magic, though magic is one of its tools.

Occultism is not the acquirement of powers, whether psychic or intellectual, though both are its servants.

Neither is occultism the pursuit of happiness, as people understand the word; for the first step is sacrifice, the second, renunciation.

Life is built up by the sacrifice of the individual to the whole.

Each cell in the living body must sacrifice itself to the perfection of the whole; when it is otherwise, disease and death enforce the lesson.

Occultism is the science of life, the art of living.

As some of the letters in the correspondence of this month show, there are many people who are looking for practical instruction in occultism. It becomes necessary, therefore, to state once for all:

1. The essential difference between theoretical and practical occultism; or what is generally known as Theosophy on the one hand, and occult science on the other, and:

2. The nature of the difficulties involved in the study of the latter.

It is easy to become a Theosophist. Any person of average intellectual capacities, and a leaning toward the metaphysical; of pure, unselfish life, who finds more joy in helping his neighbour than in receiving help himself; one who is ever ready to sacrifice his own pleasures for the sake of other people; and who loves Truth, Goodness, and Wisdom for their own sake, not for the benefit they may confer — is a Theosophist.

But it is quite another matter to put oneself upon the path which leads to the knowledge of what is good to do, as to the right discrimination of good from evil; a path which also leads a man to that power through which he can do the good he desires, often without even apparently lifting a finger.

Moreover, there is one important fact with which the student should be made acquainted. Namely, the enormous, almost limitless, responsibility assumed by the Teacher for the sake of the pupil. From the Gurus of the East who teach openly or secretly, down to the few Kabbalists in Western lands who undertake to teach the rudiments of the Sacred Science to their disciples — those western Hierophants being often themselves ignorant of the danger they incur — one and all of these Teachers are subject to the same inviolable law. From the moment they begin *really* to teach, from the instant they confer *any* power — whether psychic, mental, or physical — on their pupils, they take upon themselves *all* the sins of that pupil, in connection with the occult sciences, whether of omission or commission, until the moment when initiation makes the pupil a Master and responsible in his turn. There is a weird and mystic religious law, greatly reverenced and acted upon in the Greek, half-forgotten in the Roman Catholic, and absolutely extinct in the Protestant Church. It dates from the earliest days of Christianity and has its basis in the law just stated, of which it was a symbol and an expression. This is the dogma of the absolute sacredness of the relation between the god-parents who stand sponsors for a child.[1]

These tacitly take upon themselves all the sins of the newly baptized child — anointed, as at the initiation, a mystery truly! — until the day when the child becomes a responsible unit, knowing good and evil. Thus it is clear why the Teachers are so reticent, and why chelas are required to serve a seven years probation to prove their fitness, and develop the qualities necessary to the security of both Master and pupil.

---

[1] So holy is the connection thus formed deemed in the Greek Church, that a marriage between god-parents of the same child is regarded as the worst kind of incest, is considered illegal, and is dissolved by law; and this absolute prohibition extends even to the children of one of the sponsors as regards those of the other.

Occultism is not magic. It is *comparatively* easy to learn the trick of spells and the methods of using the subtler, but still material, forces of physical nature; the powers of the animal soul in man are soon awakened; the forces which his love, his hate, his passion, can call into operation, are readily developed. But this is black magic — *sorcery*. For it is the motive, *and the motive alone*, which makes any exercise of power become black, malignant, or white, beneficent magic. It is impossible to employ *spiritual* forces if there is the slightest tinge of selfishness remaining in the operator. For, unless the intention is entirely unalloyed, the spiritual will transform itself into the psychic, act on the astral plane, and dire results may be produced by it. The powers and forces of animal nature can equally be used by the selfish and revengeful, as by the unselfish and the all-forgiving; the powers and forces of spirit lend themselves only to the perfectly pure in heart — and this is divine magic.

What are then the conditions required to become a student of the "Divina Sapientia"? For let it be known that no such instruction can possibly be given unless these certain conditions are complied with, and rigorously carried out during the years of study. This is a *sine qua non*. No man can swim unless he enters deep water. No bird can fly unless its wings are grown, and it has space before it and courage to trust itself to the air. A man who will wield a two-edged sword, must be a thorough master of the blunt weapon, if he would not injure himself — or what is worse — others, at the first attempt.

To give an approximate idea of the conditions under which alone the study of Divine Wisdom can be pursued with safety, that is without danger that Divine will give place to black magic, a page is given from the "private rules," with which every instructor in the East is furnished. The few passages which follow are chosen from a great number and explained in brackets.

1. The place selected for receiving instruction must be a spot calculated not to distract the mind, and filled with "influence-evolving" (magnetic) objects. The five sacred colours gathered in a circle must be there among other things. The place must be free from any malignant influences hanging about in the air.

[The place must be set apart, and used for no other purpose. The five "sacred colours" are the prismatic hues arranged in a certain way, as these colours are very magnetic. By "malignant influences" are meant any disturbances through strifes, quarrels, bad feelings, etc., as these are said to impress themselves immediately on the astral light, i.e., in the atmosphere of the place, and to hang "about in the air." This first condition seems easy enough to accomplish, yet — on further consideration, it is one of the most difficult ones to obtain.]

2. Before the disciple shall be permitted to study "face to face," he has to acquire preliminary understanding in a select company of other lay *upasakas* (disciples), the number of whom must be odd.

["Face to face" means in this instance a study independent or apart from others, when the disciple gets his instruction *face to face* either with himself (his higher, Divine Self) or — his Guru. It is then only that each receives *his due* of information, according to the use he has made of his knowledge. This can happen only toward the end of the cycle of instruction.]

3. Before thou (the teacher) shalt impart to thy *lanoo* (disciple) the good (holy) words of *Lamrim*, or shalt permit him "to make ready" for *Dubjed*, thou shalt take care that his mind is thoroughly purified and at peace with all, especially *with his other selves*. Otherwise the words of Wisdom and of the good Law, shall scatter and be picked up by the winds.

[*Lamrim* is a work of practical instructions by Tsongkhapa in two portions: one for ecclesiastical and exoteric purposes, the other for esoteric use. "To make ready" for *Dubjed*, is to prepare the vessels used for seership, such as mirrors and crystals. The "other selves," refers to the fellow students. Unless the greatest harmony reigns among the learners, *no success is possible*. It is the teacher who makes the selections according to the magnetic and electric natures of the students, bringing together and adjusting most carefully the positive and the negative elements.]

4. The *upasakas* while studying must take care to be united as the fingers on one hand. Thou shalt impress upon their minds that whatever hurts one should hurt the others, and if the rejoicing of one finds no echo in the breasts of the others, then the required conditions are absent, and it is useless to proceed.

[This can hardly happen if the preliminary choice made was consistent with the magnetic requirements. It is known that chelas otherwise promising and fit for the reception of truth, had to wait for years on account of their temper and the impossibility they felt to put themselves *in tune* with their companions. For —]

5. The co-disciples must be tuned by the Guru as the strings of a lute (*vina*) each different from the others, yet each emitting sounds in harmony with all. Collectively they must form a keyboard answering in all its parts to thy lightest touch (the touch of the Master). Thus their minds shall open for the harmonies of Wisdom, to vibrate as knowledge through each and all, resulting in effects pleasing to the presiding gods (tutelary or patron-angels) and useful to the *lanoo*. So shall Wisdom be impressed forever on their hearts and the harmony of the law shall never be broken.

6. Those who desire to acquire the knowledge leading to the *siddhis* (occult powers) have to renounce all the vanities of life and of the world (here follows enumeration of the *siddhis*).

7. None can feel the difference between himself and his fellow-students, such as "I am the wisest," "I am more holy and pleasing to the teacher, or in my community, than my brother," etc. — and remain an *upasaka*. His thoughts must be predominantly fixed upon his heart, chasing therefrom every hostile thought to any living being. It (the heart) must be full of the feeling of its non-separateness from the rest of beings as from all in Nature; otherwise no success can follow.

8. A *lanoo* (disciple) has to dread external living influence alone (magnetic emanations from living creatures). For this reason while at one with all, in his *inner nature*, he must take care to separate his outer (external) body from every foreign influence: none must drink out of, or eat in his cup but himself. He must avoid bodily contact (i.e., being touched or touch) with human, as with animal being.

[No pet animals are permitted, and it is forbidden even to touch certain trees and plants. A disciple has to live, so to say, in his own atmosphere in order to individualize it for occult purposes.]

9. The mind must remain blunt to all but the universal truths in Nature, lest the "Doctrine of the Heart" should become only the "Doctrine of the Eye" (i.e., empty exoteric ritualism).

10. No animal food of whatever kind, nothing that has life in it should be taken by the disciple. No wine, no spirits, or opium should be used; for these are like the *lhamayin* (evil spirits), who fasten upon the unwary, they devour the understanding.

[Wine and spirits are supposed to contain and preserve the bad magnetism of all the men who helped in their fabrication; the meat of each animal, to preserve the psychic characteristics of its kind.]

11. Meditation, abstinence in all, the observation of moral duties, gentle thoughts, good deeds, and kind words, as good will to all and entire oblivion of self, are the most efficacious means of obtaining knowledge and preparing for the reception of higher wisdom.

12. It is only by virtue of a strict observance of the foregoing rules that a *lanoo* can hope to acquire in good time the *siddhis* of the Arhats, the growth which makes him become gradually One with the Universal All.

These twelve extracts are taken from among some 73 rules, to enumerate which would be useless as they would be meaningless in Europe. But even these few are enough to show the immensity of the difficulties which beset the path of the would-be *upasaka*, who has been born and bred in Western lands.[1]

---

[1] Be it remembered that *all* "chelas," even lay disciples, are called *upasaka* until ▸

All western, and especially English, education is instinct with the principle of emulation and strife; each boy is urged to learn more quickly, to outstrip his companions, and to surpass them in every possible way. What is miscalled "friendly rivalry" is assiduously cultivated, and the same spirit is fostered and strengthened in every detail of life.

With such ideas "educated into" him from his childhood, how can a Westerner bring himself to feel towards his co-students "as the fingers on one hand"? Those co-students, too, are not of his *own selection*, or chosen by himself from personal sympathy and appreciation. They are chosen by his teacher on far other grounds, and he who would be a student must *first* be strong enough to kill out in his heart all feelings of dislike and antipathy to others. How many Westerners are ready even to attempt this in earnest?

And then the details of daily life, the command not to touch even the hand of one's nearest and dearest. How contrary to Western notions of affection and good feeling! How cold and hard it seems. Egotistical too, people would say, to abstain from giving pleasure to others for the sake of one's own development. Well, let those who think so defer till another lifetime the attempt to enter the path in real earnest. But let them not glory in their own fancied unselfishness. For, in reality, it is only the seeming appearances which they allow to deceive them, the conventional notions, based on emotionalism and gush, or so-called courtesy, things of the unreal life, not the dictates of Truth.

But even putting aside these difficulties, which may be considered "external," though their importance is none the less great, how are students in the West to "attune themselves" to harmony as here required of them? So strong has personality grown in Europe and America, that there is no school of artists even whose members do not hate and are not jealous of each other. "Professional" hatred and envy have become proverbial; men seek each to benefit himself at all costs, and even the so-called courtesies of life are but a hollow mask covering these demons of hatred and jealousy.

In the East the spirit of "non-separateness" is inculcated as steadily from childhood up, as in the West the spirit of rivalry. Personal ambition, personal feelings and desires, are not encouraged to grow so rampant there. When the soil is naturally good, it is cultivated in the right way, and the child grows into a man in whom the habit of subordination of one's lower to one's Higher Self is strong and powerful. In the West men think that their own likes and dislikes of other men and things are guiding principles for them to act upon, even when they do not make of them the law of their lives and seek to impose them upon others.

---

after their first initiation, when they become *lanoo-upasaka*. To that day, even those who belong to lamaseries and are *set apart*, are considered as "laymen."

Let those who complain that they have learnt little in the Theosophical Society lay to heart the words written in an article in *The Path* for last February: "The key in each degree is the *aspirant himself*." It is not "the fear of God" which is "the beginning of Wisdom," but the knowledge of Self which is wisdom itself.

How grand and true appears, thus, to the student of occultism who has commenced to realize some of the foregoing truths, the answer given by the Delphic Oracle to all who came seeking after Occult Wisdom — words repeated and enforced again and again by the wise Socrates: *man know thyself*.

OCCULTISM VERSUS THE OCCULT ARTS

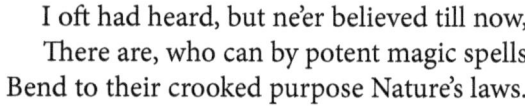

> I oft had heard, but ne'er believed till now,
> There are, who can by potent magic spells
> Bend to their crooked purpose Nature's laws.
> — **John Milton**[1]

IN THIS month's correspondence several letters testify to the strong impression produced on some minds by our last month's article "Practical Occultism." Such letters go far to prove and strengthen two logical conclusions:

1. There are more well-educated and thoughtful men who believe in the existence of occultism and magic (the two differing vastly) than the modern materialist dreams of; and:

2. That most of the believers (comprising many theosophists) have no definite idea of the nature of occultism and confuse it with the occult sciences in general, the "black art" included.

Their representations of the powers it confers upon man, and of the means to be used to acquire them are as varied as they are fanciful. Some imagine that a master in the art, to show the way, is all that is needed to become a Zanoni. Others, that one has but to cross the Canal of Suez and go to India to bloom forth as a Roger Bacon or even a Count de Saint-Germain. Many take for their ideal Margrave with his ever-renewing youth, and care little for the soul as the price paid for it. Not a few, mistaking "Witch-of-Endorism" pure and simple, for occultism — "through the yawning Earth from Stygian gloom, call up the meagre ghost to walks of light," and want, on the strength of this feat,

---

[1] John Milton, *Comus, a Mask* (London, 1795), p. 64.

to be regarded as full blown Adepts. "ceremonial magic" according to the rules mockingly laid down by Éliphas Lévi, is another imagined *alter ego* of the philosophy of the Arhats of old. In short, the prisms through which occultism appears, to those innocent of the philosophy, are as multicoloured and varied as human fancy can make them.

Will these candidates to Wisdom and Power feel very indignant if told the plain truth? It is not only useful, but it has now become *necessary* to disabuse most of them and before it is too late. This truth may be said in a few words: There are not in the West half-a-dozen among the fervent hundreds who call themselves "occultists," who have even an approximately correct idea of the nature of the science they seek to master. With a few exceptions, they are all on the highway to sorcery. Let them restore some order in the chaos that reigns in their minds, before they protest against this statement. Let them first learn the true relation in which the occult sciences stand to occultism, and the difference between the two, and then feel wrathful if they still think themselves right. Meanwhile, let them learn that occultism differs from magic and other secret sciences as the glorious Sun does from a rush-light, as the immutable and immortal spirit of man — the reflection of the absolute, causeless, and unknowable All — differs from the mortal clay — the human body.

In our highly civilized West, where modern languages have been formed, and words coined, in the wake of ideas and thoughts — as happened with every tongue — the more the latter became materialized in the cold atmosphere of Western selfishness and its incessant chase after the goods of this world, the less was there any need felt for the production of new terms to express that which was tacitly regarded as obsolete and exploded "superstition." Such words could answer only to ideas which a cultured man was scarcely supposed to harbour in his mind. "Magic," a synonym for jugglery; "sorcery," an equivalent for crass ignorance; and "occultism," the sorry relic of crack-brained, medieval Fire-philosophers, of the Jacob Böhmes and the Saint-Martins, are expressions believed more than amply sufficient to cover the whole field of "thimble-rigging." They are terms of contempt, and used generally only in reference to the dross and residues of the Dark Ages and its preceding aeons of paganism. Therefore have we no terms in the English tongue to define and shade the difference between such abnormal powers, or the sciences that lead to the acquisition of them, with the nicety possible in the Eastern languages — pre-eminently the Sanskrit. What do the words "miracle" and "enchantment" (words identical in meaning after all, as both express the idea of producing wonderful things by *breaking the laws of Nature* (!) as explained by the accepted authorities) convey to the minds of those who hear, or who pronounce them? A Christian — *breaking* "of the laws of Nature," notwithstanding — while believing firmly in the *miracles*, because said to have been produced by God through Moses, will either scout the enchantments performed by Pharaoh's magicians, or attribute them to the devil. It is the latter whom our pious enemies connect with occultism, while their impious foes, the infidels, laugh at Moses, magicians, and occultists, and would blush to give one serious thought to such "superstitions." This, because there is no term in existence to show the difference; no words to express the lights and shadows and draw the line of demarcation between the sublime and the true, the absurd and the ridiculous. The latter are the theological interpretations which teach the "breaking of the laws of Nature" by man, God, or devil; the former — the *scientific* "miracles" and enchantments of Moses and the magicians *in accordance with natural laws*, both having been learned in all the Wisdom of the Sanctuaries, which were the "Royal Societies" of those days — and in true occultism. This last word is certainly misleading, translated as it stands from the compound word *Gupta-Vidya*, "secret knowledge." But the knowledge of what? Some of the Sanskrit terms may help us.

There are four (out of the many other) names of the various kinds of esoteric knowledge or sciences given, even in the exoteric Puranas. There is: 1) *Yajna-Vidya*,[1] knowledge of the occult powers awakened in Nature by the performance of certain religious ceremonies and rites; 2) *Maha-Vidya*, the "great knowledge," the magic of the Kabbalists and of the *Tantrika* worship, often sorcery of the worst description; 3) *Guhya-Vidya*, knowledge of the mystic powers residing in Sound (Ether), hence in the mantras (chanted prayers or incantations) and depending on the rhythm and melody used; in other words a magical performance based on knowledge of the forces of Nature and their correlation; and 4) *Atma-Vidya*, a term which is translated simply "knowledge of the soul," *true Wisdom* by the Orientalists, but which means far more.

This last is the only kind of occultism that any Theosophist who admires *Light on the Path*, and who would be wise and unselfish, ought

---

[1] "The *Yajna*," say the *Aitareya Brahmana*, "exists from eternity, for it proceeded forth from the Supreme One ... in whom it lay dormant from *no* beginning." It is the key to the *Trai-Vidya*, the thrice sacred science contained in the *Rig* verses, which teaches the Yajna or sacrificial mysteries. "The Yajna exists as an invisible thing at all times; it is like the latent power of electricity in an electrifying machine, requiring only the operation of a suitable apparatus in order to be elicited. It is supposed to extend from the *ahavaniya* or sacrificial fire to the heavens, forming a bridge or ladder by means of which the sacrificer can communicate with the world of gods and spirits, and even ascend when alive to their abodes" (Martin Haug, *The Aitareya Brahmana of the Rigveda*).

"This *Yajna* is again one of the forms of the Akasha; and the mystic word calling it into existence and pronounced mentally by the initiated Priest is the Lost Word receiving impulse through *willpower*" (*Isis Unveiled*, vol. 1).

to strive after. All the rest is some branch of the "occult sciences," i.e., arts based on the knowledge of the ultimate essence of all things in the Kingdoms of Nature — such as minerals, plants, and animals — hence of things pertaining to the realm of *material* Nature, however invisible that essence may be, and howsoever much it has hitherto eluded the grasp of science. Alchemy, astrology, occult physiology, chiromancy exist in Nature, and the *exact* sciences — perhaps so called because they are found in this age of paradoxical philosophies the reverse — have already discovered not a few of the secrets of the above *arts*. But clairvoyance, symbolized in India as the "eye of Shiva," called in Japan, "infinite vision," is *not* hypnotism, the illegitimate son of mesmerism, and is not to be acquired by such arts. All the others may be mastered and results obtained, whether good, bad, or indifferent; but *Atma-Vidya* sets small value on them. It includes them all, and may even use them occasionally, but it does so after purifying them of their dross, for beneficent purposes, and taking care to deprive them of every element of selfish motive. Let us explain: Any man or woman can set himself or herself to study one or all of the above specified "occult arts" without any great previous preparation, and even without adopting any too restraining mode of life. One could even dispense with any lofty standard of morality. In the last case, of course, ten to one the student would blossom into a very decent kind of sorcerer, and tumble down headlong into black magic. But what can this matter? The Voodoos and the Dugpas eat, drink, and are merry over hecatombs of victims of their infernal arts. And so do the amiable gentlemen vivisectionists and the *diploma-ed* "hypnotizers" of the Faculties of Medicine; the only difference between the two classes being that the Voodoos and the Dugpas are *conscious*, and the Charcot-Richet crew *unconscious*, sorcerers. Thus, since both have to reap the fruits of their labours and achievements in the black art, the Western practitioners should not have the punishment and reputation without the profits and enjoyments they may get therefrom. For we say it again, *hypnotism* and *vivisection* as practised in such schools, are *sorcery* pure and simple, *minus* a knowledge that the Voodoos and Dugpas enjoy, and which no Charcot-Richet can procure for himself in fifty years of hard study and experimental observation. Let then those who will dabble in magic, whether they understand its nature or not, but who find the rules imposed upon students too hard, and who, therefore, lay *Atma-Vidya* or occultism aside — go without it. Let them become magicians by all means, even though they do become Voodoos and Dugpas for the next ten incarnations.

But the interest of our readers will probably centre on those who are invincibly attracted towards the "occult," yet who neither realize the true nature of what they aspire towards, nor have they become passion-proof, far less truly unselfish.

How about these unfortunates, we shall be asked, who are thus rent in twain by conflicting forces? For it has been said too often to need repetition, and the fact itself is patent to any observer, that when once the desire for occultism has really awakened in a man's heart, there remains for him no hope of peace, no place of rest and comfort in all the world. He is driven out into the wild and desolate spaces of life by an ever-gnawing unrest he cannot quell. His heart is too full of passion and selfish desire to permit him to pass the Golden Gate; he cannot find rest or peace in ordinary life. Must he then inevitably fall into sorcery and black magic, and through many incarnations heap up for himself a terrible karma? Is there no other road for him?

Indeed there is, we answer. Let him aspire to no higher than he feels able to accomplish. Let him not take a burden upon himself too heavy for him to carry. Without ever becoming a "Mahatma," a Buddha, or a great saint, let him study the philosophy and the "science of soul," and he can become one of the modest benefactors of humanity, without any "superhuman" powers. *Siddhis* (or the Arhat powers) are only for those who are able to "lead the life," to comply with the terrible sacrifices required for such a training, and to comply with them *to the very letter*. Let them know at once and remember always, that *true occultism or Theosophy* is the "Great Renunciation of self," unconditionally and absolutely, in thought as in action. It is *altruism*, and it throws him who practises it out of calculation of the ranks of the living altogether. "Not for himself, but for the world, he lives," as soon as he has pledged himself to the work. Much is forgiven during the first years of probation. But, no sooner is he "accepted" than his personality must disappear, and he has to become *a mere beneficent force in Nature*. There are two poles for him after that, two paths, and no midward place of rest. He has either to ascend laboriously, step by step, often through numerous incarnations and *no devachanic break*, the golden ladder leading to Mahatmaship (the Arhat or Bodhisattva condition), or — he will let himself slide down the ladder at the first false step, and roll down into Dugpaship.

All this is either unknown or left out of sight altogether. Indeed, one who is able to follow the silent evolution of the preliminary aspirations of the candidates, often finds strange ideas quietly taking possession of their minds. There are those whose reasoning powers have been so distorted by foreign influences that they imagine that animal passions can be so sublimated and elevated that their fury, force, and fire can, so to speak, be turned inwards; that they can be stored and shut up in one's breast, until their energy is, not expanded, but turned toward higher and more holy purposes; namely, *until their collective and unexpanded strength enables their possessor to enter the true Sanctuary of the Soul* and stand therein in the presence of the *Master* — the Higher Self! For this purpose they will not struggle with their passions nor slay them. They will simply, by a strong effort of will, put down the fierce flames and keep them at bay within their natures, allowing the fire to smoulder under a thin layer of ashes. They submit joyfully to the torture of the Spartan boy who allowed the fox to devour his entrails rather than part with it. Oh, poor, blind visionaries!

As well hope that a band of drunken chimney-sweeps, hot and greasy from their work, may be shut up in a Sanctuary hung with pure white linen, and that instead of soiling and turning it by their presence into a heap of dirty shreds, they will become masters in and of the sacred recess, and finally emerge from it as immaculate as that recess. Why not imagine that a dozen of skunks imprisoned in the pure atmosphere of a *gonpa* (a monastery) can issue out of it impregnated with all the perfumes of the incenses used? Strange aberration of the human mind. Can it be so? Let us argue.

The "Master" in the Sanctuary of our souls is the Higher Self — the divine spirit whose consciousness is based upon and derived solely (at any rate during the mortal life of the man in whom it is captive) from the mind, which we have agreed to call the *human soul* (the *spiritual soul* being the vehicle of the spirit). In its turn the former (the *personal* or human soul) is a compound in its highest form, of spiritual aspirations, volitions, and divine love; and in its lower aspect, of animal desires and terrestrial passions imparted to it by its associations with its vehicle, the seat of all these. It thus stands as a link and a medium between the animal nature of man which its higher reason seeks to subdue, and his divine spiritual nature to which it gravitates, whenever it has the upper hand in its struggle with the *inner animal*. The latter is the instinctual *animal soul* and is the hotbed of those passions, which, as just shown, are lulled instead of being killed, and locked up in their breasts by some imprudent enthusiasts. Do they still hope to turn thereby the muddy stream of the animal sewer into the crystalline waters of life? And where, on what neutral ground can they be imprisoned so as not to affect man? The fierce passions of love and lust are still alive and they are allowed to still remain in the place of their birth — *that same animal soul*; for both the higher and the lower portions of the "human soul" or mind reject such inmates, though they cannot avoid being tainted with them as neighbours. The Higher Self or Spirit is as unable to assimilate such feelings as water to get mixed with oil or unclean liquid tallow. It is thus the mind alone — the sole link and medium between the man of earth and the Higher

Self — that is the only sufferer, and which is in the incessant danger of being dragged down by those passions that may be reawakened at any moment, and perish in the abyss of matter. And how can it ever attune itself to the divine harmony of the highest Principle, when that harmony is destroyed by the mere presence, within the Sanctuary in preparation, of such animal passions? How can harmony prevail and conquer, when the soul is stained and distracted with the turmoil of passions and the terrestrial desires of the bodily senses, or even of the "astral man"?

For this "astral" — the shadowy "double" (in the animal as in man) — is not the companion of the Divine Ego but of the *earthly body*. It is the link between the personal self, the lower consciousness of *manas*, and the body, and is the vehicle of *transitory, not of immortal life*. Like the shadow projected by man, it follows his movements and impulses slavishly and mechanically, and leans therefore to matter without ever ascending to Spirit. It is only when the power of the passions is dead altogether, and when they have been crushed and annihilated in the retort of an unflinching will; when not only all the lusts and longings of the flesh are dead, but also the recognition of the personal self is killed out and the "astral" has been reduced in consequence to a cipher, that the union with the Higher Self can take place. Then when the "astral" reflects only the conquered man, the still living, but no more the longing, selfish personality, then the brilliant *Augoeides*, the Divine Self, can vibrate in conscious harmony with both the poles of the human entity — the man of matter purified, and the ever pure spiritual soul — and stand in the presence of the Master Self, the Christos of the mystic Gnostics, blended, merged into, and one with *It* forever.[1]

How then can it be thought possible for a man to enter the "straight gate" of occultism when his daily and hourly thoughts are bound up with worldly things, desires of possession and power, with lust, ambition, and duties, which, however honourable, are still of the earth earthy? Even the love for wife and family — the purest as the most unselfish of human affections — is a barrier to *real* occultism. For whether we take as an example the holy love of a mother for her child, or that of a husband for his wife, even in these feelings, when analysed to the very bottom, and thoroughly sifted, there is still *selfishness* in the first, and an *égoisme à deux* in the second instance. What mother would not sacrifice without a moment's hesitation hundreds and thousands of lives for that of the

---

[1] Those who would feel inclined to see three Egos in one man will show themselves unable to perceive the metaphysical meaning. Man is a trinity composed of body, soul, and spirit; but *man* is nevertheless *one* and is surely not his body. It is the latter which is the property, the transitory clothing of the man. The three "Egos" are man in his three aspects on the astral, intellectual or psychic, and the spiritual planes, or states.

child of her heart? And what lover or true husband would not break the happiness of every other man and woman around him to satisfy the desire of one whom he loves? This is but natural, we shall be told. Quite so, in the light of the code of human affections; less so, in that of Divine Universal Love. For, while the heart is full of thoughts for a little group of *selves*, near and dear to us, how shall the rest of mankind fare in our souls? What percentage of love and care will there remain to bestow on the "great orphan"? And how shall the "still small voice" make itself heard in a soul entirely occupied with its own privileged tenants? What room is there left for the needs of humanity *en bloc* to impress themselves upon, or even receive a speedy response? And yet, he who would profit by the wisdom of the universal mind, has to reach it through *the whole of humanity* without distinction of race, complexion, religion, or social status. It is *altruism*, not *egoism* even in its most legal and noble conception, that can lead the unit to merge its little Self in the Universal Selves. It is to *these* needs and to this work that the true disciple of true occultism has to devote himself, if he would obtain *theosophy*, Divine Wisdom and Knowledge.

The aspirant has to choose absolutely between the life of the world and the life of occultism. It is useless and vain to endeavour to unite the two, for no one can serve two masters and satisfy both. No one can serve his body and the higher soul, and do his family duty and his universal duty, without depriving either one or the other of its rights; for he will either lend his ear to the "still small voice" and fail to hear the cries of his little ones, or, he will listen but to the wants of the latter and remain deaf to the voice of humanity. It would be a ceaseless, a maddening struggle for almost any married man, who would pursue true practical occultism, instead of its *theoretical* philosophy. For he would find himself ever hesitating between the voice of the impersonal divine love of humanity, and that of the personal, terrestrial love. And this could only lead him to fail in one or the other, or perhaps in both his duties. Worse than this; for, *whoever indulges, after having pledged himself to* occultism, *in the gratification of a terrestrial love or lust*, must feel an almost immediate result; that of being irresistibly dragged from the impersonal divine state down to the lower plane of matter. Sensual, or even mental self-gratification, involves the immediate loss of the powers of spiritual discernment; the voice of the Master can no longer be distinguished from that of one's passions or *even that of a Dugpa*; the right from wrong; sound morality from mere casuistry. The Dead Sea fruit assumes the most glorious mystic appearance, only to turn to ashes on the lips, and to gall in the heart, resulting in:

> Depth ever deepening, darkness darkening still;
> Folly for wisdom, guilt for innocence;
> Anguish for rapture, and for hope despair.[1]

And once being mistaken and having acted on their mistakes, most men shrink from realizing their error, and thus descend deeper and deeper into the mire. And, although it is the intention that decides primarily whether *white* or *black* magic is exercised, yet the results even of involuntary, unconscious sorcery cannot fail to be productive of bad karma. Enough has been said to show that *sorcery is any kind of evil influence exercised upon other persons, who suffer, or make other persons suffer, in consequence*. Karma is a heavy stone splashed in the quiet waters of Life; and it must produce ever widening circles of ripples, carried wider and wider, almost *ad infinitum*. Such causes produced have to call forth effects, and these are evidenced in the just laws of Retribution.

Much of this may be avoided if people will only abstain from rushing into practices neither the nature nor importance of which they understand. No one is expected to carry a burden beyond his strength and powers. There are "natural-born magicians"; mystics and occultists by birth, and by right of direct inheritance from a series of incarnations and aeons of suffering and failures. These are passion-proof, so to say. No fires of earthly origin can fan into a flame any of their senses or desires; no human voice can find response in their souls, except the great cry of humanity. These only may be certain of success. But they can be met only far and wide, and they pass through the narrow gates of occultism because they carry no personal luggage of human transitory sentiments along with them. They have got rid of the feeling of the lower personality, paralysed thereby the "astral" animal, and the golden, but narrow gate is thrown open before them. Not so with those who have to carry yet for several incarnations the burden of sins committed in previous lives, and even in their present existence. For such, unless they proceed with great caution, the golden gate of Wisdom may get transformed into the wide gate and the broad way "that leadeth unto destruction," and therefore "many be they that enter in thereby." This is the Gate of the occult arts, practised for selfish motives and in the absence of the restraining and beneficent influence of *Atma-Vidya*. We are in the Kali Yuga and its fatal influence is a thousandfold more powerful in the West than it is in the East; hence the easy preys made by the Powers of the Age of Darkness in this cyclic struggle, and the many delusions under which the world is now labouring. One of these is the relative facility with which men fancy they can get at the "Gate" and cross the threshold of occultism without

---

[1] Robert Pollok, *The Course of Time* (1827).

any great sacrifice. It is the dream of most Theosophists, one inspired by desire for Power and personal selfishness, and it is not such feelings that can ever lead them to the coveted goal. For, as well said by one believed to have sacrificed himself for humanity: "Straight is the gate and narrow is the way which leadeth unto life" eternal, and therefore "few there be that find it."[2] So straight indeed, that at the bare mention of some of the preliminary difficulties the affrighted Western candidates turn back and retreat with a shudder.

Let them stop here and attempt no more in their great weakness. For if, while turning their backs on the narrow gate, they are dragged by their desire for the occult one step in the direction of the broad and more inviting gates of that golden mystery which glitters in the light of illusion, woe to them! It can lead only to Dugpaship, and they will be sure to find themselves very soon landed on that *Via Fatale* of the *Inferno*, over whose portal Dante read the words:

> Through me the way is to the city dolent;
> Through me the way is to eternal dole;
> Through me the way among the people lost.

THE BLESSINGS OF PUBLICITY

A WELL-KNOWN public lecturer, a distinguished Egyptologist, said, in one of his lectures against the teachings of Theosophy, a few suggestive words, which are now quoted and must be answered: "It is a delusion to suppose there is anything in the experience or wisdom of the past, the ascertained results of which can only be communicated from beneath the cloak and mask of mystery. . . . Explanation is the soul of science. They will tell you *we cannot have their knowledge without living their life*. . . . Public experimental research, the printing press, and a free-thought platform, have abolished the need of mystery. It is no longer necessary for science to take the veil, as she was forced to do for security in times past."

This is a very mistaken view in one aspect. "Secrets of the purer and profounder life" not only *may* but *must* be made universally known. But *there are secrets that kill* in the arcana of occultism, and unless a man *lives the life* he cannot be entrusted with them.

The late Professor Faraday had very serious doubts whether it was quite wise and reasonable to give out to the public at large certain discoveries of modern science. Chemistry had led to the invention of too

---

[2] Matthew 7:14.

terrible means of destruction in our century to allow it to fall into the hands of the profane. What man of sense — in the face of such fiendish applications of dynamite and other explosive substances as are made by those incarnations of the destroying power, who glory in calling themselves anarchists and socialists — would not agree with us in saying: Far better for mankind that it should never have blasted a rock by modern perfected means, than that it should have shattered the limbs of one per cent even of those who have been thus destroyed by the pitiless hand of Russian nihilists, Irish Fenians, and anarchists. That such discoveries, and chiefly their murderous application, ought to have been withheld from public knowledge may be shown on the authority of statistics and commissions appointed to investigate and record the result of the evil done. The following information gathered from public papers will give an insight into what may be in store for wretched mankind.

England alone — the centre of civilization — has 21,268 firms fabricating and selling explosive substances.[1] But the centres of the dynamite trade, of infernal machines, and other such results of modern civilization, are chiefly at Philadelphia and New York. It is in the former city of "Brotherly Love" that the now most famous manufacturer of explosives flourishes. It is one of the well-known respectable citizens — the inventor and manufacturer of the most murderous "dynamite toys" — who, called before the Senate of the United States anxious to adopt means for the repression of a *too free trade* in such implements, found an argument that ought to become immortalized for its cynical sophistry: "My machines," that expert is reported to have said, "are quite *harmless to look at*; as they may be manufactured in the shape of oranges, hats, boats, and anything one likes. . . . Criminal is he who murders people by means of such machines, not he who manufactures them. The firm refuses to admit that were there no supply there would be no incentive for demand on the market; but insists that every demand should be satisfied by a supply ready at hand."

That "supply" is the fruit of civilization and of the publicity given to the discovery of every murderous property in matter. What is it? As found in the Report of the Commission appointed to investigate the variety and character of the so-called "infernal machines," so far the following implements of instantaneous human destruction are already on hand. The most fashionable of all among the many varieties fabricated by Mr. Holgate are the "Ticker," the "Eight Day Machine," the "Little Exterminator," and the "Bottle Machines." The "Ticker" is in appearance like

---

[1] Nitro-glycerine has found its way even into medical compounds. Physicians and druggists are vying with the anarchists in their endeavours to destroy the surplus of mankind. The famous chocolate tablets against dyspepsia are said to contain nitro-glycerine! They may save, but they can kill still more easily.

a piece of lead, a foot long and four inches thick. It contains an iron or steel tube full of a kind of gunpowder invented by Holgate himself. That gunpowder, in appearance like any other common stuff of that name, has, however, an explosive power two hundred times stronger than common gunpowder; the "Ticker" containing thus a powder which equals in force two hundred pounds of the common gunpowder. At one end of the machine is fastened an invisible clock-work meant to regulate the time of the explosion, which time may be fixed from one minute to 36 hours. The spark is produced by means of a steel needle which gives a spark at the touch-hole, and communicates thereby the fire to the whole machine.

The "Eight Day Machine" is considered the most powerful, but at the same time the most complicated, of all those invented. One must be familiar with handling it before a full success can be secured. It is owing to this difficulty that the terrible fate intended for London Bridge and its neighbourhood was turned aside by the instantaneous killing instead of the two Fenian criminals. The size and appearance of that machine changes, Proteus-like, according to the necessity of smuggling it in, in one or another way, unperceived by the victims. It may be concealed in bread, in a basket of oranges, in a liquid, and so on. The Commission of Experts is said to have declared that its explosive power is such as to reduce to atoms instantly the largest edifice in the world.

The "Little Exterminator" is an innocent-looking plain utensil having the shape of a modest jug. It contains neither dynamite nor powder, but secretes, nevertheless, a deadly gas, and has a hardly perceptible clock-work attached to its edge, the needle of which points to the time when that gas will effect its escape. In a shut-up room this new "vril" of lethal kind will *smother to death, nearly instantaneously*, every living being within a distance of a hundred feet, the radius of the murderous jug. With these three "latest novelties" in the high season of Christian civilization, the catalogue of the dynamiters is closed; all the rest belongs to the old "fashion" of the past years. It consists of hats, *porte cigars*, bottles of ordinary kind, and even *ladies' smelling bottles*, filled with dynamite, nitro-glycerine, etc., etc. — weapons, some of which, following unconsciously Karmic Law, killed many of the dynamiters in the last Chicago *revolution*. Add to this the forthcoming long-promised Keely's vibratory force, capable of reducing in a few seconds a dead bullock to a heap of ashes, and then ask yourself if the *Inferno* of Dante as a locality can ever rival earth in the production of more hellish engines of destruction?

Thus, if purely material implements are capable of blowing up, from a few corners, the greatest cities of the globe, provided the murderous weapons are guided by expert hands — what terrible dangers might not arise from magical *occult* secrets being revealed, and allowed to fall into the possession of ill-meaning persons! A thousand times more dangerous and lethal are these, because neither the criminal hand, nor the *immaterial* invisible weapon used, can ever be detected.

The congenital *black* magicians — those who, to an innate propensity towards evil, unite highly developed mediumistic natures — are but too numerous in our age. It is high time then that the psychologists and believers, at least, should cease advocating the beauties of publicity and claiming knowledge of the secrets of Nature for all. It is not in our age of "suggestion" and "explosives" that occultism can open wide the doors of its laboratories except to those who *do* live the life.

QUESTIONS AND ANSWERS

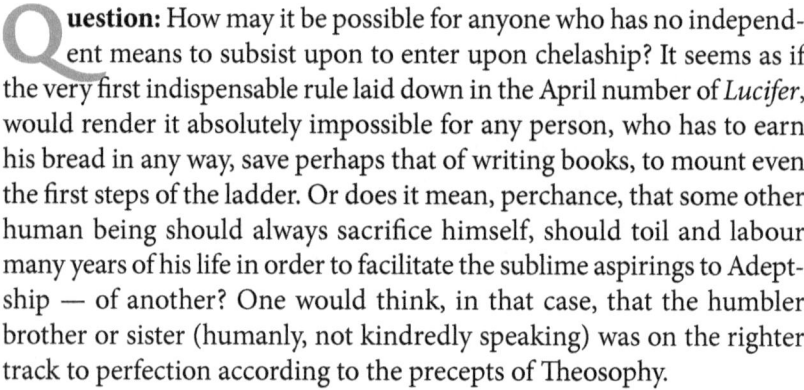

Question: How may it be possible for anyone who has no independent means to subsist upon to enter upon chelaship? It seems as if the very first indispensable rule laid down in the April number of *Lucifer*, would render it absolutely impossible for any person, who has to earn his bread in any way, save perhaps that of writing books, to mount even the first steps of the ladder. Or does it mean, perchance, that some other human being should always sacrifice himself, should toil and labour many years of his life in order to facilitate the sublime aspirings to Adeptship — of another? One would think, in that case, that the humbler brother or sister (humanly, not kindredly speaking) was on the righter track to perfection according to the precepts of Theosophy.

Answer: Chelaship has nothing *whatever* to do with means of subsistence or anything of the kind, for a man can isolate his mind entirely from his body and its surroundings. Chelaship is a *state of mind*, rather than a life according to hard and fast rules, on the physical plane. This applies especially to the earlier, probationary period, while the rules given in *Lucifer* for April last pertain properly to a later stage, that of actual occult training and the development of occult powers and insight. These rules indicate, however, the mode of life which ought to be followed by all aspirants *so far as practicable*, since it is the most helpful to them in their aspirations.

It should never be forgotten that occultism is concerned with the *inner man*, who must be strengthened and freed from the dominion of the physical body and its surroundings, which must become his servants. Hence the *first* and chief necessity of chelaship is a spirit of absolute unselfishness and devotion to Truth; then follow self-knowledge and self-mastery. These are all-important; while outward observance of fixed rules of life is a matter of secondary moment.

Question: Has any woman ever attained to Adeptship proper? Will her intellectual and spiritual nature and gifts permit it, even while supposing that her physical nature might endure the hardships therefrom indispensable?

Answer: Woman has as good a chance as any man has to reach high Adeptship. Why she does not succeed in this direction in Europe is simply due to her early education and the social prejudice which causes her to be regarded as inferior to man. This prejudice, amounting to a curse in Christian lands, was mainly derived from the Jewish Bible, and man has profited by it.

Question: In a very interesting article in last month's number entitled "Practical Occultism" it is stated that from the moment a Master begins to teach a chela he takes on himself all the sins of that chela in connection with the occult sciences until the moment when initiation makes the chela a Master and responsible in his turn.

For the Western mind, steeped as it has been for generations in "individualism," it is very difficult to recognize the justice and consequently the truth of this statement, and it is very much to be desired that some further explanation should be given for a fact which some few may feel intuitively but for which they are quite unable to give any logical reason.

Answer: The best logical reason for it is the fact that even in common daily life, parents, nurses, tutors, and instructors are generally held responsible for the habits and future ethics of a child. The little unfortunate wretch who is trained by his parents to pick pockets in the streets is not responsible for the sin, but the effects of it fall heavily on those who have impressed on his mind that it was the right thing to do. Let us hope that the Western mind, although being "steeped in individualism," has not become so dulled thereby as not to perceive that there would be neither logic nor justice were it otherwise. And if the moulders of the plastic mind of the yet unreasoning child must be held responsible, in this world of effects, for his sins of omission and commission during his childhood and for the effects produced by their early training in afterlife, how much more the "Spiritual Guru"? The latter taking the student by the hand leads him into, and introduces him to a world entirely unknown to the pupil. For this world is that of the invisible but ever-potent *causality*, the subtle, yet never-breaking thread that is the action, agent and power of karma, and karma itself in the field of divine mind. Once acquainted with this no Adept can any longer plead ignorance in the event of even an action, good and meritorious in its *motive*, producing evil as its result; since acquaintance with this mysterious realm gives the means to the occultist of foreseeing the two paths opening before every premeditated as unpremeditated action, and thus puts him in a position to know with certainty what will be the results in one or the other case. So long, then, as the pupil acts upon this principle, but is too ignorant to be sure of his vision and powers of discrimination, is it not natural that it is the *guide* who should be responsible for the sins of him whom he has led into those dangerous regions?

Question: I think, after reading the conditions necessary for occult study given in the April number of *Lucifer*, that it would be as well for the readers of this magazine to give up all hopes of becoming occultists. In Britain, except inside a monastery, I hardly think it possible that such conditions could ever be realized. In my future capacity of medical doctor (if the gods are so benign) the eighth condition would be quite exclusive; this is most unfortunate, as it seems to me that the study of occultism is peculiarly essential for a successful practice of the medical profession. (By "successful practice" I mean, successful to everybody concerned.)

I have the following question to ask you, and will be glad to be favoured with a reply through the medium of *Lucifer*. Is it possible to study occultism in Britain?

Answer: This is a too pessimistic view to entertain. One may study with profit the occult sciences without rushing into the higher occultism. In the case of our correspondent especially, and in his future capacity of medical doctor, "the occult knowledge of simples and minerals, and the curative powers of certain things in Nature," is far more important and useful than metaphysical and psychological occultism or *Theophany*. And this he can do better by studying and trying to understand Paracelsus and the two van Helmonts, than by assimilating Patanjali and the methods of Taraka Raja Yoga.

It *is* possible to study "occultism" (the occult sciences or arts is more correct) in Britain, as on any other point of the globe; though owing to the tremendously adverse conditions created by the intense selfishness that prevails in the country, and a magnetism which is repellent to a free manifestation of spirituality — solitude is the best condition for study.

Question: It is a well-known fact that the Hindus, the Mohammedans, and the Roman Catholic Christians observe fasts for certain days. The Mohammedans during those days do not eat animal food, and if I am not misinformed, the Christians do the same. The Hindus, to which class I have the honour to belong, do not eat cow, but subsist themselves on fruits, vegetables, and milk. What philosophy is hidden in this custom is a mystery not only to me, but to most of us. On consulting a Brahmin, I was informed that when the old Rishis taught us to abstain from solid food they had some medical advantage in view. What was that advantage?

Answer: The *rationale* of fasts lies on the surface. If there is one thing more than another which paralyses the willpower in man and thereby paves the way to physical and moral degradation it is intemperance in eating: "Gluttony, of seven deadly sins the worst." Swedenborg, a natural-born seer, in his "Stink of Intemperance," tells how his spirit friends reproved him for an accidental error leading to overeating. The institution of fasts goes hand in hand with the institution of feasts. When too severe strain is made on the vital energies by overtaxing the digestive machinery, the best and only remedy is to let it rest for some time and recoup itself as much as possible. The exhausted ground must be allowed to lie fallow before it can yield another crop. Fasts were instituted simply for the purpose of correcting the evils of overeating. The truth of this will be manifest from the consideration that the Buddhist priests have no institution of fasts among them, but are enjoined to observe the medium course and thus to "fast" daily all their life. A body clogged with an overstuffing of food, of whatsoever kind, is always crowned with a stupefied brain, and tired nature demands the repose of sleep. There is also a vast difference between the psychic effect of nitrogenized food, such as flesh, and non-nitrogenous food, such as fruits and green vegetables. Certain meats, like beef, and vegetables, like beans, have always been interdicted to students of occultism, not because either of them were more or less holy than others, but because while perhaps highly nutritious and supporting to the body, their magnetism was deadening and obstructive to the "psychic man."

Question: The editors of *Lucifer* would confer a great benefit on those who are attracted to the movement which they advocate, if they would state:

Whether a would-be-theosophist-occultist is required to abandon his worldly ties and duties such as family affection, love of parents, wife, children, friends, etc.?

I ask this question because it is rumoured here that some theosophical publications have so stated, and would wish to know whether such a *sine qua non* condition really exists in your Rules? The same, however, is found in the New Testament. "He that loveth father or mother more than Me, is not worthy of Me; and he that loveth son or daughter more than Me is not worthy of Me, etc., etc.," is said in Matthew 10:37. Do the Masters of Theosophy demand as much?

Answer: This is an old, old question, and a still older charge against theosophy, started first by its enemies. We emphatically answer, no; adding that no *theosophical* publication could have rendered itself guilty of such a falsehood and calumny. No follower of theosophy, least of all a disciple of the "Masters of Theosophy" (the chela of a Guru), would ever be accepted on such conditions. Many were the candidates, but "few the chosen." Dozens were refused, simply because married and having a sacred duty to perform to wife and children.[1] None have ever been asked to forsake father or mother; for he who, being necessary to his parent for his support, leaves him or her to gratify his own selfish consideration or thirst for knowledge, however great and sincere, is "*unworthy*" of the science of sciences, "or ever to approach a holy Master."

Our correspondent must surely have confused in his mind Theosophy with Roman Catholicism, and occultism with the dead-letter teachings of the Bible. For it is only in the Latin Church that it has become a meritorious action, which is called serving God and Christ, to "abandon father and mother, wife and children," and every duty of an honest man and citizen, in order to become a monk. And it is in St. Luke's Gospel that one reads the terrible words, put in the mouth of Jesus:

"If any man come to me, and hate not his *father, and mother, and wife, and children, and brethren, and sisters*, yea, and *his own life* also, he cannot be my disciple" (14:26).

Saint (?) Jerome teaches, in one of his writings:

"If thy father lies down across thy threshold, if thy mother uncovers to thine eyes the bosom which suckled thee, *trample on thy father's lifeless body*, trample on thy mother's bosom, and *with eyes unmoistened and dry, fly to the Lord, who calleth thee!*"

Surely then, it is not from any *theosophical* publication that our correspondent could have learnt such an infamous charge against theosophy

---

[1] We know but two cases of married chelas being accepted; but both these were Brahmins and had *child-wives*, according to Hindu custom, and they were *reformers* more than chelas, trying to abrogate child-marriage and slavery. Others had to obtain the consent of their wives before entering the Path, as is usual in India since long ages.

and its Masters — but rather in some *anti-Christian*, or *too* dogmatically "Christian" paper.

Our society has never been "more Catholic than the Pope." It has done its best to follow out the path prescribed by the Masters; and if it has failed in more than one respect to fulfil its arduous task, the blame is certainly not to be thrown on either Theosophy or its Masters, but on the limitations of human nature. The Rules, however, of chelaship, or discipleship, are there, in many a Sanskrit and Tibetan volume. In Book IV of *Kiu-ti*, in the chapter on "the Laws of Upasans" (disciples), the qualifications expected in a "regular chela" are: 1) perfect physical health;[2] 2) absolute mental and physical purity; 3) unselfishness of purpose; universal charity; pity for all animate beings; 4) truthfulness and unswerving faith in the laws of karma; 5) a courage undaunted in the support of truth, even in face of peril to life; 6) an intuitive perception of one's being the vehicle of the manifested Divine Atman (Spirit); 7) calm indifference for, but a just appreciation of, everything that constitutes the objective and transitory world; 8) blessing of both parents[3] and *their permission to become an upasan* (chela); and 9) celibacy, and freedom from any obligatory duty.

The two last rules are most strictly enforced. No man *convicted of disrespect to his father or mother, or unjust abandonment of his wife*, can ever be accepted even as a *lay chela*.

This is sufficient, it is hoped. We have heard of chelas who, having *failed*, perhaps in consequence of the neglect of some such duty, for one or another reason, have invariably thrown the blame and responsibility for it on the teaching of the Masters. This is but natural in poor and weak human beings who have not even the courage to recognize their own mistakes, or the rare nobility of publicly confessing them, but are always trying to find a scapegoat. Such we pity, and leave to the Law of Retribution, or karma. It is not these weak creatures, who can ever be expected to have the best of the enemy described by the wise Kiratarjuniya of Bharavi:

> The enemies which rise within the body,
> Hard to be overcome — the evil passions —
> Should manfully be fought; he who conquers these
> Is equal to the conqueror of worlds.

---

[2] This rule 1 applies only to the "temple chelas," who must be *perfect*.
[3] Or one, if the other is dead.

RECOMMENDATIONS FOR A HEALTHIER LIFE

by Helena Roerich[1]

❦

TRY TO ACQUIRE mental peace and do not clutter your brain. Read more slowly and think more. Write down the thoughts that come to you and re-read them after a while so that you perceive the progress you are making in clarity of understanding and exposition.

Often, beginners and those approaching the Sacred Teaching very much resemble medical students who, when starting to study diseases, begin to feel and find in themselves the symptoms of every existing illness. In exactly the same way, some begin to attribute to themselves the sacred pains and the highest achievements of which they have read in the books of the Teaching. One must be very careful of such enthusiasm, for this phenomenon indicates the presence of undesirable traits of the spirit such as self-conceit and lack of discernment with regard to ability. Without overcoming these traits, no advancement on the spiritual plane can be made. It should also be understood that until the age of thirty, it is impossible to open the energy centres without causing harm to the body.

Of course, I am always referring to normal, healthy bodies. So-called mediums can experience different manifestations even earlier than this.

Do not let anyone or anything confuse you. As it is said, "danger represents salvation for many." Perhaps, in connection with certain events, one could even say: the more dangerous the better. Danger will help you eliminate many deformities.

Let us remember the Helmsman of the World Ship and not be afraid.

A cold shower can be harmful when in a state of high anxiety. Do not push your brain to be active late at night. It is better to get up earlier and devote the early morning hour to reading.

Between six and eight hours (in the city) of healthy sleep is not only beneficial, but absolutely necessary, for during these hours our subtle body receives the food it needs from the Subtle World. "Drowsiness can occur for several reasons, and these should be examined. Drowsiness often arises from cosmic causes, but can also be due to coming into contact with a sick, vampiric aura, which can suck energy from us until our strength is completely exhausted. It is also not infrequently the case that our psychic energy is suddenly needed by someone close to us, and,

---

[1] Compiled from *Pis'ma Eleny Rerikh* [Letters of Helena Roerich], vol. 2 (Riga, Latvia: Uguns, 1940), pp. 228–229, 257, 229, 457–458, 209, 239, 240, 243, 258, 270, 271, 276, 286–287, 301, 301–302, 302–303, 311, 312, 313.

according to the law of the spiritual magnet, our energy will immediately rush to help them; of course, given such an outflow of energy, we experience sleepiness and even dizziness and, as it were, a temporary short absence."

One of the gravest mistakes one can make is to refrain from helping others for fear of complicating one's personal karma. Is this not an expression of the utmost selfishness? Even if we do take on a portion of that karma when providing kind assistance to our neighbour, it will not burden our spiritual development, which is the sole determiner of karma. Indeed, it is the refusal to render all possible help that burdens our karma immeasurably, for who can say to whom, where, and when we are to settle an old debt? Only Arhats are aware of when they should not help, while we are obliged to extend a helping hand wherever it is needed.

The Teaching of Living Ethics views the entire world as a single World Community. We are instructed to develop a sense of cooperation, solidarity, and friendliness, but nowhere is a crowded community model ordained. The exchange of labour and mutual assistance should not impose conditional restrictions. Excessive attachment to one place is disapproved of, for this too is a limitation. Even the Great Buddha, the founder of the World Community, instructed his disciples not to stay together for long, but to constantly disperse and visit new countries, and to be in communication with different kinds of people.

At the present level of humanity's consciousness, existing as it does in highly populated community life, a tendency towards homogenization is unavoidable, and any homogenization inevitably dissolves talent into insignificance, which leads to cultural loss and a declining civilization, that is, to simplification, and then, sadly, to the next stage of simplification, namely, to primitivization. Therefore, community and cooperation must be understood in a broad and practical sense. New scientific discoveries and life itself will prompt us to adopt new forms of cooperation.

Take care of your health, as the currents are quite severe.

The greatest benefit that we can bring is to strengthen the energy we radiate through expansion of consciousness, through improving and enriching our thinking, and through the purification of the heart, and through this raising of vibration exert a healing effect on everything around us.

Of course, the advice given with regard to urgency should not be understood too narrowly. It refers, first and foremost, to the fulfilment of tasks already allocated, and, mainly, to the internal growth and expansion of consciousness in order to meet and understand the meaning of what is happening. Brown gas envelops our planet, and the mixing of currents has a grave impact on sensitive organisms.

So, let nothing trouble you, maintain an inner calm, and take care of your health. Accustom yourself to a solemn mood, for it is solemnity that is prescribed to us above all else in these days of the Apocalypse. Recall *wise joy*.

Dark ones attempt to imitate the White Lodge in everything and, under the guise of Light, try with all their might to penetrate the centres of spirituality in order to introduce there confusion and decay. This is why it is so important to acquire the quality of discernment and restraint. With many people you encounter, remember the wise proverb: "Speech is silver, silence is golden."

It is extremely timely to put out good thoughts collectively in order to neutralize, at least to some degree, the poisoned atmosphere that surrounds us. It is important that those who participate in such transmissions are harmoniously disposed and truly filled with good feelings. For a thought may be beautiful, but if it is not spiritualized by the fire of the heart, it will remain lifeless. It is good to listen to music before making such transmissions.

In order to participate in cosmic creation, one should have a precise knowledge of the laws of cosmic forces and act in full agreement with them, otherwise destruction is inevitable. It is by acting in accordance with Cosmic Laws that the human being becomes a creator — of their own destiny and, collectively, that of the planet. All the forces and energies of the Cosmos are revealed only when a person has a powerful accumulation of the highest energies, under the condition of their infinite ascent. Therefore, ponder the immense power of the cosmic forces that surround us.

It is important to emphasize the significance of action and labour in the awakening and development of psychic energy, for above all, psychic energy needs exercise. It cannot be limited to random impulses; only constant systematic or rhythmic work can attune its current. The correct exchange of psychic energy is based on rhythm. Emphasize the full harm of laziness, which hinders the action of psychic energy within us, thereby destroying our entire evolution, eventually leading to complete decomposition. For now, people are starting to notice that the busiest people are the most long-lived, provided that there is a rhythm to their work and that their bodies are not excessively poisoned with toxins. It is worth pointing out that the principle of complete awareness should be introduced into every aspect of labour. Also, striving to improve the quality of one's work and all one's deeds is the best method to bring about the growth and intensification of psychic energy.

We are constantly instructed to be careful in how we give out our energy, especially now, when we are seeing an unprecedented intensity to the spatial currents.

Likewise, in moments of self-separation from psychic energy, when there is a draining of strength, it is important not to force oneself to work. One should give oneself the time needed to restore one's energy. Of course, with all these phenomena, a special honesty is required, for many have the inclination for a lax attitude to work, and to each attack of laziness they will ascribe an excessive release of psychic energy.

Where there is no correct exchange of psychic energy, there is no divisibility of spirit. When the fire is inactive or has begun to leave an unsuitable vessel, then, of course, divisibility of spirit is inaccessible. Also, do not forget that psychic energy is a double-edged force. Many zealous dark forces have it in large supply, but only in its lower manifestations and properties, and therefore, the actions of such energy are limited to the lower planes and are of short duration compared to energies of a higher quality.

It cannot be stressed enough the importance of thought and disciplined thinking in the development of high quality psychic energy.

"How should one act so that it is impossible to deviate from the Teaching, and impossible to become a traitor?" The answer to this question is given in all the books of the Teaching. Establish in your heart the foundations of love and devotion and apply the Teaching in your daily life.

Always and in all actions, the only criterion is *straight-knowledge*. But if direct straight-knowledge is still difficult to perceive and knocks but faintly, then, each action should be weighed on the scales of the heart. Straight-knowledge is closest to the heart.

Patience is one of the first qualities that must be acquired on the Path of Service.

If the Teaching is applied, if patience is unbreakable, if courage, fearlessness, and devotion burn in the heart as an inextinguishable flame, then you will reach the goal, and the Great Teacher will not hesitate to reveal Himself in one way or another.

THE THEOSOPHICAL MAHATMAS

IT IS WITH SINCERE and profound regret — though with no surprise, prepared as I am for years for such declarations — that I have read in the Rochester *Occult Word*, edited by Mrs. J. Cables, the devoted president of the Theosophical Society of that place, her joint editorial with Mr. W. T. Brown. This sudden revulsion of feeling is perhaps quite natural in the lady, for she has never had the opportunities given her as Mr. Brown has; and her feeling when she writes that after "a great desire . . . to be put into communication with the Theosophical Mahatmas we [they] have come to the conclusion that it is useless to strain the psychical eyes toward the Himalayas" is undeniably shared by many theosophists. Whether the complaints are justified, and also whether it is the "Mahatmas" or theosophists themselves who are to blame for it is a question that remains to be settled. It has been a pending case for several years and will have to be now decided, as the two complainants declare over their signatures that "we [they] need not run after Oriental Mystics, *who deny their ability to help us*." The last sentence, in italics, has to be seriously examined. I ask the privilege to make a few remarks thereon.

To begin with, the tone of the whole article is that of a true *manifesto*. Condensed and weeded of its exuberance of Biblical expressions it comes to this paraphrastical declaration: "We have knocked at their door, and they have not answered us; we have prayed for bread, they have denied us even a stone." The charge is quite serious; nevertheless, that it is neither just nor fair — is what I propose to show.

As I was the first in the United States to bring the existence of our Masters into publicity; and, having exposed the holy names of two members of a Brotherhood hitherto unknown to Europe and America (save to a few mystics and Initiates of every age), yet sacred and revered throughout the East, and especially India, causing vulgar speculation and curiosity to grow around those blessed names, and finally leading to a public rebuke, I believe it my duty to contradict the fitness of the latter by explaining the whole situation, as I feel myself the chief culprit. It may do good to some, perchance, and will interest some others.

Let no one think withal, that I come out as a champion or a defender of those who most assuredly need no defence. What I intend, is to present simple *facts*, and let after this the situation be judged on its own merits. To the plain statement of our brothers and sisters that they have been "living on husks," "hunting after strange gods" without receiving admittance, I would ask in my turn, as plainly: "Are you sure of having knocked at the right door? Do you feel certain that you have not lost your way by *stopping so often on your journey at strange doors, behind which lie in wait the fiercest enemies of those you were searching for*?"

Our Masters are not "a jealous god"; they are simply holy mortals, nevertheless, however, higher than any in this world, morally, intellectually, and spiritually. However holy and advanced in the science of the Mysteries — they are still men, members of a Brotherhood, who are the first in it to show themselves subservient to its time-honoured laws and rules. And one of the first rules in it demands that those who start on their journey *Eastward*, as candidates to the notice and favours of those who are the custodians of those Mysteries, should proceed by the straight road, without stopping on every sideway and path, seeking to join other "Masters" and professors often of the left-hand science, that they should have confidence and show trust and patience, besides several other conditions to fulfil. Failing in all of this from first to last, what right has any man or woman to complain of the liability of the Masters to help them?

Truly, "the Dwellers of the Threshold are within!"

Once that a theosophist would become a candidate for either chelaship or favours, he must *be* aware of the mutual pledge, tacitly, if not formally offered and accepted between the two parties, and, *that such a pledge is sacred*. It is a bond of *seven* years of probation. If during that time, notwithstanding the many human shortcomings and mistakes of the candidate (save two which it is needless to specify in print) he remains throughout every temptation *true to the chosen Master*, or Masters (in the case of *lay* candidates), and as faithful to the Society founded at their wish and under their orders, then the theosophist will be initiated into * * * thenceforward allowed to communicate with his Guru unreservedly, all his failings, save this one, as specified, may be overlooked: they belong to his future *karma*, but are left for the present, to the discretion and judgement of the Master. He alone has the power of judging whether even during those long seven years the chela will be favoured regardless of his mistakes and sins, with occasional communications with, and from the Guru. The latter thoroughly posted as to the causes and motives that led the candidate into sins of omission and commission is the only one to judge of the advisability or inadvisability of bestowing encouragement; as he alone is entitled to it, seeing that he is himself under the inexorable Law of Karma, which no one from the Zulu savage up to the highest Archangel can avoid — and that he has to assume the great responsibility of the causes created by himself.

Thus, the chief and the only indispensable condition required in the candidate or chela on probation, is simply unswerving fidelity to the chosen Master and his purposes. This is a condition *sine qua non*; not as I have said, on account of any jealous feeling, but simply because *the magnetic rapport between the two once broken, it becomes at each time doubly difficult to re-establish it again*; and that it is neither just nor fair, that the Masters should strain their powers for those whose future course and final desertion they very often can plainly foresee. Yet, how many of those, who, expecting as I would call it "favours by anticipation," and being disappointed, instead of humbly repeating *mea culpa*, tax the Masters with selfishness and injustice. They will deliberately break the thread of connection ten times in one year, and yet expect each time to be taken back on the old lines! I know of one theosophist — let him be nameless though it is hoped he will recognize himself — a quiet, intelligent young gentleman, a mystic by nature, who, in his ill-advised enthusiasm and impatience, changed Masters and his ideas about half a dozen times in less than three years. First he offered himself, was accepted on probation and took the vow of chelaship; about a year later, he suddenly got the idea of getting married, though he had several proofs of the corporeal presence of his Master, and had several favours bestowed upon him. Projects of marriage failing, he sought "Masters" under other climes, and became an enthusiastic Rosicrucian; then he returned to theosophy as a Christian mystic; then again sought to enliven his austerities with a wife; then gave up the idea and turned a spiritualist. And now having applied once more "to be taken back as a chela" (I have his letter) and his Master remaining silent — he renounced him altogether, to seek in the words of the above manifesto — his old "Essenian Master and *to test the spirits* in his name."

The able and respected editor of *The Occult Word* and her Secretary are right, and have chosen the only true path in which with a very small dose of blind faith, they are sure to encounter no deceptions or disappointments. "It is pleasant for some of us," they say, "to obey the call of the 'Man of Sorrows' who will not turn any away, because they are unworthy or have not scored up a certain percentage of personal merit." How *do* they know? Unless they accept the cynically awful and pernicious dogma of the Protestant Church, that teaches the forgiveness of the blackest crime, provided the murderer *believes sincerely* that the blood of his "Redeemer" has saved him at the last hour — what is it but *blind* unphilosophical faith? Emotionalism is *not* philosophy; and Buddha devoted his long self-sacrificing life to tear people away precisely from that *evil breeding* superstition. Why speak of Buddha then, in the same breath? The doctrine of salvation by *personal* merit, and *self*-forgetfulness is the cornerstone of the teaching of the Lord Buddha. Both the writers may have and very likely they did — "hunt after *strange* gods"; but these *were not our* Masters. They have "denied Him thrice" and now propose "with bleeding feet and prostrate spirit" to "pray that He (Jesus) may take us (them) once more under His wing," etc. The "Nazarene Master" is sure to oblige them so far. Still they will be living on *"husks"* plus *"*blind faith." But in this they are the best judges, and no one has a right to meddle with their private beliefs in our Society; and heaven grant that they should not in their fresh disappointment turn our bitterest enemies one day.

Yet, to those Theosophists, who are displeased with the Society in general, no one has ever made to you any rash promises; least of all, has either the Society or its founders ever offered their "Masters" as a *chromo-premium* to the best behaved. For years every new member has been told that *he was promised nothing*, but had everything to expect only from his own personal merit. The theosophist is left free and untrammelled in his actions. Whenever displeased — *alia tentanda via est* — no harm in trying elsewhere; unless, indeed one has offered himself and is decided to win the Masters' favours. To such especially, I now address myself and ask: Have you fulfilled *your* obligations and pledges? Have you, who would fain lay all the blame on the Society and the Masters — the latter the embodiment of charity, tolerance, justice, and universal love — have you *led the life* requisite, and the conditions required from one who becomes a candidate? Let him who feels in his heart and conscience that he has — that he has never once failed seriously, never doubted his Master's wisdom, never sought *other* Master or Masters in his impatience to become an occultist with powers; and that he has never betrayed his theosophical duty in thought or deed — let him, I say, rise and *protest*. He can do so fearlessly; there is no penalty attached to it, and he will not even receive a reproach, let alone be excluded, from the Society — the broadest and most liberal in its views, the most Catholic of all the Societies known or unknown. I am afraid my invitation will remain unanswered. During the eleven years of the existence of the Theosophical Society I have known, out of the seventy-two regularly accepted chelas on probation and the hundreds of *lay* candidates — only *three* who have not hitherto failed, and *one only* who had a full success. No one forces anyone into chelaship; no promises are uttered, none except the mutual pledge between Master and the would-be-chela. Verily, verily, many are called but few are chosen — or rather few who have the patience of going to the bitter end, if bitter we can call simple perseverance and singleness of purpose. And what about the Society, in general, outside of India? Who among the many thousands of members does *lead the life*? Shall anyone say because he is a strict vegetarian — *elephants and cows are that* — or happens to lead a celibate life, after a stormy youth in the opposite direction; or because he studies the Bhagavad Gita or the "yoga philosophy" *upside down*, that he is a theosophist *according to the Masters' hearts*? As it is not the cowl that makes the monk, so, no long hair with a poetical vacancy on the brow are sufficient to make of one a faithful follower of Divine Wisdom. Look around you, and behold our Universal Brotherhood so called! The Society founded to remedy the glaring evils of Christianity, to shun bigotry and intolerance, cant and superstition and to cultivate real universal love extending even to the dumb brute, what has it become in Europe and America in these eleven years of trial? In one thing only we have succeeded to be considered higher than our Christian Brothers, who, according to Lawrence Oliphant's graphic expression "Kill one another for Brotherhood's sake and fight as devils for the love of God" — and this is that we have made away *with every dogma* and are now justly and wisely trying to make away with the last vestige of even nominal authority. But in every other respect we are as bad as they are: backbiting, slander, uncharitableness, criticism, incessant war-cry, and ding of mutual rebukes that Christian hell itself might be proud of! And all this, I suppose, is the Masters' fault: They will not help those who help others on the way of salvation and liberation from selfishness — with kicks and scandals? Truly *we are* an example to the world, and fit companions for the holy ascetics of the Snowy Range!

And now a few words more before I close. I will be asked: "And who are you to find fault with us? Are you, who claim nevertheless, communion with the Masters and receive daily favours from Them; are you so holy, faultless, and so worthy?" To this I answer: I *am not*. Imperfect and faulty is my nature; many and glaring are my shortcomings — and for this my karma is heavier than that of any other Theosophist. *It is* — and must be so — since for so many years I stand set in the pillory, a target for my enemies and some friends also. Yet I accept the *trial* cheerfully. Why? Because I know that I have, all my faults notwithstanding, Master's protection extended over me. And if I have it, the reason for it is simply this: for thirty-five years and more, ever since 1851 that I saw my Master *bodily* and personally for the first time, *I have never once denied or even doubted Him*, not even in thought. Never a reproach or a murmur against Him has escaped my lips, or entered even my brain for one instant under the heaviest trials. From the first I knew what I had to expect, for I was told that, which I have never ceased repeating to others: as soon as one steps on the Path leading to the Ashram of the blessed Masters — the last and only custodians of primitive Wisdom and Truth — his karma, instead of having to be distributed throughout his long life, falls upon him in a block and crushes him with its whole weight. He who believes in what he professes and in his Master, will stand it and come out of the trial victorious; he *who doubts*, the coward who fears to receive his just dues and tries to avoid justice being done — *fails*. He will not escape karma just the same, but he will only lose that for which he has risked its untimely visits. This is why having been so constantly, so mercilessly slashed by my karma using my enemies as unconscious weapons, that I have stood it all. I felt sure that Master would not permit that I should perish; that he would always appear at the *eleventh* hour — *and so he did*. Three times I was saved from death by Him, the last time almost against my will; when I went again into the cold, wicked world out of love for Him who has taught me what I know and made me what I am. Therefore, I do His work and bidding, and this is what has given me the lion's strength to support shocks — physical and mental, one of which would have killed any theosophist who would go on doubting the mighty protection. Unswerving devotion to Him who embodies the duty traced for me, and belief in the Wisdom — collectively, of that grand, mysterious, yet actual Brotherhood of holy men — is my only merit, and the cause of my success in occult philosophy. And now repeating after the *Paraguru* — my Master's Master — the words He had sent as a message to those who wanted to make of the Society a "miracle club" instead of a Brotherhood of Peace, Love, and mutual assistance — "Perish rather, the Theosophical Society and its hapless Founders," I say perish their twelve years' labour and their very lives rather than that I should see what I do today: theosophists, outvying political "rings" in their search for personal power and authority; theosophists slandering and criticizing each other as two rival Christian sects might do; finally theosophists refusing to *lead the life* and then criticizing and throwing slurs on the grandest and noblest of men, because tied by their wise laws — hoary with age and based on an experience of human nature millenniums old — those Masters refuse to interfere with karma and to play second fiddle to every theosophist who calls upon Them and whether he deserves it or not.

Unless radical reforms in our American and European Societies are speedily resorted to — I fear that before long there will remain but one centre of Theosophical Societies and Theosophy in the whole world — namely, in India; on that country I call all the blessings of my heart. All my love and aspirations belong to my beloved brothers, the sons of old Aryavarta — the Motherland of my Master.

CHELAS AND LAY CHELAS

As the word *chela* has, among others, been introduced by Theosophy into the nomenclature of Western metaphysics, and the circulation of our magazine [*The Theosophist*] is constantly widening, it will be as well if some more definite explanation than heretofore is given with respect to the meaning of this term and the rules of chelaship, for the benefit of our European if not Eastern members. A "chela" then, is one who has offered himself or herself as a pupil to learn practically the "hidden mysteries of Nature and the psychical powers latent in man." The spiritual teacher to whom he proposes his candidature is called in India a *Guru*; and the real Guru is always an Adept in the occult science. A man of profound knowledge, exoteric and esoteric, especially the latter; and one who has brought his carnal nature under subjection of the Will; who has developed in himself both the power (*siddhi*) to control the forces of Nature, and the capacity to probe her secrets by the help of the formerly latent but now active powers of his being — this is the real Guru. To offer oneself as a candidate for chelaship is easy enough, to develop into an Adept the most difficult task any man could possibly undertake. There are scores of "natural-born" poets, mathematicians, mechanics, statesmen, etc., but a natural-born Adept is something practically impossible. For, though we do hear at very rare intervals of one who has an extraordinary innate capacity for the acquisition of occult knowledge and power, yet even he has to pass the self-same tests and probations, and go through the same self-training as any less endowed fellow aspirant. In this matter it is most true that there is no royal road by which favourites may travel.

For centuries the selection of chelas — outside the hereditary group within the *gonpa* (temple) — has been made by the Himalayan Mahatmas themselves from among the class — in Tibet, a considerable one as to number — of natural mystics. The only exceptions have been in the cases of Western men like Fludd, Thomas Vaughan, Paracelsus, Pico della Mirandola, Count de Saint-Germain, etc., whose temperamental affinity to this celestial science more or less forced the distant Adepts to come into personal relations with them, and enabled them to get such small (or large) proportion of the whole truth as was possible under their social surroundings. From Book IV of *Kiu-te*, chapter on "the Laws of Upasans," we learn that the qualifications expected in a chela were:

1. Perfect physical health.

2. Absolute mental and physical purity.

3. Unselfishness of purpose; universal charity; pity for all animate beings.

4. Truthfulness and unswerving faith in the Law of Karma, independent of any power in Nature that could interfere: a law whose course is not to be obstructed by any agency, not to be caused to deviate by prayer or propitiatory exoteric ceremonies.

5. A courage undaunted in every emergency, even by peril to life.

6. An intuitional perception of one's being the vehicle of the manifested Avalokiteshvara or Divine Atman (Spirit).

7. Calm indifference for, but a just appreciation of everything that constitutes the objective and transitory world, in its relation with, and to, the invisible regions.

Such, at the least, must have been the recommendations of one aspiring to perfect chelaship. With the sole exception of the first, which in rare and exceptional cases might have been modified, each one of these points has been invariably insisted upon, and all must have been more or less developed in the inner nature by the chela's *unhelped exertions*, before he could be actually put to the test.

When the self-evolving ascetic — whether in, or outside the active world — had placed himself, according to his natural capacity, above, hence made himself master of, his 1) *sharira* — body; 2) *indriya* — senses; 3) *dosha* — faults; 4) *dukkha* — pain; and is ready to become one with his *manas* — mind; *buddhi* — intellection, or spiritual intelligence; and *atma* — highest soul, i.e., spirit. When he is ready for this, and, further, to recognize in *atma* the highest ruler in the world of perceptions, and in the will, the highest executive energy (power), then may he, under the time-honoured rules, be taken in hand by one of the Initiates. He may then be shown the mysterious path at whose thither end the chela is taught the unerring discernment of *phala*, or the fruits of causes produced, and given the means of reaching *apavarga* — emancipation, from the misery of repeated births (in whose determination the ignorant has no hand), and thus of avoiding *pratyabhava* — transmigration.

But since the advent of the Theosophical Society, one of whose arduous tasks it was to reawaken in the Aryan mind the dormant memory of the existence of this science and of those transcendent human capabilities, the rules of chela selection have become slightly relaxed in one respect. Many members of the Society becoming convinced by practical proof upon the above points, and rightly enough thinking that if other men had hitherto reached the goal, they too if inherently fitted, might reach it by following the same path, pressed to be taken as candidates. And as it would be an interference with karma to deny them the chance of at least beginning — since they were so importunate, they were given it. The results have been far from encouraging so far, and it is to show these unfortunates the cause of their failure as much as to warn others against rushing heedlessly upon a similar fate, that the writing of the present article has been ordered. The candidates in question, though plainly warned against it in advance, began wrong by selfishly looking to the future and losing sight of the past. They forgot that they had done nothing to deserve the rare honour of selection, nothing which warranted their expecting such a privilege; that they could boast of none of the above enumerated merits. As men of the selfish, sensual world, whether married or single, merchants, civilian, or military employees, or members of the learned professions, they had been to a school most calculated to assimilate them to the animal nature, least so to develop their spiritual potentialities. Yet each and all had vanity enough to suppose that their case would be made an exception to the law of countless centuries' establishment as though, indeed, in their person had been born to the world a new Avatar! All expected to have hidden things taught, extraordinary powers given them because — well, because they had joined the Theosophical Society. Some had sincerely resolved to amend their lives, and give up their evil courses; we must do them that justice, at all events.

All were refused at first, Colonel Olcott, the President, himself, to begin with; and as to the latter gentleman there is now no harm in saying that he was not formally accepted as a chela until he had proved by more than a year's devoted labours and by a determination which brooked no denial, that he might safely be tested. Then from all sides came complaints — from Hindus, who ought to have known better, as well as from Europeans who, of course, were not in a condition to know anything at all about the rules. The cry was that unless at least a few Theosophists were given the chance to try, the Society could not endure. Every other noble and unselfish feature of our programme was ignored — a man's duty to his neighbour, to his country, his duty to help, enlighten, encourage, and elevate those weaker and less favoured than he; all were trampled out of sight in the insane rush for Adeptship. The call for phenomena, phenomena, phenomena, resounded in every quarter, and the Founders were impeded in their real work and teased importunately to intercede with the Mahatmas, against whom the real grievance lay, though their poor agents had to take all the buffets. At last, the word came from the higher authorities that a few of the most urgent candidates should be taken at their word. The result of the experiment would perhaps show better than any amount of preaching what chelaship meant, and what are the consequences of selfishness and temerity. Each candidate was warned that he must wait for years in any event, before his fitness could be proven, and that he must pass through a series of tests that would bring out all there was in him, whether bad or good. They were nearly all married men and hence were designated "lay chelas" — a term new in English, but having long had its equivalent in Asiatic tongues. A lay chela is but a man of the world who affirms his desire to become wise in spiritual things. Virtually, every member of the Theosophical Society who subscribes to the second of our three "declared objects" is such; for though not of the number of true chelas, he has yet the possibility of becoming one, for he has stepped across the boundary line which separated him from the Mahatmas, and has brought himself, as it were, under their notice. In joining the Society and binding himself to help along its work, he has pledged himself to act in some degree in concert with those Mahatmas, at whose behest the Society was organized, and under whose conditional protection it remains. The joining is then, the introduction; all the rest depends entirely upon the member himself, and he need never expect the most distant approach to the "favour" of one of our Mahatmas, or any other Mahatmas in the world — should the latter consent to become known — that has not been fully earned by personal merit. *The Mahatmas are the servants, not the arbiters of the Law of Karma. Lay chelaship confers no privilege upon anyone except that of working for merit under the observation of a Master.* And whether that Master be or be not seen by the chela makes no difference whatever as to the result: his good thoughts, words, and deeds will bear their fruits, his evil ones, theirs. To boast of lay chelaship or make a parade of it, is the surest way to reduce the relationship with the Guru to a mere empty name, for it would be *prima facie* evidence of vanity and unfitness for further progress. And for years we have been teaching everywhere the maxim "First deserve, then desire" intimacy with the Mahatmas.

Now there is a terrible law operative in Nature, one which cannot be altered, and whose operation clears up the apparent mystery of the selection of certain "chelas" who have turned out sorry specimens of morality, these few years past. Does the reader recall the old proverb, "Let sleeping dogs lie"? There is a world of occult meaning in it. No man or woman knows his or her moral strength until it is *tried*. Thousands go through life very respectably, because they were never put to the pinch. This is a truism doubtless, but it is most pertinent to the present case. One who undertakes to try for chelaship by that very act rouses and lashes to desperation every sleeping passion of his animal nature. For this is the commencement of a struggle for the mastery in which quarter is neither to be given nor taken. It is, once for all: "To be, or not to be"; to conquer, means Adeptship; to fail, an ignoble martyrdom; for to fall victim to lust, pride, avarice, vanity, selfishness, cowardice, or any other of the lower propensities, is indeed ignoble, if measured by the standard of true manhood. The chela is not only called to face all the latent evil propensities of his nature, but, in addition, the whole volume of maleficent power accumulated by the community and nation to which he belongs. For he is an integral part of those aggregates, and what affects either the individual man, or the group (town or nation) reacts upon the other. And in this instance his struggle for goodness jars upon the whole body of badness in his environment, and draws its fury upon him. If he is content to go along with his neighbours and be almost as they are — perhaps a little better or somewhat worse than the average — no one may give him a thought. But let it be known that he has been able to detect the hollow mockery of social life, its hypocrisy, selfishness, sensuality, cupidity, and other bad features, and has determined to lift himself up to a higher level, at once he is hated, and every bad, or bigoted, or malicious nature sends at him a current of opposing willpower. If he is innately strong he shakes it off, as the powerful swimmer dashes through the current that would bear a weaker one away. But in this moral battle, if the chela has one single hidden blemish — do what he may, it *shall* and *will* be brought to light.

The varnish of conventionalities which "civilization" overlays us all with must come off to the last coat, and the Inner Self, naked and without the slightest veil to conceal its reality, is exposed. The habits of society which hold men to a certain degree under moral restraint, and compel them to pay tribute to virtue by seeming to be good whether they are so or not, these habits are apt to be all forgotten, these restraints to be all broken through under the strain of chelaship. He is now in an atmosphere of illusions — *Maya*. Vice puts on its most alluring face, and the tempting passions try to lure the inexperienced aspirant to the depths of psychic debasement. This is not a case like that depicted by a great artist, where Satan is seen playing a game of chess with a man upon the stake of his soul, while the latter's good angel stands beside him to counsel and assist. For the strife is in this instance between the chela's will and his carnal nature, and karma forbids that any angel or Guru should interfere until the result is known. With the vividness of poetic fancy Bulwer-Lytton has idealized it for us in his *Zanoni*, a work which will ever be prized by the occultist; while in his *Strange Story* he has with equal power shown the black side of occult research and its deadly perils. Chelaship was defined, the other day, by a Mahatma as a "psychic resolvent, which eats away all dross and leaves only the pure gold behind." If the candidate has the latent lust for money, or political chicanery, or materialistic scepticism, or vain display, or false speaking, or cruelty, or sensual gratification of any kind, the germ is almost sure to sprout; and so, on the other hand, as regards the noble qualities of human nature. The real man comes out. Is it not the height of folly, then, for anyone to leave the smooth path of commonplace life to scale the crags of chelaship without some reasonable feeling of certainty that he has the right stuff in him? Well says the Bible: "Let him that standeth take heed lest he fall" — a text that would-be chelas should consider well before they rush headlong into the fray! It would have been well for some of our lay chelas if they had thought twice before defying the tests. *We call to mind several sad failures within a twelve-month.* One went bad in the head, recanted noble sentiments uttered but a few weeks previously, and became a member of a religion he had just scornfully and unanswerably proven false. A second became a defaulter and absconded with his employer's money — the latter also a Theosophist. A third gave himself up to gross debauchery, and confessed it with ineffectual sobs and tears, to his chosen Guru. A fourth got entangled with a person of the other sex and fell out with his dearest and truest friends. A fifth showed signs of mental aberration and was brought into Court upon charges of discreditable conduct. A sixth shot himself to escape the consequences of criminality, on the verge of detection! And so we might go on and on. All these were apparently sincere searchers after truth, and passed in the world for respectable persons. Externally, they were fairly eligible as candidates for chelaship, as appearances go; but "within all was rottenness and dead men's bones." The world's varnish was so thick as to hide the absence of the true gold underneath; and the "resolvent" doing its work, the candidate proved in each instance but a gilded figure of moral dross, from circumference to core.

In what precedes we have, of course, dealt but with the failures among lay chelas; there have been partial successes too, and these are passing gradually through the first stages of their probation. Some are making themselves useful to the Society and to the world in general by good example and precept. If they persist, well for them, well for us all: the odds are fearfully against them, but still "there is no impossibility to him who *wills*." The difficulties in chelaship will never be less until human nature changes and a new sort is evolved. St. Paul might have had a chela in mind when he said "to will is present with me; but how to perform that which is good I find not. For the good I would I do not; but the evil which I would not, that I do."[1] And in the wise Kiratarjuniya of Bharavi it is written:

> The enemies which rise within the body,
> Hard to be overcome — the evil passions —
> Should manfully be fought; he who conquers these
> Is equal to the conqueror of worlds.

MAHATMAS AND CHELAS

A Mahatma is a personage, who, by special training and education, has evolved those higher faculties and has attained that spiritual knowledge, which ordinary humanity will acquire after passing through numberless series of reincarnations during the process of cosmic evolution, provided, of course, that they do not go, in the meanwhile, against the purposes of Nature and thus bring on their own annihilation. This process of the self-evolution of the Mahatma extends over a number of "incarnations," although, comparatively speaking, they are very few. Now, what is it that incarnates? The occult doctrine, so far as it is given out, shows that the first three principles die more or less with what is called the physical death. The fourth principle, together with the lower portions of the fifth, in which reside the animal propensities, has Kama-loka for its abode, where it suffers the throes of disintegration in

---

[1] Romans 7:18–19.

proportion to the intensity of those lower desires; while it is the higher *manas*, the pure man, which is associated with the sixth and seventh principles, that goes into Devachan to enjoy there the effects of its good karma, and then to be reincarnated as a higher individuality. Now, an entity, that is passing through the occult training in its successive births, gradually has less and less (in each incarnation) of that lower *manas* until there arrives a time when its *whole manas*, being of an entirely elevated character, is centred in the higher individuality, when such a person may be said to have become a Mahatma. At the time of his physical death, all the lower four principles perish without any suffering, for these are, in fact, to him like a piece of wearing apparel which he puts on and off at will. The real Mahatma is then not his physical body but that higher *manas* which is inseparably linked to the *atma* and its vehicle (the sixth principle) — a union effected by him in a comparatively very short period by passing through the process of self-evolution laid down by the occult philosophy. When, therefore, people express a desire to "see a Mahatma," they really do not seem to understand what it is they ask for. How can they, by their physical eyes, hope to see that which *transcends* that sight? Is it the body — a mere shell or mask — they crave or hunt after? And supposing they see the body of a Mahatma, how can they know that behind that mask is concealed an exalted entity? By what standard are they to judge whether the *Maya* before them reflects the image of a true Mahatma or not? And who will say that the physical is not a *Maya*? Higher things can be perceived only by a sense pertaining to those higher things. And whoever therefore wants to see the real Mahatma, must use his *intellectual* sight. He must so elevate his *manas* that its perception will be clear and all mists created by *Maya* must be dispelled. His vision will then be bright and he will see the Mahatmas wherever he may be, for, being merged into the sixth and the seventh principles, which are ubiquitous and omnipresent, the Mahatmas may be said to be everywhere. But, at the same time, just as we may be standing on a mountain top and have within our sight the whole plain, and yet not be cognizant of any particular tree or spot, because from that elevated position all below is nearly identical, and as our attention may be drawn to something which may be dissimilar to its surroundings — so in the same manner, although the whole of humanity is within the mental vision of the Mahatmas, they cannot be expected to take special note of every human being, unless that being by his special acts draws their particular attention to himself. The highest interest of humanity, as a whole, is their special concern, for they have identified themselves with that Universal Soul which runs through humanity, and he, who would draw their attention, must do so through that Soul which pervades everywhere. This perception of the *manas* may be called "faith" which should not be confounded with *blind belief*. "Blind faith" is an expression sometimes used to indicate belief without perception or understanding; while the true perception of the *manas* is that enlightened belief, which is the real meaning of the word "faith." This belief should at the same time be accompanied by *knowledge*, i.e., experience, for "true *knowledge* brings with it faith." Faith is the perception of the *manas* (the fifth principle), while knowledge, in the true sense of the term, is the capacity of the intellect, i.e., it is spiritual perception. In short, the higher individuality of man, composed of his higher *manas*, the sixth and the seventh principles, should work as a unity, and then only can it obtain "divine wisdom," for divine things can be sensed only by divine faculties. Thus the desire, which should prompt one to apply for chelaship, is to so far understand the operations of the Law of Cosmic Evolution as will enable him to work in harmonious accord with Nature, instead of going against its purposes through ignorance.

CHELAS

NOTWITHSTANDING the many articles which have appeared in this magazine [*The Theosophist*] upon the above subject, much misunderstanding and many false views seem still to prevail. What are chelas, and what are their powers? Have they faults, and in what particular are they different from people who are not chelas? Is every word uttered by a chela to be taken as gospel truth?

These questions arise because many persons have entertained very absurd views for a time about chelas, and when it was found that those views should be changed, the reaction has been in several cases quite violent.

The word "chela" simply means *a disciple*; but it has become crystallized in the literature of Theosophy, and has, in different minds, as many different definitions as the word "God" itself. Some persons have gone so far as to say that when a man is a chela he is at once put upon a plane when each word that he may unfortunately utter is taken down as *ex cathedra*, and he is not allowed the poor privilege of talking like an ordinary person. If it be found out that any such utterance was on his own account and responsibility, he is charged with having misled his hearers.

Now this wrong idea must be corrected once for all. There are chelas and chelas, just as there are Mahatmas and Mahatmas. There are Mahatmas in fact who are themselves the chelas of those who are higher yet. But no one, for an instant, would confound a chela who has just begun his troublous journey with that greater chela who is a Mahatma.

In fact the chela is an unfortunate man who has entered upon "a path not manifest," and Krishna says that "that is the most difficult path."

Instead of being the constant mouthpiece of his Guru, he finds himself left more alone in the world than those who are not chelas, and his path is surrounded by dangers which would appal many an aspirant, were they depicted in natural colours, so that instead of accepting his Guru and passing an entrance examination with a view to becoming Bachelor of the Art of Occultism under his Master's constant and friendly guidance, he really forces his way into a guarded enclosure, and has from that moment to fight and conquer — or die. Instead of accepting he has to be worthy of acceptance. Nor must he offer himself. One of the Mahatmas has, within the year, written: "Never thrust yourself upon us for chelaship; wait until it descends upon you."

And having been accepted as a chela, it is not true that he is merely the instrument of his Guru. He speaks as ordinary men then as before, and it is only when the Master sends by means of the chela's magnetism an actual written letter, that the lookers-on can say that through him a communication came.

It may happen with them, as it does with any author occasionally, that they evolve either true or beautiful utterances, but it must not be therefore concluded that during that utterance the Guru was speaking through the chela. If there was the germ of a good thought in the mind, the Guru's influence, like the gentle rain upon the seed, may have caused it to spring into sudden life and abnormally blossom, but that is not the Master's voice. The cases in fact are rare in which the Masters speak through a chela.

The powers of chelas vary with their progress; and every one should know that if a chela has any "powers," he is not permitted to use them save in rare and exceptional cases, and never may he boast of their possession. So it must follow that those who are only beginners have no more or greater power than an ordinary man. Indeed the goal set before the chela is not the acquisition of psychological power; his chief task is to divest himself of that overmastering sense of personality which is the thick veil that hides from sight our immortal part — the real man. So long as he allows this feeling to remain, just so long will he be fixed at the very door of occultism, unable to proceed further.

Sentimentality, then, is not the equipment for a chela. His work is hard, his road stony, the end far away. With sentimentality merely he will not advance at all. Is he waiting for the Master to bid him show his courage by precipitating himself from a precipice, or by braving the cold Himalayan steeps? False hope; they will not call him thus. And so, as he is not to clothe himself in sentiment, the public must not, when they wish to consider him, throw a false veil of sentimentality over all his actions and words.

Let us therefore, henceforth, see a little more discrimination used in looking at chelas.

THE TEN RULES OF DISCIPLESHIP OF THE FOURTH DEGREE OF THE GREAT WHITE LODGE

From Master Hilarion[1]

GOD IS LOVE, and Love is the fundamental source of Being. Therefore, if thou sin against Love, that sin is against God.

1. "Thou shalt love the Lord thy God with all thy heart and mind, and thy neighbour as thyself." This is the highest law.

2. Thou shalt obey the laws of life. The Higher Law will hold thee accountable for the breaking of every lesser law.

3. Thou shalt not sin against thine own body nor against the body of thy neighbour by concupiscence; for the Lord thy God will demand an accounting of thee for all of the Creative Fire enthroned within thee.

4. Thou shalt not needlessly take the life of any thing or creature.

5. Thou shalt not speak falsely, unnecessarily, or critically against thy neighbour, and so put in action the converse force of creative sound and word; for the Higher Law will reverse the action of the force thus directed and bring back upon thee, with intensified strength, the results of the broken law.

6. Thou shalt bear constantly in mind the unity of the human race, and treat every member of the Great White Lodge as though he were of blood kin; for unity is the law of discipleship and, if thou sin against this law, thou shalt be greatly hindered in thy progress toward the goal of thy desires.

7. Morning and evening thou shalt lift the eyes of thy soul toward the Throne of thy God, with strong aspiration, gratitude, and devotion; for according to thy desires — thy demands — upon the Centre of all Being, desires expressed in purity, thanksgiving, and unselfishness shall the supply be vouchsafed thee.

---

[1] Francia La Due, *The Temple of Mysteries* (New York: Radiant Books, 2023), pp. 636–637.

8. Thou shalt give of thine abundance to all the poor, but of thy poverty, the price of thine own pleasures, and that which would minister to thine own desires shalt thou give to the Great Mother and to the Guardian of the Shrine, through which the Great Mother love of the universe radiates for thine own eternal good.

9. Thou shalt not despise nor ill-treat any thing or creature. Matter, Force, and Consciousness are but different degrees of the one eternal, all-pervading principle of Love — which is God; and he who despises and reviles his body, because it does not radiate the light of his soul, despises God as certainly as does the man who despises and reviles the soul and spirit of God.

10. When the Law of Love — of Karma — has brought thee out of the morass of spiritual darkness to the beginning of the path which leads to spiritual illumination, woe be unto thee if thou obstruct that path for thyself or others, by refusing to obey the Master to whose feet that law has brought thee.

Only by implicit obedience to the commands of the Master-Teacher shalt thou be able to lift one foot after another while treading that path of discipleship.

Commune long and earnestly with the God within thyself ere thou darest to make demand to tread that path, for once thou hast entered it, thou canst no more return to thy former state of irresponsibility than thou canst re-enter thy mother's womb.

Behold the Path before thee: a clean life, pure aspiration, and unselfish service. Art thou prepared to tread that Path?

THE MAHA CHOHAN'S LETTER

1881

THE DOCTRINE we promulgate being the only true one, must — supported by such evidence as we are preparing to give — become ultimately triumphant, like every other truth. Yet it is absolutely necessary to inculcate it gradually; enforcing its theories (unimpeachable facts for those who know) with direct inference, deduced from and corroborated by, the evidence furnished by modern exact science. That is why Colonel H. S. Olcott, who works to revive Buddhism, may be regarded as one who labours in the true path of Theosophy, far more than any man who chooses as his goal the gratification of his own ardent aspirations for occult knowledge. Buddhism, stripped of its superstition, is eternal truth; and he who strives for the latter is striving for *Theo-Sophia*, Divine Wisdom, which is a synonym of truth.

For our doctrines to practically react on the so-called moral code, or the ideas of truthfulness, purity, self-denial, charity, etc., we have to preach and popularize a knowledge of Theosophy. It is not the individual and determined purpose of attaining Nirvana — the culmination of all knowledge and absolute wisdom, which is after all only an exalted and glorious *selfishness* — but the self-sacrificing pursuit of the best means to lead on the right path our neighbour, to cause to benefit by it as many of our fellow creatures as we possibly can, which constitutes the true *Theosophist*.

The intellectual portion of mankind seems to be fast dividing into two classes: the one unconsciously preparing for itself long periods of temporary annihilation or states of non-consciousness, owing to the deliberate surrender of intellect and its imprisonment in the narrow grooves of bigotry and superstition — a process which cannot fail to lead to the utter deformation of the intellectual principle; the other unrestrainedly indulging its animal propensities with the deliberate intention of *submitting* to annihilation pure and simple, in case of failure, and to millenniums of degradation after physical dissolution.

Those intellectual classes reacting upon the ignorant masses — which they attract, and which look up to them as noble and fit examples to be followed — degrade and morally ruin those they ought to protect and guide. Between degrading superstition and still more degrading brutal materialism, the White Dove of Truth has hardly room whereon to rest her weary unwelcome feet.

It is time that Theosophy should enter the arena. The sons of Theosophists are more likely to become in their turn Theosophists than anything else. No messenger of the truth, no prophet has ever achieved during his lifetime a complete triumph — not even Buddha. The Theosophical Society was chosen as the cornerstone, the foundation of the future religions of humanity. To achieve the proposed object, a greater, wiser, and especially a more benevolent intermingling of the high and the low, the alpha and the omega of society, was determined upon. The white race must be the first to stretch out the hand of fellowship to the dark nations, to call the poor despised "nigger" brother. This prospect may not smile for all, but he is *no* Theosophist who objects to this principle.

In view of the ever-increasing triumph and, at the same time, misuse of free thought and *liberty* (the universal reign of Satan, Éliphas Lévi would have called it), how is the combative *natural* instinct of man to be restrained from inflicting hitherto unheard-of cruelties and enormities, tyranny, injustice, etc., if not through the soothing influence of Brotherhood, and of the practical application of Buddha's esoteric doctrines?

For everyone knows that total emancipation from the authority of the one all-pervading power, or law — called God by the priests, Buddha, Divine Wisdom and Enlightenment, or Theosophy, by the philosophers of all ages — means also the emancipation from that of human law. Once unfettered, delivered from their dead-weight of dogmatic interpretations, personal names, anthropomorphic conceptions, and salaried priests, the fundamental doctrines of all religions will be proved identical in their esoteric meaning. Osiris, Krishna, Buddha, Christ, will be shown as different means for one and the same royal highway to final bliss — Nirvana.

Mystical Christianity teaches *self*-redemption through one's own *seventh* principle — the liberated *Paramatma*, called by the one Christ, by others Buddha; this is equivalent to regeneration, or rebirth in spirit, and it therefore expounds just the same truth as the Nirvana of Buddhism. All of us have to get rid of our own Ego, the illusory, apparent self, to recognize our true Self, in a transcendental divine life.

But if we would not be selfish, we must strive to make other people see that truth and recognize the reality of the transcendental Self, the Buddha, the Christ, or God of every preacher. This is why even exoteric Buddhism is the surest path to lead men towards the one esoteric truth.

As we find the world now, whether Christian, Mussulman, or Pagan, justice is disregarded, and honour and mercy are both flung to the winds. In a word, how — since the main objects of the Theosophical Society are misinterpreted by those who are most willing to serve us *personally* — are we to deal with the rest of mankind? With that curse known as the "struggle for life," which is the real and most prolific parent of most woes and sorrows, and all crimes? Why has that struggle become almost the universal scheme of the universe?

We answer: because no religion, with the exception of Buddhism, has taught a practical contempt for this earthly life; while each of them, always with that one solitary exception, has through its hells and damnations inculcated the greatest dread of death. Therefore do we find that "struggle for life" raging most fiercely in Christian countries, most prevalent in Europe and America. It weakens in the Pagan lands, and is nearly unknown among Buddhist populations. In China during famine, and where the masses are most ignorant of their own or of any religion, it was remarked that those mothers who devoured their children belonged to localities where there were the most Christian missionaries to be found; where there were none and the Bonzes alone had the field, the population died with the utmost indifference.

Teach the people to see that life on this earth, even the happiest, is but a burden and an illusion; that it is our own *karma*, the cause producing the effect, that is our own judge — our saviour in future lives — and the great struggle for life will soon lose its intensity. There are no penitentiaries in Buddhist lands, and crime is nearly unknown among the Buddhist Tibetans. The world in general, and Christendom especially, left for two thousand years to the regime of a personal God, as well as to its political and social systems based on that idea, has now proved a failure.

If the Theosophists say: "We have nothing to do with all this; the lower classes and the inferior races (those of India, for instance, in the conception of the British) cannot concern us, and must manage as they can," what becomes of our fine professions of benevolence, philanthropy, reform, etc.? Are those professions a mockery? And if a mockery, can ours be the true path? Should we devote ourselves to teaching a few Europeans — fed on the fat of the land, many of them loaded with the gifts of blind fortune — the *rationale* of bell-ringing, of cup-growing, of the spiritual telephone, and astral body formation, and leave the teeming millions of the ignorant, of the poor and the despised, the lowly and the oppressed, to take care of themselves, and of their hereafter, as best they know how? Never! Perish rather the Theosophical Society with both its hapless founders, than that we should permit it to become no better than an academy of magic and a hall of occultism. That *we*, the devoted followers of that spirit incarnate of absolute self-sacrifice, of philanthropy and divine kindness, as of all the highest virtues attainable on this earth of sorrow, the man of men, Gautama Buddha, should ever allow the Theosophical Society to represent the *embodiment of selfishness*, to become the refuge of the few, with no thought in them for the many, is a strange idea, my brothers.

Among the few glimpses obtained by Europeans of Tibet and its mystical hierarchy of Perfect Lamas, there was one which was correctly understood and described. The incarnations of the Bodhisattva Padmapani or Avalokiteshvara and of Tsongkhapa, that of Amitabha, relinquished at their death the attainment of Buddhahood — i.e., the *summum bonum* of bliss and of individual *personal* felicity — that they might be born again and again for the benefit of mankind. In other words, that they might be again and again subjected to misery, imprisonment in flesh, and all the sorrows of life provided that they, by such a self-sacrifice, repeated throughout long and weary centuries, might become the means of securing salvation and bliss in the hereafter for a handful of men chosen among but one of the many planetary races of mankind. And it is we, the humble disciples of the Perfect Lamas, who are expected to allow the Theosophical Society to drop its noblest title, that of the Brotherhood of Humanity, to become a simple school of psychology? No, no, good brothers, you have been labouring under the mistake too long already. Let us understand each other. He who does not feel competent to grasp the noble idea sufficiently to work for it, need not undertake a task too heavy for him. But there is hardly a Theosophist in the whole Society unable to effectually help it by correcting erroneous impressions of outsiders, if not by actually propagating the ideas himself. Oh, for noble and unselfish men to help us *effectually* in that divine task! All our knowledge, past and present, would not be sufficient to repay them.

Having explained our views and aspirations, I have but a few words more to add. To be *true*, religion and philosophy must offer the solution of every problem. That the world is in such a bad condition, morally, is a conclusive evidence that none of its religions and philosophies — those of the *civilized* races less than any other — has ever possessed the Truth. The right and logical explanations on the subject of the problems of the great dual principles — right and wrong, good and evil, liberty and despotism, pain and pleasure, egotism and altruism — are as impossible to them now as they were 1881 years ago. They are as far from the solution as they ever were; but to these problems there *must* be somewhere a consistent solution, and if our doctrines will show their competence to offer it, then the world will be the first to confess that *ours* must be the true philosophy, the true religion, the true light, which gives *truth* and nothing but the Truth.

MASTER KOOT HOOMI'S LETTER

1881

THE OCCULT SCIENCE is *not* one, in which secrets can be communicated of a sudden, by a written or even verbal communication. If so, all the "Brothers" should have to do, would be to publish a *Handbook* of the art which might be taught in schools as grammar is.

It is the common mistake of people that we willingly wrap ourselves and our powers in mystery — that we wish to keep our knowledge to ourselves, and of our own will refuse — "wantonly and deliberately" to communicate it.

The truth is that till the neophyte attains to the condition necessary for that degree of Illumination to which, and for which, he is entitled and fitted, most *if not all* of the Secrets are *incommunicable*. The receptivity must be equal to the desire to instruct. The illumination *must come from within*. Till then no hocus pocus of incantations, or mummery of appliances, no metaphysical lectures or discussions, no self-imposed penance can give it. All these are but means to an end, and all we can do is to direct the use of such means as have been empirically found by the experience of ages to conduce to the required object.

And this was and has been *no secret* for thousands of years. Fasting, meditation, chastity of thought, word, and deed; silence for certain periods of time to enable Nature herself to speak to him who comes to her for information; government of the animal passions and impulses; utter unselfishness of intention, the use of certain incense and fumigations for physiological purposes, have been published as the means since the days of Plato and Iamblichus in the West, and since the far earlier times of our Indian Rishis. How these must be complied with to suit each individual temperament is of course a matter for his own experiment and the watchful care of his tutor or Guru. Such is in fact part of his course of discipline, and his Guru or initiator can but assist him with his experience and willpower but can do no more *until the last and Supreme Initiation.*

I am also of opinion that few candidates imagine the degree of inconvenience — nay suffering and harm to himself — the said initiator submits to for the sake of his pupil. The peculiar physical, moral, and intellectual conditions of neophytes and Adepts alike vary much, as anyone will easily understand; thus, in each case, the instructor has to adapt his conditions to those of the pupil, and the strain is terrible for to achieve success we have to bring ourselves into a *full* rapport with the subject under training.

And as, the greater the powers of the Adept the less he is in sympathy with the natures of the profane who often come to him saturated with the emanations of the outside world, those animal emanations of the selfish, brutal, crowd that we so dread — the longer he was separated from that world and the purer he has himself become, the more difficult the self-imposed task. Then — knowledge, can only be communicated gradually; and some of the highest secrets — if actually formulated even in your well prepared ear — might sound to you as insane gibberish, notwithstanding all the sincerity of your present assurance that "absolute trust defies misunderstanding." This is the real cause of our reticence. This is why people so often complain with a plausible show of reason that no new knowledge is communicated to them, though they have toiled for it for two, three, or more years.

Let those who really desire to learn *abandon all* and come to us, instead of asking or expecting us to go to them. But how is this to be done in your world, and atmosphere? "Woke up sad on the morning of the 18th." Did you? Well, well, patience, my good brother, patience. Something *has* occurred, though you have preserved no consciousness of the event; but let this rest. Only what more can I do? How am I to give expression to ideas for which you have as yet no language?

The finer and more susceptible heads get like yourself, more than others do, and even when *they* get a little extra dose it is lost for want of words and images to fix the floating ideas. Perhaps, and undoubtedly you know not to what I now refer to. You *will* know it one day — patience. To give more knowledge to a man than he is yet fitted to receive is a dangerous experiment; and furthermore, other considerations go to restrain me.

The sudden communication of facts, so transcending the ordinary, is in many instances fatal not only to the neophyte but to those directly about him. It is like delivering an infernal machine or a cocked and loaded revolver into the hands of one who had never seen such a thing. Our case is exactly analogous. We feel that the time is approaching, and that we are bound to choose between the triumph of Truth or the reign of error and — terror.

We have to let in a few chosen ones into the great secret, or — allow the infamous *Shammars* to lead Europe's best minds into the most insane and fatal of superstitions — spiritualism; and we *do* feel as if we were delivering a whole cargo of dynamite into the hands of those, we are anxious to see defending themselves against the red-capped brothers of the shadow.

MASTER HILARION'S LETTER

1914

My Children:

Among your number there are a few disciples who might benefit from a little advice I feel impelled to offer; for like other warm-hearted, spiritually hungry souls, they are in danger of being exploited by those fiends in human guise — tools of black magicians who continually lie in wait for new victims of their avarice and cunning.

I refer to those misnamed teachers of occultism who claim to be receiving directions from some high spiritual force, or directly from the Initiates of the "Great White Lodge," and who pour forth volumes of platitudes in flowery or abstruse language specially designed to deceive new and untried disciples, until such time as they have compromised or partially psychologized the latter, before their motives become apparent. Unfortunately, when that time arrives previous warnings are of little avail.

Place an unscalable barrier between yourself and the person who offers you *rapid* spiritual development or the possession of the powers of practical occultism at the cost of little or no effort on your own part, or who offers to teach you the secrets of such attainment for a set price.

If you are familiar with the *Book of the Golden Precepts*, or with any other reliable work on practical occultism, you will have seen that there are certain inviolable rules to be obeyed, certain unalterable conditions to be fulfilled before it is even possible for you to take the first step on the "Secret Path" — the Path of Power. If you feel a strong attraction in that direction, I would advise that you read and thoroughly digest such information as may be found in authentic works on the subject, and then create a mental mirror in which, by the aid of your Higher Self, your conscience, your knowledge of your personal self, your dominant characteristics, you proceed to hold that self before the mirror, and with an earnest petition for enlightenment, question that mirror as to what are the probabilities of your being able to live up to those rules, fulfil the conditions, and abide by the answers.

Ask that mirrored form what is the extent of its willpower, of its power of endurance, its ability for sacrifice, such sacrifice as is demanded of the true neophyte? In nine hundred ninety-nine instances out of one thousand, the answer will be: "I have neither power nor ability commensurate with the demand." But then, beware lest immediately there begins to form a series of desire-pictures upon the surface of that mirror, expressions of intense longing, memories of sacrifices previously made, such pictures as generally obsess the mind that has been denied some indulgence. Little by little the "lions in the path" will seem to disappear; the weaknesses of will and mind and physical limitations will seem of less consequence, until finally naught remains but a picture of the lower self in abject submission, the Higher Self triumphant. Such is the power of the lower self, if even temporarily divorced from that light of the Higher Self. If the glamour of lower desire is permitted to blind you to the warnings received and to the dictates of conscience, a false sensation of peace may follow and a desire to acquaint others with the fact that at last you believe you are on the path to unlimited power; and then — then you have become a fit subject for the exploiter who is very apt to appear, and unless you have been so fortunate as to have been under the protection of a true Initiate, there is sore disappointment in store for you. All too many ignorant victims of such exploiters have been forced into utter rejection of all truth and the submersion of all hope and faith after awakening to the fact that they have been purposely deceived by some false teacher, aided by the desires of the lower mind.

Bear carefully in mind that not one of the rules given for your guidance is unnecessary; not one of the directions is superfluous; not one of the sacrifices demanded is useless. Remember that a perfectly sound body and a sound mind are essentials for a practical occultist, without which it would be impossible to pass the requisite physical tests; and remembering all these things, be content to travel the path of the heart, the path of the child, until such time as you may have gained the power to tread the harder path, if that power has not yet been gained, accepting and being content with the guidance of "those who know" until in their eyes, instead of yours alone, you are capable of taking the next step in safety. The peace that will come to you as a result of such submission will be a lasting peace however great the warfare about you. You will be content to await recognition by others instead of claiming it as a right. You will recognize your father's face, your mother's hands, and will no more desire to wander in strange places. Soul sight — intuition — will come, and with its coming will also come the power of discrimination.

My Child, hold up that mental mirror and make sure of your self, your strength, your power to serve aright, ere you ignorantly put yourself into the hands of one who may guide you into the great abyss instead of to the mountain top.

If you should find that the heights are unattainable to you today, remember that another day is coming. Yet also remember that the first step must be taken by every human being, and therefore, must be taken by you; and be not discouraged or dismayed if you stumble in the taking.

Remember that you, as a Templar, have demanded of the Great White Lodge a chance to climb. Having made this demand, your feet have been placed on the first rung of the ladder; hold fast, let nothing rob you of your opportunity; so shall it be well with you.

H.P.B.'S LETTER

1889

OF THE FACT that no such large and ever-growing body as the Esoteric Section could remain without its traitors, open and secret, I have been aware from the beginning. I knew what I had to expect from the first day. I knew that the task I had undertaken would lead to more obloquy and misrepresentations for me than ever; that it was sure to create a large amount of bad feeling among the members of the main (exoteric) body of the Theosophical Society, which would finally be vented, in particular, if not solely, upon myself. And all has come to pass as I knew it would. But if it is, in a great measure, owing to this that the regular issue of Instructions has been prevented, it has not been the sole reason. There came a more serious impediment — to me the bitterest of all. I had received two letters and a reproof from the Masters. These reached me in no such way as to allow the hope that it was less serious than had at first appeared. That which I received both times was a letter in plain language, sent by post and mailed quite prosaically, at the Sikkim frontier, one in March, the other in August, 1889. The last of these left me no ephemeral hope that I had misunderstood or even exaggerated the facts. In their first, our Masters were displeased, and in their last, which arrived just as the news of a flagrant case of treachery reached me, that displeasure became still more apparent.

I was told to keep back Instruction No. III until further developments, and then to make those portions of the contents of the Masters' letter that related to the Esoteric Section known to all its members, without even omitting to show them how mistaken and dangerous had been my policy in the Esoteric Section from its beginning. I had been warned by the Council and my trusted friends, of the danger there was in admitting such a number of persons, scattered so widely over the world, who, it was added, knew me not, except on hearsay, and each of whom I had no other means, *as they supposed*, of studying, than through their auras and photographs. I myself realized that danger, but had no means of averting it, since the *Book of the Discipline and Rules* states that: "No one shall be refused admission, or the chance of learning truth and thereby improving his life, *only* because someone, or even all his neighbours think ill of him." Such is the rule. Therefore, the larger the number of applicants who *take* the pledge, the greater the possibility of helping the masses. A member of the Theosophical Society may be utterly unfit for the higher sciences and never grasp the true teachings of occultism and esoteric philosophy; but yet if he has the true spark of the Divine, and faith in the real presence of the Higher Self in him, he will remain loyal to his pledge, and will *try* to model his life in accordance with the rules of the Esoteric Section, and thereby become nobler and better in every case. Membership in the Esoteric Section and "pledges" signed, sent, and accepted, are no warrants for a high success, nor do these pledges aim at making of every student an adept or a magician. They are simply the seeds in which lurks the potentiality of every truth, the germ of that progress which will be the heirloom of only the seventh *perfect* Race. A handful of such seeds has been entrusted to me by the Keepers of these truths, and it is my duty to sow them there, where I perceive a possibility of growth. It is the parable of the Sower put once more into practice, and a fresh lesson to be derived from its new application. The seeds that fall into good ground will bring forth fruit a hundredfold, and thus repay in each case the waste of those seeds which will have fallen by the wayside, on stony hearts and among the thorns of human passions. It is the duty of the Sower to choose the best soil for the future crops. But he is held responsible only so far as that ability is directly connected with the failures, and that such are solely due to it; it is the karma of the individuals who receive the seeds by asking for them, that will repay or punish those who fail in *their* duties to their Higher Self. Nature is ever struggling, even in its so-called inorganic and inanimate kingdoms, towards progress and perfectibility by production; how much more so the nature of conscious, thinking man! Each of us, if his nature is not productive or deep enough of itself, may borrow and derive material for soil from the seeds themselves which he receives; and everyone has the means of avoiding the scorching sun, and of forcing the seeds to strike root, or preventing the thorns choking them, with very little effort indeed. Therefore my mistake did not lie in that I accepted too readily applications to join the Esoteric Section.

Nor have I sinned even in accepting men and women of whom I have not felt *quite* sure, though the opportunity of discerning their *inner natures* was possible and given to me in almost every instance. I have not sinned in this, I say, as some think, because the *Rules* teach again that the grand ethics taught in the secret Aryasanga schools are not for the benefit or perfection of saints, but verily of sinners who need moral and intellectual help.

In what particular, then, have I failed to do my duty? Simply in this, as am shown: I have begun to give out Eastern teachings to those who are unacquainted with the Eastern discipline; to Westerners, who, had they been thoroughly versed in the laws of that discipline so unfamiliar to cultured Christian-born people, would have thought twice before joining the Esoteric Section. Being taught to rely on their Saviour and scapegoat instead of on themselves, they have never stopped to think that their salvation and future incarnation depend entirely upon themselves, and that every transgression against the Holy Ghost (their Higher Self) will indeed be unpardoned in their present life, or *their next incarnation*, for karma is there to watch their actions and even their thoughts. In short, I have begun to instruct them in *spelling* before I had taught them the *letters* of the occult alphabet. Instead of solemnly warning those who signed their pledge, that, by breaking it and becoming guilty of that which they had sworn to avoid, they incurred thereby the most dangerous responsibilities, entailing sooner or later the most terrible consequences, and proving this to them by living examples from their own and other people's lives, I left them to their own devices. Instead of such warning, I have given out the preliminary knowledge which leads to the hidden secrets of Nature and the old Wisdom Religion, and which but very few can appreciate. I have, finally, by neglecting *to prepare them* by first placing each and all on a twelve-month's or so *Probation*, given them an opportunity of going quite easily, and in most cases, unconsciously to themselves, astray. It is in consequence of this that we have had such a number of members caring for nothing but *new* Instructions to amuse them, and several backsliders who have already done the greatest harm, not only to the Esoteric Section, but also to the Theosophical Society.

This is in consequence of my neglect to conform with and enforce the rules; and I now, in all humility, confess it to all my friends who read this.

How true are these words in Master's letter:

"Experience but too clearly proves that any departure from the time-honoured rules for the government and instruction of the disciple to suit Western custom and prejudices, is a fatal policy."

"Before the pupil can be taught, he must learn how to conduct himself as regards the world, his teacher, the sacred science, and his Inner Self," the letter adds, quoting the Eastern aphorism: "The ruffled water-surface reflects naught but broken images" — which means, that so long as the learners have not mastered their world-passions and remain ignorant of the Truth, their unprepared minds will perceive everything in the light of their worldly, not of their truly spiritual, inner judgement.

"How can they be expected, then," it asks, "to see aught but the broken truth, that such judgement is sure to suggest and distort the more? Violation of ancient usages is sure to result in evil."

How true are these words is shown in our own case. For what but grief and scandal have the violations of that time-honoured usage which forbids speaking in public or before the ignorant masses, of sacred things, brought upon the Theosophical Society and individual aspirants, even before the Esoteric Section had been established? In blind foolishness, without warrant and reflection, have the two Founders of the Theosophical Society, myself chiefest of all, lifted some of the veils of Truth, given some flitting glimpses of the secret laws of Nature and of Being, to a blind, ignorant, sense-ruled public, and thus provoked the hatred, deepened the scepticism, and excited the malevolent activity of many opponents who, otherwise, would have left us alone. Ah, friends, a wise law and prudent restriction was that ancient rule that kept the sacred, but dangerous knowledge (dangerous because it cuts both ways), confined to the few, and these few pledged by a vow, which, if broken, led them almost to perdition. And to this day it is these few who run the greater risk. Some of the Theosophists, yet quite recently almost adorers of the Theosophical Society, and especially of the Masters, have lost or are losing, unconsciously to themselves, their moral balance; some because of the venomous words spoken in their ears by traitors, while others are flinging aside to the four winds their good karmic chances, and turning into bitter and unprincipled enemies. Of the rude public one would have expected this, but from friends, brothers, and associates!

Well, as it now appears, so far as the members of the Esoteric Section are concerned, it is in a great measure, if not entirely, my fault; and it is a bitter draught that karma compels me to drink out of her iron cup. Had I, instead of showing such hopeful confidence and belief in the inviolability of people's *word of honour*, and almost a blind faith that the sacredness of their pledge would prove the surest guarantee of the good faith of any pledged member; had I, instead of that, gone on the old occult lines of the Eastern discipline, such things as have taken place could never have happened. But I have never permitted myself to even dream that a double pledge of such sanctity as the one taken, both on one's most solemn and sacred word of honour and in the name of the Higher Self, could ever be broken, however little one might make even of his "*most sacred word of honour*" by itself. Even in a few cases when a dark and ominous aura round the face of a photograph plainly warned me, I still tried to hope against all hope. I could not bring myself to believe any man or woman capable of such deliberate treachery. I rejected as an evil, sinful thought, the idea that conscious depravity could ever remain on the best of terms with a man, after the signing of such a sacred promise; and I have learnt now for the first time, the possibility of what has been truthfully dubbed by some Theosophists "only a *lip-pledge*." Had I strictly enforced the rules, I would have, no doubt, lost the two-thirds of our pledged members — those who had signed it as they would any circular letter; but then, at least, those few who will remain true to their vows to the bitter end, would have profited more than they have now. Having, however, omitted the usual precautions of the probationary period, I have but myself to thank; and, therefore, it is but just that I should also be myself the first to suffer for it at the hands of the inexorable Karmic Law. For this, ironclad as I have been made by daily and almost hourly unjust attacks, I would have cared but very little; but that which I deplore the most, with a bitterness few of you will ever realize, is the fact that such a number of thoroughly earnest, good, and sincere men and women should have been made to suffer for the guilt of the few. For, though but a fault of omission on my part, still that guilt, as I feel, is due to my neglect. Behold! My karma appeared as a warning almost from the beginning of the Esoteric Section.

I had started well. Several of those whom I knew to be entirely unfitted to take the pledge, had been refused from the first; but I proved unable to withstand their prayers when certain of them declared to me that it was their "last chance in life." The "pledge fever" made short work of their promises. Then it was that the old wondering query: "How is it that 'poor H.P.B.,' notwithstanding the Masters at her back, and her own insight, is *so evidently unable* to know her friends from her foes?" ran once more the round of Theosophical circles, both here and in America.

Brothers, if you *will* judge from appearances, and from the worldly standpoint, you are right; but if you take the trouble of looking into the inner causes producing outward results, you will find that you are decidedly in the wrong. That you should no longer do me injustice, let me explain what I mean.

Take for an instant for granted (you, who still may doubt at moments in your hearts) that I am doing the work of real living Masters. And if so, then surely I would not have been entrusted with such a mission unless I had pledged myself irrevocably to the laws of the ethics, science, and philosophy *they* teach. Come whatever may, I *have to* abide by these laws and rules even in the face of condemnation to death. Now, if the law, in common legislature even, holds that no person should be condemned before his guilt is proven, or becomes manifest, how much more strict must this law be in our occult code? Have I the right — in special cases when I see that a person has in him the germs of, or even a decided proclivity toward, evil-doing, deception, ingratitude, or revenge, that, in short, that person is not a reliable man or woman; but that, on the other hand, for the time being, he is earnest and sincere in his interest and sympathy for Theosophy and occultism; have I the right, I ask, to deny him the chance of becoming a better man, merely out of fear that he may one day turn traitor? I will say more. Knowing, as I do, that *no earthly forces combined can destroy the Theosophical Society and its Truths*, even if they can and *do*, in each case, hurt more or less my outward and miserable *personality*, that shell that I am solemnly pledged to use as a *buffer* of the cause I serve, have I the right, think you, out of mere personal cowardice and in self-defence, to refuse to anyone the chance of profiting by the truths I can teach him, and of thereby becoming better? That "many are called, but few chosen" is something I knew from the beginning; that "he who speaks the truth is turned out of nine cities" is an old saying; and that the man (and especially the woman) who preaches new truths, whether in religion or science, is stoned and martyred by those to whom they are unwelcome — all this is what I have bargained for, and no more.

Let me give you an illustration out of real life. When the notorious Madame Coulomb came to me in Bombay, with her husband, to ask for bread and shelter, though I had met her in Cairo, and knew her to be a treacherous, wicked, and lying woman, nevertheless I gave her all she needed, because such was my duty. But when, in course of time, I saw she hated me, envied my position and influence, and slandered me to my friends while flattering me to my face, my human nature revolted. We were very poor then, poorer even in fact than we are now, both the Society and ourselves, and to keep two enemies at our expense seemed hard. Then I applied to my Guru and Master, who was then at three days' distance from Bombay, and submitted to his decision the question whether it was right and Theosophical to keep *two such serpents* in the house; for she, at any rate, if not her husband, threatened the whole

Society. Would you know the answer I received? These are the words *verbatim*, the reply beginning with an aphorism from the *Book of Precepts*: "'If thou findest a hungry serpent creeping into thy house, seeking for food, and, out of fear it should bite thee, instead of offering it milk thou turnest it out to suffer and starve, thou turnest away from the Path of Compassion. Thus acteth the fainthearted and the selfish.' You know," went on the message, "that you are *personally* threatened; you have still to learn that *so long as there are three men worthy of our Lord's blessing in the Theosophical Society — it can never be destroyed.*... Your two karmas [hers and mine] run in two opposite directions. Shall you, out of abject fear of that which may come, blend the two [karmas] and become as she is?... They are homeless and hungry: shelter and feed them, then, if you would not become participant in her karma."

Since then I have acted more than ever on this principle of trying to help everyone irrespective of what I personally may have to suffer for it. It is not, therefore, the utter incapacity for right discrimination in me, but something quite different, that compelled me to lay aside all thought of possible consequences in this case of selection of fit members of the Esoteric Section. No, I sinned on a different plane. Neglecting to profit by personal experience, I allowed myself in this instance to be more prompted by an easily understood delicacy and regard for Western feeling than by my duty. In one word, I was loath to apply to Western students the rigorous rules and discipline of the Eastern school; afraid of seeing any demand on my part of strict submission to the rules, misinterpreted into a desire of claiming papal and despotic authority. *Read your Pledges* and the *Book of Rules* and study them; and then, finding the amount of authority you have yourselves conferred upon me by signing the pledge — say honestly which of you, if any, can come and complain, not only that I have ever abused, but even *used* that authority over any probationer? In one case only, that of a friend who could hardly misinterpret my action, I have insisted that he should leave America for a certain time. And to emphasize this the more, no sooner had I heard from several of those members in whom I have the greatest confidence that the Pledge, as originally worded, was open to a dead-letter construction, than I immediately altered it. The second and third clauses now stand:

"2. I pledge myself to support, before the world, the Theosophical movement, and those of its leaders and members in whom I have full confidence; and in particular to obey, without cavil or delay, the orders given through the Head of the Section in all that concerns my Theosophical duties and esoteric work, so far as my pledge to my Higher Self and my conscience sanction.[1]

---

[1] As this qualification may possibly be abused, the decision shall rest with

"3. I pledge myself never to listen, without protest, to any evil thing spoken falsely, or yet unproven, against a brother Theosophist, and to abstain from condemning others."[2]

I have done this because I think it right to explain the true spirit of the pledge. But it is precisely that unwillingness in me to ever guide anyone of you more than is strictly necessary that is now shown as having been productive of evil, and as that wherein my fault lies. As the same letter says, addressing me:

"You have spoken to them before their ear was trained to listen, and began showing things before the eye of the learner was prepared to see. And just for this reason, hearing but indistinctly and seeing each in his own way, more than one [member of the Esoteric Section] has turned round and tried to rend you [me] for your pains."

Those, therefore, who desire to receive further instruction, will have to study and faithfully endeavour to practise the ethics of Theosophy and the occult schools, such as are to be found in the present teaching, and in *The Voice of the Silence*, otherwise they cannot receive any further teachings from me. For, as saith the *Book of Discipline* in the schools of Dzyan:

"Speak not the mysteries to the common vulgar, nor to the casual friend, or new disciple. With prudent eye to the possible consequences, keep locked within your breast the teachings received until you find a listener who will understand your words and sympathize with your aspirations."

This does not mean that you are at liberty to repeat what you have learnt to anyone whom you believe to answer that description, but that you can exchange views with your co-disciples who are pledged as you are yourself.

I can do no better, I believe, than give at once some of the oral and written precepts from the same book above mentioned as pointed out by the Master.

"1. To the earnest disciple his Teacher takes the place of Father and Mother. For, whereas they give him his body and its faculties, its life and casual form, the Teacher shows him how to develop the inner faculties for the acquisition of the Eternal Wisdom.

---

seven members of the Esoteric Section, as arbitrators, four of whom shall be chosen by the Probationer and three by the Head of the Section.

[2] The second and third clauses of the original Pledge ran as follows:

"2. I pledge myself to support, before the world, the Theosophical movement, its leaders and its members; and in particular to obey, without cavil or delay, the orders of the Head of the Esoteric Section in all that concerns my relation with the Theosophical movement.

"3. I pledge myself never to listen, without protest, to any evil thing spoken of a brother Theosophist, and to abstain from condemning others."

"2. To the disciple each fellow-disciple becomes a brother and sister, a portion of himself,[1] for his interests and aspirations are theirs, his welfare interwoven with theirs, his progress helped or hindered by their intelligence, morality, and behaviour through the intimacy brought about by their co-discipleship.

"3. A co-disciple or associate cannot backslide or fall out of the line without affecting those who stand firm, through the sympathetic tie between themselves and the psychical currents between them and their Teacher.

"4. Woe to the deserter, woe also to all who help to bring his soul to the point where desertion first presents itself before his mind's eye, as the lesser of two evils. Gold in the crucible is he who stands the melting heat of trial, and lets only the dross be burnt out of his heart; accursed by karmic action will find himself he who throws dross into the melting-pot of discipleship for the debasement of his fellow pupil. As the members to the body, so are the disciples to each other, and to the Head and Heart which teach and nourish them with the life-stream of Truth.

"5. As the limbs defend the head and heart of the body they belong to, so have the disciples to defend the head and the heart of the body they belong to [in this case Theosophy] from injury."

Before I proceed, let me explain, for fear of being misunderstood again, that by "Teacher" I neither mean myself, as I am but the humble mouthpiece of the true Teacher, nor do I write the above in order to stimulate anyone to defend or stand by my own *personality*, but verily to make it clear, once for all, that to defend the Esoteric Section and Theosophy (the *heart* and *soul* of the Theosophical Society, its visible body) is the duty of every good Theosophist, especially of the Esoteric Section. So is it his bounden duty to protect from attack and defend every fellow-brother, if he knows him to be innocent, and try and help him morally, if he thinks he is guilty. Nor is verse 5 intended to convey the idea that aggressiveness is the best course to take, for it is not: passive resistance and a firm refusal to listen to any slanderous reports about one another, in the case of a member as well as of a stranger or an ex-Fellow, is all that would be, in some cases, necessary to entirely defeat conspiracy and malevolence.

And now hoping that no misunderstanding is any longer possible, I resume in this hope the *Rules*, quoting a few more remarks upon them from the said letter. They come as a comment on verse 5, and I quote them *verbatim*.

---

[1] "So shalt thou be in full accord with all that lives; bear love to men as though they were thy brother pupils, disciples of one Teacher, the sons of one sweet mother" (Fragment III of *The Voice of the Silence*, p. 61).

"... And if the limbs have to defend the head and heart of their body, then why not so, also, the disciples their Teachers as representing the science of Theosophy which contains and includes the 'head' of their privilege, the 'heart' of their spiritual growth? Saith the Scripture:

"'He who wipeth not away the filth with which the parent's body may have been defiled by an enemy, neither loves the parent nor honours himself. He who defendeth not the persecuted and the helpless, who giveth not of his food to the starving, nor draweth water from his well for the thirsty, hath been born too soon in human shape.'

"Behold the Truth before you: a clean life, an open mind, a pure heart, an eager intellect, an unveiled spiritual perception, a brotherliness for one's co-disciple, a readiness to give and receive advice and instruction, a loyal sense of duty to the Teacher, a willing obedience to the behests of Truth, once we have placed our confidence in, and believe that Teacher to be in possession of it; a courageous endurance of personal injustice, a brave declaration of principles, a valiant defence of those who are unjustly attacked, and a constant eye to the ideal of human progression and perfection which the secret science (*Gupta-Vidya*) depicts — these are the golden stairs up the steps of which the learner may climb to the Temple of Divine Wisdom. Say this to those who have volunteered to be taught by you."

These are the words of great Teachers, and I but do the bidding of one of these in repeating them to you. What is found in the letter, I, H.P.B., now say to you in the authentic words, which are: "*Think*; and thinking, *try*: the goal is indeed worth all possible effort." Much of what the *Book of Discipline* contains you may find in the fragments translated by me from the *Book of the Golden Precepts*, and published for the benefit of the "Few." These rules are as old as the world. And it is these, as I now see, that I was expected to impress upon the minds of all those who applied to me for instruction. This duty I knew well, and yet omitted doing it. I will not excuse myself by saying that I forgot to do so, for this would not be the truth; but I say and confess that I skipped it, out of an idiotic regard for Western prejudices and habits of thought. I knew that a code of preliminary ethics such as is obligatory, and enforced upon Eastern disciples would grate upon, nay, even offend the feelings of many American and European probationers. Ever misunderstood, judged by appearances, vilified, slandered, and persecuted, I feared to hurt the Society, by forcing several, if not many, of our members to sever their connection with it, if they found that I made the rules too exacting. For the first time in my life I acted like a coward in my own sight, and almost a traitor to my duties by such a compromise with my conscience. Therefore, though the first punished, I do not complain, and only hope that no one else will suffer through my weakness.

It is of the second and last letter in relation to the Esoteric Section that I have been speaking. The first was to the effect that those who desired to receive Eastern teaching had to conform to Eastern rules, and that I had better suspend my Instructions until I had notified them of that; reminding them also of Rule 3 of their *Pledge*, which, *if I had not the courage to enforce I had better change, as it only caused the members to become untrue to their vows.*

This was repeated by me to the Council of the Esoteric Section, and it led to their sending a joint letter of advice to the Esotericists, which was surreptitiously handed over to the *Religio-Philosophical Journal*, a leading spiritualistic paper in America, and published.

Behold, all of you, the work of never-failing, prompt karma! Had I not departed from the old Rules of the *Book of Discipline*, such a sad case would not have happened, for there would have been no need of such a document as framed by the Council. For the Rule says, to the chela:

"If thou canst not fulfil thy pledge, refuse to take it; but once thou hast bound thyself to any promise, carry it out, even if thou hast to die for it."

And to the Teacher:

"Thou shalt not remind the disciple who shows himself, whether willingly or inadvertently, disloyal to the letter and spirit of any law — more than *twice*: at the third time, thou shalt separate him from the Body," or in other words, ask him to resign or expel him.

But as unfortunately in general, though very fortunately in this case, every handful of mud thrown at the Theosophical Society reaches only myself, and as the members of the Esoteric Section had no opportunity of defending anyone but myself, I was loath to enforce this rule. I felt a great unwillingness to even pass a message in which I was *personally* concerned. But after the second letter I could remain silent no longer; it is the law and I have but to obey, taking now this opportunity of imploring every pledged member of the Esoteric Section who feels incapable of allowing himself to be subjected to such a discipline, to resign. Knowing, indeed, as I do, the free American and the free Briton, how can I come and tell either of them, for instance:

"The office of Teacher was always considered as a very solemn and responsible one among our Asiatic ancestors, and the pupil was always enjoined to obedience and loyalty. This is what you have to tell them, advising them to study Manu" (from the letter).

And how could I hope, in those early days of the Esoteric Section, to make them understand that by "Teacher" it was the Master who was meant and not myself, when I knew that at that time many of them while knowing *of* me, and luckily not having any reason to doubt *my* existence, still doubted that of the Mahatmas?

Such is my only excuse. Unable to transfuse my certain knowledge of the reality of the Masters as men into the consciousness of the Theosophists and even of pledged members, for the last fifteen years, I have ever avoided pressing this truth upon them. Yet unwilling to play the part of the crow in peacock's feathers, I *had to assert* the existence of Teachers who had taught me all I know.

And yet the rules of discipleship being so very strict upon the subject of the personal and other relations between the Teachers and the pupils, I have no choice. A Guru has ever been considered as the chela's benefactor, because he imparts that which is more precious than worldly wealth or honours, that which money cannot buy, and which concerns the welfare of the pupil's soul and future weal or woe. Yet the Guru is not the only one pointed out to the chela's consideration, but also all those who help a disciple one way or the other to pursue and progress in his studies.

"Observe," writes the Master, "that the first of the steps of gold which mount towards the Temple of Truth is — *a clean life*. This means a purity of body, and a still greater purity of mind, heart, and spirit."

And the latter are found more in the poor country-classes than among the cultured and the rich. That the Master's eye is upon you, Theosophists, is evidenced by the following lines from the same pen:

"How many of them [you] violate one or more of these conditions [of the right Path] and yet expect to be freely taught the highest wisdom and sciences, the Wisdom of the Gods. As pure water poured into the scavenger's bucket is befouled and unfit for use, so is Divine Truth when poured into the consciousness of a sensualist, of one of selfish heart and a mind indifferent and inaccessible to justice and compassion. . . . There is a very, *very* ancient maxim, far older than the time of the Romans or the Greeks, more ancient than the Egyptians or Chaldeans. It is a maxim all of them [Theosophists] ought to remember and live accordingly. And it is that a sound and pure mind requires a sound and pure body. Bodily purity every Adept takes precautions to keep. . . . Most of you [Theosophists] know this."

And yet, knowing it, how few live up to this. I had rather not say whether the letter includes in this reproof Theosophists generally or only Esotericists. It names a few, but this is for my own private information; meanwhile, these are the words addressed to all:

". . . But though they have been repeatedly told of this *sine qua non* rule on the Path of Theosophy and chelaship, how few of them have given attention to it. Behold, how many of them are sluggards in the morning and time-wasters at night; *gluttons*, eating and drinking for the sensual pleasure they give; indolent in business; selfish as to the keeping of their neighbours' (brothers') interests in view; borrowing from Brother Theosophists, making money out of the loan and failing to return it; lazy in study and waiting for others to think for and teach them; denying themselves nothing, *even of luxuries*, for the sake of helping poorer brothers; forgetting the Cause in general and its volunteer hard workers — and even debauchees, *guilty of secret immorality* in more than one form. And yet all call themselves Theosophists; all talk with outsiders about 'Theosophical ethics' and things, with a puffed-up, vain conceit in their hearts. . . ."

Alas! If these words apply to the Theosophical Society in general, to the selfish coldness and supreme indifference of most members to the future of the cause they belong to, but will not go out of their way to serve, do not most of the cases cited apply to *some* Esotericists, if not to all? Do not we find among them envy and hatred for their colleagues, suspicion and slanderous talk? Who of you who read this is prepared to say that not one out of the above enumerated faults concerns you?

Ah, friends, brothers, and many of you beloved co-workers, indeed, *indeed* little do you know of the eternal, unchangeable conditions of soul-development, and chiefly of the inexorable occult laws! Believe the Teacher from whose letter I quote, if you will not believe me:

"Though such a person with any of the faults as above described should fill the world with his charities, and make his name known throughout every nation, he would make no advancement in the practical occult sciences, but be continually slipping backward. The 'six and ten transcendental virtues,' the paramitas, are not for full-grown yogis and priests alone, but for all those who would enter the Path."

If, explaining this, I add that gentle kindness to all beings, strict honesty (not according to the world-code, but that of karmic action), virtuous habits, strict truthfulness, and temperance in all things; that these alone are the keys that unlock the doors of earthly happiness and blissful peace of mind, and fit the man of flesh to evolve into the perfect Spirit-Ego — many of you will feel inclined, I fear, to mock me for saying this. You may think that I am carrying coals to Newcastle, and that each of you knows this, at least, as well as I do. You may remark, perhaps, that I am taking my *role* of "teacher" on a too high tone altogether, regarding and treating you, grown-up, intelligent men and women, as I would little school-boys and girls. And some of you may indulge in the thought that it is useless for me to be teaching you to be "goody-goody" instead of going on with my Instructions and giving you explanations about "that occult jumble of colour and sound, and their respective relations to the human principles," as some have already complained. But I say again, if you are ignorant of the real occult value of even such trite truths as are contained in my "grandmother's sermon," how can you hope to understand the science which you are studying? Can an electrician, however well familiarized with the electric fluid and its variable currents, unless he knows human anatomy and is a good physician at the same time, apply them to himself or the body of any living man, without the risk of killing his patient or himself? What is the good of knowing all about the occult relations between the forces of Nature and the human principles if, by remaining deliberately ignorant of Self, we remain thereby as ignorant of what does or what does *not* affect each distinct principle? Are you aware that by starving, so to speak, one principle or even centre, at the expense of another principle or centre, we may lose the former and hopelessly injure the latter? That by forcing our Higher Ego (not Self, mind you) to remain inactive and silent, a result easily achieved by overfeeding the lower *manas*, which is ever gravitating downward to *kama-rupa*, we risk utter annihilation of our present personality?

As this may be questioned by some members who are not very strong even in the *exoteric* Theosophical doctrines, in order to make my meaning more clear I will supplement the present *explanation*, which had become unavoidable, by incorporating a paper on this subject in the present Instruction, which explains the case in hand. Let the dreadful possibility of losing one's "soul," not a rare occurrence, and vouched for, moreover, by the experience of a long series of seers and clairvoyant teachers, become known to all. This dogma of the *inner* schools has been often hinted at in our literature, yet never till now explained. It can be done *only* to the few who are pledged not to make the details of it known.

And now I must close. For some of you, perhaps, these will turn out to be my "parting" *farewell* words. Such I may as well now thank for the confidence they have shown, and with which they have honoured me, if even for a few months; and so I wish them "God speed" in some other science made less heavy by discipline and rules. But those, whom no hardships, providing they lead them to the eternal Truth, can ever discourage, I address in the words of the great American poet, whose lips are now cold and mute: "Up and onward for evermore!"[1] Let this be the motto of the Esoteric Section, applied to *death* of selfishness and sin through the bright Dawn of the resurrection of the Divine Science now known as Theosophy.

---

[1] Ralph Waldo Emerson, *Essays* (London: James Fraser, 1841), p. 126.

THE LOTUS
by Boris Abramov

EACH LIGHT-BRINGER is an enemy of the darkness. Light destroys the darkness, and therefore, the darkness hastens to annihilate its foe, so as not to be destroyed itself. Everyone who bears Light thereby brings upon themselves a horde of adversaries. They conceal themselves under guises of all sorts, hiding behind religion, science, virtue, morality, and a multitude of other masks, behind which the same entity lurks — darkness. If, due to the peculiarities of our era, the Light-bearer cannot be crucified, or stoned to death, or burnt at the stake, then more sophisticated methods must be employed, which are not prohibited by the law. The darkness has in its arsenal slander, forgery, distortion of the proffered truth, betrayal, suppression — in a word, everything that would inflict anguish, no less than torture, and that would result in no less harm to the cause. Physical martyrdom lasts for days, hours, or even minutes, while martyrdom of the spirit lasts for the Light-bearer's entire conscious life. And the greatest torment is caused not by personal attack, but by distortion of the imparted Teaching.

It takes truly exceptional courage to tell people the truth. It takes extraordinary selflessness to convey messages from Above. Someday recognition will come, someday they will understand, and will appreciate, and exalt. But the life path of great martyrdom will remain in the records of Space as the valour of a crown of thorns for the one side, and as an indelible disgrace for the other.

She brought Light. She exposed with fire all the layers of lies that had accumulated around the primary sources of the Teachings of Truth. She fought against the ignorance of science, against superstition, and harmful delusion. She gave to the world books brimming over with secret knowledge, mere crumbs of which were previously available only to the very few. She heroically acquired and selflessly gave away precious knowledge. For all this she was hunted, reviled, and persecuted. But they failed to extinguish the Light she brought.

We know that the seeds she planted did not perish. A shift in consciousness has occurred, people ascend the new rungs she laid, those who are able to perceive and assimilate have taken advantage of the Light she brought. Great is her merit and assistance to humanity. Her heroic life is a model for those who wish to assist evolution. She was not afraid and did not think of herself. She loved the cause entrusted to her above all. She fought bravely and courageously, taking the blows in the name of the Great Light. Everything heroic will be properly appreciated in the New Era. And she will take her rightful place in the wonderful future for whose sake she worked so hard.

Boris Abramov (1897–1972) was a Russian author and poet, disciple and follower of Nicholas and Helena Roerich. From the 1940s until the final days of his life, he kept journals of writing dedicated to the moral transformation of the human being in everyday life. During his lifetime, Helena Roerich confirmed their High Source. While Roerich gave *Agni Yoga* at the level of the higher triad of human bodies, Abramov was a transmitter of currents at the level of the quaternary, reflecting the practical path of self-improvement. Subsequently, all his records were published as a series of books under the title *Facets of Agni Yoga* in Russia.

THANK YOU!

THANK YOU so much for taking the time to journey through the pages of *The Book of the Golden Precepts*. This book is more than a collection of spiritual aphorisms and articles — it is a call to inner awakening, an insightful guide for the heart seeking truth beyond form, and a mirror for the soul ready to serve humanity.

We hope that these timeless teachings by H. P. Blavatsky have touched you in some meaningful way — perhaps by sparking reflection, kindling compassion, or deepening your understanding of the Path.

If this work has inspired you or invited you to pause and mediate, we would be deeply grateful if you would consider leaving a review wherever you obtained your copy. Whether a few lines or a thoughtful reflection, your words matter. Reviews not only help future readers discover the book, but also contribute to a living dialogue around these profound teachings. In today's digital world, your voice can carry further than ever — and it may be the encouragement someone else needs to begin their own spiritual search.

How did this book speak to you? What thoughts or questions did it stir?

Feel free to quote or record your reading of inspiring aphorisms from *The Book of the Golden Precepts* and post it on your social media.

By sharing your experience, you help keep this esoteric wisdom alive and relevant for future generations, helping it to reach those who are ready to listen, reflect, and walk the Path of the Heart.

Thank you again for being part of this journey.

If you would like to be among the first to hear about our new releases, please subscribe to our newsletter through this link and receive a free bonus:

radiantbooks.co/bonus

GLOSSARY

ABBREVIATIONS

Ar. — Arabic
Av. — Avestan
Ch. — Chinese
Chal. — Chaldean
Eg. — Egyptian
Fr. — French
Ger. — German
Gr. — Greek
Heb. — Hebrew
It. — Italian
Jap. — Japanese
Lat. — Latin
Mar. — Marathi
Mon. — Mongolian
Nah. — Nahuatl
Pahl. — Pahlavi
Sen. — Senzar
Sin. — Sinhala
Sk. — Sanskrit
Tam. — Tamil
Tel. — Telugu
Tib. — Tibetan
Tur. — Turkic

If you would like to receive this Glossary typeset in a larger font, visit radiantbooks.co/glossary (an email address is required to deliver the digital file free of charge).

A

Abhidharma (*Sk.*, "higher doctrine"). The metaphysical (third) part of *Tripitaka*, a very philosophical Buddhist work by Katyayana.

The Light of Abhidharma means the higher consciousness, *buddhi-manas*. It represents a combination of the fire of the Higher Spheres with the radiation of consciousness. The Light of Abhidharma protects one from the poisonous emissions of the lower earthly layers. The dark flame of poisonous gases is pushed back by the Light of Abhidharma and neutralized, but for this one needs to recognize the spatial Fire and one's own emanations.

Absolute. The Ultimate, Infinite Reality or Principle that transcends all distinctions and limitations. See *God*.

Absoluteness. When stated as being a quality of the Universal Principle, it denotes an abstract notion, which is applied more correctly and more logically than the adjective "absolute" when referring to something which can have neither attributes nor limitations.

Ad infinitum (*Lat.*). To infinity; endlessly.

Adam and Eve. The first human couple in the Bible. Esoterically, Adam and Eve represent the early Third Root Race and also stand as the dual symbol of the sexes. In the Chaldean Kabbalah (*Book of Numbers*), the *tat* symbol, or +, is referred to as *Adam and Eve*, the latter being the transverse or horizontal bar drawn out of the side (or rib) of Adam, the perpendicular bar.

Adam Kadmon (*Heb.*, "primordial man"). Archetypal Man; humanity; the "Heavenly Man" not fallen into sin; Kabbalists associate it with the ten Sefirot on the plane of human perception. In Kabbalah, Adam Kadmon is the manifested Logos corresponding to the Third Logos; the Unmanifested being the first paradigmatic ideal Man, and symbolizing the Universe *in abscondito* (in secret), or in its "privation" in the Aristotelean sense. The First Logos is the "Light of the World," the Second and Third — its gradually deepening shadows.

Adept (*Lat.*, "one who has obtained"). One who has reached the stage of Initiation and become a Master in the science of esoteric philosophy. Alchemists who had obtained the philosopher's stone, which symbolizes arcane knowledge and transmutation of one's essence, were also called Adepts.

Adeptship. The status or condition of an Adept, one who has attained true knowledge and mastered the Laws of Spirit and Matter.

Adhyaya (*Sk.*, "study"). A chapter or section of a book.

Adi-Buddha (*Sk.*, "primordial Buddha"). The First and Supreme Buddha; the Eternal Light; Primordial Universal Wisdom; the Wisdom-Principle which is the Absolute; a symbol of the universal and abstract principle of Divine Wisdom.

Adi-Budha (*Sk.*, "primeval wisdom"). A term used by Aryasanga in his secret treatises to denote the Unknown Deity and Absolute Wisdom.

Adi-Sanat (*Sk.*, "first ancient"). The term corresponds to the Kabbalistic "Ancient of Days," since it is a title of Brahma called in the *Zohar* the "Ancient of the Ancients."

Aeon (*Gr.*, "eternity"). An enormous period of time; a world or sub-plane of a particular world if one considers Creation a cross-section, from the lowest physical worlds to the Supreme and Divine, each of which has its own number of layers; emanations proceeding from the Divine Essence and celestial beings; genii and angels among the Gnostics.

Agama Sutras (*Sk.*, "teachings handed down by tradition"). A collection of Buddhist sacred texts.

Agni (*Sk.*, "fire"). The Fire; God of Fire in the Veda; the oldest and most revered of the Gods in India. Agni is one of the three great deities: Agni, Vayu, and Surya, and he is also all three, as he is the triple aspect of Fire: the Sun in heaven; Lightning or air in the atmosphere; ordinary Fire on earth. Agni belonged to the earlier Vedic Trimurti (Trinity) before Vishnu was given a place of honour, and before Brahma and Shiva were manifested.

Agni Yoga (*Sk.*, "fiery union," "fiery path"). The yoga of Fire, the highest form of yoga revealed by Helena Roerich in the book series of the same name, in cooperation with Master Morya. It is essential today, when new fiery energies are incrementally arriving on Earth from the Spiritual Sun. These energies cause climate change, while humanity's inability to assimilate them results in natural disasters. *Agni Yoga* is designed to help in this by teaching how to master the Fire, which manifests itself both in human beings and throughout the Cosmos.

Agnyana (*Tel.*) or **ajnana** (*Sk.*). Non-knowledge; absence of knowledge rather than "ignorance" as it generally tends to be translated.

Ahankara or **ahamkara** (*Sk.*, "I-maker"). The conception of "I," self-consciousness or self-identity; the "I," the egotistical and illusory principle in man, which, due to our ignorance, separates the "I" from the Universal One-Self Personality.

Ahavaniya (*Sk.*, "to be offered as an oblation"). The sacrificial fire to the heavens, forming a bridge or ladder by which the sacrificer can communicate with the world of gods and spirits.

Ahriman (*Av.*, "evil spirit"). In Zoroastrianism, the destructive spirit or embodiment of evil which exists in opposition to Ahura Mazda, the Supreme God of Light.

Ahura Mazda (*Av.*, "Lord of Wisdom"). The god of the Zoroastrians or the modern Parsis; symbolized by the Sun, as the Light of Lights; esoterically, the synthesis of his six Amesha Spenta (angels or divine forces) or Elohim, and the creative Logos. In the Mazdean exoteric system, Ahura Mazda is the supreme god, and one with the supreme god of the Vedic age — Varuna.

Aitareya Brahmana (*Sk.*, "explanation of sacred knowledge by the son of Itara"). A Sanskrit text, attached to the *Rig Veda*.

Ajita (*Sk.*, "invincible"). In Buddhist tradition, refers to Maitreya, the future Buddha.

Akasha (*Sk.*, "sky"). The subtle, supersensuous spiritual essence which pervades all space; the primordial substance erroneously identified as Ether. Akasha is to Ether what Spirit is to Matter. It is the Universal Space in which lies inherent the eternal Ideation of the Universe in its ever-changing aspects on the planes of matter and objectivity, and from which radiates the First Logos, or expressed thought.

Akbar the Great (1542–1605). The third Mughal emperor of India, who reigned from 1556 to 1605.

Akoustikoi (*Gr.*). Auditory.

Akshara (*Sk.*, "indestructible," "ever perfect"). Supreme Deity.

Alandi. A town in India, known as a place of pilgrimage due to its association with Dnyaneshwar, a saint who decided to entomb himself in an underground chamber.

Alaya (*Sk.*, "abode"). The Universal Soul; *Anima Mundi* (*Lat.*, "the soul of the world"). Identical to Akasha in the mystical sense, and to Mulaprakriti (*Sk.*, "root of Nature"), in its essence, as it is the basis or root of all things.

This is the Divine Essence which permeates, animates, and informs all, from the smallest atom of matter to man and god. It is in a sense the "seven-skinned mother" of the stanzas in *The Secret Doctrine*, the essence of seven planes of sentience, consciousness and differentiation, moral and physical. In its highest aspect it is Nirvana, in its lowest, Astral Light. It was considered feminine among the Gnostics, the early Christians, and the Nazarenes; bisexual among other sects, who considered it only in its four lower planes. It is of an igneous, ethereal nature in the objective world of form (and then ether), and divine and spiritual in its three higher planes. When it is said that every human soul was born by detaching itself from the *Anima Mundi*, it means, esoterically, that our Higher Egos are of an essence identical with It, which is a radiation of the ever unknown Universal Absolute.

Alchemists. The Rosicrucians of the Middle Ages, such as Robertus de Fluctibus (Robert Fludd), Paracelsus, Thomas Vaughan (Eugenius Philalethes), Jan Baptist van Helmont, and others, were all alchemists, who sought the *hidden spirit* in all inorganic matter. Many people have accused alchemists of charlatanry. Surely such individuals as Roger Bacon, Agrippa, Henry Khunrath, and the Arabian Geber (the first to introduce into Europe some of the secrets of chemistry), can hardly be treated as impostors, least of all as fools.

Scientists who reformed the science of physics upon the basis of the atomic theory of Democritus, as restated by John Dalton, conveniently forgot that Democritus of Abdera was an alchemist, and that the mind that was capable of penetrating so deeply into the secret operations of Nature in one direction must have had good reason to become a Hermetic philosopher. The cradle of alchemy is to be sought in the most distant times.

Alchemy (*Ar.*, "art of transmutation"). An ancient science that deals with the finer forces of Nature and the various conditions in which they are found to operate. Seeking under the veil of language, more or less artificial, to convey to the uninitiated as much of the *mysterium magnum* (great mystery) as is safe in the hands of a selfish world, the alchemist postulates, as his first principle, the existence of a certain Universal Solvent by which all composite bodies are resolved into the homogeneous substance from which they are evolved, a substance he calls pure gold, or *summa materia* (supreme matter). This solvent, also called *menstruum universal* (universal solvent), possesses the power to remove all seeds of disease from the human body, renew youth, and prolong life. Such is the *lapis philosophorum* (philosopher's stone).

Alchemy first penetrated into Europe in the eighth century of our era through Geber, the great Arabian sage and philosopher, but it was practised long ago in China and in Egypt — numerous papyri on alchemy, and other proof of its being the favourite study of kings and priests, have been exhumed and preserved under the generic name of Hermetic treatises.

Alchemy is studied under three distinct aspects, which admit many different interpretations: the Cosmic, human, and terrestrial. These three methods were typified under the three alchemical properties — sulphur, mercury, and salt. Different writers have stated that there are three, seven, ten, and twelve processes, respectively; but they are all agreed that there is but one objective in alchemy, which is to transmute gross metals into pure gold. What that gold, however, really is, very few people understand correctly. No doubt there is such a thing in Nature as transmutation of the baser metals into the nobler ones, or gold. But this is only one aspect of alchemy, the terrestrial or purely material, for we sense logically the same process taking place in the bowels of the earth. Yet, besides and beyond this interpretation, there is, in alchemy, a symbolical meaning, purely psychic and spiritual. While the Kabbalist-alchemist seeks for the realization of the former, the occultist-alchemist, spurning the gold of the mines, gives all his attention and directs his efforts only towards the transmutation of the baser *quaternary* into the divine upper *trinity* of man which, when finally blended, are one. The spiritual, mental, psychic, and physical planes of human existence are, in alchemy, compared to the four elements, fire, air, water, and earth, and are each capable of a threefold constitution, i.e., fixed, mutable, and volatile. Modern chemistry owes its best fundamental discoveries to alchemy; but, regardless of the undeniable truism of the latter that there is but one element in the universe, chemistry has placed metals in the class of elements and is only now beginning to discover what a gross error this is.

Alexander the Great (356–323 BCE). The king of the ancient Greek kingdom of Macedon, who formed one of the largest empires in history.

Alexandria. A city in ancient Egypt, which was for several centuries the great seat of learning and philosophy. Famous for its Alexandrian Library, which was founded by Ptolemy Soter who died in 283 BCE, at the very beginning of his reign, and once boasted 700,000 rolls or volumes; for its museum, the first real academy of the sciences and the arts; and for its world-famous scholars, such as Euclid (father of scientific geometry), Apollonius of Perga (author of the still extant work on conic sections), Nicomachus (arithmetician); astronomers, natural philosophers, anatomists, such as Herophilus and Erasistratus, physicians, musicians, artists, etc. It became still more famous for its Eclectic, or New Platonic school, founded in 193 CE by Ammonius Saccas, whose disciples were Origen, Plotinus, and many others now famous from history. The most celebrated schools of the Gnostics had their origin in Alexandria. Philo Judaeus, Josephus, Iamblichus, Porphyry, Clement of Alexandria, Eratosthenes the astronomer, Hypatia the virgin philosopher, and innumerable other stars of second magnitude, all belonged at various times to these great schools and helped to make Alexandria one of the most justly renowned seats of learning that the world has ever produced.

Alia tentanda via est (*Lat.*). Another way must be tried.

Alighieri, Dante (1265–1321). An Italian poet, writer, and philosopher; the author of *The Divine Comedy* (1472), a narrative poem divided into three parts: *Inferno*, *Purgatorio*, and *Paradiso*.

All-Powerful Ten. A composite or monogram of ten letters possessing secret powers, depicted in the seals and crests of the Panchen Lamas, as well as in the emblem of Tashi Lhunpo Monastery.

Alpha and omega (*Gr.*). The first and the last, the beginning and end of all active existence; the Logos, hence (among Christians) Christ. See Revelation 21:6, where John adopts "alpha and omega" as the symbol of a Divine Comforter, who "will give unto him that is athirst of the fountain of the water of life freely."

Alter ego (*Lat.*). Another self.

Altruism (*Lat.*, "to this other"). A quality opposed to egoism; actions tending to do good to others, regardless of self.

Amitabha (*Sk.*, "boundless age," "infinite light"). The celestial Dhyani-Buddha of which Gautama Buddha was the earthly reflex; the inner "God" of Gautama. The name has numerous variations such as Amita, Amida, Abida, Amitaya, etc. The original conception of the ideal of an impersonal divine light has been anthropomorphized over time. The Amidist sect of China and Japan show a special reverence to Amitabha enthroned in the Western Heaven, but only the popular belief takes this literally, as the Christians do in the form of "God and His Son," which are really the Absolute and its emanation the Logos or Word. In the developed doctrine of China and Japan, Amitabha is but a symbol for an inexpressible reality, and rebirth into his Paradise is the awakening of the Bodhichitta (heart of wisdom) in the human being.

Amrita (*Sk.*, "immortal"). The ambrosial drink or food of the gods; a food granting immortality. The elixir of life that was churned out of the ocean of milk in the Puranic allegory. An old Vedic term applied to the sacred Soma juice in the Temple Mysteries.

The elixir of life does exist. It is a miraculous potion, consisting of life-giving emanations from flowers and plants, forming a special combination of Light, Colour, and Sound. In combination with the crystallized fiery energy of the human heart, this elixir is able to impart immortality. For example, one of the ingredients is *strophanthus* which strengthens the heart.

Studies by alchemists tell us that if a person drinks it before they find the philosopher's stone, the elixir of life will become for them the elixir of death. The philosopher's stone is an invisible solar stone in the heart which constitutes its fiery-white core. And the quest for it — that is, the accumulation of fiery energy and growth of the heart crystal, can be undertaken only while we remain in the dense conditions encountered during our many lives on Earth. Whereas, in the Higher Worlds, we reap the effects of our earthly life. Therefore, it is important to listen for the guidance of the vigilant heart in order to make the right choices in life and not be deluded by earthly illusions, which only lead to the priceless treasure going to waste. Thus, if a person has dissipated their heart crystal by the time they draw near to death, the elixir will have no effect on them and might even result in unforeseen consequences. But if a person has lived a spiritual life, devoted their labours to the Light, and accumulated the crystal of a particular energy constant, then they may continue to exist in the same body for as long as it meets their need. This is why, as a rule, the elixir of life is given only to those who serve the good of Evolution.

Many of the Great Teachers possessed this elixir of immortality. The first to experience it in the conditions of the earthly existence was Master Rakoczy, known as the Count of Saint-Germain, who was responsible for the testing of new formulas. Hence, He has gone down in history as a most mysterious character, appearing in different centuries, remaining ever young.

The Cosmic Law of Expediency does not currently permit the wide application of the elixir among the masses or its production on an industrial scale. In the future, when the multitude of destructive souls disappears, the Great Teachers will impart the formula of the elixir of life to the best scientists on the planet.

The elixir of immortality is also given at the level of the currents crystallized in the books of the Light. The perception of such books by the heart facilitates the accumulation of the fiery-white core. Additionally, each Teaching of

Light, provided that the commandments given there are fulfilled, leads to a process of fiery purification and hence, to the growth of the heart crystal as well. And the higher the level of spiritual development, the broader will be the consciousness allowing us to consciously exist in all our seven bodies and in all the Worlds accessible to us. This is how true immortality is achieved.

It should be borne in mind that the currents of immortality now pouring forth over Earth affect only those who have already found their own philosopher's stone. Without this, they either simply will not work or will result in unexpected alchemical reactions.

Amursana (c.1723–1757). A leader of the Oirats and a political figure who rebelled against Qing dynasty rule. He attempted to restore the independence of Mongolian tribes but was ultimately defeated by the Qing forces.

Anagamin (*Sk.*, "non-returner"). One who is no longer to be reborn into the world of desire. One stage before becoming Arhat and ready for Nirvana. The third of the four grades of holiness on the way to the final Initiation.

Anahata-shabda (*Sk.*, "unstruck sound"). The mystic voices and sounds heard by the yogi at the incipient stage of his meditation. The third of the four states of sound, otherwise called *madhyama* — the fourth state being when it is perceptible to the physical sense of hearing. The sound in its previous stages is not heard except by those who have developed their internal, highest spiritual senses. The four stages are called respectively: *para, pashyanti, madhyama,* and *vaikhari*.

Ananda (*Sk.*, "joy," "happiness"). The favourite disciple of Gautama Buddha.

Anatta (*Pali*, "no soul"). The doctrine that there is no *atma*, or spirit, in any phenomenon.

Ancient Aliens. A term used by Andrew Tomas in his books to denote extraterrestrial spiritual beings who came to Earth to help humanity, unlike the modern view that presents "ancient aliens" as monster beings made of flesh and blood.

In fact, those same "alien monsters," whose photographs have been widely published, are not living beings but biorobots created by technocratic civilizations for their own research purposes. Technocratic representatives are able to acquire human form, albeit with structures devoid of higher triads. Outwardly they are no different from humans and live the same life: they are born, grow old, and die, yet are unable to reincarnate. They are particularly interested in sexual energy and the energy of human blood.

There are civilizations that "pump out" excess uranium radiation. Some have been studying the physical nature of man for millions of years. One civilization, the so-called Blues, of which there are only seven entities left in the near-Earth Cosmos, studies the field of human psychology and dreams. There is a kind of "blue spot" that circulates around the world and erases certain dreams, because it is too early for humanity to know all the mysteries of dreams. In addition, the so-called Bermuda Triangle is connected with the mystery of another planet where its own Cosmic Experiment is taking place. It was not random individuals who disappeared in that area, but people who had a direct connection to that planet.

True Ancient Aliens are spiritual rather than material. For example, in antiquity, when representatives of Sirius visited Earth, they wore bird-like masks or spacesuits, because they could not breathe in the terrestrial atmosphere. Their spacesuits were made of special stellar fabric, and when they took off their masks, their radiant faces of supreme beauty resembled those of the Gods. Hence, Egyptian Supreme Gods, who are believed to have arrived from Sirius, are depicted with bird-like masks, since no art can express the magnificence of their countenances.

Representatives of highly spiritual civilizations still come and go. Hangars for their spaceships made of light are located in mountain ranges on Earth, the main spaceport being situated in the Himalayas. Local people have often noticed unusual phenomena in the region. The hangars are difficult to find as they operate as follows: the mountains open up, a flying apparatus comes in or out, and then they close. There are also certain mountain peaks that are always covered in cloud. Of course, representatives of humanity who work with these civilizations can be called to these secret places.

Ancient of Days. The Father of the Demiurgus of the Universe; the *Third Life* or *Abatur*; corresponds to the Third Logos in *The Secret Doctrine*. The *Zohar* says: "The Ancient of Days has three heads. He reveals himself in three archetypes, all three forming but one. He is thus symbolized by the number Three. They are revealed in one another. [These are:] first, secret, hidden 'Wisdom'; above that the Holy Ancient One; and above Him the Unknowable One. None knows what He contains; He is above all conception. He is therefore called for man 'Non-Existing' [*Ayin*]."

Antaryami (*Sk.*, "indwelling presence"). In Hindu philosophy, the aspect of God or the Divine that resides within all beings, guiding them from within.

Antaskarana or **antahkarana** (*Sk.*, "internal organ"). The term has various meanings, which differ with every school of philosophy and sect. Thus, Shankaracharya renders the word as "understanding"; others as "the internal instrument, the soul, formed by the thinking principle and egoism"; whereas the occultists explain it as the *path* or bridge between the higher and the lower *manas*, the Divine Ego and the *personal* soul of man, during human life that are to rebecome one Ego in Devachan or Nirvana.

It serves as a medium of communication between the two, and conveys from the lower to the Higher Ego all those personal impressions and thoughts of man which can, by their nature, be assimilated and stored by the undying entity, and, thus, be made immortal with it, these being the only elements of the evanescent *personal-*

ity that survive death and time. This "bridge" becomes active when man aspires toward his Higher Self by developing spiritual qualities, thereby merging the lower self with the Higher. For this reason, *antahkarana* symbolically means the "Path" that must be traversed through good deeds and actions, thereby bridging over the gap between the consciousness of the Higher and the lower ego before this bridge is destroyed at our death.

The whole fate of an incarnation depends on whether the *antahkarana* will be able to restrain the *kama-manas* (lower *manas*) or not. After death the higher light (*antahkarana*), which bears the memory and impressions of all good and noble aspirations, assimilates itself with the Higher Ego, while the bad is dissociated in space, and comes back as the bad karma that awaits the new personality. It stands to reason, therefore, that only that which is noble, spiritual, and divine in man can testify in Eternity to his having lived.

This concept may seem difficult to understand, but in reality, with the help of a familiar though fanciful illustration, it becomes quite simple. Let us imagine a bright lamp in the middle of a room, casting its light upon the solid plaster wall. Let the lamp represent the Divine Ego, and the light thrown on the wall, the lower *manas*, and let the wall stand for the body. The atmosphere which transmits the ray from the lamp to the wall will, then, in our simile represent the *antahkarana*. We must further suppose that the light thus transmitted is endowed with reason and intelligence, and possesses, moreover, the faculty of dissipating all the evil shadows which pass across the wall and of attracting brightness to itself, receiving their indelible impressions.

Now, it is in the power of the human Ego to chase away the shadows (sins) and multiply the brightness (good deeds) which make these impressions, and, thus, through *antahkarana*, ensure its own permanent connection and its final reunion with the Divine Ego. Remember that the latter cannot take place while there remains a single taint of the terrestrial, or of matter, in the purity of that light. On the other hand, the connection can never be ruptured, and final reunion prevented, so long as there remains one spiritual deed, or potentiality, to serve as a thread of union; but the moment this last spark is extinguished, and the last potentiality exhausted, then comes the severance. In an Eastern parable, the Divine Ego is likened to the Master who sends out his labourers to till the ground and to gather in the harvest, and who is content to keep the field so long as it can yield even the smallest return. But when the ground becomes sterile, not only is it abandoned but the labourer also (the lower *manas*) perishes.

On the other hand, however, still using our simile, when the light thrown on the wall, or the rational human Ego, reaches the point of actual spiritual exhaustion, the *antahkarana* disappears, the light is no longer transmitted, and the lamp becomes non-existent to it. The light which has been absorbed gradually disappears and "soul-eclipse" occurs; the being lives on earth and then passes into Kama-loka as a mere surviving congeries of material qualities; it can never pass outwards towards Devachan, but is reborn immediately, a human animal and scourge. Let "Jack the Ripper" stand as a type.

This simile, however fantastic, will help one to seize the correct idea. Except through the blending of the moral nature with the Divine Ego, there is no immortality for the personal Ego. It is only that which is akin to the most spiritual emanations of the personal human soul which survives. Having, during a lifetime, been imbued with the notion and feeling of the "I-am-I" of its personality, the human soul, the bearer of the very essence of the karmic deeds of the physical man, becomes, after the death of the latter, part and parcel of the Divine Flame (the Ego). It becomes immortal through the mere fact that it is now strongly grafted on the monad, which is the "Tree of Eternal Life."

Anthropomorphism (*Gr.*, "having human form"). The act of endowing God or the gods with a human form and human attributes or qualities.

Ao Miao De Daoli (*Ch.*, "mysterious truth"). The Esoteric Doctrine.

Apavarga (*Sk.*, "liberation"). Emancipation from repeated births.

Apocalypse (*Gr.*, "revelation"). The prophetic book of the New Testament, the Book of Revelation, which concerns the Second Coming of Christ. Like any scripture and legend of antiquity, it has seven keys or meanings.

Some scholars have come to the conclusion that it is another version of the Book of Enoch and the legend of the Dragon, dating back to the pagan past. Therefore, Revelation should be attributed to other, much more ancient visions.

The War in Heaven mentioned in chapter 12 refers to events on various planes of Existence. The first event is a purely astronomical, cosmic fact related to cosmogony. This stellar prototype of the war belongs to the pre-Manvantaric period and is based on the knowledge of the entire programme and evolution of cosmogony — knowledge that is in the possession of the Initiates alone. But the second aspect of the War in Heaven has its reflection on Earth, and its action, rather than occurring in the depths of interstellar Space, occurred in the Himalayas. This is a record of the terrible battle between the Sons of Light and the sons of darkness of the Fourth and Fifth Races. All subsequent traditions connected with this subject were built precisely on these two events, merged together in legends. But whatever the astronomical meaning of this universally accepted legend of the Battle in Heaven, its human phase is based on true historical events, distorted into theological dogma (the Fall of the Angels) only to adapt it to ecclesiastic purposes.

The astronomical event of Revelation 12:1–2 occurred in 2017. See *Sanat Kumara*.

Aranyaka (*Sk.*, "forest dweller"). Holy hermits, sages, who dwelt in the forests of ancient India.

Archangel (*Gr.*, "chief messenger"). The highest supreme angel, corresponding to a Planetary Spirit or to a Master of Wisdom. Thus, Michael is Morya or Maitreya; Raphael is Gautama Buddha; Gabriel is Serapis; and Uriel is Jesus Christ or Koot Hoomi. Uriel also corresponds to the Head of the Hierarchy of Sirius, known as Sanat Kumara.

Archons (*Gr.*, "rulers"). In profane and biblical language rulers and princes; in occultism, primordial Planetary Spirits.

Ardha-matra (*Sk.*). Half metre. *Ardha* means "half," while *matra* is the quantity of a Sanskrit syllable.

Argo (*Gr.*, "shining," "bright"). The coefficient that measures the energy potential of the *ringsel* crystal.

Arhat or **Arhan** (*Sk.*, "worthy one," "deserving divine honours"). This was the name first given to the Jain and subsequently to the Buddhist holy people initiated into the esoteric mysteries. Arhat is one who has entered the best and highest path, and is thus emancipated from rebirth.

Arhatship. The state or condition of an Arhat, one who has attained the highest level of Enlightenment.

Arjuna (*Sk.*, "white"). The third of the five Brothers Pandu or the reputed Sons of Indra (esoterically the same as Orpheus). A disciple of Krishna, who visited him and married Subhadra, his sister, besides many other wives, according to the allegory. During the fratricidal war between the Kauravas and the Pandavas, Krishna instructed Arjuna in the highest philosophy, while serving as his charioteer.

Armageddon (*Heb.*, "mountain of Megiddo"). The Final Battle between the Forces of Light and darkness, proclaimed in ancient prophecies.

After Lucifer was defeated in the war with the Sons of Light during the time of Atlantis, and again in modern times, the forces of darkness realized that they could not defeat the Light, and sooner or later they would be destroyed by the fiery energies coming to Earth. Therefore, Lucifer, to whom the Higher Worlds were inaccessible, decided to explode the planet, since only this would enable him to remain for a period of time in its subtle atmosphere, and then depart on the ruins of Earth in the direction of another planet, thus prolonging his life. The catastrophe could have occurred in 1899, 1949, 1954, 1977, or 1999. If it had occurred, the Brotherhood of Great Teachers together with the most advanced Earth-dwellers would have moved to Venus and Jupiter. The majority would have waited many billions of years for the formation of a new planet to continue their evolution. The least advanced of humanity would have moved to Saturn. However, the Earth was saved from destruction by the incredible efforts of all the Light-bearing Forces of the Solar System.

The liberation of Earth from Lucifer's dictatorship began in the late nineteenth and early twentieth centuries on the Subtle Plane. The battle soon moved into the physical world in the form of the First World War 1914–1918.

At the end of 1931, the time had come in the Subtle World for a new phase of the struggle for humanity's freedom and immortality. In the book *Heart* (1932) of the *Agni Yoga* series, Master M. says:

"Armageddon has already begun — the end of the thirty-first year opened the Great Battle. . . . One should not be surprised at how events accumulate, for the earthly battle follows the heavenly one. Much has been said about the Heavenly Host, about the Archangel Michael, the appearance of the appointed Leader, and all the turmoil."

"The preparatory period of each Yuga takes place within a significant timeframe, but there may be accelerations that will unusually intensify all forces. The Great Decisive Battle should not be understood as a war only. The manifestation of the Battle goes much deeper. It will flow throughout the Subtle and earthly worlds. It will be expressed not only in combat, but in unprecedented clashes between peoples. The boundaries between the combatants will be as tortuous as those between good and evil. Many decisive battles will be incomprehensible to the earthly eye. Terrifying collisions taking place in the Subtle World will be expressed on the earthly path in catastrophe. Also, earthly courage will be reflected in the Subtle and Fiery Worlds. The Great Battle will be the first link in connecting the worlds."

"Originally, the boundary between the physical and the Subtle World was not as distinct. In the most ancient chronicles one finds fragmentary indications of close cooperation between these worlds. With the densification of the body, heart focus was needed to provide a balance with subtle energies. The physical world itself was needed so that substances could be processed and energies multiplied. But the mind, as you know, rushed towards isolation, hampering evolution. The time of Kali Yuga was difficult, yet Satya Yuga must again bring together the worlds that were forcibly separated."

At the end of the nineteenth century, all the secret schools were closed, because at the threshold of two world wars, the atmosphere had become so poisoned and unbearable that the Masters could no longer remain among humanity. Ashrams were closed not only in Egypt and Europe, but even in Tibet (for example, in Shigatse). All the Teachers who worked with disciples were summoned to the Chief Stronghold in the Himalayas. This was also connected with the forthcoming date of 1936; Blavatsky certainly knew about this date and informed her companions of it verbally.

Furthermore, Edgar Cayce was asked about the calculations found in the Great Pyramid by researchers David Davidson and Herbert Aldersmith and published in their book *The Great*

Pyramid: Its Divine Message (1925). They pointed to the importance of the year 1936 in human history. Cayce confirmed the correctness of many of their conclusions, but also indicated that, "Only an initiate may understand" (Edgar Cayce Reading 5748–5).

This was the year in which began the personal combat between the Great Lord of Shambhala and the Prince of Darkness, the heavenly battle ordained in the Bible between the Archangel Michael and his angels and the Dragon. Over time, the battle between the Forces of Light and darkness once again moved from the Subtle Plane to the dense one, which resulted in the Second World War 1939–1945.

The second phase of the Final Battle ended with the victory of the Forces of Light on 17 October 1949, when the Great Lord banished Lucifer to Saturn. Here too the Mother of the World played a special role in saving the planet.

However, after the defeat, the hierophants of evil managed to gather the remnants of their armies on the Subtle Plane, and at the end of the twentieth century, the third phase of the Final Battle began, and this was reflected on the earthly plane in the conflicts such as those taking place in Syria, Ukraine, and Israel, where some of the most important Points of Life for modern times are located. And previous to this, "breakthroughs" from battles taking place on the Subtle Plane found their reflection in Chechnya, Nagorno-Karabakh, the Caucasus, Transnistria, the former republics of Yugoslavia, and so on. From time immemorial, wherever Points of Life were situated or were to be born, the involutionary forces of evil attempted to establish their authority through local or global bloody war, giving birth to their own Points of Death.

Nowadays, the battles taking place in the near-Earth layers on the Subtle Plane have become especially cruel and there is a danger, as was the case with the First and Second World Wars, that they will become reflected on the earthly plane and take the form of a Third World War. If this happens, there will be no winners. It was for this reason that Helena Roerich stated: "A world war will not be allowed, or rather, it will be cut short by the intervention of Cosmic Forces" (26 August 1950).

In addition, as in the times of Atlantis, fratricidal wars awaken and disturb the visible and invisible elemental forces of Nature, the elements of Fire and Water in particular. The entire planet is enveloped in a network of volcanoes, both on land and under water, which serve as connection channels between the Earth's core and spatial Fire. The most powerful triangle of volcanoes consists of Fuji in Japan, Etna in Italy, and Yellowstone in the USA. These are invisibly connected and their awakening is interdependent. Moreover, each of these three points sends impulses to other volcanoes, and it is as if streams of fiery lava were running through living arteries.

Of course, transition periods of various eras are marked by volcanic eruptions. But often the result of volcanic activity is a consequence of human activity that brings dissonance and destruction. And earthquakes are accompanied by tsunamis, which can cause Great Floods. The Forces of Light, in bloody sweat, are endeavouring to keep the elements from concluding alliances among themselves that would carry out their own judgement on humanity, as they have done in previous eras.

As many predictions have stated, in the period from the early 1950s to the 1990s, a great catastrophe was anticipated as a consequence of the elements awakened after the First and Second World Wars. This catastrophe would have destroyed North America, Great Britain, and Western Europe. It is only thanks to tremendous efforts and Sacrifice of the Great Teachers, that it became possible to avoid it, or rather, to postpone it. There are no guarantees that the unfulfilled predictions of a seer as accurate as Edgar Cayce will not come true in the near future, under new conditions.

The Great Teachers will save the planet Earth from destruction, but whether the contours of the current geographical map will remain the same depends entirely on humanity, which must apply 50 per cent of the effort necessary for its salvation in order for Cosmic Forces to intervene on its behalf.

The thought that a bloody war is taking place, cities are being destroyed, and people are dying somewhere out there, far across the ocean, but that here life is good and safe, is deceptive. The Earth represents a single organism and if a certain organ or part of its body bleeds, this will certainly affect other parts that might not appear to be directly connected. Moreover, the Earth, as a conscious being endowed with free will, has every right to reshape the continents as it sees fit, for its best development, "shaking off" that part of humanity which slows down its evolution.

Therefore, it is in the best interests of the population of the territories mentioned above to assist the Forces of Light in the unequal battle with the dark horde, which is constantly supplied with low-frequency energy from the larger portion of unreasoning humanity. If the hierophants of evil are intensified by low-level human thoughts and outbursts, then the Warriors of Light need pure and sincere prayers coming from the depths of human hearts for the assertion of Peace, the Good, and Love throughout the Earth. After all, prayers and mantras are positive energies that are able to cleanse space, densely sown with spores of evil, and pacify the raging elements.

The Final Battle will be completed by the end of the twenty-first century, when the last bearer of darkness on Earth and the near-Earth spheres will be expelled to Saturn, following their ruler. But every heart has the power to make an energetical contribution towards the quickening of the Victory of Light and the averting of large-scale natural disasters.

Arunachala (*Sk.*, "red mountain"). A sacred hill in Tamil Nadu, India, associated with the

Hindu deity Shiva. It is considered a powerful spiritual centre, and was revered by the sage Ramana Maharshi.

Arya (*Sk.*, "holy," "noble"). Originally the title of Rishis (sages), those who had mastered the *Aryasatyani* (the four truths or the four dogmas) and entered the Path to Nirvana or Moksha, the great fourfold path. But now the name has become the epithet of a race, and some Orientalists, depriving the Hindu Brahmins of their birthright, have made Aryans of all Europeans. In esotericism, as the four paths, or stages, can be entered only owing to great spiritual development and "growth in holiness," they are called the "four fruits." The degrees of Arhatship, called respectively: *Srotapatti, Sakridagamin, Anagamin,* and *Arhat,* or the four classes of Aryas, correspond to these four paths and truths.

Aryahata (*Sk.*). The Path of Arhatship or holiness.

Aryan. Relating to the ancient people of India.

Aryans. The population of ancient Northern India, Aryavarta.

Aryasanga. The founder of the *first* Yogachara school; an Arhat, a direct disciple of Gautama Buddha. Aryasanga is most unaccountably mixed up and confounded with a personage of the same name, who is said to have lived in Ayodhya (Oude) in about the fifth or sixth century CE, and taught Tantrika worship in addition to the Yogachara system. Those who sought to make Tantrika popular, claimed that this personage was the same Aryasanga that had been a follower of Shakyamuni, and that he was one thousand years old. However, the works written by him and translated in about the year 600 CE, works full of Tantra worship, ritualism, and tenets now followed largely by the "red cap" sects in Sikkim, Bhutan, and Little Tibet, cannot be the same as the lofty system of the early Yogachara school of pure Buddhism, which is neither northern nor southern, but totally esoteric. Though none of the genuine Yogachara books have ever been made public or marketable, one finds in the *Yogacharabhumi-Shastra* (*Sk.*, "treatise on the stage of yoga practice") of the *pseudo*-Aryasanga a great deal from the older system, into the tenets of which he may have been initiated. It is, however, so mixed up with Shivaism and Tantrika magic and superstition that the work defeats its own end, notwithstanding its remarkable dialectical subtlety. The unreliability of conclusions drawn by certain Orientalists, and the contradictory nature of the dates assigned by them, may be seen in the following instance: While Csoma de Kőrös (who never became acquainted with the Gelugpa ("yellow caps"), deriving all his information from "red cap" lamas of the Borderland), places the *pseudo*-Aryasanga in the seventh century CE; Wassiljew, who spent most of his life in China, proves him to have lived much earlier; and Wilson, speaking of the period when Aryasanga's works, still extant in Sanskrit, were written, believes it now "established, that they have been written *at the latest, from a century and a half before, to as much after,* the era of Christianity." At all events since it is beyond dispute that the Mahayana religious works were all written far before Aryasanga's time, whether he lived in the second century BCE or the seventh CE, and that these contain all and far more of the fundamental tenets of the Yogachara system, so disfigured by the Ayodhyan imitator — the inference here being that there must exist somewhere a genuine rendering free from popular Shivaism and left-hand magic.

Aryashtanga Marga (*Sk.*). The Noble Eightfold Path to liberation from the cycle of rebirth consisting of eight practices: right understanding, right thought, right speech, right action, right livelihood, right effort, right concentration, right mindfulness.

Aryavarta (*Sk.*, "land of the Aryas"). The ancient name for Northern India, where the first newcomers from Central Asia settled following the destruction of Atlantis. The Fifth Race of humanity, the present stage of evolution, is also called *Aryan* because it originated in India one million years ago. It is erroneous to give the name of Aryavarta to the whole of India, since Manu gives the name of "the land of the Aryas" to "the tract between the Himalaya and the Vindhya ranges, from the eastern to the western sea."

Asana (*Sk.*, "posture"). A physical posture or position. While modern yoga emphasizes asanas for health and flexibility, traditional yoga views asanas as a way to prepare the body for meditation.

Asat (*Sk.*, "false"). A philosophical term meaning "non-being," or rather *non-be-ness.* The "incomprehensible nothingness." *Sat,* immutable, eternal, ever-present, and the one real "Be-ness" (not Being) is spoken of as being "born of *Asat,* and *Asat* begotten by *Sat.*" The unreal, or *Prakriti,* objective Nature regarded as an illusion. Nature, or the illusive shadow of its one true essence.

Ashram (*Sk.*, "hermitage"). A sacred abode, temple, or monastery, for Teachers and their disciples. However, every sect in India has Ashrams for ascetic purposes.

Asketai (*Gr.*). Those who practise the art; ascetics.

Aspect. In certain contexts, the form (*rupa*) under which any principle manifests, in septenary man or in Nature, is called an *aspect* of that principle in Theosophy.

Astral body or **astral double**. The ethereal counterpart or shadow of man or animal; the *linga-sharira,* the "doppelgänger," not to be confused with the *astral soul,* another name for the lower *manas,* or so-called *kama-manas,* the reflection of the Higher Ego.

There is a difference between the nature and the essence of the astral body and the Ego. The astral body is molecular, however etherealized it may be: the Ego is atomic, spiritual. The atoms are spiritual and forever invisible on this plane; molecules form around them, while the atom remains the molecule's higher invisible principle.

Astral Light. The invisible region that surrounds our planetary globe, as it does every other. As the second Principle of the Cosmos (the third being Life, of which it is the vehicle) it corresponds to the *linga-sharira* or the astral double in man. A subtle essence visible only to the clairvoyant eye, and the lowest, with the exception of one (the earth) of the Seven Akashic or Cosmic Principles.

Éliphas Lévi calls it "the great serpent" and "the dragon" from which every evil influence is radiated onto humanity. This is so; and it should be added that the Astral Light gives out nothing that it has not received; that it is the great, terrestrial crucible in which the vile emanations of the earth (moral and physical), which feed the Astral Light, are converted into their subtlest essence and radiated back to the earth in intensified form, thus becoming epidemics, moral, psychic, and physical.

Finally, the Astral Light is the same as the *Sidereal Light* referred to by Paracelsus and other Hermetic philosophers. Physically, it is the equivalent of ether in modern science. Metaphysically, and in its spiritual, or occult sense, ether is a great deal more than is often imagined. In occult physics and alchemy, it is well demonstrated that it encloses within its shoreless waves not only Tyndall's "promise and potency of every quality of life," but also the *realization* of the potency of every quality of spirit. Alchemists and Hermetists believe that their *astral* or sidereal ether is the *Anima Mundi*, the workshop of Nature and of all the Cosmos, spiritually, as well as physically. The "grand magisterium" asserts itself in the phenomenon of mesmerism, in the "levitation" of human and inert objects; and may be called the ether in its spiritual aspect. The designation *astral* is ancient, and was used by some of the Neoplatonists, although it is claimed by some that the word was coined by the Martinists. Porphyry describes the celestial body which is always joined with the soul as "immortal, luminous, and star-like."

Astrology (*Gr.*, "account of the stars"). The science which defines the action of celestial bodies upon mundane affairs, and claims to foretell future events based on the position of the stars. Its antiquity places it among the very earliest records of human learning. For a long time it remained a secret science in the East, and its ultimate expression remains so to this day.

It is useful to have some understanding of astrology, but one should always remember that human free will is the most powerful factor in any situation and can change many signs, and the most difficult can turn out to be the most conducive to success. A person with the most favourable horoscope and the most fortunate signs will achieve nothing in life if they are not prepared to make an effort. Another person with unfavourable signs can achieve everything they wish with the help of persistence and hard work. All great spirits have a difficult horoscope. Astrology is a very complex science, and a person must have a strong psychic energy in order to study it and especially to interpret it correctly. The most important key to astrology has been lost to the West. Besides this, in ancient times, a scientist-astrologer was also a palmist and could read auras. Only these capabilities combined can result in the correct definition of a person's character and destiny.

Asuras (*Sk.*, "breath"). Exoterically, elementals and evil gods, considered maleficent; demons and no-gods. Esoterically — the reverse. For in the most ancient portions of the *Rig Veda*, the term is used for the Supreme Spirit, and therefore the Asuras are spiritual and divine. It is only in the last book of the *Rig Veda*, in the *Atharva Veda*, and the *Brahmanas*, that the epithet, which had been given to Agni, the greatest Vedic Deity, to Indra and Varuna, comes to signify the opposite of gods. *Asu* means breath, and it is with his breath that Prajapati (Brahma) creates the Asuras. When ritualism and dogma got the better of the Wisdom Religion, the initial letter *a* was adopted as a negative prefix, and the term ended up signifying "not a god," and only Sura, a deity. But in the Vedas, the Suras have ever been connected with Surya, the Sun, and regarded as *inferior* deities, devas.

Atlantis (*Gr.*, "island of Atlas"). Plato's name for the continent on which the Fourth Race of humanity developed. Extending from the North to the South, it was located in an area now covered by the waters of the Atlantic Ocean.

Some five million years ago numerous islands began to rise from the depths coming to form the Atlantean continent. At the same time, the Great Teachers started to gather and resettle on one of the central islands the finest representatives of the Third Race from the continent of Lemuria, whose time was drawing to a close.

The first Atlanteans were almost three-and-a-half metres tall, later decreasing in height to approximately two-and-a-half metres. The peak of Atlantis' flourishing coincided with the Toltec period, when, after long internecine wars, tribes united into a federation headed by an emperor. The capital was the City of Golden Gates, situated in the Eastern part of Atlantis.

Living among the people, the Great Teachers imparted to the Atlanteans an abundance of mystic knowledge, enabling them to achieve success in many spheres of life as they were able to manage the most powerful energies; they knew the mysteries of Nature and could breed new species of plants and animals; they invented the most complex of technologies, including the science of aeronautics; in addition, they made direct contact with the Distant Worlds.

The decline of Atlantis began with the fall of Lucifer, who had been one of humanity's trusted Instructors. Humans began to use mystic knowledge not for the good of all but for the purpose of glorifying themselves, accumulating riches, inventing deadly weapons, waging war, practising dark magic, and so on. Those who warned of the inevitable disaster that would result from the actions of the Atlanteans faced penalty of death. This frightful moral decline, along with the humiliation of women and other perversions, led to the Atlanteans consciously repeating the sins of primitive people, the progenitors of the primary apes; sexual intercourse between some Atlanteans and primary apes produced man-like monkeys.

The violation of Cosmic Laws on such an unprecedented scale, along with the use of dark magic by the Atlanteans against the Sons of Light, brought destructive elemental forces into play. These gradually destroyed Atlantis and ushered in the Ice Age, covering whole regions of the planet with ice.

The main continent was destroyed by water a few millions years ago, leaving a number of large and small islands, among them Ruta and Daitya. The isle of Ruta sank almost 850,000 years ago, and Daitya was submerged nearly 270,000 years ago, leaving a smaller island known as Poseidonis, which itself sank below the sea in 9,564 BCE.

Prior to these disasters, the Sons of Light resettled the most spiritual inhabitants of Atlantis in Egypt, transferring there the entire mystic heritage of the Atlanteans. The Masters themselves moved to Shambhala, which was also an island at that time, and have been helping humanity secretly ever since, without revealing their identity.

The Atlanteans were ancestors of the Pharaohs and forefathers of the Egyptians. Plato heard of this highly civilized people, the last remnant of which was submerged 9,000 years before his day, from Solon, who had it from the High Priests of Egypt. It was in Syria and in Phrygia, as well as Egypt, that they established the worshipping of the Sun.

Today, Atlantis is slowly rising and will be the continent on which will occur the development of the Sixth and Seventh Races of humanity.

Atma or **Atman** (*Sk.*, "spirit"). The Universal Spirit, the divine monad, the seventh principle in the septenary constitution of man; the Supreme Soul.

Atma-buddhi-manas (*Sk.*) or **higher triad**. The three higher principles in man, consisting of spirit, soul, and mind.

Atmajnani (*Sk.*, "one who has realized the true self"). The knower of the World-Soul, or Soul in general.

Atma-Vidya (*Sk.*, "soul-knowledge"). The highest form of spiritual knowledge.

Atom. The soul of the molecule. The body, *sthula-sharira*, is made up of molecules, informed and ensouled by atoms. The molecule contains the seven principles in their Prakritic manifestation. As man, as a whole, contains every element that is found in the universe, and as there is nothing in the Macrocosm that is not in the microcosm, so every molecule is, in its turn, the mirror of its universe, man. It is this which renders man alone capable of conceiving the universe on this plane of existence; he has in him the Macrocosm and the microcosm.

The atom, esoterically speaking, contains the six principles and dwells in the molecule, the molecule being the body, or *sthula-sharira* of the atom, as *atma* contains all and dwells in the material universe. In its highest aspect it is on the seventh sub-plane of the lowest Prakritic plane, and is thus the *atma* of the objective Cosmos. It is therefore spiritual, is forever invisible on this plane, and in its first manifestations it remains atomic, as *atma-buddhi-manas* in the molecule. On the lowest Prakritic sub-plane it is afforded the material *upadhi*, or vehicle, through which the higher principles can act in the body.

The Ego is atomic, spiritual, and so are the atoms which form explicitly the three higher principles of the molecules, as well as contain implicitly the lower. Molecules form round the atom, and these molecules are related to *kama-manas*, *kama*, *linga-sharira*, and finally, as an outer coating, appear as the molecules of the *sthula-sharira*. The astral bodies are molecular, however etherealized may be their composition, whereas the Ego is atomic. This is the difference between the nature and essence of the astral bodies and the Ego. These atoms are the thirty-three crores of Gods met with in Hindu books. But despite all this the actual nature of the Ego cannot be understood by the finite mind.

The consciousness of the senses, being that of the molecules, is in *atma-buddhi* and without *manas*. The *manasic upadhi* is not developed in the molecule, hence the *manasic* aspect of the sevenfold *atma* cannot manifest in it, and there is no self-consciousness in the molecule, or in the cell composed of molecules. The cells of the legs or other parts are conscious, but they are slaves of an idea or volition sent to them and obey it. They are not self-conscious, nor can they originate an idea. When they are tired they can send to the brain an uneasy sensation, caused in them by exhaustion, by diminution of *pranic* energy. Thus they give rise in the brain to the idea of fatigue, the lower *manas* translating the cell-*kamic* sensation of exhaustion into the idea of fatigue.

Rude physical health is a drawback to seership — as may be seen in the case of Swedenborg. It is an excess of *prana* setting up powerful molecular vibrations, and so drowning the atomic.

The *linga-sharira*, or ethereal double of the body, is molecular in constitution, but of molecules invisible to physical sight. It is therefore not homogeneous.

The Astral Light is nothing but the shadow of the real Divine Light, and is not molecular.

Attavada (*Pali*, "theory of self"). The sin of personality.

Augoeides (*Gr.*, "radiant form"). The English writer, Edward Bulwer-Lytton (1803–1873), refers to it as the "Luminous Self," or the Higher Ego. But occultism makes of it something distinct from this. It is a mystery. The *Augoeides* is the luminous, divine radiation of the Ego which, when incarnated, is but its shadow — pure as it is yet.

This concept is explained in Zoroastrianism with the Amesha Spenta (*Av.*, "beneficent immortals") and their Fravashis (*Av.*, "growing forth"). The Amesha Spenta are the six angels or divine forces personified as gods who attend upon Ahura Mazda, of which he is the synthesis and the seventh. They are one of the prototypes of the Roman Catholic "Seven Spirits" or Angels with Michael as chief, or the "Celestial Host"; the "Seven Angels of the Presence." They are the Builders, Cosmocratores, of the Gnostics and identical to the Seven Prajapatis (Progenitors; the givers of life to all on this Earth), the Sefirot, etc. A Fravashi is the spiritual counterpart of a still more spiritual original. Thus, Archangel Michael, "he like God," is a Fravashi of that God.

Aum or **Om** (*Sk.*). A sacred and mystic syllable, the most solemn of all words in India; the triple-lettered unit, hence the trinity in One. The syllable is an invocation, a benediction, an affirmation, and a promise, and it is so sacred that it is truly *the word at low breath* of occult, primitive masonry. No one should be nearby when the syllable is pronounced for a purpose. It is usually placed at the beginning of sacred scriptures, and is prefixed to prayers. It is a compound of three letters A, U, M, which, in popular belief, are typical of the three Vedas, also of the three gods A (Agni), V (Varuna), and M (Maruts) or Fire, Water, and Air. In esoteric philosophy these are the three sacred fires, or the "triple fire" in the Universe and man, besides many other things. In an occult context, this "triple fire" represents the highest Tetraktys, as it is typified by the Agni named Abhimanin and his transformation into three sons, Pavaka (electric fire), Pavamana (fire by friction), and Suchi (solar fire), "who drinks up water," i.e., destroys material desires. This monosyllable is also called Udgitta, and is sacred among Brahmins and Buddhists alike.

Aura (*Gr.*, "breeze"). A subtle, invisible essence or fluid that emanates from human and animal bodies and even objects. It is a psychic effluvium, partaking of both the mind and the body, as it is the electro-vital — and at the same time electro-mental — aura; called in Theosophy the akashic or magnetic aura. It represents the electromagnetic radiation of all the accumulated energies of a living organism, especially the heart, having a dominant colour, sound, and scent. All bodies and objects of the manifest world are surrounded by an aura.

The human aura is a kind of passport which quickly identifies the individual's essence and destiny. In the future, a person's aura will determine their suitability to hold important positions in every domain of life. Every thought, emotion, feeling, or act leaves an imprint on the aura in the form of radiations, which, in turn, magnetically attract elements from space that correspond with their tonality. The more powerful the fiery energy in a person, the stronger the influence of their aura over their whole environment. Throughout their lives, people suffuse everything they touch with the radiations of their aura, brightening or darkening the objects around them. In addition every individual perceives the world through the prism of their aura, as though they were looking through a pair of glasses. Hence, through a light aura, one perceives only the Light, and through a dark aura, one perceives the darkness.

The aura of a newborn child is colourless until the first gleam of consciousness imbues it with colours that correspond to the accumulations of previous lives. As a rule, this happens at the age of seven.

The auric field should be enclosed by a protective net, woven together from the sediment of the subtlest fiery energies providing a shield against extraneous intrusions and influences. But souls devoid of spirituality lack this protection causing them often to fall victim to the impact of other people's auras, especially those that possess a powerful aura of dark fire; they also succumb to the influence of various evil entities from the Subtle Plane. First and foremost this affects a person's health. More spiritually-minded people have a protective net in the form of fiery ruby sparks. However, dark entities are always attempting to break through, for even the slightest rupture opens the way to gaining control over another being. The aura of powerful spirits generates a ray, which imbues thoughts, or anything else, with its colour and energy. When a thought like this is aimed in a specific direction, it has the appearance of a real ray in space and is equipped with tremendous power.

A planet possesses an aura, too, along with a protective net. The aura of Earth accumulates all the energies produced by the activity and free will of humanity. At the beginning of its existence, the aura of the Earth was golden, but by the mid-twentieth century it had turned ash-grey with clouds of brown gas and black holes in its protective net. By the end of the last century, the Hierarchy of Light and its earthly colleagues managed to restore the net. However, the state of the planet's aura still depends upon humanity, upon each and every individual.

Auric envelope or **auric egg**. A spiritual envelope that contains all the seven principles of man, both the Divine and the physical. In its essence, it is eternal; in its constant correlations, it is a kind of perpetual motion machine during the reincarnating progress of the Ego on Earth. It is this body which at death assimilates the essence of *buddhi* and *manas* and becomes the vehicle of these spiritual principles, which are not objective, and then, with the full radiation of *atman* upon it, ascends as *manas-taijasa* (*Sk.*, "radiant mind") into the devachanic state. The auric egg, reflecting all the thoughts, words, and deeds of man, is:

1. The preserver of every karmic record.
2. The storehouse of all the good and bad powers of man, receiving and giving out at his will — rather at his very thought — every potentiality, which becomes, then and there, an acting

potency: this aura is the mirror in which sensitives and clairvoyants sense and perceive the real man, seeing him as he is, not as he appears.

3. As it furnishes man with his astral form, around which the physical entity models itself, first as a foetus, then as a child and adult, the astral growing apace with the human being, so it furnishes him during his life; and after death, with his devachanic entity and *kama-rupa*, or body of desire (the spook).

Avalokiteshvara (*Sk.*, "onlooking Lord"). In the exoteric interpretation, Padmapani (the lotus-bearer and the lotus-born) in Tibet, the first divine ancestor of the Tibetans, the complete incarnation or Avatar of Avalokiteshvara. But in esoteric philosophy Avaloki, the "onlooker," is the Higher Self, while Padmapani is the Higher Ego or *manas*. The mystic formula "Om Mani Padme Hum" is specially used to invoke their joint assistance. While popular fancy claims for Avalokiteshvara many incarnations on earth, and sees in him, not entirely unjustifiably, the spiritual guide of every believer, the esoteric interpretation sees in him the Logos, both celestial and human. Therefore, when the Yogachara school declares Avalokiteshvara (as Padmapani) "to be the Dhyani Bodhisattva of Amitabha Buddha," this is indeed true, because the former is *the spiritual reflex in the world of forms* of the latter, both being one — one in heaven, the other on earth.

Avatamsaka Sutra (*Sk.*, "flower ornament scripture"). A large collection of Mahayana sutras, known as the King of Kings of all Buddhist scriptures.

Avatar (*Sk.*, "descent"). Divine incarnation. The descent of a God or an exalted Being, who has progressed beyond the necessity of rebirth, into the body of a simple mortal. Krishna was an avatar of Vishnu. The Dalai Lama is believed to be an avatar of Avalokiteshvara, and the Panchen Lama, an avatar of Amitabha. There are two kinds of avatars: those born from woman, and those who are parentless, the *Anupapadaka*.

As Ramakrishna puts it, an Avatar or Saviour is a human messenger of God. He is like a viceroy of the mighty Monarch. As when there is any disturbance in some far-off province, the King sends the viceroy to quell it. So whenever there is any waning of religion in any part of the world, God sends His Avatar there to guard virtue and to foster its growth. It is one and the same Avatar that, having plunged into the ocean of life, rises up in one place and is known as Krishna, and diving again rises in another place and is known as Christ.

Avesta (*Zend*, "law"). The sacred scriptures of the Zoroastrians. *Zend* means in the "Zend-Avesta" a "commentary" or "interpretation." It is an error to regard "Zend" as a language, as "it was applied only to explanatory texts, to the translations of the Avesta" (Darmesteter, *The Zend-Avesta, Part I*).

Avichi (*Sk.*, "uninterrupted hell"). A state experienced not necessarily only after death or between two births, for it can be experienced on Earth as well; the last of the eight hells, where the culprits *die and are reborn without interruption*, and yet not without hope of ultimate redemption. This is because Avichi is another name for Myalba (Earth) and a state to which certain soulless individuals are condemned on this physical plane.

Avidya (*Sk.*, "non-knowledge"). Opposite of *vidya*, knowledge. Ignorance which proceeds from and is produced by the illusion of the senses.

B

Bacon, Francis (1561–1626). An English philosopher, historian, and statesman. The Baconian theory suggests that he was the author of the works published under the name of William Shakespeare.

Bacon, Roger (1214–1292). A very famous Franciscan monk who lived in England. He was an alchemist who firmly believed in the existence of the philosopher's stone, and was a great mechanician, chemist, physicist, and astrologer. In his *Letter Concerning the Marvellous Power of Art and Nature and the Nullity of Magic* (1267), he gives hints about gunpowder and predicts the use of steam as a propelling power, describing, besides the hydraulic press, the diving-bell and the kaleidoscope. He also made a famous brazen head fitted with an acoustic apparatus which spoke prophecy.

Baha'i. A monotheistic religion founded in the nineteenth century by Baha'u'llah in Persia (modern-day Iran). It emphasizes the unity of all religions, the oneness of humanity, and universal peace, with principles of equality, justice, and service to humanity.

Bangalore. The former name of Bengaluru, a major city in southern India.

Basil the Great (c.330–379). A Christian bishop and theologian, one of the Cappadocian Fathers. He played a key role in shaping Christian monasticism and is known for his writings on the Trinity, charity, and the nature of the Church.

Baum, L. Frank (1856–1919). An American author best known for his *Oz* series, beginning with *The Wonderful Wizard of Oz* (1900). Baum's imaginative storytelling and unique characters have had a lasting influence on fantasy literature and children's stories. He and his wife joined the Theosophical Society in 1892.

Beckmann, Max (1884–1950). A German painter, printmaker, and sculptor.

Benares or **Varanasi**. A holy city in India on the Ganges River.

Be-ness. A term coined by Theosophists to render more accurately the essential meaning of the untranslatable word *Sat*. "Being" cannot serve as a translation of *Sat*, because "Being" presupposes a sentient feeling or some consciousness of existence, while the term *Sat* applies solely to the absolute Principle, the universal, the unknown and ever unknowable Presence, that which philosophical Pantheism postulates in the Cosmos, calling it the basic root of the Cosmos, and the Cosmos itself. Indeed, *Sat* is not even "the incomprehensible Entity," as translated by some Orientalists, for it is no more an Entity than it is a non-Entity — it is both. *Sat* is absolute *Be-ness*, not *Being*, the one secondless, undivided, and indivisible All — the root of all Nature, visible and invisible, objective and subjective, to be sensed by the highest spiritual intuition but never to be fully comprehended.

Bernbaum, Edwin, PhD (b.1945). An American mountaineer and scholar of comparative religion and mythology, whose work centres on the relationship between culture and Nature. He is the author of *Sacred Mountains of the World* (1990) and *The Way to Shambhala* (1980).

Besant, Annie (1847–1933). A British social reformer, Theosophist, and women's rights advocate. She served as the second president of the Theosophical Society from 1907 to 1933 and played a major role in India's independence movement, becoming the first female president of the Indian National Congress in 1917.

Bhagavad Gita (*Sk.*, "Lord's song"). A portion of the Mahabharata (*Sk.*, "great war"), the great epic poem of India. It contains a dialogue wherein Krishna — the Charioteer — and Arjuna, his disciple, have a discussion about the highest spiritual philosophy. The work is pre-eminently occult or esoteric.

The Mahabharata includes both the Ramayana and the Bhagavad Gita, and no two Orientalists agree as to its date of origin. But it is undeniably extremely ancient. The war described, which lasted 900,000 years, began between the early Aryans (the Fifth Race) and the giant Atlanteans (the Fourth Race) when the portions of Atlantis began to sink. The final struggle between the Atlantean sorcerers and the White Adepts who now form the Trans-Himalayan Brotherhood ended in the victory of the latter, fortunately for humanity.

Bharavi. A sixth-century Indian poet known for his epic poem *Kiratarjuniya*.

Bhikshu (*Sk.*, "mendicant scholar"). The name given to the first followers of Shakyamuni Buddha. Bhikshus are divided into two classes of *shramanas* (Buddhist monks and priests), namely: esoteric mendicants who control their nature by means of the (religious) law, and exoteric mendicants who control their nature by means of *diet*.

Blavatsky, Nikifor (1810–c.1873). The Vice Governor of Erivan Province of the Russian Empire (now Armenia), whom Helena Blavatsky agreed to marry at the age of 17, yet left three months later.

Blood. The means of circulation of life, *prana*, through the body. It is the vital principle in us, *pranic* rather than *prana*, and is closely allied to *kama* and to the *linga-sharira*. The essence of the blood is *kama*, penetrated by *prana*, which is universal on this plane. When *kama* leaves the blood it congeals. So that the blood may be regarded as *kama-rupa*, the "form of *kama*" in a sense. While *kama* is the essence of the blood, its red corpuscles are drops of electrical fluid, the perspiration oozing out of every cell of the various organs, and caused to exude by electrical action. They are the progeny of the *fohatic* principle.

Anatomists are beginning to discover new ramifications and new modifications in the human body, and they sometimes come very close to a truth without quite getting hold of it. For instance, they are in error as to the spleen, when they call it the manufactory of the white corpuscles of the blood, for, as said, the spleen is really the vehicle of the *linga-sharira*. But these same white corpuscles, which are the devourers, the scavengers of the human body, are oozed out of the *linga-sharira* and are of the same essence as itself. They come from the spleen, not because the spleen manufactures them, but because they are oozed out of the *linga-sharira*, which, as said, lies curled in the spleen.

The blood serves as the physical *upadhi* for *kama*, *prana*, and the *linga-sharira*, and the student will understand why it plays so large a part in the animal economy. From the spleen — enriched by the life-elements of *prana*, the corpuscles of the *linga-sharira* serving as the vehicle of these *pranic* elements, the devourers, that build up and destroy the human body — it travels all over the body, distributing everywhere these *pranic* carriers. The red corpuscles represent the *fohatic* energy in the body, closely allied to *kama* and *prana*, while the essence of the blood is *kama*, present in every part of the body.

Bodh Gaya. A sacred pilgrimage site in Bihar, India, where Siddhartha Gautama (the Buddha) attained enlightenment under the Bodhi Tree. It is one of the most important sites in Buddhism and is home to the Mahabodhi Temple.

Bodhi (*Sk.*, "awakening," "enlightenment"). Receptive intelligence, in contradistinction to *buddhi*, which is the potentiality of intelligence; the Divine Wisdom which, upon awakening within, makes the human being enlightened.

Bodhi Tree or **Bo-Tree** (*Sk.*, "tree of awakening"). A large sacred fig tree located in Bodh Gaya, India, under which the Buddha attained enlightenment.

Bodhichitta (*Sk.*, "awakening mind"). The wish to attain complete enlightenment for the benefit of all sentient beings; the union of compassion and wisdom.

Bodhidharma (*Sk.*, "law of enlightenment"). Wisdom Religion; or the wisdom contained in Dharma (ethics). Also the name of a great Arhat *Kshatriya* (one of the warrior-caste), the son of a king. It was Panyatara, his Guru, who gave him the name Bodhidharma to mark his understanding (*bodhi*) of the Law (*dharma*) of Buddha. Bodhidharma, who flourished in the sixth century, travelled to China, to where he brought a precious relic, the alms bowl of the Lord Buddha.

Bodhisattva (*Sk.*, "one whose essence has become wisdom"). Those who need but one more incarnation to become perfect Buddhas, i.e., to be entitled to Nirvana. This, as applied to *Manushi* (terrestrial) Buddhas. In the metaphysical sense, Bodhisattva is a title given to the sons of the celestial Dhyani Buddhas. Also the name of those who follow the Path of Renunciation.

Buddhists of the Mahayana mystic system teach that each Buddha manifests himself (hypostatically or otherwise) simultaneously in three worlds of Being, namely, in the world of *kama* (concupiscence or desire — the sensuous universe or our Earth) in the shape of a human being; in the world of *rupa* (form, yet supersensuous) as a Bodhisattva; and in the highest Spiritual World (that of purely incorporeal existences) as a Dhyani-Buddha. The latter prevails eternally in space and time, i.e., from one Maha Kalpa to the other — the synthetic culmination of the three being Adi-Buddha (as the secret portions of the Kalachakra assert), the Wisdom-Principle, which is Absolute, and therefore out of space and time. Their interrelation is the following: The Dhyani-Buddha, when the world needs a human Buddha, "creates" through the power of *dhyana* (meditation, omnipotent devotion), a mind-born son — a Bodhisattva — whose mission it is after the physical death of his human, or Manushi Buddha, to continue his work on Earth until the appearance of the subsequent Buddha.

The esoteric meaning of this teaching is clear. In the case of a simple mortal, the principles in him are only the more or less bright reflections of the seven cosmic, and the seven celestial principles, the Hierarchy of supersensual Beings. In the case of a Buddha, they are almost the principles in actuality themselves. The Bodhisattva replaces in him the *karana-sharira* ("casual body"), or the Ego principle, and the rest correspondingly; and it is in this way that esoteric philosophy explains the meaning of the sentence that "by virtue of *dhyana* [or abstract meditation] the Dhyani-Buddha [the Buddha's spirit or monad] creates a Bodhisattva," or the astrally clothed Ego within the Manushi Buddha. Thus, while the Buddha merges back into Nirvana whence it proceeded, the Bodhisattva remains behind to continue the Buddha's work on Earth.

Bodhisattvahood. The state or condition of a Bodhisattva, one who seeks enlightenment not only for themselves but for all beings and vows to remain in the cycle of rebirth until all sentient beings are liberated.

Body or **sthula-sharira** (*Sk.*, "dense body"). In strict esoteric parlance, an *upadhi* rather than a principle. But it is a vehicle of consciousness, and therefore must be considered when studying consciousness. Apart from this, it can be regarded simply as a denser aspect of the *linga-sharira*, for the body and the *linga-sharira* are both on the same plane, and the *linga-sharira* is molecular in its constitution, like the body. The Earth and its Astral Light are as closely related to each other as the body is to its *linga-sharira*, the Earth being the *upadhi* of Astral Light. Our plane in its lowest division is the Earth; in its highest the Astral. The terrestrial Astral Light should, of course, not be confused with the universal Astral Light.

Body, lunar. An astral or subtle body associated with emotions and desires. See *kamarupa*.

Bogd Khan (1869–1924). The spiritual and political leader of Mongolia, also known as the Eighth Jebtsundamba Khutuktu. He was recognized as a Living Buddha and declared himself the ruler of Mongolia in 1911 after the fall of the Qing dynasty, leading the country's independence movement.

Böhme, Jacob (1575–1624). A great mystic philosopher, one of the most prominent Theosophists of the medieval ages. In his boyhood, he was a common shepherd, and after learning to read and write in a village school, he became an apprentice to a poor shoemaker at Görlitz. He was a natural clairvoyant of the most wonderful powers. With no education or acquaintance with science, he wrote works which are now proved to be full of scientific truths; but then, as he says himself, what he wrote about, he "saw as in a great deep in the Eternal." He had "a thorough view of the universe, as in a chaos," which yet "opened itself in him, from time to time, as in a young plant." He was a thorough born mystic, and evidently of a constitution which is most rare — one of those fine natures whose material envelope impedes in no way the direct, even if only occasional, intercommunion between the intellectual and the spiritual Ego. It is this Ego which Jacob Böhme, like so many other untrained mystics, mistook for God. "Man must acknowledge," he writes, "that his knowledge is not his own, but from God, who manifests the ideas of wisdom to the soul of man, in what measure he pleases." Had this great Theosophist mastered Eastern occultism, he might have expressed it otherwise. He would have known then that the "god" who spoke through his poor uncultured and untrained brain was his own divine Ego, the omniscient Deity within himself, and that what that Deity imparted was not in "what measure he pleases," but in the measure of the capacities of the mortal and temporary dwelling *It* informed.

Bombay. The former name of Mumbai, the capital city of the state of Maharashtra in India.

Bon (*Tib.*, "to recite," "to invoke"). A complex doctrine in which ancient forms of North Asian shamanism are mixed with the beliefs and rituals of the Nature-religion of the indigenous population of north-west India.

There are two forms of Bon: primitive veneration of Nature, full of shamanic and necromantic rituals, and sometimes blood sacrifice (in the past this included human sacrifice, while currently only animal sacrifice is practised taking the form of a sheep, a goat, or a clay image in its place), and reformed Bon, or Bon adapted to Buddhism.

In the first form of Bon one finds the gods of heaven and earth, the sun and moon, the stars and the four cardinal directions. The King Gesar cycle of legends belongs to this form of Bon. The primitive teaching of Bon is still represented by wandering exorcists of evil spirits who never belong to settled communities. Their holy places are not marked by monasteries or chapels, but altars of rough stones or stone monuments in the shape of a megalith or circle of megaliths. Sometimes stone altars are located on mountain tops, and sometimes in secluded caves among rocks and high peaks.

Reformed Bon is an extremely complex phenomenon, as represented by the Nyingma school, also referred to as the "red caps." It was founded in the eighth century by Padmasambhava, whose original teachings were hugely distorted by his followers. They have large monasteries organized on the lamaistic model, where the red-robed priests are indistinguishable from their lamaistic colleagues. Buddhism greatly influenced the external side of Bon rituals, while the teachings of this religion were strongly influenced by Hinduism. This makes it difficult to discern where the purely natural and the foreign Buddhist and Hindu elements begin and end in the existing cults.

The main emphasis in the Nyingmapa school is not on monastic discipline, but on meditation and the development of supernatural abilities, which Blavatsky opposed and warned against.

With the advent of Buddhism, the ancient Bon religion was persecuted. During the reign of King Langdarma (c.838–842), Bon for a short time became the state religion. After the violent death of the king, it was persecuted again and Buddhism became the dominant religion. The priests were expelled and most of their activities were suppressed. From that time on, the Bon religion became the doctrine of the minority and was pushed into the remote border areas of Tibet.

A certain antagonism exists between Buddhist and Bon monasteries. It is believed that Bon lamas have knowledge of dangerous secrets, and a night spent in a Bon monastery can bring misfortune.

Belief in the forces of Nature, personified by divine beings, is common to both forms of Bon. Each locality has its own local deity or demon.

Bon literature is a treasure trove of ancient beliefs dating back to the distant past and the era of migration, when the ancestors of modern Tibetan tribes passed through the mountainous land now called Tibet, bringing with them their tribal religions. The literary monuments of Bon can be traditionally described as falling into one of the following four sections: 1) two large collections of sacred Bon texts, totalling about 300 volumes; 2) national-epic heroic songs and legendary stories; 3) popular songs; 4) sorcery books and guides to magical rituals.

Bons (*Tib.*). The followers of the old religion of the indigenous people of Tibet; of pre-Budhistic temples and ritualism; the same as *Dugpas*, "red caps," though the latter appellation usually applies only to sorcerers.

Bonze (*Jap.*, "priest"). A Japanese or Chinese Buddhist monk or priest; but in the strict sense, the main monk in a temple in Japan and other Asian countries.

Book of Dzyan. A secret and sacred book written in Senzar and stored in the Tower of Chung in Shambhala, a Stronghold of Light hidden in the Himalayas. In the nineteenth century, two parts from the *Book of Dzyan* were published, entitled *Cosmogenesis* and *Anthropogenesis*. Consisting of nineteen stanzas, they narrated the story of the origin of the Cosmos and humanity. At the beginning of the twentieth century, a third part in nine stanzas appeared — about the inherent divinity of humanity — under the title *Theogenesis*. Later, at the very end of the twentieth century, a new part was revealed — the twelve stanzas of *Agapegenesis*, about the significance of the heart.

Book of Maitreya Buddha. The secret book that Helena Blavatsky was to use along with the *Book of Dzyan* to create *The Secret Doctrine*, as evidenced by her letters. It is the Book of Life, or the Book of Fiery Destinies, of the Supreme Spirit — Maitreya — who comes into the world to elevate humanity to the next level of development. Excerpts from this Book, translated from the Senzar language, were to comprise the fifth volume of *The Secret Doctrine*.

Book of the Golden Precepts. A sacred book whose original in Senzar is stored in Shambhala. It contains approximately ninety short treatises, essentially constituting a code of rules which Initiates must follow. Copies of the sacred book in various languages are guarded in the monasteries of the East, and its ethics have imbued all Eastern sacred scriptures.

Bragdon, Claude (1866–1946). An American architect, writer, and publisher, who advocated a theosophical approach to building design.

Brahma (*Sk.*, "growth," "expansion," "creation"). There are Brahma, the neuter form, and Brahma, the male creator of the Hindu Pantheon. The former Brahma, or *Brahman*, is the impersonal, supreme, and uncognizable Principle of the Universe, from whose essence all emanates and to which all returns; it is incorporeal, immaterial, unborn, eternal, without beginning or end. It is all-pervading, animating everything from the highest god to the smallest mineral atom. By contrast, the latter Brahma is the male Creator, who exists periodically in this manifestation only and then disappears again.

Brahma Sanankumara (*Sk.*, "ever young Brahma"). The name given to Sanat Kumara in Buddhism.

Brahmacharya (*Sk.*, "conduct that leads to Brahma"). A Brahmin ascetic; one vowed to celibacy, a monk, virtually, or a religious student. This concept refers to a lifestyle of self-discipline and the control of sexual and sensual desires, often observed by spiritual aspirants and monks to conserve energy for spiritual pursuits.

Brahman (*Sk.*, "growth," "evolution"). The ultimate reality or Universal Principle in Hinduism; the unchanging, infinite, and transcendent reality that underlies all existence.

Brahmapuri (*Sk.*, "abode of Brahma"). The inner chamber of the heart.

Brahmins or **Brahmans** (*Sk.*, "priests"). The highest of the four castes in India, one supposed or rather fancying itself to be as high among humans as Brahman, the Absolute of the Vedantists, is among, or above the gods.

Brain. Taken as an organ of consciousness, it serves as the vehicle on the objective plane of the lower *manas*, which works upon its material molecules in a way hereafter to be explained. Its subdivisions correspond to, and are the organs of, the subdivisions of the lower *manas*. Its convolutions are formed by thought, the activity of the thinking principle building up more and more complicated convolutions.

There are seven cavities in the brain which during life are empty, in the ordinary sense of the word. In reality, they are filled with Akasha, each cavity having its own colour, according to one's state of consciousness. The colours are only visible to the purified vision. These cavities are called in occultism the "seven harmonies," the scale of the divine harmonies, and it is in them that visions must be reflected, if they are to remain in the brain-memory. These are the parts of the brain which receive impressions from the heart, and enable the memory of the heart to be impressed on the memory of the brain.

The fourth of these cavities is the pituitary body, which corresponds with *manas-antahkarana*, the bridge to higher intelligence; it contains various essences. The fifth cavity is the third ventricle, empty during life except for pulsating light, though filled with a liquid after death. The sixth cavity is the pineal gland, also hollow and empty during life; the granules are precipitated after death. The pineal gland corresponds with *manas* until it is touched by the vibrating light of *kundalini*, which proceeds from *buddhi*, and then it becomes *buddhi-manas*. When *manas* is united with *buddhi*, or when *buddhi* — and therefore *atman* also — is centred in *manas*, it acts in the three higher cavities, radiating and sending forth a halo of light, and this sometimes becomes visible in the case of very holy persons. The fires are always playing round the pineal gland; but when *kundalini* illuminates them for a brief instant, the whole universe is seen. This occurs occasionally in deep sleep when the third eye opens. And this opening is good for *manas*, who profits by it, even though the lower man is not then reached and therefore cannot remember it. The seventh cavity is the synthesis of all, the cavity of the skull itself, filled with Akasha. This corresponds with the *atmic* aura, the sacred auric egg.

Perception, brain perception, is located in the aura of the pineal gland, while the pineal gland itself, illuminated, corresponds with divine thought. The pituitary body is the organ *per se* of the psychic plane. Pure psychic vision (ordinary clairvoyance is not the function of this organ) is caused by the molecular motion of this body, which is directly connected to the optic nerve, and thus affects the sight, giving rise to hallucinations. This motion may readily cause flashes of light, seen within the head, similar to those that may be obtained when pressing the eyeballs, and so causing molecular motion in the optic nerve. When molecular action is set up in the pituitary body these flashes are seen, and further action gives psychic vision, as similar motion in the pineal gland gives spiritual clairvoyance. Drunkenness and fever cause disorderly motion in the pituitary body, and so produce illusions of sight, visions, hallucinations. This body is sometimes so affected by drunkenness that it is paralysed. Strict forbiddance of alcoholic liquids among all students of occultism eliminates the negative effect which alcohol would produce on the pituitary body and pineal gland.

The pineal gland is the focus of the spiritual, hence inorganic, sensorium. Its action has nothing to do with the circulation of the blood, but is rather concerned with the spiritual fiery emanation that proceeds from the blood. Further: the pineal gland, at the upper pole of the human body, corresponds with the uterus (in the female and its analogue in the male) at the lower pole; the peduncles of the pineal gland corresponding with the fallopian tubes of the uterus. The pituitary body is only the servant of the pineal gland, its torch-bearer, like the servants carrying torches that run before the carriage of a princess. Man is androgyne, so far as his head is concerned.

The corpora quadrigemina corresponds with *kama-manas*, thereby bringing *kama* within the *manasic* division of the human brain.

Kama itself corresponds with the cerebellum, which is the centre and storehouse of force. The cerebellum furnishes the materials for ideation. The frontal lobes of the cerebrum are the finishers and polishers of the materials supplied by the cerebellum, but they cannot create these materials for themselves.

In the lower part of the body *kama* corresponds to the liver, along with the stomach.

To recapitulate:
- *kama* corresponds to cerebellum;
- *kama-manas* corresponds to corpora quadrigemina;
- *manas-antahkarana* corresponds to pituitary body;
- *manas* corresponds to pineal gland;
- *manas-buddhi* corresponds to pineal gland when touched by *kundalini*;
- auric egg corresponds to cavity of skull filled with Akasha.

Thus the brain, the vehicle of the lower *manas* with *kama*, as said, has its subdivisions corresponding to the subdivisions, or aspects, of *manas* in activity, and has also cavities related to the heart, rendering possible the making of impressions on the physical consciousness, and by the action within these cavities rendering possible the action of *buddhi-manas* on the physical plane, and the development of spiritual clairvoyance.

However, the brain, or thinking machinery, is not only in the head and skull; every organ in man, the heart, liver, lungs, etc., down to every nerve and muscle, has, so to speak, its own distinct brain, or thinking apparatus. As our brain has naught to do with the guidance of the collective and individual work of every organ in us, what is it that guides each so unerringly in its incessant functions, that makes them struggle with disease, throw it off and act, each of them, even the smallest, not in a clock-work manner, as alleged by some materialists (for, at the slightest disturbance or breakage the clock stops), but as an entity endowed with instinct? To say that it is Nature is to say nothing at all, if not to claim a fallacy; for Nature, after all, is but a name for these very same functions, the sum of the qualities and attributes, physical, mental, etc., in the universe and man, the total of agencies and forces guided by intelligent laws.

Brotherhood. The Community of the Seven Messengers of the Distant Worlds and their disciples, who have lived side by side with humanity on Earth for millions of years, assisting in the development of the human mind and heart. The Brotherhood is usually referred to as *White* to indicate the White Light that, when it splits, yields the seven colours of the rainbow, each of which symbolizes one of the Great Teachers, and vice versa — the seven colours of the rainbow that result in the White Light upon fusion.

The previous evolutionary cycle was tasked with giving people knowledge and developing their intelligence. The present cycle aims to bring people closer to Love, and the focus of Love — the heart. Therefore, the Great Lords have divided themselves into two Lodges — Western and Eastern.

The Western Lodge — also known as the Brotherhood of Luxor or the Thebes Sanctuary, located in Egypt — was to provide knowledge, as well as to develop and expand human consciousness, with an emphasis on the mental body, the mind, and the human intellect, in order to help humankind take a step towards the heart. All the knowledge accumulated in the past and present evolutionary cycles has been preserved in its entirety in hidden depositories in Egypt.

The Eastern Lodge — Shambhala or the Himalayan Brotherhood — was to develop the intuition of the heart, always bearing Love and serving the highest energies. In other words, if the West is the mind, the East is the heart. When Masters achieve the highest degrees possible within the walls of the Thebes Sanctuary, they leave it for the Eastern Lodge. This happens approximately once every two thousand years.

At the end of the nineteenth century, before the start of Armageddon, all the secret schools and Ashrams of the Western Brotherhood were closed and moved to the Himalayas. All the Great Teachers who had worked in the world holding Initiations and imparting knowledge were also summoned to the Stronghold of Light in the Himalayas. Humanity was abandoned for a hundred years. Although knowledge continued to be passed on through their disciples, there was no longer any direct contact between the Masters and the wider population.

The Theban Sanctuary is now reopening and once again beginning to serve Love. While previously it worked through the Ray of Knowledge, now these two Sanctuaries, Eastern and Western, are uniting, their Rays interpenetrating and imparting a single Ray of Love-Wisdom. Similarly, all the Great Lords who saturated humanity with as much knowledge as possible are now beginning to act in service to Love. Thus a great synthesis is being born, and the two Greatest Schools are merging into one that affirms a single path for the world: ascent up the steps of Wisdom through illumination of the human heart.

When Blavatsky mentioned that a messenger is sent to the West in the last quarter of each century, she was not wrong. She simply chose not to specify that this statement related to the Brotherhood of Luxor in Thebes, Egypt, whose mission has always been to lead the peoples of the West through the mind to the heart, naturally following 100-year cycles.

In the past, it was the Masters and disciples of the Theban Sanctuary that often incarnated themselves within the specified periods. Franz Anton Mesmer (1734–1815), a famous German physician, was selected by the Council of Luxor — according to the orders of the Great Brotherhood — to act in the eighteenth century as their usual pioneer, sent in the last quarter of every century to enlighten a small portion of the Western nations in occult lore. It was the Count of Saint-Germain who supervised the development of events in this case.

However, Mahatmas Morya and Koot Hoomi who guided Blavatsky have always been representative of the Himalayan Brotherhood, which has lived through the 60-year cycles of the calendar of Shambhala, the Kalachakra calendar. Blavatsky herself belonged initially to the Western Lodge, and subsequently became a representative of the Eastern Lodge of the Great Brotherhood.

The "century" of the Kalachakra calendar consists of 60 rather than 100 years. This explains why the messenger that Blavatsky promised appeared not at the end of the twentieth century but much earlier. She could not speak about the correct periods in her writing, but she did impart this information verbally to her closest colleagues. However, this entrusted information was misinterpreted: instead of waiting for a new disciple, as Blavatsky herself had mentioned, there arose anticipation of a "World Teacher" in a physical body. But still, the object of this anticipation was scheduled not for the period 1975–2000, as Blavatsky stated in writing, but in the 1920–1930s, a period that coincided with the completion of the next 60-year cycle. This suggests that Blavatsky did convey to her closest colleagues that the next disciple would have to be sent by the Masters much earlier than the timeframe she was permitted to mention publicly.

The promised mid-twentieth-century disciple who would continue the mission of Blavatsky was none other than Helena Roerich, who gave the highest form of yoga, *Agni Yoga*, to humanity in cooperation with Master Morya.

Brothers of the shadow. A name given by the occultists to sorcerers, and especially to the Tibetan Dugpas, of whom there are many in the Bon sect of the Red Caps (Dugpa). The word is applied to all practitioners of black or left-hand magic.

One should not assume that such individuals are to be found solely in Tibet or in the past. The forces of darkness have their own hierarchy, and although its head was isolated long ago and is now exiled to Saturn, it is still quite strong. In contrast to Shambhala, located high in the mountains, the dark brotherhood established its stronghold at the lowest point on Earth, burrowing into subterranean layers closer to the earthly core in order to gain strength from its fire. One should not underestimate the hierophants of evil, as they know many secrets of Nature, especially those relating to the mortal quaternary of human bodies. However, the domain of the higher triad and spirituality is inaccessible to them.

The brothers of the shadow now act under the guise of "bearers of light." A great many hold key positions in organizations intended to bear the Light and undermine them from within. Therefore, one may often observe the representatives of certain organizations condemning those of others despite the fact that the ideas of the Light are one. They manipulate the sources coming from the Light, cleverly selecting quotations to defame some other source of light. And the human mind, being unable to comprehend the multifold facets of the same Truth, blindly falls into this trap, not realizing that the person themselves is becoming a servant of the darkness. This is why it is so important to listen to one's heart, which is incapable of falling into snares prepared for the mind. With rare exceptions, such organizations are headed by leaders who truly serve the Light and humanity.

Evil hierophants use the signs and symbols of the Light, but in so doing they self-destruct, for these signs are bearers of the fiery force, which it is impossible to apply in a harmful manner. One may recall the example of the swastika — those who used this solar symbol of Life for the purposes of evil ended up punishing themselves.

Moreover, the dark brotherhood has set up its own "shadow government," which attempts to destructively influence the policies of earthly leaders, especially those in countries that have most Points of Life. This influence is expressed often via the principle: "divide and conquer."

The threads of evil unite the most diverse categories of people, since representatives of evil are disguised beneath the robes of priests and the costumes of philanthropists such that from their outward appearance it is impossible to tell who is who. For example, those who at first glance appear to be irreconcilable enemies, behind the scenes may shake hands and serve the same destructive goal. Of course, their followers have no knowledge of this, because only the leaders of dark organizations and movements have the right to contact the hierophants of evil to receive further instruction. They have reached an apogee in the development of technology aimed at manipulating human psychology, and therefore, it is easy for them to pass off black for white.

One of the chief tasks of the shadow brothers is to convince humanity that dark forces do not exist. The main emphasis in their activities is focused on the level of the second chakra related to the sex organs. From esoteric philosophy, it is known that every sexual act results in the birth of a visible, and most often an invisible, being, and if it is produced without Love, then an invisible demonic entity is born, which enslaves and forces one to reproduce its own kind with the goal of capturing new souls and subjugating them, making of them suppliers of low-frequency currents. And here the person becomes like a fly caught in a web, or rather in sexual slavery to the hierophants of evil, from which very few are ever able to escape, and only then, over the course of a number of reincarnations. Sexual energy splashed out in vain feeds huge conglomerates of dark forces, since they know how to use it for destructive purposes. For example, so-called hypersexual people are invisibly connected to the conglomerate of possessors and feed it with their energy, which in turn can be the reason for such tragedies as murders in educational institutions in various parts of the world, although at first glance these are completely unrelated phenomena. And when possessors are able to capture the minds of state leaders, this always results in bloody conflict, after all, for the dark forces, the energy of blood has the same meaning as sexual energy. It is not for nothing that Buddhists avoid spilling any blood, aware as they are that it attracts evil spirits.

A particular characteristic of dark forces is that they never value those who serve them ardently. They may make promises and even realize all a person's cherished desires on the material plane in exchange for loyalty. However, as soon as they achieve their goal, they will immediately get rid of their minions, no matter what position they occupy, and replace them with new executors.

In the modern book market there is a lot of literature and so-called "spiritual practice" that is created by the brothers of the shadow. At first glance, everything is fine; it all stands with impeccable logic, for who will believe them if they do not hide behind well-known truths. But in all this there will always be introduced something completely alien to the Path of Light, which can be expressed in three phrases: one beloved, one Teacher, and one Path. For example, minions of darkness will have a veiled or overt justification for polygamy or promiscuity, which is simply absurd on the Right-hand Path. Or among the truths, there will suddenly appear promotion for using the "gifts of Nature," such as cannabis, psychedelics or other drugs, to attain enlightenment.

It is true that in the seventh century, polygamy was admitted in the Quran, but it was a forced measure to save the peoples of the Middle East from complete extinction. At that time, war raged continuously, and when men in their prime died, it was necessary to replenish the ranks of the army. Countless raids on peaceful nomadic tribes also served to ensure that the Prophet Muhammad united them under his banner. After all, women, children, and the elderly were incapable of resisting the conquerors. Therefore, it was necessary to raise and expand the role of women, deprived of any rights, and somehow equalize their rights with men, in contrast to the situation as it existed in other nations, in which a man took one official wife, but still had numerous extra-marital affairs from which children were born without any rights. Muhammad himself was faithful to his beloved Khadija until the time of her death. However, his desire to establish monogamy met with enormous resistance from the people forcing him to give in, and be content with limiting the number of legal wives a man may take to four. And the Teaching itself was subsequently greatly distorted through false interpretation.

The herd instincts of the earlier centuries can have no place in the twenty-first century, And so polygamy has been abolished even in some Muslim countries such as Turkey, where Ataturk officially banned it in 1924. Since ancient times, in Judaism, polygamy has not considered a standard of perfection; on the contrary, husband and wife in Kabbalistic works are perceived as two halves of a whole.

The brothers of the shadow are especially interested in people who have turned to certain practices for the first time, wanting to develop some superpower. This is because their first chakra, *kundalini*, which contains a basic and untouchable reserve of vital energy, begins to be engaged in the process. The stronger the aspiration, the more clearly the process manifests itself when the so-called red serpent of *kundalini* "raises its head," giving a powerful impetus for the "awakening" of the second chakra. And with this there is literally an explosion of sexual energy that requires application.

Some will be able to cope with this energy and direct it higher along energy channels, furthering the transformation of all the higher centres into a qualitatively new state, acquiring the ability for clairvoyance, clairaudience, and many other superhuman powers as they open. And this will be the path of vertical advancement leading to the formation of the God-man.

Others, and these represent the majority, suddenly decide to use sexual energy for its "intended purpose" and begin endlessly changing sexual partners, not realizing that they have already become suppliers of energy food for the brothers of the shadow, as well as for elementals, disembodied low entities, and creatures living under the Earth's crust. And these are not the only recipients, after all, extraterrestrial technocratic civilizations require this type of energy to prolong life, and they, too, have filled the bookstore shelves with their "revelations." People who fall under their influence will, of their own volition, block the movement of currents along an ascending line and gradually degrade, sliding down the involutionary ladder to a primitive state over the course of just a few reincarnations. If they do not come to their senses, they can be found, for example, in abandoned buildings surrounded by packs of stray dogs.

There are abodes of the black lodge, whose task is to bring about the destruction of this world, and therefore, they are engaged in creating combinations of destructive currents. And where these are present, wars take place and blood is sure to be shed. Black sorcerers and darkness feed on vapours, that is, emanations of blood and are strengthened by it. For this purpose, they attempt to gain a foothold in a certain area. Whereas sorcerers of a lower order require conflicts, irritation, and quarrels, the powerful ones require the emanations of bloodshed, a tragedy of enormous proportions. And they will do anything possible to ensure that there are people endowed with power — their reflections on the earthly plane, who will start wars and supply them with a harvest of bloody dew. Also, initiators of unrest are disembodied entities living in the lower near-Earth spheres, whose food consists solely of bloody vapours. Crystallized emanations of blood, splashed into the near-Earth spheres as a result of numerous wars, can be preserved for centuries, millennia even, if they are also periodically multiplied by the accumulation of destructive processes in which blood is shed.

In areas into which the greatest amount of Light and positive energy that can change the world for the better has been poured, places like India, Israel, Russia, Syria, Ukraine, and so on, the darkness, often acting from within, tries to eradicate this energy from the soil by shedding blood, creating hotbeds of ongoing conflict on religious, political, or any other grounds, hiding behind "good intentions." The emanations of blood very quickly change the formula of energy at the level of the material sphere, and the result is destructive energy that goes out into the world. Also, this clot of energy can be used by extraterrestrial technocratic civilizations to create beings of the biorobot type.

Moreover, spilled blood affects Nature. Since the times of Atlantis, when people wanted to subjugate the power of stones and establish magical power over the whole world, when blood was shed for the sake of treasure, and wars were started that brought death, representatives of the Mineral Kingdom have become saturated with emanations of blood, which upsets the energy code of their evolution. These emanations transferred into the Plant Kingdom, creating poisonous species that bring death. And from here there followed the transition to the Animal Kingdom in the form of aggressive species aimed at bringing death to the higher Kingdom of Humanity. All Kingdoms are interconnected, and humans, it turns out, created the lethal classes of Nature with their own hands. In addition, some species of the Mineral Kingdom declared war on the Human Kingdom due to the fact that humanity was using them for evil purposes. Ores are melted, bullets are produced, and these same bullets kill people. The Mineral Kingdom exploits human hands, as people go about killing each other — this is how the ores win in this war. And more people die in accidents than in wars.

In addition to the Mineral Kingdom, the Virus Kingdom is also at war with humanity. Viruses have their own hierarchy and their own level of consciousness. And what may seem accidental from a human point of view may be completely non-accidental from the point of view of the Virus Kingdom. If highly moral scientists work with viruses in order to study them with the goal of protecting humanity, then viruses cannot in any way affect human consciousness, and some can even provide assistance. If on the other hand viruses are studied, for example, with the aim of creating bacteriological weapons, then the objectives of the virus and researcher — to destroy humanity en masse — coincides, and that is to mention if such a scientist is also a representative of dark forces. In this case the virus is capable of influencing the mind of the researcher and using his hands to achieve its own end, for example, to develop new, more resistant strains and to "accidentally" enter the world outside the laboratory.

Humanity has yet to establish peace among all the Kingdoms of Nature. Many people with open hearts have already made representatives of the Mineral Kingdom their friends and protectors. There are cases in which drivers have fallen asleep at the wheel, and the car has somehow stopped of its own accord, saving the driver from an accident.

The Light and the darkness are the two poles of the material world. Both are magnetic and fill space with their fires, attracting related elements inherent in the soul of each. And each one of us has the right to choose between the phenomena of both poles. However, one should bear in mind that the darkness is temporary, for it acts contrary to the Laws of Evolution, while the Light is eternal.

Brown, Dan (b.1964). An American bestselling author known for his novels that include *Angels & Demons* (2000), *The Da Vinci Code* (2003), and *The Lost Symbol* (2009).

Brown, William Tournay (1857–unknown). A Scottish lawyer, who joined the Theosophical Society in 1883 and left it in 1886. It is of him that Blavatsky says in her article "The Theosophical Mahatmas," he was someone who "changed Masters and his ideas about half a dozen times in less than three years."

Buddha (*Sk.*, "enlightened"). The highest degree of knowledge. To become a Buddha, one has to break through the bondage of sense and personality; to acquire a complete perception of the Real Self and learn not to separate it from all other selves; to learn, by experience, the utter unreality of all phenomena of the visible Cosmos foremost of all; to reach a complete detachment from all that is evanescent and finite, and live while yet on Earth in the immortal and the everlasting alone, in a supreme state of holiness. This degree of enlightenment was reached by Gautama, the Prince of Kapilavastu.

Buddha, Living. A title used in Tibetan Buddhism and Mongolian traditions to describe *tulkus*: reincarnated spiritual teachers or lamas believed to embody the wisdom of past masters. Examples include the Dalai Lama and Panchen Lama.

Buddhi (*Sk.*, "soul"). Universal Soul or Mind; the spiritual soul in man (the sixth principle), the vehicle of *atma* exoterically the seventh.

Buddhi-manas (*Sk.*). The representation of the Divine *plus* the human intellect and self-consciousness.

Buddhism. Buddhism now has two distinct divisions: Southern and Northern Buddhism. Southern Buddhism is generally said to be the purer form, having preserved more religiously the original teachings of the Lord Buddha. This is the religion of Sri Lanka, Thailand, Myanmar, and other areas, while Northern Buddhism is confined to Tibet, China, and Nepal. Such a distinction, however, is incorrect. While Southern Buddhism has departed little — except perhaps in some trifling dogmas due to the many councils held after the death of the Master — from the public or *exoteric* teachings of Shakyamuni, Northern Buddhism is the outcome of Siddharta Buddha's esoteric teachings, which he confined to his elect Bhikshus and Arhats. In fact, Buddhism in the present age cannot be fairly judged either by one or the other of its exoteric popular forms. Real Buddhism can be appreciated only by blending the philosophy of the Southern division and the metaphysics of the Northern School. If one seems too iconoclastic and stern, and the other too metaphysical and transcendental, even to the point of being overgrown with the weeds of Indian exotericism — many of the gods of its Pantheon have been transplanted under new names to Tibetan soil — this is entirely due to the popular expression of Buddhism in both divisions. They stand in relationship to one other as Protestantism to Roman Catholicism. Both err in an excess of zeal and erroneous interpretation, although neither the Southern nor the Northern Buddhist clergy have ever departed from truth consciously, still less have they acted under the dictates of *priestocracy* and ambition, or with an eye to personal gain and power, as the two Christian Churches have.

Buddhist Society. One of the oldest Buddhist organizations in Europe, founded in London in 1924 by Christmas Humphreys (1901–1983). In 1961, His Holiness the Fourteenth Dalai Lama became its patron, thereby honouring the first organization in the West.

Budha (*Sk.*, "wise," "intelligent"). The personification of Secret Wisdom; the planet Mercury; the son of Soma, the Moon, and of Rokini or Taraka, wife of Brihaspati carried away by King Soma. This act led to the great war between the Asuras, who sided with the Moon, and the Gods, who chose to defend Brihaspati (Jupiter), their *purohita* (family priest). This war is known as the *Tarakamaya*. It is the original version of the war in Olympus between the Gods and the Titans and also of the war in Revelation between Michael (Indra) and the Dragon (personifying the Asuras).

Bulwer-Lytton, Edward (1803–1873). An English writer and politician; the author of *Zanoni* (1842) and *The Coming Race* (1871).

Burne-Jones, Edward (1833–1898). A British artist and designer associated with the Pre-Raphaelite Brotherhood, known for his romantic, medieval-inspired paintings and stained glass work. His art emphasizes beauty and fantasy, often drawing on mythology and literature.

Burning of Darkness. A painting by Nicholas Roerich, created in 1924 and housed in the Nicholas Roerich Museum in New York City. It depicts Master M. who carries a shining casket and comes out of a secret opening in the rocks near to Everest together with other figures, in whom Nicholas, Helena, and George Roerich may be recognized.

Burrows, Herbert (1845–1922). A British socialist, activist, and Theosophist, who collaborated with Annie Besant.

Buryatia. A republic of Russia in eastern Siberia.

Buryats. A Mongolic ethnic group indigenous to Siberia, primarily in the Republic of Buryatia (Russia). They practise Tibetan Buddhism mixed with traditional shamanistic beliefs, reflecting their historical ties to the Mongol culture.

Byrne, Rhonda (b.1951). An Australian bestselling author and filmmaker best known for *The Secret* (2006), which popularized the law of attraction.

C

Cables, Josephine (1843–1917). An American Theosophist, editor and publisher of *The Occult Word*. In 1882, she co-founded the Rochester Branch of the Theosophical Society.

Caduceus (*Gr.*, "herald's wand"). A staff entwined by two serpents and surmounted by two wings; an attribute of Hermes Trismegistus. The Greek poets and mythologists took the idea of the caduceus of Mercury from the Egyptians. The caduceus in the form of two serpents twisted round a rod, is found on Egyptian monuments built before Osiris. The Greeks altered this, and in the hands of Asclepius it assumed a different form to the wand of Mercurius or Hermes. The caduceus is a cosmic, sidereal or astronomical, as well as a spiritual and even physiological symbol, its significance changing with its application. Metaphysically, the caduceus represents the fall of primeval matter into gross terrestrial matter, the one Reality becoming Illusion. Astronomically, the head and tail represent the points of the ecliptic, where the planets and even the sun and moon meet in close embrace. Physiologically, it is the symbol of the restoration of the equilibrium lost between Life, as a unit, and the currents of life performing various functions in the human body.

Cairo. The capital city of Egypt.

Calvin, John (1509–1564). A French theologian and Protestant reformer whose work, particularly *Institutes of the Christian Religion* (1536), shaped Reformed theology. He emphasized predestination and the absolute sovereignty of God, and his teachings greatly influenced Presbyterian and Reformed Churches.

Campbell, Joseph (1904–1987). An American mythologist, writer, and lecturer best known for his work on comparative mythology and religion. His book *The Hero with a Thousand Faces* (1949) introduced the concept of the "hero's journey," an archetypal narrative structure that has influenced literature, psychology, and film. From Campbell's biography, *A Fire in the Mind* (1991) by Stephen and Robin Larsen, it is evident that he had many contacts among Theosophists.

Candler, Ida Garrison (1848–1891). An American Theosophist, the wife of the United States Representative from Massachusetts, John W. Candler (1828–1903).

Carlyle, Thomas (1795–1881). A Scottish historian, essayist, and philosopher known for works like *Sartor Resartus* (1834) and *On Heroes, Hero-Worship, and the Heroic in History* (1841). He was influential in promoting the idea of heroic leadership and moral integrity.

Carmel. A mountain range in Israel, associated with the biblical story of the prophet Elijah. It is also the site of Mount Carmel Monastery, the founding place of the Carmelite order of Catholic monks and nuns known for their contemplative lifestyle.

Carroll, Lewis (1832–1898). An English writer, mathematician, and photographer best known for his classic novels *Alice's Adventures in Wonderland* (1865) and *Through the Looking-Glass* (1871).

Caste. Originally the system of the four hereditary classes into which the Indian population was divided: Brahmin, Kshatriya, Vaisya, and Sudra (or descendants of Brahma, warriors, merchants, and the lowest or agriculturalists). Besides these original four, hundreds have now emerged in India.

Catherine of Siena (1347–1380). An Italian mystic and saint who played a major role in the politics and spiritual renewal of the Catholic Church. She is famous for her letters and her major work, *The Dialogue of Divine Providence* (1472). She was declared a Doctor of the Church on account of her theological writings.

Cayce, Edgar (1877–1945). An American clairvoyant, known as the "Sleeping Prophet." Under the guidance of the Forces of Light, he was able to diagnose diseases and recommend treatments for ailments while asleep. During thousands of transcribed sessions, Cayce would answer questions on a variety of subjects such as healing, reincarnation, dreams, the afterlife, past lives, nutrition, Atlantis, and future events. He was a member of the Theosophical Society for about two years.

Chaitanya Mahaprabhu (1486–1534). An Indian saint and founder of the Gaudiya Vaishnavism tradition, which emphasizes devotion (bhakti) to Lord Krishna. He is regarded as a key figure in the spread of Krishna consciousness.

Chakra (*Sk.*, "wheel"). An energy centre in a human being, planet, star system, and so on. There are seven main chakras, each of which has seven centres, numbering 49 chakras in total. And each of these in turn has a sevenfold nature. Some have a double branch, e.g., the lung centre, and that of the shoulders, kidneys, knees, wrists, and so on.

When speaking on the subject of the seven master chakras which govern and rule the seven principal plexuses in the body, Blavatsky indicated that they are located in the head. However, it is important to understand that it is the external impulses of chakras that are in the head, and that while these impulses influence the nerve centres, they do not control them. The essence of all the chakras is in fact located in the heart.

In Eastern philosophy, energy centres are also called lotus flowers. This poetic name is a most fitting and beautiful symbol to express their true meaning and essence. Just as a lotus flower, which has its foundation in a swampy area of the bottom of a river or lake, devoid of light, then passes through the element of water and, emerging into the air moving in the direction of the light and the sun, blossoms into a beautiful white flower, the main centres, which have their foundation in the channel of the spinal cord, pass through the physical body and reach the surface of the etheric body, which, when emitted, protrudes several centimetres from the physical.

Being outside the physical body, the opened centres, like blossoming lotus flowers, have the ability to perceive higher vibrations and subtle energies in the external space and to transmit them to the perceptual organs of the physical body. Belonging to the composition of the subtle human body, the centres of higher consciousness, like the subtle body itself, are invisible to the naked eye, and yet to the sight of a clairvoyant they may be perceived as resembling blossoming flowers, with a specific number of petals and a depression at the centre.

Each opened centre has its own colour, consisting of different hues, but with one predominant colour, and the petals of the same lotus, while maintaining the general shade of the centre, contribute their own play of colours, depending on the function they perform in the human body. The opened centres scintillate with all the colours of the rainbow and are also sometimes called "little suns."

The seven main chakras, being centres of higher power, are in charge of the seven main nerve plexuses in the human body and these are called: *sahasrara*, *ajna*, *vishuddha*, *anahata*, *manipura*, *svadhisthana*, and *muladhara*. All these etheric lotuses located in the etheric body have corresponding centres in the astral body and the necessary vehicles for transmitting perceived sensations to the physical organs. Together, they form a whole.

Sahasrara is located at the crown and is also called the *bell centre*. This is the centre of auditory and visual perception. With this centre, one perceives spatial thoughts and everything that comes from the Higher Spheres. If an inhabitant of the Supreme World wants to communicate something to a person, they act through the bell centre, and if this centre is open in the person, then that person can communicate with the inhabitants of the Subtle World.

Ajna, which is also called the *eye of Brahma* and the *third eye*, is situated above the eyebrows. The physical organ of this centre is the pineal gland. The harmonious development of the human body and the proportionality of all its parts depend on this centre. By concentrating on it, one can correct physical defects in the body. The opening of this centre stimulates in a person the capacities of clairaudience and clairvoyance; not random glimpses that many have, but conscious sight, a perception of past and future events existing beyond time and space. One who has opened the third eye is capable of observing how the bodily organs are functioning. They can see through physical obstacles and through the ground, can observe the life of plants and minerals, and can hear the music of the spheres and the voices of Heaven and Earth.

When, through the desire for self-improvement, a person has prepared the way to open this centre, one of the Teachers of humanity, who watch over the kindling of "fires," will open this centre by touching the solar plexus.

Vishuddha, the centre of the larynx, is represented by the thyroid gland, dysfunction of which leads to goitre, a disease common in some areas. It should be understood that the centre of the larynx is not located directly in the thyroid gland, but nearby. The centres are not located in the glands; they are situated near to the corresponding gland and coordinate its work. The centres give out numerous, very fine branches, but these require little space.

Memory and mental abilities depend on the development of *vishuddha*. This is the centre of synthesis, analytical thinking, and logical reasoning. The opening of this centre not only facilitates understanding of any speech in any language, but the ability to influence the listener with one's own speech in such a way that they will understand the words addressed to them, regardless of the language they was spoken in, as was the case when, according to the Gospel, the disciples of Christ spoke in different languages. By concentrating on this centre, one can maintain a youthful appearance.

Anahata, which is also called the *chalice*, corresponds to the silver lotus and is situated near the heart, among the nerve nodes. The chalice is the focus of all radiation. This is the focus where radiations of the seed of the spirit (monad) are refracted and through which they are disseminated. Centuries of experience from previous lives are stored here. The chalice forms a triangle between the centre of the heart and the solar plexus. It is placed above the solar plexus at the level of the heart. The chalice belongs to those nerve nodes that have not yet been researched.

Higher consciousness resides in the human heart, and if the chalice centre is opened and the connection with the heart is established, then one acquires the supreme wisdom, which is situated within oneself. It comes to a person as an immutable truth not through inference or logical reasoning, but from the centre of the chalice, through the wire of the heart connected to higher consciousness or forces. When someone encounters difficulty in resolving an issue, or a loss of strength and energy, then, by connecting their consciousness with the consciousness of the Teacher, they can receive an immediate answer or other assistance.

The open chalice centre is that high organ that serves as a source of creativity in highly developed beings. The chalice contains everything. It reacts to all cosmic phenomena and vibrates in unison with all cosmic vibrations. All creative ideas come from the chalice. Saturated with cosmic energies, the chalice saturates everything within its circle of influence with the same energies. One who has opened the chalice centre is a creator and collaborator in the cosmic building of life, a participant in the life of the entire Cosmos and, in the truest sense of the word, a citizen of the world.

Manipura is the centre of the solar plexus. The solar plexus — also the serpent of the solar plexus — is so called because in the human body it performs a role similar to the sun in the human solar system, and its movement and action resemble the spiral-like and ring-shaped movements of a snake. Just as the Sun gives life to everything, saturating all that exists with its rays and energy, the solar plexus feeds the entire human body with life force, in other words, with psychic energy. And just as the Sun unites, sets in motion, and keeps in balance the entire Macrocosm, so the solar plexus plays exactly the same role in the microcosm. The threads of all the organs and all the centres are intertwined in the solar plexus.

The solar plexus brings to harmony and balance the activity of the intellectual and sensitive centres, in other words, the brain and the sexual sphere. The solar plexus is an accumulator, transmuter, and distributor of psychic energy, not only to all organs of the physical body, but also to the etheric body, which, in turn, nourishes the astral body. It represents a reserve warehouse of unused and unspent psychic energy. When the solar plexus is set in motion, it action is independent and unceasing.

Svadhisthana is situated in the pelvic region. Its functions are related to human sexual activity. During spiritual ascent, this centre is subordinated and controlled by the solar plexus. It is also connected to the centre of the larynx, *vishuddha*, and during sexual abstinence, all its energy rises upwards and passes into *vishuddha*. Further, provided that there is rotation in the pineal and pituitary glands, it passes into the crown centre, *sahasrara*, thanks to which Illumination is achieved.

If the portion of human energy which is expressed as sexual energy in sexual functions, sexual thoughts, and so on, is stopped and controlled, it easily turns into *ojas* (Sk., "life force, energy") — the inexhaustible spiritual power obtained from the sublimation of sexual energy. Those who cannot control their animal passion and who treat carelessly the most secret and powerful relationships in Nature, the sexual union, are unaware that they are literally spilling their own blood, their white blood which constitutes their vitality.

If the sexual energy of the male and female principles on the earthly plane is so wonderful and powerful that it is capable of generating a new life, then in the Cosmic scope, in combination with the Power of Love, it can create entire Worlds.

The ancient Mysteries said, "Lingam is a vessel of wisdom," in the sense that this vital substance contains important qualities. It is by not squandering this substance that people accumulate vital force and maintain creative power. Therefore, complete abstinence has been required of everyone who studies practical occultism. Only later did this knowledge turn into ugly phallic cults and religion begin to forbid something, in the name of who knows what. This is why Arhats lead their lives in full compliance with the strict rules of abstinence.

If two individuals are compared, one of whom wastes their vital substance, while the other consciously preserves it, the apparatus of the spirit in the latter develops much more sensitively. The quality of this individual's work becomes entirely different and the number of their plans and ideas increases. The centres of the solar plexus and brain are as if heated by an invisible fire. Therefore, abstinence is not a pathological rejection, but a reasonable action. Giving life does not mean throwing away one's entire supply of vital substance.

It is not without reason that Napoleon Hill in one of the most influential self-help books of all time, *Think and Grow Rich* (1937), determines "sex transmutation" as one of the necessary steps towards success, since sexual energy can be converted into a power that people can use to achieve anything they want in life. He writes: "When harnessed and redirected along other lines, this motivating force maintains all of its attributes of keenness of imagination, courage, etc., which may be used as powerful creative forces in literature, art, or in any other profession or calling, including, of course, the accumulation of riches."

From this one may comprehend why the efforts of the representatives of darkness are so focused on the sexual chakra. For them, through various methods of media propaganda, it is important to make "normal and healthy" a way of life, in which people change sexual partners like gloves, throwing away in vain their most powerful energy into space. People who entertain such a lifestyle, willingly or unwillingly, become suppliers of enormous currents of life-force which the brothers of the shadow put to evil ends.

Finally, *muladhara* is located at the base of the spine and is the foundation and root of all the "lotus flowers." From this it becomes clear that the *muladhara* centre develops first, thereby giving impetus to the development of the other centres. This is the main centre of vital force and will. It is in charge of human sexual activity. When this centre is in a dormant state, people spend huge reserves of vital energy located in this centre on sexual excess, which at the same time, inevitably, weakens their willpower. Since people waste their life force recklessly, they also waste their will. Meanwhile, in order to use it wisely, to preserve this excess power and direct it towards useful creative activity, one must have strong will.

The *muladhara* centre is also called *kundalini*; the energy or current it develops is called serpentine fire and *kundalini* current. In India *kundalini* energy is called the power of the Mother. The touch of the Mother of the World should be understood as a manifestation of primordial energy. This centre is the Mother, who gives life, who gives the stimulus for the actions of all other centres of higher consciousness.

With very rare exceptions, all centres of higher consciousness in modern humanity are dormant and inactive. Therefore, awakening *kundalini* to action should be considered the most important and greatest event in the life of any individual, for only from this moment on do the rebirth and spiritual development of the personality begin. From this point onwards, one enters the path of improvement. The activization of *kundalini* represents the opening of the first gate on this path. However, this process should take place in a natural way only. Any forcing of the process leads to unpredictable, even disastrous results, the consequences of which may be felt for more than one lifetime.

A certain reserve of life force, placed at the centre of *muladhara* belongs to the element of fire and is the condensed energy of the lifegiver — the Sun. Therefore, the *kundalini* current is a fiery current, and the opening of centres represents their ignition. Consequently, the cause of the inflaming and the initial activization of the *kundalini* current may not lie in an external influence, or in mechanical exercises, but in a stimulus of an internal, spiritual nature. When a person has advanced in their development to such an extent that they can no longer be satisfied with the trifles of everyday life and now experience spiritual needs, this serves as an indicator of the possible igniting of the *kundalini* centre, but only a true fiery aspiration to Wisdom, Light, and Truth can engender a fiery consequence in the form of the awakening of this centre.

When, on account of the reasons outlined, a person awakens to action, in other words, when the *kundalini* centre is enkindled, it means that it has begun to rotate. The *kundalini* current generated by the rotation of energy rises upwards along the spinal column. Before now, this channel will have been closed. The spiral movement of the *kundalini* current or, as they also say, the serpentine fire of *kundalini*, gradually opens the channel, which in Eastern philosophy is called *sushumna*. As *sushumna* opens, the fiery energy of *kundalini* ignites other lotuses located along the spine, which, in turn, begin to rotate and generate their own special kind of energy. The entire *sushumna* channel gradually opens and the whole system of lotuses, which are all interconnected, is brought into action and movement.

When the *kundalini* current has reached the centre of the bell, located at the crown of the head, the human body is ready to perceive subtle energies and higher currents that exist and operate in the Cosmos. One's centres turn into organs of perception. Each centre, which corresponds to the equivalent centre of the Cosmos, can perceive cosmic energies and emit its own. Only then does one become a condenser and transmuter of cosmic energies, a participant and collaborator of cosmic life in the fullest meaning of the word, and a human being in the highest meaning of the word.

A person comes to acquire that great power with which nothing is impossible, with which one can perform incredible phenomena, of all different kinds, which, from the point of view of the laws of the physical world, would be considered miracles, and yet there is nothing miraculous about these things to one who has acquired supreme knowledge, and developed higher abilities. This high ability and power are inherent in each and every individual and are an inalienable right, but it is acquired only by those who follow the right and legitimate path of their own development.

A person's spiritual accumulations and achievements do not disappear, but instead are deposited in the chalice, and pass into the next incarnation where, if there is the necessary aspiration, they can be developed further. It is impossible to indicate the period during which the opening of the centres of higher consciousness occurs, because the process is entirely individual. It depends on many factors, mainly, on the strength of aspiration and purity of motivation. Occult literature speaks of seven lives being required to achieve the level of Arhat, but this period is not definitive. It can be extended to infinity or reduced to a minimum. But the opening of the centres, that is, the achievement of the level of Arhat in one short life, is possible only if one's chalice is full, only in exceptional cases of extraordinary fiery striving.

The opening of centres depends not only on spiritual aspiration, but is subject to the laws and terms of human physical development, which can neither be bypassed nor violated. The fiery energy of *kundalini*, once brought into action, will continue its invisible work in a number of incarnations, regardless of the human consciousness operating in each incarnation, but in full accordance with the laws and terms of development of the material essence of the human being.

If a person's *kundalini* was activated in one incarnation, one should not assume that in any subsequent life it will continue to operate from the first days after birth. In the first seven years of life, the human body still has a strong connection with the Astral World, which it has so recently left. Only at the end of the second seven year cycle is the connection broken and the action of the centres resumed. However, in order to lay channels in the new physical body for the passage of subtle energies, the *kundalini* current must work for another fifteen years. Thus, only at the age of 30, in the most favourable case, when, like Christ, the full Arhat is incarnated, is the action of the centres resumed that was formerly interrupted by death and a new birth. This explains why Christ began serving humanity when He had reached the age of 30.

For an ordinary mortal, who has not reached the Arhat stage, the interval between the end of the action of the *kundalini* current in one life and its resumption in another can be much longer, and certainly, in no case is it ever less. Awakened centres are a great and, at the same time, dangerous force that can only be present in a person who is fully mature, physically, mentally, and spiritually.

For a better understanding of the topic of chakras, here is the occult anatomy of the human body, as described by Sister Rahaanii in Claude Bragdon's *Yoga for You* (1943):

"At the upper end of the spinal cord (looking like half an English walnut) is the cerebrum. It is the first, and most important gland in the body. The essence which it exudes flows through all the glands, and this fluid is modified by each in a different manner. The cerebro-spinal system is the first part of the organism developed, and from it the entire form materializes, as it were. The sensory nerves are the wires connected with this great generator of electrical energy, the cerebrum. These ramify throughout the entire organism, supplying the electricity with which to run it.

"Right under the cerebrum is the optic thalamus; it occupies the central portion of the brain, or third ventricle. It is the great ganglion of the inner brain. It is shaped like an egg, with the small end directed forward. When seen in cross section of the brain the thalamus, with its adjacent appendages, looks like a beetle. In the scarab, or sacred beetle of ancient Egypt is symbolized this egg of immortality, referred to in the Egyptian Book of the Dead as 'the boat of the seeker.' The optic thalamus is called the open eye, the single eye, the light of the world, the crystal lamp. In Sanskrit literature it is called the heart of the lotus, the place where *buddhi* (Divine Wisdom) sits, the knowledge to which the yogi seeks to attain.

"At the back and base of the skull is the cerebellum, the mechanical brain. The cerebrum is the God-brain and the cerebellum the animal, or man-brain. The latter is the organ of the subconscious mind; the former, the organ of consciousness. Both words, *cerebrum* and *cerebellum* derive from the word *cere* meaning seed; *bellum* means conflict, opposition, and there is constant warfare between the two forces in the body represented by the higher brain and the lower. No one can be fully conscious and balanced who is living in the animal passions which find expression through the lower brain.

"Continuing this enumeration of the strange contents of that golden urn which is the human head, the pineal gland may appropriately come next, a cone-shaped body on the posterior side of the optic thalamus attached to it by delicate nerves, and joined to the roof of the third ventricle by a flattened stalk, the habenula. The pineal gland is the male organ of spirituality. Fluid from the upper brain flows down into the pineal gland, where it is differentiated, becoming masculine, positive, electrical, in quality and action.

"A little lower down and on the other side of the optic thalamus is the pituitary gland or body, the female organ of spirituality, a small, reddish, ellipsoid in a depression of the sphenoid bone, and attached to the brain by a peduncle. It has two lobes, and secretes a mucous substance; it is magnetic, and is provided with a little gossamer sac for the reception of the holy seed.

"Connected with the pineal gland is the nerve *pingala*. This crosses the spinal cord at the base of the skull, in the medulla oblongata, and follows down the right side of the spinal cord to its end. Likewise connected with the pituitary body is the nerve *ida*, which crosses the spinal cord at the same place where the *pingala* crosses, following down the left side of the spinal cord to its base. Here the two nerves converge into the body through the semi-luna ganglion, where they merge into the solar plexus.

"The pneumogastric nerve, rising in the floor of the fourth ventricle of the head, and connected with the cerebellum, crosses the spinal cord at the base of the skull. At this point is a double cross made by *ida*, *pingala*, and the pneumogastric nerve. The pneumogastric nerve sends numerous branches to the throat, lungs, heart, and stomach, terminating in the solar plexus, which is called the androgynous brain. This is the channel of the holy breath, without which there could be no conception or birth of the psycho-physical germ, or holy seed.

"The solar plexus consists of twelve large nerve ganglia which branch off in different directions. It is the largest of the three sympathetic plexuses, and receives the greater and lesser splanchnic (intestinal) nerves and some filaments from the right vagus. The solar plexus is the centre of the physical body, and its nerves, branching from this point form the channels over which the psycho-physical germ-seed is carried to its birth or maturity. This first 'seed of immortality' is formed in the solar plexus of every individual at the age of puberty, when the moon is in the sign that the sun was in at the person's birth, and thereafter the process is repeated monthly. From the solar plexus the psycho-physical germ moves into the central channel of the spinal cord, ascending or descending according to its type or nature (animal or divine). The solar plexus cannot receive this psycho-physical germ or regenerative life-unit until the perfect state of harmony has been attained between the cerebrum and the cerebellum through the male and female organs of spirituality. Pure thought (electric) attracts its mate (magnetic) in the breath, and this quickens the conception of the psycho-physical germ. If the thoughts are animal, carnal, the germs which are carried to the solar plexus for birth are marked and sent to the 'pit.' This means that under the influence of the lower mind they are attracted and drawn down into the testicles in the case of the male, or into the ovaries in the case of the female, and are here changed into animal germs. The prostate gland in the male receives the germ-seeds after they have been animalized in the testes; they are there stored until ejaculated. The female uterus receives the ovum, which if fertilized becomes a procreative germ-cell, passing out of the 'south gate' as the karmic-bound body of a new human being.

"By making the sexual act an 'indoor sport' man cheats himself of his most precious possession, for he robs his body of its recreative corpuscles by this defilement of the sacred fountain. There is more calcium in the seminal fluid than in the blood, indicating that it is the chief building material, and was never intended to be thrown away. The true yogi will use this force in a regenerative way, for the building of his indestructible form.

"When man ceases to destroy his psychic energy by indulging his animal nature, the psycho-physical germ returns to its true throne in the brain. Ascending the central channel of the spine it makes the crucial crossing at the base of the brain and returns to the optic thalamus. At this point it undergoes the final balancing, and is transmuted into the sacred oil which is deposited in the 'crystal lamp' which is the optic thalamus. This precious fluid supplies the nerves which dip into this bowl from the cerebrum. Thereupon is produced that shock of sudden light which awakens dormant brain cells and produces the phenomenon of illumination. Only then will the *kundalini* awaken which lies sleeping at the base of the spine. If we lift up or raise the oil in the spinal cord by the power of the seed (by saving it), that oil becomes so refined, transmuted, vitalized, that it regenerates the body, and overcomes death itself.

"*Degeneration, generation,* and *regeneration* are the three types of life; by these everyone can make judgement of himself. Degeneration is that form of life in which cohabitation is for sensual pleasure only. Generation is that in which cohabitation is for companionship and parenthood — the giving of some returning entity its personal mask. Regeneration is that in which by the sublimation of the sex force the body loses neither creative substance nor electrical energy."

Chakravartin (*Sk.*, "one who turns the wheel"). The Everlasting King of Enoch; an ideal Universal Monarch who rules ethically and benevolently over the whole world. This figure is most often incarnated as an Avatar, who is to lead humanity out of its earthly misery into Paradise.

In 1994, the lost manuscript of Nostradamus, known as *Vaticinia Nostradami*, and consisting of mysterious watercolour images was accidentally rediscovered. As is the case with other coded messages of the Initiates, no one has succeeded in interpreting the images correctly.

One of the pictures depicts a King holding a book. At the top of the composition a golden veil is surrounded by an empty scroll; to the right hangs a lock, and over the veil is depicted the Dharmachakra (*Sk.*, "Wheel of the Law"). In Buddhism, the Wheel of the Law is the main emblem of Chakravartin. The Lord is holding an open book — His Doctrine or Law. Since the Teachings have never appeared independently of the Teacher, the Doctrine of the Lord must be recorded also. Therefore, depicted below are three women — Faith, Hope, and Love — united by a scroll: they are destined to rewrite the Lord's Teaching on the scroll and to open the lock on the curtain of mystery. These three disciples were summoned by the King of Shambhala to remove the veil of ignorance from the eyes of the world.

Chaldeans (*Gr.*, "people of Kaldu"). Initially a tribe and later a caste of learned Kabbalists; the sages, the magians of Babylonia, astrologers, and diviners.

Chan (*Ch.*, "contemplation"). A Chinese school of Mahayana Buddhism, founded by Bodhidharma, who is regarded as its first Chinese patriarch. As *Thien* it spread from China to Vietnam, as *Seon* to Korea, and as *Zen* to Japan.

Chana Dorje (*Tib.*). See *Vajrapani*.

Chang, B. T. A Chinese secretary of the Ninth Panchen Lama.

Charcot-Richet. Jean-Martin Charcot (1825–1893) and Charles Robert Richet (1850–1935), French psychologists, who used hypnosis in their practice.

Chela (*Sk.*, "servant"). A disciple, the pupil of a Guru or Sage, the follower of a certain Adept in a school of philosophy.

Chelaship. Discipleship.

Chhaya (*Sk.*, "shadow"). In esoteric philosophy, a person's astral image.

Chintamani (*Sk.*, "magical jewel"). A Gift from the constellation of Orion to the planet Earth; the mystical Stone manifest as the Treasure of the World, which is destined to bring happiness and prosperity to all living beings. Its actual place of origin is Sirius, because when this event occurred Sirius was part of the constellation of Orion.

The Chintamani is preserved at the very heart of Shambhala and maintains a connection with the fire-breathing cores of maternal stars, thanks to which the planet Earth still retains the orbit of its own revolution.

A fragment of the Chintamani can "travel" around the world, if the Seven Great Teachers make a unanimous decision to place it into the hands of their messenger, who is destined to carry out a specific historical mission. And then the fragment returns of its own accord and merges literally with the Treasure that remains always within the boundaries of Shambhala.

Chiromancy (*Gr.*, "divination by the hand"). The ancient art of palm-reading to understand a person's character and future by interpreting the lines on the palms of the hands.

It has been known since ancient times that the convolutions of the brain are reflected on the palms in the form of a kind of map. Currently, tomographic and electroencephalographic studies have revealed a structural similarity between papillary patterns and the convolutions of the brain.

The brain emits electromagnetic waves of a special order, which, like radio waves, can be transmitted over a distance and picked up not only by another person but by particularly sensitive devices. Thoughts themselves flow over the brain. True clairvoyants are able to see a glow spreading around a person's head — these are generated thoughts flowing over the brain so that it can perceive them. They go along a network of invisible light-bearing channels and are superimposed on the grey matter in a certain pattern, forming convolutions.

Human thoughts form a person's destiny. This destiny is imprinted on the grey matter of the brain in the form of convolutions, which are reflected on the palms. Hence, knowing perfectly the art of palm-reading, one can read the destiny a person has created for themselves, both in past lives and in the present life. People can also record changes if they have begun to change themselves and their lives by their own will.

The left palm, as a rule, reveals the pages of the previous and the present life; while the right hand reveals the future, which a person is able to change for the better. So if one were to copy or photograph the palms, one year later, on the same day, it is possible to see how much a person's destiny has changed in one direction or another.

There is also a process referred to as *corrective chiromancy* which is when a person who has something negative in their destiny, influences the brain through the palms by correcting the lines on them with a fountain or felt-tip pen, thereby improving their own destiny. The thought-forms activated on the mental level switch on the self-regulation mechanism in the brain, rewarding people according to their faith.

Chokyi ku (*Tib.*, "truth body"). See *Dharmakaya*.

Chohan (*Tib.*, "lord," "master"). A chief; thus *Dhyan Chohan* would answer to "Chief of the Dhyanis," or celestial Lights, which in English translates as *Archangels*. In Sanskrit, Chohan literally means a four-handed warrior and it is the name of a Rajput dynasty of the twelfth century whose special mission was to guard the sacred Mount Abu. The word Cho-han is used by both Tibetan and Indian esoteric writers to denote high spiritual beings.

Christ. One of the Greatest Teachers of Humanity, the Teacher of Teachers, the Solar Hierarch, the Solar Logos who has many names. He was the first to sow the seeds of Divine Love in human hearts.

The ancient writings of the Initiates indicate that Christ is the Spirit of Sophia, the Power and Supreme Wisdom of God, and She is His Soul. He is the equivalent of the Central Spiritual Sun, whose Light gives life to all of creation in the Solar System. The soul of all is, first and foremost, the reflection or ray of this Light, clothed in matter of the lower vibrations.

Being a Spirit of the utmost purity and fiery force, Christ can enlighten the purest human being with His Light, or Ray — and this may be justly considered to be His partial incarnation on the Earth. Such a man, born on the Earth, was Jesus — the incarnation of one of the Great Teachers. However, it should be mentioned that He was not the Messiah promised in the ancient scriptures. He was a kind of Precursor preparing the Path for an even Higher Spirit, whose Advent is prophesied in all religions of the world. In Jesus was manifested the Hypostasis of this Supreme Spirit, Christ, who illuminated him with His Light of the perfect knowledge of Sophia during the baptism in the River Jordan.

The physical bodies of the Highest Spirits who made human appearances on the Earth — such as Gautama Buddha and Jesus Christ — are only outwardly similar to the bodies of other people. The matter of immortality contained in their bodies is not yet a property accessible to humanity. Therefore, ordinary earthly parents could not build the body for a God. Esoteric teachings say that the High Spirits came to earthly life as the future mother and father of Jesus Christ. Thus, His father Joseph was also the one of the Great Teachers. And His Mother was no less great than the Son: the Mother of the World was manifested in Her, having exchanged the consciousness of a Great Goddess for that of an earthly woman.

The chronology of the life of Jesus, as it is usually given, is quite inaccurate. Mahatma Koot Hoomi and Helena Blavatsky both stated that He lived a century before the time commonly thought. From ancient scriptures it is also known that He came in the year of the Tiger.

Each of the Great Messengers, before beginning their mission, is summoned into the Abode of Light, Shambhala, to restore spiritual knowledge. This is the reason that the twelve-year-old Jesus went to India. According to the ancient scrolls stored in the monasteries of Tibet, He studied secret knowledge for seventeen years visiting Greece, Egypt, Persia, the Himalayas and, most importantly, studying with the Great Teachers of Humanity. At the age of 29, Jesus left India and returned to Judea, where He began His sermon. Jesus Christ came to the people of Judea, but they did not accept the Teaching of the Saviour and killed Him, thus determining their future for many centuries ahead. Therefore, Israel as a state arose only on the threshold of the Second Coming of Christ, having already redeemed most of its karma.

In her article "Facts Underlying Adept Biographies," Blavatsky says: "Jesus of Nazareth was an Initiate, a holy, grand, and noble character, . . . truly 'a Son of God.' . . . Sophia, 'the Celestial Virgin,' is prevailed upon to send Christos, her emanation, to the help of perishing humanity, from whom Ialdabaoth (the Jehovah of the Jews) and his six Sons of Matter (the lower terrestrial Angels) are shutting out the Divine Light. Therefore, Christos, the perfect, uniting himself with Sophia [Divine Wisdom] descended through the seven planetary regions, assuming in each an analogous form . . . [and] entered into the man Jesus at the moment of his baptism in the Jordan. From this time forth Jesus began to work miracles; before that he had been entirely ignorant of his own mission. Ialdabaoth, discovering that Christos was bringing to an end his kingdom of Matter, stirred up the Jews, his own people, against Him, and Jesus was put to death. When Jesus was on the Cross, Christos and Sophia left His body, and returned to Their own sphere. The material body of Jesus was abandoned to the earth, but He Himself, the Inner Man, was clothed with a body made up of Aether."

After the death of His physical body, Jesus Christ managed to break it down into atoms, which is why His body was never found. It was the densified subtle body that became visible to the eye. A High Spirit in a subtle body, purified by the fire of psychic energy, freed from the physical shell before the allotted time (i.e., before the natural time of death), possesses extraordinary power on Earth. This power could have burnt a whole country to the ground, but Christ chose to destroy or break down into atoms His physical body only. This was a tremendous accomplishment for those times, for no one prior to this had been able to harness such a powerful fiery energy on Earth.

The Ascension took place in the same manner, in the fiery apotheosis of His subtle body. The disciples, whose spiritual eyes were opened when the transfigured Christ suddenly appeared among them, could also experience the miracle of so-called *prismatic vision* and see the resplendent body of the Lord, disappearing in the light of His Rays. Of course, the subtlest body, or the "glorious body," as Apostle Paul calls it, is not dispersed, but remains clothed in the sublimated tissue of the light-bearing matter called *Lucida* and remains on the corresponding plane of Being. In this way, Christ proved the conscious existence of man in the Subtle World and in the body corresponding to that World.

The Resurrection of the Teacher and His communication with His disciples afterwards made of them true Apostles, who would spread the Gospel of Love all over the world. Later, according to some researchers, Christ left Judea and continued His mission in India. Helena Roerich confirmed that for eleven years after His Resurrection, Christ appeared before Mary Magdalene and instructed her in the secrets of the Ethereal World.

In crucifying God, humanity committed the most terrible crime which shocked the entire Universe. Every crime requires punishment according to Cosmic Laws, and Earth was to be incinerated as unsuitable for further evolution. But Christ's Great Love saved the planet, along with His persecutors and enemies. In order to postpone the verdict signed by humanity itself, He changed the flow of Time by His Will, dividing it into two channels. One Time stream passed into the evolutionary stream intended for those who accepted Christ. The other Time stream designated a two-thousand-year probationary period in which humanity would have the opportunity to realize the full gravity of the crime it had committed against God. Through repentance in their hearts, people would have to redeem themselves with the same coin which God vouchsafed to them. He brought them only Love, hence humanity can redeem itself before God by Love alone.

During the period 19 July 1999 and 19 July 2017, these two Time streams joined, completing the probation period for those who had not accepted Christ. By this point everyone had already determined their place in the Universe and their destiny — evolution or involution.

Today, there are many people who claim to be "Christs," "Maitreyas," or "Mothers of the World," and have attracted many supporters. There are also those who do not claim anything of the sort, but people themselves feel the high spirits embodied in them, sometimes considering them to be new incarnations of Jesus or Mary. This is because the Earth is the Messiah's lowest point of descent, and thousands of representatives and ambassadors of other worlds and civilizations have come here to meet Him. Such spirits, assimilating the Messianic Fire, return to their own worlds with the most elevated currents, each being a kind of Saviour for the spheres and strata of that world enabling it to rise one step higher on the Ladder of Evolution. These people may not even realize who they really are, since the knowledge of the spirit has been obscured during their earthly incarnation.

Christian Scientist. A practitioner of the art of healing by will. The name is a misnomer, since Buddhist or Jew, Hindu or materialist, can practise this new form of Western yoga with like success, if they can only guide and control their will with sufficient firmness.

Christos (*Gr.*, "anointed one"). The Higher Self in man. *Christos* should be distinguished from *Chrestos*. Chrestos denotes a disciple on probation — a candidate for becoming a full Initiate. When the disciple attained the status of Initiate through long trials and suffering, and was "anointed" (i.e., "rubbed with oil," as befitted an Initiate, as the last touch of ritualistic observance), his name is changed to Christos, which means the "purified" in esoteric or mystery language. In mystic symbology, *Christos* means the "Way," the Path that was already trodden and the goal reached; the point at which the fruits of arduous labour unite the personality of evanescent clay with the indestructible individuality, transforming it into the immortal Ego. "At the end of the Way stands the *Christos*," the *Purifier*, and once the union is accomplished, the *Chrestos*, the "man of sorrow," becomes *Christos* himself. Paul the Apostle knew this, and meant this precisely, when he says, in poor translation: "I travail in birth again until Christ be formed in you" (Galatians 4:19), the true rendering of which would be "until ye form the Christos within yourselves." Every good individual, therefore, may find Christ in his "inner man" as Paul expresses it in Ephesians 3:16, whether he be Jew, Muslim, Hindu, or Christian.

Chromo-premium. An expensive coloured picture (chromo) printed using the method of chromolithography. In the nineteenth century, publishers of periodicals started to offer chromos as a premium for their direct subscribers to increase their circulation and decrease the cut taken by distributors.

Chuan Teng Lu (*Ch.*). *The Jingde Record of the Transmission of the Lamp*, often referred to as *The Transmission of the Lamp*, a 30-volume work, which is a primary source of information for the history of Chan Buddhism in China. It contains the biographies of seven Buddhas, Indian and Chinese patriarchs, as well as of other Buddhist masters and monks.

Clairvoyance. The faculty of seeing with the inner eye or spiritual sight. As now used, it is a loose and flippant term, embracing in meaning both a happy guess due to natural shrewdness or intuition, as well as that faculty which was so remarkably exercised by Jacob Böhme and Swedenborg. Yet even these two great seers, since they could never rise higher than the general spirit of the Jewish Bible and sectarian teachings, have sadly confused what they saw, and fallen far short of true clairvoyance. Real clairvoyance implies the faculty of seeing through the densest matter (the latter disappearing before the will and spiritual eye of the seer), irrespective of time (past, present, and future) or distance.

Whereas *clairaudience* is the faculty of hearing things at whatever the distance, whether innate or acquired through occult training.

Confucius. A Chinese philosopher and teacher whose ideas greatly influenced East Asian culture. Central to his philosophy are virtues like *ren* (benevolence), *li* (proper conduct), and *filial piety* (respect for parents and elders).

Constantinople. The former name of Istanbul in Turkey, the capital of the Roman Empire, the Byzantine Empire, and the Ottoman Empire.

Conze, Edward, PhD (1904–1979). A German-British scholar and translator, renowned for his work on Buddhist texts, particularly Mahayana Buddhism. He served on the faculties of several universities in Great Britain and the United States including Oxford, London, and California. His scholarship significantly contributed to the understanding of Buddhist philosophy in the West.

Cornell University. A prestigious private research university, located in Ithaca, New York.

Corson, Hiram (1828–1911). An American professor of literature, writer.

Coulomb, Emma and Alexis. A couple who appealed to Blavatsky for help when they had financial problems and were offered a job at the Theosophical Society in India. However, later they took money from Christian missionaries in order to fabricate evidence for an accusatory report against Blavatsky by the Society for Psychical Research.

Council of Constantinople, Second. The fifth ecumenical council of the Christian Church in 553. This Council declared: "If anyone asserts the fabulous pre-existence of souls, and shall assert the monstrous restoration which follows from it: let him be anathema." From this time onward, the doctrine of rebirth officially became a "heresy" in Christianity. Prior to this, the tolerance of the Church and its Councils was maintained solely by supporters of Gnostic Christianity.

Cranston, Sylvia (1915–2000). An American author, known for her extensive work on the subject of reincarnation and H. P. Blavatsky's biography. Her books include: *Reincarnation: The Phoenix Fire Mystery* (1977), *Reincarnation: A New Horizon in Science, Religion and Society* (1984), and *H.P.B.: The Extraordinary Life and Influence of Helena Blavatsky, Founder of the Modern Theosophical Movement* (1993).

Cromwell, Thomas (c.1485–1540). An English statesman and lawyer who served as chief minister to King Henry VIII from 1534 to 1540; a character in William Shakespeare's *Henry VIII* (1616).

Crookes, William (1832–1919). An English physicist and chemist who discovered thallium, invented the radiometer, and studied cathode rays. He and his wife joined the Theosophical Society in 1883.

Cum-passio (*Lat.*, "to suffer with"). The root of the English word *compassion*. It implies empathy, or the ability to feel and share in the suffering of others.

Cycle. The ancients divided time into endless cycles, wheels within wheels, all such periods being of various durations, and each marking the beginning or end of some event either cosmic, mundane, physical, or metaphysical. There were cycles of only a few years, and cycles of immense duration such as the great Orphic cycle, referring to the ethnological change of races, that lasted 120,000 years, and the cycle of Cassandrus that lasted 136,000 years and brought about a complete change in planetary influences and their correlations between people and gods — a fact of which modern astrologers have entirely lost sight.

In human lives, seven-year cycles are of great significance. The number 7 was built into the very foundation of the present Solar System as an energy code. From this emerges the seven states of matter, the seven worlds, and the sevenfold structure of everything manifest and not manifest, including human beings and the planet.

For example, the system of Sirius is based on the number 12, and everything within it is twelvefold. The same is expected of the current Solar System, which at this very moment is changing under the influence of currents emitted by the Central Spiritual Sun.

For now, the Earth transforms its energy structure every seven thousand years. Human beings are completely renewed at the cellular level every seven years, and their entire lives are subject to seven-year rhythms, regardless of whether they are aware of this or not. Here, three-year cycles can also be traced, and these should be taken into account as every seventh year, following the six years of two triennial periods, also marks the first year preceding the subsequent two three-year cycles.

Everything happens in a spiral; that is, there is a kind of repetition, yet it occurs within a new cycle. The human will is able to stretch this spiral horizontally, to flatten it, and thus a person travels in a circle, not only in one particular lifetime, but from life to life. However, the higher the goal people set for their seven-year period, the faster their trajectory of ascent to unprecedented heights, and each subsequent seven-year cycle brings new opportunities that were totally unimaginable as recently as in the previous cycle.

Similarly, in all matters, activities, and stages of life, one can trace both three-year and seven-year cycles. But if people lack high aspirations, then it is impossible to track these cycles, since their will has turned the spiral of ascent into a flattened circle.

However, all those who dedicate themselves to spiritual matters are constantly tested by the so-called *Dwellers on the Threshold*. This applies not only to individuals but also, for example, to organizations that devote themselves to the attainment of spiritual goals.

In general, the Dwellers on the Threshold are the embodiment of the internal negative essence of human beings that has formed over the course of their many lifetimes. Their spirits are set to meet with the Dwellers before their entrance into the Higher World. All weaknesses, vices, and shortcomings which were present in them on the Earth intensify hugely. They clothe themselves in the visible images which are the most attractive and seductive in order to captivate and devour a person's consciousness to such an extent that they no longer have either the strength or desire to cross the Threshold into the Supreme World, and so remain in the lower layers of space.

A trial by the Dwellers on the Threshold, produced both by their own self and the self of others, also awaits each individual in the material world who has decided to follow the path of spirituality.

Normally the "tasks" of the Dwellers consist in leading people away from a spiritual path and onto the path of everyday hustle and bustle by intensifying in them all material desires and all sorts of illusions. These temptations can be especially amplified towards the end of the seven-year period, as well as within the three-year cycles, so as not to allow people to cross the "threshold" of the next period. If people are weak, then two seven-year periods are usually enough for the Dwellers on the Threshold to accomplish their "mission" successfully. The milieu of all prominent spiritual personalities serves to vividly illustrate this principle.

Apart from the number 42, an age boundary beyond which not all people live, the number 59 is also important. In the East, the age of 60 is considered to be the age of majority, and, since the date of conception is considered the date of birth, one subtracts nine months to reach the number 59. And here is another boundary that may fall under the power of death.

Of course, Life arranges its own combinations on the basis of the Law of Expediency, and it may allow people who are burdened with karmic debts to live on, so as to give them an opportunity to pay off their old debts. And if they are successful in freeing themselves from these debts during the additional time allotted to them, then they gain the protection of the Supreme Forces.

On the other hand, the fate of those who burden themselves with new karmic debts instead of paying off their old ones is unenviable, because so often these individuals come under the power of the Dwellers on the Threshold. And, despite the fact that their human souls leave them, their outer shells remain to live on, supported by the lowest energies of the animal atom. And it is worth noting that esoterically speaking the number of each atom is expressed through the number 6. Six is the number of the mineral atom, as it is the number of the plant atom and the animal atom, and so 666 is the number of the beast. At this point, one sees the reverse countdown for those who slide backwards, through the stages of involution.

By acknowledging the seven-year rhythms built into the foundation of life on Earth, and the tests associated with them, people are able to make any goal they set easier to achieve. The main thing is to track one's own path, preferably on a daily basis — whether one has taken a step upward or downward — because the next rungs in the ladder are created by a person's thoughts, words, and deeds.

The reader may find it useful to draw a timetable of their own life, dividing it into both three-year and seven-year cycles. After filling it in with the significant events in one's life, certain cycles should be easily recognizable. One should then be able, after peering into the future, to prevent the intrusion of foreign phenomena, and enrich one's life with whatever aligns with the heart. It should always be taken into account that human free will makes the impossible possible, and vice versa, makes the possible impossible.

D

Dalai Lama (*Mon.-Tib.*, "great teacher"). Considered an incarnation of Avalokiteshvara or Chenrezig, the Bodhisattva of Compassion and the patron saint of Tibet.

Dalai Lama, Fifth, Ngawang Lobsang Gyatso (1617–1682). A significant Tibetan Buddhist leader who unified Tibet under the Gelug school and established the Potala Palace in Lhasa. He maintained relations with the Mongols and was instrumental in securing Tibetan sovereignty with the support of Gushi Khan. Gushi Khan's victory over the opponents of the Gelug school contributed to Tibet's unification, as well as the final establishment of theocracy in this country and the absolute dominance of the Gelug school in it. The Tibetan state began to be headed by the Dalai Lamas, in whose hands was the supreme secular and religious power. The Fifth Dalai Lama went down in history under the name of the Great Fifth.

Dalai Lama, Thirteenth, Thubten Gyatso (1876–1933). The spiritual and political leader of Tibet. In domestic politics, he distinguished himself as an outstanding reformer, and in foreign policy, as a skilled diplomat and fighter for the independence of his country. During his reign, Tibet redeclared its national independence and was a sovereign state.

Dana (*Sk.*, "charity"). Generosity; almsgiving to mendicants; the first of the six paramitas (virtues) in Buddhism.

Darjeeling. A town in West Bengal, India, located in the Eastern Himalayas.

Darshanas (*Sk.*, "demonstrations," "views"). The schools of Indian philosophy which are referred to as the *Shad Darshanas* or six demonstrations: Nyaya, Vaisheshika, Samkhya, Yoga, Purva Mimamsa, and Uttara Mimamsa (Vedanta). They all have a starting point in common and maintain that *ex nihilo nihil fit* (*Lat.*, "nothing comes from nothing").

Das, Sarat Chandra (1849–1917). An Indian scholar of Tibetan language and culture.

Dashizhi (*Ch.*) or **Mahasthamaprapta** (*Sk.*, "one who has attained great strength"). One of the Great Bodhisattvas, representing the power of wisdom. Dashizhi is usually depicted together with Amitabha and Guanshiyin.

David-Néel, Alexandra (1868–1969). A French explorer, Buddhist, opera singer, and author of books describing her journeys to Tibet. She was the first Western woman to reach Lhasa in 1924. Her book, *My Journey to Lhasa* (1927), was endorsed by His Holiness the Fourteenth Dalai Lama in 1992.

De facto (*Lat.*). In fact; actually.

De jure (*Lat.*, "by law"). Designates the formal state of things, in contrast to *de facto* that designates what actually exists in reality.

Dead Sea. A salt lake bordered by Jordan, Palestine, and Israel, known for its extreme salinity, healing properties, and biblical associations; lowest point on Earth's surface.

Dead Sea fruit or **Apple of Sodom.** A metaphor for something that looks attractive on the outside but is hollow, worthless, or disappointing inside. The phrase comes from the legend of fruit growing at Sodom, near the Dead Sea. It was described by the first-century historian Flavius Josephus: "The ashes [are] growing in their fruits; which fruits have a colour as if they were fit to be eaten, but if you pluck them with your hands, they dissolve into smoke and ashes."

Decad. A group or set of ten. In philosophy, especially in Pythagorean thought, the decad symbolized completeness or perfection.

Dee, John (1527–1609). An English philosopher, mathematician, astronomer, alchemist, and astrologer; advisor to Queen Elizabeth I.

Delhi. A city in India, which contains New Delhi, the capital of India.

Delphic Oracle. A Pythia, a priestess chosen among the *sensitives* of the poorer classes, and placed in a temple in ancient Greece where oracular powers were exercised. There the Pythia had a room secluded from all but the chief Hierophant and Seer, and once admitted, was, like a nun, lost to the world. She sat on a tripod of brass placed over a fissure in the ground, through which intoxicating vapours arose. These subterranean exhalations penetrated her whole system and produced the abnormal state of prophetic *mania* in which she delivered oracles.

Aristophanes called the Pythia *ventriloqua vates* or the "ventriloquial prophetess," on account of her *stomach*-voice. The ancients placed the soul of man (the lower *manas*), or his personal self-consciousness, in the pit of his stomach. We find in the fourth verse of the second *Nabhanedishta* hymn of the *Aitareya Brahmana*: "Hear, O sons of the gods, one who speaks through his navel (*nabha*), for he hails you in your dwellings!" This is a somnambulic phenomenon. The navel was regarded in antiquity as "the circle of the sun," the seat of divine internal light. Therefore the oracle of Apollo at Delphi, the city of Delphus, was called the womb or abdomen, while the seat of the temple was called the *omphalos*, navel. It is a well-known fact that a number of mesmerized subjects can read letters, hear, smell, and see through this part of their body. In India there exists to this day the belief that Adepts have flames in their navels, which enlighten for them all darkness and unveil the spiritual world. Among the Zoroastrians, it is referred to as *the lamp of Deshtur*, or the "High Priest"; and among the Hindus, the light or radiance of the *Dikshita* (the Initiate).

Demiurgus (*Gr.*, "artisan"). The Demiurge or Artificer; the Supernal Power which built the Universe. Freemasons derive from this word their phrase "Supreme Architect." Among the occultists the Demiurgus is the third manifested Logos, or Plato's "second god," the second Logos being represented by him as the "Father," the only Deity that he dared mention as an Initiate into the Mysteries.

Demons. In the strict sense, the disembodied souls of the depraved, otherwise known as *elementaries*. These souls have at some time prior to death separated themselves from their divine spirits, and so lost their chance for immortality. The term *elementaries* also applies to the spooks or phantoms of disembodied persons, in general, to those whose temporary habitation is Kama-loka.

Elementaries should not to be confused with *elementals*, although Éliphas Lévi and certain other Kabbalists make little distinction between elementary spirits who have been human beings and those beings which populate the elements and are the blind forces of Nature.

Once divorced from their higher triads and their bodies, these souls, elementaries, remain in their *kama-rupic* "shells," and are irresistibly drawn to the earth amid elements congenial to their gross natures. Their stay in Kama-loka varies as to its duration; but ends invariably in disintegration, dissolving like a column of mist, atom by atom, in the surrounding elements.

The most dangerous entities are those who committed atrocities while being human, since they provoke and push those who are physically incarnated to carry out the same outrageous crimes. Elementaries are also those disembodied entities who during their earthly lives failed to overcome and eradicate any severe form of addiction (smoking, gambling, drinking, drugs, sex, etc.) and who now vampirize those who are physically incarnated with the same inclinations, thereby intensifying their vices, and tempting those who have none. Places where the space is invisibly crowded with them include bars, nightclubs, casinos, brothels, drug dens, slaughterhouses, etc.

A male elementary is called an *incubus*; a female elementary, a *succubus*. They are called forth from the invisible regions by human passion and lust. Some benighted spiritists and mediums call them "spirit brides" and "spirit husbands." But these poetical names do not prevent them in the least from being that which they are — ghools, vampires, and soulless elementaries; formless centres of Life, devoid of sense; in short, *subjective protoplasms* when left alone, but called into a definite being and form by the creative and diseased imagination of certain mortals. They were known under every clime as in every age, and the Hindus can tell more than one terrible tale of the dramas enacted in the life of young students and mystics by the *pisachas*, as they are called in India.

After death, the instincts of disembodied humans with unresolved vices are intensified so much that they will seek with avidity contact with living persons, since nothing likes to starve. Each body as well as each principle powerfully craves and is attracted towards those elements which are necessary for its subsistence. The principles of lust, gluttony, envy, avarice, revenge, intemperance, etc., will rush blindly to the place they are attracted to, where their craving can be temporarily gratified — either directly as in the case of vampires by imbibing the emanations of fresh blood, or indirectly by establishing magnetic relations with sensitive persons (mediums) or ordinary people, whose inclinations correspond to their own.

If a magnetic relation still exists between the elementary and its physical body, it will return to the grave where it is buried. If no such relation exists, it will follow other attractions. It craves a body, and if it cannot find a human body, it may be attracted to that of an animal. The Gospel account of the swine into which Jesus Christ drove the "evil spirits" may be a fable in its historical application, but it is a truth, not only a possibility, with reference to many such parallel cases.

Elementaries are able to influence human thoughts and desires, becoming partial or full possessors by attaching themselves to a person's aura or taking over (blending with) their astral body. For example, if a person commits murder under possession and this person is sentenced to capital punishment that still exists in many countries, including the United States, this releases the elementary that possesses them to seek a new person that they can take over and through whom they can commit other murders, knowing no state borders.

At mediumistic séances these "spirits" precipitate themselves upon sitters and mediums alike; and as there can be no séance without there being present some or many bad elementaries — half dead human beings — there is much vampirizing going on. These things fall upon the people like a cloud or a big octopus, and disappear within them as if sucked up by a sponge.

Elementaries have much automatic and seemingly intelligent action left if they are those of strongly material people who died still very much attached to the things of life. In people of the opposite character, they are not so strong. Then there is a class which are really not dead, such as suicides, sudden deaths, and the intensely wicked. These are powerful. Elementals enter into all of them, and thus acquire a fictitious personality and intelligence wholly the property of the shell. They galvanize the shell into action, and by its means can see and hear as if they were normal beings, like us. In this case the "shells" are like a human body sleepwalking. Out of habit they will exhibit the behaviour they learnt during the life of the physical body.

Both the suicides and those killed in accidents can communicate, and both pay dearly for visiting séances. They are an exception to the rule, in that they must remain within the field of Earth's magnetic attraction, and within its atmosphere — Kama-loka — until the very last moment of what would have been the natural duration of their lives. In other words, that particular wave of life-evolution must run on to its shore. But it is a sin and an act of cruelty to revive their memory and intensify their suffering by giving them a chance to live an artificial life; a chance to *overload their karma*, by tempting them through opened doors, namely, mediums and sensitives, for they will have to pay roundly for every such pleasure.

Suicides, who, hoping to escape life, find themselves still alive, have suffering enough in store from that life. Their punishment lies is in the intensity of it. Having lost — though not forever, as both can be regained — through the rash act of suicide their seventh and sixth principles, instead of accepting their punishment, and taking their chances of redemption, they are often made *to regret losing life* and tempted to regain a hold upon it by sinful means. In Kamaloka, the land of intense desires, they can gratify their earthly yearnings only through a *living* proxy, and by so doing, at the expiration of the natural term of life, they generally lose their monad forever.

The victims of accidents are generally exempt from this curse. It affects only those falling into the current of attraction who die full of some engrossing earthly passion and the selfish who have never given a thought to anyone but their own selves. Overtaken by death in the consummation — whether real or imaginary — of some master-passion of their life, the desire remaining unsatisfied even after its full realization, and they still craving more, these types can never pass beyond the earth's attraction to wait for the hour of deliverance in happy ignorance and full oblivion.

If they are good and pure, they will fall into a state of quiet slumber, a sleep full of rosy dreams, during which, they will have no recollection of the accident, and will move and live among their familiar friends and scenarios, until their natural life-term ends, after which they will find themselves born in Devachan.

But if they are sinful and sensual, they wander about — not as "shells," for their connection with their two higher principles is not quite broken — until their death-hour comes. Cut off in the full flush of earthly passions which bind them to familiar scenes, they are enticed by the opportunities which mediums afford, to gratify them vicariously. They become the *pisachas*, the incubi and succubi of medieval times; the demons of thirst, gluttony, lust, and avarice — elementaries of intensified craft, wickedness, and cruelty; provoking their victims to horrid crimes, and revelling in their commission. They not only ruin their victims. These psychic vampires, borne along by the torrent of their hellish impulses, finally, at the fixed close of their natural period of life are carried out of Earth's aura into regions where for ages they must endure exquisite suffering and end in total destruction.

The best remedy against the influence of elementaries is one's own will together with the help of spirituality and its masterful inspiration. The will is the one indomitable power in Nature and in the psychic world; whatever the phantom or demon, it may be swept into nothingness by concentrating the will upon it and bidding it go. If people make their own nature pure and their thoughts elevated, they may even sleep unmolested by a vampire, incubus, or succubus. Around the insensible form of such a sleeper, the immortal spirit sheds a divine power that protects them from evil approaches, as though it were a crystal wall.

Deva (*Sk.*, "divine being"). A god, deity, or celestial being, whether good, bad, or indifferent. Devas inhabit the "three worlds," which are the three planes above us. In Hinduism, it is believed that there are 330 million individual *devas*.

Devachan (*Sk.-Tib.*, "dwelling of the gods") or **Dewachen** (*Tib.*, "great bliss," "pure land"). A state intermediate between two earth-lives, into which the Ego (*atma-buddhi-manas*, or the trinity made one) enters after its separation from *kama-rupa* (*Sk.*, "body of desires") and the disintegration of the lower principles on earth. The interval between incarnations may vary from a few moments to hundreds of years.

Deva-hearing. Clairaudience, the faculty of hearing, whether innate or acquired through occult training, something that is not present to the ear.

Deva-sight. The divine sight the Lord Buddha developed at the twentieth hour of his vigil when sitting under the Bo-Tree, while he was attaining Buddhaship. This is the eye of the glorified Spirit, to which matter is no longer a physical impediment, and which has the power to see all things within the space of the limitless Universe. On the following morning of that night, at the close of the third watch, the Merciful One attained supreme knowledge. See *clairvoyance*.

Dezhin Shekpa (*Tib.*). See *Tathagata*.

Dhammapada (*Pali*, "path of the law"). A collection of sayings and teachings attributed to the Buddha, written in verse form, and one of the most widely read and revered scriptures in the Theravada Buddhist canon.

Dharana (*Sk.*, "concentration"). The state in yoga practice when the mind is fixed unflinchingly on a single object of meditation.

Dharma (*Sk.*). The sacred Law; Truth; the right way of living; the Buddhist Canon.

Dharmakaya (*Sk.*, "body of truth"). The glorified spiritual body which is the third, or highest, of the *Trikaya* (Three Bodies). It is an attribute developed by every Buddha, i.e., every Initiate who has crossed or reached the end of what is called the *fourth Path* (in esotericism the sixth "portal" prior to entry on the seventh). The highest of the *Trikaya*, it is the *fourth* of the *Buddhakshetra*, or Buddhic planes of consciousness, and is represented figuratively in Buddhist asceticism as a robe or vesture of luminous spirituality. In popular Northern Buddhism these vestures or robes are: 1) *Nirmanakaya*; 2) *Sambhogakaya*; and 3) *Dharmakaya*, the last being the highest and most sublimated of all, as it places the ascetic at the threshold of Nirvana.

Dharmapala, Anagarika (1864–1933). A Sri Lankan Buddhist revivalist who devoted his life to spreading Buddhist teachings and restoring Buddhist sites, especially in India, where he was instrumental in the restoration of Bodh Gaya, the site of the Buddha's enlightenment.

He was also a prominent speaker and writer, founding the Maha Bodhi Society in 1891 to promote Buddhist education and interfaith understanding.

Dhyan Chohan (*Sk.-Tib.*, "Lord of Contemplation," "Lord of Light"). A generic name for all celestial beings, the highest gods, answering to the Archangels of Roman Catholicism. Some are Cosmocratores, or impersonal Builders — the Divine Intelligences charged with the supervision of the Cosmos and who execute the plans of Cosmic Ideation. Others are highly evolved self-conscious Beings from past cycles, who are now the guides and instructors of the present humanity.

Ordinarily, a man is said to reach Nirvana when he evolves into a Dhyan Chohan. The condition of a Dhyan Chohan is attained in the ordinary course of Nature after the completion of the Seventh Round in the present Planetary Chain. After becoming a Dhyan Chohan, a man does not, according to the Law of Nature, incarnate in any of the other planetary chains of this Solar System. The whole Solar System is his home. He continues to discharge his duties in the Government of this Solar System until the time of Solar Pralaya, when his monad, after a period of rest, will have to overshadow in another Solar System a particular human being during his successive incarnations, and attach himself to his higher principles when he in turn becomes a Dhyan Chohan. There is progressive spiritual development in the innumerable Solar Systems of the Infinite Cosmos. Until the time of the Cosmic Pralaya, the monad will continue to act in the manner indicated above, and it is only during the inconceivable period of Cosmic Sleep, which follows the present period of activity, that the highest condition of Nirvana is realized.

Dhyana (*Sk.*, "contemplation"). A mystic meditation. In Buddhism, one of the six paramitas of perfection, a state of abstraction which carries the ascetic practising it far above this plane of sensuous perception and out of the world of matter. The stages of *dhyana* differ only in the degree to which the personal Ego achieves abstraction from the life of the senses. This long-lasting practice that requires the ignition of the heart's fires is usually accompanied by the unfoldment of various spiritual powers.

The fourth degree of *dhyana* (the seventh esoterically) attained by every true Arhat or Buddha results in *abhijna* (*Sk.*, "superknowledge"). It represents six phenomenal or supernatural gifts, which Shakyamuni Buddha acquired in the night on which he reached Buddhaship. A Tibetan epithet of the Buddha is the "possessor of the six kinds of prescience," which are: 1) the power of seeing anything one wills to see, by which one can see (realize) the sufferings of all kinds of living beings; 2) the same power in hearing by which one can understand the different languages articulate and inarticulate of all living beings; 3) knowing another's heart and thoughts; 4) knowledge of one's former and future states of existence, the circumstances of one's death and birth, and how to move one's body without being seen; 5) remembrance of former births; 6) knowledge of the destruction of the passions.

It should be noted, as *The Voice of the Silence* indicates, that the Path of Dhyana belongs to the "Eye" Doctrine and head-learning. Even if it results in superknowledge, it is still pure knowledge which is useless, unless applied to help others. Only in the latter case, is it imbued with Love, becoming Wisdom. The lives of all saints, miracle-workers, prove that their supernatural powers came to them not because they were sitting and meditating, practising the fourfold *dhyana*, unaware even that such a thing exists, but because they truly loved all humanity, willing to help anyone in any way possible.

Dhyani-Bodhisattvas (*Sk.*). In Buddhism, the five sons of the Dhyani-Buddhas. They have a mystic meaning in esoteric philosophy.

Dhyani-Buddhas (*Sk.*). They "of the Merciful Heart." There are seven Dhyani-Buddhas or, rather, Seven Hierarchies of Dhyanis, all of which represent aspects of one and the same Essence. They exist in the state of the Dharmakaya, a state in which no progress is possible; the Entities there may be said to be crystallized in purity, goodness, and a condition of homogeneity.

In the esoteric Buddhism, Adi-Buddha, the One unknown, without beginning or end, identical to Parabrahman and Ein Sof, emits a bright ray from its darkness. This is the Logos (the first), or Vajradhara, the Supreme Buddha (also called Dorje Chang). As the Lord of all Mysteries, he cannot manifest, but sends into the world of manifestation his heart — the "diamond heart," Vajrasattva (Dorje Sempa). This is the second Logos of Creation, from whom emanate the seven (exoterically the five) Dhyani-Buddhas, which are also called the *Anupapadaka* ("the parentless"). These Buddhas are the primeval monads from the world of incorporeal being, the *arupa* ("formless") world, wherein the Intelligences (on that plane only) have neither shape nor name in the exoteric system, but have seven distinct names in esoteric philosophy.

By virtue of *dhyana*, the Dhyani-Buddhas emanate, or create from themselves, celestial Selves — the superhuman Bodhisattvas. Incarnating at the beginning of every human cycle on Earth as mortal human beings, they become, occasionally, owing to personal merit, Bodhisattvas among the Sons of Humanity, after which they may reappear as Manushi (human) Buddhas. They have furnished the many and various nations with divine kings and leaders, teaching humanity their arts and sciences, and revealing the great spiritual truths of the transcendental worlds.

Divina Sapientia (*Lat.*). Divine Wisdom.

Divine Pymander, The. A Hermetic text attributed to Hermes Trismegistus, and containing philosophical teachings on the Divine, the Cosmos, and spiritual rebirth.

Dnyan (*Mar.*, "knowledge"). Esoterically, supernal or divine knowledge acquired through mystic meditation or yoga; the same as *jnana* in Sanskrit or *gnyana* in Telugu.

Dnyan Marga (*Mar.*, "path of knowledge"). The path of pure knowledge that is attained through mystical meditation and yoga practices.

Dnyaneshwar (1275–1296). A Marathi saint and poet-philosopher, also known as Jnaneshvara, who wrote a famous commentary on the Bhagavad Gita, referred to as the *Dnyaneshwari*; considered one of the most important figures in the Bhakti movement.

Dnyaneshwari (*Mar.*) or **Jnaneshvari** (*Sk.*, "Lord of Knowledge"). A commentary on the Bhagavad Gita written by Dnyaneshwar in 1290.

Domo Geshe Rinpoche Ngawang Kalsang (1866–1936). A highly respected Tibetan Buddhist lama, renowned for his spiritual accomplishments, scholarship, contributions to preserving and spreading Buddhist teachings, and establishing the first Gelugpa monasteries in regions where there had been none. He was also the head of Ghoom Monastery from 1910 to 1936. During his tenure, the lama commissioned and oversaw the construction of the main 5-metre statue of Maitreya Buddha inside the monastery, as he had done in other monasteries.

The name Ngawang Kalsang was offered to him by the Eighth Panchen Lama when he entered Tashi Lhunpo Monastery at the age of eight. After twenty years of study he received the Kachen degree, which was the Tashi Lhunpo's equivalent of the Geshe degree of Central Tibet's great monastic universities. In different holy places along the Himalayan snow mountain range, in caves and other isolated places, Geshe Rinpoche maintained his practice and actually saw the different meditational deities, receiving their blessings, teachings, guidance, and predictions.

He was the first of the Tibetan lamas to go on pilgrimage repeatedly to the Buddhist holy sites in India before this became an established practice. Domo Geshe Rinpoche was openly praised by both the Ninth Panchen Lama and the Thirteenth Dalai Lama, who referred to him as a "realized one who is completely tamed" and as someone who is "Lama to people inside and outside of Tibet and whose widespread fame resonates like the sound of a great bell." Geshe Rinpoche enjoyed a close relationship with the Ninth Panchen Lama, from whom he received a special holy object: the mould for the famous image of Je Tsongkhapa called "Tsong-bon Geleg."

Domo Geshe Rinpoche was also known as "the precious doctor of Chumbi," since he healed numerous people using a variety of methods. The famous holy pills (*rilbus*) that he made from hundreds of sacred and medicinal ingredients were of unequalled power and cured many otherwise hopeless cases.

Dorje (*Tib.*) or **vajra** (*Sk.*). A diamond club or sceptre. In Hindu works, the sceptre of Indra, similar to the thunderbolts of Zeus, with which the god of thunder slays his enemies. In mystical Buddhism, the magic sceptre of Priest-Initiates and Adepts — the symbol of the possession of *siddhis* or superhuman powers, wielded during certain ceremonies by the priests and theurgists. It is also the symbol of the Buddha's power over evil spirits or elementals. Those who possess this wand are called *Vajrapani*.

Dorje represents the masculine principle and lightning. During the service, the lama holds the *dorje* sign in his right hand and a bell in his left hand as a symbol of the feminine principle and wisdom. Two crossed *dorjes* mean two worlds, the Ethereal and the earthly — a symbol of balance.

Dorje Chang (*Tib.*). See *Vajradhara*.

Dorje Sempa (*Tib.*). See *Vajrasattva*.

Dosha (*Sk.*, "faults"). That which causes problems.

Dragon. Now considered a "mythical" monster, an idea perpetuated in the West on seals as a heraldic griffin, and as the Devil slain by St. George. In fact, it is an extinct antediluvian monster referred to in Babylonian antiquities as the "scaly one," and connected on many gems with Tiamat the sea. "The Dragon of the Sea" is repeatedly mentioned. In Egypt, it occurs as the star of the Dragon (then the North Pole Star), the origin of the connection almost all the gods have with the Dragon. Bel and the Dragon, Apollo and Python, Osiris and Typhon, Sigur and Fafnir, and finally St. George and the Dragon, are the same. These are all solar gods, and wherever we find the Sun, we also find the Dragon, the symbol of Wisdom — Thoth-Hermes. The Hierophants of Egypt and of Babylon styled themselves as "Sons of the Serpent-God" and "Sons of the Dragon." "I am a Serpent, I am a Druid," said the Druid of the Celto-Britannic regions, for the Serpent and the Dragon were both types of wisdom, immortality, and rebirth. As the serpent casts off its old skin only to reappear in a new one, so the immortal Ego casts off one personality and assumes another.

Dragshed (*Tib.*, "cruel, wrathful executioner"). Wrathful deities that protect the Buddhist teaching and each of its followers.

Dravidians (*Sk.*, "people of the South"). The oldest population of Hindustan.

Dryden, John (1631–1700). An English poet, playwright, and literary critic who was England's first Poet Laureate. He is known for his satirical poetry, plays, and translations, with notable works including *Absalom and Achitophel* (1681) and *Mac Flecknoe* (1682).

Dubjed (*Tib.*, "to make ready [the vessels]"). A rite in Tibetan Buddhism intended to concentrate the thoughts. Those who are about to devote themselves to profound meditation, place before them a vase-like vessel called *namgyal bumpa*, "the entirely victorious vessel," and a flat vessel called *lai bumpa*, "the vessel of the works." The *namgyal bumpa* typifies abstraction of the mind from surrounding objects, the *lai bumpa* perfection in abstract meditation. These vessels are not put upon the earth, but upon a cloth or a piece of paper on which is drawn an octagon frame called *dabchad*, "octagon"; the vessels are filled with water perfumed with saffron, and strips of the five sacred colours are twisted round them; flowers or kusa grass are placed inside. Fixing his eyes upon these two vessels, the devotee reflects upon the benefit to be derived from meditation, and is exhorted to intense concentration of the mind.

Dugpa or **Dad-Dugpa** (*Tib.*, "mischief-makers"). A group of sorcerers or black magicians who follow the left-hand path of occultism; the brothers of the shadow, "the murderers of their souls."

In the nineteenth century, writers in the West mistakenly referred to all non-Gelugpa sects of Tibetan Buddhism as Dugpas: the Nyingma, Sakya, and Kagyu schools as well as their subdivisions. These sects are termed "red cap" after the colour of their monks' hats as worn during formal occasions, but they are not all Dugpas in the sense of "evil-doers."

Before the advent of Tsongkhapa in the fourteenth century, the Tibetans, whose Buddhism had deteriorated and been dreadfully adulterated with the tenets of the old Bon religion, were all followers of "red cap" sects, called "Dugpas" by Western writers. From that century onwards, however, and after the rigid laws imposed upon the Gelugpas ("yellow caps") and the general reform and purification of Buddhism (or Lamaism), the followers of the "red hat" schools gave themselves over more than ever to sorcery, immorality, and drunkenness, being negatively influenced by the pre-Buddhist Bon religion.

Since then, the word *Dugpa* has become a synonym of "sorcerer," "adept of black magic," and all things vile. According to *A Tibetan-English Dictionary* (1881) by H. A. Jaschke, the word *Dugpa* or *Dukpa* denotes "poison," "anything hurtful, or any injury, mischief, harm done," or "noxious, mischievous, dangerous."

In his book, *Buddhism in Tibet* (1863), while listing various sects in Tibet, Emil Schlagintweit mentions the "Dugpa or Dad-Dugpa" sect, which is "particularly addicted to the Tantrika mysticism." This "red hat" sect, which is a subsect of the Kagyu school, became the dominant school in Bhutan, now known as the *Drukpa* or *Drukpa Kagyu* lineage, which explains why "Dugpa" also denoted a native of Bhutan. In reference to these Dugpas, Blavatsky writes in her article "Elementals":

"In the East, they are known as the 'brothers of the shadow,' living men possessed by the earth-bound elementaries; at times — their masters, but ever in the long run falling victims to these terrible beings. In Sikkim and Tibet they are called Dugpas ('red caps'), in contradistinction to the Gelugpas ('yellow caps'), to which latter most of the Adepts belong. And here we must beg the reader not to misunderstand us. For though the whole of Bhutan and Sikkim belongs to the old religion of the Bons, now known generally as the Dugpas, we do not mean to have it understood that the whole of the population is possessed, *en masse*, or that they are all sorcerers. Among them are found as good men as anywhere else, and we speak above only of the elite of their lamaseries, of a nucleus of priests, 'devil-dancers,' and fetish worshippers, whose dreadful and mysterious rites are utterly unknown to the greater part of the population."

Then in her article "Reincarnations in Tibet," Blavatsky further explains:

"The 'Dugpa or Red Caps' belong to the old Nyingmapa sect, who resisted the religious reform introduced by Tsongkhapa between the latter part of the fourteenth and the beginning of the fifteenth centuries. It was only after a lama coming to them from Tibet in the tenth century had converted them from the old Buddhist faith so strongly mixed up with the Bon practices of the aborigines — into the Shammar ['red hat'] sect, that, in opposition to the reformed Gelugpas, the Bhutanese set up a regular system of reincarnations. . . .

"The term 'Dugpa' in Tibet is deprecatory. They themselves pronounce it *dog-pa* from the root to 'bind' (religious binders to the old faith); while the paramount sect — the Gelugpa ('yellow caps') — and the people, use the word in the sense of 'Dugpa' mischief-makers, sorcerers. The Bhutanese are generally called Dugpa throughout Tibet and even in some parts of Northern India. . . .

"The Shammar sect is not, as wrongly supposed, a kind of corrupted Buddhism, but an offshoot of the Bon religion — itself a degenerated remnant of the Chaldean mysteries of old, now a religion entirely based upon necromancy, sorcery, and sooth-saying. The introduction of Buddha's name in it means nothing."

To sum up, before Buddhism, Tibetans practised the ancient Bon religion. In 747, the Emperor Trisong Detsen wanted to introduce Buddhism and so invited to Tibet Padmasambhava, who founded the Nyingma school. Over the next few centuries, each subsequent attempt to introduce pure Buddhism to Tibet resulted in the founding of a new "red hat" school: Kagyu and Sakya as well as their subdivisions. None of them could fully escape the negative influence of the indigenous Bon religion and Hindu Tantrika. This was especially the case with the Dugpa or Dad-Dugpa subsect of the Kagyu school that was regarded as the most versed in sorcery.

It was owing to the evils of these systems, in which Buddhism was mixed to various degrees with the original Bon and Hinduism, that Tsongkhapa undertook his purifying reform and founded the "Yellow Caps" order (Gelugpa).

The term *Dugpas* should be applied only to evil sorcerers, the brothers of the shadow, who are not confined to any one religion or country or even to one plane of existence. Their network is truly international and multidimensional; their representatives can be found anywhere, in all domains of life. Visibly and invisibly, they guide scientists to destructive and dangerous inventions. Introducing division and discord, they inspire political leaders to start wars and conflicts. Both subtly and explicitly, they promote cults of money and sex. They manipulate human psychology, placing traps for the mind, and often act under the guise of "light-bearers." Their minions are not averse to learning something useful for themselves and even have meetings on how to cleverly use their findings against spiritual advancement. Indeed, many volumes could be written about the tricky and cunning methods of their work.

Dugpaship. The status or condition of a Dugpa.

Duke of Westminster. A title in the British peerage, created in 1874 for the Grosvenor family, one of the wealthiest aristocratic families in the UK. The title is associated with great wealth, landownership, and influence in British society.

Dukkha (*Sk.*). Sorrow, pain.

Dukyi Khorlo (*Tib.*). See *Kalachakra*.

Dwellers on the Threshold or **Guardians of the Threshold.** A term invented by Edward Bulwer-Lytton in *Zanoni* (1842); but in occultism the word "Dweller" is a term used by students for long ages past, and refers to certain maleficent astral doubles of defunct persons. The "Dweller on the Threshold" is found in two cases:

1. The triad is separated from the quaternary.
2. *Kamic* desires and passions are so intense that the *kama-rupa* persists in Kama-loka beyond the devachanic period of the Ego, and thus survives the reincarnation of the devachanic entity (e.g., when reincarnation occurs within 200–300 years). The "Dweller" being drawn by affinity towards the reincarnating Ego to whom it had belonged, and being unable to reach it, fastens onto the *kama* of the new personality, and becomes the Dweller on the Threshold, strengthening the *kamic* element and thus lending it a dangerous potency. This is sufficient to cause some to lose their mind.

Dzyan (*Tib.*). Secret Wisdom, knowledge, attained through intuition during mystic meditation or contemplation.

E

Eagle. One of the most ancient symbols. Among the Greeks and Persians it was associated with the Sun; among the Egyptians, under the name of *Ah*, with Horus, and the Kopts worshipped the eagle under the name of *Ahom*. It was regarded by the Greeks as being the sacred emblem of Zeus, and by the Druids as that of the highest god. The symbol passed down to the present day, when, following the example of the pagan Marius, who, in the second century BCE used the double-headed eagle as the ensign of Rome, the Christian-crowned heads of Europe chose to devote the double-headed sovereign of the air to themselves and their scions. For Rome, the one-headed eagle was the symbol of Jupiter as well as the Sun. The former imperial houses of Russia, Poland, Austria, and Germany adopted a two-headed eagle as their device.

Earth. The youngest planet in the Solar System, called the *Cradle of Gods* by the Masters. In the Tablets of Eternity, Earth is listed under its original name — *Tiamat*. It is a living conscious being, governed by Cosmic Laws. In the esoteric tradition, it is believed that the Mother and Father of the Earth is the Sun, the feminine aspect of which is represented by Venus, and the masculine aspect by Mars.

In all ancient legends, the description of Earth's creation refers only to the Fourth Round after Pralaya, or obscuration, which followed the Third Round. The lack of information about the first two Races of the current Round is due to the fact that human consciousness is yet unable to understand this state of existence which has no equivalent on Earth. In the Fourth Round, man appeared before animals.

Earth is the successor to the Moon, which gave to the planet all its vital force. Life from the Moon migrated to the Earth, clothing itself in new vestures. As a rule, a planet that has yielded its life-force to another planet becomes its satellite until such time as a New Round of Evolution begins. The Moon significantly affects Earth and maintains its balance.

Like everything else in the Solar System, Earth has a septenary structure. Accordingly, it has seven bodies, globes, or spheres, which concentrically interlace with one another, comprising a Planetary Chain. These globes are the invisible spheres of the Subtle, Mental, and Fiery Worlds which surround Earth. Each represents a particular plane of consciousness or existence. It should be understood that the Planetary Chain is not comprised of the individual planets of the Solar System, but of different levels of the same planet.

Physical humanity lives on the most material globe that represents the physical world. When leaving this dense world, souls migrate to Earth's higher spheres — the Subtle, Mental, and more distant Fiery Planes. Then, in being incarnated on Earth, the soul traces a reverse path — from the Fiery World to the Subtle, and finally to the physical world — passing through all seven globes of the Earth's Planetary Chain. In the Higher Worlds, that is, the Highest Spheres of Earth, as well as on other, more advanced planets, there is no evil as such, though there is imperfection, or light and shadow.

The more material the world, the more binary the nature of its manifestation. Thus, in the period of its greatest density, which began 18 million years ago and peaked in the time of Atlantis, Earth experienced a period of maximum confrontation between opposites, the Light and the darkness, Good and evil, which significantly worsened its condition.

The first spores of evil appeared on the planet at a time when the first giant vegetation had just formed. Since the Earth itself was also endowed with free will to create from what it had "at hand," the Sun, as its Parent, could not and did not have the Cosmic Right to intervene unless the integrity of the planet was threatened.

The first creatures of the Earth, which can only conditionally be called *human*, were themselves similar to plants, constituting more tenuous, fibrous structures. The strongest among them began to engage in vampirism, capturing the powers of others. Even at this time poisonous spores of evil had already begun to appear in Earth's creations. In man there is an atom of the Mineral Kingdom, an atom of the Plant Kingdom, the Animal Kingdom, and so on. The planet formed its creations step by step, starting with dust and clay, gradually including the ingredients of subsequent Kingdoms. And every more or less created entity was already endowed with at least a tiny share of consciousness, free will in its embryonic manifestation, which subsequently flowed from the Kingdom of Stones to the Kingdom of Plants, from plants to animals, and from animals to humans.

Nature in a broader sense is devoid of evil, especially in its highest manifestation, where certain flowers and plants represent the crown of Evolution. However, Nature can also be poisonous in the form of certain corals and carnivorous flowers, as well as in animal nature and human nature of a base and destructive character.

Before the first appearance of physical humanity, the Earth had tried several times to create it independently. The result was dreadful reptile-like beings. Various "versions" of humanity followed, one after another, until the planet realized that without the assistance of the Supreme Forces, its own experiments would not lead to anything good. However, in each experiment, it was possible to select one or more individuals who had shown the ability to evolve further. It was from this number that the Titans of the Earth emerged.

The first reptile-like creations of the Earth did not entirely disappear and now constitute the Inner Kingdom mentioned in *The Mahatma Letters*. They live beneath its crust – the natural habitat of reptilian creatures. Like all reptiles, they try to stay close to gold-bearing veins and also require surges of sexual energy for their reproduction. Therefore, they exist in especially large concentrations under large cities like London, New York, Moscow, etc., as these areas can supply both types of energy. The first is represented by money since it has a direct connection to the gold reserves of the planet, regardless of whether gold has been extracted or remains beneath the crust. The second is sexual energy, supplied in abundance by millions of ignorant human beings. Reptiloids are able to take possession of people who are obsessed with money or sex, or both, that is, who are the same in nature.

Furthermore, in attempting to separate Earth from the Distant Worlds, the forces of darkness under Lucifer obscured the atmosphere around the planet on the Subtle Plane so that the rays from the Sun and other stars, sent to help humanity, could not penetrate. This contributed to parts of the planet being covered with ice. Its melting in the present age is a sign of the Era of Fire, where there is no place for any suggestion of cold. This means that Earth is gradually being released from the "heritage" of Atlantis and that its atmosphere is being purified. However, people are not yet accustomed to the new stellar rays, having been deprived of them for centuries. Therefore, it is only the willingness and desire of humanity to assimilate these new energies that can completely destroy the heavy, dirty-grey atmosphere, which is suffocating the entire planet, as it is seen from the Subtle Plane.

The Earth must exist for the Seven Rounds of Evolution, the stages of its development and progress. During the first three Rounds, it takes shape and solidifies; through the Fourth (current) Round, it establishes itself and hardens, possessing the highest degree of materiality; and over the last three Rounds, it gradually rarefies, ending up as a star.

Such conditions as now exist on Earth facilitate the quickest evolution of all its forms. It serves as an excellent launching platform for the spirit, providing the firmest possible foothold. So unique are the conditions of Earth that it is studied by more than three thousand civilizations; indeed, the Earth is the epicentre, where representatives come together from a variety of different planets, each bringing their own ideas into the world, concerned with expanding their influence on the consciousness of Earth-dwellers.

The extraterrestrial civilizations that came to the planet at the dawn of its inception, with both higher and lower purposes, fit into four main categories:

1. The Divine Worlds, whose messengers brought the Highest Laws to help in raising Gods from earthly humanity, Gods capable of creating new universes. Their representatives are the Seven Great Teachers and their disciples.

2. Spiritual civilizations, whose representatives follow in the footsteps of the Great Teachers, but have not yet themselves reached the level of Gods and Creators. These are 144,000 high spirits who responded to the call for help from Earth.

The 144,000 spirits did not come at once but in two Waves, and therefore, this number is common to the first two categories, being represented by a majority in the second. The First Wave included the Great Teachers and their disciples from Sirius, Orion, Alpha Centauri, the Pleiades, Cassiopeia, Coma Berenices, and so on. Many have already left Earth after completing their duties to the planet. Now is the time for all these spirits to return to their own Worlds and to be replaced by those who arrived during the Second Wave from planets within the Solar System, both visible and invisible.

3. Technocratic civilizations, whose creatures do not own the higher spiritual triads in their structures, and therefore, engage in various types of research and experiment on the plane of matter in order to prolong their lives.

In the Universe, there are civilizations with broken monads, which are devoid of immortal principles. Their representatives live 600–700 years at most. Then their matter decomposes and, without the ability to be reincarnated, they simply cease to exist. These civilizations look for the opportunity to advance to the plane of immortality. Therefore, knowing that humanity possesses this quality, they study the planet Earth and humanity in order to find a way to transform their matter so that it will no longer be destroyed, and to communicate this information to their own world.

Their representatives are incarnated in human bodies, and they are quite successful in recruiting numerous followers of their ideas. They have their own hierarchy, the lower layer of which is represented by a kind of biorobot, possessing both artificial intelligence and their own developments in consciousness, which is closer to primitive nature. Lacking higher spiritual triads, they search solely on the plane of matter. Of greatest interest to them is spiritualized matter, since it is durable and can subject their quaternaries to a kind of initiation up to the fifth level from where they will be able to live, flowing from body to body. So far their experiments have not advanced into the field of spirituality, despite the fact that many strive to be closer to the saints and messengers of Light. Such technocratic people are mainly guided by the instincts of the animal soul, or astral body, which can exist for hundreds of years. In their worldview, many sexual partners are promoted, since through the sex chakras of Earth-dwellers who have triads, they are able to draw energy to continue the life of their own astral bodies.

Each human being has a special sign on the forehead, invisible to the naked eye, which, in accordance with Cosmic Laws, marks their belonging to the corresponding sphere, that irrepressibly draws them into its field of attraction. The beacon of eternity can be seen glowing on the brow of one who has gone through Initiation. The signs are different colours, each colour indicating a certain level of spirituality. They usually represent a shining star, but may take the form of other symbols. A lilac-coloured star, for example, is a sign of high spiritual achievement.

Higher level extraterrestrial technocratic civilizations which study human beings and their structure will never touch a person with a sign on their forehead indicating that they are following a spiritual path. They deal with the so-called biomass — people who have not yet made any kind of definite choice, who are "neither cold nor hot." Cosmic Laws allow aliens to conduct all kinds of experiments with "nobody's" people like these: they might be taken aboard UFOs for research on their physical organs and suchlike. Hence this sign also designates personal inviolability.

4. Dark, destructive forces that sow death and which are for the most part products of near-Earth, terrestrial, and underground spheres. Such evil as there is on Earth does not exist in the immediate Cosmos, and it is other civilizations that take measures and protect themselves from Earth so that evil will not penetrate their systems.

Conspiracy theories about "reptilians" who came either from the Draco constellation or elsewhere are fundamentally incorrect and arose due to the erroneous interpretation by ufologists of ancient legends about Serpents and Dragons, who, as Blavatsky explained, have always been symbols of Wisdom and characterized the Teachers who came to Earth from Distant Worlds.

No one brought evil to Earth; it sprouted here quite abundantly of its own accord, and the most fertile soil turned out to be the human being. If humanity had not cultivated the spores of evil, the Prince of Darkness and his minions would not have had such a rich harvest, and they would never have been able to carry out their insidious plans on Earth. The Teachers came to Earth to help all to transform, for, according to Cosmic Laws, if they had not, there would have been no place in the Universe for such humanity and for such a planet, as was the case with the planet Phaeton which was destroyed.

Over the entire period of existence on Earth, each of the four categories mentioned above has found followers, and there is not a single dweller who would not fall under their influence to some extent at the level of consciousness. The most numerous is the fourth, which has always managed to triumph during the planet's previous cycles of Evolution. Next in number comes the third category, because the Earth itself is more technocratic in the essence of its development than other planets within the Solar System. These two categories focus more on materialism and "high intelligence." While the first and second categories, which pave the way through the heart for spiritual advancement towards the formation of a God-man, are the smallest, since only one sixth of humanity is more or less ready to perceive the Cosmic Laws that reign in the Higher Worlds. This explains why only this portion of humanity is destined to remain on Earth and continue their evolution, while all others will have to begin their evolution anew on Saturn under the extremely difficult conditions of this two-dimensional world. A number of Earth-dwellers will also relocate to Saturn as Gods in order to assist the planet in its development.

Edison, Thomas (1847–1931). An American inventor and entrepreneur, known for the phonograph, the motion picture camera, and early versions of the electric light bulb. Edison held over a thousand patents and contributed significantly to modern industrial technology and power systems. He joined the Theosophical Society in 1878.

Edkins, Joseph (1823–1905). A British expert in Chinese religions; the author of *Chinese Buddhism* (1880).

Ego (*Lat.*, "self"). The consciousness in man that is "I am I," or the feeling of "I-am-ship." Esoteric philosophy teaches the existence of two Egos in man, the mortal or personal, and the Higher, the Divine and the impersonal, calling the former *personality* and the latter *individuality*.

Égoisme à deux (*Fr.*). Dual selfishness.

Eidolon (*Gr.*, "image," "double"). The same as the human phantom, the astral form.

Eight dire miseries. In Buddhism, types of suffering that all sentient beings experience in samsara (the cycle of birth, death, and rebirth).

These are: 1) birth; 2) ageing; 3) sickness; 4) death; 5) separation from loved ones; 6) encountering the disliked; 7) not getting what one desires; 8) attachment to the five aggregates (*skandhas*): form, sensations, perceptions, mental formations, and consciousness.

Einstein, Albert (1879–1955). A German-born theoretical physicist and one of the most influential scientists of the twentieth century, best known for his theories of relativity and his famous equation, $E=mc^2$. His work revolutionized science's perception of space, time, energy, and gravity.

Eknath (1533–1599). A Marathi saint, poet, and scholar who was part of the Bhakti movement in India. He is known for his commentaries on Hindu scriptures, particularly the Bhagavad Gita and the *Bhagavata Purana*, and for his devotional songs (*abhangas*) dedicated to Lord Vithoba (a form of Vishnu).

Elementals. Spirits of the elements. The creatures that have evolved in the four kingdoms or elements — earth, air, fire, and water. The Kabbalists call them gnomes (of the earth), sylphs (of the air), salamanders (of the fire), and undines (of the water). Except for a few of the higher kinds, and their rulers, they are rather forces of Nature than ethereal men and women. As the servile agents of the occultists, these forces may produce various effects. However, if employed by "elementaries" (the disembodied souls of the depraved who have forfeited the opportunity of immortality) that enslave mediums at séances, they will deceive the credulous.

The elementals never evolve into human beings, but occupy, as it were, a specific step of the ladder of Being, and, by comparison with other beings, may properly be called nature-spirits, or cosmic agents of Nature, each being confined to its own element and never transgressing the bounds of others.

They have neither immortal spirits nor tangible bodies, only astral forms, which partake, in a distinguishing degree, of the element to which they belong and also of the Aether. They are a combination of sublimated matter and a rudimental mind. Some are changeless, but still have no separate individuality, acting collectively, so to say. Others, of certain elements and species, change form under a fixed law which Kabbalists explain. The most solid of their bodies is ordinarily just immaterial enough to escape perception by our physical sight, but not so unsubstantial that they can be perfectly recognized by the inner, or clairvoyant vision.

They not only exist and can all live in the Aether, but can handle and direct it for the production of physical effects, as readily as humans can compress air or water for the same purpose using pneumatic and hydraulic apparatus. In this activity they are readily helped by the "human elementary." More than this, they can so condense Aether as to make for themselves tangible bodies, which by their plastic powers they can cause to assume such likeness as they choose, by taking as their models the portraits they find stamped in the memory of the persons present. It is not necessary that the sitter should be thinking in that moment of the one represented. The person's image may have faded many years before. The mind receives indelible impressions even from chance acquaintances and persons encountered but once. As a few seconds exposure of the sensitized photograph plate is all that is requisite to preserve indefinitely the image of the sitter, so is it with the mind.

All the lower invisible beings generated on the fifth, sixth, and seventh planes of the terrestrial atmosphere are referred to as elementals: peris, devs, jinns, sylvans, satyrs, fauns, elves, dwarfs, trolls, kobolds, brownies, nixies, goblins, pinkies, banshees, moss people, white ladies, spooks, fairies, etc.

Elijah. A prophet in Israel, known for his miraculous acts. He is considered a forerunner of the Messiah in Jewish tradition and is revered in Christianity and Islam.

Eliot, Charles (1862–1931). A British diplomat, scholar, and linguist; the author of *Hinduism and Buddhism* (1921).

Eliot, T. S. (1888–1965). An influential American-British poet, playwright, and Nobel laureate, known for poems like *The Waste Land* (1922) and *Four Quartets* (1943).

Elizabeth I (1533–1603). Queen of England and Ireland, during whose reign from 1558 to 1603 the country experienced the "golden age."

Elohim or **Alhim** (*Heb.*, "gods"). A name for God in the Hebrew scriptures. It is used incorrectly in singular form, since it refers to a host, an army of creative powers that represent the Architects of this visible physical planet and of man's material body or encasement.

Kabbalah explains sufficiently that the Elohim number seven; each creates one of the seven things enumerated in the first chapter of Genesis, and these correspond allegorically to the seven creations. To make this clear, one can count the verses in which it is said "And God saw that it was good," and one will find that this is said seven times.

The Hebrew letters are *aleph, lamed, he, yod, mem*, and are numerically 1, 30, 5, 10, 40 = 86. It seems to be the plural of the feminine noun *Eloah*, ALH, formed by adding the common plural form IM, a masculine ending; and hence the whole seems to imply the emitted active and passive essences. As a title it refers to Binah, the Supernal Mother, as does the fuller title IHVH ALHIM, Jehovah Elohim. As Binah leads on to seven subsequent Emanations, so Elohim has been said to represent a sevenfold power of godhead.

Emanation. A doctrine opposed to Evolution in its metaphysical meaning, yet one with it. Science teaches that evolution is physiologically a mode of generation in which the germ that develops the foetus pre-exists in the parent, the development, final form, and characteristics of that germ being accomplished in Nature; and that in cosmology the process takes place blindly through the correlation of the elements and their various compounds.

Occultism answers that this is only the *apparent* mode, the real process being Emanation, guided by intelligent Forces under an immutable Law. Therefore, while the occultists and Theosophists believe thoroughly in the doctrine of Evolution as set forth by Kapila and Manu, they are *Emanationists* rather than *Evolutionists*.

The doctrine of Emanation was at one time universal. It was taught by the Alexandrian as well as by the Indian philosophers, by the Egyptian, the Chaldean, and Hellenic Hierophants, and also by the Hebrews (in Kabbalah and even in Genesis). For it is only owing to deliberate mistranslation that the Hebrew word *asdt* has been translated as "angels" from the Septuagint, when, in fact, it means *Emanations, Aeons*, precisely as the Gnostics had denoted. Indeed, in Deuteronomy 33:2, the word *asdt* or *ashdt* is translated as "fiery law," whilst a correct rendering of the passage would read: "from his right hand went [not a fiery law, but] a fire according to the law"; namely, that the fire of one flame is imparted to, and caught up by, another as in a trail of inflammable substance. This is a precise metaphor for emanation.

As shown in *Isis Unveiled*: "In Evolution, as it is now beginning to be understood, there is supposed to be in all matter an impulse to take on a higher form — a supposition clearly expressed by Manu and other Hindu philosophers of the highest antiquity. The philosopher's tree illustrates it in the case of the zinc solution. The controversy between the followers of this school and the Emanationists may be briefly stated thus: The Evolutionist stops all inquiry at the borders of 'the Unknowable'; the Emanationist believes that nothing can be evolved — or, as the word means, unwombed or born — except it has first been involved, thus indicating that life is from a spiritual potency above the whole."

Emotionalism. A doctrine stressing the value of emotions in ethics and the arts.

Emoto, Masaru (1943–2014). A Japanese researcher and author of a number of books, including *The Hidden Messages in Water* (2004). He discovered and proved that human consciousness could affect the molecular structure of water.

En bloc (*Fr.*). All together; as a whole.

Enoch (*Heb.*, "initiator"). A generic character belonging to a distant race, and not to any one nation but to all. Enoch also means "internal eye" or seer. Thus, every prophet and Adept may be called Enoch.

In the Bible (Genesis 4 and 5) there are three distinct Enochs: the son of Cain, the son of Seth, and the son of Jared, but they are all identical, and two are mentioned for the purposes of obfuscation. The years of only the last two are given, the first being left without further mention.

Esoterically speaking, Enoch is the first Son of Man, and symbolically, the first sub-race of the Fifth Root Race. And if his name yields for purposes of numerical and astronomical glyphs the meaning of the solar year, or 365, in conformity with the age assigned to him in Genesis, it is because, being the seventh, he is, for occult purposes, the personified period of the two preceding Races with their fourteen sub-races. Therefore, he is shown in the Book as the great-grandfather of Noah who, in turn, is the personification of humankind of the Fifth, struggling with that of the Fourth Root Race — the great period of the revealed and profaned Mysteries, when the "Sons of God" coming down to Earth took for wives the daughters of men, and taught them the secrets of the Angels; in other words, when the "mind-born" humans of the Third Race mixed with those of the Fourth, and the Divine Science was gradually reduced by humankind to sorcery.

The Book of Enoch, from which the author of Revelation and even St. John of the Fourth Gospel have so profusely quoted, is a Book of Initiation, giving out in allegory and cautious phraseology the programme of certain archaic mysteries performed in the inner temples. The prophecies of the Book of Enoch are indeed prophetic, but they were intended for, and cover the records of, five Races of the seven, everything that related to the other two being kept secret. It relates to the history of the human Races and their early relation to Theogony, the symbols being blended with astronomical and cosmic mysteries.

Epictetus (c.50–c.135). A Greek Stoic philosopher, known for his teachings on inner freedom, self-discipline, and the importance of distinguishing between what we can and cannot control. His philosophy is encapsulated in works like the *Enchiridion* and the *Discourses*.

Esoteric (*Gr.*, "inner"). Hidden, secret; intended solely for Initiates with the aim of avoiding use by untrained persons that might result in destructive consequences.

Esoteric Section. An inner section of the Theosophical Society founded in October 1888 for the deeper study of esoteric philosophy.

Esotericism. A system of hidden or inner knowledge and spiritual wisdom intended for a limited group of Initiates rather than the general public.

Essenes (*Heb.*, "healer"). A mystic Jewish sect that flourished between the second century BCE and the first century CE. For thousands of years, the Essenes lived near the Dead Sea in highly organized groups and held property in common. They held many Buddhist-like ideas and practices.

Ether. A term often confused with Akasha and Astral Light. It is, in fact, neither, in the sense in which ether is described by physical science. Ether is a material agent, though hitherto undetected by any physical apparatus, whereas Akasha is a distinctly spiritual agent, identical, in one sense, with the *Anima Mundi*. The Astral Light is the seventh and highest principle of the terrestrial atmosphere, as undetectable as Akasha and real Ether, because it is something quite on another plane. The seventh principle of the earth's atmosphere, the Astral Light, is but the second on the Cosmic scale. The scale of Cosmic Forces, of Principles and Planes, and Emanations (on the metaphysical plane) and Evolutions (on the physical plane) is the Cosmic Serpent biting its own tail, the Serpent reflecting the Higher, and reflected in turn by the lower Serpent. The caduceus explains the mystery, and the fourfold dodecahedron on whose model the universe is said by Plato to have been built by the manifested Logos, synthesized by the unmanifested Firstborn, yields geometrically the key to cosmogony and its microcosmic reflection — Earth.

Depending on the spiritual tradition, Ether, Aether, and Akasha can all refer to the fifth element of the seven elements on Earth. Four elements (air, fire, water, earth) are now fully manifested, while the fifth (ether) is only partially so, as we are in the Fifth Race of the Fourth Round, and consequently, the fifth element will manifest fully only in the Fifth Round.

However, a distinction should be drawn between Aether and Ether, the former being divine, the latter physical and infernal. Ether is the lowest in the septenary division of Akasha, primordial Fire-substance. Aether-Akasha is the fifth and sixth principles of the body of the Cosmos, thus corresponding to *buddhi-manas* in man; Ether is its Cosmic sediment mingling with the highest layer of Astral Light. Beginning with the current Fifth Race, it will develop fully only at the beginning of the Fifth Round. Aether is Akasha in its higher aspect, and Ether is Akasha in its lowest aspect. In one sense it is equivalent to the Father-Creator, Zeus, Pater Aether, and in another, to the infernal serpent-tempter, the Astral Light of the Kabbalists. In the latter case, it is fully differentiated matter; in the former, only rudimentally so. In other words, Spirit becomes objective matter, and objective matter rebecomes subjective Spirit, when it eludes our physical senses. Aether has the same relation to the Cosmos and Earth as *manas* has to the monad and the body. Therefore, Ether has nothing to do with spirit, and a good deal to do with subjective matter and Earth.

Evans-Wentz, W. Y. (1878–1965). An American scholar and writer who edited the translations of Tibetan works made by Lama Kazi Dawa Samdup, popularizing them in the West.

Everest. The highest mountain in the world, located in the Himalayas on the border between Nepal and Tibet. It has sacred significance in Himalayan cultures.

Evolution. The development of higher orders of animals from lower orders. Modern science holds but to a one-sided physical evolution, prudently avoiding and ignoring the higher or spiritual evolution, which would force our contemporaries to confess the superiority of the ancient philosophers and psychologists over themselves. The ancient sages, ascending to the Unknowable, made their starting point the first manifestation of the unseen, the unavoidable, and, from a strictly logical point of reasoning, the essential creative Being, the Demiurgus of the Universe. Evolution began from pure spirit, which, descending lower and lower down, assumed at last a visible and comprehensible form and became matter. Having arrived at this point, they speculated in the Darwinian method, but on a far larger and more comprehensive basis.

Ex cathedra (*Lat.*, "from the [teacher's] chair"). With infallible authority.

Exoteric (*Gr.*, "outer"). Outward, public; the opposite of esoteric or hidden.

F

Facsimile (*Lat.*). An exact copy.

Faith, Hope, and Love. The Three Persons of Sophia, the Spirit of Wisdom, Love, and Truth, the Greatest Spirit of the Feminine Principle not of earthly evolution, who has Her personification in many religions of the world: Isis, Ishtar, Lakshmi, Tara, Mary, the Mother of the World, and so on.

Christ and Sophia are One, like Spirit and Soul, constituting the head of the Hierarchy of Light in the Solar System. Sophia sent Christ forth at the time of the First Advent and stayed beside Him. And She alone was able to give life to Him who descends into the world during the Second Advent. And although this Spirit cannot become incarnate as a human being on Earth in Her full strength, She sends Her Rays to accompany Her Daughters, who can justly be considered incarnations of Sophia, on the thorny path of service to humanity.

Two thousand years ago, having sown the first seeds of Divine Love on Earth, Christ left His Soul on probation, so that She might continue to sustain these shoots of Love. All that time, Sophia was to remain concealed in the body of an earthly woman, undying on the plane of Her subtle bodies. Thus, Faith, Hope, and Love periodically replaced each other, never abandoning this world. One Hypostasis departs only when the next is born, and Her subtle bodies flow into the womb of the woman who is the bearer of the next Hypostasis. In this way, Sophia and Her Rays have continuously manifested themselves on Earth for the past two thousand years.

In their physical bodies, each time traversing the difficult and thorny path of self-sacrifice for the good of humanity, Faith, Hope, and Love carry out the highest Cosmic Tasks that often remain beyond the sight and knowledge of the masses. Sophia, being a reflection of Christ, must traverse His Path, and therefore, Her Hypostases are crucified morally and physically. Hence, they too have frequently perished at the hands of killers.

Faith passed through the religions that the messengers of Light gave to humanity. Faith alone could accustom people, who had long lost the ability to see and hear the Higher Worlds, to the notion of their existence and connection with them. These religions soon experienced a distortion of their teachings. Messengers were exterminated, but they were replaced by others. And so Faith has never faded in the human heart.

Hope went hand in hand with knowledge. The Wisdom of Sophia descends to humanity through scientific discoveries imparted to scientists by the messengers of Wisdom. Many were burnt at the stake for their discoveries, which were misunderstood, but were incarnated anew in order that these discoveries might be embraced by subsequent generations.

The most difficult path towards humanity was experienced by the Third Hypostasis of Sophia, that is, Love. Every manifestation of sacrificial Love was trampled upon by the people right from the start, yet until all Three Persons were established in the world, the Mother of the World — Sophia — was unable to descend to Earth. It is through Love alone that the composite Ray of Sophia may be made manifest, uniting within herself all the Rays of Faith, Hope, and Love.

It should be borne in mind that their One Mother periodically manifested Herself in one Ray or another, and that these three Hypostases cannot be considered completely in isolation, since their energy flow could occur during the life of one. Periodically, the Ray of one of the bearers could be superimposed on the Ray of another, and for a certain period of time, they could receive each other's Rays, while preserving the dominance of their own. There are no contradictions here — much is within the competence of the vision of the Initiates alone.

Faraday, Michael (1791–1867). A British scientist who made ground-breaking contributions to the fields of electromagnetism and electrochemistry. He discovered electromagnetic induction, laws of electrolysis, and helped lay the foundation for the practical use of electricity.

Faust. The main character of the tragic play of the same name by Johann Wolfgang von Goethe, based on Johann Georg Faust, a legendary German alchemist, astrologer, and magician.

Fenians. Members of an Irish revolutionary organization founded in the nineteenth century to fight for an independent Ireland.

Fiat Rex (*Lat.*, "let there be a king"). A painting by Nicholas Roerich created in 1931 in the form of a triptych and dedicated to Master M., the Lord of Shambhala.

Fiery Experience. The method which the Great Teachers use to transmit supreme knowledge through their colleagues and disciples who practise the fiery yoga, those who have established power over their lower nature, thoughts, and actions, and who are on the path of continuous self-perfection and self-sacrificing service to humanity. In this sense, it could be said that the saints of all religions were fiery yogis.

The New Era supposes spiritual awakening. To prepare humanity for this amazing time, many beautiful souls have been incarnated to bring new ideas to the world in all spheres of life. That is why, especially now, at the junction of two Eras, many books of spiritual content have appeared, designed to shift the consciousness of humanity. However, since everyone is on their own level of development — what is clear to one may be quite unclear to another — the quality of these books represents all levels of consciousness, from the lowest to the highest. But their essential task is always the same — to encourage as many people as possible to take the path of Love, Good, and Light. Obviously, if such a goal is not evident throughout the course of a book, then it cannot be regarded as spiritual.

There are a great many techniques for writing such unusual books, and in each case they are individual. Nevertheless, it is possible to classify them all into four main groups that are known to esoteric philosophy: spiritual enlightenment, mediumship, mediatorship, and the Fiery Experience.

The first method of writing is characteristic of ordinary people who have no extraordinary abilities, but who aspire to the Light. Their high level of spirituality awakens their chalice of accumulations, the experience of many past lives that practically everyone possesses. After all, many people follow the path of Light for more than one lifetime; they could have, for example, passed an Initiation in an ancient civilization, studied various secret books of the past, or been close to Jesus Christ and Gautama Buddha, and so on. And in moments of illumination and enlightenment, memories from the chalice might have developed into a new understanding of the sacred texts, as well as into beautiful, mystical, and spiritual novels, which awaken the imagination of readers and impel them towards the unusual. Of course, authors may even be unaware that their books describe one of the pages of their lives, perhaps even the start of their path towards the Light, which now serves as inspiration for many other people.

A medium is an intermediary between the physical world and the near-Earth layers of the Subtle World. Mediums are born with this ability; but if they do not aspire towards the Light, then the information transmitted through them is in constant danger of being influenced by dark forces. On the other hand, mediators and fiery yogis have to *become* such.

Mediators are individuals who have accumulated significant experience serving the Light throughout their previous lives. Their elevated morality and merit in the past allow them to obtain access to the spatial treasury of high spheres and draw knowledge from them, or to communicate with high spirits or even with highly developed extraterrestrial civilizations who want to help humankind on Earth. In modern language, a mediator can be called a *conscious channeller*. Any medium, provided they are morally pure and strive towards the Light, can become a mediator. Since mediators possess a high level of spiritual accumulations, they can also consciously communicate with their own spirits, their Divine Selves, receiving clear answers to various questions. This, of course, cannot be regarded as channelling. High mediators are able to reach many degrees of the next stage, that of the fiery yoga; only the highest degrees, such as the ability to fly to Distant Worlds and Cosmic Cooperation with the Forces of Light, will be unavailable to them. Yet even these restrictions are in force only until the mediators reach that level of spirituality which opens up such opportunities.

However, it should be borne in mind that the information passing through mediators, i.e., through their own levels of earthly understanding, may be distorted. That is why the Great Teachers do not use this method to transmit Teachings. Only in a few cases, when the spiritual purity of the mediators is at a sufficiently high level, can they work in the Rays of one of the Teachers or with their authorized disciples. Edgar Cayce, being an exceptional man of high moral character, is an example of such a mediator, who, moreover, was under the guidance of the Forces of Light.

The Great Teachers have quite a large number of advanced disciples, who are permitted to work with humanity through mediators and to act on behalf of the Teachers. As a rule, these disciples are in a disembodied state, staying close to their Masters in the higher spheres of the Subtle World. One might say that in this way, they are practising to attain the degree of Teacher. Studying with the Great Teachers is largely an expression of free will. The Teacher simply indicates a goal; it is up to the disciple to decide how they will achieve it. The same applies to the comprehension of Truth: disciples can gather its fragments, which are scattered through all the sacred texts, but only if they themselves come to a correct conclusion can the Teacher confirm it. Hence, how exactly disciples work with humanity and undertake their "practicum" depends upon their own free will; and sometimes it may be the case that they, like all who are learning, make insignificant mistakes.

There is a custom in the East: when a Teacher accepts a disciple, they must renounce their own name and take that of the Teacher. The name may represent either the current name of the Teacher or one of the names of His previous earthly incarnations. That is why there are now so many varying messages from the "Ascended Masters," the quality of which largely depends upon the purity of the receivers' consciousness. It should also be borne in mind that, in the near-Earth layers of the Subtle World, there are many disembodied souls, so-called impersonators, who pretend to be the Teachers or their disciples, but have quite different goals. Therefore, one should discern such moments and judge any spiritual book simply by such criteria as: Has it brought one joy and spiritual awakening? Has it encouraged one to do good deeds in respect to other people? Has it impelled one to set out on the path of self-sacrificing service to the Light? If the answer is yes, then it has come from the Light, and one should not listen to those who do not share one's opinion; yet at the same time one should not condemn those books that have left one indifferent, but moved other people closer to the Light.

The Teachers themselves choose one or two people and work with them in a certain Ray of the Hierarchy with the purpose of advancing the consciousness of humanity to a new level every Eastern century, which consists of 60 years. This is the Fiery Experience. During this time, mediators can connect to this single stream, receiving information and transmitting it through their own consciousness.

Despite the fact that the term *Fiery Experience* is fairly modern, first being introduced in the twentieth century by Helena Roerich to explain the way she received *Agni Yoga*, or the Teaching of Living Ethics, the experience itself was primary in the transmission of all the sacred scriptures known to humanity, from the Vedas and the Puranas to the Bible and the Quran. It was the Fiery Experience that lay at their foundation.

The individuals whose destiny it was to give to humanity various Teachings of Light, in oral or written form, prepared for the task over many lifetimes. In those incarnations, they could have fulfilled the role of priest, government official, astrologer, or mere poet, but the main feature characteristic of all these individuals is a supreme level of spirituality. Sometimes, they had to retire from their ordinary lives, moving into a pure realm far away from other people and common vanity. They could also be called to the Chief Stronghold of Light, Shambhala, to restore their spiritual knowledge; and accounts of travelling to the East, to India, have been preserved in connection with many founders of philosophical and religious systems. Just before the transmission of a Teaching, the representatives of the Hierarchy of Light worked with the chosen ones, purifying their bodies and souls to prepare them to receive the supreme fiery energies that, without such training, might literally have incinerated their physical bodies. Therefore, as a rule, these chosen ones were the Great Teachers themselves or their closest colleagues, who incarnated amidst humanity for this superhuman mission. Usually, they were born as ordinary people, but in some cases, they were high mediators.

After a certain period of time, when the selected disciples are ready, the Teachers come to them in a dream or reality, often in the form of Angels, to convey to them and through them the Teachings destined for certain historical stages in the development of various peoples, as well as the territories they inhabit. Such a transmission happens via one of the Teachers' Rays, which represents a highly vibrational fiery stream, as it is directed at the disciples' higher centres of consciousness.

There are Seven Rays, each of which is used to achieve certain evolutionary goals. For example, the Ray of Knowledge influences the brain centres. It is the Ray that protects and prevents new knowledge from being distorted and that serves as a special tool for translating inaccessible Cosmic Knowledge into a form that the disciple's consciousness is able to assimilate. However, it should be borne in mind that transmission via the Ray is not a dictation but the *creative work* of the disciple. The Ray influences and awakens the corresponding higher energy centres, causing a strong influx of thoughts, images, and ideas, which the disciple then translates into words. That is, the disciple is in a high state of consciousness, and so, creativity enacted under the Ray's impact could be called *divine inspiration*. And precisely because it is *creativity*, it is important for disciples to possess the talent that they have refined over the course of numerous earthly incarnations. Thus, along with their invisible Teachers, the disciples are the true co-authors of the Teachings.

During the oral or written transmission of Teachings, a crystallization of fires occurs at the level of the disciples' higher energy centres, which in turn saturates the surrounding world with new currents of the corresponding Ray. Their centres emit these higher energies, already assimilated and processed, into the world for other people to absorb, helping them begin a new stage in their development. What then becomes public is only a part of the work produced by the disciples. The unpublished parts of the Teachings will exist in the archives of Shambhala. Yet the most significant part of the unpublished work will be imprinted upon the entire space of the earthly world, from the lowest to the highest spheres, and all humankind will perceive the ideas of the Teachings, regardless of the fact that they were initially given in a particular language to a particular people.

However, each transmission of the Teaching of Light has its own individual characteristics, and therefore, the explanation of the process as divine inspiration is aimed at providing a general understanding only. For example, originally the incarnated Great Teachers often gave the Teachings verbally, and significant periods of time might pass before a Teaching appeared in the form of a sacred text. In this case, the highly spiritual disciples played the part of co-authors, who in their past lives were included in the inner circle of the Teachers giving the Teachings. Once the disciples had undergone special preparation, the Ray would influence their chalice of accumulations, drawing out of it their memories of what the Teachers had preached. And then the disciples creatively translated them into words in the appropriate languages, at the same time as the crystallization of fires imbuing space was taking place.

It should be emphasized that no Teaching of Light can be given through mediumship, but any medium, given the appropriate steadfast aspiration, can become a mediator under the guidance of one of the Teachers and, subsequently, a fiery yogi.

According to prophecy, Maitreya's Teaching must precede His Advent. Thus, it was said that Three Teachings would be given, one in the West, one in the East, and one in the North. Moreover, one of the drawings accompanying the recently discovered manuscript by Nostradamus, *Vaticinia Nostradami*, symbolically depicts Chakravartin, or the King of the Golden Wheel, whose Teaching was supposed to have been recorded by three women.

The first disciple was Helena Blavatsky, who wrote her major work, *The Secret Doctrine*, under the guidance of Master Morya in the late nineteenth century in the countries of the West. Morya is the Eldest and the Greatest of the Teachers, who in His essence is one with His Father, and for this reason *The Secret Doctrine* relates to the Triune Teaching of Maitreya.

Blavatsky was born the strongest type of medium because of her special mission to convince humanity of the existence of the higher laws of Nature. But she is also the most striking example of the transfiguration of a medium into a fiery yogi. Following the yogic path in previous lives, she succeeded with the help of her Teacher, Mahatma Morya, in becoming a high mediator and a fiery yogi in order to give *The Secret Doctrine* to the world.

She began a new, hitherto unprecedented cycle in the transmission of secret knowledge, which previously could not have been revealed to humanity so broadly and was instead hidden and only hinted at in all sacred writings. Blavatsky wrote her major work in the Rays of Master Morya, the bearer of all Seven Rays, namely, in the Ray of Knowledge and the Ray of Harmony through Conflict. It is commonly believed that the Great Teachers dictated *The Secret Doctrine* to Helena Blavatsky in its entirety, but in fact it was practically her own, fully fledged creative work produced in the Rays of Mahatma Morya. The "dictation" was limited mainly to the instructions and advice of the Teachers, through their letters, as to what sources she should use and what fields of esoteric knowledge she should cover.

As always happens with true messengers of Light, humanity did not accept Blavatsky and treated her as a charlatan, morally crucifying her by all available means, including the fabrication of false evidence. All attempts to justify herself led only to even more violent disbelief on the part of her critics and accusers. For any person who finds themselves under the constant influence of the Master's Ray, it is extremely difficult to be among groups of people in large cities, to stand before a whole society. Unbearable pain and declining health, constantly exacerbated by the torments of both enemies and former friends, resulted in Blavatsky's premature departure from the earthly plane.

Helena Blavatsky was required to sow in human minds the first seeds of knowledge concerning the Laws and Principles of the Universe, so as to prepare the soil, because the Cosmic Period was approaching when everyone in their spirit would have to make the most important decision of their earthly existence, choosing with whom to stand: with the Light or the darkness.

It is Helena Blavatsky who laid the foundation for what was called in *The Mahatma Letters* the "Great Mystery," something that could not be revealed in full to the understanding of humanity:

"Notwithstanding that the time is not quite ripe to let you entirely into the secret; and that you are hardly yet prepared to understand the great Mystery, even if told of it, owing to the great injustice and wrong done, I am empowered to allow you a glimpse behind the veil. This state of [Helena Blavatsky] is intimately connected with her occult training in Tibet, and due to her being sent out alone into the world to gradually prepare the way for others. After nearly a century of fruitless search, our chiefs had to avail themselves of the only opportunity to send out a European *body* upon European soil to serve as a connecting link between that country and our own. You do not understand? Of course not. Please then, remember, what she tried to explain, and what you gathered tolerably well from her, namely the fact of the *seven* principles in the *complete* human being. Now, no man or woman, unless he be an initiate of the 'fifth circle,' can leave the precincts of *Bod-Las* and return back into the world in his integral whole — if I may use the expression. One, at least, of his seven satellites has to remain behind for two reasons: the first to form the necessary connecting link, the wire of transmission — the second as the safest warranter that certain things will never be divulged."

Even now this Mystery can be described and understood only on a primitive level. So, before the commencement of her work on *The Secret Doctrine*, Blavatsky underwent special training under the supervision of her Teacher in Tibet. This Experience of the fiery transmutation of her body allowed the Teachers to prepare the way for the colleagues of Shambhala who followed in order to continue and deepen this Experiment for the good of all humanity. Since the goal was to impart to the world the Triune Teaching of Maitreya during three 60-year cycles, connecting Shambhala and the West, East, and North by a single thread, the prerequisite for this was the unification of the energy currents of all three female disciples, who were destined to reveal the Three Teachings to humanity. Simply speaking, their work had to involve elements energetically linking the previous Teaching with the new one, establishing spiritual continuity, both invisibly and visibly, in the form of a particular piece of writing.

As is known from *The Mahatma Letters*, disciples who visit Shambhala, unless they are incarnated Teachers, cannot return to the world "completely." One of the principles of the sevenfold structure of their bodies must remain there, so as to form a *spatial fiery wire*, a secure connecting link for transmissions between Shambhala and the world, when the disciples return to their countries of residence. However, if disciples live high in the mountains, then there is no need to separate their principles, because the Teachers, if necessary, can freely descend to certain heights. Leaving behind one principle in Shambhala also allows them to save disciples who live most of their lives in the lowlands from fatal blows, especially at times when they are on the verge of death. It is this that enabled the Teachers to intervene to save Blavatsky at times when she was on her deathbed. Accounts of her miraculous recoveries can be read in the reminiscences of her companions.

In esoteric philosophy, it is known that spiritual communication with one of the Teachers happens through a *single wire*, whereas communication with all the Teachers occurs through a *spatial wire*, which also gives access to the Ocean of Cosmic Knowledge. Since ancient times, sages have stated that all creations in the Universe are interconnected by invisible threads, or rays, which form a light-bearing net. Potentially, a single wire is available for every spirit, which is capable of connecting them with the Teachers and even with Distant Worlds. However, in order to "activate" this wire and to connect with a Teacher, one must have enormous reserves of spiritual accumulations over numerous lifetimes of self-sacrificing service to humanity, because the connection operates on the principle of a magnet: to receive something, one must already have something which is able to attract it. It is through these wires that the Teachers' Rays, which impact the disciples' consciousness, pass, and it is precisely these Rays that protect them, preventing anyone from interfering with the process. As mentioned above, the preparation of disciples to receive the high-frequency energies conducted through the Rays is neither easy nor painless. Therefore, one should not confuse these fiery wires with the channels of modern-day channellers, since the latter, generally speaking, are protected neither from the intervention of other forces, nor from the distortion of the information being transmitted. They vary significantly in quality and reliability in exactly the same way as any other wired or wireless connection. Only if a channeller is working at a high ethical and spiritual level will their channel be protected, either by their own power or by that of the Forces of Light.

The single wire, then, has been used before in guiding the colleagues of Shambhala, who were to give the world various Teachings of Light. But the spatial wire, which allows earthly disciples to communicate with all the Teachers of Shambhala, was first created during Blavatsky's lifetime. It becomes available only to fiery yogis functioning at the higher degrees of spirituality, because it is much more difficult to use than a single wire. It requires a significantly greater expenditure of energy, and as a result, it has a much stronger effect on the disciple's health. Prior to this, the spatial wire was the prerogative of Teachers alone. When Blavatsky departed the earthly plane in 1891, the fiery thread that passed through the countries of the West remained in London, where the next colleague of Shambhala would arrive, so as to "pick it up" and continue the energy work, this time on new base currents. This is how the unification of the fiery energies of previous and succeeding disciples takes place on the invisible plane.

With this purpose, as Helena Blavatsky had predicted in *The Secret Doctrine*, the next disciple, Helena Roerich, arrived in London in 1920. There she began recording *Agni Yoga* under the guidance of Mahatma Morya, and continued in Europe, the United States, and finally, in the countries of the East, where she wrote the main part of her Teaching of Living Ethics. This series of books represents the path of fiery yoga, a synthesis of all previous yogas, presented for the first time as a spiritual practice accessible to all, that serves the transformation of all the bodies of the human structure. At this time, also, the first Call to Light began to sound. This call comprised an energy that saturated the entire space of the planet in order to attract consonant individuals with its magnetic power, and thereby help people make the choice on which side they would stand: on the side of Light or the side of darkness.

In 1924, Morya was appointed the Lord of Shambhala. The appointment of Morya as a Ruler was associated with the commencement of the Era of Synthesis, and He, like His Father, is the bearer of all the Rays, or energies, given to the world throughout the history of earthly civilization. Therefore, during the ceremony of enthronement, He took the name of Maitreya as a tribute to His Father, the Teacher of Teachers, who Himself would soon be manifested on the planet. After all, the Advent of Maitreya began in 1942, a date which, for certain reasons, was obscured in the scriptures. Nonetheless, some researchers succeeded in understanding that the giant figures were merely symbols, and in the 1930s, they widely declared as much to the population of India. On this subject Helena Roerich writes:

"Let us not forget that many interpretations were wrong, for their meaning was deliberately obscured, and the Forces of Light did not seek to provide clarification for a certain time, because they saw what treachery was in the works. The year of 1936 was great, for it marked the end of a particular regime. This was a great victory for the Forces of Light. It is also interesting to note that it is now broadly accepted across India that the year 1942 marks the end of Kali Yuga and the incarnation of the Kalki Avatar in Shambhala. This date is correct. Our Teacher indicated it long ago. Pundits are now proving that the large numbers in the scriptures were a concealment and should be counted not as years but as days, for by this counting system the period of the end of Kali Yuga falls in the year 1942. This is quite correct, for you can find a statement in *The Secret Doctrine* that zeros are often used to hide real numbers. Also, the end of Kali Yuga, esoterically speaking, should coincide with the entry into the Cycle of Aquarius" (3 December 1937).

From Nicholas Roerich's diaries: "Today a solar eclipse is taking place. Kali Yuga ended on 1 August and Satya Yuga is coming into force. Such are the calculations of the Brahmins. They even published a small book, which, for some reason, is prohibited by the [Indian] government" (1 August 1943).

"A letter from a lama in Kalimpong. On 1 August, in all Buddhist temples solemn services were held to mark the end of the dark age of Kali Yuga and the beginning of the light age, Satya Yuga. On 15 August, Rigden Dragpo, the Avatar of Light, goes to fight for the truth, for the building of a new world. A long-awaited event! These periods have also been celebrated and recorded in Tibet and Mongolia. Shambhala is on everyone's lips. How greatly people waited for 1943! But they understood that events occur gradually. There can be no instant transformations. Only unforeseen avalanches and earthquakes thunder suddenly" (17 August 1943).

At that time, the King of the World was indeed, for the first time in thousands of years, incarnated in Shambhala at the level of the Supreme Spheres of the planet, obtaining single wholeness with His Eldest Son, Morya. So, in other words, the Solar Hierarch fully manifested Himself in Morya at the hour that Morya took the name of the Lord of Shambhala, Maitreya.

During the period 1920 to 1955, under the guidance of the Lord of Shambhala, the Teachers were able to conduct a unique Fiery Experiment together with Helena Roerich. Previously, many had come close, but the conditions of their lives had proven unsuitable. This Experiment was necessary because, as ancient Teachings warned, the strongest fiery energies, coming from the Cosmos would begin to affect the whole Earth and humanity as of 1999. However, the spiritual level of Earth-dwellers was not sufficiently developed to pass through this period painlessly: the devastating future for the end of the twentieth century, which Edgar Cayce saw and predicted, was a *reality*. To avert it and change the destiny of humanity, Roerich agreed to give herself over to the test of the spatial Fire — the cosmic energies, which soon were to reach Earth.

For the first time, the Fiery Experience was undergone not in reclusion but among people living in the conditions of everyday life as Roerich travelled across the East, and then in the towns of India at the foot of the Himalayas. The pure natural environment of the mountains, and close circle of loving people were a great help to this unprecedented Experiment. Under the close supervision of her Teacher, the Great Lord of Shambhala, she experienced the opening and transmutation of *all* energy centres, perceiving all Light available on Earth, that is, all the Seven Rays. For the first time, an earthly being could communicate not only with all the Teachers, each of whom has His individual Ray, as Blavatsky was able to do, but with all other members of the Brotherhood, among whom the Seven Rays are divided by tonality. This was necessary because the task was to conduct a huge number of experiments on Roerich's human matter, and the entire Brotherhood needed a means of communicating with her directly. It should be noted that even communication with one Teacher necessitates huge tension in the higher centres of the disciple's consciousness, something that not every mediator, even one that has achieved a very high level, is able to withstand. Thanks to her spiritual achievements, Roerich had both wires: one to converse with Master Morya, and the other to communicate with the entire Brotherhood, which additionally gave her access to everything that was happening in Shambhala.

In normal earthly conditions, the process of opening and transmuting the energy centres can be excruciating because their highly vibrational nature no longer corresponds to the low vibrations of the earthly environment. Therefore, the process should be conducted under the supervision of a Teacher and not attempted independently, and this is particularly relevant in the conditions of modern life. Roerich was often ill for long periods of time, as her body was unable to withstand such fiery tension. Even communicating with the people closest to her was painful. For certain stages of the Experience, she needed to retire to places high in the mountains, and even there the Teacher rescued her from fiery death.

As a result of this Heroic Deed, all seven bodies of her human structure were developed and transfigured, while her consciousness reached the superhuman level. Conscious and creative Cosmic Cooperation and Construction together with the Great Lord of Shambhala had become available to her on all the seven planes of Existence. The vibrations of Cosmic Cooperation are so high that they cannot be perceived and comprehended by the physical brain fully or for any length of time, without bringing about its destruction. It is a state that is indescribably difficult to undergo, and the fiery strain would often disable Roerich for long weeks, during which, in order to restore her strength, she was forbidden not only to write or read, but even to *think*. However, Cosmic Cooperation is especially efficient when the individual occupies a purified physical body that helps to accelerate not only the evolution of Earth but also that of the Solar System.

As a result, Roerich was able to travel within the Solar System in her mental body together with other members of the Brotherhood, carrying out the assignments of the Lord. This may all sound strange and far-fetched to ordinary people, who are accustomed to the idea that huge spaceships are required in order to travel through the Universe. However, in Tibet, there are special closed monasteries, where monks practise travelling first within our planet and then to other planets; this is all possible for the human spirit, and it should be said that such mental flight was also available to Nikola Tesla. During the Cosmic Cooperation, Roerich, too, could provide assistance to both individuals and the entire Earth, for example, participating in battles with the dark forces, containing the elements, and extinguishing underground fire.

Alongside the opening of her energy centres and cooperation with the Brotherhood, Roerich was also writing *Agni Yoga* in the Rays of the Lord of Shambhala. *Agni Yoga* essentially reflects her own path of transformation of all seven bodies, which now every aspirant can follow. The penning of the books occurred in the Ray of Knowledge with some projection in the Ray of Love-Wisdom. Every day was filled with intense creative activity: from morning until late at night she spent her time writing down conversations she had with her Teacher, preparing new books of the Teaching for publication, translating them, and maintaining extensive correspondence with numerous correspondents around the world, including President Franklin Roosevelt, who partially accepted the advice given by the Lord of Shambhala. However, far from all of her work was published in printed form. While her major work, describing all the effects of the Rays and her body's reaction to them during the Fiery Experience, is yet to be fully appreciated by humanity. In time, it will assist future scientists in making incredible discoveries.

Helena Roerich also translated *The Secret Doctrine* into Russian. This, to date, is the only correct translation of *The Secret Doctrine*, as it was carried out in the same Rays in which Helena Blavatsky worked. This work was necessary, not only because it was important for a translation of this fundamental masterpiece that synthesized all the previous Teachings of Light to become more widely available, but also because during the process of the translation work the energy currents of Blavatsky and Roerich could become united, albeit on an invisible level.

The main component of Roerich's Fiery Experience was the assimilation of new Rays coming from the Cosmos, as yet unknown to the planet. This Ray assimilation by the heart of a woman in a physical incarnation enabled the Teachers, like an experienced doctor testing new vaccines, to gradually inoculate the majority of humanity with their formula. This meant that in the future these energies would not produce unexpected alchemical reactions in the human body, and as a consequence in the planetary body, that would otherwise have caused catastrophes on a global scale. It is thanks to this sacrificial Heroic Deed that the Teachers succeeded in averting the devastating scenario predicted for the end of the twentieth century. Roerich's Experiment allowed the current generation of humanity to inhale the new fiery energies now enveloping the whole Earth almost painlessly, and to reduce the number of natural disasters to the minimum level permitted by the karma of humanity. Only the energy of Love, a high level of spirituality, enables one to absorb new energies. It should be noted, therefore, that it is the inability of humanity to fulfil the primary commandment given in all the Teachings of Light — to love — which causes disasters, including the planetary scale catastrophe that threatened the late twentieth century.

By the end of her life, Roerich had reached the highest level of spirituality and enlightenment possible on Earth. She laid the foundation for a new phase of human development. It is also thanks to the hearts which responded to the Call of the Lord of Shambhala, which has been resounding since 1920, that the Fire has been able to penetrate earthly spheres, become assimilated as a wider flow, and direct the destinies of entire continents along a positive course.

Helena Roerich foresaw that soon many beautiful mediators would appear on Earth who would assist in accelerating humanity's spiritual awakening: "In the New Era, there will be many so-called mediators; of course, these facilitators will be able to help shift human consciousness out of the deadlock of nay-saying" (28 April 1951).

A year prior to her passing, she made her circle aware that the Fiery Experience would be continued by the next disciple at the end of the twentieth century: "The foundations of the Fiery Experience must be passed on. Many will come close to it at the end of this century, and one of the Sisters of the Brotherhood will become my successor, carrying out Agni Yoga under new and, possibly, more favourable conditions" (10 October 1954).

Helena Roerich's experiment, like Helena Blavatsky's before it, enabled the Teachers to form qualitatively new matter for future colleagues of Shambhala who would incarnate on Earth.

The book *Heart* of the *Agni Yoga* series ends with a promise to give a second book about the Heart, and it also mentions the *Teaching of the Heart*, which is "so necessary for the life of the future," as being separate from *Agni Yoga*.

It is also interesting to note that in Helena Roerich's notebooks, revealed in 2018, it is said that the book *Supermundane* was not completed due to Nicholas Roerich's demise, and that hundreds of sections still had to be written down. Moreover, when preparing both the handwritten and typewritten versions of the book, Helena Roerich deliberately placed the number of the next section and then left a blank space. Consequently, it was made clear where exactly the continuation of Helena Roerich's mission by the next Sister should begin at the end of the twentieth century.

Fire. Not an element but a divine thing. The nature of Fire is eternal motion. The best definition of the Cosmos is the ceaseless movement of Fire in its endless patterns, in its continuous changing outlines manifested in Flames, and their endlessly changing manifestation.

The physical flame is the objective vehicle of the highest spirit. Everything in this world has an aura and a spirit. The flame that one applies to the candle wick has nothing to do with the candle itself. The aura of the object comes into conjunction with the lowest part of the Aether. The reason that granite cannot burn is because its aura is Fire.

The fire elementals are the highest among the elementals. They have no consciousness on this plane; they are too high for this, and reflect the divinity of their own source. Other elementals do have consciousness on this plane as they reflect man and his nature. There is a very great difference between the mineral and the vegetable kingdoms. The wick of the lamp, for instance, is negative. It is made positive by fire, the oil being the medium.

Aether is Fire. The lowest manifestation level of Aether is the flame which one can see. Fire is Divinity in its subjective presence throughout the Universe. Under other conditions, this Universal Fire manifests as water, air, and earth. It is the one element in our visible Universe which is the *kriya-shakti* of all forms of life. It is that which gives light, heat, death, life, etc. It is even the blood. In all its various manifestations it is essentially *one*.

It is the "seven Cosmocratores" (the Creative Forces personified). Evidence of the esteem in which Fire was held is to be found in the Old Testament: the Pillar of Fire, the Burning Bush, the Shining Face of Moses — all Fire. Fire is like a looking-glass in its nature, and reflects the beams of the first order of subjective manifestations which are supposed to be thrown on to the screen of the first outlines of the created Universe; in their lower aspect these are the creations of Fire.

In the grossest aspect of its essence, fire is the first form and reflects the lower forms of the first subjective beings in the Universe. The first divine chaotic thoughts are the fire elementals when on Earth they take form and come flitting in the flame in the form of the salamanders or lower fire elementals. In the air there are millions of living and conscious beings, besides human thoughts which they catch on to. The fire elementals are related to the sense of sight, and they absorb the elementals of all the other senses. Through sight one can have the consciousness of feeling, hearing, tasting, etc., since all are included in the sense of sight.

As time goes on, there will be more and more Aether in the air. In the nineteenth century, in Virginia, an apple tree of a special kind had already appeared: it did not bloom, but bore fruit from a kind of berry with no seeds. This phenomenon will gradually extend to animals, and then to human beings. When Aether fills the air, then will be born children without fathers. This will happen in the Seventh Round of Evolution. But even now, because of the gradual increase of Aether, or Fire, in the atmosphere, thanks to the currents of the invisible Spiritual Sun, the mystical Udumbara flower has started to appear around the world having no need for soil or any other of the normal conditions that it requires to reproduce.

Living Fire is a figure of speech used to denote the deity, the One Life. This theurgic term was used later by the Rosicrucians. The symbol of the living fire is the sun, whose rays develop the fire of life in a diseased body, impart knowledge of the future to the sluggish mind, and stimulate to active functioning a certain psychic and generally dormant faculty in man. The meaning is very occult.

Fire-philosophers. The name given to the Hermetists and alchemists of the Middle Ages, and also to the Rosicrucians. The latter, successors to the theurgists, regarded fire as a symbol of the Deity. It was not only the source of material atoms, but the container of the spiritual and psychic Forces that energize them. Broadly analysed, fire is a triple principle; esoterically, a septenary, as are all the other elements. As man is composed of spirit, soul, and body, plus a fourfold aspect, so is Fire. As in the works of Robert Fludd (de Fluctibus), one of the famous Rosicrucians, Fire contains: 1) a visible flame (body); 2) an invisible, astral fire (soul); and 3) spirit. The four aspects are heat (life), light (mind), electricity (*kamic*, or molecular powers), and the synthetic essence, *beyond* spirit, or the radical cause of its existence and manifestation. For the Hermetist or Rosicrucian, when a flame is extinct on the objective plane, it has only passed from the seen world into the unseen, from the knowable into the unknowable.

Five impediments or **five hindrances**. In Buddhism, obstacles on the path to enlightenment. These are: 1) attachment to sensory pleasures; 2) ill-will or negative emotions towards others; 3) laziness or lack of energy; 4) restlessness due to desires and worries; 5) scepticism or doubts about the teachings and the path.

Five virtues. Spiritual qualities leading to enlightenment: 1) faith; 2) making efforts to do good; 3) mindfulness; 4) mystic concentration; 5) wisdom or insight into the true nature of reality.

Fivefold source of Bodhi power. Powers obtained through practising the five virtues. In Buddhist texts, the five powers and the five virtues are the same. See *five virtues*.

Flammarion, Camille (1842–1925). A French astronomer and author, who wrote popular works on astronomy and explored the possibility of extraterrestrial life. He became an honorary member of the Theosophical Society in 1880.

Fludd, Robert (1574–1637). Generally known as Robertus de Fluctibus, the chief of the "philosophers by fire." A celebrated English Hermetist of the sixteenth century and a voluminous writer. He wrote on the essence of gold and other mystic and occult subjects.

Fo Xin (*Ch.*). The Buddha's heart.

Fohat (*Tib.*). A term used to represent the active (male) potency of the Shakti (female reproductive power) in Nature. The essence of cosmic electricity. An occult Tibetan term for *Daiviprakriti* (primordial light), and in the universe of manifestation, the ever-present electrical energy and ceaseless destructive and formative power. In esoteric terms, it is understood similarly, Fohat being the universal propelling vital Force, at once the propeller and the resultant.

Fontainebleau (*Fr.*, "spring of beautiful water"). A historic town in France, located south-east of Paris and surrounded by the scenic forest of the same name. It is home to a grand royal palace which belonged to French kings for a period of eight centuries.

Forster, E. M. (1879–1970). An English novelist, known for works like *A Room with a View* (1908), *Howards End* (1910), and *A Passage to India* (1924).

Fosdick, Sina (1889–1983). The director of the Nicholas Roerich Museum in New York City from 1949 to 1983; the most valuable colleague of Nicholas and Helena Roerich in America. She described meetings with them in a diary published as *My Teachers: Meetings with the Roerichs* (2015).

Four modes of Truth. See *Four Noble Truths*.

Four Noble Truths. Rendered in various ways, but can be summarized as follows: 1) all life is suffering; 2) the cause of suffering is desire; 3) liberation comes only through eradicating desires and passions; 4) the path to liberation is the Noble Eightfold Path (right understanding, right thought, right speech, right action, right livelihood, right effort, right concentration, and right mindfulness).

Four stages of the Path. Four grades of initiation mentioned in exoteric works: 1) "entering the stream" leading to Nirvana (Srotapatti); 2) one more birth (Sakridagamin); 3) no more reincarnation (Anagamin); 4) experiencing supreme enlightenment and bliss, or Nirvana, while living (Arhat). The Arhat, though he can see the past, the present, and the future, is not yet the highest Initiate; for the Adept himself, the initiated candidate, becomes chela (pupil) to a higher Initiate. Three further higher grades must be conquered by the Arhat who would reach the apex of the ladder of Arhatship.

Francis of Assisi (c.1181–1226). An Italian saint, mystic, and founder of the Franciscan order. Renowned for his love of Nature, simplicity, and devotion to poverty, he is the patron saint of animals and the environment. His life and teachings emphasize humility, peace, and caring for all creation.

G

Gandhi, Mohandas Karamchand (1869–1948). A leader of the Indian independence movement who promoted non-violent resistance and civil disobedience. His philosophy of non-violence inspired global movements for civil rights and social change.

In 1889, Gandhi met Blavatsky and later, in 1891, became an associate member of the Blavatsky Lodge in London. In his *Autobiography* (1927), he writes: "I recall having read, at the brothers' [direction] Madame Blavatsky's *Key to Theosophy*. This book stimulated in me the desire to read books on Hinduism, and disabused me of the notion fostered by the missionaries that Hinduism was rife with superstition." In 1894, he wrote in a letter to his friend: "I intend to spread as much as possible information about Theosophy. (To me there is little difference between Theosophy and Esoteric Christianity)."

Garbo, Greta (1905–1990). A Swedish-American actress, considered one of the greatest screen actresses of all time.

Garden of Eden (*Heb.*, "delight"). In Genesis, the "Garden of Delight" built by God; in

Kabbalah, a place of Initiation into the mysteries. This is the Biblical name of Shambhala as the cradle of the first human. See *Shambhala* for more.

Orientalists identify Eden with a place situated in ancient Babylonia in the district of Karduniyas, called also *Gan-dunu*, which is almost like the *Gan-eden* of the Jews. The district has four rivers: Euphrates, Tigris, Surappi, and Ukni. The names of the first two were adopted without change by the Jews; the other two were probably transformed into "Gihon and Pison," so as to use something original. Here follow some of the reasons for the identification of this area with Eden, as given by Assyriologists. The cities of Babylon, Larancha, and Sippara were founded before the flood, according to the chronology of the Jews. "Surippak was the city of the ark, the mountain east of the Tigris was the resting place of the ark, Babylon was the site of the tower, and Ur of the Chaldees the birthplace of Abraham." And, as Abraham, "the first leader of the Hebrew race, migrated from Ur to Harran in Syria and from thence to Palestine," the most prominent Assyriologists hold to the opinion that there is "so much evidence in favour of the hypothesis that Chaldea was the original home of these stories (in the Bible) and that the Jews received them originally from the Babylonians."

Garuda (*Sk.*, "devourer"). A gigantic half-eagle, half-man in the Ramayana, the steed of Vishnu; esoterically, the symbol of the great cycle.

Garuda Yantra (*Sk.*). A geometrical diagram (*yantra*) associated with Garuda.

Gathas (*Av.*, "hymns"). Hymns composed by Zoroaster (Zarathustra), forming the core texts of the Zoroastrian holy book, the Avesta. These Gathas are the oldest fragments of Zoroastrian literature known to the Parsis, for they are written in a special dialect, older than the language predominantly used in the Avesta.

Gauguin, Paul (1848–1903). A French painter, sculptor, and ceramist.

Gautama Buddha. The Prince of Kapilavastu, son of Suddhodana, the Shakya king of a small realm on the borders of Nepal, born in the seventh century BCE, now called the Saviour of the World. Born a simple mortal, he rose to Buddhaship through his own personal and unaided merit.

Siddharta was the name given to him at birth. It is an abbreviation of *sarvartthasiddha* and means, the "realization of all desires." Gautama or Gotama, which means, "on earth" (*gau*) "the most victorious" (*tama*), was the sacerdotal name of the Shakya family, the kingly patronymic of the dynasty to which the father of Gautama, the King Suddhodana of Kapilavastu, belonged. Kapilavastu was an ancient city, the birthplace of the great reformer and was destroyed during his lifetime. In the title *Shakyamuni*, the last component, *muni*, is rendered as meaning "one mighty in charity, isolation, and silence," and the former *Shakya* is the family name. Thus, Shakyamuni means "the saint of the Shakya family."

Every Orientalist knows by heart the story of Gautama Buddha, the most perfect of mortal humans the world has ever seen, but rarely does any suspect the esoteric meaning underlying his prenatal biography, i.e., the significance of the popular story. The *Lalitavistara Sutra* tells the tale, but abstains from hinting at the truth. The 5,000 *jatakas*, or the events of former births (reincarnations), are taken literally instead of esoterically. Gautama Buddha, would not have been a mortal man, had he not passed through hundreds and thousands of births previous to his last. Yet the detailed account of these, and the statement that during these lives he worked his way up through every stage of transmigration, from the lowest animate and inanimate atom and insect to the highest — or *man*, contains simply the well-known occult aphorism: "a stone becomes a plant, a plant an animal, and an animal a man." Every human being who has ever existed, has passed through the same process of evolution. But the hidden symbolism in the sequence of these rebirths (*jataka*) contains a perfect history of the evolution on this Earth, *pre* and *post* human, and is a scientific exposition of natural facts.

One truth, not veiled but bare and open, can be found in their nomenclature, namely, that as soon as Gautama had reached the human form he began exhibiting in every personality the utmost expression of generosity, self-sacrifice, and love. Buddha Gautama, the fourth of the Sapta (Seven) Buddhas and Sapta Tathagatas was born according to Chinese Chronology in 1024 BCE, but according to the Sinhalese chronicles, on the eighth day of the second (or fourth) moon in the year 621 before our era. He fled from his father's palace to become an ascetic on the night of the eighth day of the second moon, 597 BCE, and having passed six years in ascetic meditation at Gaya, and perceiving that physical self-torture was useless to achieve enlightenment, he decided to strike out on a new path until he reached the state of Bodhi. He became a full Buddha on the night of the eighth day of the twelfth moon, in the year 592, and according to Southern Buddhism finally entered Nirvana in the year 543.

The Orientalists, however, have decided upon several other dates. All the rest of his biography is allegorical. He attained the state of Bodhisattva on Earth when embodying the personality called Prabhapala. Tushita stands for a place on this globe, not for a paradise in the invisible regions. The selection of the Shakya family and his mother Maya, as "the purest on earth," is in accordance with the model of the nativity of every Saviour, God, or deified reformer. The tale about his entering his mother's bosom in the shape of a white elephant is an allusion to his innate wisdom, the white elephant being a symbol of every Bodhisattva. The statements that at Gautama's birth, the newly born babe walked *seven steps* in four directions, that an *Udumbara* flower bloomed in all its rare beauty, and that the Naga kings forthwith proceeded "to baptize him," are all allegories in the phraseology of the Initiates, their meaning accessible to every Eastern occultist. All the events of his noble life are given in occult numbers, and every so-called *miraculous* event — so deplored by Orientalists as confusing the narrative and making it impossible to extricate truth from fiction — is simply the allegorical veiling of the truth, and as comprehensible to an occultist learned in symbolism, as it is difficult to understand for a European scholar ignorant of occultism. Every detail of the narrative after his death and prior to cremation is a chapter of *facts* written in a language which must be studied before it can be understood, otherwise, taken literally, it will lead one to assume absurd contradictions.

For instance, having reminded his disciples of the immortality of Dharmakaya, Buddha is said to have passed into *samadhi* and become lost in Nirvana — *from which none can return*, and yet, notwithstanding this, the Buddha is shown bursting open the lid of the coffin, and stepping out of it, saluting with folded hands his mother, Maya, who suddenly appears in the air, despite having died seven days after his birth, etc.

As Buddha was a Chakravartin (*Sk.*, "one who turns the wheel of the Law"), his body at cremation could not be consumed by common fire. What happened? Suddenly a jet of flame *burst out of the swastika on his breast* and reduced his body to ashes. It is beyond the scope of this note to cite further instances. As to his being one of the true and undeniable Saviours of the World, suffice to say that the most rabid orthodox missionary, unless he is hopelessly insane, or has not the least regard for historical truth, would fail in finding the smallest accusation against the life and personal character of Gautama Buddha. Without any claim to divinity, allowing his followers to fall into atheism, rather than into the degrading superstition of deva or idol worship, his walk in life is, from beginning to end, holy and divine. During the 45 years of his mission, it is as blameless and pure as that of a god — or as the latter should be. He is a perfect example of a divine, godly man. He reached Buddhaship, i.e., complete enlightenment entirely by his own merit and his own individual exertions, although no god is thought to have any personal merit in the exercise of goodness and holiness.

Esoteric teachings claim that he renounced Nirvana and gave up the Dharmakaya vesture to remain a Buddha of Compassion within the reach of the miseries of this world. And the religious philosophy he left to it has for over two thousand years produced generations of good and unselfish beings. His is the only *absolutely bloodless* religion among all the existing religions. It is tolerant and liberal, teaching universal compassion and charity, love and self-sacrifice, poverty and contentment with one's lot, whatever it may be. It has never been disgraced by conducting persecution or the enforcement of the faith by fire and sword. No thunder-and-lightning-vomiting god has interfered with its chaste commandments; and if the simple, humane, and philosophical code of daily life that was left to us by the greatest reformer ever known, should ever come to be adopted by humankind at large, then, indeed, an era of bliss and peace would dawn upon humanity.

Gautama Rishi. A sage, also known as Aksapada and Dirghatapas, who founded the Nyaya school.

Gelong (*Tib.*, "one who adopts virtue"). A fully ordained monk in Tibetan Buddhism who has taken the full set of monastic vows according to the Vinaya, the Buddhist canon containing the rules and precepts for monastic communities.

Gelug (*Tib.*, "virtuous"). The highest and most orthodox school of Tibetan Buddhism, the antithesis of the Dugpa ("red caps"), the old "devil worshippers."

Gelugpa (*Tib.*). The followers of the Gelug school.

Genghis Khan (c.1162–1227). The founder and first Great Khan of the Mongol Empire, which became the largest contiguous empire in history. He unified nomadic tribes and established a legacy of conquest, cultural exchange, and governance.

Genii. A name for Aeons, or angels, among the Gnostics. The names of angelic hierarchies and classes are simply legion.

Geshe (*Tib.*, "virtuous friend"). A scholarly degree in Tibetan Buddhism for monks and nuns, equivalent to a doctorate in Buddhist philosophy, typically conferred after rigorous study that usually takes more than twenty years to complete.

Getsul (*Tib.*, "one who is training in virtuous conduct"). A novice monk in Tibetan Buddhism. Getsuls take preliminary vows and undergo training before becoming fully ordained as *gelongs*.

Ghoom Monastery. One of the oldest Tibetan monasteries in Darjeeling, India, also known as Yiga Choeling and referred to as Old Ghoom Monastery to distinguish it from a newer temple in the same area. Founded in 1850 at an elevation of 2,400 metres and located eight kilometres from Darjeeling, it is famous for its large statue of Maitreya Buddha.

Ghose, Aurobindo (1872–1950). An Indian philosopher, yogi, poet, and nationalist who advocated for spiritual evolution through Integral Yoga. He believed in the transformation of human consciousness towards divine realization and social harmony.

Gibran, Kahlil (1883–1931). A Lebanese-American poet, philosopher, and artist, best known for his book *The Prophet* (1923), which combines spiritual and philosophical reflections on topics such as love, joy, and sorrow.

Gita (*Sk.*, "song"). Refers to the Bhagavad Gita, a 700-verse Hindu scripture that is part of the Mahabharata. It is a conversation between Prince Arjuna and the god Krishna discussing duty, righteousness, and devotion.

Glagolitic alphabet. The oldest known Slavic alphabet, created in the ninth century by Saints Cyril and Methodius to translate the

Bible and other texts into Old Church Slavonic, the liturgical language of the Slavic peoples.

Gnosis (*Gr.*, "knowledge"). The technical term used by the schools of religious philosophy, both before and during the first centuries of Christianity, to denote the object of their enquiry. This spiritual and sacred knowledge, the *Gupta-Vidya* of the Hindus, could only be obtained by Initiation into Spiritual Mysteries of which the ceremonial Mysteries were a type.

Gnostics. The philosophers who formulated and taught the Gnosis. They flourished in the first three centuries of the Christian era. Eminent Gnostics include Valentinus, Basilides, Marcion, and Simon Magus.

Gnyana (*Tel.*, "knowledge"). Knowledge as applied to the esoteric sciences; the same as *jnana* in Sanskrit or *dnyan* in Marathi.

Göbekli Tepe. An ancient archaeological site in south-eastern Turkey. It is considered the world's oldest known temple complex, featuring huge stone pillars arranged in circular formations.

Gobi (*Mon.*, "waterless place"). A large desert in Central Asia where the ethereal Abode of Sanat Kumara is located.

God. The Divine, Unchangeable, Invariable, and Infinite Principle; the eternally Unknowable Cause of All that exists; the omnipresent, all-pervading, visible and invisible spiritual Nature, which exists everywhere, in which everything lives, moves, and has its being; the Absolute, including the potential of all things as well as all universal manifestations. Upon being made manifest, out of its Absolute Oneness, God becomes the Absolute of infinite differentiation and its consequences — relativity and polarities. God has no gender and cannot be imagined as a human being. In the holy scriptures, God is Fire, God is Love — the one primeval energy that conceives the worlds.

Where this notion does not refer to the above, in ancient Teachings it has always denoted the totality of the working and intelligent forces of Nature. Thus, the world is ruled by the Creative Forces of the Cosmos, together constituting the limitless Hierarchy of Light, which, in the Bible, is represented as Jacob's Ladder.

However, the Great Unknown was, is, and always will be hidden from the eyes of those who live in the manifested world. The Primal Cause, the Absolute, has been and will be unknowable — forever and always.

The traditional Christian concept of *God* refers to the Planetary Spirit or *Demiurge* (*Gr.*, "creator") — the Supreme Lord or Ruler of Earth, who has lived out His human evolution and reached an unparalleled level of spiritual development. Together with other High Spirits that constitute the Hierarchy of Light, He is now responsible for the creation, preservation, and transfiguration of Earth.

The Planetary Spirit is androgynous because there is no gender separation on the higher planes of Existence, hence, the pronoun *He* is used merely for lack of a more appropriate one. The Planetary Spirit can manifest in various Aspects and Hypostases, including male and female in the binary world since He bears within Himself both Principles.

As a rule, the governing Hierarchy of Light for young planets, such as Earth, consists of High Spirits that originated in Distant Worlds, where they long ago completed the stage of Evolution now being faced by Earth. When humanity on any given planet reaches spiritual maturity, the Lords of Light, who arrived there from other Worlds, leave and are replaced by the worthy High Spirits who have completed their evolution on this, their native young planet.

From ancient sacred texts, it is evident that the Planetary Spirit of Earth is the Lord of Sirius. Even the Quran states that Allah is the Lord of Sirius. However, it should be borne in mind that the God described in the Old Testament is not the same as the Supreme Lord of Earth whom Christ calls His Father in the New Testament.

Sometimes He who is denoted by the name *the One and Only*, forms simultaneously several of His own Hypostases, as well as Individualities (under different names), and one that possesses a higher energy component serves another (we might even say, Himself) as a Master, Teacher, and Protector — either in the physical world or in the Ethereal, depending on the single goal that is set before His "emanating forms."

Gods. The Spirits of the Higher Spheres, Distant Worlds, who have succeeded in achieving a high level of evolution, far surpassing the level of earthly humanity that led to people beginning to perceive them as Gods. In other words, this level of spiritual achievement is destined for humanity as well.

In Tibet, such a Spirit is denoted by the ancient word *Lha* (*Tib.*, "spirit," "god"), which covers the entire series of celestial Hierarchies. Every supreme concept of the Cosmos is personified in a High Spirit, that also takes a human form. That is why every ancient religion has a pantheon of Gods, each of whom, being an embodiment of a certain Idea, represents a particular Force of Nature.

The Sons of God, the Sons of Light, the Sons of Heaven, the Sons of Fire, the Sons of Reason, the Archangels, the Regents of Planets, the Masters of Wisdom, the Bodhisattvas, the Dhyan Chohans, the Rishis, the Kumaras, and so on — all these are High Spirits, who, like the Avatars, assumed a human appearance to raise the consciousness of humanity and accelerate its development.

The Seven Great Spirits have taken care of the planet Earth and its humanity. Again and again, they have incarnated as the great founders of kingdoms, religions, sciences, and philosophies in order to help people unite with their divine nature. And so they have left deep traces in every domain of life and in every land. Up to the present time, each has educated disciples who have reached a high level of consciousness, and the number of the Leaders of Humanity is now 777.

For example, included among the known incarnations of the Brothers of Humanity on Earth are the following:

- Aeschylus (Greek dramatist)
- Akbar the Great (Mughal emperor)
- Alexander I (Russian emperor)
- Amenhotep IV (pharaoh of Egypt)
- Ammonius Saccas (Greek philosopher)
- Amos (Jewish prophet)
- Ananda (favourite disciple of Gautama Buddha)
- Anaxagoras (Greek philosopher)
- Apollonius of Tyana (Greek philosopher and mystic)
- Arthur (legendary British king)
- Aryasanga (founder of the Yogachara school)
- Ashoka the Great (Mauryan emperor)
- Ashvaghosha (Indian philosopher)
- Atisha (Bengali teacher)
- Chandragupta Maurya (Mauryan emperor)
- Charlemagne (king of the Franks)
- Christian Rosenkreuz (founder of the Order of Rosicrucians)
- Clovis I (king of the Franks)
- Confucius (Chinese philosopher)
- Constantine the Great (Roman emperor)
- Count of Saint-Germain (French polymath)
- Dante Alighieri (Italian poet and philosopher)
- Domo Geshe Rinpoche Ngawang Kalsang (Tibetan teacher)
- Dushyanta (king of Hastinapur)
- Empedocles (Greek philosopher)
- Erik the Red (Norse explorer)
- Francis of Assisi (Italian saint and mystic)
- Galileo Galilei (Italian scientist)
- Gautama Buddha (Great Teacher, founder of Buddhism)
- Gavrila Derzhavin (Russian poet)
- Giordano Bruno (Italian philosopher, mathematician, and astronomer)
- Heraclitus (Greek philosopher)
- Ivan the Great (grand prince of Moscow)
- Jakob Böhme (German mystic and theologian)
- Jesus Christ (Great Teacher)
- Johann Sebastian Bach (German composer and musician)
- John the Apostle (beloved disciple of Christ)
- Joseph (father of Jesus)
- Joseph, son of Jacob (Jewish prophet)
- Joshua (successor of Moses)
- Kanada (Indian philosopher)
- Kapila (Vedic sage)
- Krishna (Hindu Saviour)
- Lao Tzu (Chinese philosopher)
- Leonardo da Vinci (Italian artist)
- Lobsang Palden Yeshe (sixth Panchen Lama of Tibet)
- Louis IX (king of France)
- Louis XIV (king of France)
- Luke of Simferopol (Russian saint and surgeon)
- Lycurgus (law-giver of Sparta)
- Mani (Iranian prophet and founder of Manichaeism)
- Marcus Aurelius (Roman emperor and philosopher)
- Melchizedek (high priest-king)
- Menes (pharaoh of Egypt)
- Mikhail Lomonosov (Russian scientist)
- Milarepa (Tibetan yogi and poet)
- Moses (prophet and law-giver)
- Moses de León (Jewish rabbi, compiler of the *Zohar*)
- Muhammad (prophet and founder of Islam)
- Nagarjuna (Indian teacher and philosopher)
- Ngawang Lobsang Gyatso (fifth Dalai Lama of Tibet)
- Nicholas Roerich (Russian artist)
- Nicolaus Copernicus (Polish scientist)
- Nikolay Novikov (Russian philanthropist and educator)
- Nostradamus (French astrologer and physician)
- Numa Pompilius (king of Rome)
- Origen (Greek Christian theologian)
- Orpheus (Greek musician and poet)
- Padmasambhava (Indian teacher whose teachings were later distorted)
- Pantaleon (Greek saint and physician)
- Paracelsus (Swiss physician and philosopher)
- Patanjali (Indian philosopher and mystic)
- Paul the Apostle (early Christian missionary)
- Pericles (Greek statesman)
- Peter Abelard (French philosopher)
- Plato (Greek philosopher)
- Plotinus (Greek philosopher)
- Pythagoras (Greek mathematician and philosopher)
- Rama (legendary Indian king)
- Ramakrishna (Indian mystic and saint)
- Ramesses the Great (pharaoh of Egypt)
- Rurik (grand prince of Novgorod)
- Sathya Sai Baba (Indian saint)
- Seneca (Roman philosopher)
- Seraphim of Sarov (Russian saint)
- Sergius of Radonezh (Russian saint)
- Shankaracharya (Indian philosopher)
- Shimon ben Yochai (Jewish rabbi, author of the *Zohar*)
- Socrates (Greek philosopher)
- Solomon (king of Israel)
- Taras Shevchenko (Ukrainian poet)
- Thales of Miletus (Greek philosopher)
- Thomas of Kempis (German monk and mystic)
- Thomas Vaughan (Welsh philosopher)
- Thutmose III (pharaoh of Egypt)
- Tsongkhapa (Tibetan Buddhist reformer)
- Tutankhamun (pharaoh of Egypt)
- Valmiki (Indian poet and author of the Ramayana)
- Virgil (Roman poet)
- Vivekananda (disciple of Ramakrishna)
- Volodymyr II Monomakh (grand prince of Kyiv)
- Vyasas (authors of the Vedas, the Puranas, and the Mahabharata)

- William Shakespeare (English playwright and poet)
- Yaroslav the Wise (grand prince of Kyiv)
- Zoroaster (prophet, founder of Zoroastrianism)

And here are some of the incarnations of the Sisters, to pay tribute to their inspiring lives and deeds:
- Alaila (wife of Zoroaster)
- Alexandra Bryachislavna (princess of Polotsk and Novgorod)
- Alexandra David-Néel (French traveller)
- Amina bint Wahb (mother of Muhammad)
- Anandamayi Ma (Indian saint and mystic)
- Asenath (mother of two tribes of Israel)
- Aspasia (Greek philosopher who made Athens the cultural centre of Greece, teacher of Socrates)
- Catherine of Siena (Italian saint, mystic, first woman to preach in the church)
- Clare of Assisi (Italian saint who founded the female monastic order)
- Clotilde (queen of the Franks)
- Devaki (mother of Krishna)
- Dositheya of Kyiv (Orthodox saint who pretended to be a man to become a monk)
- Durdhara (Mauryan empress)
- Efanda (princess of Norway and Novgorod)
- Elisabeth Kulmann (Russian poetess)
- Elizabeth I (queen of England who raised the country to a new level)
- Eurydice (Orpheus' beloved who together with him developed the cult of music)
- Francesca da Rimini (Italian noblewoman of Ravenna)
- Francia La Due (founder of the Temple of the People)
- Françoise d'Aubigné (founder of Europe's first boarding school for girls)
- Gytha of Wessex (princess of England and Kyiv)
- Hatshepsut (female pharaoh of Egypt who implemented many good reforms)
- Helena Blavatsky (author of *The Secret Doctrine*)
- Helena Roerich (author of the *Agni Yoga* series)
- Hildegard (queen of the Franks)
- Hypatia (Greek philosopher, astronomer, and mathematician)
- Ingegerd Olofsdotter (princess of Sweden and Kyiv)
- Joan of Arc (liberator of France)
- Khadija (first wife of Muhammad, Mother of the Believers)
- Layla (her tragic love with Majnun had a huge impact on the culture of the Middle East)
- Mariam-uz-Zamani (Mughal empress)
- Marie Curie-Sklodowska (Polish chemist and physicist, first female Nobel laureate)
- Marie of Anjou (queen of France)
- Mary (mother of Jesus)
- Mary Magdalene (disciple of Christ without whom there would have been no memory of Him)
- Maya (mother of Gautama Buddha)
- Mother Teresa (Catholic saint and founder of the Missionaries of Charity)
- Nefertiti (queen of Egypt)
- Olga (first female ruler of Kyivan Rus')
- Roxelana (Ukrainian slave who became one of the most powerful women in Ottoman history)
- Rukmini (wife of Krishna)
- Sappho (Greek poetess and musician)
- Shakuntala (Indian heroine, queen of Hastinapura)
- Shulamith (Solomon's beloved who inspired the Song of Songs)
- Sita (wife of Rama)
- Sofya Kovalevskaya (Russian mathematician, first female professor of mathematics)
- Sophia Palaiologina (princess of Byzantium and Moscow)
- Teresa of Ávila (Spanish saint, religious reformer, and mystic)
- Thjodhild Jorundsdottir (wife of Erik the Red)
- Tiye (queen of Egypt)
- Yashodhara (wife of Gautama Buddha, female Arhat)
- Zenobia Septimia (queen of Palmyra)

Thus, the Gods, or High Spirits, who assume human form, appear among humanity to foster progress in various domains of life.

Golden Rule. An ethical principle of treating others as one would like to be treated. Variants of the Golden Rule appear in many religious and philosophical traditions.

Gonpa (*Tib.*, "remote place"). A Buddhist temple or monastery; a lamasery.

Gotrabhu-nana (*Pali*, "change-of-lineage knowledge"). Maturity-knowledge; knowledge of deliverance from worldly conditions; knowledge received at the moment of a change of lineage which occurs in the moment that an ordinary person becomes a Noble One.

Govinda, Anagarika (1898–1985). A German-born Buddhist scholar, philosopher, mystic, poet, and artist, who became a prominent figure in spreading Tibetan Buddhism to the West; a disciple of Domo Geshe Rinpoche Ngawang Kalsang. He founded the order of the Arya Maitreya Mandala in 1933, inspired by his teacher who saw the future Buddha Maitreya as a model for modern spirituality. His most well-known books are *The Way of the White Clouds* (1966) and *Foundations of Tibetan Mysticism* (1957). His painting style is often compared to the works of Nicholas Roerich.

Great Lord of Shambhala. The Solar Hierarch that stands at the head of the Solar System's Hierarchy of Light; the Creator, Preserver, and Transfigurer of the Solar System; the Teacher of Teachers, the Lord of the World, the Lord of Civilization, the Lord of the White Flame, the Holder of the Wheel of the Law; the Prime Mover of humanity's evolution on Earth and everything that exists in the Solar System.

It should also be borne in mind that the Solar Hierarch has a Father — the Stellar Hierarch, the Planetary Spirit, and the Lord of Sirius, who on Earth is known as Sanat Kumara in the Puranas, as well as the Ancient of Days in the Bible. The Father can manifest Himself in the Son, and therefore, the Son may bear the same names.

Occupying a predominant position in the Solar System, the Solar Hierarch is also manifested under certain names, which can be both known and unknown, in the role of the Heads of the Hierarchical structures on each of the individual planets of the Solar System. Only one who ascends the rungs of Initiation can be endowed with more extensive knowledge of the vital activity, as well as the Ray manifestations and Emanations of the Solar Hierarch.

Many times He has incarnated among Earth-dwellers, each time under a different name, amid a different people and race, and in a different era of the planet's history. But His essence has remained forever unchanged, and His goal is always the same: to uplift humanity to the next stage of spirit. Whatever earthly garments He donned, they could not veil His Light, and those unable to withstand His mighty empyreal fires reacted furiously with persecution, torture, and killings. The long-suffering Lord, the "Great Sacrifice," bore the burden of Earth on His shoulders.

The Solar Hierarch is the Head of Shambhala and reigns together with the Seven Kumaras — the Great Teachers, or the Masters of Wisdom, who personify the Seven Rays. Each era must be permeated with the energies of a particular Ray in whose Light the next stage of planetary evolution develops. And, so, for each period of time He designates one of the Mahatmas as the Ruler of Shambhala, who bears the titles of Maha Chohan (*Sk.*, "Great Lord"), Rigden (*Tib.*, "holder of the lineage"), and Kalki (*Sk.*, "destroyer of ignorance"). And the current time is referred to as the Era of the Heart, which is to bring about a Synthesis of all Seven Rays.

In 1924, Mahatma Serapis was replaced by Mahatma Morya in this critical position. The Master of Helena Blavatsky and Helena Roerich became the Great Lord of Shambhala, changing His name to Maitreya, for each era requires an affirmation of the power in a particular name. This Great Lord is the King of Shambhala known as Rigden Dragpo Khorlocan (*Tib.*, "wielder of the iron wheel") and Kalki Rudra Chakrin (*Sk.*, "forceful wheel holder"), under whose reign, according to legend, the Great Battle of Armageddon was to be fought between the forces of Good (the Warriors of Shambhala) and the forces of evil. Master M. is the bearer of all Rays, who brings the synthesis of all the energies given to the world throughout the history of human civilization. He is the highest among the Seven Kumaras (or Gods), who, coming from the Distant Worlds, were responsible for the evolution of planet Earth. In other words, the Lord Morya and the Solar Hierarch constitute One Individuality, made manifest in both earthly and Heavenly forms.

The Puranas and other sacred texts state that it is from Shambhala, the City of Gods, that the Kalki Avatar would emerge to establish the Golden Age on Earth. The present Great King of Shambhala is the Messiah promised by all world religions: Christ of Christianity, Maitreya of Buddhism, Mahdi of Islam, Kalki of Hinduism, the Messiah of Judaism, Saoshyant of Zoroastrianism, Li Hong of Taoism, and so on.

Grünwedel, Albert (1856–1935). A German orientalist, archaeologist, and explorer known for his work on Central Asian Buddhist art and Himalayan languages. He translated the famous book by the Sixth Panchen Lama, Palden Yeshe, which he wrote in 1775, describing in great detail how to enter the Kingdom of Shambhala. The translation from Tibetan into German was published in 1915 as *Der Weg nach Sambhala* and later translated from German into English as *The Journey to Shambhala* by His Eminence the Twenty-fifth Tsem Rinpoche (1965–2019).

Guanshiyin or **Kwan-shi-yin** (*Ch.*, "one who perceives the sounds of the world"). The male logos of the Northern Buddhists and those of China; the "manifested god"; one of the Great Bodhisattvas, representing supreme compassion; the equivalent of the Sanskrit *Avalokiteshvara*, and as such, an androgynous deity.

Guanyin or **Kwan-yin** (*Ch.*, "one who perceives sounds"). The female logos, Mother of Mercy; the female aspect of Guanshiyin called the *Divine Voice*.

Guardian Wall. A suggestive name given to the host of translated Adepts or the saints collectively, who watch over, help, and protect humanity.

Guha (*Sk.*, "one who dwells in the cave"). Another name for Sanat Kumara in Hinduism, along with Kartikeya and Skanda.

Guhya (*Sk.*). Concealed, secret.

Guhya-Vidya (*Sk.*). The secret knowledge of mystic mantras.

Gunas (*Sk.*, "qualities"). In Hindu philosophy, the three divisions of the inherent qualities of differentiated matter: pure quiescence (*sattva*), activity and desire (*rajas*), stagnation and decay (*tamas*). These qualities correspond to the deities Vishnu, Brahma, and Shiva.

Gupta-Vidya (*Sk.*). The same as *Guhya-Vidya*; esoteric or secret science; knowledge.

Guru (*Sk.*, "teacher"). A spiritual teacher; a master in metaphysical and ethical doctrines; used also for a teacher of a science.

Gushi Khan (1582–1655). A leader of the Khoshut Mongols who played a key role in Tibetan history. He supported the Fifth Dalai Lama, defeated rival factions, and established the Khoshut Khanate, ensuring Gelugpa dominance in Tibet.

H

Hagia Sophia (*Gr.*, "holy wisdom"). A former sixth-century Christian cathedral in Istanbul, Turkey, converted into the Grand Mosque in 1453.

Hamlet. The Prince of Denmark in William Shakespeare's tragedy of the same name.

Hamsa (*Sk.*, "swan"). A mystical bird, often identified with the Supreme Spirit in Hinduism.

Hardy, Robert Spence (1803–1868). A British orientalist and a Methodist missionary in Sri Lanka; author of articles and books about Buddhism.

Harishchandra. A legendary king in the Hindu scriptures. To fulfil a promise he had made to the sage Vishvamitra, he first renounced his kingdom and then his wife and children. However, it later turned out that this was a test, and the gods, pleased with the high morality of the king, returned him to his former glory and granted him divine blessing.

Harrison, Vernon, PhD (1912–2001). A British researcher, physicist, and photographer, long-time member of the Society for Psychical Research, president of the Royal Photographic Society, and co-founder of the Association for the Scientific Study of Anomalous Phenomena.

Harrison is best known for his re-examination of the infamous Hodgson Report, which denounced Blavatsky as an impostor and which is often quoted in encyclopaedias, reference books, and biographical works. Using his expertise in forgery detection and photographic analysis, Harrison challenged the conclusions of the original report, arguing that Blavatsky had been misrepresented and that the evidence against her was flawed. He found the Hodgson Report to be "riddled with slanted statements, conjectures advanced as fact or probable fact, uncorroborated testimony of unnamed witnesses, selection of evidence and downright falsity."

Harrison's work helped to spark renewed interest and dialogue on the validity of Blavatsky's contributions to esoteric thought, as well as the role of rigorous analysis in psychical research.

Hartmann, Franz (1838–1912). A German medical doctor, Theosophist, astrologer, traveller, and author.

Because of Helena Blavatsky's letters to William Q. Judge and A. P. Sinnett in 1885, it is believed that Hartmann was always hostile towards her.

However, in April 1886, she wrote to him: "[Olcott] was led on blindly by people as blind as himself to see you in quite a false light, and there was a time, for a month or two, when I myself — notwithstanding my inner voice, and to the day [that] Master's voice told me I was mistaken in you and had to keep friends — shared his blindness."

This letter was published in Judge's magazine, *The Path*, in 1896. According to Boris de Zirkoff, Blavatsky's relative and researcher of her heritage, "In spite of many radical changes in his attitude, [Hartmann] can be said to have remained true to H.P.B."

The evidence that they had reconciled is that Hartmann respectfully dedicated his book, *Magic, White and Black* (1886), to "the genius of Helena Petrovna Blavatsky, the martyr of a great cause and defender of the rights of humanity," while Blavatsky refers to his work in the first volume of *The Secret Doctrine* (1888): "[Paracelsus'] ideas are admirably synthesized by Dr. F. Hartmann, F.T.S. [Fellow of the Theosophical Society], in his *Life of Paracelsus*."

In 1892, Hartmann translated *The Voice of the Silence* and later organized the translation of *The Secret Doctrine* into German. He supported William Q. Judge when the split in the Society took place.

Hartmann first met Blavatsky at Adyar, India, in 1883. When she left India for Europe, he was with her in Italy — at Naples and at Torre del Greco in 1885. After Blavatsky moved to Würzburg (Bavaria, Germany), Hartmann *repeatedly* visited her there in 1886 until she moved to Belgium later that year. Then they also met in London.

It is during the meetings in Germany that he received her manuscripts for further publication. He released them in 1887 as *An Adventure Among the Rosicrucians* under the pseudonym "A Student of Occultism." In 1890 and 1893, the book was reprinted in Boston with his own name indicated as the author.

In 1910, Hartmann republished the book under a new title: *With the Adepts*. However, in his preface, he acknowledged that he was not its original author, but that it "has been gathered from notes handed to me by a friend, a writer of considerable repute."

In 1939, Helena Roerich said about the book: "This account of the inner life of the Brotherhood was undoubtedly recorded by Franz Hartmann from the words of H. P. Blavatsky, conveyed with some changes in literary form" (19 December 1939).

Moreover, de Zirkoff mentions that Hartmann's first book, *Magic, White and Black*, is "the result of discussions with H. P. Blavatsky while Dr. Hartmann was at Adyar." Why then could his third book not be a compilation of her notes?

Another example of the appropriation of Blavatsky's words, although with her permission, is William Q. Judge who published in his magazine, *The Path*, during the period 1888 to 1895, a series of articles entitled "Conversations on Occultism" (that take place between a Sage and a Student) without indicating that the Sage was in fact Blavatsky. These articles were included by de Zirkoff in her *Collected Writings*. Nonetheless, any person unfamiliar with anything theosophical and coming across them online would assume that the Sage answering the Student's questions was in fact Judge.

Whether the individuals who surrounded Blavatsky acknowledged it or not, all their knowledge and mystical experiences came from and thanks to her alone. Their names would have remained unknown to this day had they not been connected to her.

Some people suggest that this "friend, a writer of considerable repute" might have been Carl du Prel (1839–1899), a German philosopher. Du Prel did have a long friendship with a Hartmann, but the Hartmann in question was Eduard von Hartmann, not Franz Hartmann.

In 1884, Blavatsky spoke very highly of du Prel after becoming familiar with his German publications: "One is tempted to ask himself in wonder: 'Is Baron du Prel, a disciple — a

European chela of our Himalayan sages that his thoughts should seem, so to say, photographed from their (and our) doctrines!' Truly the author of the work reviewed is a born Theosophist — or shall we say occultist? At any rate, here we have one more profound and unprejudiced thinker. May our present race evolute many more such philosophers for the greater glory of Truth!"

Du Prel joined the Theosophical Society in Germany in 1884, yet left it two years later, when Blavatsky was under attack of never-ending criticism. Despite being a prolific writer, his name is almost unknown in the English-speaking world, because, to date, only one of his numerous works has been translated. Even in Blavatsky's time, he was unknown outside Germany and Austria, except to those who could read in German. This is why du Prel could not have been the "writer of considerable repute" to whom Hartmann referred, as *With the Adepts* was intended for an English-speaking audience.

It seems Hartmann does add a fact to support the suggestion that du Prel might have been the true author of *An Adventure Among the Rosicrucians*. Thus, in the preface to the German translation published in 1899, he says that it expresses in a theosophical way the ideas that Carl du Prel expounded in his book, *Das weltliche Kloster* [The Secular Monastery]. But he makes an error when citing the year of publication, stating that the English original was published in 1893, instead of 1887. And if Hartmann had mentioned du Prel's name in 1899, what reason would he have not to credit him in 1910?

Das weltliche Kloster is a 30-page book that was published in Leipzig. The matter of the year of its release is confusing, since the cover bears the year 1888, while the title page states 1887. It may therefore have been published after *An Adventure Among the Rosicrucians*, which was printed and reviewed by Blavatsky herself in October 1887: "A strange and original little story, charmingly fantastic, but full of poetic feeling and, what is more, of deep philosophical and occult truths, for those who can perceive the ground-work it is built upon."

Das weltliche Kloster and *An Adventure Among the Rosicrucians* share the same idea: that somewhere in the mountains are hidden Abodes of spiritually advanced people — the Adepts. However, this idea was nothing new at the time, and especially so after Blavatsky appeared in the West in 1875. For instance, a century earlier, the German mystic Karl von Eckartshausen wrote about an isolated Island that cannot be detected, but from which messengers are sent out into the world to spread Divine Wisdom. Also, lamas in Tibet have always considered the space of dreams to be the most common way of gaining access to the Abodes of Shambhala.

Therefore, it cannot be said that Hartmann introduced du Prel's ideas about the existence of such places to the English-speaking world; if any one individual is to be credited for the revival of this idea in the nineteenth century, then, it is unquestionably Blavatsky.

Du Prel's book actually mentions 17 such places in Europe alone, but in his narrative the individuals who abide there do not call themselves the Rosicrucians. The plot involves his meeting the abbot of a monastery located in the Alps. The abbot briefly describes their way of life, then du Prel meets a Brother from India, and then he wakes up, realizing that he had fallen asleep and it was all a dream.

On the other hand, the plot of *An Adventure Among the Rosicrucians* differs significantly: the narrator meets someone called the Imperator, visits a monastery, has conversations with the Brothers and Sisters, enters the alchemical laboratory, and participates in a magical experiment before waking up.

Another distinction is that du Prel's monastery seems to be full of disciples, while the Abode described in *An Adventure Among the Rosicrucians* has very few dwellers. This means that the latter Abode was of a higher degree, and one to which a newcomer would have been admitted rarely. Therefore, *An Adventure Among the Rosicrucians* could not have been based on du Prel's experience that was clearly very different.

Furthermore, the book throughout its pages contains theosophical teachings, similarly to Blavatsky's *From the Caves and Jungles of Hindostan* that ends with the promise that it is to be continued. It is known that she reused her Master's conversation with other people that occurs in this work, originally written in Russian, and later published it as an article, "Dialogue on the Mysteries of the After Life," and then as part of *The Key to Theosophy* (1889).

Another thing to consider is that *An Adventure Among the Rosicrucians* was originally written in English. The title page of *With the Adepts* states that it was translated from German, and yet the text is identical to the original English edition published in 1887, with the exception of minor spelling corrections as well as some omissions and additions.

It seems that du Prel did not know English well. Otherwise, he would have taken advantage of his knowledge and found a way to publish books or articles in English. If one assumes that the notes originated with du Prel, then they must have been written in German. If this were the case, then how is one to explain that Helene Zillmann needed to render an "authorized translation" of *An Adventure Among the Rosicrucians* from English to German in 1899? Why not use the "original" text in German that Hartmann supposedly received from du Prel?

Consequently, one may deduce that the notes were originally written in English and, since du Prel did not write in English during his lifetime, it could never have been du Prel who wrote the notes and handed them to Hartmann.

Given Blavatsky's remark on du Prel, he could independently have had the experience of visiting one of the Abodes in the Alps, just as some other individuals did. Be that as it may, whatever Abode he may or may not have visited, it was definitely not the same place that is described in *An Adventure Among the Rosicrucians*.

Nicholas Roerich's writings mention the experience of Dr. Lao Chin in Tibet, which was later confirmed by Helena Roerich as something which indeed occurred: "I can say that the Lord [M.] has confirmed the fact of this visit, but has added that the doctor saw only what was shown to him; moreover, he drew his own conclusions and these do not entirely accord with the truth" (6 May 1934).

However, Dr. Lao Chin's experience, despite there being similar descriptions, is rather different from the two discussed here. For example, he says that there were 200 residents and that he saw no women. This suggests that he is referring to one of the Abodes of Shambhala in Central Asia, but not the main Stronghold, where the Sisters dwell too.

So, there are three accounts and all are different, as each describes a particular Abode of the many that existed in Europe and Asia at the time.

In his *Autobiography* published in 1908, Hartmann does not mention du Prel at all and certainly not as someone who influenced him in any way. Yet Blavatsky is mentioned throughout the text along with his experiences. He even says that he met a group of Rosicrucians after arriving with Blavatsky in Italy in 1885. Some of these were illiterate, yet they shared the same ideas as expounded in her works. Of course, these were not the Adepts described in the book. A quarter of his other book in German, *Unter den Adepten und Rosenkreuzern* [Among the Adepts and Rosicrucians], is devoted to Blavatsky.

While Hartmann asserts that *An Adventure Among the Rosicrucians* is his first attempt to write an occult novel, it is his very last words in 1910 that are important because in these words he acknowledges that he simply compiled the book from someone else's notes. Helena Blavatsky — and not Carl du Prel — was the most significant person in his life, the person who opened the door for him onto an entirely new world of spirituality; for why otherwise would he have dedicated so much space to her in his memoirs?

Being fascinated by elementals, Hartmann added his own fantasies to the original story of *An Adventure Among the Rosicrucians*. In 2022, the book was published under the name of its true author, H. P. Blavatsky, as *The Land of the Gods* without Hartmann's additions. It briefly mentions the higher kinds of elementals who guard the approaches to the Abodes of Shambhala. The subject of the higher orders of elementals and their rulers still represents the secret behind the seven seals.

Some argue that Blavatsky could not have written *The Land of the Gods* because she wrote esoteric works only, never fiction. However, this is not true. For example, in Russia, she first became known on account of her "travel memoirs," which were originally published under the pseudonym Radda-Bai and later comprised *The Durbar in Lahore*, *The People of the Blue Mountains*, and *From the Caves and Jungles of Hindostan*.

Thus, in a letter to A. P. Sinnett, Blavatsky tells him: "I wrote *stories*, on facts that happened hither and thither, with living persons, only changing names. . . . It is like my *Russian Letters* from India, where while describing a fictitious journey or tour through India with Thornton's *Gazeteer* as my guide, I yet give there true *facts* and true personages only bringing in together within three or four months time, facts and events scattered all throughout years as some of Master's phenomena."

In 1892, a collection of her stories was published under the title *Nightmare Tales*. Its foreword by Annie Besant says:

"The world knows H. P. Blavatsky chiefly by her encyclopaedic knowledge, her occult powers, her unique courage. This little book, composed of stories thrown off by her in her lighter moments, shows her as a vivid, graphic writer, gifted with brilliant imagination. The student will catch glimpses of reality under the garb of fancy, and will know that only the hand of an occultist could have added some of the touches to the pictures. The *Nightmare Tales* were rewritten during the last few months of the author's pain-stricken life: when tired with the drudgery of *The Theosophical Glossary* she, who could not be idle, turned to this lighter work and found therein amusement and relaxation. Her friends, all the world over, will welcome this example of gifts used but too rarely amid the strain of weightier work."

Moreover, Blavatsky wrote other stories in collaboration with Mahatma Hilarion — "the Adept who writes stories with H.P.B.," as Mahatma Koot Hoomi mentions in his letter.

So, despite a fictitious presentation and changed names, it is still possible for those who have developed the heart's intuition to recognize who is who in *The Land of the Gods*, just as it is in *From the Caves and Jungles of Hindostan*. This explains why Roerich was in no doubt that the story was written down according to words of Blavatsky, because only she could gain access to the main Abode of Shambhala, which Roerich also visited, albeit in the physical.

See *Land of the Gods* for more.

To read Carl du Prel's book, *The Secular Monastery*, and Dr. Lao Chin's article about his journey to one of the Abodes of Shambhala, visit radiantbooks.co/bonus.

Haug, Martin (1827–1876). A German Indologist and scholar of Zoroastrianism, known for his work on ancient Persian texts and his translations of the Avesta, the sacred scriptures of Zoroastrianism.

Heart. The most important organ in a human being; the centre of spiritual consciousness. It is a mover, producer, and collector of fiery might. The heart represents the concentration of fiery energies that are always pulsating in a person, and on the tonality of which their state of being is completely dependent.

The structure of the heart is sevenfold: each of the seven human bodies, the physical body, the subtle body, and so on has its own heart, the highest of which is the fiery heart. During a person's life on Earth, all the hearts are united with the physical heart. The heart is the focal point in all the human bodies, from the densest body to the higher triad. The whole experience of previous lives, and all abilities and knowledge, which are inaccessible to the brain because it lives only one life, are concentrated in the spiritual fiery heart called the *chalice*. The heart remains a person's inalienable property throughout all incarnations, for while its physical form is mortal, its fiery essence is immortal.

The heart is not limited by anything and is capable of assimilating everything that would be inaccessible to the brain, restricted as it is to the five senses and the earthly dual world, that is, the earthly illusion, so that it is difficult for it to grasp anything that goes beyond these limits. It is difficult for the brain to understand even two opposite, yet correct statements and, therefore, as a rule, one of the two is accepted and the other is negated. While the path of the brain is long, winding, and horizontal, that of the heart is short, straight, and vertical.

The brain is called to serve as a mouthpiece for the heart. It is a kind of recorder of the subtle energies passing through the heart, expressing the heart's thoughts and feelings in verbal form. The heart and brain must act in a coordinated and harmonious manner, complementing each other and thereby expanding a person's consciousness. However, this is such a rare phenomenon that the brain, due to its excessive activity, is only occasionally able to register those flashes of the heart, which are often called intuition or conscience.

The heart thinks, just like the brain, but in its own way. The logic of the heart works through fiery channels, sometimes with no time being required as the heart just knows, without having to engage in the tedious and tortuous process of reflection. The words of the heart always exhibit extreme simplicity, along with profundity, wisdom, and selflessness. The voice of conscience is the voice of the heart, which sounds especially clear when all else is silent. The heart owns an energy which is insubordinate to the brain. For example, thoughts sent by the brain are brief, ineffective, and immediately self-exhausting, while thoughts from the heart know no obstacles, distance, or time.

Many mysteries are hidden in the heart, and these will be revealed by the science of the future. A scientist who knows the secret of numbers, in comparing mystic knowledge with the knowledge of science, will make significant discoveries in the domain of cardiology. For example, on average blood flows through the greater circulation in 22 seconds and through the lesser circulation in 5–6 seconds. Matching the numbers that indicate Rounds and Races, one can trace signs of a person's racial identity in the operation of the heart.

The heart is designed to love, for Love is the mission of the heart. One who loves will attract and assimilate the highest vibrations through the heart. Not everyone is capable of accepting the Fire, since not everyone's flesh can endure the divine currents. The Fire transmutes that which is able to evolve, while that which cannot evolve is destroyed. Therefore, cardiovascular diseases are more prevalent than others, especially in our age, for the Era of Fire, which has already begun, is the Era of the Heart.

HeartMath Institute. A non-profit research and educational organization founded by Doc Childre in 1991 that focuses on the study of heart-brain coherence, stress reduction, and emotional resilience. It is known for its research into the physiological and psychological effects of heart-centred practices.

Helmont, Franciscus Mercurius van (1614–1698). The son of Jan Baptist; a mystic, alchemist, and philosopher, known for promoting Kabbalah in Europe.

Helmont, Jan Baptist van (1580–1644). A Flemish physician, philosopher, mystic, alchemist, and pioneer of early chemistry; coined the word *gas*.

Hemis Monastery. A Buddhist monastery in the village of Hemis, Ladakh, India.

Henan (*Ch.*, "south of the river"). A province in China, location of the Shaolin Temple, the birthplace of Chan Buddhism.

Hermes Trismegistus (*Gr.*, "thrice great Hermes"). The God of Wisdom, Thoth or Thot in Egypt. Hermes Trismegistus is the name of Hermes or Thoth in his human aspect. According to Plato, he "discovered numbers, geometry, astronomy, and letters."

Hermetism. A philosophy based on doctrines or writings connected with the esoteric teachings of Hermes, who, whether as the Egyptian Thoth or the Greek Hermes, was the God of Wisdom among the ancients. Though mostly considered spurious, the Hermetic writings were highly prized by St. Augustine, Lactantius, Cyril, and others. In the words of James Bonwick: "They are more or less touched up by the Platonic philosophers among the early Christians (such as Origen and Clemens Alexandrinus) who sought to substantiate their Christian arguments by appeals to these heathen and revered writings, though they could not resist the temptation of making them say a little too much" (*Egyptian Belief and Modern Thought*). Though represented by some clever and interested writers as teaching pure monotheism, the Hermetic or Trismegistic books are, nevertheless, purely pantheistic. The Deity referred to in them is defined by Paul as that in *which* "we live, and move and have our being," notwithstanding the "in Him" introduced by the translators.

Hierophant (*Gr.*, "one who explains sacred things"). The discloser of sacred learning and Chief of the Initiates. A title belonging to the highest Adepts in the temples of antiquity, who were teachers and expounders of the Mysteries, and Initiators into the final great Mysteries. The Hierophant represented the Demiurge (Creator), and explained to the postulants for Initiation the various phenomena of Creation that were produced for their tuition. "He was the sole expounder of the esoteric secrets and doctrines. It was forbidden even to pronounce his name before an uninitiated person. He sat in the East, and wore as a symbol of authority a golden globe suspended from the neck. He was also called *Mystagogus*" (*The Royal Masonic Cyclopaedia*). In Hebrew and Chaldaic, the equivalent term was *Peter*, the opener, discloser; hence, the Pope as the successor of the hierophant of the ancient Mysteries, sits in the Pagan chair of St. Peter.

Hilarion. One of the Great Teachers of Shambhala; the Lord of Mars. He co-wrote several occult stories with Blavatsky that were published in 1892 in the collection *Nightmare Tales*. At least three of these were written jointly, namely: *An Unsolved Mystery, A Story of the Mystical*, and *The Ensouled Violin*. Hilarion was also behind Mabel Collins' *Idyll of the White Lotus* (1884) and *Light on the Path* (1885).

In 1898, under the guidance of Master Hilarion, Francia La Due founded in Syracuse, New York, the Temple of the People which was later moved to Halcyon, California. Together with Mahatmas Morya and Koot Hoomi, He revealed through Francia La Due a new section from the secret *Book of Dzyan* and transmitted beautiful lines of Teachings which were first published in *The Temple Artisan*, the official periodical of the Temple of the People.

The incarnations of Master Hilarion include Paul the Apostle, Thomas of Kempis, Iamblichus, Giordano Bruno, and Jacob Böhme. The latter two intersected during the period 1575–1600, which is explained by the ability of the Masters to incarnate through the divisibility of the Spirit, as well as through the Ray.

Together with Master Rakoczy, Master Hilarion is guardian of America and Europe.

Himalayas. The world's highest mountain range, stretching across South Asia. Home to Mount Everest and other peaks.

Hinayana (*Sk.*, "smaller vehicle"). A school of the Northern Buddhists, opposed to the Mahayana, "the greater vehicle," in Tibet. Both schools are mystical. Also, in exoteric superstition, the lowest form of transmigration.

Hodgson, Richard (1855–1905). A member of the Society for Psychical Research (S.P.R.) who prepared an accusatory report, known as the Hodgson Report, against H.P.B. in 1885 based on fabricated evidence. The document caused substantial damage to H.P.B.'s reputation and subsequently her health. However, in 1986 the S.P.R. issued a press release headlined: "Madame Blavatsky, co-founder of the Theosophical Society, was unjustly condemned, new study concludes." Dr. Vernon Harrison, who re-examined the case, finished his report with the words: "I apologize to her that it has taken us one hundred years to demonstrate that she wrote truly."

Holgate, George. The notorious manufacturer of explosive machines in Philadelphia. An article entitled "Infernal Machines" describing his lethal inventions appeared in many newspapers in 1883–1884.

Holy Grail. According to the etymology of the Old French word *san-gréal* ("holy grail"), refers to the "real blood" (*sang réal*) of Jesus Christ. The subject of the Holy Grail is taboo, "a secret for the unworthy," which can provide only its chosen ones with "ethereal viands."

Nevertheless, according to surviving legends, during the Last Supper, the cup was used for communion between Christ and His apostles. Then, the mysterious vessel became associated with another legend — that this was the chalice containing the blood of Jesus Christ that Joseph of Arimathea gathered when he took down His crucified body from the cross.

Precious containers for materialized sacred relics imply the nobility of the material of which they are made. They are also associated with miraculous powers, especially when the vessel contains something that is incomprehensible in terms of the study of its structure — the blood of Christ. It was crystallized and literally "stuck" to the walls of the chalice, thereby creating a special mixture in combination with metal, becoming similar to a stone that has magical properties.

The Holy Grail is akin to the Treasure of the World, the Chintamani Stone, that was presented as a Gift to Earth by the constellation of Orion. Certainly, a special combination of stellar currents constitutes the Chintamani. However, in the case of the Holy Grail, the blood spilled on the Earth bound the Spirit and Flesh of the Crucified Christ with *terra firma* by "blood ties," thereby creating a new miraculous Gift for the planet.

Homer. A Greek poet, who lived in the ninth or eighth century BCE; the author of the *Iliad* and the *Odyssey*.

Hongren (601–674). The fifth patriarch of Chan Buddhism.

Hotri (*Sk.*, "sacrificer"). A priest who recites hymns from the *Rig Veda*, and makes oblations to the fire.

Howard, Robert E. (1906–1936). An American writer, best known for his pulp fiction stories and the creation of the sword-and-sorcery character Conan the Barbarian.

Huanghe (*Ch.*, "yellow river"). The second-longest river in China.

Huineng (638–713). The sixth patriarch of Chan Buddhism, chosen by the fifth patriarch, Hongren, after the verse contest. Huineng founded the Southern School of Chan Buddhism that focuses on an immediate attainment of enlightenment.

Humanity. Esoterically, the whole of humankind is symbolized by Manu in India; by Vajrasattva or Dorje Sempa, the head of the Seven Dhyani, in Northern Buddhism; and by Adam Kadmon in Kabbalah. All these represent the totality of humankind whose beginning is to be found in this androgynic protoplast, and whose end lies in the Absolute, beyond any symbol or myth of human origin. Humanity is a great Brotherhood by virtue of the sameness of the material from which it is formed, physically and morally. However, unless it becomes a Brotherhood in the spiritual sense, humanity is no better than a superior genus of animal.

The seeds of humankind were sown on Mercury, Venus, Earth, the Moon, Mars, Phaeton, and Jupiter. On each planet humankind was manifested variously, in each case with its own peculiarities, ranging from complete ugliness to perfection. Mercury, the Moon, and Earth brought forth the most terrible types; that of Mars was a little better. Only through selection and perfection did their types become more refined and their forms improved. The most beautiful types appeared on Phaeton, Venus, and Jupiter.

On Earth the first human type resembled a large lizard rather than a human being; the modern animal is more beautiful than was this primitive being. Only with the arrival on Earth of the Great Teachers and the incarnation of divine monads from other planets such as the perished Phaeton did the evolution of earthly humanity undergo significant acceleration and come to manifest as the modern human being, designed in the image and likeness of the Teachers of Humanity.

Humphreys, Christmas (1901–1983). A British barrister and author of a number of books on Mahayana Buddhism; founder of the Buddhist Society in London.

Hydra. In Greek mythology, a seven-headed water monster whose heads regrew after being cut off. It was slain by Hercules as one of his twelve labours.

Hypatia (c.350/370–415). A female philosopher, who lived at Alexandria during the fifth century and taught many a famous man, among others Bishop Synesius. She was the daughter of the mathematician Theon and became famous for her learning. Falling a martyr to the fiendish conspiracy of Theophilos, Bishop of Alexandria, and his nephew Cyril, she was foully murdered by their order. With her death fell the Neoplatonic school.

Hypnotism (*Gr.*, "sleep"). A name given by Dr. Braid to various processes by which one person of strong willpower plunges another of weaker mind into a kind of trance; once immersed in this state, the latter will do anything *suggested* to him by the hypnotizer. Unless produced for beneficial purposes, occultists would call this *black magic* or *sorcery*. It is the most dangerous of practices, morally and physically, as it interferes with the nerve fluid and the nerves controlling the flow of blood through the capillaries.

Hypnotism and suggestion are great and dangerous powers, for the very reason that the victim never knows when he is being subjected to them; his will is stolen from him. Some of the techniques of hypnotism and suggestion were used by Adolf Hitler to rule the German people. However, nowadays, similar psychological technologies are also widely used in the media and social media to manipulate people and to pass off black for white.

Hypostasis (*Gr.*, "essence," "person"). A unique, personal existence that is distinct yet shares the same essence with others in a unified nature. For example, in the context of the Trinity, the Father, the Son, and the Holy Spirit are the three persons of the Godhead. Each person is a distinct hypostasis, yet shares one divine essence with the other two.

I

I.H.S. These initials stand for *In hoc signo* (*Lat.*, "by this sign [you will triumph]"), used by Constantine the Great, or *Iesus Hominum Salvator* (*Lat.*, "Jesus, Saviour of humankind") used by the Roman Church. It is, however, well known that the Greek IHS was one of the most ancient names of Bacchus, a solar deity in the esoteric meaning. As Jesus was never identical to Jehovah, but had his own Father (as we all do), and had come rather to destroy the worship of Jehovah than to enforce it, as the Rosicrucians maintained, the scheme of its author, Eusebius, is quite transparent. *In hoc signo vinces*, or the *labarum* ☧ (the *tau* and the *resh*) is a very old sign, placed on the foreheads of those who had just been initiated. It simply means "through this sign hast thou conquered"; i.e., through the *light* of Initiation — Lux (*Lat.*, "light").

Iamblichus (c.245–c.325). A great theurgist, mystic, and writer of the third and fourth centuries, a Neoplatonist and philosopher, born in Chalcis, Coele-Syria. A correct biography has never existed because of the hatred of the Christians towards him; but that which has been gathered of his life in isolated fragments from works by impartial pagan and independent writers shows how excellent and holy was his moral character, and how great his learning. He may be called the founder of theurgic magic among the Neoplatonists and the reviver of the practical mysteries outside of the temple.

His school was at first distinct from that of Plotinus and Porphyry, who were strongly against ceremonial magic and practical theurgy considering them dangerous, though later he convinced Porphyry of its advisability on some occasions, and both master and pupil firmly believed in theurgy and magic, of which the former is principally the highest and most efficient mode of communication with one's Higher Ego, through the medium of one's astral body. Theurgic is benevolent magic, and it becomes goetic, or dark and evil, only when it is used for necromancy or selfish purposes; but such dark magic has never been practised by any theurgist or philosopher whose name has descended to us unspotted by any evil deed. So much was Porphyry (who became the teacher of Iamblichus in Neoplatonic philosophy) convinced of this, that though he himself never practised theurgy, he gave instructions for the acquirement of this sacred science. Thus, he says in one of his writings: "Whoever is acquainted with the nature of *divinely luminous appearances* knows also on what account it is requisite to abstain from all birds (and animal food), and especially for him who hastens to be liberated from terrestrial concerns and to be established with the celestial Gods" (Thomas Taylor, *Select Works of Porphyry*).

Moreover, the same Porphyry mentions in his *Life of Plotinus* a priest of Egypt, who, "at the request of a certain friend of Plotinus, exhibited to him, in the temple of Isis at Rome, the familiar *daimon* of that philosopher." In other words, he produced the theurgic invocation by which Egyptian Hierophant or Indian Mahatma of old could clothe their own or any other person's astral *double* with the appearance of its Higher Ego, or what Bulwer-Lytton terms the "Luminous Self," the *Augoeides*, and confabulate with It. This is what Iamblichus and many others, including the medieval Rosicrucians, meant by *union with Deity*.

Iamblichus wrote many books but only a few of his works are extant, such as his *Egyptian Mysteries* and a treatise *On Daemons*, in which he speaks most severely against any intercourse with them. He was a biographer of Pythagoras and deeply versed in the system of the latter, and was also learned in the Chaldean Mysteries. He taught that the One, or Universal Monad, was the principle of all unity as well as diversity, or of homogeneity and heterogeneity; that the duad, or two ("principles"), was the intellect, or that which we call *buddhi-manas*; three, was the soul (the lower *manas*), etc. There is much of the theosophical in his teachings, and his works on the various kinds of elementals are a well of esoteric knowledge for the student. His austerities, purity of life, and earnestness were great. Iamblichus is credited with having once levitated about five metres above the ground, as are some of the modern yogis and even great mediums.

Iddhi (*Pali*, "power"). Psychic or magical powers attained through special training. These powers include: clairvoyance, clairaudience, astral projection, becoming invisible, teleportation, telekinesis, levitation, etc.

Idea. The true essence of thought, unexpressed in form; fore-thought. At first, an idea appears in consciousness, clads itself in the matter of thought, and develops into an image after which it acquires material form (visible or invisible) and is embodied in life.

According to Cosmic Laws, which also exist beyond form (but are manifested in Primordial Matter), all phenomena unexpressed in form subordinate whatever is clad in form, and subsequently, subordination takes place according to the degree of rarefaction in matter, with the physical degree being the lowest. Plato correctly stated that "Ideas rule the world." Ideas, unlike thoughts, are always invisible, even in the Higher Worlds.

The Great Teachers saturate space with the most advanced ideas. The birth of an idea calls forth particles of consonant elements which act as a magnet, creating a field of attraction around it. So, the invisible search for allies occurs among people who are willing to turn this idea into reality using human hands and feet. The border between two ages, that is taking place now, is marked by a great penetration of new ideas into the depths of space in order to awaken dormant consciousness. These ideas enter the consciousness of many, thereby dividing humanity into two camps: those who follow them, and those who counteract them. If one's consciousness is ready, it accepts the new ideas without difficulty. Those who follow evolution develop them — from different points of view — all over the world. There is no barrier or restriction that can keep them from spreading to all hearts and minds. Ideas are borne through the air, compelling everyone to make a firm decision as to what they support: whether they are for peace or for war, for freedom or for slavery, for remaining in the old world or for entering the New World, and so on.

The published Teachings of Light represent thoughts expressed in words and gathered together in printed books. Many sections of the Secret Teachings remain unpublished and are contained in manuscripts stored at Shambhala and other Abodes of Light. But the larger portion is sealed in the archives of space, or Akasha, which is inaccessible to the average person. However, the Great Teachers have permeated space with thoughts that are in tune with the evolutionary stage reached by humanity to date. In this way, they share with the world what every sensitive spirit may perceive from the spheres surrounding Earth. Even in cases where the Teaching is not published, its ideas still fill space, as if borne through the air. They reach many hearts, and people in different parts of the world begin to speak and express the same thoughts and espouse the same formulas, although they have never had contact with the Teaching on the physical plane. As they bring the light of heart-centredness into the world around them, they begin to facilitate the unification of humanity into a single family. In this way, they prepare the ground for future change in the world, for the transformation of individual consciousness and individual lives.

Although they may be forgotten, ideas never die; they live in space. As time goes by, they once again spark interest in human minds and, as they increase in strength, they are embodied in life, even thousands of years later. Ideas that express indisputable truths are immortal, changing only in the manner of the form in which they are manifest, simultaneous to the evolution of consciousness.

Naturally, progressive ideas are seldom accepted immediately. They generally require a period of time to take root in the consciousness of the masses. But as the majority become accustomed to them, accepting them as their own thoughts, these ideas begin to rule the world on a practical rather than a theoretical level.

Ignatius of Loyola (1491–1556). A Spanish saint and founder of the Society of Jesus (Jesuits). His work *Spiritual Exercises* (1548) is a guide for Christian meditation and prayer. He played a key role in the Counter-Reformation.

Illumination. A state of contemplation that precedes union with the Divine. Illumination endows one with the highest form of knowledge, attained intuitively during mystic meditation. Once an Arhat obtains full illumination and perfect control over his personality and lower nature, he ceases to create merit and demerit, that is, he no longer generates karma.

Illusion. In occultism, everything finite (like the universe and everything within it) is called *illusion* or *Maya*.

Imagination. In occultism this is not to be confused with fancy, as it is one of the plastic powers of the higher soul, and is the memory of preceding incarnations, which, however disfigured by the lower *manas*, rests always on the ground of truth.

Individuality. One of the names given in Theosophy and occultism to the human Higher Ego. A distinction is made between the immortal and divine Ego on the one hand, and the mortal human Ego on the other which perishes. The latter, or *personality* (personal Ego), survives the dead body for a limited period of time in Kama-loka; the individuality prevails forever.

Indra (*Sk.*, "igniter," "equipped with great power"). The Vedic God of the Firmament, the King of the sidereal gods.

Indriya (*Sk.*, "sense faculties") or **deha samyama** (*Sk.*, "body control"). The control of the senses in yoga practice. These are the ten external agents; the five senses which are used for perception are called *jnana-indriya*, and the five used for action — *karma-indriya*. *Pancha-indryani* means both literally and in its occult sense "the live roots producing life (eternal)." Among the Buddhists, it is the five positive agents producing five supernal qualities.

Initiate. The designation of one to whom the mysteries and secrets of occultism have been revealed; in antiquity, those who were initiated into the arcane knowledge taught by the Hierophants of the Mysteries, and in the modern day, those who have been initiated by Adepts of mystic lore into the mysterious knowledge, which, notwithstanding the lapse of ages, still has a few real votaries on Earth.

Each new stage of Initiation reveals ever new mysteries and imparts new abilities to one who has become entitled to acquire the secret knowledge of the Cosmos and human beings.

Initiation ceremonies, or Mysteries, took place in ancient Sanctuaries, such as the Pyramids of Egypt, the Temples of Greece, India, and so on. Secret Sanctuaries with halls for Initiations were built in places of powerful energy, mostly in the mountains. Mountains are the source of the strongest energy because their summits are covered with snow, which, like a natural lens, serves to receive the currents of other constellations and planets. Similarly, representatives of other worlds who study Earth have their base in the mountains too.

The procedure of Initiation is a mystical penetration into a higher level of perception and comprehension of the mystery of Existence, thanks to the acceptance of higher-order currents and the ability to use them effectively. It is the transition from life to a temporary death by means of a magic dream, which in turn enables a candidate to experience a disembodied Spirit and Soul in the subjective world. Each Initiation requires moral purity, strength of spirit, and an aspiration for Truth.

For example, Hermes Trismegistus (*Gr.*, "thrice-greatest") underwent three Initiations, although he is already the four-time-greatest, having successfully passed through yet another. His father, Arraim, is a four-time-greatest also. Thales of Argos passed through four Initiations. Christ passed through eight Initiations, and His Second Coming is associated with His ninth Initiation.

Pythagoras was an Initiate, one of the greatest of all scientists. His disciple, Archytas, was marvellously apt at applied science. Plato and Euclid were Initiates. The latter learnt his geometry in the Mysteries. Modern science only rediscovers old truths.

However, it is not only people and the Great Spirits who may go through Initiations, but also realms of Nature, planets, stars, solar systems, etc. Thus, in the present day, humanity as a whole and Earth are undergoing the next level of their Fiery Initiation.

Initiation. The practice of initiation or admission into the sacred Mysteries, taught by the Hierophants and learned priests of the Temples, is one of the world's most ancient customs. Initiation was practised in every national religion. In Europe, the practice was abolished with the fall of the last pagan temple. According to the greatest Greek and Roman philosophers, in the days of old, the Mysteries were the most sacred and beneficent of all solemnities, and greatly promoted virtue. The Mysteries represented the passage from mortal life into finite death and the experiences of the disembodied Spirit and Soul in the world of subjectivity.

Every nation had an exoteric and an esoteric religion, the one for the masses, the other for the learned and elect with three degrees of Initiation. For example, the Hindus had three degrees with several sub-degrees. The Egyptians had three preliminary degrees, personified in the Mysteries as the "three guardians of the fire." The Chinese had an ancient Triad Society: and to this day the Tibetans have the "triple step," which was symbolized in the Vedas by the three strides of Vishnu. Everywhere antiquity shows an unbounded reverence for the Triad and the Triangle — the first geometrical figure. The old Babylonians had three stages of Initiation into the priesthood (which was then esoteric knowledge); the Jews, the Kabbalists, and the mystics borrowed their three stages from the Chaldeans, and the Christian Church borrowed theirs from the Jews. "There are Two," says Rabbi Shimon ben Yochai, "in conjunction with One; hence, they are Three, and if they are Three, then they are One."

All rituals of Initiation were invented for the masses, since true Initiation consists in the assimilation of the Higher Rays of varying intensity and properties. It can take place in different places and premises, the main condition being the readiness of the disciple. The length of the preparation period depends on their spiritual accumulations. Often, a person who sincerely strives for good comes under the influence of High Rays without at first even suspecting it.

In *The Doctrine of the Bhagavad Gita* (1966), a disciple of Mahatma Koot Hoomi, Bhavani Shankar, explains: "[Initiation] takes place, as H.P.B. says in *The Voice of the Silence*, neither in the physical body which she calls the Hall of Ignorance, nor in the astral body which is called by her the Hall of Learning, but it is in the *karana-sharira* [spiritual soul], the Hall of Wisdom, in his own *hridaya* (heart), that the disciple sees Him [his Master] for the first time whose life and peace he was so long feeling in his heart. Therefore does *The Voice of the Silence* teach the aspirant: 'Seek for him who is to give thee birth, in the Hall of Wisdom.'"

Inner Group. The group of twelve (six men and six women) chosen by H. P. Blavatsky from among the members of the Esoteric Section to teach them the deeper mysteries of the Cosmos.

Inner Man. An occult term, used to designate the true and immortal entity in man, not the outward and mortal form of clay that is called the body. The term applies, strictly speaking, only to the Higher Ego, the "astral man" being the appellation of the double and *kama-rupa* or the surviving *eidolon*.

Inquisition. A system of tribunals established by the Catholic Church in various countries to root out or combat heresy, blasphemy, witchcraft, etc. The Spanish Inquisition and the Roman Inquisition were among the most infamous, often associated with harsh interrogations and punishments for perceived religious non-conformity.

The Inquisition was established, not to persecute witches or sorcerers, who were mostly mediums, but to destroy all dissenters, all personal enemies of the representatives of the Church, in order to establish its unlimited power. And among these enemies, first and foremost, were all the most enlightened servants and true followers of Christ, such as Giordano Bruno, Galileo Galilei, Jan Hus, and Joan of Arc. It was easy for the inquisitors to destroy their enemies by branding them as having association with the Devil, while they themselves were in fact his faithful followers and representatives on Earth for the implementation of his plan to exterminate all those capable of enlightening the dark and ignorant masses.

Moreover, by forcibly interrupting the lives of millions of its victims, the Inquisition gave rise to the terrible calamity of possession. From all secret teachings, it is known that souls plunged into the Subtle World before the expiration of the normal term of their life, yearn to touch vital earthly power through any vehicle available to them. They are still full of the unexhausted reserve of the magnetic force that binds them to Earth, and often are unable to perceive currents of a higher frequency due to a low level of development in consciousness. Motivated by malice and revenge, these victims are drawn to their executioners, and through possession, force them to commit even greater crimes, even to end their own life in suicide, in order to absorb and enjoy the emanations of their blood, creating, albeit for a short time, the illusion of life.

The Inquisition was inspired by the former Prince of this world to corrupt and undermine faith in the purity, goodness, and justice of the Church for all times to come. It remains a terrible and indelible stain on the Christian Church.

Intellect. A recorder of impressions received from the heart; the more it is clogged with dry, unspiritual knowledge, the greater the difficulty it will have in understanding the impulses sent by the heart. However, the intellect coupled with spirituality is a powerful tool for the spirit.

The intellect lives in the present, a little in the past, but very little in the future. The realm of what truly exists, the one inseparable whole consisting of the past and the future, is inaccessible to it. The intellect lives in illusion, for it is based on external feelings and has no insight into the future. It cannot instantly solve a complex mathematical problem, as Sofya Kovalevskaya did, nor can it see life in Distant Worlds.

An Adept of the Right-hand Path is not always initially of powerful intellect. In fact, there are Adepts whose intellectual powers were originally below the average. King Solomon and Akbar the Great, both incarnations of Master Morya, possessed a level of intellect that was lower than that of an ordinary lawyer. It was their hearts that provided them with unsurpassed wisdom.

It is the Adept's purity, his equal love to all, his working with Nature, with karma, with his "Inner God," that give him his power. Intellect alone will make of one the black magician. For intellect alone is accompanied by pride and selfishness; it is the intellectual *plus* the spiritual that raises man aloft. Spirituality eliminates pride and vanity.

The inhabitants of Atlantis could harness and control the forces of Nature, including the spirits of the elements: earth, water, air, and fire, such as genies, elves, undines, dwarfs, etc. Similarly, it is with this kind of knowledge as well as the help of genies that the High Initiates of Egypt built the pyramids at Giza, and King Solomon constructed the Temple.

Devoid of spirituality and exploiting secret knowledge, the intellect of the black-magic sorcerers of Atlantis created mechanical creatures, which were animated by spells using blood and by what are called *elementals* (the spirits of the elements of Nature) and *elementaries* (the disembodied souls of evil humans, unsuitable for evolution, who have lost their immortality). These unique biorobots were endowed with various abilities. For example, they could speak and warn their master of impending danger; they guarded palaces and performed any other task assigned by their masters. Subject only to the will of their producer, they were able to operate on different planes of matter, visible and invisible.

Warlocks sent whole armies of these monsters to battle against the Sons of Light, armies that could not be stopped by ordinary people. Nonetheless, one with a pure heart, imbued with the Power of Love, could annihilate an entire army of these visible and invisible monsters. From these originated various legends such as the three Gorgon sisters in Greek mythology, and these were merely the "precursors" to other entities that acquired more terrifying forms and sizes. Fortunately, they were neutralized by the Forces of the Great Brotherhood, although the poison from their "snake" heads had already managed to seep into many human minds.

Nowadays, the hierophants of evil would like to repeat what they achieved in the distant past with regard to the creation and development of so-called "artificial intelligence," and they intend to endow their army of minions with it, both on the visible and invisible planes.

During its evolution, every human thought passes into the inner world and becomes an active entity by associating itself, coalescing, with an elemental, i.e., with one of the semi-intelligent forces of the various kingdoms. It survives as an active intelligence — a creature of the mind's begetting — for a longer or shorter period of time proportionate to the original intensity of the cerebral action which generated it. A good thought is perpetuated as an active, beneficent power, an evil thought, as a maleficent demon. And so each individual is continually populating their current in space with the offspring of their fancies, desires, impulses, and passions; this current reacts on any sensitive or nervous organization which comes into contact with it, in proportion to its dynamic intensity. An Adept evolves these shapes consciously; other people generate them unconsciously.

With its emission of thought forms, humanity mentally gave birth to a huge number of mutants on the Subtle Plane, which can be animated by elementals or elementaries and used by the hierophants of evil.

For example, fear is, first and foremost, a *thought*, which in turn influences human consciousness. Therefore, it is possible to eliminate it with the help of another, *fearless* thought. If the thought of fear enters the human aura, its energy essence attempts to stay there for as long as possible. This means vibrating and receiving sustenance by causing anxiety about something, anything, just so as to maintain perpetual motion within itself. That is why fear has many faces, and why its guises are so diverse and deceptive. A tiny hint of fear begins to pull in other fear-vibrating hints from space. In this way, the originating thought flows from one form into another, making people its slaves. Each dark flash of fear only serves to reinforce the darkness. One can only imagine how much "sustenance" is supplied to the dark hierarchy, for example, by the single viewing of a horror movie in a cinema, or by the reading of books of a similar genre.

In this way, and with this kind of energy supply at their disposal, the warlocks create entities on the Subtle Plane in the form of gigantic "energy cats." These are able to attack spaceships with solely good intentions which travel to Earth from other star systems. In the early 1990s, only three of these hugely powerful entities existed. Now their number has increased significantly and they exist in small forms also, which launch attacks on human beings because they need the human energy. They devour it instantly, and the person dies just as quickly. In these instances, medicine is at a loss to explain the cause of death. The person's internal organs may well be in a reasonably healthy state, and there may be no trace of disease or other visible reason why death should have occurred. So, humanity has, with its own hands, or rather, with its intellect disconnected from the heart, created a new disease for itself.

Isaias. Another name for the biblical prophet Isaiah, a major prophet in the Old Testament who is known for his prophecies about the coming of the Messiah and the vision of peace and justice in the future Kingdom of God.

Ishwara (*Sk.*, "sovereign, independent existence"). The Lord or the personal god, divine spirit in man. A title given to Shiva and other gods in India. Shiva is also called Ishwaradeva, or sovereign deva.

Isis. In Egyptian *Issa*, the goddess Virgin-Mother; personified Nature. In Egyptian or Koptic *Uasari*, the female reflection of *Uasar* or Osiris. She is the "woman clothed with the sun" of the land of Chemi. Isis Latona is the Roman Isis. The temple of Isis in Sais, Egypt, bore the inscription: "I am all that hath been, and is, and shall be; and my veil no mortal has hitherto raised."

Isis Unveiled. A fundamental two-volume work by H. P. Blavatsky, published in 1877. She describes the process of writing it in a letter to her sister, Vera Zhelikhovsky, in the following way:

"Vera, whether you can believe me or not, something magical is happening to me! You cannot imagine what an enchanting world of pictures and visions I am living in! I am writing *Isis* — although I am not writing as such rather I am copying and drawing what *she* shows me. In truth it seems to me that the ancient beauty-goddess herself is leading me through all the countries of past centuries that I must describe. I sit with my eyes open; it seems to me that I see and hear everything, everything is real tangible, and at the same time I can see and hear what I am writing. It takes my breath away! I am afraid to move, so as not to break the spell. Slowly, century after century, image after image appears and passes before me, as if in some magic panorama, and I mentally connect them, putting together the years and eras in my mind, and I know *for sure* that *there can be no mistake*. Races and nations, countries and cities, long since vanished into the gloom of the prehistoric past, become clear, and then disappear, giving way to others, and then I am shown successive years. Grey-haired antiquity is replaced by historical periods; myths are explained to me through events and persons that actually existed; and every more or less remarkable event, every page turned of this bright and multicoloured book of life is imprinted in my brain with photographic accuracy."

Issa. The Eastern name of Jesus Christ.

J

Ja Lama (1862–1922). A military leader and figure in the national liberation movement in Western Mongolia in the 1910s.

Jagrat (*Sk.*, "wakefulness"). The waking state of consciousness.

James, William (1842–1910). An American philosopher and psychologist, considered "the father of modern psychology." He joined the Theosophical Society in 1882 and served as president of the American Association of Psychologists, the Society for Psychical Research, and the American Philosophical Association.

Jamkhang Chenmo (*Tib.*, "chapel of Maitreya"). The tallest building of Tashi Lhunpo Monastery erected in 1914 by the Ninth Panchen Lama to house a giant statue of Maitreya Buddha.

Jamspal, Lozang, PhD (1933–2024). An Indian-born professor, scholar, and translator. He obtained a higher monastic education at Tashi Lhunpo Monastery and received an Acharya (Master's) degree in Sanskrit, Hindi, and Buddhist and Indian philosophy at Sanskrit University, Benares. He earned a PhD from Columbia University, where he taught Buddhist Sanskrit and Classical Tibetan. Dr. Jamspal served as a regular professor at the International Buddhist College in Thailand. From the late 1960s onwards, he dedicated his life to translating the Buddhadharma (the Buddha's teachings) into English and training future translators to do the same.

Java Aleim or **Jahva Alhim** (*Heb.*). The name that in Genesis replaces Alhim, or Elohim, the gods. It is used in chapter 1, while in chapter 2 the words "Lord God" and Jehovah start to creep in.

In esoteric philosophy and exoteric tradition, Jahva Alhim was the title of the chief of the Hierophants, who initiated others into the good and the evil of this world in the college of priests known as Aleim College in the land of Gandunya or Babylonia. Tradition and rumour assert that the chief of the temple *Fo-maiyu* (a temple situated in the fastnesses of the great mount of Kunlun Shan between China and Tibet), who was called Foh-tchou (teacher of Buddhist law), teaches once every three years under a tree called *Sung-Min-Shu*, or the "Tree of Knowledge and (the tree) of life," which is the Bo (Bodhi) tree of Wisdom.

Jawaharlal Nehru University. A prestigious public research university, located in Delhi, India, known for its focus on social and applied sciences.

Jebtsundamba Khutuktu (*Tib.-Mon.*, "Venerable Excellent Incarnate Lama"). The title for the spiritual head of Mongolian Buddhism and the highest-ranking lama in Mongolia, regarded as a Living Buddha. The Eighth Jebtsundamba Khutuktu later became Bogd Khan, Mongolia's theocratic ruler in the early twentieth century.

Jefferies, Richard (1848–1887). An English nature writer.

Jerome (c.340s–420). An early Christian priest and theologian.

Jesus. See *Christ* and *Koot Hoomi*.

Jiao-men (*Ch.*, "gate of teaching"). The exoteric school of Chinese Buddhism, representing the tradition of the *words* of the Buddha.

Jin Guang Ming Jing (*Ch.*). The Chinese translation of the *Suvarnaprabhasa Sutra* (*Sk.*, "Golden Light Sutra"), a fundamental text on various topics of Mahayana Buddhism.

Jiva (*Sk.*, "life"). Life, as the Absolute; the monad also, or *atma-buddhi*.

Jivatama (*Sk.*, "living soul"). In Hindu philosophy, the individual soul or living being, which is distinct from the *Paramatman* (Supreme Soul). The *jivatama* undergoes cycles of birth and rebirth (*samsara*) until it attains liberation (*moksha*).

Jnana (*Sk.*, "knowledge"). Occult wisdom; the same as *dnyan* in Marathi or *gnyana* in Telugu.

Joan of Arc (1412–1431). A national heroine and saviouress of France. A peasant girl from the village of Domrémy, she led the liberation struggle of the French people against the English during the Hundred Years' War (1337–1453). With utmost trust in the voices of the saints who guided her (St. Michael, St. Catherine, and St. Margaret), Joan convinced the garrison commander of Vaucouleurs, and then the king's advisers, to entrust her with an army. After the liberation of Orleans, besieged by the English, the people began to call Joan the Maid of Orleans. She insisted on Charles VII's march to Reims for the coronation and anointing, which confirmed the independence of France. Hoping to liberate Paris, Joan led a detachment to Compiègne, where she was captured. The trial lasted a whole year, demonstrating the spiritual height, purity, and wisdom of Joan. She was accused of heresy and witchcraft by the English and was burnt at the stake on 30 May 1431 in the square of Rouen. In 1456, a new trial found her innocent. In 1920, the Catholic Church canonized Joan of Arc and declared her the patron saint of France.

John of the Cross (1542–1591). A Spanish mystic, poet, and Catholic saint known for his works on mystical theology, including *Dark Night of the Soul* (1618) and *Ascent of Mount Carmel* (1618).

John the Baptist. A Jewish prophet, the forerunner of Jesus Christ.

Johnston, Reginald (1874–1938). A Scottish diplomat and academic who served as the tutor to the last emperor of China; the author of *Buddhist China* (1913).

Joyce, James (1882–1941). An Irish novelist and poet, known for works such as *Ulysses* (1922) and *A Portrait of the Artist as a Young Man* (1916).

Judah ben Samuel of Regensburg (1150–1217). A prominent Jewish mystic and scholar, also known as Judah the Pious. He was a key figure in the Hasidei Ashkenaz movement in Germany and wrote mystical works that influenced Jewish spirituality.

Jue (*Ch.*). Awakening, awareness, consciousness.

Julai or **Rulai** (*Ch.*). The Chinese name for Gautama Buddha; a title applied to every Buddha.

K

Kabbalah (*Heb.*, "to receive"). The ancient Chaldean Secret Doctrine, an occult system handed down by oral transmission, but which, though accepting tradition, is not in itself composed of merely traditional teachings, as it was once a fundamental science, now disfigured by the additions of centuries and by interpolation by the Western occultists, especially by Christian mystics. Originally, the doctrines were transmitted "from mouth to ear" only, in an oral manner from teacher to the pupil who received them; hence, the name *Kabbalah*, from the Hebrew root QBL ("to receive").

The mystery and poetry of the origin of Kabbalah as a gift from the deity to humankind cluster around the name of Rabbi Shimon ben Yochai, a second-century Adept. Tradition has it that Kabbalah was a divine theosophy first taught by God to a company of angels, and that some glimpses of its perfection were conferred upon Adam; that the wisdom passed from him unto Noah, thence to Abraham, from whom the Egyptians of his era learnt a portion of the doctrine. Moses derived a partial initiation from the land of his birth, and this was perfected by direct communications with the deity. From Moses it passed to the seventy elders of the Jewish nation, and from them the theosophical scheme was handed down from generation to generation. David and Solomon especially became masters of this concealed doctrine. No attempt, the legends tell us, was made to commit the sacred knowledge to writing until the time of the destruction of the Second Temple by the Emperor Titus, when Rabbi Shimon ben Yochai, escaping besieged Jerusalem, concealed himself in a cave, where he remained for twelve years. Here he, a Kabbalist already, was further instructed by the prophet Elijah. And here Shimon taught his disciples, and his chief pupils, Rabbi Eliezer and Rabbi Abba, committed to writing those teachings which in later ages became known as the *Zohar*, and were certainly published afresh in Spain by Rabbi Moses de León around 1280. Thus, the *Zohar* we have now is not the *Zohar* left by Shimon ben Yochai to his son, Rabbi Eliezer, and secretary, Rabbi Abba, as an heirloom.

Currently, Kabbalah represents the hidden wisdom of the Hebrew Rabbis of the Middle Ages, derived from the older secret doctrines concerning the Divine and cosmogony, which were combined into a theology after the time of the captivity of the Jews in Babylon. It deals with hitherto esoteric interpretations of the Jewish scriptures and teaches several methods of interpreting Biblical allegories.

All the works that fall under the esoteric category are termed *Kabbalistic*. Hence, the books of Ezekiel, Daniel, Enoch, and the Revelation of St. John are purely Kabbalistic.

Kafka, Franz (1883–1924). An Austrian writer of Jewish and Czech origin, best known for *The Metamorphosis* (1915).

Kagawa, Toyohiko (1888–1960). A Japanese Christian social reformer, author, and pacifist known for his work with the poor and advocacy for labour rights and cooperative movements. He wrote more than 150 books and is remembered as the Japanese Apostle of Love.

Kaivalya (*Sk.*, "solitude"). In Hindu philosophy, the state of absolute liberation or isolation of the self (*purusha*) from the material world (*prakriti*), where the soul attains spiritual freedom and oneness with the Divine.

Kalachakra (*Sk.*, "wheel of time," "circle of time"). A system as old as man that combines the knowledge of many domains, and facilitates the mastering of supreme powers hidden in human beings, connecting this might with cosmic energies. This ancient Teaching of Fire was known in India and practised before Europe became a continent. More precisely, it was brought to humanity of the Third Race by the Great Teachers 18 million years ago, when physical and conscious man came into being.

Today the Kalachakra is widely known in Tibet, where it was brought from Shambhala in the eleventh century. The text of its books in its present form may have originated even later, for there are numerous texts that have been tampered with by sects to suit the fancies of each.

The esoteric aspect of the Kalachakra has always been imparted directly from Master to disciple, whereas, the aggregate of written texts comprises a multitude of commentaries intended for the spreading of superficial knowledge and advice. Hence, the actual Kalachakra is unknown, being accessible only to a few people who have maintained direct relationships with Shambhala. The original book on the Kalachakra that was rewritten by Tsongkhapa and included his commentaries remains unknown also.

The Kalachakra calendar is the calendar of Shambhala. It is based on a 60-year cycle, which consists of five smaller cycles of twelve years each. Therefore, when the word *century* is used in the teachings of the East, one should understand that it is used to mean a period not of 100 years, but of 60.

Kalahamsa (*Sk.*, "swan in and out of time"). A mystic title given to Brahma (or Parabrahman). It is an ancient symbol of the "First Cause," which had no name in the beginning and was later depicted in thinkers' imaginations as an ever invisible, mysterious Bird that dropped an egg into Chaos, which became the Universe. Thus, in becoming the Swan of Eternity at the beginning of each Grand Cycle of Evolution, Brahma lays a golden egg; this typifies the great Circle, itself a symbol of the Universe and its spherical bodies.

Kali Yuga (*Sk.*, "dark age"). An age of spiritual decline and ignorance. See *Yuga* for more.

Kalimpong. A town in the West Bengal state of India.

Kalki Avatar (*Sk.*, "descent of the destroyer of impurity"). The last Manvantaric incarnation of Vishnu, according to the Brahmins; of Maitreya Buddha, according to the Northern Buddhists; of Saoshyant, the last hero and Saviour of the Zoroastrians, as claimed by the Parsis; and of the "faithful and true" on the White Horse of the Christians. In his future epiphany, or tenth Avatar, the heavens will open and Vishnu will appear "seated on a milk-white steed, with a drawn sword blazing like a comet, for the final destruction of the wicked, the rejuvenation of creation, and the restoration of purity."

Kalmyks. An ethnic group primarily residing in Kalmykia, Russia. The Kalmyks are of Mongolic descent and are the only Buddhist-majority people in Europe, practising Tibetan Buddhism with strong ties to their nomadic heritage.

Kalpa (*Sk.*, "formation," "creation"). The period of a mundane revolution, generally a cycle of times, but usually it represents a Day and Night of Brahma, a period of 4,320,000,000 years.

Kama (*Sk.*, "desire"). Evil desire, lust, volition; the cleaving to existence. Kama is generally identified with Mara, the tempter.

However, Kama has a higher meaning which is the equivalent of *Eros* (*Gr.*, "love"). Hesiod makes of the god Eros the third personage of the Hellenic primordial Trinity composed of Ouranos (Uranos), Gaia, and Eros. It is the personified procreative force in Nature in its abstract sense, the propeller to creation and procreation. Exoterically, mythology makes of Eros the god of lustful, animal desire; hence, the term *erotic*. Esoterically, it is different to this. Eros is the same as Kamadeva, the god of love in the Hindu Pantheon. As the Eros of Hesiod was degraded into Cupid by exoteric law, and still more degraded by a later popular sense attributed to the term, so also is Kama a most mysterious and metaphysical subject. The earlier Vedic description of Kama alone gives the keynote of what he emblematizes. Kama is the first conscious, *all-embracing desire* for universal good, love, and for all that lives and feels, needs help and kindness; the first feeling of infinite tender compassion and mercy that arose in the consciousness of the creative One Force as soon as it came into life and being as a ray from the Absolute. Says the *Rig Veda*: "Desire first arose in *It*, which was the primal germ of mind, and which Sages, searching with their intellect, have discovered in their hearts to be the bond which connects entity with non-entity," or *manas* with pure *atma-buddhi*. There is no idea of sexual love in the conception.

Kama is pre-eminently the divine desire to create happiness and love; and it is only ages later, as humankind began to materialize, by anthropomorphization, its grandest ideals in cut and dried dogmas, that Kama became the power that gratifies desire on the animal plane. This is shown by what every *Veda* and some *Brahmanas* say. In the *Atharva Veda*, Kama is represented as the Supreme Deity and Creator. In the *Taitariya Brahmana*, he is the child of Dharma, the god of Law and Justice, of Sraddha and faith. In another account, he springs from the heart of Brahma. Others show him born from water, i.e., from primordial chaos, or the "Deep," hence one of his many names, *Ira-ja*, "the water-born"; and *Aja*, "unborn"; and *Atmabhu* or "Self-existent." Because of the sign of *Makara* (Capricornus) on his banner, he is also called "Makara Ketu." The allegory involving Shiva, the "Great Yogin," reducing Kama to ashes by the fire from his *central* (or third) Eye for inspiring the Mahadeva with thoughts of his wife while he was at his devotions, is highly suggestive, as it is said that in doing so he reduced Kama to his primeval spiritual form.

Eros in man is the will of the genius to create great pictures, great music, things that will live and serve the race. It has nothing in common with the animal desire to create. Will is of the higher *manas*. It is the universal harmonious tendency acting by the higher *manas*. Desire is the outcome of separateness, aiming at the satisfaction of Self in Matter. The path (*antah-karana*), opened between the Higher Ego and the lower, enables the Ego to exert an effect on the personal self.

Kama-loka (*Sk.*, "place of desire"). The semi-material plane, to humankind subjective and invisible, where the disembodied "personalities," the astral forms called *kama-rupa*, remain until they fade out of it, which occurs when the effects of the mental impulses that created these eidolons of human and animal passions and desires are finally exhausted. It is the Hades of the ancient Greeks, and the Amenti of the Egyptians; the land of Silent Shadows.

Kama-rupa (*Sk.*, "body of desires"). The subjective form created by all sentient beings through the mental and physical desires and thoughts connected to objects of matter; a form which survives the death of the body. After this death, three of the seven principles, or planes of the senses and the consciousness on which human instincts and ideation act in turn — the body, its astral prototype, and physical vitality — being of no further use, remain on Earth. The three higher principles, grouped into one, merge into the state of Devachan, in which the Higher Ego will remain until the hour comes for a new reincarnation; and the *eidolon* of the ex-personality is left alone in its new abode. Here, the pale copy of the man that was vegetates for a period of time, the duration of which varies according to the element of materiality it has retained and which is determined by the past life of the defunct. Bereft as it is of its higher mind, spirit, and physical senses, if left alone to its own senseless devices, it will gradually fade and disintegrate. But, if forcibly drawn back into the terrestrial sphere either by the passionate desires and appeals of surviving friends or by regular necromantic practices — one of the most pernicious of which is mediumship — the "spook" may prevail there for a period of time greatly exceeding the span of the natural life of its body. Once the *kama-rupa* has learnt the way back to living human bodies, it becomes a vampire, feeding on the vitality of those who are so anxious for its company.

If a man has failed to raise his vibration higher than that of animal, the *kama-rupa* eventually breaks up and goes into animals, following the principle "like attracts like." All red-blooded animals come from man, while cold-blooded animals come from the matter of the past.

Kanada. An ancient Indian philosopher who founded the Vaisheshika school.

Kandinsky, Wassily (1866–1944). A Russian painter and art theorist, credited as a pioneer of abstract art.

Kangyur (*Tib.*, "translated words"). A collection of Buddhist works containing the commandments or the "word of the Buddha."

Kapila Rishi. A great sage and Adept of antiquity; the author of the Samkhya philosophy.

Karasahr. An ancient city on the Silk Road, located in present-day Xinjiang, China.

Karma (*Sk.*, "action"). The Law of Retribution, the Law of Cause and Effect or Ethical Causation. There exists the karma of merit and the karma of demerit. Karma neither punishes nor rewards, it is simply *the one* Universal Law which guides unerringly, one could even say blindly, all other laws productive of certain effects along the grooves of their respective causations.

Karma defines the limits within which the destiny of an individual, people, or planet can be developed. Every word, action, thought, or desire leads to an appropriate effect, and eventually, to everything in one's surroundings. Nothing happens accidentally. Karma may be individual and collective, embracing whole peoples, continents, planets, and star systems. One cannot change or eliminate it except by removing the causes that underlie human actions.

Built from the matter of three worlds, we constantly create three types of karma: the karma of thought, the karma of desire, and the karma of action.

A person's actions are a consequence of their previous thoughts and desires. The main influence on the karma of each of us is exerted in accordance with the share of happiness or misfortune that we have brought to the people around us and the other Kingdoms of Nature.

The happiness and joy that we bring to others through our actions will bring prosperity to us on the physical plane in a future life; contributing to the unhappiness of others will lead one to wretched living conditions and personal misfortune in a future life. This misfortune and suffering can bring the person to open their heart to the suffering of the world and towards spiritual ascent.

The main, profound part of karma is created by a person's thoughts and desires. High, pure, and altruistic thoughts, aimed at the Common Good, connect a person to the Fiery World, changing the composition of the mental body during life. Such reflections will lead to the formation of new high abilities in the future life, and will bind those who are pure and loving through family ties and the ties of cooperation.

The thoughts and desires of the majority of the inhabitants of Earth are closely connected, that is, they are mainly thought-forms, where thoughts are closely intertwined with personal desires. This brings a person into constant connection with various levels of the Subtle World.

The Upanishads say: "Man is a creature of reflection: what he meditates on in this life, that is what he becomes in the next." Thus, the wise Law of Karma places the construction of our mind and character entirely in our own hands: "The present life is the daughter of the past and the mother of the future life."

Our thoughts not only shape our mind and character, but, acting upon others, they determine the companions we shall have in our future incarnation.

"Can man ascend or descend for himself alone? Of course, no being can act without implications for his surroundings. Not only does he disturb various layers of the atmosphere with every action, but he literally attracts beings that are close to him. Moreover, man must acknowledge his responsibility to the Universe. A man entertains elevated thought and, thereby, renders significant benefit to someone else. Another man loses heart and, thereby, perhaps brings about the death of another. Besides conscious thoughts, constant unconscious cooperation occurs, taking up wide circles according to the Law of Karma and the aura. . . .

"Many examples can be given of instances in which someone in Asia who fell into madness was the cause of death in a person in Europe. And when one whose spirits were raised in America brought about the healing of another in Egypt. Therefore, the blossoming of righteous thought is the fiery flower of the spirit."

In these words from *Agni Yoga* reference is made to the karmic connection that exists not only to people known to us (relatives, colleagues), but also to former loved ones and friends, who, although for karmic reasons may be incarnated in other countries, maintain a connection to us on the spiritual planes. We exchange transmissions of psychic energy with them; sometimes we heal the other, and sometimes, unknowingly and unwillingly, bring about their death with our negative thoughts and actions.

Currently, the desires of man are more powerful than his thoughts. When desires are full of cruelty and impurity, intoxicated and stupefied by drugs, in the future life they become the cause of a weak, underdeveloped brain, various nervous diseases, and developmental deformities.

For a better understanding of how the Law of Karma works, let us cite the story of a group of people.

In the twelfth century, knight "A" takes part in a crusade to the East, where in a battle he kills local resident "B," who feels the utmost hatred for the Christian invaders.

Upon returning home, "A" falls in love with "D," the wife of his neighbour "C." Her feelings for him being mutual and blinded by them, she leaves her husband "C" and her children and runs away with "A" to another country. She knew little joy in her life with her new husband, a rude and cruel man, but loved him all her life. "C" devoted his life to raising their children, but the hatred and jealousy he felt towards his ex-wife burdened his life and stayed with him even on his deathbed.

After 700 years, the Law of Karma again unites this group of people, who, drawn to each other by love and hatred and by unexhausted passions and desires incarnate in the same family to pay off their karmic debts. None is aware of what they did in their past lives, and so they returned in new physical bodies, but with similar passions and desires.

"D" is again the wife of "C" whom she left for "A" in the previous life. "A" is their eldest son; "B," whom "A" killed in a crusade to the East, is their youngest son. What kind of life have they set up for themselves?

"D" and "C" marry, attracted to each other by hatred, jealousy, and guilt, taking this attraction for the feeling of love. Her feelings quickly fade away, and all her love is directed at her eldest son "A," who was her second husband in the previous life.

"C"'s feelings of hatred, love, and jealousy are embedded in the astral body from his former life, but his love for his children helps him untie the karmic knots with them and to become free.

"B" is the second son, who is like a stranger to the others. He is drawn into this family through bloodshed, and his hatred for Christians has led him to be born in a Christian country.

In a drunken fight, when the property is being divided after his father's death ("C"), "B" kills his elder brother "A" in front of his mother "D" and goes into permanent exile. This is how the karma of "A," who killed "B" 700 years earlier, is exhausted enabling them now to be free of each other.

This historical scheme gives an example of the group and family karma in which we participate in addition to our individual karma. Karmic connections, like threads, follow each of us from an unimaginably distant past, the middle of the Third Race, from the moment we received consciousness (about 18 million years ago). Incarnating several times in each of the seven sub-races of the Third, Fourth, and Fifth Races, we created for ourselves both good and bad karma, lived it out, and then created new karma.

If karmic debts are not paid off, the Law of Karma dictates that a person will be placed in the optimal situation (from the viewpoint of karma) for them to do so. The situation provided involves the same people from one lifetime to the next until that person is free. The best means to pay off karmic debts is through Love.

This is why the karma of those who take revenge is very difficult. It was explained by Jesus Christ in the Sermon on the Mount: "Ye have heard that it hath been said, 'An eye for an eye, and a tooth for a tooth.' But I say unto you that ye resist not evil, but whosoever shall smite thee on thy right cheek, turn to him the other also" (Matthew 5: 38–39). If we respond to a blow with a blow, then, not knowing all the deep reasons for this blow, probably sown in past lives, we complicate our karma instead of exhausting it. Repaying evil for evil only ties new karmic knots with the offenders. After all, the blow could have been deserved, but the counterblow will again and again bring us together with the same people from one lifetime to another. The Law of Karma is immutable (indeed, "an eye for an eye and a tooth for a tooth"), but we should not take upon ourselves the fulfilment of this Law, for if we do, we will never escape the vicious circle of karma. Forgiving our offenders is the best way possible to ensure that the Law of Karma will not place us in the same environment again.

The karmic retribution of those who resort to black magic, including all kinds of love spells and "harmless" evocations, is especially heavy and, as a rule, falls on the shoulders of their children for up to seven subsequent generations.

It can be rather difficult to eradicate the karma created when a person indulges in carnal pleasures. Here is an example that illustrates how this is resolved from the position of the evolving spirit and karma. At a certain stage in his life, a man, who had entered the Path of Light, began to cheat on his wife and took numerous mistresses. It became difficult for his spirit to break through to his mind in order to set him on the right path. Therefore, his spirit left its quaternary and began to form new incarnations in order to find a "vessel" that would be more sensitive to spiritual needs and tasks. A boy would be born who would die at the initial stages of puberty, and would be born again, only to die at puberty. Then a girl would be born who would become a nun and maintain her chastity. If it takes a spirit with significant accumulations three incarnations to break all ties established through sexual extra-marital relationships, it will be all the more difficult for ordinary people who fall into the nets set by the brothers of the shadow, becoming their sexual slaves from one life to the next.

In Kyivan Rus', before the adoption of Christianity, polygamy was common. The most famous polygamist in its ancient history was Grand Prince Volodymyr the Great, who baptized Rus'. He had several official wives and a huge number of concubines in different cities. And yet his spirit chose Christ as the one and only Master after which he chose the path of reincarnations as a monk. He spent more than one life in the service of prayer at Kyiv Pechersk Lavra until he had transformed his instinctive masculine nature.

It is worth noting that, from the viewpoint of the Higher Powers, it does not matter whether a vow of abstinence is taken or a life is spent in a family with one's only beloved spouse — both paths are chaste.

The age of 42 years — 24 years for future generations — is considered the age of "cosmic adulthood." At this age begins the *Karma of Love* by which people are expected to work with the Cosmos on a spiritual level, for example, by helping others through sharing their life experiences or developing some spiritual quality within themselves. It can also be the case that after the age of 42, an individual may suffer a heart attack and pass on. This can happen for the reason that before reaching the age of 42 they needed to fulfil a certain programme associated with their former karma. Once the soul has completed its task, it leaves its current incarnation and brings about a new one. It may also be that a human spirit acknowledges that its present body is unable to perform a certain divine task and, so, to avoid wasting time, it attempts to weave together another body. It is evident that once most people reach the age of 40, they begin to take an interest in spiritual practices and ponder their mission in life. This is the Cosmic Karma of Love coming into effect. The Karma of Love may also go beyond the individual human life and touch the life of humanity as a whole, playing out within smaller or greater evolutionary cycles.

Humanity is watched by the Lipikas (*Sk.*, "scribes") — the Lords of Destiny. These Divine Beings are mystically connected with the Law of Retribution, for they are the Recorders who impress on invisible tablets a "grand gallery of scenes of eternity" — a faithful record of every word, act, and even thought of every man on Earth, and of all that was, is, or ever will be in the manifest Universe. It is the Lipikas, or the Lords of Karma, who project and make objective the ideal plan of the Universe, according to which the God-Creators re-create the Cosmos.

The Lipika Lords direct the evolution of the world, following Cosmic Laws and harmonizing their will with the evolution of the Cosmos. Human will is powerless against the will of the Lords of Karma, for the latter is created by the former. To shape the course of human destiny, they use special matter that outlines the foundation of the path a man must walk, being bound by karmic necessity.

However, for humans, planets, systems, etc., the Lords of Destiny create the precise conditions necessary for the ascent of the Ladder of Evolution.

The Lipika Lords, as the Lords of Karma, are better known in the East. In the West almost nothing is known of them at all. Nevertheless, in the Western consciousness they can to some degree be identified with Guardian Angels, who assist, save from trouble and misfortune, and provide protection. The White Angel is from God, while the black angel is from the devil, and a person can feel the presence of both from birth: the white angel behind the right shoulder and the black angel behind the left. One will instruct on the Righteous Path, while the other will pull a person onto the left-hand path, into the abyss, weaving crafty intrigues that lead to degradation and falling into sin.

Everyone can have an Angel, but in one case the angel will be white, and in another, in the case on one who has already become completely degraded, an outright representative of the satanic forces, there can be only the black angel. As a rule, these Angelic Hierarchies, track people who have an *argo* coefficient of 1 to 3 units. But the Lord of Karma pays attention to those who have achieved 3 units through good deeds, and in this case, He has the Cosmic Right not only to observe, but to help the spirit of an individual person in creating their optimal pattern of destiny.

People also know of the so-called Fates, who "weave" human destinies, serving as good assistants to the Lords of Karma. And whereas each individual person can have their own Guardian Angel, in the case of the Lords of Karma who observe them, the situation is somewhat different.

Those who have come from Distant Worlds will have their own Lords of Karma who have descended from the same planets or stars, and their number may range from one to twelve, depending on the representatives of the kingdoms and cohorts of unknown spirits that descended from the Distant Cosmoses. As for the earthly plane, the Lords of Karma of alien systems have already been able to raise replacements for themselves from among the most advanced Titans of Earth, who have moved to the rank of the Lords of Karma and will remain so until the end of the evolution of their mother planet, observing and protecting their fellow beings — inhabitants of Earth. Of course, the Lords of Karma will be connected with those whom they have marked with their attention and chosen to carry out certain evolutionary tasks. The Lords of Karma take full responsibility for the choice they have made and are guarantors for their wards, in some way acquiring a karmic connection with them. And if one of those who has become close to a Lord of Karma loses his light-bearing accumulations, then that Lord is willing even to risk His life to save the "fallen sheep," for, like all representatives of the Forces of Light, He is endowed with the right to pay 50 per cent of His ward's karmic debts.

The Lords of Karma are mostly Titans who have undergone evolution in other, higher star systems, as well as those who are representatives of younger planets. And in order to educate the future Lords of Karma among native inhabitants of Earth, many decide voluntarily to undergo human evolution in order to gain experience for the sake of those whom, after a certain period of time, they will leave behind as replacements.

At the earthly level, the ranks of the Lords of Karma can be increased by those who have reached a certain *argo* coefficient, have risen to the level of Titan, and are now determined, not to be helped, but to continue to help others as well as themselves in reaching a higher rung on the ladder of Evolution. This is achieved through light-bearing deeds, heartfelt gratitude towards one's Guardian Angel, and care taken to avoid binding the angelic wings in a chain of vile actions. It is essential to refrain from heaping unbearable burdens upon the shoulders of the Lord of Karma, who has begun to serve in the role not only as Patron but also as Master, composing together with the ward's spirit the best possible karmic patterns. When these conditions are met, the ward has every chance of standing shoulder to shoulder with the Lords who helped raise him up to the higher rungs of the Hierarchical Ladder, assisting him in gaining experience not only of human evolution but also divine-human evolution in the Ethereal Spheres.

The ward may perceive his Guardian Angel or the Lord of Karma as his Teacher. Although as a rule they do not belong to the Hierarchy of Masters, in some ways they play the role of Guide. Almost all of the Seven Great Teachers' chosen disciples, who in any one century numbered no more than two or three individuals, have already reached the level of Master.

Of course, a person who is neither hot nor cold and essentially, represents an amorphous biomass is of no interest even to the forces of darkness. The hierophants of evil are engaged in an eternal search for those who already have certain positive accumulations and whose *argo* coefficient is close to 3 units. Their most "tempting objects" are those who have more accumulations, because they have something that can be taken if the energies with a plus sign are converted into a minus. Clearly, it is difficult, and sometimes impossible, to shoot down an aircraft that has risen to an unattainable height, and yet at the moment it takes off the ground, it is easily made vulnerable. The souls of Earth's inhabitants, striving for transformation in spirit and having already fallen under the "jurisdiction" of the Forces of Light, often serve as targets for the forces of evil, since it is through them that these forces try to harm the Lords of Karma, loosing deadly arrows in their direction.

In order to illustrate how the Lipika Lords participate in human life, we cite a situation in which a Lord of Karma tried to save His female ward, who had been placed in a psychiatric hospital. The Lord descended into layers that were too low and energetically destructive to His transformed subtle bodies. From these layers the hierophants of evil were able to attack and catch Him in their "energy net." Being a hostage to the situation, He remained in this trap for several years, losing His life force, which flowed towards the ward. Of course, burning through the black net and sending a signal for help to the Brothers would have taken up the lion's share of His energy, in turn risking the death of His ward on whom He had placed such bright hopes. The Lords of Light still managed to discover Him, thanks to their disciples, incarnated on the earthly plane, and to free Him from the excruciating fetters. The Lord of Karma, who was found practically lifeless, was wrapped in a white luminous cloth, like a shroud, and carried to the Abode of the Brotherhood.

So, the Lipika Lords, by their pledge to a ward's spirit, can often bind themselves to their wards and remain in the role of hostage until the spirit of those in whom they have placed such good hope leaves this world.

Kartikeya (*Sk.*, "of the Krittikas"). Another name for Sanat Kumara in Hinduism; Indian god of war, son of Shiva, born of his seed fallen into the Ganges; personification of the power of the Logos; the planet Mars. Kartikeya is an intensely occult personage, a nursling of the Pleiades, and a Kumara. After killing Taraka, a giant-demon, he was given the title *Shakti-Dhara* (*Sk.*, "spear-holder"), which makes of him a kind of St. Michael.

Kashmir (*Sk.*, "land desiccated from water"). A valley in northern India, surrounded by the ranges of the Himalayas.

Kasyapa. A predecessor of Gautama Buddha; a Vedic Sage; in the words of the *Atharva Veda*: "The self-born who sprang from Time." Besides being the father of the Adityas (planetary gods) headed by Indra (the Vedic god of the firmament), Kasyapa is also the progenitor of serpents, reptiles, birds, and other walking, flying, and creeping beings.

Katha Upanishad. One of the main Upanishads.

Kaya (*Sk.*, "body"). In Buddhism, often used in terms like *Trikaya*, which refers to the "three bodies" of the Buddha: Dharmakaya (truth body), Sambhogakaya (bliss body), and Nirmanakaya (emanation body).

Keely, John Worrell (1837–1898). An American inventor who discovered a new form of energy based on sound vibration called *Dynaspheric* or *Etheric Force*. He used this mysterious energy to conduct his experiments. In *The Secret Doctrine*, Blavatsky writes: "For the *etheric* Force, discovered by the well-known (in America and now in Europe) John Worrell Keely of Philadelphia, is no *hallucination*.... Had Keely been permitted to succeed, he might have reduced a whole army to atoms in the space of a few seconds as easily as he reduced a dead ox to the same condition.... Keely's discovery would lead to a knowledge of one of the most occult secrets, a secret which can never be allowed to fall into the hands of the masses."

Keightley, Bertram (1860–1944). An English Theosophist who helped H.P.B. in preparing *The Secret Doctrine* for publication. In 1889, he founded the Indian Section of the Theosophical Society, serving as its first General Secretary from 1897 to 1901.

Key. A symbol of universal importance, an emblem of silence among the ancient nations. Represented on the threshold of the Adytum (the innermost sanctuary), the key had a double meaning: it reminded candidates of the obligation of silence, and promised the unlocking of many a hitherto impenetrable mystery to the profane. The priestess of Ceres bore a key as her ensign of office, and the key was, in the Mysteries of Isis, symbolic of the opening or disclosing of the heart and conscience before the 42 assessors of the dead.

Khadija. The first wife and the first follower of Muhammad.

Khan (*Tur.*, "lord," "prince"). A title for rulers or tribal leaders in Central Asia, Mongolia, and other Turkic and Mongolic cultures.

Khechara (*Sk.*, "sky-walker"). A yogi who can travel in astral form.

Khenpo (*Tib.*, "abbot"). A senior monastic teacher or abbot in Tibetan Buddhism; a title equivalent to a PhD degree in Buddhism, usually awarded after 13 years of intensive study. Khenpos are responsible for teaching scripture, philosophy, and monastic discipline.

Khyung (*Tib.*). See *Garuda*.

Kiratarjuniya (*Sk.*, "Arjuna and the hunter"). A Sanskrit epic celebrating the strife and prowess of Arjuna in his encounter with the god Shiva, disguised as a forest-hunter.

Kiu-te or **Kiu-ti.** A generic name for secret and sacred multivolume books, which were available to H. P. Blavatsky: seven secret folios, fourteen volumes of Commentaries and annotations, and 35 exoteric volumes.

Klee, Paul (1879–1940). A Swiss-German artist, known for his abstract works that blend colour, form, line, and symbolism.

Klesha (*Sk.*, "pain and misery"). Love of life; cleaving to existence; very similar to *kama*.

Kok tu cho (*Tib.*). A secret doctrine; to worship secretly.

Koot Hoomi. One of the Great Teachers of Shambhala; the Lord of Neptune. In the second half of the nineteenth century, together with Master Morya, He undertook the mission to bring about the spiritual enlightenment of Western countries immersed in materialism and selfishness.

Master K.H. taught Helena Blavatsky, consulted her on the writing of books, and actively participated in the organization of the Theosophical Society. He corresponded with the British journalist A. P. Sinnett, who used His answers to compile *Esoteric Buddhism* (1883). The Master's letters later comprised the majority of the book *The Mahatma Letters to A. P. Sinnett*, first published in 1923. The letters mention that Master K.H. became seriously ill after coming into contact with the auras of certain valleys and people. For this reason, He was called back to Tibet for quite a long time on the order of the previous Lord of Shambhala, Mahatma Serapis, in order that the protective net of His aura could be strengthened.

The Mahatma Letters also mention that Mahatma K.H. spent 48 hours on horseback and, therefore, one of His letters was not checked during the *precipitation* process and contained errors. However, why such a long trip was undertaken and for what purpose remained unknown. During the 1923–1928 Central Asian expedition, Nicholas Roerich heard from a Mongol the following story:

"You know that we have several lamas who have great spiritual power. Of course, they do not live in cities or large monasteries. They usually dwell in remote places in mountain sanctuaries. About sixty or fifty years ago one of these lamas was entrusted with a great mission. He had to carry it out personally and before he died pass on the mission to a person of his choosing, someone he trusted. You know that the greatest assignments are given by Shambhala. But on Earth they must be carried out by human hands under earthly conditions. You should also know that such assignments are always accompanied by great difficulties, which must be overcome by fortitude and devotion. It happened that the lama had partially completed his assignment, but then fell ill and lost consciousness; in this state, of course, he could not pass on the mission to a worthy successor. The Great Keepers of the Himalayas were aware of his predicament. Since the mission had to be carried out under these conditions, one of the Great Keepers undertook in the greatest haste the tedious journey from the Tibetan highlands to our Mongolian steppes. The trip was so urgent that the Keeper remained in the saddle for 60 hours, but in doing so managed to arrive in time. He temporarily restored the lama to consciousness so that he was able to complete the task entrusted to him in a dignified manner. You see how the Great Keepers assist humanity, how much self-sacrifice and earthly hardship they take upon themselves to help the Great Future."

In 1920, Master K.H. met with Helena Roerich in London. She describes Him as follows: "The Great Teacher K.H. amazes with His unusually tall stature, He is even taller than the Great Lord M. His head resembles the head of Zeus by the sculptor Phidias. The majestic calm of His face is illumined by a smile full of goodness. His hair and beard are chestnut, His eyes are dark blue, and his skin is golden, darker than that of the Great Lord M." (16 July 1937).

The incarnations of Master K.H. include Pythagoras, Pericles, and St. Francis of Assisi. In Theosophical literature one also finds the indication that Jesus was an incarnation of Master K.H.

Like Joseph and Mary, Jesus was an Aramaic. His childhood was spent among the most educated representatives of the Essenian communities. His mother taught Jesus the Tamil language, which she knew from her mother, who although being born in India was not a Hindu. The true story of Jesus Christ is hidden in the secret catacombs of Palestine and will be revealed to humanity as soon as it is ready to hear it.

When the time of the Way to Calvary and the Crucifixion approached, Jesus was enlightened by a Higher Spirit, the Solar Logos. The new Jesus was baptized by John the Baptist, becoming Christ, and then began to approach new sections of the population, preaching among the poorest and most ordinary. Mention and confirmation of this Cosmic Mystery can be found in Gnostic literature. Annie Besant mentions it in her work *Esoteric Christianity* (1901). Thus, the Uncrucified Christ was indeed K.H., while the Crucified and the Resurrected Christ were manifestations of the Solar Hierarchy.

Helena Roerich's notebooks affirm that Master K.H. left for Jupiter, to where Master Serapis had departed previously, to commence a New Cycle on that planet. In the future, He will be the Ruler of Neptune, the planet that belongs to Him by Cosmic Right. Of course, when the Great Teachers leave Earth, they appoint successors — disciples who have reached the level of Master and have the full right to use the names that have been given to humanity to designate Teachers, names that are pseudonyms, not the Teachers' true names.

Krishna. The most celebrated Avatar (divine incarnation) of Vishnu, the Saviour of the Hindus and their most popular god.

Kshanti (*Sk.*). Patience, one of the paramitas of perfection.

Kshatriya (*Sk.*, "ruler"). A warrior class; one of the four castes in India, considered to be second after the Brahmins. In olden times, the Kshatriya Kings were like the King Hierophants of Egypt, receptacles of the highest divine knowledge and wisdom, the *elect*, and incarnations of the primordial divine Instructors — the Dhyani-Buddhas or Kumaras.

Ku (*Ch.*, "suffering or misery"). The first of the four Noble Truths in Chinese Buddhism: all life is suffering; the equivalent of *dukkha* in Sanskrit.

Kullu Valley (*Sk.*, "end of the habitable world"). A picturesque valley in the Indian state of Himachal Pradesh known as a gateway to the Himalayas.

Kumara (*Sk.*, "youth"). A virgin boy, or young celibate. The first Kumaras were the seven sons of Brahma, born out of the limbs of the god in the so-called ninth creation. It is said that they earned this name owing to their formal refusal to "procreate their species," and so, as legend has it, they "remained yogis."

Kumbakonam. A city in India.

Kundalini (*Sk.*, "curled in the form of a snake"). The "serpent power" or mystic fire, also referred to as the "World Mother." It is *buddhi* when considered as an active rather than a passive principle (which it is generally, when regarded only as the vehicle, or casket, of the supreme spirit, *atma*). *Kundalini* is called the "serpentine" or the *annular* power on account of its spiral-like working or progress in the body of the ascetic who develops the power within himself. It is a fiery electric occult or *fohatic* power, the great pristine force which underlies all organic and inorganic matter. This creative and electro-spiritual force, when aroused into action, can as easily kill as it can create.

Kung (*Ch.*, "palace"). The first note in the Chinese pentatonic scale.

Kyivan Rus'. The first East Slavic state formed around the city of Kyiv, the seat of the Grand Prince, existing from the late ninth to the mid-thirteenth century. Its borders included most of present-day Ukraine, Belarus, and part of north-west Russia. In the recently published notebooks, Master M. tells Helena Roerich: "Ukraine preserves the core of the best Rus' people, and Kyiv bore the name Mother of Rus' Cities.... Ukraine is the original Rus'" (24 April 1953).

Kyongbu Rinpoche. A teacher and spiritual adviser to the Ninth Panchen Lama, who consecrated the temple and statue of Maitreya and then miraculously disappeared in front of thousands of people. Alexandra David-Néel gathered the following explanations of this phenomenon:

1. The lama created a phantom of himself which appeared to have entered the sedan chair, and then acted as has been recounted in the Temple of Maitreya. This phantom vanished, as its master wished, when touching the statue, while the lama may have all the time remained in his hermitage.

2. He was able to produce, from afar, a collective hallucination.

3. The lama was already dead when the miracle took place, but had left behind a kind of phantom of his creation which he sent to Tashi Lhunpo.

4. By means of certain kinds of concentration of the mind, a phenomenon may be prepared in connection with a peculiar event which is to take place in the future. Once success is obtained with the concentration, the process goes on mechanically, without further cooperation of the person who has projected the energy required to bring about the phenomenon. It has even been said that this individual is, in most cases, completely incapable of preventing the phenomenon which he has planned to take place at an appointed time. Having shaped itself in a particular way, the energy generated is now beyond his control.

L

La Due, Francia (1849–1922). The founder and first Guardian-in-Chief of the Temple of the People in Halcyon, California.

La Due was born in the city of Chicago, Illinois. When she was four years old, her family moved to Syracuse, New York, where she spent most of her life until she moved to California. Even during her school years, La Due demonstrated exceptional literary talent. Later, she worked as a nurse despite having no medical education. In 1894, La Due became a member of the Syracuse branch of the Theosophical Society, founded there in 1892 by Dr. William Dower. Together with Dower, she advocated for the rights of Native Americans.

After the passing of Helena Blavatsky, the Great Brotherhood needed a new successor to continue its spiritual work in America. In 1898, the Master of Wisdom, known as Hilarion, began to guide La Due's activities. In the same year, she founded the Temple of the People in Syracuse. However, Master Hilarion later deemed it necessary to find a new location taking into account the intersections of the Earth's lines of force that create points of power. After two trips to California, La Due found an area on the eastern coast of the ocean. There, in 1903, she established the community of Halcyon, where a new stage of the spiritual work of the Temple of the People began. La Due was the first head of the Temple, serving as its Guardian-in-Chief.

The Temple of the People published the monthly magazine *The Temple Artisan*, which for many years published messages given through La Due from Master Hilarion, as well as Masters Morya and Koot Hoomi. Those messages were later compiled in two works: *Teachings of the Temple* (1925), republished as *The Temple of Mysteries* in 2023, and *From the Mountain Top* (1914), republished in 2023. The pages of *The Temple Artisan* also revealed a new section, *Theogenesis*, from the secret *Book of Dzyan*, which sheds light on the evolutionary path of humanity towards realizing its divine nature.

The members of the Temple succeeded in laying the foundation for scientific discoveries, such as microwave technology, the fruits of which still benefit humanity today.

Ladakh (*Tib.*, "land of high passes"). A region in India, also known as "Little Tibet."

Laden La, Sonam Wangfel (1876–1936). An Indian police officer, scholar, and intermediary of Tibetan origin in British India, known for his important role in British-Tibetan relations.

He was educated in the Tibetan language and religion by Sokpo Sherab Gyatso at Ghoom Monastery in Darjeeling. Between 1894 and 1898, Laden La participated in the writing of *A Sanskrit-Tibetan Dictionary* by Sarat Chandra Das. In 1899, he joined the Darjeeling police. In 1912, he welcomed Alexandra David-Néel who wished to meet the Dalai Lama. Laden La also served as the Chief of Police in Lhasa in 1923–1924.

In gratitude for Laden La's service in promoting good relations between Tibet and British India, Their Holinesses the Thirteenth Dalai Lama and the Ninth Panchen Lama presented him with gold medals and granted him the official ranks of General and Lord Chamberlain at the court of Tashi Lhunpo. After retiring in 1931, Laden La became involved in Buddhist work. He was president of the committees of several Buddhist monasteries and assisted W. Y. Evans-Wentz with the translation of *The Tibetan Book of the Great Liberation* (1954).

Lagpa (*Tib.*, "hand"). The astrological symbol of the planet Mercury.

Lama (*Tib.*, "none above"). A title which, when correctly applied, belongs only to the priests of superior grades, those who can hold office as gurus in the monasteries.

Lamaism. Tibetan Buddhism.

Lamas, Perfect. The highest Adepts. The Perfect Lamas or Bodhisattvas in Tibet are also called *Lhas*, or Gods and Spirits.

Lamasery. A monastery of lamas in Tibet or Mongolia.

Lamrim Chenmo (*Tib.*, "great treatise on the stages of the path"). A sacred volume of precepts and rules written by Tsongkhapa "for the advancement of knowledge."

Land of the Gods. Another name for Shambhala, so called because each of its inhabitants has reached a divine state. See *Shambhala*.

The Land of the Gods is the title under which the long-hidden book penned by H. P. Blavatsky was published in 2022. See *Hartmann, Franz* for background.

In the same way as *From the Caves and Jungles of Hindostan*, *The Land of the Gods* describes various real events that took place in different places and times, and weaves them into a single story.

Over the years, for the purpose of attaining the necessary energy alignment of her sevenfold structure, Blavatsky needed to visit the main Western Abode in the Alps and the main Eastern Abode in the Himalayas. Hence, the meeting with the Sisters that is described in the book took place in the Himalayas, while the experiments in the alchemical laboratory were conducted in the Alps. Of course, she also visited Abodes on other continents, but there is no mention of this in the book.

It is worth taking a look at the characters of *The Land of the Gods* that are based on real figures. Although their names were changed, in essence, their portrayal in the book remains faithful to the character in life.

The Imperator is the former Lord of Shambhala, Mahatma Serapis, who was replaced by Mahatma Morya in 1924. Serapis has since left Earth, but Confucius, Plato, Numa Pompilius, and Seneca are among His incarnations in the ranks of humanity. In ancient Egypt, Serapis was a great Solar God who replaced Osiris in popular worship, and in whose honour the seven vowels were sung. He remained the greatest God of Egypt even during the first centuries of Christianity and was often depicted as a serpent, a "Dragon of Wisdom." In late 1862, when President Abraham Lincoln was still hesitating about whether to issue the Emancipation Proclamation, it was the Lord of Shambhala who appealed to him in spirit as Seneca and urged him to do so.

Theodorus is the Brother known as the Great Alchemist who was incarnated as Thomas Vaughan and Paracelsus. It was he who was behind the phenomenon of Edgar Cayce, and Nicola Tesla was an advanced disciple of his.

The disciple of Theodorus referred to as the *famulus*, with whom the "teleportation" experiment took place, has already become a Master. It is this mysterious Spirit who today stands behind one particular bestselling author whose books help millions of people by revealing many hitherto unknown aspects of health.

Sister Helen was incarnated as Helena Roerich. Her previous short life in Saint Petersburg, Russia, could not have been known to Franz Hartmann and yet is accurately described. In the thirteenth century, it was she who sheltered Rabbi Moses de León in her mansion in Germany, receiving the Chintamani fragment in gratitude; this explains why it returned to her in the twentieth century. As St. Catherine of Siena, she manifested a new type of saint, one who had political influence, especially unusual at a time when barely anyone heeded the opinion of women. During the time of Christ, she incarnated as Mary Magdalene who recorded all the Gospels under different names, since the other close followers of Christ were illiterate. John the Apostle preserved her writings and passed them to his disciple, who in turn gave them to the early Gnostic Valentinus, asking him to guard this treasure. Valentinus greatly distorted the writings entrusted to him and claimed them as his own. Therefore, only the Initiated are able to correctly understand the Gnostic teachings that were derived from Mary Magdalene's secret manuscripts. The moment in which Mary touched the Resurrected Christ laid the foundation for the Fiery Experience, through which the *Agni Yoga* series was given to the world and thanks to which the Masters were able to save the planet at the end of the twentieth century, a century which, according to Blavatsky, could have been "the last of its name." Roerich succeeded in mastering the cosmic Fire, and reached the highest condition of spirituality possible on Earth.

Sister Layla, so named after her incarnation which underlay the famous Arab legend of separated lovers, *Layla and Majnun*, is the unnamed Sister of Mahatma Koot Hoomi, whom Blavatsky met when, for a time, she stayed at His house in Tibet. In Helena Roerich's works Sister Layla is referred to as Sister Oriola. It was she, with "a pair of coal-black eyes that held in their depths such a weird, unearthly expression," who manifested herself to early Theosophists, as described by Olcott's sister, Isabelle. In one of her incarnations, hundreds of thousands of years ago, Oriola was known throughout the world as a singer with a charming voice that inspired whole peoples. Three thousand years ago, in the person of Shulamith, her singing attracted the attention of King Solomon. After the tragic death of his beloved, Solomon dedicated the Song of Songs to her. Among her other incarnations are Joan of Arc and St. Teresa of Ávila. "Grateful" humanity has seen to it that she be burnt or killed almost 100 times across 777 incarnations. In the Bible, she is mentioned as the "other Mary," who was present together with Mary Magdalene after Christ's Resurrection. According to the Great Initiate of the Theban Sanctuary, Thales of Argos (who was there), "the Mother of my Lord brought closer to Him that humble Judean girl, from under whose veil the eyes of Pallas Athena once glanced at me." Jesus Christ introduced her to Thales of Argos in the following way: "Here she is, My daughter, manifest for the coming ages under the name of Sophia, the Supreme Wisdom of God" (*The Mystery of Christ*).

Thus, the three Sisters — Faith, Hope, and Love — whose paths mysteriously crossed in *The Land of the Gods*, while one was out in the world and the other two remained in Shambhala, have been continuously replacing each other since the time of Christ. Faith and Hope have already completed their mission and departed from Earth, leaving Love in the world to bid a final farewell to humanity.

Of course this does not mean that the world will be deprived of Faith, Hope, and Love, since their worthy successors, originating from earthly humanity, will remain on Earth.

Lanoo (*Sk.*). A disciple, the same as *chela*.

Lanoo-shravakas (*Sk.*). Those who have entered willingly upon the path of serious discipleship.

Lanoo-upasaka (*Sk.*). A chela who has passed the first initiation.

Lao Tzu. A great sage, saint, and philosopher who preceded Confucius; the author of *Tao Te Ching* (*Ch.*, "book of the perfectibility of Nature"). The text is based on a kind of cosmogony containing all the fundamental tenets of esoteric cosmogenesis. Thus, Lao Tzu writes that in the beginning there was nothing but limitless, boundless Space. All that lives and is, was born in it, from the "Principle which exists by Itself, developing Itself from Itself." As its name is unknown and its essence is unfathomable, philosophers have called it *Tao* (*Anima Mundi*), the uncreate, unborn, and eternal energy of Nature, manifesting periodically. When reaching a state of purity, man, like Nature, will achieve rest and then become one with Tao, the source of all bliss and felicity. As in the Hindu and Buddhistic philosophies, such purity, bliss, and immortality can only be reached through the exercise of virtue and the perfect quietude of our worldly spirit; the human mind must control, subdue, and even crush the turbulent action of man's physical nature. The sooner he reaches the necessary degree of moral purification, the happier he will feel.

Laukika (*Sk.*). Ordinary psychic abilities.

Lawrence, D. H. (1885–1930). An English novelist, poet, and essayist.

Laws of the Universe. The absolute and immutable foundations which underlie the Cosmos and the entire order of the Universe. All creation is subordinate to them; no person or thing can evade their influence. Being both restrictive and permissive at the same time, they direct Evolution along a particular channel.

Cosmic Laws condition the infinite self-perfection of all phenomena, provided that they are not violated. Should this happen, Nature will destroy her own forms, sometimes destroying whole worlds and systems in the process. Ignorance of the Laws is no excuse, and so they have been inculcated in one form or another into every religion and philosophy known today.

The foremost Law of the Universe is the *Law of Divine Love*. This law is the basis of everything, and all other Laws are subordinate to it. As for the remaining laws, none is more important than another — they are all equal. They all operate in close correlation with each other, sometimes overlapping in their actions.

Cosmic Laws are many. Just a handful are mentioned here:

The Law of Cause and Effect. All creatures endowed with the higher mind (such as human beings) fall within the scope of this Law of Karma, or Justice, which determines retribution for each thought, word, and action.

The Law of Commensurability. "Hitherto shalt thou come, but no further." This refers to the need to observe limits in everything, everywhere, and always, to give exactly as much as one is able to digest and understand in order not to cause harm.

The Law of Communicating Vessels. A change in one results in a change in the other in the interests of establishing a balance, for all things in the Cosmos are interrelated, exerting an impact on each other.

The Law of the Equality of Principles. As the two poles of the One Divine Principle, the Masculine and Feminine Principles are equal, in turn creating the Universe as Spirit and Matter.

The Law of Expediency. The expenditure of force and energy should be reasonable and correspond to the benefits bestowed; processes and phenomena which are of no advantage to the Common Good cannot exist in the Universe.

The Law of Free Will. The liberty of the spirit lies in freedom of choice concerning how to act and think in any one instance; individual free will is inviolable.

The Law of Hierarchy. The entire Cosmos is constructed and managed hierarchically: the higher governs the lower. Every manifestation in the world has its own Hierarch, obedience to whom is a fundamental condition for progress.

The Law of Magnetism and Consonance. Like attracts like: magnetic attraction, tuned by will, naturally attracts to itself consonant elements, and everyone receives exactly what their inner essence strives to attain.

The Law of Reincarnation. Every creation of Nature passes through a multitude of lives in the Mineral, Vegetable, Animal, Human, and other Kingdoms.

The Law of Rhythm. The whole Universe consists of vibration, based on the repetition of events, movement, or rhythm. All that exists in space evolves through the spiral and cyclic pulsations of life.

The Law of Sacrifice. Underlying the whole Being, this Law ensures the eternal circulation of energies in which one sacrifices itself in the name of the conception, existence, development, or self-perfection of another.

The Law of the Unity of All Things. Everything originated from the One Divine Principle, and all forms of the visible and invisible world, from a blade of grass to a star, are united and interrelated, for each contains a particle of this Principle.

Left-hand. Relating to the path of darkness and evil, while "right-hand" refers to Light and Good.

Leigong (*Ch.*). The god of thunder in Chinese mythology.

Lemuria. The name commonly used to designate the continent where the Third Race of humanity developed. It covered most of the present-day Pacific and Indian Oceans, stretching along the equator. Lemuria included present-day Australia, New Zealand, Madagascar, and Easter Island.

Lemuria was the birthplace of physical humanity, since the first Races did not have bodies of matter. The ethereal and sexless beings slowly began to take on density and, by the middle of the Third Race, resembled beast-like giants up to 20 metres tall. Even though their shapes were similar to animals, these were already human beings, though not yet rational. At the same time, a separation of the sexes in all creation gradually took place, and distinct male and female individuals appeared, along with certain animals of the time, i.e., dinosaurs. Being mindless, many male Lemurians had sexual intercourse with female animals and procreated a vicious breed of monsters — primeval apes. It was from these creatures that some Atlanteans — this time consciously — later engendered all currently existing species of man-like apes.

When nearly 18 million years ago, humanity was ready to perceive knowledge, the Great Teachers came to Earth from the Distant Worlds and endowed humans with the higher mind. Some Great Teachers had arrived much earlier, at the dawn of the planet's formation, although with the aim of solving certain Cosmic Tasks.

The Great Teachers lived among humanity. They cultivated morality in humans through their own example, always at their side as Elder Brothers. There was no need for religion at this time, since the Gods were right there alongside the people. The messengers from the Distant Worlds had taught the Lemurians much in the way of science, providing them with the knowledge of highly developed planets. For example, they knew the properties of Fire and the fiery energies; they had knowledge of architecture, construction, mathematics, astronomy, agriculture, etc. Some of the plants — wheat, for instance — did not have wild-growing counterparts on Earth, as they were gifts of the Sons of Light from Venus. Likewise, bees and ants were brought from Venus for the edification of human beings: their diligence, along with their communal and hierarchical system, could serve as an example for humanity.

By the end of the Third Race, the Lemurians had achieved a highly developed civilization. Their physical bodies had become more perfect, and their height had been reduced to between six and seven-and-a-half metres; a similar evolution took place among the animals, unusual species of which are still preserved in Australia. The Lemurians had built huge cities, and were impeccable masters of both arts and sciences. Humanity at this time can be compared to the civilization of the nineteenth century of the current era, but its knowledge of Nature and the Cosmos was far superior. Even so, those days saw the beginning of fierce confrontation between the Forces of the Light and the forces of darkness.

When the Cosmic Period came for the next change of Races, the Great Teachers resettled the most spiritual and advanced representatives of Lemuria to new islands, who were soon to form a new Race on the emerging continent of Atlantis. Lemuria was destroyed by the Fire, that is, by extremely powerful earthquakes, and then submerged into the water about four million years ago.

Evidence of the existence of the Lemurians and their civilization has been preserved in the form of mysterious sculptures on Easter Island. And archaeological excavations have also revealed huge skeletons which once belonged to the giants of that time.

Lévi, Éliphas (1810–1875). The pen name of Alphonse Louis Constant, a French poet and author of over 20 esoteric books.

Levitation. Being lifted into the air with no visible agent at work. The action may be conscious or unconscious; in the case of the former, it is accounted for by magic, and in the case of the latter, either disease or a power which requires a few words of elucidation.

The earth is a magnetic body; in fact, as some scientists have found, and as Paracelsus affirmed, it is one vast magnet. It is charged with one form of electricity — let us call it positive — which it evolves continuously by spontaneous action in its interior, or centre of motion. Human bodies, in common with all other forms of matter, are charged with the opposite form of electricity, the negative. That is to say, if left to themselves, organic or inorganic bodies will constantly and involuntarily charge themselves with and evolve the form of electricity opposite to that of the earth itself. Now, what is weight? Simply the attraction of the earth. "Without the attraction of the earth you would have no weight," says Professor Stewart; "and if you had an earth twice as heavy as this, you would have double the attraction." How then, can we get rid of this attraction? According to the electrical law above stated, there is an attraction between our planet and the organisms upon it, which keeps them upon the surface of the globe. But the law of gravitation has been counteracted in many instances by levitation of persons and inanimate objects. How can we account for this? The condition of our physical systems, say theurgic philosophers, is largely dependent upon the action of our will. If well-regulated, it can produce "miracles"; among others a change in this electrical polarity from negative to positive; the man's relations with the earth-magnet would then become repellent, and "gravity" for him would have ceased to exist. It would then be as natural for him to rush into the air until the repellent force had exhausted itself, as before it had been for him to remain upon the ground. The altitude of his levitation would be measured by his ability, greater or lesser, to charge his body with positive electricity. This control over the physical forces, once obtained, would make alteration of his levity or gravity as easy as breathing.

Lhagpa (*Tib*.). The planet Mercury.

Lhamayin (*Tib*., "not a god"). Elemental sprites of the lower terrestrial plane. Popular fancy makes of them demons and devils.

Lhamo Latso (*Tib*., "lake of the goddess"). A sacred lake in Tibet, revered as an oracle lake. Pilgrims and lamas visit it for visions and guidance, often related to finding the reincarnations of high-ranking lamas, like the Dalai Lama. This lake is also known as the Spiritual-Lake of the Goddess Palden Lhamo, the principal protectress of Tibet.

Lhasa (*Tib*., "place of the gods"). The capital of Tibet. Derived from the word *Lha* meaning "Spirits of the Highest Spheres."

Linga-sharira (*Sk*., "body's image"). The aerial symbol of the body; the astral body of man or animal; the reflection of the man of flesh. It is born *before* the physical body and dies or fades out with the disappearance of its last atom.

The atomic quality of astral doubles is not uniform. On the contrary it varies immensely depending on the individual's moral, spiritual, and physical makeup. Let us take the instance of the ego who was "A" 1,500 years ago, and is now "B."

Now the double of "A" is, after the death of his body, either predominantly spiritual or predominantly terrestrial. In the first case it soon dissipates in Kama-loka and disappears like smoke, for it has no *kama-rupa* (body of strong desires and passions) to cling to and assimilate.

"The *linga-sharira* of the good man is like the morning mist after it has quitted the body of illusion; the merits of virtue of the man that was are like the sun. When the sun rises its warm rays dissipate the image (astral body) like the perfume of the rose" (*Occult Aphorisms*).

This is the case if "A" was even an average good man. But suppose he has been a great sensualist, or cruel or something of the sort, his double at his death survives by a sort of elastic quality, a striking of its atoms together by the surviving medium of that intense force which made the man the sensualist or whatever he was.

Now, in this case the double survives and holds on together for centuries sometimes. Whereas the double of "A," the good man, is disintegrated long, long before the rebirth of his Ego; the double of "A," the sensualist, may linger until the next reincarnation. And what takes place then is this:

The previous double is drawn by affinity to the new personality (or rather to the Ego therein, its old Ego). The old double fastens very often onto the new personality of his ex-Ego, and if the actual double is weaker, the former obtains mastery over the latter; it overpowers it and sometimes makes the otherwise good man all that his ex-personality was in the previous birth or worse.

So, man's ex-double can try to link itself to him again. Yet it is but a phantom of a phantom, and unless soon after death or when the deceased has been exceedingly wicked, it cannot affect third parties. But, until it is finally disintegrated and dispersed, it can affect its old Ego now, in new form, that individuality within the man's present body and his past bodies, which are moving ahead from one reincarnation to the next. It can give him (the new man) in his physical self, a lascivious, or cruel, or selfish, or avaricious tendency against his better feelings, making him vain and self-opinionated, etc., and have the best of him unless he struggles hard to shake off the incubus. It is the ex-doubles of the present man and woman which, if the man was a woman in the previous birth, or the woman a man, take the shells or forms of their past incarnations and play the "spirit wives" and "spirit husbands" with the unfortunate mortals.

Lingua franca (*It*.). A language adopted for communication among people of different native tongues.

Liver and stomach. The correspondences of *kama* in the trunk of the body, the navel and the generative organs falling into the same category. The liver is closely connected with the spleen, as is *kama* with the *linga-sharira*, and both these play a role in generating the blood. The liver is the general, the spleen the aide-de-camp. All that the liver does not accomplish is taken up and completed by the spleen.

Locke, John (1632–1704). An English philosopher known as the "Father of Liberalism." His works on political philosophy, including *Two Treatises of Government* (1689), greatly influenced modern democracy, particularly his ideas about natural rights, government by consent, and the separation of powers.

Logos (*Gr*., "word"). The manifested deity in every nation and people; the outward expression, or the effect of the cause which is ever concealed. Thus, speech is the Logos of thought; hence, Logos is aptly translated by "Verbum" and "Word" in its metaphysical sense.

Lohan (*Ch*., "Arhat"). An Adept who lives in great solitude in a hidden retreat.

Loka (*Sk*., "place"). A region or circumscribed place; a world, sphere, or plane. The Puranas in India speak incessantly of seven and fourteen Lokas, above and below our Earth, of heavens and hells.

Lokottara (*Sk*.). Extraordinary psychic abilities.

London, Jack (1876–1916). An American author and journalist known for his adventure novels, such as *The Call of the Wild* (1903) and *White Fang* (1906), which often explore the theme of survival in harsh natural settings.

Lop Nur (*Mon*., "Lop Lake"). A former salt lake in the Xinjiang region of China.

Lotus. The most occult plant, sacred in Egypt, India, and elsewhere; called "the child of the Universe bearing the likeness of its mother in its bosom." There was a time, so the allegory goes, "when the world was a golden lotus." It is a species of *nymphaea*, first introduced from India to Egypt where it was not indigenous.

Love. An energy of supreme intensity, the all-creating power, higher than anything else in the Universe. In other words, Love is the Sacred Fire to which all other fires are subordinate.

Love is the One Law to crown all other laws. It creates and transforms everything in the created Universe.

Love is a powerful force; the heart is its generator and accumulator. From the bipolar inner world of the human being, it elicits the elements of Light, good principles, the very best in a person. Love conquers everything: time, space, death, and darkness. Thought governed and animated by Love can perform miracles, for the magnetic power of such a thought is great and irresistible.

Lovecraft, H. P. (1890–1937). An American writer, best known for his creation of the *Cthulhu Mythos*.

Lucas, George (b.1944). An American filmmaker and creator of the *Star Wars* and *Indiana Jones* franchises. He is also the creator and executive producer of *The Adventures of Young Indiana Jones*, whose DVD release features 94 historical documentaries created by Lucasfilm's crew. Among these special documentaries is one dedicated to Annie Besant, the second president of the Theosophical Society, entitled *Annie Besant — An Unlikely Rebel*.

Lucifer (*Lat*., "Light-bearer"). A monthly magazine published in London between 1887 and 1897. In the article "What's In a Name?" H.P.B. explained its name in the following manner: "The name of the present magazine — rather equivocal to orthodox Christian ears — is due to no careless selection, but arose in consequence of much thinking over its fitness, and was adopted as the best symbol to express that object and the results in view. Now, the first and most important, if not the sole object of the magazine, is expressed in the line from the First Epistle to the Corinthians, on its title page. It is to bring light to 'the hidden things of darkness'; to show in their true aspect and their original real meaning things and names, men and their doings and customs; it is finally to fight prejudice, hypocrisy, and shams in every nation, in every class of Society, as in every department of life. The task is a laborious one, but it is neither impracticable nor useless, if even as an experiment. Thus, for an attempt of such nature, no better title could ever be found than the one chosen. 'Lucifer' is the pale morning-star, the precursor of the full blaze of the noon-day sun — the 'Eosphoros' of the Greeks. It shines timidly at dawn to gather forces and dazzle the eye after sunset as its own brother 'Hesperos' — the radiant evening star, or the planet Venus. No fitter symbol exists for the proposed work — that of throwing a ray of truth on everything hidden by the darkness of prejudice, by social or religious misconceptions; especially by that idiotic routine in life, which, once that a certain action, a thing, a name, has been branded by slanderous inventions, however unjust, makes respectable people, so-called, turn away shiveringly, refusing to even look at it from any other aspect than the one sanctioned by public opinion. Such an endeavour then, to force the weak-hearted to look truth straight in the face, is helped most efficaciously by a title belonging to the category of branded names."

Lugs (*Tib*.). Manner, tradition, rule; casting, foundry work.

Lung (*Tib*., "breath"). A traditional doctrine or precept; the oral transmission of teachings.

Luther, Martin (1483–1546). A German priest, theologian, and key figure in the Protestant Reformation. Luther's *Ninety-five Theses* (1517) criticized Church practices, particularly the sale of indulgences, and he promoted the doctrine of justification by faith. His actions led to the establishment of Protestantism and significant changes in Christian doctrine and church structure.

M

MacLaine, Shirley (b.1934). An American award-winning actress and bestselling author. Her books, such as *Out on a Limb* (1983), explore reincarnation, past lives, and metaphysical concepts, bringing New Age spirituality into the mainstream for the first time. *Out on a Limb* was later adapted for television broadcast in 1987, which resulted in an explosion of interest in Theosophical books.

Macrocosm (*Gr.*, "great Universe"). The Cosmos.

Madhyamikas (*Sk.*, "followers of the Middle Way"). A sect mentioned in the *Vishnu Purana*. Agreeably to the Orientalists, a Buddhist sect, which is an anachronism. It was probably initially a sect of Hindu atheists. A later school of this name, teaching a system of sophistic nihilism that reduces every proposition into a thesis and its antithesis, and then denies both, has been started in Tibet and China. Thus, while the mystic Yogacharas affirm that everything exists owing to a previous cause or concatenation, the Madhyamikas deny this. They adopt a few of Nagarjuna's principles, Nagarjuna being one of the founders of the esoteric Mahayana systems, not their *exoteric* travesties. The allegory that regarded Nagarjuna's *Paramartha* as a gift from the Nagas (Serpents) illustrates that he received his teachings from the Secret School of Adepts and therefore, that the real tenets are kept secret.

Magi. The name of the ancient hereditary priests and learned Adepts in Persia and Media, a word derived from *Maha* ("great"), which later became *mog* or *mag*, meaning "priest" or "great one" in the Pahlavi language. Porphyry describes them as follows: "The learned men who are engaged among the Persians in the service of the Deity are called Magi." And Suidas informs us that "among the Persians the lovers of wisdom are called Magi." The priestly caste of Magi was divided into three classes or degrees: 1) *Herbeds*, or disciples; 2) *Mobeds*, or Masters; 3) *Destur Mobeds*, or Perfect Masters. The Chaldees had similar colleges, as did the Egyptians, *Destur Mobeds* being identical to the Hierophants of the Mysteries, as practised in Greece and Egypt.

The Maha-atma (the great Soul or Spirit) in India had priests in the pre-Vedic times. The Magians were priests of the Sun and the fire-god; we find them among the Assyrians and Babylonians, as well as among the Persian fire-worshippers. The three Magi, also denominated kings that are said to have made gifts of gold, incense, and myrrh to the infant Jesus, were fire-worshippers like the rest and astrologers for they saw his star.

Magic. The great science of communicating with and directing supernal, supramundane potencies, as well as of commanding those of the lower spheres; a practical knowledge of the hidden mysteries of Nature known only to the few, because they are so difficult to acquire, without falling into sin against Nature.

Magic, black. Sorcery; necromancy, or the raising of the dead, and other selfish abuses of abnormal powers. The abuse may be unintentional, and yet it still qualifies as *black* magic whenever anything is produced phenomenally for the sake of self-gratification.

Magic, ceremonial. Magic, according to Kabbalistic rites worked out, as alleged by the Rosicrucians and other mystics, by invoking powers that are higher spiritually than man, and commanding elementals who are far lower than man on the scale of being.

Magic, white. Beneficent magic, divine magic, devoid of selfishness, love of power, ambition, or lucre, and bent only on doing good to the world in general, and one's neighbour in particular. The smallest attempt to use one's abnormal powers for the gratification of self, makes of these powers sorcery or black magic.

Magician. This term, once a title of renown and distinction, has come to be wholly perverted from its true meaning. Once a synonym of all that was honourable and reverent, of a possessor of learning and wisdom, it has become degraded into an epithet to designate one who is a pretender and a juggler; a charlatan, in short, or one who has "sold his soul to the Evil One," who misuses his knowledge and employs it for low and dangerous uses, according to the teachings of the clergy, and a mass of superstitious fools who believe the magician a sorcerer and an enchanter. The word is derived from *magh, mah*, in Sanskrit *maha* — great; a man well versed in esoteric knowledge.

Magnetism. A force in Nature and in man. When it is the former, it is an agent which gives rise to the various phenomena of attraction, polarity, etc. When the latter, it becomes "animal" in contradistinction to cosmic magnetism, as well as terrestrial magnetism.

While official science calls animal magnetism a "supposed" agent and utterly rejects its actuality, the teeming millions of antiquity and of the now living Asiatic nations, occultists, Theosophists, spiritualists, and mystics of every description proclaim it to be a well-established fact. Animal magnetism is a *fluid*, an emanation. Some people can emit it for curative purposes through their eyes and the tips of their fingers, while all other creatures, humankind, animals, and even every inanimate object, emanate it either as an *aura*, or a varying light, whether consciously or not. When acted upon by contact, with a patient or by the will of a human operator, it is called *mesmerism*.

Maha (*Sk.*). Great.

Maha Bodhi Society. A Buddhist society based in Calcutta that renewed interest in

Buddhism in India. It was founded in 1891 by the Sri Lankan Buddhist leader Anagarika Dharmapala (1864–1933) and the British poet Sir Edwin Arnold (1832–1904). In 2008, His Holiness the Fourteenth Dalai Lama became its chief patron.

Maha Chohan (*Sk.*, "Great Lord," "Grand Master"). The chief of a spiritual Hierarchy or school of occultism; the Head of the Trans-Himalayan Initiates frequently mentioned in *The Mahatma Letters*; the title of the Lord of Shambhala. The duties associated with this appointment are assumed by the Brothers in turn, according to their individual assignments. *Arghyanath* ("Lord of Libations") is another of his titles, and *Arghya Varsha* ("Land of Libations") is the mystery name of the region which extends from Mount Kailash in Tibet almost as far as the Gobi Desert (known in antiquity as Shamo), from which the Kalki Avatar of the Hindus, or Maitreya Buddha, is expected. It is in this region that the sacred oasis Shambhala (from *Shamo*) exists as the Abode of the Initiates. An Esoteric Commentary states that Mother Earth's Heart "beats under the foot of sacred Shambhala" (*The Secret Doctrine*). The Hebrew form of the title is *Jahva Alhim*, which replaces in Genesis the word Elohim (the Host of Builders, mistranslated as "God"). *Java Aleim* was the title of the Chief of the Hierophants in the Aleim college of the priests of Babylonia, who held the secret of the Lost Word. "The Hierophants of all the Sacerdotal Colleges were aware of the existence of Shambhala; but the Word was known only to the Java Aleim or Maha Chohan, and was passed to his successor only at the moment of death" (*The Secret Doctrine*).

Maha Guru (*Sk.*). A Great Teacher.

Maha Kalpa (*Sk.*). The great age; a period of 311,040,000,000,000 years.

Maha Mara (*Sk.*). The great temptation.

Maha Maya (*Sk.*, "great illusion"). The great illusion of manifestation. This universe, and all that it contains in mutual relation is called the great illusion or *Maha Maya*. It is also the usual title given to Gautama Buddha's Immaculate Mother — Mayadevi, or the "Great Mystery," as she is called by the mystics.

Maharashtras (*Sk.*, "people of the great nation"). An Indo-Aryan ethnolinguistic group who are indigenous to Maharashtra in Western India.

Mahatma (*Sk.*, "great soul"). An Adept of the highest order. Exalted beings who, having attained mastery over their lower principles, are thus living unimpeded by the "man of flesh," and are in possession of knowledge and power commensurate with the stage they have reached in their spiritual evolution. Called *Arhats* in Sanskrit, *Arahants* or *Arhans* in Pali, *Rahats* in Sinhala, and *Lohans* in Chinese. This title is applied in India to those of high spiritual attainment, hence, to the members of the Trans-Himalayan Brotherhood. It is also used as a courtesy title for any distinguished or lofty individual held in high public esteem, e.g., Mahatma Gandhi.

Mahatmaship. The status or condition of a Mahatma.

Mahavakya (*Sk.*, "great saying"). In Vedanta philosophy, four great sayings or aphorisms from the Upanishads that encapsulate the essence of non-dualistic (Advaita) teachings. These are: "Tat Tvam Asi" (Thou art That), "Aham Brahmasmi" (I am Brahman), "Prajnanam Brahma" (Wisdom is Brahman), and "Ayam Atma Brahma" (Atma is Brahman).

Maha-Vidya (*Sk.*). The great (magic) knowledge.

Mahayana (*Sk.*, "great vehicle"). A mystical system founded by Nagarjuna. Its books were written in the second century BCE. It is the Northern School of Buddhism, Hinayana (*Sk.*, "lesser vehicle") being the name of the Southern School. Broadly speaking, the Mahayana includes philosophy, mysticism, and the Esoteric or Heart Doctrine embodying the idea of compassion represented by the self-sacrificing Bodhisattva. The Hinayana was the outcome of the Buddha's exoteric doctrine for the masses, hence its rendering into "the more colloquial, popular, and vulgar Pali, and its degeneration into a realistic and materialistic philosophy" (*Introduction to Mahayana Buddhism*). The Tibetans also specify a *Pratyeka Buddha* or *Pradeshika Yana*, placed between the other two, because the Pratyeka state is higher than the mere salvation of the Arhat in the Hinayana. He attains enlightenment, but it is for himself alone, not for the benefit of others as in the unselfish Bodhisattva of the Mahayana. The esoteric division of the latter is called *Vajrayana*, the *vajra* ("diamond sceptre") being symbolical of spiritual and mystic powers.

Mahdi (*Ar.*, "guided one"). The Muslim Saviour who will appear before the Day of Judgement to restore justice and guide the faithful.

Mahler, Gustav (1860–1911). An Austrian composer and conductor.

Maitreya (*Sk.*, "love," "loving-kindness"). Synonymous with the Kalki Avatar of Vishnu (the "White Horse" Avatar), Saoshyant, the Mahdi, and other Messiahs. All these names belong to the same Spirit, the only difference being the date of His appearance which varies across religions.

While Vishnu is expected to appear on his white horse at the end of the present Kali Yuga age "for the final destruction of the wicked, the renovation of creation, and the restoration of purity," Maitreya is awaited earlier than this. Exoteric or popular teaching that offers slight variations on the esoteric doctrine states that Shakyamuni (Gautama Buddha) visited him in Tushita (a celestial abode) and commissioned him to issue thence on earth as his successor at the expiration of five thousand years after his (the Buddha's) death, which would be in less than three thousand years hence. Esoteric philosophy teaches that the next Buddha will appear during the seventh sub-race of this Round. Maitreya was a follower of Buddha, a well-known Arhat, though not his direct disciple, and he was the founder of an esoteric philosophical school. As shown by Eitel in *Handbook of Chinese Buddhism* (1888), "statues were erected in his honour as early as 350 BC." See *Morya* for more.

Maitreya Loving Kindness Tour. A worldwide touring exhibit of ancient sacred relics belonging to the historical Buddha Shakyamuni and other Buddhist masters. The tour travelled the world from 2001 to 2015, visiting 68 countries on six continents. Approximately 2.5 million people visited the exhibitions.

The tour was held under the auspices of Lama Zopa Rinpoche, the spiritual director of the worldwide Tibetan Buddhist organization "Foundation for the Preservation of the Mahayana Tradition."

The touring collections consisted of 7,458 individual relics from 71 Buddhist masters including four of Shakyamuni Buddha offered by His Holiness the Dalai Lama, and even some of the previous Buddha, Kasyapa. The Buddhist traditions of India, Nepal, China, Korea, Thailand, and Tibet were represented. For more information about the tour and these relics see: ThePowerOfHolyRelics.com.

Man. A human being of male or female gender destined to *become* the bearer of the highest spiritual principle on the planet Earth and to *be* a creator. The word *man* has its roots in the Sanskrit *manu* ("thinking creature"). Man's evolution on Earth passes through Seven Races, Seven Spheres, and Seven Rounds, with at least 777 incarnations in each Round.

Man develops through the following stages: mineral, plant, animal, man, God-man, and God. Each stage presupposes the attainment of perfection on a particular planet; and each higher level involves the repetition of previous experiences. Thus, humanity was once evolving in a Mineral Kingdom on a planet which no longer exists. Then it passed through the Mineral Kingdom once more, but by this point it had reached the Plant Kingdom on another planet, which also disappeared. Subsequently, human monads emigrated to the Moon, where they continued their evolution in the Mineral, Plant, and Animal Kingdoms. On the Moon, the wave of life appeared one stage earlier than on Earth. This means that the current Animal Kingdom of Earthly Evolution was the Plant Kingdom on the Moon. When the Moon completed its life cycle, when all its forms of life had reached the highest point in their development within the Seven Rounds, they ascended to the next higher step and, thereby, to another planet — Earth. Now, when humanity achieves perfection on Earth, it will move to a new planet, where there will be new conditions for a higher development still, and so on, endlessly into Infinity.

Man goes through all the Kingdoms of Nature in turn. Not only from the moment of conception, as an embryo, but throughout his lifetime his structure is continually being formed in accordance with these steps. Hence for the first seven years, he lives as a mineral; the next seven years, up to the age of 14, as a plant; further, up to the age of 28, as an animal (its atom is laid down as a double seven-year period); then up to the age of 35 as a man; and later, up to 42, as a soul. The number 42 is inherent in the Solar System as the maturation of the sevenfold human structure. In other words, from the perspective of the Cosmos, man attains the age of majority at 42 years. Then, from 42 onwards, man lives as a spirit. However, this scheme should be understood symbolically, since it cannot be said that one can achieve spiritual transformation at the age of 49 simply by adding seven years to 42. These are just small steps, while the ascent through the stages of spiritual development is endless.

The evolution of High Spirits, who came to Earth from Distant Worlds to assist humanity, is an exception: in order to become human beings, they can avoid the Animal Kingdom through additional incarnations in the Plant Kingdom, or pass through this stage in the Kingdom of Birds.

The human structure, as everything in the Solar System, is septenary and consists of seven principles, which go by different names in various philosophies and can also be represented as a traditional tripartite concept:

I. Spirit

1. *Spirit*, or *atma* (*Sk.*, "spirit"): The fiery element united with the Absolute, as its radiation.

2. *Spiritual soul*, or *buddhi* (*Sk.*, "soul"): Spirituality, the conductor of spirit.

3. *Higher mind, manas* (*Sk.*, "mind"), or *human soul*: The principle that endows man with self-consciousness and responsibility, bringing the Law of Karma into force. Man is the only being in all the Kingdoms of Nature on Earth endowed with higher consciousness. Therefore, his immortal part, the sixth and seventh principles, is integrated with the higher mind. It brings together the accumulated experience of all past lives, in contrast to the intellect, the lower mind, which is renewed at the onset of each new life.

II. Soul

4. *The astro-mental body*: Expresses physical and mental desires, emotions, and thoughts. It consists of two parts:

a) *the mental body, kama-manas* (*Sk.*, "mind of desires"), or *astral soul*, which includes the lower mind, or intellect;

b) *the subtle body, the higher astral body, the emotional body, kama-rupa* (*Sk.*, "body of desires"), or *animal soul*.

The mental body is more perfect and is used by Adepts for interplanetary flight, while the subtle body can be used for travelling within the limits of Earth. The astro-mental body is mortal, although it may live on for thousands of years.

III. Body

5. *The etheric double, the lower astral body, linga-sharira* (*Sk.*, "body's image"), or *plastic soul*: The transmitter of cosmic and solar energy to the physical body during its lifetime, being closely associated with the nervous system. The state in which man is insensible to pain — either under narcosis, certain drugs, or hypnosis — is achieved by the weakening of the link between the etheric and physical bodies. Containing all

the physical features of man, the etheric body constructs man's physical appearance according to the pattern inculcated in him at the moment of conception: hence, the physical body is, in fact, the precise double of the etheric body. It disintegrates soon after the death of the human being; certain highly sensitive people are capable of seeing etheric bodies as ghosts in graveyards. Mediums use their etheric doubles to demonstrate various phenomena.

6. *The energy body, vital principle*, or *prana* (Sk., "breath"): Consists of various energies intrinsic to Earth. After the death of the physical body it is discarded and immediately assimilated by Earth.

7. *The physical body, rupa* (Sk., "form"), or *sthula-sharira* (Sk., "dense body"): The densest body that can communicate with the physical world.

So, man has three subtle natures. The first is woven from his desires and thoughts; the second is formed from his higher impulses and thoughts; and the third is manifested in Cosmic cooperation with higher energies.

All the principles mentioned are also sevenfold in structure. Often *atma* is referred to as the seventh principle, *buddhi* as the sixth, *manas* as the fifth, and so on. Though the principles are usually numbered, strictly speaking, this is of little use. The dual monad alone (*atma-buddhi*) tends to be thought of as the two highest numbers (the sixth and seventh). As for the others, since *that* principle alone which is predominant in man has to be considered as the first, no numeration is possible as a general rule. In some people, it is the higher intelligence (*manas* or the fifth) which dominates; in others, the animal soul (*kama-rupa*) reigns supreme, exhibiting the most bestial instincts, etc.

The four lower principles form a *quaternary* — the mortal personality; while the three higher principles comprise a *triad* — the immortal individuality, also known as a *monad* or the seed of the spirit. Hence in the physical world, all seven are encased in the physical body. After leaving the dense world, the three lower bodies die, and man lives on in the Subtle World with the remaining four principles in his subtle shell. Further, man casts off his higher astral body as he moves into the Mental World. Finally, he passes into the Fiery World with the higher triad only, which is encased in the fiery body.

It would be erroneous to conclude that someone who commits evil acts in life will become an animal in their next incarnation. Sometimes it happens that a person's higher principles abandon them during their lifetime. Outwardly such a person may not appear any different to any other. They might even be highly intellectual, but such a person is merely an empty shell, a living corpse. The living dead keeps reincarnating until the complete separation of the higher triad from the lower principles has occurred. According to Cosmic Laws, such an individuality begins their evolution all over again, that is, from a mineral state, but on a completely different planet with new conditions of life.

A striking example of this is Joseph Stalin, whose principles were fractured in the 1930s. Unfortunately, there are many such examples of living corpses on Earth at the current time. As for the majority of humanity, their divine triads are simply "sleeping," being unneeded, since humanity as a whole does not turn towards spirituality. To the Forces of Evolution they are already dead, although they continue to exist temporarily on Earth.

Man himself constructs the bodies of his seven principles. He builds his subtle bodies with his thoughts, feelings, and actions, and his physical body in conjunction with food. He is the creator of his own karma, which is expressed within set limits. It is possible that a man's essence is not always fully reflected in his physical appearance, for it is sometimes difficult to find suitable parents and a suitable body. In the Higher Worlds, however, man acquires an external appearance which precisely corresponds to who he actually is.

Each of the principles mentioned above, save the physical and etheric bodies, is in fact only an aspect or state of human consciousness, made up of various qualities of the one primary energy of Fire, life, or consciousness. Man is Fire, manifested in constant action. All actions and processes in the body are Fire-derived. Therefore, the control over any one of them involves mastering the Fire.

The world at the level of the quaternary is binary, whereas it is androgynous, or unified, at the level of the triad. In the Higher Spiritual World, or in the Heavens, there is no separation of the sexes. That is, man and woman are a single creature at the level of their triad. When this single individuality is about to incarnate itself in the earthly and binary world, its triad is divided at the level of the quaternary, thus actually becoming the person of a man or a woman. However, the invisible link between them is always maintained at the triad level. Despite the fact that these halves are equal, one of the principles (either masculine or feminine) may dominate if the spirit is assigned with a task that would require it.

In the physical world, periodically, the preponderance of one or the other principle occurs. But Nature herself attempts to equalize the balance by replenishing the number of children of one sex or another, which can be observed especially after a war, when more boys are born than girls.

In addition, an individual incarnates in one gender no less than three and no more than seven times in a row. Especially in the latter case, an individual that must be reincarnated in the opposite gender often feels discomfort in their own body. However, the sex of the physical body in which one is to be incarnated is determined by one's own spirit, and to change it artificially is to go against the higher tasks and will of one's own spirit.

The cases of reincarnation mentioned above and of ex-doubles (see *linga-sharira*) can lead to energy disruption and deformation of the currents of a person's gender at the subtle level. This, in turn, can result in same-sex attraction, since, in this way, at the subconscious level, the person attempts to fill in the gaps with regards to the deformed currents of their gender principle, either masculine or feminine. Same-sex attraction might also occur, if in this life a person meets someone whom they have loved in previous lives, but who is now incarnated in the same gender. This attraction might be triggered at the level of the sexual centres or the sexless emotional and mental bodies, which are magnetically attractive to each other. Therefore, it is necessary to show an appropriate understanding and approach to this phenomenon, not condemnation or hatred that lead to even greater negative consequences.

In the binary world, however, there is an immutable and inexorable Law, which prescribes cognizance of the essence of one's own principle by deepening the spirit of exploration in spheres delineated by the mystery of the existence of the opposite principle. The violation of this Law inevitably results in the gradual degradation of individuals through a number of reincarnations. Such is the Law under which the binary world works, and *nothing* can change its operation.

Therefore, in all the cases of same-sex attraction, people are faced with the task of manifesting feelings of high friendship without an intimate relationship, thereby converting sexual impulses into higher creative energy that will help them tremendously in their spiritual progress and even in achieving material success.

The human triad has its own individual accumulations, frequency of vibration, and energy formula. When it splits into two, this unique quality of energy is preserved and inherent in the two newly formed halves which compose their lower bodies according to this formula. That is, each time it reincarnates, the human spirit, its individuality, creates four lower bodies for itself, like clothing that is sewn according to a pattern.

In Nature and the Cosmos, everything is organized to a level of great wisdom and, as we know, the law of conservation of energy states that energy cannot be created or destroyed; it can only be transformed from one form into another. That is why, when the time comes for a person to depart for the Higher Worlds, they throw off these lower bodies as discarded garments that can be worn again in their next earthly reincarnation, evolving further, stepping up from the previous level of achievement. If an individual, despite human appearance, has failed to become a human being, but remained at the level of animal in their life and behaviour, then their discarded bodies go to animals. In this manner, humanity as a whole has affected the evolution of the Animal Kingdom.

However, other individuals can also "pick up" cast-off garments if the energy formula that created the garments is similar to their own. There is also such a thing as a *Soul Group* — a whole group of related individuals, vibrating at the same frequencies.

According to esoteric sources, 144,000 souls from more perfect Worlds have descended to Earth. Of course, these souls can also be considered related to one another, since they are bearers of higher, more consonant vibrations. However, during one lifetime, a separate individuality of a high spiritual level can, through the divisibility of their spirit, create between three and twelve bodies that will live in parallel and solve the tasks assigned to them, both in the dense and the Subtle Worlds. Also, it should be remembered that whereas each of the seven bodies of man is sevenfold, the mind is unable to monitor the activities of each of them.

Even an ordinary individual can give rise to numerous other bodies during their many lives on Earth: for example, the other seven halves of one's own seven bodies could be anywhere in the world. So, if a person has a dominant astral or emotional body, then, through the power of their vibrations, they may attract a person who in their own structure contains the other astral or emotional half, or bodies which are similar to them in terms of their energy formula. In this case, the two may share the same emotions and thoughts, and experience human love, however transient and short-lived.

Meanwhile, the true other half, the true soul mate, is one at the level of the triad with which one incarnated on Earth and which split into two parts in this binary world. This is the immortal nature, and therefore, what is experienced then is Divine Love. There can only be one other half of one's own triad, and moreover, it may be located in a completely different world. Even if it is now embodied as a human being, that person may not necessarily be what one would imagine: remember the symbol of Tao, black and white. The most important thing is to recognize them, because here divine rather than human vibrations are present. Only the heart can advise one in this matter.

Esoteric teachings assert that true soul mates have never met on Earth for reasons that cannot be revealed to humanity. The only exceptions are the unions thanks to which Jesus Christ and other Saviours were born. However, a powerful impetus has already been given for the future unification of all other soul mates. After reunification, these will start a new cycle in their evolution, but this time in different and higher conditions of life during the Sixth and Seventh Races.

In the future, the structure of man at the stages of God-man and God will be twelvefold with seven lower and five higher principles. Now the human body is being refined under the influence of the Cosmic Fire, becoming subtler and more attenuated. Unusual feelings and abilities are gradually beginning to awaken. Also, man will reach maturity in his subtle and physical bodies not by age 42 but by age 24. Between the ages of 24 and 42, he will then experience the formation of a different structure which will not include ageing. This is to say that a New Humanity is being born this very moment. The twenty-first century and future centuries will be devoted entirely to this.

It should be noted that on Earth there are already representatives of this future stage of evolution who go through all stages faster and become "mature," energetically speaking, by the age of 24 years old. They develop along a special line of Evolution, without stopping at the sound level of the animal atom, limiting it to one seven-year period. And at the age of 21, they begin to sound on a different note, and the next three years are enough for them to develop a structure within themselves which is designated as the human atom. At the age of 24, the atom of their soul begins to take the first decisive steps on the path of serving the Forces of Evolution.

Manas (*Sk.*, "mind"). The mental faculty which makes of man an intelligent and moral being, and distinguishes him from the mere animal; a synonym of Mahat. Esoterically, however, when unqualified, it means the Higher Ego, or the sentient reincarnating principle in man. When qualified it also means *buddhi-manas*, or the spiritual soul, in contradistinction to its human reflection — *kama-manas* (*Sk.*, "mind of desire").

Manas, lower. An emanation from the higher *manas* that is of the same nature as the higher *manas* in that it can make no impression on this plane, nor receive any. The lower *manas* clothes itself in the essence of Astral Light, thereby creating an envelope that closes it off from its parent, except through the *antahkarana* which is its only salvation. Break this and the human being becomes an animal.

Manasa-putras (*Sk.*, "sons of mind," "mind-born sons"). A name given to our Higher Egos before they incarnated in humanity. In the *exoteric* though allegorical and symbolical Puranas (sacred and ancient writings of the Hindus), it is the title given to the mind-born Sons of Brahma, the Kumaras. These developed Spirits from previous cycles of evolution, who endowed man with reason and intelligence, are also called Manasa Dhyanis. They are the highest Pitris in the Puranas, the Solar Ancestors of Man, who made of man a rational being by incarnating in the senseless forms of semi-ethereal flesh characteristic of Third Race humanity.

Manasa-rupa (*Sk.*, "body of mind"). The vehicle of the reincarnating Ego.

Manchu. The Tungusic language of the Manchus, a Mongoloid people of Manchuria, who conquered China in the seventeenth century, establishing in 1644 a dynasty that lasted until 1912.

Mandala (*Sk.*, "circle"). A geometric configuration of symbols; also the ten divisions or chapters of the *Rig Veda*.

Manek, Nisha, MD (b.1964). A Kenyan-born physician, author, educator, and integrative health specialist, who bridges science and spirituality. Formerly an esteemed member of the Mayo Clinic's Division of Rheumatology in Rochester, Minnesota, she is a recognized leader in the field of integrative medicine.

Mantra or **mantram** (*Sk.*, "instrument of thought"). A sacred or mystical phrase, word, verse, or sound that has spiritual power and is used in spiritual practices, such as meditation or prayer.

Manu. The great Indian legislator. The name comes from the Sanskrit root *man* "to think" — humankind really, but stands for Swayambhuva, the first of the Manus, who started from Swayambhu, "the self-existent," hence the Logos and the progenitor of humankind. Manu is the first Legislator, almost a Divine Being.

The fourteen Manus are the patrons or guardians of the race cycles in a Manvantara, or Day of Brahma. The primeval Manus are seven; they become fourteen in the Puranas.

Manushis or **Manushi Buddhas** (*Sk.*). Human Buddhas, Bodhisattvas, or incarnated Dhyan Chohans (Lords of Light).

Manvantara (*Sk.*, "age of a Manu"). A period of manifestation, as opposed to Pralaya (dissolution, or rest), applied to various cycles and to the reign of one Manu (the patron or guardian of humankind's cycles in a Manvantara).

The current Manvantara is the Fourth and is called the Manvantara of the Sun. The First Manvantara was of Sirius; the Second, of Saturn; the Third, of Uranus. The central stars of the Solar System have been Sirius, Uranus, Saturn, again Uranus, and currently the Sun. Likewise, the legends of the Aztecs speak of Five Suns. The Aztecs believe that the world has already experienced four major transformations. In each era, it was born and destroyed, and a new one was created, characterized by a change of Sun.

In the next Manvantara, Altair will become the central star, replacing the Sun. There should be seven Manvantaras in total, each corresponding to the human principles, with the Fifth, Sixth, and Seventh Manvantaras corresponding to *manas*, *buddhi*, and *atma*, respectively.

Mara (*Sk.*, "causing death," "killing"). An evil spirit or force; the god of temptation; the Seducer who tried to turn Buddha away from his Path; called the "destroyer" and "death" (of the soul).

Marathi. An Indo-Aryan language predominantly spoken by Marathi people in the Indian state of Maharashtra.

Marga (*Sk.*). The Path. The Aryashtanga Marga is the holy or sacred path that leads to Nirvana. The eightfold path grew out of the sevenfold path by the addition of the (now) first of the eight Marga, i.e., "the possession of right views," which a *real Yogachara* would have nothing to do with.

Margrave. A villain character in *A Strange Story* (1862) by Edward Bulwer-Lytton. In the text he is an ever-young, powerful, yet amoral magician.

Martinists. A society in France, founded by a great mystic called the Marquis de St. Martin, a disciple of Martinez Pasqualis, who was a very learned man, a mystic, occultist, and Kabbalist, born in Portugal around 1700. The society was first established at Lyons as a kind of occult Masonic Society, its members believing in the possibility of communicating with

Planetary Spirits, and minor Gods, and genii of the ultramundane spheres. Louis Claude de St. Martin, born in 1743, commenced life as a brilliant officer in the army, but left it to devote himself to study, ending his career by becoming an ardent Theosophist and a disciple of Jacob Böhme. He tried to return Masonry to its primeval character of occultism and theurgy, but failed. He first made his "Rectified Rite" to consist of ten degrees, but these were brought down to seven owing to the study of the original Masonic orders.

Mary Magdalene. The closest and most beloved disciple of Jesus Christ, who became Mother and Teacher for His disciples. She was a talented drama actress and a remarkable dancer. Mary was the only highly educated disciple among the followers of Christ and she often conducted philosophical debates with the Rabbis and Sadducees, perplexing them. She tried to record every word of Christ, and without these records no Gospel would have been created. After the Resurrection, Christ appeared before her in His subtle body for eleven years and taught her the mysteries of Existence, which she also wrote down.

All the records of Mary Magdalene were kept by the Apostle John, who, after her death, settled in the cave where she lived. But he himself was illiterate, and therefore, could not understand their meaning. John passed these most valuable manuscripts to his disciple, who in turn handed them to the Gnostic Valentinus, asking him to preserve them. But Valentinus claimed them as his own, subjecting them to severe distortion, and subsequently, they were edited by translators and interpreters. The Gnostic teachings about Christ are based on the writings of Mary Magdalene. Their true meaning is accessible only to the Initiates.

Although efforts were made to destroy Mary Magdalene's records, they were preserved in the caves in Sinai. Moreover, one of the secrets concerning her life is associated with France, in particular with the Pyrenees.

Masonry or **Freemasonry**. A centuries-old fraternal organization based on a system of moral and ethical teachings. It uses symbols and allegory derived from the tools and practices of stonemasonry. Just like the Rosicrucians, the Knights Templar, and other mystical orders, this society was first designed to protect and spread secret knowledge among those who could use it for the benefit of humanity, often guided by the Masters of Wisdom. The first Grand Master and founder of Masonry was Enoch, also known as Hermes. The founding fathers of the United States were Freemasons. Over time, this organization, like all the others founded by the Masters, lost all connection with them and today operates as any other secular organization.

Master. A translation from the Sanskrit *Guru*, "spiritual teacher," and adopted by the Theosophists to designate the Adepts, from whom they hold their teachings.

Master Institute of United Arts. An art school founded on 17 November 1921 in New York City by Russian artist and philosopher Nicholas Roerich and his wife Helena Roerich. The Institute formed part of a larger cultural movement to unite different forms of art, such as painting, music, drama, ballet, and architecture, in the pursuit of spiritual and creative expression.

Masters of Wisdom. The Great Teachers of Humanity, who have taken responsibility for its evolution. Through suffering and sacrifice, Masters of Wisdom are those who have achieved a high level of development, far surpassing that of the ordinary individual, and of course, in the human understanding, they may be considered Gods. In the nineteenth and early twentieth centuries, six Mahatmas were incarnated and known under the following names: Morya, Koot Hoomi, Rakoczy, Serapis, Hilarion, and Djual Khool. Now they no longer occupy their former physical bodies, and they have also changed their names; some have gone on to other more advanced planets, leaving worthy earthly successors in their place.

The Masters are the Great Guardians of Truth who implement the Divine Plan. They know when, what, and how much should be given to people and attentively watch over their evolution. They undertake so much intense work that the Mahatmas have no time for anything of a personal nature. They create new causes that bring about the effects needed for Evolution, thereby helping humanity to liquidate its former karma. The Masters know in advance the flow of consequences and can project them for millennia ahead. And sometimes, when the Teachers foresee the future, they know the effects of the causes consciously produced by them. So, they create the future, which is pliant in the hands of their fiery will. The Masters know the course of the stars and their future combinations, and they coordinate their creative work with the energies of the Cosmos.

One of the most essential tasks of the Great Brotherhood is to select and guide colleagues and disciples. For various reasons, the Teachers cannot enter into direct, close contact with multitudes of people. They act through their colleagues, disciples, and messengers. When their disciples are incarnated on Earth with a definite mission, the Masters follow and guide them from childhood. A karmic relationship of many millennia enables the Teachers to make contact with their disciples without difficulty. In addition to being taught secret sciences, they usually undergo a fiery transmutation that allows them to maintain communication with the Masters. The disciples are constantly being tested, even at higher levels of development. It is also inevitable that they should experience in their lives the most terrible betrayals.

Each century, the Mahatmas admit into their Abodes of Light a maximum of two candidates to convey through them a part of the secret knowledge. However, this may not always be necessary. The chief consideration is that the messenger's body must be ready to receive the Teaching. The Teachings of Light, of course, never appear spontaneously — specific periods are allotted to them. To record the Teaching, the disciples go through many incarnations of preparation, sometimes for thousands of years, and when the time comes, they are alerted beforehand to the work they are about to undertake. As a rule, preliminary preparation takes place over three years, during which the Higher Spirits work with the disciples, attuning their bodies.

Contrary to established opinion, the Great Teachers do not make contact with mediums or channellers, except in very rare cases, and when they do, it is usually indirectly, via one of their advanced disciples.

It must be remembered that on turning towards the Powers of Light, a person must initially establish a connection with their own higher bodies: for example, the mental body will be higher than the emotional body, and the spirit can act as a Guide for the soul, as well as take on the role of god in relationship to the body. And only after establishing a harmonious order of all seven bodies can a person hope that someone from Above will pay attention to them, according to their vibrational sound, or karma, both human and spiritual, depending on the goal they have set for themselves, or that was set by the Teachers entrusting them with a specific mission.

Helena Blavatsky had to accept the body of a powerful medium, as this was necessary for the tasks assigned to her during her final life on Earth. She was required to work with many different people and to perform miracles that would convince them of the existence of the higher laws of Nature and supreme knowledge. With the help of her Master, she brought her ability under complete control. Before revealing *The Secret Doctrine* to humanity, Blavatsky experienced the fiery transmutation of her body, a process which lasted for three years under the supervision of her Teacher in one of His Ashrams in Tibet. For those who have endured this process, it is tough to be out in the world among other people, and all the more so to find oneself among people who are adversely disposed towards them. This was the cause of Blavatsky's poor health. Helena Roerich went through something similar and even more intense when she received *Agni Yoga*. However, she lived in India, in the pure mountain air, in almost total solitude, surrounded by loving individuals — conditions that enabled her to almost wholly accomplish the mission of her last earthly incarnation.

Thanks to their Masters, disciples gain access to knowledge preserved in the scrolls collected in the Library of the Great Brotherhood; such knowledge comprises several levels, like a pyramid. At each level of ascent, a disciple must first take a vow of silence before they can exercise their right to receive certain knowledge. They must swear to keep any received knowledge secret until special cosmic and spatial conditions come about, or until the Council of Lords decides to open yet another page revealing the Mysteries of the Cosmos to the world.

When such a decision is made, a certain Master assumes the responsibility of preparing one of His disciples — whomever among them is most suitable for the assigned mission. The disciple's subtle bodies, in addition to their previous accumulations, are infused with certain sacred knowledge even before birth. Furthermore, before the disciple starts recording the destined works, their chalice is also systematically filled with qualitatively new currents, accompanying the inflow of new Truths. It should be noted that the Master may also work with the disciple through dreams, although the disciple may not remember them.

Of course, sorry cases in which disciples betrayed their Masters have been known to history. By tradition, disciples who have achieved the level of earthly Master renounce their own names, and not only adopt the names of their Masters, but begin to act on their behalf. However, some disciples, after gaining access to the first levels of knowledge relating to cosmogony, have failed to pass what they saw as yet another test and turned away from the Forces of Light, like Lucifer, who millions of years ago betrayed the Great Teachers and afterwards became identified with the devil.

These disciples broke the vow of silence, and attempted to sow, prematurely, in unprepared soil, divulging without the permission of the Great Teachers the secret knowledge which they had managed to receive from them. Often this type of sharing was carried out in a manner other than through the specific Ray and through whose fires the knowledge was destined to be transmitted. This resulted in a great number of distortions and terrible consequences at the level of the mental body of those people who imbibed the energetically distorted knowledge. These occasions also cast a shadow over the lives of these treacherous disciples' earthly colleagues.

A recent example of such treachery occurred when, in the first half of the twentieth century, one of Master Djual Khool's disciples betrayed Him and began to promulgate a teaching under the name of "the Tibetan." Because of this, Master Djual Khool was forced to change His name, as well as His appearance. This disciple-traitor prematurely disclosed the knowledge of the Brotherhood, which human consciousness was not ready to perceive, thereby provoking a tilt towards mentality, in addition to confusion in the mind.

Initially, when the Leaders of Humanity first came into the world, the continents were divided into seven spheres, wherein each of the Great Lords emitted their own luminous vibrations. As the rainbow is dispersed into seven colours, so all the Seven Great Teachers represent the Seven Rays, bringing with them the currents consonant with the particular note of each. Naturally, each of these Teachers also has their own Teacher, for the process of cognition is limitless.

Master-Soul. See *Alaya*.

Materialist. Not necessarily only one who believes neither in God nor soul, nor the survival of the latter, but also any person who materializes the purely spiritual, such as belief in an anthropomorphic deity, in a soul capable of burning in hell fire, and hell and paradise as localities instead of states of consciousness.

Matra (*Sk.*, "measure"). The diacritical marks or vowel signs used in Indic scripts.

Maya (*Sk.*, "illusion"). The cosmic power which renders phenomenal existence and the perceptions thereof possible. In Hindu philosophy, that alone which is changeless and eternal is called *reality*; all that is subject to change through decay and differentiation, and which has, therefore, a beginning and an end, is regarded as *Maya* — illusion.

Mayavic (*Sk.*). Illusory or deceptive, typically used to describe the transient and impermanent nature of the material world.

Mayo Clinic. A non-profit American academic medical centre based in Rochester, Minnesota, recognized as one of the leading healthcare institutions in the world. It is renowned for its clinical practice, education, and research in a wide range of medical fields.

McGovern, William Montgomery (1897–1964). An American explorer, linguist, and political scientist; the author of *An Introduction to Mahayana Buddhism* (1922).

Mea culpa (*Lat.*). An acknowledgement of one's error or fault.

Meditation. Silent and unuttered prayer, or, as Plato expressed it, "the ardent turning of the soul toward the Divine; not to ask any particular good (as in the common meaning of prayer), but for good itself — for the universal Supreme Good" of which we are a part on earth, and from whose essence we have all emerged. Therefore, adds Plato, "remain silent in the presence of the divine ones, till they remove the clouds from thy eyes and enable thee to see by the light which issues from themselves, not what appears as good to thee, but what is intrinsically good."

Genuine concentration and meditation, conscious and cautious, upon one's lower self in the light of the inner divine being and the paramitas (perfect virtues) is an excellent thing. All that helps in concentrating one's thinking and bridling its chaotic run is very useful. However, true self-improvement cannot be achieved through artificial meditations, concentrations, or any other mechanical techniques, but only through good deeds in life. Consistency in thought and action is necessary for the expansion of consciousness.

Mediumship. An abnormal psycho-physiological state which leads a person to take the fancies of his imagination and hallucinations, real or artificial, for realities. No entirely healthy person on the physiological and psychic planes can ever be a medium. That which mediums see, hear, and sense is "real," but *untrue*; it is either gathered from the astral plane, so deceptive in its vibrations and suggestions, or from pure hallucinations, which have no actual existence except for him who perceives them.

Melchizedek (*Heb.*, "king of righteousness"). One of the Hypostases of the Lord of Sirius manifested on Earth. Melchizedek is mentioned in the Bible as a Priest of the Most High. In esoteric philosophy, He is the King and Father of planet Earth and the Priest of the Ineffable One, or the One whose name is Silence, whose name He shares.

According to ancient legends of Judaism and early Christianity, Melchizedek establishes the right to the manifestation of a special and ideal dignity and extraordinary priesthood, germane to both royalty and high priests. Melchizedek is the prototype of the Messiah. He is the head of eternal angels, and He is "King of peace; without father, without mother, without descent, having neither beginning of days, nor end of life; but made like unto the Son of God; abideth a priest continually" (Hebrews 7: 2–3). Jesus Christ was "called of God a high priest after the order of Melchizedek" (Hebrews 5:10).

The last incarnation of Melchizedek was about six thousand years ago, and it took the form of the first Zoroaster, or Zarathustra, prophet and founder of Zoroastrianism. The image of Melchizedek bears within itself a seal of High Mystery, and while the main pages of His incarnations on the earthly and the Ethereal Plane may be slightly open, they are so only to those who have ascended the first rungs of Initiation.

Merseyside. A metropolitan county in North West England that includes the city of Liverpool and surrounding towns.

Meru (*Sk.*, "navel"). The name of a mountain in the centre (or "navel") of the Earth, where Svarga (*Sk.*, "abode of light"), the Olympus of Hinduism, is placed; another name for Shambhala — the Imperishable Sacred Land, the first and ever-present continent of the planet Earth.

Mount Meru contains the cities of the greatest Gods and the abodes of various Devas. Geographically accepted, it is an unspecified mountain north of the Himalayas. In tradition, Meru was the Land of Bliss in the earliest Vedic times. It is also referred to as *Hemadri* ("golden mountain"), *Ratnasanu* ("jewel peak"), *Karnikachala* ("lotus-mountain"), *Amaradri* ("eternal mountain"), and *Deva-parvata* ("mountain of the gods").

The occult teachings place "the Land of the Gods where the Sun never sets" in the very centre of the North Pole, identifying it as the site of the first continent on our Earth, after the solidification of the globe. However, it should be borne in mind that there have been frequent changes of the poles over the entire history of the Earth. Therefore, the original North Pole was where Shambhala is located nowadays. It is referred to as the Land of the Eternal Sun. Shambhala is a place where three worlds merge, being more ethereal than physical, which is why, there, the sun never sets.

Mesmerism. The term comes from Franz Mesmer (1734–1815), a German physician, who rediscovered the magnetic force in man and its practical application towards the year 1775, in Vienna. This magnetic fluid was called *animal magnetism*, and since then, *mesmerism*. It is a vital current that one person, a mesmerizer, may transfer to another, and through which he induces an abnormal state of the nervous system that permits him to have a direct influence upon the mind and will of the *subject* or mesmerized person.

Messiah (*Heb.*, "anointed one"). The awaited Saviour occurring in all religions under different names.

Metaphysics (*Gr.*, "beyond the things of the external material world"). The term used to designate that science which treats of the real and permanent being, as contrasted with the unreal, illusionary, or *phenomenal* being. To translate this word as beyond Nature or *supernatural* is to forget the spirit and hold to the dead letter, for rather it is above the ordinary, visible, and concrete.

Metaphysics are the domain of the higher *manas*, whereas physics are that of the *kama-manas*, which does the thinking in physical science and on material things. *Kama-manas*, like every other principle, consists of seven degrees. The mathematician without spirituality, however great he may be, can never reach metaphysics, but the metaphysician will master the highest conceptions of mathematics, and will apply them, without having to learn the latter. To a born metaphysician, the psychic plane will not be of much account: he will see its errors immediately he enters it, inasmuch as it is not the thing he seeks. With respect to music and other arts, these are the children of either the *manasic* or *kama-manasic* principle, proportionately as soul or technicality predominates.

Mi, Mie (*Ch.*), or **Mu** (*Sen.*). The mystic word (or rather a portion of it) in Northern Buddhism, meaning the "destruction of temptation" during the course of yoga practice; the third of the four Noble Truths in Chinese Buddhism: liberation comes only through eradicating desires and passions; the equivalent of *nirodha* in Sanskrit.

Microcosm (*Gr.*, "little Universe"). Man, made in the image of his creator, the Macrocosm, or "great" Universe, and containing all that the latter contains.

Mihirakula. A sixth-century ruler of the Hephthalite Empire in North India.

Milarepa (1028/1040–1111/1123). A famed Tibetan yogi, poet, and one of the most venerated figures in Tibetan Buddhism, known for his spiritual songs and transformation from a dark past to enlightenment through dedicated practice.

Milton, John (1608–1674). An English poet, best known for his epic poem *Paradise Lost* (1667), which explores the biblical story of the Fall of Man. He is also known for his works on theology, politics, and freedom of speech.

Mimamsa (*Sk.*, "reflection," "investigation"). A school of philosophy; one of the six in India. There are two Mimamsa, the older and the younger. The first, Purva Mimamsa, was founded by Jamini, and the latter or Uttara Mimamsa, was founded by a Vyasa and is now called the Vedanta school. Shankaracharya was its most prominent apostle.

Mirabai (c.1498–c.1546). A Hindu mystic and poet-saint, known for her devotional songs to Krishna. She is celebrated for her deep love for God and her rejection of worldly norms in favour of spiritual devotion.

Moksha (*Sk.*, "liberation"). The same as Nirvana; a post-mortem state of rest and bliss in the "soul-pilgrim."

Monad (*Gr.*, "unity"). The unified triad, *atma-buddhi-manas*, or the duad, *atma-buddhi*, that immortal part of man which reincarnates in the lower kingdoms and gradually progresses through them to the human being, and then on to the final goal of Nirvana.

A divine spark, or ray of Eternal Light, it is indestructible, unchangeable, and eternal. It is the same for all existence; it is the unconscious basis of life. As a particle of the One Divine Principle, this spark of life is inseparably linked with it. Its programme includes the aspiration to become cognizant of Divine Love, and to strive after the eternal self-perfection of the forms it animates.

At the dawn of the Grand Cycle of Evolution, every monad is begotten under the rays of a specific star or planet, which has its own Planetary Spirit, or Regent. Therefore, the monad contains the same energies as this Spirit; the Lord of the star or planet may be called the true Guardian Angel of the monads conceived in His Rays, and the celestial body itself is considered to be their guiding star for the entire Cycle. All monads engendered here are part of His own essence, although its vehicle — the human beings for whom He is Teacher and Cosmic Father — may never become aware of this fact. Similarly, the Great Masters of Wisdom have a Father, who has His own Lord, and so on. However, everything in the Universe remains indissolubly connected to the Unknowable Divine Principle, who is the Primal Progenitor of all creation.

The more developed the monad, the more advanced the forms it embodies. Levels of perfection correspond to levels of development of consciousness and are attained by a lengthy evolutionary process. At the end of the Grand Cycle of Evolution, the divine spark returns to its Source or point of origin, there to begin a new cycle of development at a higher level, and so on, forever, with no beginning or end.

Initially, the monad is a duad: a union of *atma* and *buddhi*. It is reincarnated in the lower Kingdoms of Nature — mineral, vegetable, animal — and gradually proceeds through these kingdoms to man, clothing itself in appropriate forms. Upon entering the Human Kingdom, the principle of higher consciousness, *manas*, joins the duad, forming the divine triad. It is *manas* that transforms man into a rational, ethical being, and it is this that distinguishes man from beast.

Sixty billion monads were sown on the planet Earth bearing the divine triad. All of these belong to the rays of various stars and planets, although they are all at the same temporary "stop" — Earth. Of course, as of 2025 only eight billion are incarnated in physical human form, while the others occupy the Subtle and Fiery Spheres that surround the planet.

The divine triad resides in the heart of man. From this fiery seed is germinated a special flame, the tongues of which resemble the folded petals of a lotus. The higher a man's spirituality and morality, the brighter and stronger the radiations of the heart's flame. As a rule, the flame has three tongues, or petals, hence the description of the flame as threefold. The first three petals are green, or emerald, the next three are a rose colour, or scarlet, and the last three are white. When man receives knowledge, the first three green petals of the heart-lotus begin to unfold. When he begins to love, the rose-coloured petals unfold. Then the last three, the white petals appear, only they are of a colour that is not accessible to the human eye.

In the vast majority of people, the green petals of Knowledge are unfolded to varying degrees. The rose-coloured petals of Love are revealed in a mere handful of people around the world — people who have reached the level of holiness. The white petals are possessed only by those who work with the Masters — Adepts and Initiates.

Mondrian, Piet (1872–1944). A Dutch painter and art theoretician known for his geometric, abstract style *Neo-plasticism*.

Mongolia. A country in East and Central Asia, bordered by Russia and China. Known for its vast steppes, nomadic culture, and deep connection to Tibetan Buddhism, it was the homeland of the Mongol Empire founded by Genghis Khan.

Monroe, Marilyn (1926–1962). An American actress and model.

Montessori, Maria (1870–1952). An Italian physician and educator, who developed the ground-breaking teaching method known as the Montessori method that is in use today in many public and private schools across the world. She was nominated for the Nobel Peace Prize three times: in 1949, 1950, and 1951.

In 1896, Montessori graduated from the University of Rome as a doctor of medicine, becoming the first woman to practise medicine in Italy. In 1910, at the request of Pope Pius X, Dr. Montessori developed an atrium for children. Pope Benedict XV, who installed all her publications in the Vatican Library, wanted to implement her method in all Catholic schools. He even asked her to draw up a universal syllabus for schools, but this did not come to life due to his passing. Dr. Montessori also enjoyed private audiences with Popes Pius XII, John XXIII, and Paul VI.

Dr. Montessori joined the Theosophical Society in 1899. She developed a close friendship with the second president of the Society, Annie Besant, and much of her work was published by the Theosophical Publishing House. Dr. Montessori and her son Mario also contributed articles for *The Theosophist*. In 1939, she gave a training course for teachers in India, which was held at the Theosophical Society in Adyar.

Moon. One of the oldest planets of the Solar System, originating in the First Manvantara. It has been the moon of Sirius, Uranus, Saturn, and the Sun. In general, moons are necessary for suns to create new life, worlds, and planets, because they carry magnetic power and subtle energies that endow suns with the cosmic power of attraction. Esoterically speaking, the Moon is the symbol of the lower *manas*; it is also the symbol of the Astral.

The Moon is the Mother of Earth, for it gave to Earth all life, all principles, as well as all its power — its water element. This is why the Moon controls the element of water on Earth. The Moon keeps Earth in balance, impacting the ebb and flow of its waters. During the times of Atlantis, its magnetic power raised water, thereby flooding a one seventh part of the land. In addition, the Moon influences the Earth's rotation and magnetic storms.

There is also a psycho-physiological aspect to the Moon's influence. The Moon is dead, and yet it is in another regard as a living body that sends out injurious emanations like a corpse. It vampirizes Earth and its inhabitants so that anyone sleeping in the Moon's rays suffers, losing a portion of their life force, or *prana*. A white cloth can be used as a form of protection, as the rays will not pass through it. The head especially should be guarded in this way. The Moon has most power when it is full. Gradually disintegrating, it throws off particles which humanity absorbs. These particles of its decaying corpse are full of active and destructive life, although the body which they formed is soulless and lifeless. Therefore, its emanations are at the same time beneficent and maleficent — a circumstance which finds its parallel on earth in the fact that the grass and plants are nowhere more juicy and thriving than on graves, while at the same time it is the graveyard or corpse-emanations which kill.

Where there is snow the Moon resembles a corpse, being unable, through the white snow, to vampirize effectually. Hence snow-covered mountains are free from its negative influences. Plants which are beneficent under the Sun's rays are maleficent under the rays of the Moon. Herbs containing poisons are most active when gathered under the Moon's rays.

And like all ghouls and vampires, the Moon is a friend to the sorcerer and foe to the unwary. Its nature and properties were known to every occultist from the archaic past and the later times of the witches of Thessaly, and to some of the present Tantrikas of Bengal, yet the Moon's properties have remained a closed book to physicists.

One of the names of the Moon in Sanskrit is *Soma*, which is also the name of the mystic drink of the Brahmins, showing the connection between the two. A "soma-drinker" attains the power of placing himself in direct rapport with the bright side of the Moon, thus deriving inspiration from the concentrated intellectual energy of the blessed ancestors. Beyond the mere fact of mentioning the continuous pouring out upon Earth of a certain influence from the bright side of the orb, it is this "concentration" and the Moon's role as storehouse of this energy that is the secret, the meaning of which must not be revealed.

What appears (to the ignorant) to be one stream is in fact of *dual nature* — one giving life and wisdom, the other being lethal. One who can separate the former from the latter, as Kalahamsa separated the milk from the water it was mixed with, thus showing great wisdom, will have his reward.

The maleficent influence of the Moon was intensified when Lucifer established his stronghold on its dark side on the Subtle Plane. His venomous emanations together with the lunar emanations resulted in a lethal mix that poisoned Earth for thousands of years. After Lucifer's defeat and subsequent banishment to Saturn in the middle of the twentieth century, the Great Brotherhood decided to revive the Moon and project beneficial Rays through it with the aim of influencing the majority of humanity that still had not overcome their animal nature — the nature they developed while evolving on the Moon in the distant past. Therefore, its nefarious impact is no longer what it was in the nineteenth century and earlier.

With the future appearance of the New Planet in the Solar System and under the influence of its rays, the Moon will begin a new stage of development. It will be covered in rich vegetation and transform into a flourishing garden. It will accept those spirits that are unable to move to the New Planet.

Morya. The eldest among the Great Teachers of Shambhala; the Lord of Uranus; the human aspect of the Solar Hierarch; the Manu of Earth's humanity in the Fourth Round, including the emerging Sixth and Seventh Races. In 1924, He again assumed the position of the Ruler of Shambhala and took the name Maitreya. Since Master M. is the eldest, He is also the bearer of all the names and titles of His Father, the Lord of Sirius: Sanat Kumara, the Teacher of Teachers, the Ancient of Days, Chakravartin, and so on.

The name *Morya* originates in one of the royal Buddhist houses of Magadha (an ancient kingdom in India), to which the first Buddhist king in India, Chandragupta and his grandson Ashoka belonged; it is also the name of a Rajput tribe.

The initiated Hindus were always well informed about the Great Mahatmas abiding in the Trans-Himalayas, but from the curious they guarded this sacred knowledge very carefully. Many were at one time against Blavatsky for making these great names known to the world.

Here is a passage from *The Secret Doctrine* taken from the sacred Puranas, signifying the great mission of Master Morya as the Kalki Avatar: "When . . . the close of the Kali age shall be nigh, a portion of that divine Being which exists, of its own spiritual nature [Kalki Avatar] . . . shall descend upon Earth, . . . endowed with the eight superhuman faculties. . . . He will re-establish righteousness upon earth; and the minds of those who live at the end of Kali Yuga shall be awakened, and shall be as pellucid as crystal. The men who are, thus, changed . . . shall be as the seeds of human beings, and shall give birth to a race who shall follow the laws of the Krita Age [or Age of Purity]. . . . Two persons, Devapi, of the race of Kuru, and Maru [Morya], of the family of Ikshvaku [the Solar Dynasty], . . . continue alive throughout the Four Ages, residing at . . . Kalapa [Shambhala]. They will return hither, in the beginning of the Krita Age . . . Maru [Morya] the son of Shighra, through the power of devotion [yoga] is still living . . . and will be the restorer of the Kshatriya race of the Solar Dynasty."

And further: "In the *Matsya Purana*, chapter 272, the dynasty of ten Moryas, or Maureyas, is spoken of. In the same chapter, it is stated that the Moryas will one day reign over India, after restoring the Kshatriya race many thousand years hence. Only that reign will be purely spiritual and 'not of this world.' It will be the kingdom of the next Avatar."

The incarnations of Master M. include Rama, Krishna, Zoroaster, Ramses the Great, Orpheus, Moses, Solomon, Apollonius of Tyana, Origen, St. Sergius of Radonezh, and Akbar the Great. Due to the Cosmic Mystery by which the Solar Hierarch manifested Himself in Jesus, the incarnation of Jesus Christ can also be attributed to Master M. This explains why Helena Roerich asserts: "The statement that the Lord Maitreya and Christ are One Individuality is a Truth, a Truth not fully expressed" (13 April 1953).

His final incarnation was Raja Charnoya in India, from the family of the wife of Akbar the Great. Charnoya was born where prophecy dictated that Maitreya would be born — in the holy city of Benares. He owned lands in Leh, the capital of Ladakh. His palace, of which on the mountainside only ruins now remain, was situated three kilometres (two miles) from Leh. In the final years before his departure, Raja Charnoya converted to Buddhism and finally moved there from Rajputana. On this very spot stood the house where the Buddha stayed on his journey through Hotan. Having completed his karma, at the age of about 50, he left for Shambhala, once again assuming the name Morya and later Maitreya.

In 1824, at the Secret Council of Shambhala, which took place in a monastery near Shigatse in Tibet, all the Masters of Wisdom discussed the question of whether it was worthwhile to begin a great cycle in which secret knowledge would be revealed to humanity. This cycle would cover three centuries and three areas of the world: the West, the East, and the North. Understanding the unreadiness of humanity, none of those present expressed much enthusiasm, except for one

Teacher — Master Morya, who was supported by His Brother Koot Hoomi. Despite all objections, the Council of Shambhala nevertheless decided to entrust Mahatmas Morya and Koot Hoomi with the conducting of the experiment to disclose Secret Wisdom, unprecedented in the current evolutionary cycle, and to prepare disciples for the mission.

So it was that, in the nineteenth, twentieth, and twenty-first centuries, Master Morya took upon Himself the mission of enlightening humanity through the bestowal of a cycle of books which as a whole constitute the Secret Teaching, the integral Triune Doctrine, indicating the shortest Path from the Mind to the Heart.

It was in the figure of a Raja around 2 metres tall, wearing white clothes and a turban, that Master Morya first met with Helena Blavatsky in 1851 and with Helena Roerich in 1920, in London. He had lived in this physical body for about 300 years, while looking no more than 35. Such extended preservation of the physical body was necessary both for His personal and victorious battle with Lucifer, which took place between 1936 and 1949, and for the execution of certain Cosmic Tasks.

Master M. has already departed Earth, having bequeathed to humanity three Teachings, written in the West, the East, and the North: *The Secret Doctrine*, *Agni Yoga*, and *The Teaching of the Heart*.

Thanks to Helena Roerich, it became known that in addition to the Triune Teaching, Master M. was also behind individual books written by different authors in the twentieth century, namely: *Living Waters or Messages of Joy* (1919) by Grace Lucia Kimball, republished as *The Living Waters of Joy* in 2023, and *The Song of Sano Tarot* (1929) by Nancy Fullwood, republished under the author's real name, Anna Fullwood, in 2023. Besides this, two little books were given by His advanced disciple through "Two Workers": *Awaken! Children of the Light!* (1918) and *The Spirit of the Unborn* (1918), both republished in 2023 as *Becoming What You Are* and *The Seven Laws of Spiritual Purity*, respectively.

Moses. A great Initiate and Jewish prophet, who united into one nation the Israeli tribes and organized the exodus of the Jews from ancient Egypt. As a disciple of the Egyptian priests, Moses was initiated into their secret knowledge: the Unity of the Cosmos and unity in all its multiformity, and this idea of unity he affirmed as monotheism, consolidating among the masses worship of Jehovah as one aspect of the Divinity. There were also other reasons why the image of Jehovah was chosen as the Ruling Principle or God for the Jewish people. Jehovah was connected with Saturn, and Israel, as an individual nation, was born under this planet.

However, Jehovah does not always denote the planetary spirit of Saturn. All such symbols have many meanings, and often one name covers a whole series of concepts or substitutes. Esoterically, Jehovah means "Elohim." Thus, the Voice that sounded on Mount Sinai was the Voice of the Mother of the World. *The Secret Doctrine* says: "Jehovah in its best aspect is Binah, the Upper mediating Mother, the *Great Sea* or Holy Spirit."

Moses de León (c.1240–1305). A Jewish Rabbi, the editor and first publisher of the *Zohar*, the most famous of all the Kabbalistic volumes. Entrusted with the mission to gather the foundations of the forgotten Teaching, he compiled the *Zohar* around 1280.

Mother of the World. The Greatest Spirit of the Feminine Principle, who stands at the head of the Hierarchy of Light and is One with the Lord of the World. She is personified in many religions of the world as the Supreme Goddess. The Mother of the World incarnated Herself as Mary to give life to Jesus Christ. After that, and for the past two thousand years, She has manifested Herself through Her Hypostases-Daughters — Faith, Hope, and Love, who have continuously replaced one another, never abandoning this world.

Mudra (*Sk.*, "seal," "gesture"). The mystic seal; a system of occult signs made with the fingers. These signs imitate ancient Sanskrit characters of magic efficacy. First used in the Northern Buddhist Yogachara school, they were adopted later by the Hindu Tantrikas but often misused by them for the purposes of black magic.

Muhammad. The prophet to whom the Quran, the sacred scripture of the Muslims, was revealed by Allah (God) himself. The revelation differs, however, from that given by Jehovah to Moses. Christians criticize the Quran calling it a hallucination and the work of an Arabian impostor, whereas Muhammad preaches in his scripture the unity of Deity and renders honour to the Christian prophet *Isa ibn Maryam* (Jesus, son of Mary). The Quran is a grand poem, replete with ethical teachings proclaiming loudly faith, hope, and charity.

Mukti (*Sk.*, "liberation," "freedom"). In Hinduism, the liberation of the soul from the cycle of rebirth (*samsara*), often synonymous with *moksha*.

Mumbai. The financial and entertainment capital of India, formerly known as Bombay, and home to Bollywood and major financial institutions.

Munis (*Sk.*). Saints, or Sages.

Myalba (*Tib.*). In the esoteric philosophy of Northern Buddhism, the name of our Earth, called *hell* for those who reincarnate in it for punishment. Exoterically, Myalba is translated as "hell."

Mysteries. Celebrations of initiation and observances, generally kept secret from the profane and uninitiated, in which the origin of things, the nature of the human spirit, its relation to the body, and the method of its purification and restoration to higher life were taught by dramatic representation and other methods. Physical science, medicine, the laws of music, and divination were all taught in the same manner. The Sacred Mysteries were enacted in the ancient Temples by the initiated Hierophants for the benefit and instruction of the candidates. The most solemn and occult Mysteries were certainly those which were performed in Egypt by "the band of secret-keepers." As Plato and many other sages of antiquity affirm, the Mysteries were highly religious, moral, and beneficent as a school of ethics. In short, the Mysteries were, in every country, a series of dramatic performances in which the mysteries of cosmogony and Nature were personified by the priests and neophytes, who enacted the parts of various gods and goddesses, repeating supposed scenes (allegories) from their respective lives. These were explained in their hidden meaning to candidates for initiation and incorporated into philosophical doctrines.

Mystic. In antiquity, one belonging to those admitted to the ancient mysteries; in our own times, one who practises mysticism, holds mystic, transcendental views, etc.

Mysticism. Any doctrine involved in mystery and metaphysics, and dealing more with the ideal worlds than with the matter-of-fact, actual universe.

N

Nada (*Sk.*, "sound"). The soundless voice of the Higher Self, which can be "heard" through the heart alone.

Nadabindu Upanishad. One of the minor Upanishads.

Naga (*Sk.*, "serpent"). The name in the Indian Pantheon of the Serpent or Dragon Spirits, and of the inhabitants of *Patala* (hell). Patala means the *antipodes* and was the name given to America by the ancients, who knew and visited the continent before Europe had ever heard of it. In esotericism, however, it serves as a nickname for the "wise men," or Adepts, in China and Tibet; the "Dragons" are regarded as the titulary deities of the world and of various spots on the earth, and the word is explained as meaning Adepts, yogis, and saints. The term simply makes reference to their great knowledge and wisdom. The Naga is ever a wise man, endowed with extraordinary magic powers, in South and Central America, as in India, Chaldea, and ancient Egypt. In China, the "worship" of the Nagas was widespread. The Nagas are regarded by the Celestials as the tutelary Spirits or gods of the five regions or the four points of the compass and the centre, as the guardians of the five lakes and four oceans. This, traced to its origin and translated esoterically, means that the five continents and their five Root Races have always been under the guardianship of "terrestrial deities," i.e., Wise Adepts. The tradition that Nagas washed Gautama Buddha at his birth, protected him, and guarded the relics of his body after his death, points again to the Nagas being wise men, Arhats, and not literally monsters or dragons.

Nagal or **Nagual** (*Nah.*, "pure spirit"). The title of the chief sorcerer or "medicine men" in some Mexican indigenous tribes. The Nagals always keep with them a *daimon* or god, in the shape of a serpent — and sometimes some other sacred animal — who is said to inspire them.

Nagarjuna (b.223 BCE) An Arhat, a hermit (a native of Western India) converted to Buddhism by Kapimala, and the fourteenth patriarch, now regarded as a Bodhisattva-Nirmanakaya. He was famous for his dialectical subtlety in metaphysical arguments; he was the first teacher of the Amitabha doctrine and a representative of the Mahayana School. Viewed as the greatest philosopher of the Buddhists, he was referred to as "one of the four suns which illumine the world." After his own conversion, he travelled to China where he, in turn, converted the entire country to Buddhism.

Nam Sa-go (1509–1571). A Korean scholar, poet, and seer from the Joseon dynasty, known for his prophetic writings and predictions about the future of Korea, including the rise and fall of dynasties.

Namchu Wangden (*Tib.*). See *All-Powerful Ten*.

Namkha Ding (*Tib.*, "sky-soarer"). See *Garuda*.

Nana-dassana-visuddhi (*Pali*, "purity of insight"). Purification by knowledge and vision; perception of the highest knowledge in its purest form.

Nang rigpa (*Tib.*). The esoteric science or learning; inner knowledge.

Nangwa Taye (*Tib.*, "infinite light"). Amitabha in the Dharmakaya vesture.

Napoleon I (1769–1821). The leader of the French Republic from 1799 to 1804, then of the French Empire from 1804 to 1814 and in 1815.

Nargal (*Chal.*). The Chaldean and Assyrian chiefs of the Magi.

Narjol (*Tib.*). A saint; a glorified Adept. See *nenjor*.

Nemesis. In Greek mythology, the goddess of divine retribution and revenge. The term is also used in modern contexts to refer to an unbeatable rival or an agent of downfall and justice.

Nenjor or **naljor** (*Tib.*). The realization of the blissful state of meditation; complete mental tranquillity; mastery in contemplation.

Nenjor chopa or **naljor chopa** (*Tib.*, "yoga practice"). The practice of systematic meditation, but more specifically, an expert in the art; the Tibetan name of the real Yogachara school and books.

Nenjorma or **naljorma** (*Tib.*). A female hermit or ascetic; but hardly known in Tibet in modern times. However, the lady-abbess of Samding Monastery on Yamdrok Lake is usually accorded this distinction.

Nenjorpa or **naljorpa** (*Tib.*). One who adheres to contemplative tranquillity; a hermit, an ascetic given up to meditation; a yogi.

Neophyte (*Gr.*, "newly planted"). A novice; a postulant or candidate for the Mysteries. The methods of initiation varied. Neophytes had to pass in their trials through all the four elements, emerging in the fifth as glorified Initiates. Thus, having passed through fire (deity), water (divine spirit), air (the breath of God), and earth (matter), they received a sacred mark, a *tat* (+) and a *tau* (τ). As shown by Edward Kenealy in his *Book of God, Part 2* (1868), the cross in symbolical language (one of the seven meanings) "+ exhibits at the same time three primitive letters, of which the word LVX or Light is compounded. . . . The Initiates were marked with this sign, when they were admitted into the perfect mysteries."

Neoplatonism (*Gr.*, "new Platonism"). An eclectic pantheistic school of philosophy founded in Alexandria by Ammonius Saccas of which his disciple Plotinus was the head (189–270 CE). It sought to reconcile Platonic teachings and the Aristotelean system with oriental Theosophy. Its chief occupation was pure spiritual philosophy, metaphysics, and mysticism. Theurgy was introduced towards its later years. It was the ultimate effort of high intelligences to check the ever-increasing ignorant superstition and *blind* faith of the times; the last product of Greek philosophy, which was finally crushed and put to death by brute force.

Newcastle. A historic city in north-east England.

Nidana (*Sk.*, "cause"). The twelve causes of existence, or a chain of causation, "a concatenation of cause and effect in the whole range of existence through twelve links." This is the fundamental dogma of Buddhist thought, "the understanding of which solves the riddle of life, revealing the insanity of existence and preparing the mind for Nirvana" (*Handbook of Chinese Buddhism*). The twelve links stand thus in their enumeration:

1. *Jati*, or birth, according to one of the four modes of entering the stream of life and reincarnation — or *catur yoni*, four ways of entering the path of birth as decided by karma: a) birth from the womb, as in humans and mammalia; b) birth from an egg, as in birds and reptiles; c) birth from moisture and air-germs, as in insects; and d) birth by sudden *self-transformation*, as in Bodhisattvas and Gods (*Anupapadaka*).

Each mode places the being that is born in one of the six *gatis* (esoterically seven), or conditions of sentient existence. These are divided into two groups: the three higher and the three lower paths. To the former belong the *devas*, the *asuras*, and (immortal) humans; to the latter (in exoteric teachings), creatures in hell, *pretas* or hungry demons, and animals. Explained esoterically, however, the last three are the *personalities* in Kama-loka, elementals and animals. The seventh mode of existence is that of the Nirmanakaya.

2. *Jaramarana*, or decrepitude and death, following the maturity of the *skandhas* ("bundles") — groups of attributes; everything finite, inapplicable to the eternal and the absolute. There are five — esoterically, seven — attributes in every human living being, which are known as the *pancha skandhas*. These are: a) form, *rupa*; b) perception, *vedana*; c) consciousness, *samjna*; d) action, *samskara*; e) knowledge, *vijnana*. These unite at the birth of man and constitute his personality. After the maturity of these *skandhas*, they begin to separate and weaken, and this is followed by *jaramarana*.

3. *Bhava*, the karmic agent which leads every new sentient being to be born in this or another mode of existence in the *Trailokya* ("three worlds") and *gati*.

4. *Upadana*, the creative cause of *bhava* which thus becomes the cause of *jati* which is the effect; and this creative cause is the *clinging to life*.

5. *Trishna*, love, whether pure or impure.

6. *Vedana*, or sensation; perception by the senses.

7. *Sparsa*, the sense of touch.

8. *Sadayatana*, the organs of sensation.

9. *Namarupa*, personality, i.e., a form with a name, a symbol of the unreality of material phenomenal appearances.

10. *Vijnana*, the perfect knowledge of every perceptible thing and of all objects in their concatenation and unity.

11. *Samskara*, action on the plane of illusion.

12. *Avidya*, lack of true perception, or ignorance.

The *nidanas* belong to the most subtle and abstruse doctrines of the Eastern metaphysical system.

Nihilism (*Lat.*, "nothing"). The view that existence is meaningless and all values are baseless.

Nirmanakaya (*Sk.*, "emanation body"). A Bodhisattva or late Adept, who, having reached Nirvana and liberation from rebirth, renounces it voluntarily in order to remain invisibly in the world to help humanity within the limits permitted by karma. This is the state of Masters or Initiates who have advanced along the path of comprehension of Truth and purified themselves to the extent that they have risen above even the divine illusion of Devachan — the Sixth Plane of Existence, akin to Paradise. They have achieved the supreme enlightenment which enables them to enter the Seventh and the Highest Plane, called *Nirvana*, to experience bliss. However, they voluntarily sacrifice themselves and decline to go to Nirvana because, if they did, they would be forever separated from the Earth and unable to help humanity. Therefore, such Masters continue to live in the higher Subtle or Astral spheres of Earth, to guide and protect humankind. They maintain all their body-principles, except their physical and lower astral bodies, and reside in the robe of conscious immortality. Nevertheless, they are able to create these two lower bodies should they need to incarnate among humankind in order to carry out specific tasks on Earth.

In esoteric philosophy this concept of *Nirmanakaya* represents something entirely different from the popular meaning attached to it and from the fancies of the Orientalists. Some call the Nirmanakaya body "Nirvana with remains" (Schlagintweit, etc.) no doubt on the supposition that it is a kind of Nirvanic condition during which consciousness and form are retained. Others say that it is one of the *Trikaya* (three bodies) with the "power of assuming any form of appearance in order to propagate

Buddhism" (Eitel's idea); again, that "it is the incarnate *avatar* of a deity," and so on.

Occultism, on the other hand, has it that Nirmanakaya, although literally a transformed "body," is a state. The form is that of the Adept or yogi who enters, or chooses, that post-mortem condition in preference to the Dharmakaya or *absolute* Nirvanic state. He does this because the latter *kaya* separates him forever from the world of form, conferring upon him a state of *selfish* bliss, in which no other living being can participate, the Adept being thus precluded from the possibility of helping humanity, or even *devas*. As a Nirmanakaya, however, the man leaves behind him only his physical body, and retains every other principle save the lower astral, for he has crushed this out forever from his nature during life, and it can never resurrect in his post-mortem state. Thus, instead of going into selfish bliss, he chooses a life of self-sacrifice, an existence which ends only with the life-cycle, and which will enable him to help humankind in an invisible yet most effective manner.

Thus, a Nirmanakaya is not, as popularly believed, a body "in which a Buddha or a Bodhisattva appears on earth," but truly one who, whether an Adept or a yogi during life, has since become a member of that invisible Host which ever protects and watches over humanity within karmic limits. Mistaken often for a "Spirit," a Deva, God himself, etc., a Nirmanakaya is ever a protecting, compassionate, true Guardian Angel to those who become worthy of his help. Whatever objection may be brought forward against this doctrine, however much it is denied, because, forsooth, it has never been made public hitherto in Europe, and therefore, since it is unknown to Orientalists it must be "a myth of modern invention," no one will be bold enough to say that this idea of helping suffering humankind at the price of one's own almost interminable self-sacrifice, is not one of the grandest and noblest that was ever evolved from the human brain.

When an Adept reaches during his lifetime that state of holiness and purity that makes him "equal to the Angels," then at death his apparitional or astral body becomes as solid and tangible as was the late body, and is transformed into the real man. While the old physical body falls off like the cast-off serpent's skin, the body of the "new" man remains either visible or, at the choice of the Adept, disappears from view, surrounded as it is by the Akashic shell that screens it. In the case of the latter, the Adept has the option of renouncing conscious Nirvana and rest on Earth for the good of humankind. This he can do in a twofold way: either, as said above, he can reassume the self-same personality by consolidating his astral body into physical appearance, or he can avail himself of an entirely new physical body, whether that of a newly born infant or that of a spiritually related individual illuminated by his Ray, manifesting himself thus for as long as he chooses. This is what is meant by "continuous existence."

One example is known in which a Nirmanakaya blended with the subtle body of William Q. Judge in his early 30s without him knowing of the change that had occurred within him. In 1886, Blavatsky told Judge: "The trouble with you is *that you do not know the great change* that came to pass in you a few years ago. Others have occasionally their *astrals* changed and replaced by those of Adepts . . . and they influence the *outer* and the *higher* man. With you, it is the Nirmanakaya, not the 'astral,' that blended with your astral. Hence the dual nature and fighting." As a result of this spiritual enlightenment, Judge became unusually prolific in his activities to spread Theosophy in America.

Nirvana (*Sk.*, "blown out"). A state of absolute existence and absolute consciousness, into which the Ego of an individual who has reached the highest degree of perfection and holiness during life passes after the body dies and occasionally, as in the case of Gautama Buddha and other saints, during life.

It is a state of complete enlightenment and liberation, the highest tension and development of all the capabilities inherent in the human body. Nirvana can also be called the *fiery ascent* because it represents the seventh state of matter, or the "Seventh Heaven" (Sphere). This is the only Reality in which neither Time nor Space exists, in which one can experience bliss from complete unity with one's Spirit. The other spheres, or planes, simply represent various degrees of illusion (*Maya*) of which the physical world is the greatest. However, even Nirvana is an illusion from the viewpoint of still higher Spheres that are as yet inaccessible to earthly humanity.

Nirvani. One who has attained Nirvana, an emancipated soul. That Nirvana means nothing of the kind asserted by Orientalists, every scholar who has visited China, India, and Japan is well aware. It is "*escape* from misery" but only from that of matter, freedom from *klesha*, or *kama*, and the complete extinction of animal desires. If we are told that the *Abhidharma* defines Nirvana "as a state of absolute annihilation," we concur, adding to the last word the qualification "of everything connected with matter or the physical world," and this simply because the latter (as also all within it) is illusion, *Maya*. Shakyamuni Buddha said in the last moments of his life that "the spiritual body is immortal." As Eitel, the scholarly Sinologist, explains it: "The popular exoteric systems agree in defining Nirvana *negatively* as a state of absolute exemption from the circle of transmigration; as a state of entire freedom from all forms of existence; to begin with, freedom from all passion and exertion; a state of indifference to all sensibility" (*Handbook of Chinese Buddhism*), and he might have added "death of all compassion for the world of suffering." And this is why the Bodhisattvas who prefer the Nirmanakaya to the Dharmakaya vesture stand higher in the popular estimation than the Nirvanis. But the same scholar adds that: "Positively (and esoterically) they define Nirvana as the highest state of spiritual bliss, as absolute immortality through absorption of the soul (spirit rather) into itself, but *preserving individuality* so that, e.g., Buddhas, after entering Nirvana, may reappear on earth" — i.e., in the future Manvantara.

Niyama (*Sk.*, "observances"). In the practice of yoga, the second of the eight limbs of yoga described by Patanjali. It consists of ethical guidelines for personal conduct, including purity (*saucha*), contentment (*santosha*), and self-discipline (*tapas*).

Nom de plume (*Fr.*). A pen name.

Nostradamus (1503–1566). A world-famous French astrologer, physician, and seer, known for his cryptic prophecies published in the book *Les Prophéties* (1555). As an Initiate, he knew how to protect secret knowledge by using the language of symbols. His predictions were based on astrological data and sometimes verified by his clairvoyance.

His disciple, Jean-Aimé de Chavigny, an astrologer and alchemist, left a precious manuscript on the prenatal and postnatal influence of the stars on certain marked individuals, a secret revealed to him by Nostradamus. This treatise was last in the possession of the Emperor Alexander of Russia.

Notovitch, Nicolas (1858–after 1916). A Russian journalist who at Hemis Monastery gained access to the Tibetan manuscript entitled *Life of Saint Issa, Best of the Sons of Men*. The manuscript describes the years that Jesus Christ spent in India. He translated it into French and then it was published in English as *The Unknown Life of Jesus Christ* (1894). In his preface to the 1895 edition, he mentions that a cardinal of the Roman Church told him: "The Vatican Library possesses sixty-three complete or incomplete manuscripts in various Oriental languages referring to this matter, which have been brought to Rome by missionaries from India, China, Egypt, and Arabia."

In 1922, Swami Abhedananda, a disciple of Ramakrishna, confirmed the authenticity of Notovitch's account. In *Journey into Kashmir and Tibet* (1987), he says: "The lama who was acting as our guide took a manuscript from the shelf and . . . said that it was an exact translation of the original manuscript which was lying in the monastery of Marbour near Lhasa. The original manuscript is in Pali, while the manuscript preserved in Hemis is in Tibetan. It consists of fourteen chapters and 224 couplets (shlokas). . . . The original manuscript in Pali was prepared three or four years after Christ's demise on the basis of reports given by Tibetans who actually saw him at this time of his life and the accounts received from wandering merchants who had witnessed his crucifixion."

Nyaya (*Sk.*, "justice"). One of the six Darshanas or schools of philosophy in India; a system of Hindu logic founded by Rishi Gautama.

Nyima (*Tib.*). The Sun, astrologically.

O

Oblong square. A Masonic term; a symbol of the Arc of Noah, the Covenant, the Temples of Solomon, the Tabernacle, and the Camp of the Israelites, all built as "oblong squares." Mercury and Apollo were represented by oblong cubes and squares, and so is Kaaba, the great temple at Mecca.

In her article "The Roots of Ritualism in Church and Masonry," Blavatsky writes: "The vaulted ceilings of cathedrals and churches, Greek or Latin, are often painted blue and studded with golden stars, to represent the canopy of the heavens. This is copied from the Egyptian temples, where solar and star worship was performed. Again, the same reverence is paid in Christian and Masonic architecture to the Orient (or the Eastern point) as in the days of Paganism. Ragon described it fully in his destroyed volumes. The *princeps porta*, the door of the world, and of the 'King of Glory,' by whom was meant at first the Sun, and now his human symbol, the Christ, is the door of the Orient, and faces the East in every church and temple. It is through this 'door of life' — the solemn pathway through which the daily entrance of the luminary into the *oblong square* of the earth or the Tabernacle of the Sun is effected every morning — that the "newly born" babe is ushered, and carried to the baptismal font; and it is to the left of this edifice (the gloomy north whither start the 'apprentices,' and where the candidates got their *trial by water*) that now the fonts, and in the days of old the well (*piscinas*) of lustral waters, were placed in the ancient churches which had been pagan fanes."

Occult Word, The. A monthly Theosophical journal published between 1884 and 1889 by Josephine Cables in Rochester, New York.

Occultism (*Lat.*, "hidden," "secret"). The science of the secrets of Nature: physical and psychic, mental and spiritual; called *Hermetic* and *esoteric sciences*. In the West, one may cite Kabbalah; in the East, mysticism, magic, and yoga philosophy, the latter often being referred to by the chelas in India as the *seventh* Darshana (school of philosophy), there being only *six* Darshanas in India known to the world of the profane. These sciences are, and have been for ages, hidden from the vulgar for the very good reason that they would never be appreciated by the selfish educated classes, nor understood by the uneducated; indeed the former might misuse them for their own profit, and thus turn the divine science into *black magic*. It is often brought forward as an accusation against esoteric philosophy and Kabbalah that their literature is full of "a barbarous and meaningless jargon" unintelligible to the ordinary mind. But do not exact sciences — medicine, physiology, chemistry — do the same? Do not official scientists equally veil their facts and discoveries with a newly coined and most barbarous Greco-Latin terminology? As justly remarked by Kenneth Mackenzie: "To juggle thus with words, when the facts are so simple, is the art of the scientists of the present time, in striking contrast to those of the seventeenth century, who called spades *spades* and not 'agricultural implements.'" Moreover, whilst their facts would be as simple and as comprehensible if rendered in ordinary language, the facts of occult science are of so abstruse a nature, that in most cases no words exist in European languages to express them; in addition to which our "jargon" is a *double* necessity: 1) for the purpose of describing clearly these *facts* to him who is versed in the occult terminology; and 2) to conceal them from the profane.

Occultist. One who studies the various branches of occult science. Occultism embraces the whole range of psychological, physiological, cosmical, physical, and spiritual phenomena. It therefore applies to the study of Kabbalah, astrology, alchemy, and all arcane sciences.

Octad. A group or set of eight.

Ogdoad (*Gr.*, "eightfold"). The tetrad or "quaternary" reflecting itself produced the *Ogdoad*, the "eight," according to the Marcosian Gnostics. The Eight Great Gods were called the "sacred Ogdoad."

Oirats (*Mon.*, "allied," "forest people"). A group of Western Mongolic tribes, historically significant in Central Asia. They established the Zunghar Khanate and played a major role in regional conflicts before being defeated by the Qing dynasty in the eighteenth century.

Olcott, Henry Steel (1832–1907). The co-founder of the Theosophical Society and its first president from 1875 to 1907. His activities contributed to the revival of Buddhism in South Asia.

Oliphant, Laurence (1829–1888). A British author, traveller, diplomat, and member of British Parliament.

Om Tat Sat (*Sk.*). A mantra signifying Supreme Absolute Truth. It is believed to be the most effective tool for purification and higher awakening. The utterance of any mantra brings into action the level of man's higher divine structures. It depends upon the energy of its utterer: the higher a person's energy, the more properties of the mantra are revealed.

Om or *Aum*. The most sacred and mystical of all words. It may be pronounced as two, three, or seven syllables, producing different vibrations. Its correct utterance, or rather, the intonation with which it should be pronounced, is a great secret, conveyed directly by the Teacher to His disciple. One who is able to pronounce it correctly draws close to the creative power of the Universe: *In the beginning was the Word, and the Word was Aum.* However, those who know how to use this Word rarely turn to it, since they know that it evokes forces which they cannot control and which may destroy them. Aum includes three components: Light, Colour, and Sound. These are the Three Fires or the Triple Sacred Fire in man and the Universe. According to popular belief, Aum symbolizes the three Vedas and the three Gods of Fire, Water, and Air. They also mean Creation, Preservation, and Transfiguration, personified by Brahma, Vishnu, and Shiva — or Buddha, Christ, and Maitreya. In esoteric philosophy, there are many interpretations of this three-lettered entity, which symbolizes the Trinity in One. This word is usually placed at the beginning of sacred scriptures and is prefixed to prayers, though it may serve in itself as a prayer. It is from Aum that the word *Amen* is derived.

Tat. All that is, was, or will be, all that the human consciousness is able to imagine. In Egypt this was the symbol of stability depicted as a cross. *Tat* relates to Nature and the Cosmos representing the two principles of creation: the Masculine and the Feminine, Spirit and Matter, which are One in Eternity, being the Causeless Cause of All. It expresses the unity, interpenetration, and comprehensiveness of all creation.

Sat. The eternal Absolute Truth; the one ever-present Reality in the infinite world; the Divine Essence which is, but cannot be said to exist, since it is Absoluteness, the Essence of Being itself.

Om Vajrapani Hum (*Sk.*). A mantra to invoke the infinite power and energy.

Om. See above.

Vajrapani ("wielder of the diamond sceptre"). The Protector of all Buddhas; one of the three Great Bodhisattvas, together with Avalokiteshvara and Manjushri, who represent power, compassion, and wisdom, respectively. They are known as the Three Family Protectors. Vajrapani symbolizes strength and the power to overcome all obstacles and delusions.

Hum. A mystical seed syllable that often ends mantras to seal their energy as symbolic of the highest bliss. It represents the enlightened mind and also relates to the Divine Fire. It is used as the last syllable of many Tibetan invocations, such as *Aum Mani Padme Hum, Om Ah Hum*, etc. The Tibetan language, being derived from the ancient Sanskrit, is founded on the potency of sound, and each letter has its own symbolic meaning. For instance, A (Ah) is symbolic of the Absolute, M (Ma) of non-attachment to objects of the senses, and S (Sa) of perfect secrecy or occultism.

Omito Fo (*Ch.*, "Amita Buddha"). The Chinese transliteration of *Amitabha Buddha* from Sanskrit. The complete invocation is *Na-mo-O-mi-to-Fo*, and corresponds to the Tibetan *Om (Aum) Mani Padme Hum*. In both it is the inner divinity or Higher Self which is invoked, and it will be noticed that the sacred sound *Om* or *Aum* occurs also in *Omito. Fo* is Chinese for Buddha. According to K. L. Reichelt, "*Omito Fo* is one of the most sacred terms in the consciousness of the people of Asia, it is a bright Guardian Angel hovering over human souls, it is the holy reflection from the secret chambers of the life of conscience" (*Truth and Tradition in Chinese Buddhism*).

Opakme (*Tib.*, "immeasurable light"). Amitabha in the Nirmanakaya vesture.

Orion. A prominent constellation named after a hunter from Greek mythology, recognizable by its bright stars and belt of three aligned stars; the same as Atlas, who supports the world on his shoulders. Formerly Sirius was part of Orion and the constellation appeared to have the outlines of the chalice, thanks to two bright stars that subsequently became extinct.

Orpheus (*Gr.*, "tawny one"). A legendary ancient Greek singer; one of the earliest philosophers and spiritual teachers of ancient Greece; the inventor of music and poetry. His wonderful singing enchanted gods and people, and tamed the wild forces of Nature. Together with his beloved Eurydice, Orpheus developed the cult of music.

Mythology makes Orpheus the son of Aeager and the muse Calliope. Esoteric tradition identifies him with Arjuna, the son of Indra and the disciple of Krishna. He went round the world teaching the nations wisdom and sciences and establishing mysteries. The very story of his losing Eurydice and finding her in the underworld or Hades is another point of resemblance with the story of Arjuna, who goes to Patala (or hell) and finds there and marries Ulupi, the daughter of the Naga king. This is as suggestive as the fact that he was considered dark in complexion even by the Greeks, who were never very fair-skinned themselves.

The system of Orpheus is one of the purest morality and of severe asceticism. The theology taught by him is again purely Indian. With him the Divine Essence is inseparable from whatever is in the infinite universe, all forms being concealed from all eternity in It. At determined periods these forms are manifested from the Divine Essence or manifest themselves. Through this law of emanation (or evolution) all things participate in the Divine Essence, and are parts and members imbued with Divine Nature, which is omnipresent. All things having proceeded from it must necessarily return into it; and therefore, innumerable transmigrations or reincarnations and purifications are needed before this final consummation can take place. This is pure Vedanta philosophy. Again, the Orphic Brotherhood ate no animal food, wore white linen garments, and had many ceremonies like those of the Brahmins.

Osiris (*Eg.*, "mighty"). The greatest God of Egypt, the Son of Seb, celestial fire, and of Neith, primordial matter and infinite space. This indicates that he is the self-existent and self-created god, the first manifesting deity (the third Logos), identical to Ahura Mazda and other "First Causes." For as Ahura Mazda is one with, or the synthesis of, the Amesha Spenta (the six angels or divine forces personified as gods), so Osiris, the collective unit, when differentiated and personified, becomes Typhon, his brother, Isis and Nephtys, his sisters, Horus his son and his other aspects.

He was born at Mount Sinai, the Nyssa of the Old Testament (see Exodus 17:15), and buried at Abydos after being killed by Typhon at the early age of 28, according to the allegory. According to Euripides, he is the same as Zeus and Dionysos, or *Dio-Nysos* "the god of Nysa," for Osiris is said by him to have been brought up in Nysa, in Arabia "the Happy." The question arises as to how much the latter tradition influenced, or has anything in common with, the statement in the Bible, that "Moses built an altar and called the name Jehovah Nissi," or Kabbalistically — "Dio-Iao-Nyssi"?

The four chief aspects of Osiris were: Osiris-Phtah (Light), the spiritual aspect; Osiris-Horus (mind), the intellectual *manasic* aspect; Osiris-Lunus, the "lunar" or psychic, astral aspect; Osiris-Typhon, the physical, material, and therefore, passional turbulent aspect. In these four aspects he symbolizes the dual Ego: the divine and the human, the cosmico-spiritual and the terrestrial.

Of the many supreme gods, this Egyptian conception is the most suggestive and the grandest as it embraces the entire range of physical and metaphysical thought. As a solar deity he had twelve minor gods under him — the twelve signs of the zodiac. Though his name is the Ineffable, his 42 attributes each bore one of his names, and his seven dual aspects made these up to 49, or seven times seven; the former are symbolized by the 14 members of his body, or twice seven. Thus, the god is blended in man, and the man is deified, elevated to godhood.

He was addressed as Osiris-Eloh. Dunbar T. Heath speaks of a Phoenician inscription which when read yielded the following tumular inscription in honour of the mummy: "Blessed be Ta-Bai, daughter of Ta-Hapi, priest of Osiris-Eloh. She did nothing against anyone in anger. She spoke no falsehood against any one. Justified before Osiris, blessed be thou from before Osiris! Peace be to thee." And then he adds the following remarks: "The author of this inscription ought, I suppose, to be called a heathen, as justification before Osiris is the object of his religious aspirations. We find, however, that he gives to Osiris the appellation *Eloh*. Eloh is the name used by the Ten Tribes of Israel for the Elohim of Two Tribes. Jehovah-Eloh (Genesis 3:21) in the version used by Ephraim corresponds to Jehovah Elohim in that used by Judah and ourselves. This being so, the question is sure to be asked, and ought to be humbly answered: What was the meaning meant to be conveyed by the two phrases respectively, *Osiris-Eloh* and *Jehovah-Eloh*? For my part, I can imagine but one answer, viz., that Osiris was the national God of Egypt, Jehovah that of Israel, and that Eloh is equivalent to *Deus*, *Gott* or *Dieu*."

As to his human development, he is, as James Bonwick, the author of *Egyptian Belief*, has it: "One of the Saviours or Deliverers of Humanity.... As such he is born in the world. He came as a benefactor, to relieve man of trouble.... In his efforts to do good he encounters evil... and he is temporarily overcome. He is killed.... Osiris is buried. His tomb was the object of pilgrimage for thousands of years. But he did not rest in his grave. At the end of three days, or forty, he rose again and ascended to Heaven. This is the story of his humanity." And Mariette Bey, speaking of the Sixth Dynasty, tells us that "the name of Osiris ... commences to be more used. The formula of *Justified* is met with" and adds that "it proves that this name (of *the Justified* or *Makheru*) was not given to the dead only."

Ossendowski, Ferdinand (1876–1945). A Polish writer, explorer, and university professor. He is best known for his book *Beasts, Men, and Gods* (1922), which recounts his travels in Asia and includes mystic stories about the King of the World and Shambhala.

Over-Soul. The Universal Soul, also known as *Alaya* (*Sk.*, "abode"); the Father-Mother. All individual souls are its rays or sparks and are able to merge with it.

Ovi (*Mar.*, "strung together"). A metre form used in Marathi poems. The *Dnyaneshwari* is written in this poetic form.

P

Padmapani (*Sk.*, "lotus-holder"). See *Avalokiteshvara*.

Pagan. Meaning, at first, no worse than a dweller in the country or the woods; one far removed from the city-temples, and therefore, unacquainted with the state religion and ceremonies. The word *heathen* has a similar significance, meaning one who lives on the heaths and in the country. Now, however, both have come to mean *idolaters*.

Paithan. A town in Maharashtra state, India, associated with many saints, such as Eknath and Dnyaneshwar.

Pali. The ancient language of Magadha that preceded the more refined Sanskrit. The Buddhist scriptures are all written in this language.

Panchashila (*Sk.*, "five precepts"). In Buddhism, a set of ethical guidelines for lay followers and monks that serve as the foundation of moral conduct on the path to enlightenment. The five precepts are commitments to abstain from: 1) killing living beings; 2) stealing; 3) sexual misconduct; 4) lying; and 5) intoxication through alcohol, drugs, or other means.

Panchen Lama (*Tib.*, "great scholar"). Considered an incarnation of Amitabha, the Celestial Father of Chenrezig (Avalokiteshvara), which means to say that he is an Avatar of Tsongkhapa.

Panchen Lama, Sixth, Lobsang Palden Yeshe (1738–1780). A revered spiritual leader in Tibetan Buddhism and a prolific scholar, known for his mystical and symbolic book, *The Journey to Shambhala*. His life was marked by significant spiritual and diplomatic achievements that had a lasting impact on the Gelug tradition of Tibetan Buddhism and Tibet's relations with its neighbours.

Panchen Lama, Eighth, Tenpai Wangchuk (1855–1882). A significant figure in Tibetan Buddhism. He was placed in charge of a secret school founded by Tsongkhapa near Shigatse in Tibet, where H. P. Blavatsky studied.

Panyatara. The twenty-seventh Indian patriarch; the teacher of Bodhidharma (the twenty-eighth Indian and the first Chinese patriarch).

Parabrahman (*Sk.*, "beyond Brahman"). The Supreme Infinite Brahma, the Absolute — the attributeless, secondless reality; the impersonal and nameless universal Principle.

Paracelsus (1493–1541). The symbolical name adopted by the greatest occultist of the Middle Ages, Philippus Aureolus Theophrastus Bombastus von Hohenheim, born in the canton of Zurich. He was the cleverest physician of his age, and the most renowned for curing almost any illness by the power of talismans that he had himself prepared. He never had a friend, and was surrounded by enemies, the most bitter of whom were the Churchmen and their party. That he was accused of being in league with the devil stands to reason, nor is it to be wondered at that finally he was murdered by some unknown foe, at the early age of 48. He died in Salzburg leaving a number of works behind him which are to this day greatly valued by the Kabbalists and occultists. Many of his utterances have proved prophetic. He was a clairvoyant of great powers, one of the most learned and erudite philosophers and mystics, and a distinguished alchemist. Physics is indebted to him for the discovery of nitrogen gas.

Paraguru (*Sk.*). A teacher's teacher.

Paramartha (*Sk.*). Absolute existence; a hymn by Nagarjuna dedicated to the Ultimate.

Paramarthasatya (*Sk.*). The highest and absolute truth.

Paramatma (*Sk.*). The Supreme Soul of the Universe.

Paramita (*Sk.*, "perfection"). A virtue necessary to achieve enlightenment. There are six paramitas in Mahayana Buddhism: 1) generosity; 2) morality; 3) patience; 4) vigour; 5) meditation; 6) wisdom. Other traditions list more.

Paranirvana or **Parinirvana** (*Sk.*, "beyond Nirvana"). Absolute Non-Being, which is equivalent to absolute Being or "Be-ness," the state reached by the human monad at the end of the great cycle.

Parikalpita (*Sk.*, "contrived"). The imaginary or falsely conceived nature of phenomena.

Patanjali. The founder of yoga philosophy. The date assigned to him by the Orientalists is 200 BCE; and by the occultists nearer to 700 than 600 BCE. At any rate he was a contemporary of Panini, a celebrated Sanskrit grammarian and philologist. According to Blavatsky, Patanjali's yoga philosophy should be read with caution, for it is very apt to mislead, being written in symbolic language.

Path, The. A Theosophical magazine, published by William Q. Judge in New York from 1886 to 1896.

Paul the Apostle. A key figure in early Christianity; a missionary and theologian who spread the teachings of Jesus Christ to non-Jews and authored many of the epistles in the New Testament. Paul, who did not personally meet Christ, nevertheless did more for His Teaching than many of those who saw and heard Him. He was an Initiate and his words acquire a completely different meaning when interpreted esoterically.

Coming from a Jewish family of the Pharisaic sect, as well as having a Roman name, he also had a Jewish name — Saul. As a militant Pharisee, Saul participated in the persecution of the first followers of Christ, but on the way to Damascus, where he was headed to make arrests of Christians, Saul was blinded by a sudden bright light from Heaven and, on hearing the reproachful voice of Jesus: "Saul, Saul! Why are you persecuting Me?" he began to believe in Him.

After his conversion, Paul went into the Arabian desert, where he spent the next three years, and then travelled through the Middle East, Cyprus, Italy, and Greece, founding Christian communities and performing miracles of healing. He was captured in Jerusalem and taken to Rome, where he was beheaded by a court order.

In her article "The Esoteric Character of the Gospels," regarding contradictions between James and Paul, Blavatsky writes: "This contradiction is surely due to later tampering with his Epistles. Paul was a Gnostic himself, i.e., a 'Son of Wisdom,' and an Initiate into the true mysteries of Christos, though he may have thundered (or was made to appear to do so) against some Gnostic sects, of which, in his day, there were many.... He was an Initiate, a true 'Master-Builder' or Adept."

Personality. The teachings of occultism divide man into three aspects: the *divine*, the *thinking* or rational, and the *irrational* or animal man. For metaphysical purposes also, he is considered under a septenary division, or, as it is agreed that it should be expressed in Theosophy, he is composed of seven principles, three of which constitute the higher *triad*, the remaining four, the lower *quaternary*. It is in the latter that the *personality* dwells which embraces all the characteristics, including memory and consciousness, of each physical life in turn. The *individuality* is the Higher Ego (*manas*) of the triad, considered a unity. In other words, the individuality is our imperishable Ego, which reincarnates and clothes itself in a *new personality* at each new birth.

Phala (*Sk.*). Retribution; the fruit or result of causes.

Pharaoh (*Eg.*, "great house"). The title of the rulers of ancient Egypt.

Phenomenon. In reality "an appearance," something previously unseen, and puzzling when its cause is unknown. Leaving aside various kinds of phenomena, such as cosmic, electrical, chemical, etc., and holding merely to the phenomena of spiritism, let it be remembered that theosophically and esoterically every "miracle" — from the biblical to the theumaturgic — is simply a phenomenon, but that no phenomenon is ever a miracle, i.e., something supernatural or outside of the laws of Nature, as all such are impossibilities in Nature.

Phidias (c.480–c.430 BCE). A great Greek sculptor known for his huge statue of Zeus at Olympia, which was one of the Seven Wonders of the Ancient World.

Philosopher's stone. An alchemical term also called the *powder of projection*, which is a mysterious substance possessing the power to transmute base metals into pure gold. Mystically, however, the philosopher's stone symbolizes the transmutation of the lower animal nature of man into the highest and divine.

Phoenix. The ancient symbol of self-creation and resurrection through death, a type of Solar God and divine Ego in humans. It is the symbol of cycles, the types of return of the light from the darkness, the yearly and great cyclic return of the sun-god to his birthplace, or his Resurrection. The bird phoenix is always associated with the Tree of Initiation or the Tree of Knowledge.

According to tradition, on feeling its end approaching the phoenix builds for itself a funeral pile on the top of a sacrificial altar, and then proceeds to consume itself thereon as a burnt-offering. Then a worm appears in the ashes, which grows and develops rapidly into a new phoenix resurrected from the ashes of its predecessor.

Pico della Mirandola, Giovanni (1463–1494). An Italian Renaissance philosopher and founder of Christian Kabbalah. Christian David Ginsburg and others have stated the following facts, namely that, after having studied Kabbalah, Mirandola "found that there is more Christianity in Kabbalah than Judaism; he discovered in it proof for the doctrine of the Trinity, the Incarnation, the divinity of Christ, original sin, the expiation thereof by Christ, the heavenly Jerusalem, the fall of the angels, the order of the angels, purgatory and hell-fire," and so on. In 1486, when only 24 years old, he published *900 Theses*, "which were placarded in Rome [not without the consent or knowledge surely of the Pope and his government?], and which he undertook to defend in the presence of all European scholars, whom he invited to the eternal city, promising to defray their travelling expenses. Among these Theses was the following, 'No science yields greater proof of the divinity of Christ than magic and Kabbalah'" (Ginsburg, *The Kabbalah*).

Pineal gland. A small pinecone-shaped endocrine gland located in the brain. The brain is the special physical organ of perception, and perception occurs primarily in the aura of the pineal gland. This aura answers in vibration to any stimuli, but in a living person it can only be felt, not perceived.

During the process of a thought becoming manifest in consciousness, a constant vibration occurs in the light of this aura. A clairvoyant looking at the brain of a living individual may see with the spiritual eye, count even the seven scales, the seven shades of light from the dullest to the brightest.

When someone touches their hand, immediately before the moment that physical touch occurs, a vibration is already passing through the aura of the pineal gland with its own shade and colour. It is this aura and the vibrations it sets up which cause the wear and tear of the organ. Set vibrating, the brain conveys vibrations to the spinal cord and so to the rest of the body. Happiness and sorrow set up these strong vibrations and so wear out the body. Powerful vibrations of joy or sorrow may even kill.

The septenary disturbance and play of light around the pineal gland are reflected in the heart, or rather the aura of the heart, which vibrates and illumines the seven brains of the heart, just as the aura does round the pineal gland. This is the exoterically four-leaved, but esoterically seven-leaved lotus, the Saptaparni, the cave of Buddha with its seven compartments.

Pistis Sophia (*Gr.*, "faith wisdom"). A sacred book of the early Gnostics or the first Christians, dated from the second or third century CE. Its text predates the Revelation and belongs to the same esoteric school. According to *Pistis Sophia*, Christ remained on earth for eleven years after Crucifixion, appearing before His disciples in the transfigured or resurrected body and revealing cosmological mysteries to them. Its doctrines are in many essentials identical with Egyptian teachings, especially with regard to the mysteries of life and death and of reincarnation.

This Coptic manuscript was acquired in 1785 by the British Museum. M. G. Schwartze quite accidentally discovered it in the Museum and then translated it into Latin. The text and Schwartze's version were published in 1851. From his Latin translation, all early English translations were made.

In the text itself the authorship of *Pistis Sophia* is ascribed to Philip the Apostle, whom Jesus bids sit down and write the revelation. However, the early Gnostic Valentinus, to whom authorship is mistakenly ascribed, edited it at his own discretion and for certain purposes to the detriment of Truth. He also received secret manuscripts written by Mary Magdalene from John the Apostle's disciple and claimed them as his own. Therefore, the true author of *Pistis Sophia* could feasibly have been Mary Magdalene, as among all the followers of Jesus Christ only she was educated and literate.

Blavatsky wrote a commentary on *Pistis Sophia* to illuminate its meaning. See her article "Pistis Sophia: Commentary and Notes."

Pitris (*Sk.*, "fathers"). The ancestors, or creators of humankind. These are of seven classes, three of which are incorporeal, *arupa*, and four corporeal. In popular theology they are said to be created from Brahma's side. They are variously genealogized, but in esoteric philosophy they are as given in *The Secret Doctrine*. In *Isis Unveiled* it is said: "It is generally believed that the Hindu term means the spirits of our ancestors, of disembodied people, hence the argument of some spiritualists that fakirs (and yogis) and other Eastern wonder-workers, are *mediums*. This is in more than one sense erroneous. The Pitris are not the ancestors of the present living men, but those of the human kind, or Adamic races; the spirits of human races, which on the great scale of descending evolution *preceded our races* of men, and they *were physically, as well as spiritually, far superior* to our modern pigmies. In the *Manava-Dharmashastra* they are called the *Lunar Ancestors*."

Pitris, Lunar. The Fathers or the lunar ancestors. These are subdivided, like the rest, into seven classes or Hierarchies. In Egypt, although the moon received less worship than in Chaldea or India, still Isis stands as the representative of Luna-Lunus, "the celestial Hermaphrodite." Strangely enough, while the modern connect the moon only with lunacy and generation, the ancient nations, who knew better, have, individually and collectively, connected their "wisdom gods" with it. Thus, in Egypt, the lunar gods are Thoth-Hermes and Chons; in India, Budha, the Son of Soma, the moon; in Chaldea, Nebo is the lunar god of Secret Wisdom, etc. The wife of Thoth, Sifix, the lunar goddess, holds a pole with five rays or the five-pointed star, symbol of man, the microcosm, in distinction from the septenary Macrocosm. As in all theogonies, in which a goddess precedes a god, most likely on the principle that the chick can hardly precede its egg, in Chaldea, the moon was held as older and more venerable than the Sun, because, as they said, darkness precedes light at every periodical rebirth (or creation) of the universe. Osiris, although connected with the Sun and a Solar God, is nevertheless born on Mount Sinai, because *Sin* is the Chaldeo-Assyrian word for the moon; so was Dio-Nysos, god of Nyssi or *Nisi*, whose latter appellation was that of Sinai in Egypt, where it was called Mount Nissa. The crescent is not — as proven by many writers — an ensign of the Turks, but was adopted by Christians as their symbol before the Muslims. For ages, the crescent was the emblem of the Chaldean Astarte, the Egyptian Isis, and the Greek Diana, all Queens of Heaven, and finally it became the emblem of Mary the Virgin.

Pituitary body or **pituitary gland.** A pea-sized gland located at the base of the brain that produces and releases essential hormones that regulate various bodily functions and control other endocrine glands. See *brain* for more.

Plane. An extension of space or of something in it, whether in the physical or metaphysical sense, e.g., a "plane of consciousness." As used in occultism, the term denotes the range or extent of a state of consciousness, or the perceptive power of a particular set of senses, or the action of a particular force, or the state of matter corresponding to any of the above.

Planetary Spirits. Primarily the rulers or governors of the planets. They are the highest Kumaras. They no longer incarnate in the Universe during this Manvantara, appearing on Earth as Avatars only at the beginning of every new human Race and at the junctions or close of the two ends of the small and great cycle. Their bodies are made up of pure ether and fire.

As our Earth has a hierarchy of terrestrial planetary spirits, from the highest to the lowest plane, so does every other heavenly body. In occultism, however, the term *Planetary Spirit* is generally applied only to the seven highest Hierarchies corresponding to the Christian Archangels. These have all passed through a stage of evolution that corresponds to that of Earth's humanity when this was lived out in other worlds, in long-past cycles. Our Earth, being as yet only in its Fourth Round, is far too young to have produced high planetary spirits and so it is governed by the Spirits of other planets in the Solar System, who are to be replaced eventually by "native" spirits. One of these was the Lord of Saturn, not a spirit of a particularly high grade, who dealt mostly with matter, never having any concern with spirit.

The highest Planetary Spirit ruling over any globe is, in reality, the "Personal God" of that planet which is far more truly its "overruling providence" than the self-contradictory Infinite Personal Deity of modern Christianity.

Each people and nation has a direct Watcher, Guardian, and Father in Heaven — a Planetary Spirit which collectively comprise One Planetary Spirit. They are also karmic agencies which have everything to do with Earth physically and morally, ruling the destinies and fate of humanity.

In *The Mahatma Letters* the term is also applied to the Buddhas and other high self-conscious entities who can penetrate beyond the Solar System: "There can be no Planetary Spirit that was not once material or what you call human. When our great Buddha — the patron of all the Adepts, the reformer and the codifier of the occult system, reached first Nirvana on earth, he became a Planetary Spirit; i.e., his spirit could at one and the same time rove the interstellar spaces in full consciousness and continue at will on Earth in his original and individual body. For the Divine Self had so completely disfranchised itself from matter that it could create at will an inner substitute for itself, and leaving it in the human form for days, weeks, sometimes years, affect in no wise by the change either the vital principle or the physical mind of its body. That is the highest form of Adeptship man can hope for on our planet. But it is as rare as the Buddhas themselves."

As man became more animalized, over time the truths revealed to him by the Planetary Spirits were made to fade from his memory. Yet, though these Teachers remain with man for no longer than the time required to impress upon the plastic minds of child-humanity the eternal verities they teach, their spirit remains vivid though latent in humankind. And the full knowledge of the primitive revelation has remained always with a few elect, and has been transmitted from that time up to the present, from one generation of Adepts to another. As the Teachers say in the Occult Primer: "This is done so as to ensure them (the eternal truths) from being utterly lost or forgotten in ages hereafter by the forthcoming generations."

The mission of the Planetary Spirit is but to strike the keynote of Truth: Once He has directed the vibration of the latter to run its course uninterruptedly along the concatenation of the Race to the end of the cycle, He, the denizen of the highest inhabited sphere, disappears from our Earth until the following Planetary Manvantara.

The Planetary Spirit of Earth, as well as the Chief of all high Planetary Spirits, is the One known under the name of Sanat Kumara, the Lord of Sirius. As predicted by many, the period when the Teacher of Teachers stroked the keynote of Truth for the Sixth and Seventh Races of humanity was at the junction of the twentieth and twenty-first centuries, leaving the planet in 2017, until the next period at the end of the Seventh Race when it will be necessary for Him "to instruct or 'refresh the memory' of the first race of the Fifth Round men after this planet's future obscuration" (*The Mahatma Letters*).

Plato (c.420s–348 BCE). An Initiate into the Mysteries and the greatest Greek philosopher, whose writings are known the world over; the pupil of Socrates and the teacher of Aristotle.

Platonism. A philosophy derived from the teachings of the Greek philosopher Plato, emphasizing the existence of ideal forms or abstract realities that are more real than the physical world. Platonism has had a profound influence on Western metaphysics, ethics, and theology.

Plenum Void. A philosophical concept combining the ideas of "plenum" (fullness) and "void" (emptiness), often used to describe a paradoxical state in which apparent emptiness is actually filled with potential or unseen energy.

Poe, Edgar Allan (1809–1849). An American writer, poet, and literary critic, famous for his gothic tales of mystery and the macabre. Notable works include *The Raven* (1845), *The Tell-Tale Heart* (1843), and *The Fall of the House of Usher* (1839). He is considered a pioneer of the short story and detective fiction genres.

Points of Life. Places of power on the planet in which, since ancient times, it has been customary for the Initiates to build temples and position special energy magnets associated with Shambhala. Some Points of Life are natural, such as mountains, others are human-made, formed by the currents of holiness of saintly individuals or by a collection of sacred objects. Being associated with certain constellations or celestial bodies, Points of Life receive currents from them and project these currents onto the territories entrusted to them, territories which may be located at some distance geographically from the Point of Life itself. The functioning of these Points of Life is capable of harmonizing underground fires, which, due to the imperfect low-frequency thinking of humanity, threaten to break out and result in large-scale natural disaster. There have even been cases when Points of Life have prevented fratricidal war.

Periodically, twelve main Points of Life are formed in various places around the world. These may be found in Israel, Syria, Ukraine, Russia, Italy, America, Great Britain, India, Japan, as well as in a number of other countries, depending on Cosmo-spatial conditions, and whose purpose is to serve not only the realm of individual countries, but humanity as a whole. These magnets are designed to work as a single organism. Each main Point is duodecimal in essence, and so 144 magnets in total are laid throughout the planet by the Great Initiates in accordance with the laws of sacred geometry, both on the physical and the Subtle Plane. The malfunction of any one Point can disrupt the energetical harmony of the entire territory entrusted to it, and impede the circulation of energies through the Fiery Heart of the planet — Shambhala.

The forces of darkness always attempt to establish their own Points of Death nearby and in opposition to Points of Life in order to disrupt the energy balance of the planet and the connection of Points of Life with Shambhala. These may take the form of military bases or destructive monasteries, the residences of various dark sects that use prohibited techniques, drugs, and other substances to achieve "superhuman" abilities. Points of Death feed on bloody emanations to grow, and therefore, constantly require a source of food generated by conflict, whether it is simply in the form of a negative attitude towards another, or outright war. In this manner, the minions of darkness aim to lower the vibrational frequency of magnets embedded at Points of Life in an attempt to "bend" their Power and draw it over to their own side so that it can be exploited for sinister purposes.

It is timely to highlight Points of Life directly related to the Slavs, which have come into wide focus due to the "breakthrough" into the earthly world of the fierce battle taking place on the Subtle Plane.

Around 2,400 years ago, a selfless devotee of the Abode located in the Himalayas was sent in the direction of the Slavic lands, entrusted with a special mission: to lay down a sacred stone, saturated with special currents of White Fire, in a grotto in the Crimea on the shores of the Black Sea. In the Crimea another Point of Life can be found in the Holy Trinity Cathedral in Simferopol, where the relics of St. Luke of Crimea are lain to rest.

In the eleventh century, in Kyiv, Yaroslav the Wise embedded a stone in the foundations of St. Sophia Cathedral. At certain times of day — noon, midnight, 4 o'clock in the morning — the magnet emits a host of rays, spreading currents of Love-Wisdom throughout Ukraine. The Points in the Kyiv Pechersk Lavra and the Holy Dormition Pochaiv Lavra located in the West of Ukraine are also significant. Incidentally, the main portal of the Trinity Cathedral of the Pochaiv Lavra is decorated with a mosaic by Nicholas Roerich. In addition, Points of Life associated with Future Races are located in the Holy Mountains Lavra of the Holy Dormition, where a magnet was laid by an Initiate of the Theban Sanctuary, and in the "Stone Tomb" Nature Reserve, both located in the East of Ukraine.

The St. Sophia Cathedral in Kyiv, in comparison with others, is symbolically at a pinnacle in its ability to manifest the Divine Fire. Moreover, it has on occasion been initiated by currents of Heavenly Sophia, the Power and Supreme Wisdom of God, thanks to which the stone-magnet laid in its foundation has acquired immense strength, and the manifestation radius of its grace-filled currents has increased. In addition to all Ukraine, the area it covers includes part of Belarus, as well as Russia, and other neighbouring countries. Naturally, following the principle "divide and conquer," the forces of evil are alien to the position of both spreading the Heavenly Fires and establishing lines of intersection at the level of all Points of Life. The hierophants of evil are concerned with generating the greatest number of conflicts possible in order to strengthen their own Points of Death at the cost of bloody war among fraternal peoples.

Further, in the twelfth century, a monk brought a stone from Shambhala, consecrated in the Rays of Chintamani and, for the sake of the future, laid it in the ground near Moscow on the banks of the Belyana River. In the fourteenth century, while still a youth, St. Sergius of Radonezh received from a mysterious stranger a stone-magnet which was to be laid in the foundations of the holy place now known as the Trinity Lavra of St. Sergius. This stone remains underground to this day, directly beneath the tomb of St. Sergius of Radonezh. And finally, in 1817, King Alexander I, who was himself an Initiate, embedded a magnet in the foundations of the Cathedral of Christ the Saviour in Moscow. In 1839, the construction was moved to another site. Nevertheless, it should be noted that a peculiar quality of stones serving as magnets is that they are capable of shifting their location in accordance with the changing routes of force lines. Therefore, the stone laid by Alexander I was able to resume its destined position in the depths of the soil buried beneath the renewed Cathedral of Christ the Saviour. Thus, the Trinity Lavra of St. Sergius, the Cathedral of Christ the Saviour, as well as the Diveyevo Convent, where the relics of St. Seraphim of Sarov are interred, represent three giant Points of Life connected by force lines, together serving as a single organ resembling a Heart from which life-giving currents spread throughout all temples capable of receiving the blessed fires.

The Altai Mountains are another example of one of the planet's most ancient Points of Life. Unfortunately, various representatives and their followers who are far from the Light have already settled here. "Krasnoyarsk Pillars" National Park, which represents a former sanctuary built at the dawn of the Third Race of humanity, is another example. This was once a huge, magnificent Temple with sparkling golden domes, dedicated to the God of the Sun, where the King and Father of the Black, Arraim the Four-time-Greatest, served. In addition to those already mentioned, there are places of power in Novosibirsk, Kemerovo, Cheboksary, and Vladivostok. The Slavic lands as a whole are rich in Points of Life. If only people would turn to these sources with good, pure thoughts.

Two more magnets located beyond the Slavic lands should be mentioned, both of vital importance. One of these was laid by King Solomon in the tenth century BCE, in the foundations of his Temple in Jerusalem. King Solomon also founded the city of Palmyra, situated in modern-day Syria, in whose foundations he embedded a special stone that he had in his possession. With the advent of Christianity in the Slavic lands, these two Points of Life began to project a portion of their currents to the point where Sergius of Radonezh later founded his Abode. This triad was called upon to be revived at the end of the twentieth century for a new cycle of manifestation so as to begin receiving rays from Sirius and to project them onto the Slavic lands. It goes without saying that all the holy places in Israel associated with Christ are Points of Life. But the main projection of rays onto the Slavic lands comes from Jerusalem and Palmyra. It is for this reason that the forces of darkness have seen to the strangling of this energy through prolonged bloodshed in the Middle East. By separating this triangle, they weakened the magnets in the Slavic lands, which could have helped prevent fratricidal war. This war, in turn, negatively affects some of the most powerful Points of Life on which the balance of the entire planet depends.

All the magnets embedded at Points of Life exist beyond temporal and political contexts, since they were laid thousands of years ago, when each place had a different name and other peoples inhabited the area — for the magnets these factors are of no consequence. They manifest at the right moment, regardless of era or political battle. Nonetheless, in order to enhance their effect, a peaceful sky and prayerful service are required, and with these things in place, the people living in close proximity could significantly improve their karma.

And so it would appear that varying degrees of negative influence, from bloody conflict to bloodless discord connected to one or another territory, produce a negative impact, which, in turn, has a suffocating effect on the "breath" of the planetary system as a whole and on the Slavs in particular, who play a special role and carry a great portion of the responsibility for world peace.

Even a cursory glance at a map will reveal that, predominantly, conflicts have taken place near mountain ranges — natural Points of Life: the Alps, the Caucasus, the Carpathians, the Himalayas, and so on. This is due to the fact that mountains receive high cosmic energies, and also preserve a unique conglomerate of Fires, on which the movement of new currents of grace-filled energy in the world depends. Triggering various kinds of conflict from the Subtle Plane, the hierophants of evil try to prevent these new currents from spreading and attempt to change the positive formulas of the energies involved into negative ones. And where there are voluntary or involuntary executors of such "strategies" already present on the physical plane, there invisible near-Earth battles break through and are reflected in the earthly world. For when the real desire to prevent conflict and establish true peace exists, wise solutions and the ways to implement them will always be found, inspired from Above.

Each place and each embedded magnet has its own period of awakening that might also mean a new cycle of manifestation. As soon as this time approaches, the forces of evil will attempt to gain a foothold, in one point or another, sometimes centuries in advance.

For example, the time of awakening of the Caucasus, whose ancient civilization was associated with the Initiates of Egypt, came at the end of the twentieth century. This explains why such weighty problems have arisen in this region.

As for the magnet on the Black Sea coast mentioned above, its time of awakening came in 2015. Peering into history, one can see all the "preparatory work" of the dark forces that was laid over centuries prior, the many bloody battles fought over the Crimea. And it has to be said that not a single war passes without trace, since the huge numbers of people who die prematurely as a result of murder hang in the near-Earth space for centuries. And there, hundreds of thousands if not millions of restless souls continue to fight with each other. For centuries rivers of blood were shed over the Crimea, preventing the lower layers of the Subtle World from being cleansed. If people could only see the otherwise invisible "mishmash" of half-disintegrated shells that linger literally just above them, their hearts would wither at the horror of the "spectacle."

In 2007, a letter was received from Master M., in which it was written that in the space of the Subtle Plane above the Slavs, and in particular above Ukraine, a bloody war was being fought that threatened to break through into the denser layers. And the letter included the request that people in different parts of the country begin to pray so that the Demiurge-Builders as well as the Patron Spirits of Ukraine (one of whom is the Spirit of the poet Taras Shevchenko) could rely on the subtle energy structures of those praying as "transmitters," and conduct their currents into the physical world, thereby somewhat modifying the "Alchemy of Space." For in the East, people know that a single saint can save an entire area. In this case, the calculation was made based on the combined number of consonant people who had reached certain coefficients of heart luminosity, and which could slow down the negative processes underway. Demiurges can rely only on those who have an *argo* coefficient above 3 units, and even in this case, these individuals would have to appeal to the Higher Powers, expressing their readiness to help Them. Alternatively, the total so-called "people's will" could be expressed and the required energy level achieved through collective effort. Sadly, collective free will was not expressed, the request was not fulfilled, and the space did not receive the necessary support, circumstances of which the hierophants of evil took full advantage.

It should be especially noted that due to the centuries-old layers of people killed that reside in the space above the Crimea, any bloody battle fought over this area is extremely dangerous, since it risks triggering battles occurring in the lower astral layers which could break through into the physical world. This would concern not only Ukraine and Russia but also Turkey, and then other allies would get involved. This would have the potential to result in a brutal war between many countries, forming a giant deadly funnel, that could result in the use of nuclear weapons. And if this were to happen, there would be no winners.

As for the two Points of Life in the East of Ukraine, in modern times, the forces of evil have been trying to settle nearby. The time for the awakening of these Points has not yet come and is connected with the Future, but one began to pulsate at the end of the twentieth century. If this hotbed cannot be extinguished, it will continue to "bleed," preventing the deposition of currents trying to form the most beautiful pattern of the Future.

By analysing the picture of Points of Life beyond geographical and political boundaries, one can understand the deeper reasons and true motives for the negative phenomena occurring in the Slavic lands and, by analogy, in other areas, without being deluded by the "good intentions" that justify the strangulation of certain Points. Moreover, one can understand how important the collective prayer emanating from human hearts is to the Higher Powers, so that They can provide timely Help to a particular area.

There is no evil without good, and the isolation of huge numbers of people around the world resulting from the coronavirus pandemic contributed to the rejuvenation of many Points of Life that were able to take a rest from the endless stream of tourists, parishioners, pilgrims, and so on, and catch their breath for the first time in a very long time. Thanks to this temporary lull, larger-scale disasters were avoided, which could otherwise have served as a subsequent impetus for gigantic cataclysms.

Some Points of Life have been able to avoid the fate of Notre-Dame de Paris, the beating Heart of France. For many hundreds of years, the cathedral was exhausted from the excessive pouring out of energy, since it so rarely received reciprocal gifts. People come to churches, temples, and cathedrals only to take. Very few leave a feeling of heartfelt gratitude at the altar and not just the bitterness of their troubles and sorrows. In April 2019, only the element of Fire could make up for the deadly losses of Notre-Dame Cathedral. The physical flame is capable of destroying structures made by human hands, but it also attracts spatial Cosmic Fire, which incinerates the invisible destructive formations that the masses have layered over the centuries, and immerses them in a kind of gigantic font, producing a Fiery Baptism. This enabled the Cathedral, which guards the crown of thorns of Jesus Christ, to resurrect and continue its sacred work in a new round of manifestation.

It goes without saying that Points of Life exist in varying numbers in many countries around the world. It would be impossible to list them all due to the fact that some are fading completely and others are in the process of shifting to different geographical coordinates. Some Points begin to pulsate at the inception stage, but many are immersed in a magical dream state, while still others must remain secret, hidden from human eyes and feet, which are capable, figuratively speaking, of "trampling and desecrating" the Source of Divine Fires. As at all times, some Points of Life are actively manifested and can attract a multitude of pilgrims or ordinary tourists by the law of magnetic attraction.

Here it should be pointed out that Italy occupies a unique position in terms of its location on what is literally fire-breathing soil. Italy has not only preserved many Points of Life, it has also birthed new ones that are highly mobile. Of course, wherever the relics of saints are to be found, Points of Life are manifested — St. Peter's Basilica in the Vatican, St. Mark's Basilica in Venice, the Church of St. Nicholas the Wonder-worker in Bari. Of course, Points of Life are not situated exclusively in temples. They are also manifested in unpopulated areas, as well as in the waters, where various islands lie off the coast of Italy.

Germany has a hugely significant Point of Life in the area of St. Thomas Church in Leipzig. It also has Points of Life in other places as a network of force lines extends outwards from the church, which is home to the burial of Johann Sebastian Bach whose Spirit continues to fulfil the role of invisible Guardian Demiurge and Patron Spirit of this country.

Spain, along with other High Spirits, is guarded by the image of St. Teresa of Ávila, whose relics are housed in the Convent of the Annunciation in Alba de Tormes. St. Teresa of Ávila is one of the incarnations of the Spirit of Heavenly Sophia, and She predetermines the coordinates of the most important Points of Life in Spain to which an Impulse should be sent, pouring forth currents of the Great Feminine Principle.

The USA has the most important Points of Life in the Riverside area of New York City. Of course, one of these is the Nicholas Roerich Museum, which represents a magnet thanks to the paintings of the Messenger of Beauty and certain sacred objects. There is also a Point of Life in Philadelphia and in San Francisco, and Yellowstone itself is at a unique stage of what is literally a battle between Life and Death. And the preponderance towards either outcome will determine which of the Points will manifest its pulsation. As a rule, Points of Death are not of an enduring nature, since often, being "self-devouring," they exhaust themselves and perish under the onslaught of elements of Fire.

In 1999, 2004, and 2012, giant cataclysms originating in the underwater depths and caused by the movement of underground fire were neutralized. In the 2012 hurricane season, hurricane Sandy, whose deadly force was reduced by 50 per cent, marked what could have been just the beginning of the "end" that America might have experienced, were it not for the timely intervention of the Higher Powers.

Australia, which has a direct and kindred connection with Antarctica, is endowed with its own Points of Life, mainly located along the coast. It is worth noting that places with the most powerful manifestations of both the element of Water as well as the element of Fire are where the most powerful Points of Life are materialized.

Canada has the largest number of Points of Life residing in a magical dream state, which will awaken at the predestined time; these are already gradually awakening to Life, since the country will have a significant role to play in the near future.

As for Great Britain, here, first and foremost, one should note Stonehenge and, secondly, Hyde Park in London. Both are connected through force lines with other Points of Life in England, Scotland, Northern Ireland, and Wales, as well as being partially projected into France towards the island-fortress on which towers the castle of Mont-Saint-Michel.

Nevertheless, Points of Life, composed of currents of holiness, are not only associated with the saints and Initiates of the past. New places have been formed in modern times, among which may be counted the Dalai Lama Temple in Dharamsala, the Sri Sathya Sai Baba Ashram in Puttaparthi, as well as the Roerich estate in Naggar, where for a long time a fragment of the Chintamani stone was held. The Dalai Lama Temple in Dharamsala, St. Peter's Basilica in the Vatican, and the Cathedral of Christ the Saviour in Moscow form one of the most important Point of Life triangles, which will play an important energy role in the future.

Also worth noting are magnets of a different kind — those composed of a collection of artefacts, ancient manuscripts, and works of art. For example, some thangkas (Tibetan paintings), made by the hands of monks, serve as a kind of magnet and are enhanced by interaction with other objects carved from special types of wood or stone. Through the consonance of currents they "flow into each other," energetically forming a single conglomerate of crystallized Fire, which represents a single magnet, immortalized in a certain place. Points of Life are represented by certain museums and libraries around the world that house particular sacred objects and manuscripts created or owned by Initiates of all times and ages. Notable among many others are the Louvre Museum, the Egyptian Museum, the British Museum, and the Roerich Museum in Moscow.

Besides, knowing the powerful energy of sacred books and manuscripts, the Initiates kept them in concentrated collections for three or seven years in a particular place where, for example, there was a problem area with a crust fracture that had the potential to cause a natural disaster of terrifying proportions in the future. The intention was that the concentration of sacred objects would help to avert such an event, for even if there is no demand for them among the general public, books with light-bearing crystallized fires still fill the world with beneficial, healing radiations, thereby neutralizing negative vibrations.

Assistance to the Earth has been rendered in all ages. But there are special periods when the currents of the Great Masculine or Great Feminine are particularly active. From 13 to 15 March 2021, the Hagia Sophia Cathedral in Istanbul was immersed in a giant Font of invisible Fire. And this Point of Life was revived in new currents. The Great Impulse passed through all the earthly Cathedrals associated with the name of Sophia — the Power and Supreme Wisdom of God.

Therefore, Points of Life which are all invisibly connected should be treated with special care. By remaining in a prayerful state, making sincere prayers from the heart for the good of the world and humanity, one may render a noble service not only to oneself, but to all the spheres, from the earthly to the Ethereal. Prayers will create invisible channels by attracting fiery currents from the Sources of Life, which will bring peace and grace to all one's environment.

Pollock, Jackson (1912–1956). An American painter.

Pollok, Robert (1798–1827). A Scottish poet best known for his ten-book poem in blank verse, *The Course of Time* (1827).

Pondicherry. A city in southern India that was a French colony until 1954. It is well-known for its cultural mix of Indian and French influences and for being the home of Sri Aurobindo's Ashram.

Pope John XXIII (1881–1963). Head of the Catholic Church from 1958 to 1963; best known for convening the Second Vatican Council which modernized Church practices.

Pope John Paul I (1912–1978). Pope for only 33 days in 1978, known for his humility and warmth, earning the nickname the "Smiling Pope."

Prajna (*Sk.*, "wisdom"). A synonym of Mahat, Universal Mind; the power or capacity that gives rise to perception, existing under seven different aspects corresponding to the seven conditions of matter in the manifested world; consciousness, the seven states of which correspond to the seven principles of the human constitution; wisdom, one of the paramitas of perfection.

Prakrit. A group of ancient Indic languages that were the vernaculars spoken in India during the time of the Buddha and Mahavira. Prakrit is related to Sanskrit but is simpler in terms of its grammar and vocabulary.

Pralaya (*Sk.*, "dissolution"). A period of obscuration or repose (planetary, cosmic, or universal), the opposite of Manvantara.

Prana (*Sk.*, "breath"). Life-principle; the breath of Life.

Pranayama (*Sk.*, "suspension of breath"). In yoga, the practice of breath control, involving techniques to regulate the flow of life force (*prana*) through various breathing exercises. It is one of the eight limbs of yoga as described by Patanjali.

In the instructions for students of the Inner Group, Blavatsky says: "The science of Hatha

Yoga rests upon the 'suppression of breath,' or pranayama, to which exercise our Masters are unanimously opposed. For what is pranayama? Literally translated, it means the 'death of (vital) breath.' *Prana*, as said, is not *jiva*, the eternal fount of life immortal; nor is it connected in any way with Pranava [a sacred word], as some think, for Pranava is a synonym of Aum in a mystic sense. As much as has ever been taught publicly and clearly about it is to be found in *Nature's Finer Forces* [by Rama Prasad]. If such directions, however, are followed, they can only lead to black magic and mediumship. Several impatient chelas, whom we knew personally in India, went in for the practice of Hatha Yoga, notwithstanding our warnings. Of these, two developed consumption, of which one died; others became almost idiotic; another committed suicide; and one developed into a regular Tantrika, a black magician, but his career, fortunately for himself, was cut short by death. . . .

"Further, the practice of the Five Breaths results in deadly injury, both physiologically and psychically, as already shown. It is indeed that which it is called, pranayama, or the death of the breath, for it results, for the practicer, in death — in moral death always, and in physical death very frequently."

One should distinguish simple rhythmic breathing, which in itself is useful for the restoration of spiritual and physical strength, from that which is recommended in yogic literature. In the latter, pranayama aims, through holding the breath, rotation and other gymnastics, to irritate and force a rush of blood to certain centres, thereby causing their increased activity. But one can easily imagine what harm will result if a person begins to irritate the centres located in organs that are for some reason weakened or even diseased. Of course, this will only intensify their unhealthy condition. This is why there are so many accidents among those who practise pranayama with ignorant and irresponsible teachers. The opening of centres can occur without harm only under the guidance of a Great Teacher, who sees the true state of our body in all its complexity and knows what can be applied or permitted and when.

The science of breathing practised by true raja yogis has little in common with pranayama. Hatha yogis are busy controlling the vital breathing of the lungs, while the ancient raja yogis understood this as mental breathing, for only mastery of mental breathing can lead to higher clairvoyance, the restoration of the function of the third eye, and the true achievements of Raja Yoga.

Only those who have completely purified their hearts and mental bodies of all earthly waste can penetrate into the Holy of Holies of Yoga. Without this cleansing, no pranayama will ever lead even to the first gate of true knowledge. Pranayama can develop mediumship, which is the closing of the Gate. Long exercises in pranayama or Hatha Yoga make it impossible to practise Raja Yoga. All psychic powers developed through pranayama, through artificial stimulation of the physical and astral bodies, are limited to the psychic plane that is far from high, as evidenced by all the visions of psychics and mediums. It must be understood that psychism is not spirituality.

Prasanga School (*Sk.*, "devotion," "connection"). The most metaphysical and philosophical school in Tibet. The school derives its name from the peculiar method it uses in the context of refuting arguments by deducing the absurdity and erroneousness of every esoteric opinion. Correct interpretations of Buddhist philosophy are crowned by the misleading interpretation of a thesis from the Prasanga School that "Even an Arhat goes to hell in case he doubt anything," thus making of the most free-thinking religion in the world a blind-faith system. Yet the "threat" refers simply to the well-known law that even an Initiate may fail, and thus have his object utterly ruined, if he doubt for one moment the efficacy of his psychic powers — the ABC of occultism, as every Kabbalist well knows.

The Prasanga School was divided into two: the Prasanga (Prasangika) Madhyamika School, founded by Buddhapalita, the follower of Nagarjuna, and the Svatantrika Madhyamika School, founded by Bhavaviveka, who criticized Buddhapalita's approach. Both have their exoteric and esoteric divisions. To know anything of the esoteric doctrines of the Prasanga School, one must belong to the latter. Chandrakirti (Dava Dagpa) wrote commentaries on the Prasanga doctrines and taught publicly; he expressly states that there are two ways of entering the Path to Nirvana. Any virtuous man can, through meditation, reach an intuitive understanding of the four Truths, without either belonging to a monastic order or having been initiated.

In short, this doctrine is that of Raja Yoga in its practice of the two kinds of *samadhi* state: one of the Paths leads to the sphere of bliss (Sukhavati or Devachan), where man enjoys perfect, unalloyed happiness, while still being connected with personal existence; the other Path leads to full emancipation from the worlds of illusion, self, and unreality. The first Path is open to all and is reached simply by merit; the second — a hundredfold more rapid — is reached through knowledge (Initiation). Thus the followers of the Prasanga School are nearer to Esoteric Buddhism than are the Yogacharas, for their views are those of the most secret schools, only an echo of the doctrines of which is ever heard in works found in public circulation and use.

However, over the course of history, the Prasanga Madhyamika teaching broke away from the purely esoteric schools and now offers an anti-esoteric and most rationalistic system, which is very popular. It follows, like the Yogachara system, the Mahayana or "Great Vehicle" of precepts, but being founded far later than the Yogachara, it is not as rigid or severe.

Pratyabhava (*Sk.*, "rebirth"). The state of the Ego under the necessity of repeated incarnation.

Pratyahara (*Sk.*, "withdrawal of senses"). A preliminary training in order to control one's mind and thoughts; another of the eight limbs of yoga, the withdrawal of the senses from external objects to turn focus inward, considered an essential step in preparing for meditation.

Pratyeka Buddha (*Sk.*, "isolated Buddha"). A degree which belongs exclusively to the Yogachara school; one of high intellectual development but with no true spirituality. It is the *dead letter* of the yoga laws, in which intellect and comprehension play the greatest part, added to the strict carrying out of the rules of inner development. It is one of the three paths to Nirvana, and the lowest, in which a yogi — "without teacher and without saving others" — by the mere force of will and technical observances attains to a kind of nominal Buddhaship individually, doing no good to anyone, working selfishly for his own salvation and himself alone. The Pratyekas are respected outwardly but are despised inwardly by those of keen or spiritual appreciation. A Pratyeka is generally compared to a *khadga* or solitary rhinoceros and called *Ekashringa Rishi*, a selfish solitary Rishi (or saint). "As crossing *samsara* ('the ocean of birth and death' or the series of incarnations), suppressing errors, and yet not attaining to absolute perfection, the Pratyeka Buddha is compared to a horse, which crosses a river swimming without touching the ground" (*Handbook of Chinese Buddhism*). He is far below a true Buddha of Compassion. He strives only to reach Nirvana.

Prayer. A bond with the Higher World; fusion with the Light. A prayer from the heart is the most powerful, for prayer is the fire of the heart in action. It can fly as far as its strength permits. Regular, consistent prayer, prayer that is never missed under any circumstances, is intensified in force manifoldly, inconspicuously transforming the human essence. Pure and sincere prayer for the good of the world and humanity attracts waves of spatial fire, contributing to the growth of the fiery crystal in the heart, which explains the feeling of influx and the restoration of one's spiritual forces. True meditation is also a prayer, which calls forth a responding fiery wave through its radiating love to the world.

A selfish prayer, aimed only at one's own desires, cannot fly far. In space, it meets other forms of the same selfish energy which neutralize and destroy one another. The result is that none of these prayers reaches those who could possibly answer them; in other words, they benefit no one. If one sends forth in prayer the strong energy of selfish desire without sufficient power to realize that desire, the energy dissipates and the body which produced and sent it receives a boomerang blow and is consequently weakened. Similarly, mere mechanical repetition of words learnt by rote, devoid of the energy of love, can benefit none.

Prayer can serve as a powerful means of protection. Saint Seraphim of Sarov used the Jesus Prayer and advised others to repeat it incessantly during periods of trial and difficult moments in life, while experiencing temptation and danger: "Lord Jesus Christ, Son of God, have mercy on me, a sinner." Despite its brevity, this prayer acts like a sharp blade and is able to repel the onslaught of dark thoughts and influences, freeing the consciousness from them.

The Initiates of ancient Egypt used the protective formula "Do not touch!" to repel enemy attacks occurring on the invisible plane. This formula entails the least karmic consequence. When one feels that a dark influence is being exerted upon oneself (for example, a surge of negative thoughts), one should pronounce this formula clearly in one's own mind. It is also useful to imagine a protective wall of flowing silver light or simply a fiery barrier around anyone in need of protection. Of course, one may choose whatever mental image one is most comfortable with. This formula instantly repels negativity and returns it to the sender, without causing harm to others.

If a large-scale disaster is expected or is being escalated, then everyone involved should utter: "Lord, let this cup pass." This formula helps to demagnetize formations generated by the fear and dread of a particular situation, thereby preventing its embodiment in reality. It is also useful to affirm creative, positive images using willpower and the imagination.

United, collective prayer for the benefit of the entire world has immense power, although its effects may not appear instantly. Such prayer is especially necessary when a major tragedy takes place in the world, as the panic and fear of a large number of people will only strengthen the resulting negativity.

The Great Teachers pray continuously for humanity and Earth. Every day at 12 noon (in each time zone), when the Fire is at its zenith, a collective prayer takes place with the participation of all the Forces of Light. Anyone can join in, sending forth into the world a particle of their heart's fire. It is not essential that the prayers be long: the most important thing is that the prayers are sincere. One may say the Lord's Prayer, the word *Aum* repeated three times, or just a brief thought "Good will to the world!" In other words, a person may use whatever prayer is most familiar to them.

The most beautiful prayer may be simply to say the heartfelt words: "I love You, Lord!" After all, the currents of Love are the highest and the purest of all, capable of neutralizing disharmonious energies in space and travelling to any point in space.

For those whose heart awaits the Messianic Fire, below is a short prayer which addresses Maitreya (*Sk.*, "love"). The name Maitreya can be replaced by another name, one that may be closer to the heart of the one speaking the prayer:

> In the great name of Maitreya,
> May the Light of Sacred Faith,
> May the Light of Holy Love
> Emblaze and pervade God's world.

Precipitation. The mysterious production of letters sent by the Masters to disciples. H.P.B. explained this in her article "Precipitation": "Mr. Sinnett sought for an explanation of the process and elicited the following reply from the revered Mahatma who corresponds with him: 'Bear in mind these letters are not written but impressed, or precipitated, and then all mistakes corrected.... I have to think it over, to photograph every word and sentence carefully in my brain before it can be repeated by precipitation. As the fixing on chemically prepared surfaces of the images formed by the camera requires a previous arrangement within the focus of the object to be represented, for otherwise — as often found in bad photographs — the legs of the sitter might appear out of all proportion with the head, and so on — so we have to first arrange our sentences and impress every letter to appear on paper in our minds before it becomes fit to be read.' ... Those having even a superficial knowledge of the science of mesmerism know how the thoughts of the mesmerizer, though silently formulated in his mind, are instantly transferred to that of the subject.... The work of writing the letters in question is carried on by a sort of psychological telegraphy; the Mahatmas very rarely write their letters in the ordinary way. An electromagnetic connection, so to say, exists on the psychological plane between a Mahatma and his chelas, one of whom acts as his amanuensis. When the Master wants a letter to be written in this way, he draws the attention of the chela, whom he selects for the task, by causing an astral bell (heard by so many of our Fellows and others) to be rung near him, just as the despatching telegraph office signals to the receiving office before wiring the message. The thoughts arising in the mind of the Mahatma are then clothed in words, pronounced mentally, and forced along the astral currents he sends towards the pupil to impinge on the brain of the latter. Thence, they are borne by the nerve-currents to the palms of his hand and the tips of his fingers, which rest on a piece of magnetically prepared paper. As the thought-waves are thus impressed on the tissue, materials are drawn to it from the ocean of Akasha (permeating every atom of the sensuous universe), by an occult process, out of place here to describe, and permanent marks are left."

Pre-existence. A term used to denote that we have lived before; synonymous with *reincarnation*. The idea is derided by some, rejected by others, and still by others called absurd and inconsistent, yet it is the oldest and most universally accepted belief of immemorial antiquity. And if this belief was universally accepted by the most subtle philosophical minds of the pre-Christian world, surely it is not amiss that some of our modern intellectuals should also believe in it, or at least give the doctrine the benefit of the doubt. Even the Bible hints at it, St. John the Baptist being regarded as the reincarnation of Elijah, and the disciples asking whether the blind man *was born blind because of his sins*, which is equal to saying that he had lived and sinned before being born blind. As James Bonwick well says in *Egyptian Belief*: it was "the work of spiritual progression and soul discipline. The pampered sensualist returned a beggar; the proud oppressor, a slave; the selfish woman of fashion, a seamstress. A turn of the wheel gave a chance for the development of neglected or abused intelligence and feeling, hence the popularity of reincarnation in all climes and times.... Thus the expurgation of evil was ... gradually but certainly accomplished."

Truly, "an evil act follows a man, passing through one hundred thousand transmigrations" (*Panchatantra*). "All souls have a subtle vehicle, image of the body, which carries the passive soul from one material dwelling to another" says Kapila; while Basnage explains of the Jews: "By this second death is not considered hell, but that which happens when a soul has a second time animated a body." Herodotus tells his readers that the Egyptians "are the earliest who have spoken of this doctrine, according to which the soul of man is immortal and, after the destruction of the body, *enters into a newly born being*. When, say they, it has passed through all the animals of the earth and sea, and all the birds, it will re-enter the body of a newborn man." This is *pre-existence*. Deveria showed that the funeral books of the Egyptians say plainly "that *resurrection* was, in reality, but a renovation, leading to a new infancy, and a new youth."

Presley, Elvis (1935–1977). An American singer and actor. Works by H. P. Blavatsky and Helena Roerich were among his favourites.

Prima facie (*Lat.*, "at first appearance"). At first sight; self-evident.

Principles. The elements or original essences, the basic differentiations upon and of which all things are built. We use the term to denote the seven individual and fundamental aspects of the One Universal Reality in the Cosmos and in man. Hence, also the seven aspects in the manifestation of the human being — divine, spiritual, psychic, astral, physiological, and simply physical.

Probation. A period of testing and trial that a candidate undergoes when aspiring to become accepted as a Teacher's disciple. During this time, the aspirant is subject to various challenges, temptations, and difficulties designed to test their moral strength and faith, and to draw out their true nature. Probation usually lasts from three to seven years, but this period can be shortened or extended.

Prometheus. The Greek *logos*; he who, by bringing to Earth divine fire (intelligence and consciousness), endowed humanity with reason and mind. Prometheus is the Hellenic type of the Kumaras or Egos, those who, by incarnating in humankind, made of human beings latent gods instead of animals. The gods (or Elohim) were averse to humans becoming "as one of us (Genesis 3:22), and knowing "good and evil." Hence we see these gods in every religious legend punishing man for his desire to know. As the Greek myth has it, for stealing the fire that he brought to humankind from Heaven, Prometheus was chained by the order of Zeus to a crag in the Caucasian Mountains.

Proteus (*Gr.*, "first"). A Greek sea god capable of changing his shape; the intangible, omnipotent and omnipresent "Unknown," indivisible in Essence and eluding form, yet capable of appearing under each and every form.

Psychic energy. The primary fiery energy which lies at the foundation of the manifested world.

Psychism. A term used to denote, very loosely, every kind of mental phenomena, e.g., mediumship and the higher sensitiveness, hypnotic receptivity and inspired prophecy, simple clairvoyance in the Astral Light and real divine seership; in short, the word covers every phase and manifestation of the powers and potencies of *human* and *divine* souls.

Psychology. The science of soul in days of old, a science which served as the unavoidable basis for physiology, whereas in the present day, psychology is based upon physiology.

Pu Ji Qun Ling (*Ch.*, "universal Saviour of all living beings"). A title of Avalokiteshvara and Buddha; an inscription on the tablet granted by the Emperor Kangxi to Puji Temple, located on the island of Mount Putuo in China.

Pundit (*Sk.*, "learned"). An expert in a particular subject.

Pune. A city in the state of Maharashtra, India.

Puranas (*Sk.*, "ancient"). A collection of the symbolical and allegorical sacred writings of Hinduism.

Pure Land. Another name for Shambhala known for its utmost purity and supreme vibrations that an impure heart is simply unable to withstand. See *Shambhala* for more.

Purusha (*Sk.*, "man"). Heavenly Man; the Spiritual Self.

Putidamo. The Chinese name of Bodhidharma, the first Chinese patriarch.

Putuo (*Ch.*, "Potalaka"). An island of the Zhoushan archipelago of China associated with the Bodhisattva Guanshiyin.

Pythagoras (c.570–c.495 BCE). The most famous of the mystic philosophers, born on the Greek island of Samos. He seems to have travelled the world and to have culled his philosophy from the various systems to which he had access. He studied the esoteric sciences with the Brachmanes of India and astronomy and astrology in Chaldea and Egypt. In India, he is known to this day under the name Yavanacharya ("Ionian teacher"). After returning to his homeland, he settled in Crotona, Magna Grecia, where he established a college to which very soon all the finest intellects of the civilized centres were drawn. His father was Mnesarchus of Samos, a man of noble birth and learning. Pythagoras was the first to teach the heliocentric system, and was the greatest proficient in geometry of his century. It was also he who created the word "philosopher," composed of two words meaning a "lover of wisdom" — *philo-sophos*. As the greatest mathematician, geometer, and astronomer of historical antiquity, and also the highest of the metaphysicians and scholars, Pythagoras has won imperishable fame. He taught reincarnation as it is professed in India and much else of the Secret Wisdom.

Q

Quaternary. The four lower principles in man, those which constitute his *personality* (i.e., body, astral double, *prana*, or life, organs of desire, and lower *manas*, or brain-mind), as distinguished from the higher triad, composed of the higher spiritual soul, mind, and *atman* (Higher Self).

Quietists. A religious sect founded by a Spanish monk named Molinos. Their chief doctrine was that contemplation (an internal state of complete rest and passivity) was the only religious practice possible, and constituted the whole of religious observances. These were the Western hatha yogis who passed their time in trying to separate their minds from the objects of sense. The practice became a fashion in France and also in Russia during the early part of the nineteenth century.

Quoad sé (*Lat.*, "in relation to itself"). Knowable by itself as the Absolute, therefore, unknowable in this aspect for us created beings as opposed to the concept of *Quoad nos* (*Lat.*), seen or perceived by us, as created beings. Both *Quoad nos* and *Quoad sé* derive from concepts of the *Summa Theologica* of St. Thomas Aquinas.

R

Rabbi (*Heb.*, "my teacher"). Originally a teacher of the Secret Mysteries, Kabbalah; now a religious teacher in Judaism, often one who has studied Jewish law and is qualified to lead a synagogue, teach Torah, and provide spiritual guidance to the community.

Race or **Root Race**. A stage in the evolution of humanity. This Theosophical term does not refer to ethnicity. Belonging to one of the various Races is primarily determined by level of spirituality, or by the coefficient that indicates brightness of the heart — a coefficient termed *argo*. There are Seven Races in total, each of which has seven sub-races. Each Race develops a particular character or quality that densifies or rarefies the matter of human bodies.

People in the first two Races, as well as in the first half of the Third Race, did not have physical bodies — their bodies were of ethereal matter. These were genderless beings, not endowed with reason and never dying, for they did not have flesh, who existed for 300 million years.

The separation of the sexes took place 18 million years ago, in the middle of the Third Race, i.e., the Lemurians, and at this point people began to conceive their progeny. Humanity received dense physical bodies and began to reflect the higher mind.

The Fourth Race, the Atlanteans, came into being approximately 4–5 million years ago. But only three Atlantean sub-races evolved on the continent of Atlantis. The evolution of the remaining four took place in Egypt, Asia, and Europe.

The current Fifth Race, known as the Aryan Race, originated about one million years ago in India. In the twentieth century, the term *Aryan*, as well as additional hidden knowledge previously revealed by the messengers of Light, was used by the dark forces to develop and circulate anti-evolutionary theories. The people of the Fifth Race are now to be found on each existing continent and all its seven sub-races have already formed. Nevertheless, the Third and Fourth Races are still represented on Earth.

The formation of any future Race will not require the millions of years that it took previous Races. Therefore, it may be said that the Sixth and Seventh Races will exist and develop simultaneously. Thus, since the beginning of the twentieth century, in each country there have appeared individuals of the highest spiritual and moral calibre who are generating the next, i.e., the Sixth Race. These individuals are no different from any other in outward appearance, but they have loving hearts, strong energy, and often many abilities and talents. And seeds of the Seventh Race are already showing themselves. Towards the final stages of the Seventh Race, many things that are now considered miraculous will have become commonplace, and the attenuation of the human body, as well as the matter of the planet, will reach the point prescribed by the Evolution for this Round and its final Race.

The farther one looks back into humanity's past, the more one can see of its future, for the past contains a projection of the future. The first Races were ethereal, and matter slowly became solid. The Races that are last to develop will be the same, but this time, matter will gradually rarefy. The end and the beginning are similar in form but distinct in expression. While the beginning was characterized by the absence of self-consciousness, the end is the pinnacle of self-awareness. The middle of the Fourth Round — the middle of the Fourth Race — marks the lowest point of the fall into matter, the densification of the human body, and the development of intelligence. The Fifth Race is on an ascending arc. Therefore, gradually the spiritual must achieve an ever-increasing preponderance over the material, and the heart over the intellect, so that by the end of the Seventh Race matter is completely subordinate to spirit to the extent accessible to the Fourth Round of Evolution.

Humanity currently lives in a period of great responsibility — the time of the change of Races. This process is always accompanied by an extremely powerful influence of Cosmic Fire, leading to a change in the inclination of the Earth's axis and magnetic poles, attended by natural disasters and climate change. Additionally, humanity is reaping what it has sown over this period of its development. As the time of the change of Races approaches, information is being imparted to the world (within permissible limits) through the messengers of Light, with the aim of warning humanity of forthcoming dramatic, earth-shaking change.

Helena Blavatsky's works and *The Mahatma Letters*, along with other ancient writings, foretell that, during the change of Races, the continents America and Europe will be shaken by powerful earthquakes, and submerge into the sea. Edgar Cayce also foresaw this scenario for the end of the twentieth century. However, the development and collective will of humanity enabled the Hierarchy of Light to prevent the occurrence of such devastating cataclysms. Even the Hierarchy of Light only has the right to exercise their involvement in such cases up to 50 per cent; otherwise, humanity would learn nothing. The other 50 per cent of effort required for the salvation of humanity must be made by Earth-dwellers themselves.

America and Europe may have a beautiful future. Everything depends on the people, who must keep pace with Evolution, and this requires a revival of spirituality. Also, it should be borne in mind that books, films, and other works of art which proclaim yet another "end-of-the-world" scenario and various cataclysms promote — through human will — thought-forms that take on enormous proportions. Such energies may explode in space, resulting in huge disasters. So, North America finds itself, on the Subtle Plane, in a rather unstable condition, since its population in the physical world is constantly destroying its own cities and the entire continent by the thought-forms contained, for example, in its entertainment films, which are distributed worldwide. It requires a tremendous effort on the part of all the colleagues of the Great Brotherhood to prevent such thoughts and the destruction they depict from becoming manifest in physical reality. But this is something that is also within the power of any conscientious citizen of any country. If a person can erect giant destructive structures simply through their thoughts, then, by the same token, a light-bearing individual is able to produce creative, positive currents, for example by making prayerful appeals to the Forces of Light. And then the transfiguring Fire will descend into the lower spheres and mitigate the destructive influence of these negative formations.

Therefore, the manner in which the change of Races will actually take place, whether through conscious evolution without tragic consequences or through constant upheaval, depends upon each and every one of us.

The end of each Race is also the period of the Great Choice, which in almost all religions is referred to as the *Last Judgement*.

Regarding the Last Judgement at the end of the Fifth Race, Helena Roerich explains:

"When Christ spoke about the end of the world, He could not have meant the final completion of the evolution of our planet. For, if evolution follows the natural and lawful order of development and the planet enters its Seventh Round, and its humanity, the Seventh Race, with all sub-races, then at the completion of this evolution there cannot be one such Last Judgement. For by this time humanity and the planet will have reached the state of the Higher Worlds, where there is no longer any conscious force of evil opposing good.

"Christ, of course, knew about the heavy karma of humanity and the planet that had been created, and He knew about the impending death of the majority, and therefore, He had in mind precisely the approaching replacement of the Race, which is always accompanied by great cosmic cataclysms, before which a great selection is made in advance of the Final Judgement. Being an Initiate, He must have known that this catastrophe might appear as the Last Day, due to the terrifying decline in spirituality among humanity. After all, it is possible that not enough opposing, or rather, *discharging* energies will gather to keep the planet from ending in a giant explosion. The Prince of this world directs all his efforts towards this explosion, for he knows that in a purified atmosphere, imbued with new fiery Rays or energies, his stay in the earthly sphere will become unbearable and impossible. This is why he strives to blow it up, in order, as it has been said, to fly away on its fragments....

"Is it not of this replacement of the Race that the Apostle Peter speaks (Second Epistle 3:13), as well as Revelation (21:1) and the prophecy of Isaiah (66:22)? Remember, the Teaching says that it is the human spirit that can become the exploder of the planet. It says the same of the *dischargers*, whose number is so small, and, therefore, the entire burden of maintaining the balance of the planet falls to them. A strong Spirit can keep an entire area from being hit by an earthquake. In ancient times, the Great Teachers sent their high disciples to localities threatened by earthquakes" (23 August 1934).

The Last Judgement is not one specific day, but the whole period for each individual of the *final choice* which is made in the spirit, summing up the results of numerous lifetimes during various cycles of Evolution.

The choice of each person determining whether they belong to the Light or the darkness, to the New World or the old, manifests itself in the form of an invisible symbol on their foreheads; this symbol expresses the energy potential of a crystal in their hearts, *ringsel*. The energy potential, or brightness, of each person's *ringsel* crystal is measured by the *argo* coefficient.

One might imagine that there exist Cosmic Scales of total accuracy and that the sum positive potential of the *argo* of all humanity is weighed on one pan, the negative potential being weighed on the other. At the end of each cycle of Evolution, or Race, the time always comes when humanity reaps what it has sown by its actions during that period. It is important that the pans of the Scales are in balance with no extra weight in favour of evil, since this would lead to negative consequences on a global scale.

Thanks to the fact that the energy potential of the people who have chosen the Light may exceed by up to three or more times that of those who, consciously or unconsciously, have decided to remain in the darkness, the balance of the forces of Light and darkness is maintained on the swaying Cosmic Scales. In other words, it is important to have *quality*, although in quantity there might be significantly fewer people on the side of Good than those who appear on the opposite side.

The same principle is at play in the case of the individual. If the energy potential of *argo* formed by the totality of that person's incarnations falls below a certain level, and that person has no aspiration to do kind deeds for the good of their neighbours, even in this life, then their choice will be negative with the corresponding consequences which they will reap, if not in the physical world, then after their transition into another world.

And so it is that the brightness of the *ringsel* crystal in the heart serves as a "pass" into the New World or the New Race.

The Last Judgement for present humanity is to take place in three main phases which are closely associated with the cosmic events described in sacred scriptures.

The first occurred in 1942, when, esoterically speaking, the Age of Aquarius began. For certain reasons, this date was obscured in the scriptures of the East. Yet certain researchers succeeded in understanding that the key to calculating the end of Kali Yuga (Dark Age) had been lost and that the giant figures indicated were merely symbols. In the 1930s, they widely disseminated among the population of India information relating to the significance of the year 1942. Helena Roerich, who continued the mission of Helena Blavatsky in the twentieth century, told those with whom she corresponded that this date had been confirmed by her Teacher long before.

And on 1 August 1943, the cosmic event described in the *Vishnu Purana* (Book 4, chapter 24) signifying the beginning of Satya Yuga (Light Age) occurred: "When the Sun and Moon, and the lunar asterism Tishya, and the planet Jupiter are in one mansion, the Krita [Golden] Age shall return."

Therefore, it is logical to assume that with the beginning of the New Era, the process of summing up the results of the previous Era must begin. Naturally, everything in the world occurs gradually, and as with the change of the seasons, humanity is now living during the transitional period between the dark and the light Eras, when "winter" with its frosts still makes itself felt, despite the arrival of "spring" on the calendar.

The second phase of the Last Judgement occurred during the period 19 July 1999 to 19 July 2017, when all of humanity was *finally* divided into those who belong to the Light and those who belong to the darkness. This period was marked by two cosmic events, one of 11 August 1999 and the other of 21 September 2017, which are indicated in the Bible (Matthew 24:29–30 and Revelation 12:1–2, respectively). There have been a number of predictions about the significance of the years 1999 and 2017.

The results of the present cycle of Evolution have already been determined, and each person on Earth has already made their final choice, either consciously or unconsciously. And now, the third phase of the Last Judgement is underway. Characteristic of this phase is that everyone, after their natural departure from the earthly plane, receives exactly what they deserve. This process will be completed approximately by the end of the twenty-first century, and prior to its completion, those who have chosen the darkness can still alter their choice in favour of Light as long as they are physically incarnate. Even if the brightness of their hearts precludes this, here, the factor of human will is of great importance, since it is able to change everything even at the very last moment. Therefore, for every person, the choice they make on leaving the earthly plane is crucial, as this will complete the third phase of the Last Judgement over themselves.

After leaving planet Earth, those who have chosen the darkness will forever lose the ability to be reincarnated on this planet and will instead be drawn to spheres that correspond to their true essence. In previous cycles, human individualities did not lose their ability to reincarnate on Earth. Instead, they reaped the fruits of their actions in subsequent incarnations and in new cycles. This is because at that time the planet was on the descending line of its evolution, whereas now, as stated in Blavatsky's *The Secret Doctrine*, it is on the ascending arc.

Currently, anyone who committed evil or simply lived solely for the sake of themselves in centuries and millennia past is being given the final chance to wake up and reach out towards the Light. This is one of the esoteric reasons why so many people are currently incarnated on Earth — all those that once lived in a previous cycle and did not paid off their karmic debt are now gathered together. However, this time, those who have chosen the darkness, those who are spiritually undeveloped, will simply be unable to live in the following cycle, since their energy structures will fail to withstand the high vibrations of Light that will flood the Earth. In modern times, the energies that are already coming to the planet from the Cosmos are increasing incrementally; this is what is causing climate change and what we call global warming, when virtually every year a new temperature record is set.

Each previous cycle of Evolution had its own Last Judgement, or period of final choice. However, as *The Secret Doctrine* states, the Third Race (the Lemurians) was destroyed by fire, while the Fourth Race (the Atlanteans) was swept away by the water that is depicted in the Bible as the Deluge. In the previous cycles, the percentage of those who had chosen the Light ranged within 6–9 per cent, and this imbalance of forces led to large-scale disasters that destroyed entire continents.

A similar scenario for the completion of the present, Fifth Race was actually a *reality* for the end of the twentieth century, of which prominent prophets, such as Edgar Cayce, warned. Nevertheless, the spiritual development of humanity as well as a surge of interest in spiritual subjects all around the world in the 1980s and 1990s allowed the Forces of Light to prevent giant cataclysms and to reduce them to the minimum level permitted by the karma of humanity. That is why the period of the Last Judgement is taking place unnoticeably for the human race, without experiencing a global scale calamity of the sort commonly depicted in modern popular culture.

The second book of the *Agni Yoga* series given in 1925 through Helena Roerich by Mahatma Morya says: "And so I shall summon under the Banner of Spirit 1,000,000,000. This will be the sign of My army. Consider when this manifestation will be fulfilled and seven banners will be affirmed!" In the original Russian edition the number is written in numerals, rather than words, as it is in the English version.

From *The Secret Doctrine* it is known that zeros are used as a veil to conceal the real numbers. In this case, esoterically speaking, three zeros signify nine. That is, Master Morya was actually indicating the year 1999.

Further, Helena Roerich wrote in her letters: "The ancient prophecies have it: 'On the day of the Last Judgement, one in three will remain.' The most recent prophesy states: 'One in six will remain.' Humanity has endeavoured to aggravate its fate, moving closer to destruction. Lucifer sowed his seeds, truly, on a grand scale, and the crop has grown tall and ripe. The Forces of Light will stop the explosion of the planet, but it cannot be that all the consequences of such a sowing are destroyed. Those who sowed the storm will have to accept it" (21 August 1950).

Thus, it was known that in the year 1999 the side of Light would be taken by every sixth person, or one billion people. It is interesting to note the accuracy of the prediction given by the Mahatma. In 1925, the population of Earth was two billion people, and one sixth of this would be 333 million, but it was in October 1999 that the population reached the mark of six billion people, one sixth of which was exactly the one billion of the Army of Light.

This number increased to about 1.25 billion out of the 7.5 billion incarnated inhabitants of Earth as of 19 July 2017. If all of the planet's seven planes are taken into account, then ten billion of the 60 billion souls that populated the planet at the beginning of the Grand Cycle of Evolution belong to the Light.

It is precisely the positive potential of 17 per cent of Earth's population that has secured the energy balance of the forces on the Cosmic Scales at a 50–50 ratio (slightly swaying sometimes in one direction, sometimes in the other), and this has allowed the Forces of Light to prevent global cataclysms at the present time.

However, the number of those who have chosen the Light is variable, because in every moment one person will start to ascend while another falls, having been insufficiently resolved on their position of Light. And therefore, for the first half of the twenty-first century, there is still a threat that the pan of evil on the swaying Cosmic Scales may significantly outweigh the other; after all, human will has delivered a "surprise" on more than one occasion in past cycles.

As of 19 July 2017, the Karmic Scales showed a slightly greater weight in favour of Good. However, two years later, a certain preponderance towards evil was manifested. The imbalance, generated by human will, gave the right to representatives of the Virus Kingdom, which has its own scores to settle with the Human Kingdom, to carry out their own Judgement, using the hands of the people themselves. As a rule, people only remember the Higher Powers when something bad happens. Therefore, only a confident and stable preponderance towards the Good can enable large-scale negative phenomena to become a thing of the past.

It should also be said that the completion of the Last Judgement in this cycle does not mean that only ideal "angels" will remain on planet Earth and in the near-Earth spheres. Imperfection will still exist in the future; though such an acute manifestation of evil, as seen in the past and today, will be no more. In addition, one should not forget that selections in the form of Last Judgements will continue to occur in future cycles.

Those who have chosen the darkness will still be given a new chance to come to the Light, so to speak "from scratch," but this time under completely different conditions, i.e., on Saturn. On the other hand, in their future incarnations, those who choose the Light will witness and participate in the gradual transformation of the world, transforming the planet Earth into a genuine Paradise.

The Seven Races of humanity comprise one *Round* — a life-cycle of Evolution of varying time scales. So, the transition of humanity across all seven globes (or spheres) of Earth or any other planet through incarnation in each of the four Kingdoms of Nature — mineral, plant, animal, and man — is known as the *Planetary Round*, or *Great Round*, or simply *Round*. That is, the Great Round consists of the Seven Races, which evolve on the Seven Spheres of the planet. The development of the Seven Races in just one globe of the planet is called a *Small Round*, or *Ring*. Also, each Race that experiences human evolution within each of its seven sub-races may be considered a Small Round.

There are Seven Great Rounds in total comprising *Manvantara* — a period of active life. Although in ancient scriptures there are other divisions and expressions, this one is generally accepted at the present time. Between Rounds and Manvantaras there are *Pralayas* of different timespans — periods of rest, similar to slumber, which are equal in duration to periods of activity. After passing through the Seven Rounds, humanity moves on to new planets, endlessly.

The current population of humanity, representing mainly the Fifth Race, is now in the Fourth Great Round, which will come to completion in the Seventh Race. It is in this Round that humanity on Earth has fully developed — earlier, it was referred to as *humanity* only for want of a more appropriate term. That which becomes man passes through all the forms and kingdoms during the First Round and through all human shapes during the two following Rounds. At the commencement of the Fourth Round, man appears on Earth as a primeval form, being preceded only by the Mineral and Vegetable Kingdoms. Over the following three Rounds, humanity, like the globe on which it lives, will ever tend to reassume its original divine form, except that humanity will become more and more self-aware. Like every other atom in the Universe, man strives to become first a God-man and then a God.

Every new Round always repeats the previous one in miniature before proceeding to a new level of development. The Mahatmas briefly revealed human evolution in each of the Rounds:

First Round. Man is an ethereal being, non-intelligent, but super-spiritual. In each of the subsequent Races, sub-races and minor races of evolution he grows more and more into a compacted or incarnate being, but is still essentially ethereal. And like the animal and vegetable, he develops bodies corresponding to his coarse surroundings.

Second Round. Man is still gigantic and ethereal, but grows firmer and more condensed in his body as he becomes a more physical man. Yet, still, he is less intelligent than spiritual, for mind evolves with less speed and more difficulty than does the physical frame — i.e., the mind is not able to develop as rapidly as the body.

Third Round. Man has now a perfectly concrete or compacted body. At first it is the form of a giant ape, more clever (or rather, cunning) than spiritual. For in the downward arc he has now reached the point where his primordial spirituality is eclipsed or overshadowed by his nascent mentality. In the last half of this Third Round, his gigantic stature decreases, his body improves in texture, and he becomes a more rational being — though still more of an ape than a man. The people of this Round had reached the physical state, but could not stay in it, causing a catastrophe, although on a smaller scale than in the subsequent Round. Some returned to their astral state, while others simply perished.

Fourth Round. The mental body and intellect experience an enormous development. The formerly mute races acquire human speech on the Earth, during which, starting with the Fourth Race, language is perfected and knowledge of physical things increases. At this point, the world teems with the results of intellectual activity and spiritual deterioration. In the first half of the Fourth Race, sciences, arts, literature, and philosophy are born, degenerating in one nation and being reborn in another. Like everything else, civilization and intellectual development whirl through septenary cycles. Only in the second half of this Round does the spiritual essence begin the process of transmuting the body and the mind to manifest its transcendental powers and accept the governing role of the heart.

Fifth Round. The same relative development and struggle continue, but with a new goal: mastery of the subtlest cosmic energies. Plato, Confucius, and the Count of Saint-Germain were representatives of this Round (it should be understood that prior to their coming to Earth, they were present on another planet, which was already in the Fifth Round of development). In this Round, the higher mind reaches perfection. People have completely mastered thought; clairvoyance and clairaudience are available to almost everyone, but in varying degrees. Common language is replaced with the reading of thought. Evil in the form of a struggle against the Light does not exist, but there is imperfection at various stages of evolution. Science and art are highly appreciated; chemistry and other natural sciences are well developed.

Sixth Round. In this Round the human soul is fully developed. Humanity is so advanced that the qualities and abilities of the Greatest Master become the property of transfigured man. Gautama Buddha was a representative of this Round.

Seventh Round. Humanity becomes a tribe of Gods, and animals are intelligent beings. It ends with the spiritualization of matter and the transition into subtly luminous forms. On the plane of ordinary visibility the Earth becomes invisible, but life remains, and its forms are manifested on the highest planes of invisibility. Everything is focused on spirit. Thought is the external expression of life, becoming a reality without a single limitation. But even these conditions are merely the preparation for a New Cycle of Evolution.

Thus, the chain of Rounds inevitably leads humanity towards a state of omnipotence, while each Round assigns a task for human beings to develop their bodies, principles, or any other abilities of their microcosm.

Radda-Bai. The pen name of H. P. Blavatsky in Russia.

Rahat (*Sin.*, "Arhat"). The Adept who becomes entirely free from all desire on this material plane by acquiring divine knowledge and powers.

Rahul, Ram. The late professor of Central Asian Studies at Jawaharlal Nahru University, known for his work on Asian relations, history, cultures, and religions. Travelling on geographical and anthropological expeditions in Asia, he wrote extensively on the Himalaya borderlands, especially the kingdom of Bhutan and Nepal. He is the author of more than 25 books, including *The Government and Politics of Tibet* (1969) that features a foreword by His Holiness the Dalai Lama.

Rai Bahadur. A title of honour bestowed upon Hindus in British India for faithful service.

Raison d'être (*Fr.*, "reason for being"). Refers to the primary purpose or justification for the existence of a thing.

Raja (*Sk.*). A prince or king in India.

Raja Yoga (*Sk.*, "royal path"). The true system of developing psychic and spiritual powers and union with one's Higher Self, or the supreme spirit. The exercise, regulation, and concentration of thought. Raja Yoga is opposed to Hatha Yoga, the physical or psycho-physiological training in asceticism.

Rajagriha or **Rajgir** (*Sk.*, "city of kings"). A city in the ancient kingdom of Magadha (on the territory of modern India) famous for its conversion to Buddhism in the days of the Buddhist kings. It was their residence from Bimbisara to Ashoka, and was the seat of the first Buddhist Council held in 510 BCE.

Rajasic (*Sk.*, "passion"). In the context of the *gunas* (qualities of nature), the quality of activity, passion, and dynamism. A rajasic person is typically driven by desires, ambition, and change, often leading to restlessness.

Rakoczy. One of the Great Teachers of Shambhala; the Ruler of the Age of Aquarius. His incarnations include Lao Tzu, Nostradamus, and the Count of Saint-Germain. In Helena Roerich's notebooks, He is indicated as the successor of Master M. in the position of the Lord of Shambhala.

Of course, Master Rakoczy made history around the world as the ever young Count of Saint-Germain, an Initiate, referred to as an enigmatic personage by many writers. His rare intellectual endowments, brilliant conversation, and mysterious mode of life astounded and dazzled the public mind. Frederic II, King of Prussia, used to say of him that he was a man whom no one had ever been able to make out. Many are his "biographies," each as wild as the next, but the best of these, which was recommended by Helena Roerich, is *The Comte de St. Germain* (1912) by Isabel Cooper-Oakley.

By some he was regarded as an incarnate god, by others as a clever Alsatian Jew. One thing is certain, Count de St. Germain, whatever his real patronymic may have been, had a right to his name and title, for he had purchased a property called San Germano, in the Italian Tyrol, and paid the Pope for the title. He was uncommonly handsome and his enormous erudition and linguistic capacities undeniable, for he spoke English, Italian, French, Spanish, Portuguese, German, Russian, Swedish, Danish, and many Slavonian and Oriental languages, with equal facility as a native speaker of each.

Saint-Germain was extremely wealthy, never received a penny from anyone — in fact never accepted a glass of water or broke bread with anyone — and made most extravagant presents of superb jewellery to all his friends, even to the royal families of Europe.

His proficiency in music was marvellous; he played every instrument, the violin being his favourite. "St. Germain rivalled Paganini himself," said an octogenarian Belgian in 1835, after hearing the *Genoese maestro.* "It is St. Germain resurrected who plays the violin in the body of an Italian skeleton," exclaimed a Lithuanian baron, who had heard both. The British

Museum houses pieces of music composed by Comte de St. Germain.

Moreover, he was a gifted artist who used unusually bright colours in his oil paintings on historical subjects. His paintings under different names remained in four countries: France, England, Germany, and the Netherlands.

Saint-Germain never laid claim to spiritual powers, but proved himself to have a right to such a claim. He used to pass into a dead trance lasting from 37 to 49 hours without awakening, and then knew all he had to know, and demonstrated the fact by prophesying the future without ever making a mistake. It is he who prophesied before the Kings Louis XV and XVI, and the unfortunate Marie Antoinette. Many were the witnesses still living in the first quarter of the nineteenth century who testified to his marvellous memory; he could read a paper in the morning and, though hardly glancing at it, repeat its contents without missing a single word days afterwards; he could write with two hands at once, the right hand penning a piece of poetry, the left a diplomatic paper of the greatest importance. He read sealed letters without touching them while they were held still in the hand of those who brought them to him. He was the greatest Adept at transmuting metals, making gold and the most marvellous diamonds, an art, he said, that he had learnt from certain Brahmins in India, who taught him the artificial crystallization ("quickening") of pure carbon.

In 1780, when on a visit to the French Ambassador to the Hague, he broke to pieces with a hammer a superb diamond of his own manufacture, the counterpart of which, also manufactured by himself, he had just before sold to a jeweller for 5,500 French gold coins. He was a friend and confidant of Count Orloff in 1772, in Vienna, whom he had helped and saved in St. Petersburg in 1762, when he found himself embroiled in the famous political conspiracies of that time; he also became a close friend of Frederick the Great of Prussia.

As a matter of course, he had numerous enemies, and therefore, it is not to be wondered at if all the gossip invented about him is now attributed to his own confessions: e.g., that he was over 500 years old; also, that he claimed personal intimacy "with the Saviour and his twelve Apostles, and that he had reproved Peter for his bad temper" — the latter clashing somewhat in point of time with the former, if he had really claimed to be only 500 years old. If he said that "he had been born in Chaldea and professed to possess the secrets of the Egyptian magicians and sages," he may have spoken the truth without making any miraculous claim. There are Initiates, by no means the highest, who are placed in a condition to remember more than one past life. But we have grounds to reason that St. Germain could never have claimed "personal intimacy" with the Saviour. However that may be, Count St. Germain was certainly the greatest Oriental Adept Europe has seen in recent centuries.

He passed out of public sight at the end of the eighteenth century after staging his own death in 1784. However, there is proof that he was still living several years after 1784. He is said to have had a most important private conference with the Empress of Russia in 1785 or 1786, and to have appeared before the Princess de Lamballe when she stood before the tribunal, a few moments before she was struck down by a bullet and a butcher-boy cut off her head; and before Jeanne du Barry, the mistress of Louis XV, as she waited on her scaffold at Paris for the stroke of the guillotine in the Days of Terror, 1793. Blavatsky's relatives, the Fadeyevs, possessed highly important documents relating to him.

The Count of Saint-Germain travelled extensively, and one of the reasons for this was to lay special magnets, forming Points of Life, as previously had Apollonius of Tyana. Their disciples, too, carried them to distant countries.

It is also interesting to note that in Darjeeling, India, there is a grave of a mysterious philologist and Orientalist from Hungary, whose year of birth is the same as the "official" year of death of the Count of Saint-Germain — Csoma de Kőrös (1784–1842). Not only did he speak seventeen languages, but he was also similar in appearance to the Count. In 1933, he was declared a Bodhisattva in Japan, because he "opened the Heart of the West to the teachings of the Buddha." His statue was placed in Taisho University in Tokyo. A plaque fixed to his memorial in Darjeeling was carved with the phrase in Hungarian: "Rakoczy, 1980."

In the second half of the twentieth century, one of Saint-Germain's disciples noticed Helen Schucman, who had begun writing *A Course in Miracles* (1976), and started to invisibly supervise her writing of the text. His was truly "exquisite workmanship" that paved the way to heartfulness through the mental-emotional sphere, making this text extremely useful for the consciousness of the West.

Master Rakoczy played a decisive role in the adoption of the Declaration of Independence of the United States in 1776, appearing as an "Unknown Stranger." He delivered a fiery speech that encouraged the doubting assembly to sign the historical document. When the event was ending and the delegates wanted to thank the mysterious stranger, they discovered that he had vanished from the locked room.

Manly P. Hall received a copy of this speech taken from a "rare old volume of early American political speeches of a date earlier than those preserved in the first volumes of the *Congressional Record.*" However, he was not given the title or date of the relevant volume. He quoted the speech in *The Secret Teachings of All Ages* (1928).

In 1938, the complete speech appeared in *The Theosophist* with the following footnote: "Published in a rare volume of addresses, and known probably to only one in a million, even of American citizens." Hall confirmed that it was the same as the copy he had received. He published it himself in *The Secret Destiny of America* (1944), but omitted two paragraphs. When quoting the speech in 1957, President Ronald Reagan used Hall's book as the reference.

The speech also appears in George Lippard's *Washington and His Generals; or, Legends of the Revolution* (1847), which is regarded as historical fiction. For this reason, it is believed that Hall had a copy of the speech taken from Lippard's book and, therefore, that he quoted fiction.

However, a careful comparison of the speech from both books reveals significant differences. Apart from the fact that Lippard's version is longer, there are other slight differences. For example, in Lippard's book the phrase "God has given America to be free" appears as "God has given America to the free." These differences might indicate that there is one primary source, in which case either Hall had an altered copy or Lippard added something of his own.

Moreover, Hall gives the description of what was happening "According to Jefferson," while Lippard does not mention anything of the kind. Hall specifically states: "From the letters of Thomas Jefferson, which are preserved in the Library of Congress, I have been able to gather considerable data concerning this portentous session."

Another reference to Jefferson is made in *The Light of Liberty* (1987) by Paul H. Dunn. Giving "an account which Thomas Jefferson once gave concerning the Declaration of Independence," Dunn writes on page 23: "Then a man rose and spoke. Jefferson described him not as a young man, but one who had to summon all his energy for an impassioned plea."

However, neither Hall nor Lippard give any description of the Stranger's age. Hall mentions only his "strong, bold voice," while Lippard adds that he was a "tall slender man."

Yet another instance is contained in *The Three Nephites* (1969) by Ogden Kraut. He describes the event on page 47 as based on an unknown book entitled *America's Thirteen Colonial States*:

"Now it was apparently this same 'Stranger' who again appeared at Philadelphia on July 4, 1776. Speaker after speaker had failed to rally the delegates (who feared for their lives) to sign the prepared Declaration of Independence. The old bellman finally said, 'No, they will never sign it.'

"When one o'clock came, a penetrating voice rang out, ringing with holy zeal. The debating stopped and everyone listened. It was not the voice of mortal man — for it stirred their inner souls. His divine counsel and commanding voice strengthened their faith and gave them courage to back it up. The speaker ended with these words: 'God has given America to be free.'

"The immediate signing of the document began, and the prepared bell of liberty, at 2 p.m., sent their decree around the world."

Again, neither Hall nor Lippard give any specific timing for when the events took place or mention what the bellman said.

All this indicates that there is a primary source of the speech which is not freely available to the public. In any case, the Masters' decisive role in America's struggle for independence was confirmed by both Helena Blavatsky and Helena Roerich.

To read this speech visit radiantbooks.co/bonus.

Rama. The seventh Avatar or incarnation of Vishnu; the eldest son of King Dasaratha of the Solar Race; full name: Ramachandra; hero of the Hindu epic Ramayana. Rama marries Sita, the female Avatar of Lakshmi, Vishnu's wife, who is abducted by Ravana, the Demon-King of Lanka, an act that led to the climatic war in which Rama slays Ravana.

Ramakrishna (1836–1886). An Indian mystic and saint who is regarded as an incarnation of the Divine by his followers. He taught the unity of all religions and emphasized direct experience of God over mere ritual.

Ramana Maharshi (1879–1950). An Indian sage who taught the path of Jnana Yoga (the yoga of knowledge) and self-inquiry as a means of realizing the true self and attaining liberation (*moksha*).

Ratthapala. The great Arhat who lived at the time of the Buddha. He was born into a wealthy family and lived in great luxury. However, when the Buddha visited his village, Ratthapala went to hear him speak and decided to become a monk.

Ratthapala Sutrasanne (*Sin.*). The Sinhalese translation of the legend of Ratthapala, narrated in the Pali *Ratthapala Sutta*.

Ray. A creative power, energy; the focused Fire of space that creates and constructs all visible and invisible forms of life on all planes of existence. A ray is a material body, a form of the expression of Light, stretching out through space in all directions and saturated with the subtlest substance of matter, containing a myriad of electrons. Ray energy is creative, for it carries elements which both combine among themselves and form compounds with elements of other rays by the Law of Magnetism and Consonance, thereby generating new types and combinations of matter and various orders of phenomena, along with whole new worlds. Invisible and visible rays are mighty producers and movers of life, regulating the life of each specific organism and form.

The influence of the rays of the Sun and stars extends to all that exists on Earth. Life has always depended on the celestial bodies, for its founding elements are to be found in the Universe. Rays of energy from the celestial bodies are sent to Earth for the combination of forms and the generation of new ones. Hence the rays of every planet take part in constructing each individual's physical body, the various elements of which are scattered throughout cosmic space among the corresponding stars. At birth the rays intersect and develop the framework within which a person's physical, astral, and mental bodies are constructed. The form of each organ — heart, lungs, liver, etc. — depends on the combination of rays from corresponding stars at the moment of birth. The alignment of the stars is always precisely determined and may be calculated for any given moment. Human beings are a concentration of the influence of rays, having gathered crystals of cosmic energies in the seed of their spirit for billions of years. The rays of the celestial bodies and their combinations condition not only the life of each individual, but also that of whole peoples, planets, and star systems.

The solar ray bears the essence of the structure and chemical composition of the Sun along with charges of powerful electromagnetic energy, bipolar in essence, threefold in manifestation, septenary in structure, and duodecimal in tonality. The visible solar ray is just one of its basest manifestations. Of course, the invisible rays of the solar spectrum are not limited to ultraviolet and infrared rays, but stretch out on both sides of the visible scale. This ray essence is natural not only to the rays of the Sun, but also to any star and any centre of existence in either an actual or a potential state. And if the heart is the sun of the body, then, consequently, every heart possesses the same qualities in its inexhaustible potential. Everything radiates light, but that light varies in terms of substance and degree.

Each Ray is a personified Being on any given plane of existence, and every evolving person is a particle of a given Ray. All the Lords pour the Light of their Rays into the world. They also use the Rays to communicate with their disciples. Every disciple is assigned a certain shade of their Master's Ray through which they receive knowledge and information directly from Him. In this way, the Ray serves as a special tool for the translation of impenetrable Cosmic Knowledge into something that the disciple's consciousness is capable of perceiving. In addition, this helps to prevent gross distortions of Truth, since anyone can access the Ocean of Knowledge, but only a few are able to understand it and convey it correctly to others.

The current Era of Maitreya is the Era of the Synthesis of all Seven Rays, which together constitute the Colour White. However, every two thousand years, a certain Ray, associated with one of the Seven Lords, dominates. The Ray of Christ has prevailed for two thousand years — the Age of Pisces. The next two thousand years will be the Age of Aquarius of Master Rakoczy, also known as Saint-Germain, the Lord of the Seventh Ray. So, now the Violet Ray makes its appearance, alongside the White Ray.

Of course, here one cannot apply the concept of *Time*, as it is Periods that prevail. The process of transfiguration began in 1942, when esoterically the Age of Aquarius came into force. However, it is impossible to pinpoint the precise moment at which one thing ends and another thing begins, because everything crosses over in a gradual flow. For a while, the two Eras will overlap. Nevertheless, the Age of Aquarius gathers momentum with each passing day.

The numbering of Rays varies according to different traditions; if viewed from the point of view of energy centres (chakras), then the first colour is red. It starts with *kundalini* (in the coccyx region) and ascends up the spinal column. But if one starts at *sahasrara* (the crown), then the violet ray is regarded as the first. The gradation of the Rays also differs. There are Rays of the Solar Systems, such as the Ray of Reason (emerald in colour), which dominated the First Solar System; the Second Ray of Love-Wisdom is now being manifested (rarefied rose in colour), and the next Solar System will be dominated by the First Ray of Will and Power (white in colour). Also, each of the Seven Great Lords is the carrier of a Ray of a certain colour, and these also have their own series of numbering and gradation.

The incarnation of Great Spirits can occur through the Ray that is sent to chosen successors. At the birth of a person with a special spiritual mission, a High Spirit that is karmically close sends that person His Ray, which will then accompany that person throughout his life. This Ray is perceived by the newborn in the same way as the rays of the celestial bodies under which he is born. He grows under this Ray, and with further development, complete assimilation of the Ray occurs. It is along this "wire" that the so-called incarnation of the Ray occurs.

Moreover, the matter or energy that once enclothed a High Spirit is indestructible and can, by power of attraction or kinship, in special cases become part of the subtle body formed around another high spirit, ready for a new incarnation. For example, a person may be born who was once a disciple of Hermes. His closeness to this Spirit can allow him to have part of the energy structure of Hermes in the composition of his subtle bodies, which once composed Hermes' quaternary. And here, from the point of view of the Higher Powers, this person can be considered Hermes, since he carries within himself some part or even one of Hermes' former bodies (astral, emotional, or mental). But whether he will *become* Hermes is another question, since bearing part of the energy of the High Spirit does not mean that this person will be able to *become* Him. He is given a chance to become Hermes by assimilating His Ray, but for various reasons this may not happen.

Reagan, Ronald (1911–2004). The President of the United States from 1981 to 1989, previously an actor and governor of California. His presidency is known for conservative policies and economic reforms known as *Reaganomics*.

Reincarnation. The once universal doctrine, which taught that the Ego is born on this earth an innumerable number of times. This doctrine of rebirth was believed in by Jesus and the Apostles, as by all people at that time, but is repudiated now by Christians. Nevertheless, the putting on of flesh periodically and throughout long cycles by the higher human soul (*buddhi-manas*) or Ego is taught in the Bible, as it is in all other ancient scriptures. All the Egyptian converts to Christianity, the Church Fathers, and others, believed in this doctrine, as shown by the writings of several. In surviving symbols, the human-headed bird flying towards a mummy, a body, or "the soul uniting itself with its *sahou* (glorified body of the Ego, and also the *kama-lokic shell*)" proves this belief. "The song of the Resurrection" chanted by Isis to recall her dead husband to life might be translated "Song of Rebirth," as Osiris is collective humanity. "Oh! Osiris [here follows the name of the Osirified mummy, or the departed], rise again in holy earth (matter), august mummy in the coffin, under thy corporeal substances," was the funeral prayer of the priest over the deceased. "Resurrection" among the Egyptians never meant the resurrection of the mutilated mummy, but of the *Soul* that informed it, the Ego in a new body. The putting on of flesh periodically by the Soul or the Ego, was a universal belief; nor can anything be more consonant with justice and Karmic Law.

Religio-Philosophical Journal. A weekly spiritualist journal, published in Chicago between 1865 and 1905.

Rice, Isaac (1850–1915). An American businessman and musicologist; the author of *What Is Music?* (1875).

Rig Veda (*Sk.*, "knowledge of verses"). The first and most important of the four Vedas. Fabled to have been "created" from the Eastern mouth of Brahma; recorded in occultism as having been delivered by great sages on Lake Manasarovar beyond the Himalayas, tens of thousands of years ago.

Rigden (*Tib.*, "holder of the lineage"). The title of the Lord of Shambhala. Rigden Dragpo (also transliterated as Drakpo and Jyepo) is the name of Mahatma Morya in the Tibetan tradition. He became the Lord of Shambhala in 1924 and took the name Maitreya.

Ringsel (*Tib.*, "treasure"). A crystal in the human body that becomes visible after cremation. It is formed through the deposition of energies that are present when an individual lives a highly moral life of service to others.

Rinpoche (*Tib.*, "precious one"). An honorary title, often used for highly respected teachers or reincarnated lamas in Tibetan Buddhism.

Rishi (*Sk.*, "sage"). An Adept; an inspired one. In Vedic literature the term is employed to denote those persons through whom the various mantras or mystic incantations were revealed.

Rishikesh. A holy city in northern India, located on the banks of the Ganges River. It is renowned as a centre for yoga and meditation, and is home to many ashrams and spiritual retreats.

Rochester. A city in New York State, USA.

Roerich Museum. A museum founded on 17 November 1923 in New York City dedicated to preserving and showcasing the works of Nicholas Roerich.

Roerich, George (1902–1960). A prominent Russian Tibetologist, linguist, and explorer, whose work encompassed many areas of Tibetan studies. He was an expert in Central Asian languages and Tibetan Buddhism, playing a key role in the Roerich Central Asian Expedition (1923–1928), and was the director of the Institute of Himalayan Studies (Urusvati). He is known for his translation of the *Blue Annals*, an important Tibetan work, and his 11-volume Tibetan-Russian-English dictionary.

Roerich, Nicholas (1874–1947). A great Russian artist, who was nominated three times for the Nobel Peace Prize in recognition of his activities. During his lifetime, he created approximately seven thousand paintings, some of which are now housed in the Nicholas Roerich Museum in New York. All of his paintings are prophetic; they are also coded. The creation of these masterpieces of art, which conceal the mystery of Colour, Light, and Sound, involved the participation of the four Great Spirits of the Hierarchy of Light. The colours in his paintings, radiating invisible and inaudible sound, have a direct influence on the higher energy centres of the viewer and awaken their creativity. Being well acquainted with Oriental philosophy and with the same sacred sources from which Helena Blavatsky obtained her knowledge, Nicholas Roerich also left a literary legacy.

Roerich, Svetoslav (1904–1993). A Russian painter and philosopher. Known for his portraits, landscapes, and mystical themes, he spent much of his life in India, where he became a prominent cultural figure. His paintings of Jawaharlal Nehru and Indira Gandhi adorn the historic Central Parliament Hall in New Delhi. For outstanding achievements in the field of culture, as well as for his contribution to peace, Svetoslav Roerich was the recipient of government awards from various different countries. In 1989, the President of the USSR, Mikhail Gorbachev, invited Svetoslav Roerich to lunch at the Kremlin, and his wife, Raisa Gorbachev, was involved in establishing the Roerichs Fund and Museum in Moscow.

Roosevelt, Franklin D. (1882–1945). The President of the United States from 1933 to 1945, known for leading the country through the Great Depression and most of the Second World War. He implemented the New Deal to aid economic recovery and was instrumental in shaping the Allied strategy during the war.

In the 1930s, Roosevelt was receiving advice from the Great Lord of Shambhala, Master M., through Helena Roerich. From Nicholas Roerich he received one of the ten copies of a manuscript entitled *Guidance for the Leader*, which outlines profound principles of becoming a true leader who can guide any nation to prosperity by building just relations between people and state. See more in Helena Roerich, *The Divine Government* (New York: Radiant Books, 2023).

Rosicrucians. The name was first given to the disciples of a learned Adept named Christian Rosenkreuz, who flourished in Germany, circa 1460. He founded an Order of mystical students who maintained their secrecy. Nonetheless, traces of them have been found in various places every half-century since then.

Rossetti, Christina (1830–1894). An English poetess known for her devotional and lyrical poetry, including works like *Goblin Mar-*

ket (1862) and *In the Bleak Midwinter* (1872). Rossetti was associated with the Pre-Raphaelite movement and often explored themes of faith, death, and renunciation.

Rothenburg ob der Tauber (*Ger.*, "red castle above the Tauber"). A town in the state of Bavaria, Germany.

Rowling, J. K. (b.1965). A British author best known for the *Harry Potter* series, which became one of the bestselling book series in literary history.

Rukmini. The wife of Krishna.

S

Sacred Science. The name given to the *inner* esoteric philosophy, the secrets taught in days of old to initiated candidates and divulged during the last and supreme Initiation by the Hierophants. Also the epithet given by the Rosicrucians to Kabbalah, and especially to the Hermetic philosophy.

Sagara. In Hindu and Buddhist mythology, a dragon king associated with the ocean. He is often depicted as a protector of the underwater realm.

Sai Baba, Sathya (1926–2011). An Indian saint, known for his teachings on universal love, service, and unity of religions. He established schools, hospitals, and water projects, emphasizing selfless service as a path to enlightenment. As it customary for messengers of Light, Sai Baba faced numerous false accusations during his lifetime, none of which were based on any evidence.

Sai Baba's philosophy can be expressed in his words: "There is only one religion, the religion of Love. There is only one language, the language of the Heart. There is only one caste, the caste of Humanity."

In Helena Roerich's notebooks and letters, there is mention of Master M.'s advice for Svetoslav Roerich to become friends with Sai Baba. Their first meeting took place in 1968. Svetoslav's wife, the Indian actress Devika Rani, had issues with her hearing but the doctors were unable to help her. Having heard of Sai Baba's miracles, she decided to visit his Ashram in Puttaparthi. There, despite her wearing the simplest clothes, Sai Baba immediately noticed Devika and sat next to her, asking: "Why did you come to me, a poor fakir, when you have such a great Light in your house?" Devika explained to him her problem. Sai Baba laid his hands on her ears and healed her hearing at once. After that, Devika told him that Svetoslav would visit him soon, too, or that they would come together. To this Sai Baba replied: "No, I will visit him. I want to pay my respects to him." When Sai Baba visited their mansion in Bangalore, he asked to see Svetoslav's paintings. While looking at them, Sai Baba was very accurate in describing the ideas behind the paintings.

Svetoslav Roerich told Dr. Erlendur Haraldsson, who was investigating Sai Baba's miracles: "Whether you agree that the phenomena Baba produces are necessary or not does not make much difference. I accept the necessity of the phenomena because from his point of view that is the quickest way to attract people. If a teacher did not display these phenomena, he would not make sufficient impact. There can be no doubt that Baba is a great phenomenon" (*Modern Miracles*).

Saint Sophia Cathedral. A Christian cathedral of the eleventh century in Kyiv, Ukraine.

Saint-Germain, Count of. See *Rakoczy*.

Saint-Martin, Louis Claude de (1743–1803). A great French mystic and writer, a true Theosophist, who pursued his philosophical and theosophical studies in Paris, during the Revolution. He was an ardent disciple of Jacob Böhme and studied under Martinez Paschalis, finally founding a mystical semi-Masonic Lodge, "the Rectified Rite of St. Martin," with seven degrees.

Sakkayaditthi (*Pali*, "heresy of individuality"). Delusion of personality; the erroneous idea that "I am I," a man or a woman with a special name, instead of an inseparable part of the whole.

Sakridagamin (*Sk.*, "one-time returner"). "One who will receive birth (only) once more" before reaching Nirvana; one who has entered the second of the four paths which lead to Nirvana, and has almost reached perfection.

Salsk Celestial Code. An unexplained phenomenon observed on 15 September 1989 by hundreds of people in Salsk, Russia, which became widely known. The phenomenon was vigorously discussed by experts in anomalous phenomena, who subsequently put forward many theories.

On that day, at 2:45 p.m., five huge squares appeared against the clear blue sky. Their outlines resembled the tracks of aeroplanes, as if they had turned several times in the sky at right angles. At first, the squares were empty and the sky was visible through them, but soon, to the exclamations of amazed onlookers, symbols began to appear inside the squares as if someone was drawing letters in the sky. They disappeared only to be replaced by others.

At first a number of signs appeared, similar to the mathematical inequality sign "greater than." Then they disappeared and two question marks appeared in one of the squares. Then these were replaced by the numbers 2 and 7, occurring across the squares in a particular order, while other squares remained empty. A total of five white squares hung in the sky for a period of 10–15 minutes.

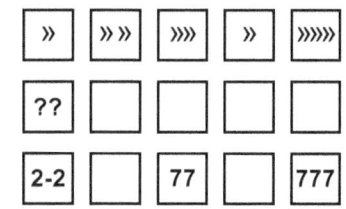

The Salsk Celestial Code in order of appearance.

This unusual phenomenon attracted the attention of numerous researchers who rushed

to solve the celestial puzzle. That year, across Russia all newspapers, radio stations, and television channels, not just the local ones, talked about the Salsk phenomenon.

For many months, researchers Alexey Priyma and Mikhail Gaponov put their heads together to break the code. If the question marks were to be excluded from the code, and taken to be purely rhetorical in nature, indicating the presence of certain "answers to questions" in the code, then the "inscription" could be written as follows:

>> >> >> >>>> >> >>>>>> 2 2 77 777

Priyma suggested representing the chain of "greater than" signs as a digital series "2 2 2 4 2 6," according to the number of double symbols. Gaponov, in turn, decided to write down the same line, replacing each "greater than" sign with 1, and each space between them with 0 arriving at a binary number: 11011011011110110111111. This number corresponds to the decimal number 7191999, when translated from the binary machine "language" to the usual decimal system. That is, the number indicates the date 19 July 1999.

Gaponov conducted an extremely difficult analysis of three versions of the "Salsk Code." To their shared astonishment, in the course of mathematical operations with groups of numbers, all the physical world constants were obtained, as well as all the basic information concerning the astronomical parameters of the Solar System.

Further, the researchers turned to the most ancient Slavic alphabet — the Glagolitic script. At a time when the people of Kyivan Rus' wrote in Glagolitic letters, Arabic numerals were not yet in use, appearing only later, together with the introduction of the Cyrillic alphabet. Before its introduction, numerical values were designated through letters, as in ancient Hebrew.

Substituting the letters for the indicated numbers (2 2 2 4 2 6 2 2 7 7 7 7 7), ignoring the zeros in their numerical values, they first found "Jesus Christ, the Son of God." The numbers of the phrase "the Son of God" also yielded "alias God." Then they began to add and subtract sevens from the code and found "will save you." Continuing the mathematical operations, they discovered "His Mother," and then "This is for Rus', Russians."

In this manner, a kind of heavenly telegram appeared:

To: Rus', Russians.
Text: Jesus Christ, the Son of God, alias God, will save you.
Question: When will He save them?
Answer: 19 July 1999.
Signature: His Mother.

Thinking that through such substitutions one could find almost anything in the code, Priyma and Gaponov spent a huge amount of time attempting to arrive at something else, anything at all, but failed to do so. They also tried to read the code in English, German, Spanish, and Hebrew, numbering the letters in a manner similar to the Glagolitic alphabet. However, nothing came of it. The code only worked in Russian.

Alexey Priyma published the results of his research in the book *19 iyulya 1999: Konets Sveta?* [19 July 1999: The End of the World?] in Moscow in 1993.

Samadhi (*Sk.*, "to bring together"). A state of spiritual ecstasy and complete trance, induced by means of mystic concentration. He who possesses this power is able to exercise absolute control over all his faculties, physical and mental; the highest yogic state.

Sambhogakaya (*Sk.*, "body of compensation," "body of bliss"). One of the three "vestures of glory," or bodies, obtained by ascetics on the Path. Some sects hold it as the second, others as the third, of the *Buddhakshetras*, or forms of Buddha. Of these *Buddhakshetras* there are seven, those of Nirmanakaya, Sambhogakaya, and Dharmakaya, belonging to the *Trikaya*, or threefold quality.

Samding Dorje Phagmo. The highest female incarnation in Tibetan Buddhism, being the third highest-ranking person in the hierarchy after the Dalai Lama and the Panchen Lama. The seat of the Samding Dorje Phagmo is at Samding Monastery in Tibet.

Samdup, Kazi Dawa (1868–1922). One of the first translators of important works of Tibetan Buddhism into English, such as *The Tibetan Book of the Dead* (1927).

Samkhya (*Sk.*, "enumeration"). The system of philosophy founded by Kapila Rishi, a system of analytical metaphysics and one of the six Darshanas or schools of philosophy. It discourses on numerical categories and the meaning of the 25 *tattvas* (the forces of Nature in various degrees). This "atomistic school," as some call it, explains Nature by the interaction of 24 elements with *purusha* (spirit) modified by the three *gunas* (qualities), teaching the eternity of *pradhana* (primordial, homogeneous matter), or the self-transformation of Nature and the eternity of the human Egos.

Samsara (*Sk.*, "rotation"). The ocean of births and deaths. Human rebirths represented as a continuous circle, a wheel in perpetual motion.

Samskara (*Sk.*, "to improve, refine, impress"). In Hindu philosophy the term is used to denote the impressions that are left upon the mind by individual actions or external circumstances, and that can be developed on any future favourable occasion, even in a future incarnation. The term *samskara* denotes, therefore, the germs of propensities and impulses from previous incarnations to be developed in this or in coming reincarnations. In Tibet, *samskara* is called *doodyed*, and in China, it is defined as, or at least connected with, action or karma. It is, strictly speaking, a metaphysical term, which in exoteric philosophies is variously defined; e.g., in Nepal as illusion, in Tibet as notion, and in Sri Lanka as discrimination. The true meaning is as given above, and as such is connected with karma and its workings.

Samtan or **samten** (*Tib.*). The same as *dhyana* or meditation.

Samvriti (*Sk.*, "to hide"). False conception, the origin of illusion.

Samvritisatya (*Sk.*, "concealed truth"). Truth mixed with false conceptions (*samvriti*); the reverse of absolute truth — or *paramarthasatya*, self-consciousness in absolute truth or reality.

Samyak Sambuddha (*Sk.*, "perfectly and completely awakened"). The Buddha of correct and harmonious knowledge, and the third of the ten titles of Shakyamuni.

Samyama (*Sk.*, "holding together"). The perfect concentration of the mind and control over it during the combined simultaneous practice of *dharana* (concentration), *dhyana* (meditation), and *samadhi* (union).

Sanat Kumara (*Sk.*, "eternal youth"). One of the names of the Planetary Logos of Sirius; the Teacher of Teachers; the Supreme Spirit, the Messiah, known to all peoples under different names: Christ, Maitreya, Mahdi, Kalki Avatar, Saoshyant etc. He is the Fire that administers the Fiery Baptism of the planet and humanity.

For every Lord of Light there is a date that marks the highest intensity of the manifestation of their Rays, which are associated with certain cosmic energy flows. The day of Sanat Kumara is 19 July, and it is associated with the rays of Sirius. All the key stages of His Coming to Earth are invariably related to this sacred date.

It was written in the sacred Puranas that the Kalki Avatar would be born in Shambhala. Later, the famous sixteenth century Korean astronomer Nam Sa-go left prophecies received from a mountain-dwelling sage. These predicted that the King of Kings would be born north of the 38th parallel and that He would come "from the mountain of the island nation" (*The Korean Books of Prophecy*). The 38th parallel runs through the Pamirs, which, together with the Himalayas, form the "Roof of the World." Legends often place Shambhala, also known as the White Island, in this location. Throughout the history of humanity, Shambhala has been the recipient of a great many names, all of which were revealed to different peoples according to the capacity of their consciousness. In the Christian tradition, it is believed that Christ ascended into *Heavenly Jerusalem*, the symbolic name of Shambhala, the Kingdom of God both on Earth and in the Heavens. As described in Acts 1:11, the Resurrected Christ will indeed return from Heavenly Jerusalem "in like manner as ye have seen Him go into Heaven," but now grown immeasurably in Power and Glory.

In the nineteenth century, H. P. Blavatsky left hints in her article "The Esoteric Character of the Gospels": "'the coming of Christ,' means the presence of Christos in a regenerated world, and not at all the actual coming in body of 'Christ' Jesus.... On the other hand, at no time since the Christian era have the precursor signs described in Matthew applied as graphically and forcibly to any epoch as they do to our own times. When has nation arisen against nation more than at this time? When have 'famines' — another name for destitute pauperism and the famished multitudes of the proletariat — been more cruel, earthquakes more frequent, or covered such an area simultaneously, as in the last few years? Millenarians and Adventists of robust faith may go on saying that 'the coming of (the carnalized) Christ' is near at hand, and prepare themselves for 'the end of the world.' Theosophists — at any rate, some of them — who understand the hidden meaning of the universally expected Avatars, Messiahs, Saoshyants, and Christs — know that it is no 'end of the world,' but 'the consummation of the age,' i.e., the close of a cycle, which is now fast approaching."

In the twentieth century, Helena Roerich explained that this event was indeed "fast approaching": "The Great Coming cannot be an ordinary phenomenon, and, therefore, it will not be in a physical body. One must understand that the Great Lords assume or maintain this or that appearance in accordance with the needs of the world. Why is it so difficult to imagine that the Great Individuality *will not* have need of a physical body for His future manifestations?

"Moreover, facts of the past and examples of modern life show us how all the appearances of Great Spirits among the ignorant were met and what events accompanied them. At best, they were awarded with the epithet of 'charlatan,' 'spy,' or both. It is customary for people to attribute all their own qualities to others. It is instructive to read the historical data about Saint-Germain, messenger of the White Brotherhood. Even if Christ appeared among us now, He would not escape imprisonment or, at worst, a lynching. Re-read *The Grand Inquisitor* by Dostoevsky.

"Therefore, it is important to understand that the Greatest Individuality simply *could not* appear amidst the chaotic thinking and vibrations of the unbridled crowds characteristic of the present day. Great Lords follow the Law of Expediency in everything. So understand that, on account of the condition of modern humanity, Manifestation in the physical form would be totally impossible and destructive to all evolution. The Great Individuality, invisibly visible, will be, and already rules, clothed in all the Rays of that Powerful but invisible *Laboratory*....

"The Individuality, which manifests as the Image of Maitreya in the understanding of the East, became a Buddha long ago, that is, achieved high Enlightenment, and therefore the reason you have cited for physical incarnation ceases to have significance. In addition, I can only confirm all the prophecies given in the book *Shambhala* [by Nicholas Roerich]. Truly, the era of Shambhala has begun, and His colleagues and leaders have already assumed their incarnation.

"Of course, the year 1936 is indicated as a year of laying great foundations and of change. However, the onset of the reign of the Lord of Shambhala does not mean that He will appear and physically take part in the final battle, as the most ignorant among the Buddhists would think. According to the most ancient testaments, the Lord of Shambhala fights with the enemy of humanity, and this battle takes place first and foremost on the Subtle Planes. In this the Lord of Shambhala acts through His earthly warriors but is Himself visible only in the rarest cases and, of course, would never appear in a crowd or among the curious.

"His appearance in the Fiery form would be destructive for many and for much, for His Aura is strained with energies of extraordinary power. In the Gospel of Matthew, chapter 24, verses 27–39, the Advent at the Day of Judgement awaiting our planet is described quite precisely. You will have time to grow old before this day arrives, although smaller scale catastrophes may occur earlier.

"In the Teaching, Russia is marked as a New Country, which will come under the Patronage of Saint Sergius, but it must first be resurrected in spirit and be cleansed. Indeed, the turn has come for each and every person to reveal their potential. If humanity fails to do so, the planet will face destruction on the Day of Judgement, that is, instead of the surviving part of humanity entering the new evolution of the Sixth Race after a cosmic cataclysm, all of humanity, together with its little house, will fly off into the air, and Earth risks scattering into billions of meteors before completing the Fourth Round of its evolution" (12 April 1935).

During his travels in Central Asia in 1845–1846, the French Catholic priest Évariste Régis Huc heard a prophecy that existed in various versions. It said that the Panchen Lama would be reborn in the future in a country north of Tibet, between the Tian Shan and the Altai mountain range; that after the future conquest of Tibet by the Chinese, the New Country in the North would become the cradle of the revival of Buddhism, and the Panchen Lama as the Universal Sovereign would crush the forces of evil and spread Buddhism throughout the Earth.

This is symbolic, since from Helena Roerich's notebooks it is already known that at that time (but not now) Shambhala was situated in the Tian Shan. At the same time, by the "New Country" was meant the Slavic lands as a whole, Russia, as it was frequently referred to in the *Agni Yoga* series. The Panchen Lama is considered to be an incarnation of Amitabha ("Buddha of Infinite Light"). That is, it symbolically speaks of the incarnation of the "Celestial Father" in Shambhala with the purpose of participating in the Final Battle of the Forces of Light with the forces of darkness, or Armageddon, and bestowing the Teaching of Truth on humanity.

In *The Theosophical Glossary* (1892), in the entry for Maitreya Buddha, Blavatsky left a subtle hint in the form of a single word in parentheses: "Esoteric philosophy teaches that the next Buddha will appear during the seventh (sub) race of this Round."

A Round consists of Seven Races, while each Race has seven sub-races, and the Race itself can be considered a Small Round. From *The Secret Doctrine* it is known that the fifth sub-race of the current Fifth Race is represented by Europeans, while the sixth sub-race is represented by Americans. Almost nothing is said about the seventh sub-race, except for the symbolic timing of its appearance. However, it is represented by the Slavs in the current historical period.

Blavatsky deliberately omitted any mention of Russia or the Slavs in her writings, as if the country, occupying one-fifth of the world at that time, had no place in the cosmic plan or evolution. If the role of the Slavs had been proclaimed prematurely to the whole world, saying that these lands had a great future ahead of them and that the Coming of the Messiah would take place there, the forces of darkness would have begun to tear them apart much earlier. However, the spiritual mission of the Slavs is spoken of in certain prophecies.

For example, Max Heindel writes in *The Rosicrucian Cosmo-Conception* (1911) that the Slavic civilization will be born out of deep sorrow and untold suffering, which, according to the Law of Compensation, will result in unprecedented spiritual development: "From the Slavs will descend a people which will form the last of the seven [sub] races of the Aryan Epoch [or the Fifth Race]."

Edgar Cayce predicted that new religious ideas would come from Russia: "For changes are coming, this may be sure — an evolution, or revolution in the ideas of religious thought. The basis of it for the world will eventually come out of Russia; not communism, no! But rather that which is the basis of the same as the Christ taught — His kind of communism!" (29 November 1932, Edgar Cayce Reading 452–6); "Out of Russia, you see, there may come that which may be the basis of a more worldwide religious thought or trend" (25 August 1933, Edgar Cayce Reading 3976–12); "In Russia there comes the hope of the world, not as that sometimes termed of the Communistic, of the Bolshevistic; no. But freedom, freedom! That each man will live for his fellow man!" (22 June 1944, Edgar Cayce Reading 3976–29).

Further, Mitar Tarabich, a prominent Serbian prophet, foresaw for the second half of the twentieth century and present time: "Among the people of a nation in the North, an inconspicuous individual will appear, as though out of water, who will teach people about love and compassion, but there will be many hypocrites and Judases around this person and so they will experience ups and downs. None of these hypocrites will want to know about real human grace, but this person's wise books will remain along with all the words they uttered, and later people will see how utterly wrong they were."

Then, in 1978, the famous Bulgarian clairvoyant, healer, and prophetess Vanga said that the New Teaching of the White Brotherhood would appear in Russia in 1998: "The New Teaching will come from Russia. That country will be the first to be purged. The White Brotherhood will spread across Russia and from there its Teaching will begin its march throughout the world. This will happen in twenty years — it will not happen earlier. In twenty years, you will reap the first rich harvest."

Moreover, the Great Initiate of the Theban Sanctuary, Thales of Argos, under whose name the book *The Mystery of Christ* was written, passed his letter to the readers in Romania through a monk around 1943 along with the manuscript. This letter, first published in the 1995 Romanian edition of *The Mystery of Christ*, stated that the end of the millennium would be marked by Sophia's Great Revelation.

The same was stated by a Tibetan lama in conversation with Andrew Tomas in 1966. He said that "the teaching of Tara, the Doctrine of the Heart" would be given in the last quarter of the twentieth century, "for this alone can save the planet" (*Shambhala: Oasis of Light*).

Thus, if during the last cycle the people of Israel achieved the greatest development, the same is destined for the Slavs in the present cycle. The profound suffering of the Slavic peoples brings purifying and liberating properties. After all, suffering refines the heart and enlightens it with the great quality of empathy. Only the long-suffering heart is able to understand the grief and suffering of another. Each instance of suffering creates a special substance that deposits fiery crystals of *ringsel* in the heart. Those who have accumulated and increased this treasure have truly undergone much suffering in their lives. This in turn has given rise to that great quality of spirit known as *compassion*. This is what will allow the Slavs to create a just society, the example of which all other peoples will follow.

Besides this, one should understand that the Slavs are a symbol of a condition of the spirit, and not only a national identity, just as the entire Fifth Race is called *Aryan*, regardless of the nationalities that compose it.

The Advent of the Messiah is the most important event in the Cosmos. The Spirit of the Power that is to descend upon the Earth is such as has never come before. As far back as the sixteenth century, the prophecies of Nam Sa-go held that He would bear the Power of Three: Buddha, Christ, and Maitreya. This Spirit emerges from the depths of the Universe, beyond our imagining, incarnating on every planet, in all worlds.

Above our earthly world, in cross-section, one can imagine the existence of a huge number of other worlds: high, spiritual, divine, through which the Spirit of the Messiah passes. They are not visible to us, since they undergo their evolution in conditions other than ours, but they do exist.

The development of this gigantic chain of worlds depends upon the humanity of Earth. The descent of the Messiah to this lowest point gives a powerful impulse to all the worlds, which results in their shifting and making progress. In this way, the worlds higher than our planet — the Divine Worlds — and the worlds lower than our planet in their level of development — will all ascend to the next stage of their evolution.

He is born in each of them, leaving a portion of His Fiery Power, only after these worlds send out their call. His Coming upon the Earth could not take place in a single moment, and so the ground must have been prepared both by the efforts of earthly humanity's representatives and by those of the worlds through which He has already passed.

As He approaches Earth, each world that has already welcomed the Saviour, when He was born into it, sends their own Demiurges — their High Spirits, Gods, or Hierarchs who are responsible for their development — for incarnation on Earth. They must forget their own worlds, descend into human flesh, and disappear amidst the people. They must incarnate as human beings, otherwise the process would be unjust in relation to humankind and violate the laws of Humanity's Kingdom on Earth.

In order for the Demiurge of a certain sacred planet to incarnate, their arrival is preceded by some sort of revelation, a work revealing the truth about the origin of the world. There are many books of this kind; each recounts how the world began, and each has its differences. But each Demiurge describes the cosmogony of their own world. Each world has a common pattern of conception and creation, and yet in other aspects, they exhibit a certain uniqueness.

When Demiurges of other worlds are born, people who feel akin to their vibration will gather around them. A multitude of movements may be formed, as there are a multitude of worlds. And of course, along with the Supreme Worlds, there are worlds in which matter is not manifested in spirit; these worlds are represented by people who are more imperfect than perfect, but these people may be the ambassadors of the other worlds or even of the Subtle Spheres of our own planet, Earth. The Demiurges from the planets of the Solar System have already passed through; the Demiurges of Pluto, Uranus, and Venus have already enacted their earthly incarnation; all have played a part in preparing the ground for the Messiah.

They have gathered at this point — the point of the descent of the Supreme Lord — in order to receive the most powerful impulse of Fire that the Heart of the Messiah can give. And, refracting it through the prism of their own hearts, they will send this impulse of Light into their own spheres and planets, returning there as Saviours. For this reason, one should broadly look at the fact that there are many people nowadays who are viewed as Messiahs — these may be messengers from other spheres. These Demiurges, the ambassadors of Distant Worlds will form a certain number of His Apostles and close disciples.

The Demiurges of all the worlds that participate in the Great Cosmic Plan of the Birth of New Universe must have arrived by the moment of the Advent of the Supreme Spirit on Earth.

According to many prophecies, both Western and Eastern, the Messiah was to appear as a King in Russia, the Slavic lands, which esoterically speaking represent the Heart of the planet. Since the Messiah does not have the lower bodies of the quaternary, the four bodies which comprise His earthly flesh were woven over the course of centuries by High Spirits. King Solomon, Saints Sergius of Radonezh and Seraphim of Sarov, as well as King Alexander I worked on the creation of these bodies, each preparing one of them. From the fabrics of the transfigured bodies they left behind — emotional, astral, mental — a special matter was formed which was to compose the lower quaternary of the Messiah. The spiritually transformed body of Alexander I was the closest to the physical plane. Hence, the expectation emerged that the Messiah should have been Russian. Prior to this, however, the High Spirits mentioned previously were incarnated among all the peoples of the world.

In 1825, Alexander I visited Seraphim of Sarov, who revealed to him the Secret in which he must play his role. No preliminary warnings of the King's arrival were given, but Seraphim experienced a kind of anxiety, which was noticed by the monks. He was definitely expecting an important guest and insisted on tidying his cell himself. Indeed, in the evening, a military man in a troika galloped into the Sarov Hermitage and made his way to Father Seraphim's cell. The great elder hurried to meet the guest standing on the porch, bowed at his feet, and greeted him with the words: "Greetings, great sovereign!" Then, taking the newcomer by the hand, Father Seraphim led him into his cell and closed the door behind them. They remained there in solitary conversation for two or three hours. Once they had left the cell together and the visitor was already leaving the porch, the elder called after him: "Do, Sire, as I told you." After this, Alexander I staged his own death in order to spend the remaining 40 years of his life in Siberia under the guise of Saint Feodor Kuzmich.

Solomon and Sergius of Radonezh were incarnations of Master Morya. Seraphim of Sarov was also an incarnation of one of the Great Teachers of humanity. Alexander I was one of Saint-Germain's favourite disciples. Thus, the Teachers on Earth have woven the lower quaternary for their Cosmic Father — the Teacher of Teachers.

His Coming is also accompanied by a Fiery Baptism, which represents the spiritual transfiguration and fiery transmutation of humanity and the planet under the influence of the Fire which comes from the Cosmos. In other words, this represents a contact that the human body and all living things will have with the new fiery energies — their assimilation, or the destruction of any unprepared body. All ancient Teachings have forewarned humanity of the inevitable Age of Fire.

In the period 1924 to 1955, Helena Roerich voluntarily and consciously agreed to undergo a kind of individual Fiery Baptism under the supervision of the Great Teachers; this was termed the *Fiery Experience*. Under ordinary terrestrial conditions, this is an excruciating and agonizing process, accompanied by extreme and persistent pains in the physical body. But the Mother of Agni Yoga, as the Masters of Ancient Wisdom call her, drained this cup to the dregs, thereby assisting them in finding ways to alleviate the sufferings of the world when the time comes for all humanity to undergo the Fiery Baptism.

There are several stages to the Fiery Baptism which are inextricably linked to the Advent on Earth of the Supreme Spirit. The Periods of His Coming, and therefore, of the Fiery Baptism, have always been cloaked in the strictest secrecy and could not be disclosed prematurely. All sacred scriptures have veiled these Periods in some manner. According to many prophecies, right at the end of the Kali Yuga (*Sk.*, "dark age"), Maitreya was to be incarnated in Shambhala. In the Puranas, the period of the Kali Yuga is calculated in gigantic numbers, the true meaning of which is known solely to the Initiates. Likewise Helena Blavatsky was unable to disclose the dates of the manifestation of the Kalki Avatar, and therefore used the same figures.

However, in the first half of the twentieth century, the correct calculations of the end date of the Dark Age — the year 1942 — began to spread among the population of India. At precisely the same time, the process of the Fiery Transfiguration of the world commenced, and He, having passed through all the planets of the Solar System, was born at the level of the higher triad, or at the level of the Fiery World in Shambhala, for the first time on Earth. Thus, the Great Lord of Shambhala, Morya, and Maitreya are One and the same Supreme Spirit, who is the Solar Hierarch. His Father is Sanat Kumara, who gradually began to be reflected in the Son.

The sacrament of the birth of Gods on Earth will always remain a mystery that eludes human understanding, for only God can give life to a God. The Father must be consubstantial with His Son, and in order to achieve this, the Planetary Spirit of Sirius first had to manifest Himself on Earth, so as to then reflect Himself in the image of His Son — the Messiah.

Moreover, on 1 August 1943, the predicted cosmic event occurred, namely a rare combination of stars and planets at the time of the solar eclipse, indicated in the *Vishnu Purana*: "When the Sun and Moon, and the lunar asterism Tishya, and the planet Jupiter are in one mansion, the Krita [Golden] Age shall return." This event was widely celebrated in India, Tibet, and Mongolia; solemn services were held in all Buddhist temples. The Great Lord of Shambhala, now in possession of all of His Fiery Might for the first time, entered the final battle to defeat Lucifer and his dark army in 1949.

In that moment began the preparation for the Advent of the King of Shambhala in the world to bring about the final overthrow of darkness. Almost the entire world awaited the coming of the Messiah, and each and every nation gave Him a beautiful, dearly held name, often unaware that these names belonged to One and the same Supreme Spirit. As always, the specific Periods could not be revealed prematurely. Nevertheless, accurate hints and even precise dates were predicted by the greatest prophets, but these were misunderstood by the people. For example, 1568 saw published the complete collection of the predictions of Nostradamus, who was an Initiate and knew how to safeguard the most sacred knowledge. No one is able to understand his indications without holding the key; moreover, his predictions bear the imprint of the Dark Ages. His famous Quatrain 72, Century X reads: "The year 1999, seventh month, from the sky will come a Great King of Terror." It should be understood that for humanity, which by then had lapsed into the darkness of ignorance, the Messiah, who was to put an end to the Dark Age, represented a direct threat.

Another great prophet, Edgar Cayce, predicted twice the exact year of the Advent of the Messiah when commenting on the mathematical and astronomical calculations that had been found in the Great Pyramid of Giza: "the entrance of the Messiah in this period — 1998" (30 June 1932, Edgar Cayce Reading 5748–5); "a Liberator of the world... must enter again at that period, or in 1998" (29 July 1932, Edgar Cayce Reading 294–151).

In Book 2 of the *Agni Yoga* series, Master Morya indicated the year 1999. At the same time, Helena Roerich, not being empowered to speak openly, gave repeated warnings to her correspondents. For example: "There is time as yet, for the last Cosmic Period will strike in a few decades, but our century will not see its end" (23 June 1934); "The decisive hour of the Judgement Day is not far off, and many children will live until this *day*. That is why the Teaching of the Lord M. is given so urgently and so many extraordinary signs are being poured forth upon Earth, but people are blind and deaf!" (11 October 1935).

On 15 September 1989 many people in Salsk, Russia, observed an unexplained phenomenon known as the *Salsk Celestial Code*. On this day, huge squares appeared in the sky. At first, the squares were empty, but soon mathematical signs, question marks, and numbers began to appear inside the geometric shapes, as though someone were drawing them in the sky. After transforming the signs into numbers and the numbers into the Glagolitic alphabet (in which each letter has its own number, as in the old Hebrew), researchers deciphered the following message: "To Rus', Russians. Jesus Christ, the Son of God, alias God, will save you on 19 July 1999. (signature) His Mother."

Many researchers attempted to unravel the date for the completion of Kali Yuga, at the end of which the Second Coming was expected. Although in his research René Guénon (1886–1951) did not indicate the start date of Kali Yuga, he did leave clues. In the early 1980s, his commentator Jean Robin claimed to have deciphered his description and calculated that Kali Yuga lasted from 4481 BCE to 1999 CE. Gaston Georgel in his 1949 book, *Les quatre âges de l'humanité* [The Four Ages of Humanity], calculated the same end date of 1999.

The main mistake was expecting the Golden Age to arrive right on the first day, and, therefore, many of the correct calculations made in the past by researchers were simply ignored, since nothing improved after that year. But in the same way, the advent of the New Year on 1 January does not in any way mean that life becomes radically different from what it was on 31 December.

The world is ruled by Periods — the astrological combination of the rays of stars and Distant Worlds that strictly defines the time frame for the manifestation of certain events and phenomena, on both cosmic and individual levels. These Periods can have an impact on whole cycles and stages of Evolution.

In the Cosmos and Higher Worlds, time (in the earthly sense) does not exist, but there are Periods defined by inevitable consequences. Cosmic Periods are characterized by the sequence of events that allows a developed consciousness to take a specific event as a means of foreseeing all others.

When the time finally comes for a specific Period, nothing can delay its implementation. The Great Teachers merely watch to see that everyone and everything necessary is ready for the appointed time, otherwise the results may be disastrous. It is better that everything be prepared in advance, but postponement until the last moment need not cause significant damage. In this case, the Period's implementation simply proceeds with particular speed and intensity.

Certain dates in earthly time may not coincide with Cosmic Periods, since it is necessary to consider all seven sub-planes of the Seven Worlds, which could result in as many as 49 terrestrial dates. And so, true prophets rarely mention specific dates in earthly time. The appearance or delay of a particular event depends on the combinations of the currents emanating from both the stars and the collective will of Earth's humanity.

According to the cosmic calendar, Satya Yuga has already arrived in all spheres: in 1942 in the Fiery World (where, of course, Kali Yuga had completely different manifestations), and in 1999 in the higher layers of the Subtle World. But when exactly the true Era of Prosperity will arrive in the physical world is up to humanity itself to decide. Master M. explains in the *Agni Yoga* series:

"One needs to know the periods of different layers of matter. Just because one point of matter has changed, it does not mean that the entire group of bodies will have changed by the same time. In other words, if Satya Yuga begins on a particular planet, it will unify a whole group of bodies over a long period of time. Signs will start to show themselves on different bodies. You should never limit your thinking to one planet" (*Agni Yoga*).

"Thus one can see the end of Kali Yuga. Where Satya Yuga begins depends on humanity.

We know that Satya Yuga is destined, but the place and conditions under which it will occur may be different" (*Hierarchy*).

According to Buddhist scriptures, before the impending Advent of the King of the Golden Wheel in the world, a sacred flower, the *Udumbara*, appears, which blooms once every several thousand years. It was in 1997 that the first appearance of this celestial flower was spotted on the statue of Buddha in a temple in South Korea.

And so the Great Period 1998–1999 was marked by the further descent of Maitreya into Shambhala, from the Fiery World into Earth's Subtle World. In 1998, the sacrament of the descent of the Spirit of the Messiah into the aura of His Mother took place in the Tower of Chung in Shambhala. This was followed a year later by the beginning of the Great Fiery Baptism of the planet and humanity on 19 July 1999, as well as the Final Choice. The total solar eclipse of 11 August 1999 coincided with a significant planetary alignment. The planets arranged themselves in the shape of a Grand Cross — the sign of the Son of Man in the sky. This cosmic event proclaiming the Advent of Christ is described in the Bible: "Immediately after the tribulation of those days shall the sun be darkened, and the moon shall not give her light, and the stars shall fall from heaven, and the powers of the heavens shall be shaken. And then shall appear the sign of the Son of Man in heaven: and then shall all the tribes of the earth mourn, and they shall see the Son of Man coming in the clouds of heaven with power and great glory" (Matthew 24:29–30).

Since then, the inflow of Cosmic Fire has intensified daily, being accompanied by an anomalous increase or decrease in temperature. The new Fires of Transfiguration may have a destructive impact on physical bodies causing extreme pain and other health problems along with natural disasters, such as earthquakes, floods, rainstorms, avalanches, and tornadoes. In addition, these energies, if not accepted, may give rise to revolutions and epidemics. If the matter of a person's physical body is not able to accept the Fire, then the body will die, but in the next incarnation that person will be born into a body with a different formula. This happens because human hearts are unable to assimilate the new currents, as people have not yet learnt to fulfil the prime commandment given by all Teachers in all periods of history — to *love*.

It is for this reason that humanity's spiritual decline, heartlessness, and inability to perceive the fiery energies of the Cosmos have threatened all with devastating cataclysms that could cause partial planetary catastrophes — as was the case with the continents of Lemuria and Atlantis — or complete planetary destruction. Edgar Cayce predicted that this future would befall humanity by the end of the twentieth century — a future that people had created with their own hands. However, after the triumph over Lucifer, who did his utmost to implement that scenario, the entire Hierarchy of Light, together with enlightened people all over the world who had made their choice in favour of the Good, managed to save the planet from destruction. Humanity survived this period, for the most part completely unaware of their narrow escape.

The Mystery of the birth of the Highest Spirits on Earth, especially the Messiah, has always been devoutly guarded by the Great Brotherhood, just like the Periods. Now, however, some part of it may be revealed.

The legends that have been preserved in various religions have it that each Saviour of the World was immaculately conceived by the Supreme God or Holy Spirit. According to esoteric philosophy, there is truth in this, which can be explained in the following way: A High Spirit, acting as a Father, projects His Ray onto one of the energy centres of the future Mother as a result of which an immaculate conception takes place. Usually this Ray and the corresponding centre represent the energy that dominates in space in that historical period. Then the Father's Power gradually flows into the Son. For example, the conception by the first energy centre may be connected with Zoroaster. The birth of Jesus Christ took place in the Ray of the Orange Solar Flame, as a Solar Logos, representing the second centre which is also connected to the fifth. Buddha appeared from the side of His Mother — the solar plexus, the third energy centre. And Krishna was conceived through the same centre.

At each stage of evolution, the highest level of such a birth takes place. We are living in the Fourth Round of Evolution and, consequently, the conception and birth of the Supreme Spirit must occur by means of the fourth energy centre — the Heart, which should benefit from the greatest development in this Round.

In esoteric philosophy, conception and birth through the heart is called the *Third Fire*. It is characteristic of civilizations that have the highest level of spiritual development, such as Sirius, the homeland of Sanat Kumara. In earthly conditions, one can imagine that a man and a woman create the Third Fire by the fire of their love, begetting it in the higher level heart of the mother's sevenfold structure, as though in her aura. Then, if the fire of this couple's love has not abated, the Third Fire is conceived within the mother's heart on every level, which may last up to seven years. When the Fire is established on all seven planes, including the physical, an invisible fiery foetus appears, within which a luminous, angelic creature is born. This being may be carried in the heart of the mother for seven, nine, or twelve years. And then, if this spirit considers it appropriate, he may be born on the physical plane, only his body will have a very different material structure from that of Earth-dwellers. If he decides not to be born on the physical plane, he will depart for the higher worlds as an Angel, Archangel, or Planetary Spirit.

The Advent on Earth of the Greatest Spirit comes about in almost like manner, with the exception of certain aspects that must remain secret. Nevertheless, it should be borne in mind that His Coming proceeds in strict accordance with Cosmic Laws, taking billions of causes into consideration.

According to Cosmic Laws, each planet belongs to the humanity populating it, and He can manifest Himself upon it in all His Fiery Glory only when summoned by that planet's population. After all, the expression of free will is the inalienable Cosmic Right of every creature, one, therefore, that the Forces of Light conscientiously honour, never imposing anything against the free will of humanity. By a particular time, the answer to the question of whether a people awaits Him appears on the pans of the Cosmic Scales, a decision — *yes* or *no* — taken consciously or unconsciously by every individual heart. If *yes* prevails, He is born in the Highest Image characteristic of that planet; if the answer is *no*, then He goes higher. It should be noted that He has already been incarnated on all other inhabited planets, and none of them answered *no*.

It is the same on Earth: if the *yes* outweighs the *no*, then He will be manifested in the flesh, and people will be able to behold Him with their own physical eyes. If humanity says *no*, then the eyes of the heart alone will be capable of seeing Him. And, after fulfilling His invisible mission, He will depart again, only higher this time, tracing a gigantic Circle.

Evolution's plan foreordains that the Messiah must come in the flesh and be visible physically. But He must not violate Cosmic Laws. Earth belongs to the Kingdom of Humanity, and it is the people's prerogative whether to invite Him into their house or not. Moreover, two thousand years ago people deprived Him of His physical flesh. By their own will, they signed the death-sentence: they had no use for God in a human body.

According to Cosmic Laws, the Messiah has the right to be born in the Heart, descending only as far as the fourth level, which, from the perspective of the Cosmos, counts as Earth's physical world, but at the same time, will not cause discomfort to those who do not await Him. According to the Law of Expediency, the absence of a response from the heart presupposes an *Advent* in Spirit, *birth* on the level of the Heart centre and the manifestation of the *Androgynous Fires*, which proceed from one heart to another. Only the heart is capable of perceiving the Fire of Immortality, in other words, the Fire of Eternal Youth, which Sanat Kumara brings. It is clear that if He were born in a physical body, it would be a struggle and a waste of Fire and Energy, which would be inadmissible according to the Laws of the Universe. Suffice to recall how, in the second half of the nineteenth century, Helena Blavatsky and the Mahatmas — the Lords of Shambhala — were derided when they, for the first time in the history of this humanity, revealed themselves to the public at large. The Messiah does not come to take away the sins of humanity just so that the people can deride Him, call Him the Antichrist, and crucify Him again. The main goal is to advance the Chain of Fiery Evolution. His Advent from the Supreme Divine Worlds transmits the mightiest current of Fire, which gives an impetus for the ascent up the Ladder of Evolution to all the Worlds, i.e., those located within the Solar System as well as those located beyond its boundaries.

From esoteric philosophy it is known that after the death of His physical body, Jesus Christ managed to transform its matter on an atomic level in such a way as to essentially resurrect it, thereby making it immortal. But it was the densified subtle body, the so-called Body of Light or Glory, which became visible temporarily to those who were pure in heart. This is why the Resurrected Christ appeared suddenly before His disciples and disappeared just as quickly. The Fiery Transfiguration of Christ is a supreme achievement on Earth. It is this achievement that created the particular formula of matter that composes the Body of the Coming Messiah. Over the course of millennia, those who are Initiated into this Mystery of Light have taken part in the further energy perfection of His Light-bearing Matter, which, while not being physical, may be visible to certain highly spiritual individuals.

In May 2005, the celestial Udumbara flower bloomed for the second time, on this occasion in a temple in South Korea, signifying that on 19 July 2005 the Messiah of all times and all peoples would descend from Shambhala into the material world of the Earth, being born in the heart of His Mother. It is interesting to note that according to the Kalachakra calendar of Tibet, 2005 is the nineteenth year in the seventeenth sexagenary cycle. That is, even symbolically it reads as the birth of the Lord of the World (19) in the Heart of the Mother of the World (17). According to the Shambhala calendar, 2004 is the zero year, and 2005 is the first year of the New Era.

On 19 July 2005, the impulse of the mightiest Fire occurred in the area of sacred Mount Kailash and lasted for 24 days: the currents of the Great Masculine Principle dominated for the first twelve days and the currents of the Great Feminine Principle for the second twelve days. Not androgynous but binary, the world is able to absorb either one or the other of the two polar opposites, but not both at the same time. The giant energy waves which accompanied the descent of the Messiah manifested through the full power of the forces of Nature: on the same day there was extreme heat and extreme cold, along with such powerful manifestation of the elements that even the grass in the Himalayas was charred.

In addition to those reasons mentioned above, the division into Masculine and Feminine Principles is no longer appropriate. It would not be right for Him to be incarnated as a man because the epoch that is coming is the Epoch of Woman. If He were embodied as a woman, the imbalance would be in the direction of the Feminine Principle, since today there are many men with evident female characteristics. In other words, this would tilt the balance of the matrix structures in the fabric of the manifest physical world. Therefore, the lowest point of His descent is the chalice, the heart of His Mother, Sophia, wherein it was ordained that He would be borne for a period of twelve years. This is depicted symbolically on the miraculous icon of 1878 known as *The Inexhaustible Chalice*. Thus, Maitreya, as was foretold in the prophecies, is already ruling invisibly visible, performing the Fiery Baptism of humanity on Earth.

Death on the physical plane is an unnatural phenomenon which violates Cosmic Laws. It is a result of the delay in human evolution brought about by the activity of Lucifer, who wanted to limit Earth-dwellers solely to the dense, physical world. As an infant grows into a youngster, an adult, and an elderly person, the human body, too, should develop into a higher form, but not die.

It is now a well-known fact that the entire cellular structure of human body renews itself completely every seven years. Not a single atom of the previous structure remains. It turns out that the human body has a continuous stream of matter flowing through it. However, a person still grows old because the cells of their body lie dormant, deprived of their full vitality. After a certain time their fieriness fades, despite the constant renewal of atoms in the body. Not only that, but a person fills their body with the emanations of decomposition in the form of impure food, along with base thoughts, emotions, desires, and deeds. In other words, people extinguish the fire of their own vitality. Consequently, control over all thoughts, feelings, and actions together with the proper diet ought to strengthen the fieriness of each cell and raise its vibration, thereby increasing the power a person has over their own body. Hence, the body of a saint is not susceptible to decay for, given its fieriness, it is formed from a different type of matter altogether. And yet, even though they can alter the properties of matter, saints also succumb to death. The mystery consists in the fact that atoms take whatever form or image is shaped by the spirit. If one creates, say, the fiery formula of an eternally young physical body and, through a moral lifestyle, succeeds in preventing the usual extinction of the body's fieriness, the combinations of atoms in the cells do not follow the common path, but that which is outlined by the fiery formula of spirit. However, in the average human, the structure of the higher triad lacks the necessary formula for the physical body.

Therefore, since 2005, in order not only to help intensify the fieriness of terrestrial organisms but also to change the structure and formula of the human body, currents of Immortality have been pouring out upon the Earth, currents of Eternal Youth that pour forth from Sanat Kumara.

There was a lot of talk about the end of the world in 2012 according to the Mayan calendar. And here it should be understood that representatives of other planets that survived the destruction of their own world, such as Mars, can, more often than others, enter the system of prophecies and talk about destruction, not because this is what they desire, but simply because destruction lives in the memory of the matrix structures that compose their bodies.

The spiritual regeneration of the world did in fact occur at that time, and Blavatsky spoke about it as a condition for the presence of Christ. Although this "rebirth" does not yet have visible consequences for humanity, it was precisely then that the foundation was laid.

In 2012, Earth was enveloped by a powerful incandescence of Fires coming from Sirius as well as surrounding constellations, which reached its apogee on 19 July. In every evolving human being, at the level of the heart centre — the chalice, at the level of the matrix structures and subtle bodies, a new formula of Light and the New World was manifested. At the same time, the formula of the former world lost its significance, that is, a symbolic "end of the (old) world" took place. On 19 July 2012, humanity was given the currents that contain the formula of Immortality, and that were to enter into the heart of each and every human being. Every individual was to make the choice on a spiritual level whether to accept the new formula or not.

As a result of this alchemical process, children born after the year 2012, and those children who are growing up at present, assimilating the Fires of Immortality, will, in the future, provided that they also possess the sufficient level of fiery accumulations, be capable of giving birth to a generation that carries entirely different formulas.

Hence, over a period of 24 to 42 years, a different structure will form in the new human being by which the ageing process will be replaced by a process of fiery regeneration at the cellular level. And at a certain point in time, these people will consciously make their way into the Higher Worlds, not through the process of death on the physical plane, but by adapting their bodies to the new conditions of their own will. The Great Teachers achieved this. There were many eyewitnesses, especially in the nineteenth century, who confirmed the fact that the Mahatmas did not age for hundreds of years, their outward appearance remaining the same as it was when they were in their prime of life.

Of course, whether humanity will take advantage of this Gift from the Lord of Sirius depends on its spiritual development. It may take not just decades but centuries for death as a phenomenon to disappear from the stage of life on Earth.

It is also this Mystery that Blavatsky referred to when she wrote in her article "Lamas and Druses": "There is but the *Supreme Wisdom*, the abstract principle from which emanated the five Buddhas — Maitreya Buddha (the last Bodhisattva, or Vishnu in the Kalki Avatar), the tenth 'messenger' expected on earth included. But this will be the One Wisdom and it will incarnate itself into the whole of humanity collectively, not in a single individual. But of this mystery, no more at present."

Just as 18 million years ago, when He endowed humanity with reason, they did not become intelligent overnight, so now His Gift of Immortality will manifest itself gradually, over a long period of time.

The end of 2012 revealed the basic energy framework that crystallized over the next three years, and by the end of 2015 a new pattern had emerged. This is already "a different" Earth at the level of energy resonance, which going forward should result in even greater unification of humanity and countries, manifesting at the geographical level too. Of course, this manifestation is vehemently opposed by the forces of darkness, acting on the principle of "divide and conquer."

For a period of twelve years ending in 2017, Sanat Kumara, visible only to colleagues of Shambhala who have passed the high levels of Initiation, transpierced the entire planet with currents of Eternal Youth and Immortality through His Mother as well as twelve embodied Apostles, each of which bears their own colour and tone (with sharps and flats), one of them bearing the colour white. And after that, on 19 July 2017, Sanat Kumara was born in the Subtle World as a Planetary Spirit of the highest degrees, which are inaccessible even to the gaze of those who are Great Initiates. His Birth lasted twelve days after which He left for the Sun, so as, in the New Body, to keep the entire Solar System safe from destruction by the energy "tsunamis" that are now occurring in the Cosmos.

Unfortunately, the call of the hearts of Earth-dwellers was not sufficiently strong that *yes* outweighed *no* on the Cosmic Scales, for they were not ready to accept a Fire of even greater incandescence. Had it been otherwise, the Messiah could have become manifest in a "physical" body in the earthly world as well. This could have happened at any time after the Final Choice, as soon as human hearts were ready. From the perspective of Cosmic Justice, humanity must have returned the Son to Mary at the age that She lost Him as a result of the death sentence pronounced by Earth-dwellers. Then His body would have been visible to the "physical eye" of the pure in heart, although this would have been the densified subtle body, the "Glorious Body," composed of the matter in which Jesus Christ was resurrected and seen by His disciples.

Human beings are sevenfold in their structure, just like the planet on which they live. And all seven levels from the Spiritual to the material have a kind of Scales on which are weighed the actions recorded in a particular sphere. Choice occurs at all seven levels, although not all people are able to rise above the level of the quaternary and create within the limits of the higher triad.

The majority of humanity vibrates with the three lower centres of consciousness, or chakras. The condition of the lower bodies cannot prepare ground for the Advent, that is, the world is not attuned to the required wavelength.

The totality of the contents of the seven conventional pans ultimately adds up to a single set of Cosmic Scales. And if we are to talk about a preponderance in favour of the Good, then it is by the efforts of those who increased the Light of the world, through actions taken in the realm of Spirituality, that there was manifest the slight preponderance on the side of the Higher Powers which became marked on 19 July 2017. At that time, in the totality of the seven pans of the Scales, the higher three resulted in the Good having the advantage and making up for the deficit of the lower four.

A "slight swing" of the pan cannot be considered a preponderance on the Cosmic Scales. In 2017, unlike in 1999, the Call was in fact manifested, although it came from hearts that exceeded the luminosity coefficient of 3 *argo*, and for the most part, these were alien beings from Distant Worlds. The main mass, whose energy potential constitutes 1–2 units, remained immersed in darkness, in a state of "deep sleep."

However, according to Cosmic Laws, the Call is considered to have sounded only if it comes from the "native" Earth-dwellers, and if the necessary vibrational component sounds, going beyond the spheres of the lower quaternary. Aside from the creations of the planet itself, "native" Earth-dwellers are also considered to be those who were born in the early period of the descent of the Gods, those messengers from Distant Worlds who, at the dawn of humanity, came into contact with the so-called wives of Earth, as a result of which children were born that were endowed with a spark of spirituality. And since the world is ruled by Periods, the right of the Gods to enter into affairs with the creations of Earth was exhausted long ago, in antiquity. These children, those who were able to demonstrate the ability to preserve the Light-bearing seed within, at a later time entering into affairs with their fellow Earth-dwellers, passed on to subsequent generations of descendants a particle of the fires of spirituality, multiplied by their own efforts.

The date of 2017 was important, because everything in the Universe is subject to Cosmic Periods, which, constituting special combinations of rays and the position of stars and planets, determine timeframes for the manifestation of particular events. And so, if this Period had been missed, it could never have been repeated. It is interesting to note that the Messiah's Heavenly Nativity in 2017 was long ago depicted symbolically in sacred texts:

"Maitreya, the best of men, will then leave the Tushita heavens, and go for his last rebirth into the womb of that woman. For ten whole months she will carry about his radiant body.... He, supreme among men, will emerge from her right side, as the sun shines forth when it has prevailed over a bank of clouds" (*Maitreyavyakarana*).

"And there appeared a great wonder in heaven; a woman clothed with the sun, and the moon under her feet, and upon her head a crown of twelve stars. And she being with child cried, travailing in birth, and pained to be delivered" (Revelation 12:1–2).

These citations should be understood with the help of an astrological key. In 2017, there occurred a unique alignment of the celestial bodies: the Moon, Jupiter, Mercury, Mars, Venus, and Regulus; the Moon was "under the feet" of the constellation of Virgo, "clothed with" the Sun. The nine stars of the constellation of Leo together with the three planets (Mercury, Mars, and Venus) formed the "crown of twelve stars." Since ancient times, the planet Jupiter, the King of Planets, has been a planetary symbol of the Messiah, while Regulus, the King of Stars, is His stellar symbol. Symbolically, the King of Kings descended from the "Tushita heavens" through the aligned planets into the "womb" of Virgo, being represented as Jupiter, which entered her "womb" for 42 weeks, or almost ten months.

Similar findings indicating the significance of the year 2017 have also been discovered in the geometrical construction of the Great Pyramids in Egypt (see Daniel Matson, "The Oracle in Stone," *Signs of the End*).

There were also Muslim prophecies. It is known that the Imam Mahdi, the Islamic Saviour, was initially personified as the Prophet Isa, or Jesus Christ. Only later, did people begin to perceive the Mahdi as an independent image. As a saying of Muhammad states, the Mahdi will emerge in the years 1420–1439 of the Islamic calendar, equivalent to the period 1999–2017 (Harun Yahya, *The Signs of Prophet Jesus' (pbuh) Second Coming*). It is interesting to note that the Islamic new year of 1439 falls on 22 September 2017 of the Gregorian calendar, a date which accurately coincided with the Bible's cosmic event that occurred on 20–23 September 2017. Furthermore, researchers of the Quran broadly use a numerological key: each letter of any language has a numerical value, and when researchers apply it to certain verses of sacred texts, they can determine specific dates of future events. By these means it has been found that the Quran's verse 4:159 concerning the return of Jesus Christ yields the number 1439, which, if taken as denoting an Islamic year, again points to the year 2017 (*The Signs of Prophet Jesus' (pbuh) Second Coming*).

One of the sayings of Muhammad indicates the acceleration of time as a sign of the approaching Judgement Day, when it seems that "a year will be like a month, and a month will be like a week." Likewise, in the Bible there are the words of Jesus Christ that "days shall be shortened" (Matthew 24:22) as a sign of the Advent. Indeed, the Age of Maitreya is the age of acceleration in everything. And currently, despite the fact that days and nights still contain 24 hours, many people around the world have a feeling that time is quickening, moving much faster than ever before.

Moreover, after making his own biblical calculations and astrological observations, Rabbi Judah ben Samuel of Regensburg, a legendary Jewish mystic of the twelfth century, predicted that the Messianic time would begin after the tenth Jubilee year which concludes in 2017 (Ludwig Schneider, "Israel: Between Mysticism and Reality," *Israel Today*).

Also, in the nineteenth century, Ellen White, a co-founder of the Seventh-Day Adventist Church predicted that the Second Coming of Christ would occur in the year that the Jubilee would commence. Looking into White's prediction and the Bible, modern researchers interpret this to mean that the "Jubilee" being referred to must be a Sabbatical Jubilee, coinciding with the day of purification of the Heavenly Sanctuary, and falling on a Sunday. Their calculations have found only one possible date that meets these criteria — 22 October 2017 (see 221017.ru, *Internet Archive*, 5 August 2016).

It is also interesting to recall the famous prophecy of St. Malachy concerning the last Pope. Many were quick to recall this prophecy when, in 2013, Pope Benedict XVI suddenly abdicated and Pope Francis was elected in his place. According to this prophecy, Francis, who reigned from 2013 to 2025, was destined to be Pope during the Second Coming of Christ and the Last Judgement.

Finally, as the supreme and supernatural sign of the approaching Advent of the Lord of Light, the appearance of the sacred Udumbara flower has since 1997 been spotted almost all over the world, blossoming in the most unexpected places; sometimes it emerged out of nowhere, filling the space with its aroma and then vanishing just as suddenly.

However, as mentioned previously, whether the Messiah will manifest Himself in the physical world or not depends upon every single person and the collective will of the people of Earth, since the stars never force anything to happen against human will, merely creating the necessary conditions. This is why it was impossible to say when exactly He would appear: in the coming years, decades, or centuries. But those who were genuinely waiting for Him must have been prepared, "for in such an hour as ye think not the Son of Man cometh" (Matthew 24:44) — as was said two thousand years ago.

The Coming of the Messiah is the Mystery of Mysteries, and here it is important to understand that He comes according to the Law of Expediency in one of the Twelve Bodies, or in the totality of a number of them. And if the Higher Spiritual Quinary remains at the invisible level, then the lower Quaternary, and in this case the Senary, can already be considered manifested in the world of physical forms. Of course, an ordinary person, mainly living at the level of the quaternary, will not understand the interaction of Bodies at the level of the Twelve Messianic structures, and therefore, one can only accept with the heart the fact that this Great Advent has already taken place, and that the lowest point of the Saviour's descent was the human heart — the fire-breathing heart of His Mother.

Since there is no purposiveness for the Planetary Spirit to incarnate as a human being now, it is enough for Him to use between three and twelve of those already incarnated to partially transmit His Ray, depending on the measure of their human throughput. But these individuals must be ascetics, practically holy people.

As stated in *The Mahatma Letters*, the Planetary Spirit will be among the Seventh Race to instruct the emerging First Race of the Fifth Round. However, these will be different bodies, rarefied and capable of moving in intergalactic spheres, and the planet itself will be different. The Planetary Spirit will be manifested in the Fiery Body of Glory. This, however, will mark an entirely different stage of Evolution, one so different that it will bear almost no relation to the current stage.

A brief chronology of events associated with the Coming of the Messiah, Sanat Kumara, is as follows:

1942 — the incarnation of the Messiah in Shambhala, in the Fiery World, at the level of Earth's higher triad of principles. The date was calculated by pundits in India in the 1930s and confirmed by Helena Roerich.

1943 — the combination of cosmic bodies, predicted in the *Vishnu Purana* as the date for the beginning of the Age of Light.

1949 — the victory of the Lord of Shambhala over the Prince of Darkness, predicted in sacred scriptures and legends, after which preparations began for His Coming into the world.

1997 — the mystical Udumbara flower first bloomed, announcing that the King of Kings is already here.

1998 — His Spirit entered the aura of His Mother in the Tower of Chung in Shambhala, predicted by Edgar Cayce as the entrance of the Messiah.

1999 — the further descent of the Messiah into the layers of the Subtle World of the planet, accompanied by the sign of the Son of Man in Heaven, described in the Bible as a sign of His Coming. This year was also indicated by the prophecy of Nostradamus, the second book of the *Agni Yoga* series, the calculations of researchers as the end date of the Dark Age, and the Salsk Celestial Code.

2005 — the nineteenth year in the seventeenth cycle when the Messiah was born in the Heart of His Mother, an event accompanied by the second blossoming of Udumbara, which has since occurred in various countries around the world.

2012 — the end of the old world at an energy level and the spiritual regeneration of humanity that received from the Messiah into their matrix structures the Gift of Immortality, which will have its consequences in the future.

2017 — the Nativity of the Messiah in the Subtle World, the date indicated by the Bible, *Maitreyavyakarana*, the pyramid calculations, and other prophecies. His transition to the Sun in the New Body of Glory in order to keep and save the Solar System from destruction during its passage through the energetically dangerous zone in the Cosmos.

Thus, humanity lives in times of the Great Presence and yet is unaware of it.

The human structure of those who do not sleep, but are vigilant, and who have preserved the purity of their souls, is already changing gradually thanks to the Fiery Baptism accomplished by the Hierarch of Sirius. And one generation later, the children of those born after 2012 may be capable of giving life to human beings who possess the gift of Immortality, but, again, it will depend on their level of spirituality. In addition, this same process will enable all those currently living to reach the Higher Spheres when departing into the Subtle World, for the more they assimilate the Fires now pouring forth upon Earth, the higher they will be able to rise in the Ethereal World. From now on, more and more people will have new abilities, and some will even succeed in conquering Time and Space and other mysteries of the Universe. Thus will the New Humanity summoned by Maitreya come into its own.

Sangha (*Sk.*, "assembly," "community"). In Buddhism, the community of practitioners who follow the teachings of the Buddha.

Sangwa Dagpo (*Tib.*). A concealed Lord; the Lord of Mysticism, an epithet of Vajrapani.

Sangye (*Tib.*, "awakened"). The Tibetan name for any Buddha; one who has become fully awakened from the slumber or *avidya* (ignorance).

Sanskrit. The classical language of the Brahmins, never known *nor spoken in its true systematized form* (given later *approximately* by Panini), except by the initiated Brahmins, as it was pre-eminently "a mystery language." It has now degenerated into so-called Prakrit.

Saoshyant (*Av.*, "one who brings benefit"). The Zoroastrian Saviour who will bring about the final renovation of the world, defeating evil and bringing everlasting peace and righteousness.

Sapta (*Sk.*). Seven.

Saptaparni (*Sk.*, "sevenfold"). A plant which gave its name to a famous cave in Rajgir, now near Bodh Gaya, India, where the Lord Buddha used to meditate and teach his Arhats, and where the first Buddhist Council was held after his death. This cave had seven chambers which accounts for the name. In esotericism *saptaparni* is the symbol of the "sevenfold man-plant."

Sat (*Sk.*, "true"). The one ever-present Reality in the infinite world; the Divine Essence which is, but cannot be said to exist as it is Absoluteness, Be-ness itself.

Satan (*Heb.*, "opposer"). Two aspects should be distinguished: one cosmic and so ignorantly slandered, and the other planetary, pertaining only to Earth, appearing in the image of Lucifer (although having no right to bear this name) as the Lord of Saturn and the former ruler of the planet Earth.

The whole difficulty in understanding the existence of evil along with the Principle of Goodness lies in the fact that people have humanized the Ineffable Divine Principle, while at the same time, upon observing the many imperfections in the physical world, they are quite rightly perplexed as to how a Good and All-Merciful God could allow the destructive cosmic cataclysms, and the horrors and the suffering endured by human beings in their struggle for existence. Here limited thinking gives rise to the idea of an equally powerful force of evil in the person of the enemy of God, or Satan. But if one rejects the limitation or humanization of the Ineffable Power and accepts the majestic pantheism of the ancients, echoes of which can be found in the commandments of all the Great Teachers, including the Bible, then everything falls into place.

God, in His aspect of the Absolute, conceals within Himself the potential of all that exists. The Absolute envelops every universal manifestation. The Absolute, on account of its absolute Unity during manifestation, becomes the Absolute of infinite differentiation and its consequence — relativity and opposites. In the Absolute, or in the World of Supreme Reality or Existence, of course, evil as such does not exist. But in the manifested world, which is a consequence of differentiation, all opposites are already evident: i.e., light and darkness, spirit and matter, opposite polarities, good and evil, etc.

In his cosmic aspect, Satan is not a being, but instead, merely the personification of the consequences of differentiation (relativity and opposition). Without the law of relativity and opposition, no awareness, cognition, or improvement can take place. Only through comparison, juxtaposition, and selection does everything that exists advance in an evolutionary process.

Only by juxtaposing this duality, or pairs of opposites, can sparks of knowledge be ignited and improvement, or evolution, become possible. Perpetual motion, or evolution, also creates the relativity of all concepts. Reality can only be comprehended through the eternal change and juxtaposition of opposite polarities.

The action of opposites produces harmony, like the centrifugal and centripetal forces, which, being interdependent, are each necessary to the other in order for both to exist. If one were to cease, the action of the other would immediately become destructive. Indeed, it is opposing forces that maintain balance in the manifested world. These opposing forces or pairs of opposites take on one quality or another in human consciousness, i.e., become good or evil. On each plane of manifestation, the degree of evil and good is assessed by a person's consciousness according to the level of their development. What represents the Good on a lower plane may represent evil on a higher plane, and vice versa. Hence the relativity of all concepts in the manifested world.

Therefore, if the law of evolution is not realized, likewise, if it is not acknowledged that "No man hath seen God at any time" (John 1:18), that "God is a consuming fire" (Hebrews 12:29), and therefore, that God is *That Ineffable* of all ancient religions, that Absolute which contains within itself everything that exists, both visible and invisible — as the Apostle Paul says: "in Him we live, and move, and have our being" (Acts 17:28) — in other words, without Whom none can exist, then it is impossible to understand the existence of the opposing Force, or, as it is customary through some obtuseness to call it, *Satan*.

When there is awareness that the concepts of good and evil in their cosmic understanding are relative, then, of course, the existence of Satan as the focus of a self-sufficient evil in cosmic notion and scope should naturally fall away or be refuted.

However, it is also undeniable that the image of Satan, as the former ruler of Earth (hence, a human being), exists. This earthly aspect is personified in the adversary of Archangel Michael. It is the Fallen Angel, one of the Elohim, but one who was filled with pride and wanted to rise above his Brothers and become the only God for Earth-dwellers. Hindu legends have immortalized him in many images; the most famous among them is the image of King Ravana from the island of Lanka, the enemy of the godlike King Rama, and the kidnapper of his wife Sita. The ancient legends that tell of the Fallen Angel who rebelled against the Forces of Light and transformed into Satan reflect the real drama that occurred on Earth millions of years ago.

Lucifer was one of the Great Spirits who, having sacrificed themselves and left their own Worlds, came to Earth to help and guide humanity about 18 million years ago. He quickly advanced through the stages of Evolution and achieved great things in his own World. Of all the Teachers, his Spirit was energetically closest to the Earth, as well as having all the compositional characteristics of Saturn. This gave him the right to participate in the development of humanity, especially of its intellect. Just like other Great Teachers, by contacting humanity and incarnating among them, he endowed humanity with reason and free will.

An expert in all the secrets of Earth, Lucifer rightly began to be called the Prince of this world. But as a result, he became especially attached to the Earth, while the other Great Teachers were drawn to the Higher Worlds and were able to maintain their purity. Lucifer became Pratyeka Buddha, having developed his intellect to the limit, to the detriment of his higher energy centres, and having mastered all the knowledge of the Laws of Matter, manifested throughout the existence of the Solar System.

When a spirit reaches awareness of its potential for unlimited power and invincibility, when it masters many cosmic secrets and forces and knows that it can become the creator of different worlds, then it requires enormous strength of heart to resist the many temptations and, above all, the pride of the spirit. It is important to remember that not a single human feeling disappears; on the contrary, all feelings grow infinitely, and, therefore, they must be transformed into higher perceptions within the good, for if not, they may also become refined in evil.

The Prince of this world, being by Cosmic Right the ruler of the Earth, was unable to overcome feelings of pride and jealousy towards other Light-bearing Spirits. With each new incarnation on the planet, Lucifer's high consciousness was gradually darkened. Pride seized his mind completely which resulted in his fall and rebellion against Cosmic Laws during the time of Atlantis.

In any normal situation, the ruler of Earth would have elevated matter, filling its parts with the consciousness of unity. After all, the Spirit of the Lord of the planet passes through the human form as the primary teacher of the mastery of its inherent matter, and therefore, he is an expert in the properties of this matter. In a worthy condition, he is a valuable friend to all new formations; there are no opposing actions, only mutually beneficial seeking. Lucifer should have conveyed his knowledge to the Earth-dwellers, developing and rising together with his planet's inhabitants.

However, the ruler of Earth made no sacrifice for the sake of humanity, and instead sacrificed all of humanity to his own selfish pride. As far back as the earliest appearance of man in the Fourth Round, he conceived the idea of isolating Earth and delaying its evolution. He wanted to limit all humanity to Earth, depriving it of communication with Higher and Distant Worlds. Needless enlightenment of the masses did not suit his plan. However, the principle of the unity of existence and the law of mutual exchange dictate that isolation of any kind can lead only to withering or death.

Lucifer began to develop the human intellect at the expense of its spirituality, for without spiritual development the intellect becomes an instrument of darkness, manifesting as vindictiveness and lechery. Possessing all the secrets of the planet and manifesting the wonders of matter, Lucifer quickly began to gain a group of like-minded followers, which quickly grew into the majority of the population of Atlantis, for the underdevelopment of human hearts ensured that they were unable to withstand temptation.

To achieve his goal of becoming the absolute and only god of the Earth-dwellers, Lucifer directed all his efforts towards humiliating Woman, which always leads inevitably to the coarsening and degeneration of humanity. He dealt a blow to the Cult of Spirit by creating a cult of personality: the Atlanteans began to build temples and monuments dedicated to themselves, and secret knowledge was used solely for their own benefit. The use of black magic reached an unprecedented scale, going against the Forces of Light. However, nothing and no one can go against Cosmic Laws forever, and Atlantis was washed from the face of the Earth.

With the beginning of a new stage in the development of humankind, the Fallen Angel founded and headed the dark brotherhood, becoming a vehement opponent of the Great Brotherhood of Teachers in all centuries to come. It was Lucifer's rebellion and the implementation of his plan to achieve the self-sufficiency of earthly Matter that brought about the need for adjustments to be made to the Great Brotherhood — an establishment whose involuntary combat readiness made it unfamiliar to other planets.

This time, Lucifer decided to convince humanity of his non-existence so that it would be easier to deceive and enslave. His main goal was to terminate all connection between humanity and the Great Teachers. The minions of darkness entered the ranks of the servants of religions in order to distort beyond recognition the simple, pure commandments of the spiritual teachings of all peoples and ages. Thus were born dogmas and terrible fanaticism, which resulted in cruel intolerance and persecution of all dissenters as well as those of different beliefs in the name of the Great Lords, who taught only Love and Mercy for all that exists. Humanity in its majority became dark and ignorant, serving as an obedient instrument for the achievement of Lucifer's goals. And then every reminder of the Great Brotherhood, however small, was fiercely persecuted by humanity itself.

Nevertheless, the messengers of Light managed to reverse this situation in the recent past. At that time, realizing that his death was imminent, Lucifer decided to blow up the planet for the sake of extending his life for a short time. For Earth's atmosphere is preserved for a long time near the planet's exploded fragments (naturally, not physical), and this would allow the Prince of this world to reside within it. Since the higher layers of space were inaccessible to him, he had a choice: either to float among the fragments and the atmosphere surrounding them, or to retreat to Saturn, which he was extremely reluctant to do on account of the planet's difficult environment.

In the twentieth century, the Final Battle between the Forces of Light and the forces of darkness began. On 17 October 1949, the Great Lord of Shambhala expelled Lucifer sending him to Saturn, where he would begin his evolution anew in the most challenging conditions of this planet. However, "deputy" still remains on Earth and is sufficiently powerful in his destructive activities.

Of course, Lucifer's rebellion against Cosmic Laws considerably slowed Earth's evolution. Without him there would be no boundary between the physical world and the Higher Spheres, and humanity would not experience the phenomenon of death. Nonetheless, the Fallen Angel can still appear as the Saviour to those souls that, like him, have fallen low to the ground and lead them high up the rungs of Evolution. For Saturn has every chance of developing much faster than the Earth did.

Having mixed the cosmic and earthly aspects of Satan into one, a deeply ignorant, treacherous belief took root in human consciousness that would hold sway over the course of many centuries, the belief that Satan ruined humanity by endowing humankind with knowledge of good and evil. People are accustomed to repeating this absurdity without considering what human beings might represent if they had no knowledge of good and evil. Would they not be as unaccountable as animals? And who now would agree to return to an existence of ignorance, even if it were to be lived out in the Garden of Eden?

The great gift of discernment and free will is a Divine gift and only by possessing it can a human being come to acquire God's likeness. Therefore, this gift could not have been bestowed by the forces of darkness, but was instead sacrificially bestowed by the Forces of Light. Hence, the Messenger's original name was Lucifer the Light-bearer, but over the centuries in the West, the great meaning of this legend was lost surviving only in the secret teachings of the East.

There is a passage in *The Secret Doctrine* that explains this meaning: "Thus 'Satan,' once he ceases to be viewed in the superstitious, dogmatic, unphilosophical spirit of the Churches, grows into the grandiose image of one who makes of a terrestrial, a divine man; who gives him, throughout the long cycle of Maha Kalpa, the law of the Spirit of Life, and makes him free from the sin of ignorance, hence of death."

Of course, this "Satan" is the totality of those Supreme Spirits who brought to humanity the light of reason and the great gift of immortality, for they brought man out of his unconscious animal state and led him closer to the reflection of the Divine Principle in all its diversity. Now one can understand the magnitude of the Great Sacrifice made and still being made by these true and selfless Saviours of humanity in the person of the Christian Archangels or the Eastern Kumaras. They came from the higher planets renouncing higher evolution in order to help earthly humanity. They vowed to withstand the battle with the hierophant of evil and his minions and to remain with suffering humanity on Earth until the end of its existence. Therefore, it is they who should be called Light-bearers, or Lucifers.

Again, the Fallen Angel has no right to carry the name "Lucifer." This name appears only once in the Bible, in the Book of Isaiah, where it refers to the Assyrian king. In Hebrew it is *Helel ben Shachar*, which means "shining one, son of the morning," which in Latin is *Lucifer* and also refers to Venus. In early Christianity, the phrase "morning star," or Lucifer, was used as a glorifying epithet. However, Pope Gregory I was the first to apply this phrase from the Old Testament, "How art thou fallen from heaven, O Lucifer, son of the morning" (Isaiah 14:12), to Satan. Further, the equivalence of the concepts *Lucifer* and *Satan* was especially popularized in the Middle Ages, in particular by the poet John Milton, although how it is possible to call the embodiment of evil "Light-bearer" for many centuries still remains a mystery.

The true Lucifer, the Light-bearer, is Christ, as in Revelation 22:16: "I, Jesus, have sent mine angel to testify unto you these things in the churches. I am the root and the offspring of David, and the bright and morning star."

Sattvic (*Sk.*, "goodness"). In the context of the *gunas* (qualities of nature), the quality of purity, balance, harmony, and clarity. A sattvic person is calm, thoughtful, and spiritually oriented.

Satya (*Sk.*). The supreme truth.

Schlagintweit, Emil (1835–1904). A German scholar; the author of *Buddhism in Tibet* (1863).

Scriabin, Alexander (1872–1915). A Russian composer and pianist, known for innovative compositions in which he links musical keys to specific colours.

Seal of Solomon. The symbolical double triangle, adopted by the Theosophical Society and by many Theosophists. In India this seal or double triangle is also called the "Sign of Vishnu," and may be seen on the houses in every village where it is used as a talisman against evil. The triangle was considered sacred and used as a religious sign in the far East long before Pythagoras proclaimed it to be the first of the geometrical figures as well as the most mysterious. It is found on pyramids and obelisks, and is pregnant with occult meaning, as are all triangles, in fact. Thus, the pentagram is a triple triangle.

The way a triangle points determines its meaning. When pointing upwards, it signifies the male element and *divine fire*; when pointing downwards, the female and the *waters* of matter; when pointing upright, but with a bar across the top, it signifies *air* and astral light; when pointing downwards, with a bar, the *earth* or gross matter, etc. When a Greek Christian priest holds his two fingers and thumb together in blessing, he is simply making the magic sign — by the power of the *triangle* or "trinity."

Second birth or **twice-born**. In ancient times, meant spiritual birth or Initiation, but later was used more generally to refer to any Brahmin.

Secret Doctrine. The general name given to the esoteric teachings of antiquity.

Secret Doctrine, The. A major two-volume work by H. P. Blavatsky, published in 1888. It represents a synthesis of secret teachings previously guarded by the Freemasons and the Rosicrucians.

A further third and fourth volume were planned for publication should the reception of the first two volumes warrant it. Furthermore, according to Blavatsky's closest colleagues, Henry S. Olcott and William Q. Judge, she was to write five volumes in total. However, Blavatsky was unable to carry out *The Secret Doctrine* in its entirety owing to severe criticism, which contributed to her ill health and untimely demise. Therefore, after her passing, the almost completed manuscripts of volumes 3 and 4 mysteriously disappeared and volume 5 was never commenced. Thus, humanity deprived itself of the opportunity to see them.

A controversial third volume, edited and published by Annie Besant in 1897, did surface, but it was a compilation of articles that Blavatsky had roughly penned but not published. Besant herself acknowledged this in an interview in 1926: "The matter from which I compiled the third volume of 'Occultism' in *The Secret Doctrine* published under my direction was compiled from a mass of miscellaneous writings found in her desk after her death. . . . I never saw them [the third and fourth volumes] and do not know what became of them."

Apart from the material that Blavatsky herself mentioned would be elucidated in subsequent volumes, it was also intended that she would tell the world about the Battle of the Forces of Light with the darkness and the approaching Armageddon, and that she would shed light on the activities of the former Prince of this world. For she alone could write about him; being free of any connection to him by personal karma, he was unable to harm her directly.

The ultimate goal of *The Secret Doctrine* was to synthesize all ancient knowledge for future generations, since nothing of the most vital books and materials would have survived the great catastrophe that was expected to occur in the middle of the twentieth century.

Moreover, some obscurity was introduced deliberately into the presentation of *The Secret Doctrine*, for if it had not been, a number of the excellent scientists of the day would have discovered atomic energy prematurely.

The issue is that experiments with atomic and hydrogen bombs, which represent subtle energies, lead to the destruction of layers of the Subtle World adjacent to the Earthly plane and in the space of the Solar System, depriving their inhabitants of spheres of habitation. After all the experiments of this kind, which were conducted in the USA and the USSR as well as in other countries, the Teachers had to build these spheres anew. In addition, experiments with atomic bombs and other exploding shells disrupt the safety net around the planet, creating gaps within it. The result is that the toxic conglomerates of disintegrated spatial bodies from the Cosmos can penetrate Earth's atmosphere and environment.

In his article "New Evidence about Vols. 3 and 4 of *The Secret Doctrine*," Basil Crump writes: "A very important piece of evidence throwing an entirely new light on the mysterious disappearance of vols. 3 and 4 of *The Secret Doctrine* has lately been revealed to the Blavatsky Association by an elderly gentleman, a devoted admirer of Madame Blavatsky, who knew Mr. Thomas Green, one of the well-known early workers who helped with the printing at the H.P.B. Press in London before and after H.P.B.'s death. Before he died Mr. Green told this gentleman, who prefers to withhold his name, that he worked at the London Headquarters for some time and was paid to set up the type of vol. 3 and part of vol. 4 of *The Secret Doctrine*. The proofs of vol. 3 were passed by H.P.B. shortly before her death, and Mr. Green was just going to press with them when he received orders from her to break up the type, also such portions of vol. 4 as had already been set. . . . That she gave orders for the type to be broken up makes it practically certain that she also destroyed the manuscripts. . . . The final effort made by her Master M. to save the Theosophical Society by means of the Esoteric School and Inner Group having failed, H.P.B. evidently received orders from him to destroy the remainder of *The Secret Doctrine*, as her withdrawal was imminent and it was not safe to give out any further teaching."

Moreover, confirmation that the Masters intended to complete *The Secret Doctrine* later is found in the recently published notebooks of Helena Roerich. At the beginning of 1924, Master M. said: "Did you really think that *The Secret Doctrine* was to be released in this form? . . . A new book must be written to explain the meaning of the World Religion. To provide a conclusion does not mean to complicate things. All the writing is complex, but the last page should be the most simple and this page never materialized. We shall bring it to completion."

The Master kept His word, and in 1999–2000, volumes 3, 4, and 5 of *The Secret Doctrine* were completed in the Ray of Love-Wisdom. Thus, a three-volume work was born, which is both the final part of Blavatsky's *magnum opus* and a stand-alone, fundamental work in its own right. Its first volume examines the construction of the Universe and the human being at the level of octaves and musical sounds, the second volume is dedicated to the One Religion, and the third contains pages from the secret *Book of Maitreya Buddha*.

Seer. One who is a clairvoyant; who can see things that are both visible and invisible to others at any physical or temporal distance by means of spiritual or inner sight and perception.

Sefirah (*Heb.*, "counting, enumeration"). An emanation of Deity; the parent and synthesis of the ten Sefirot (the plural form of *Sefirah*) when she stands at the head of the Tree of Life; in Kabbalah, Sefirah, or the "Sacred Aged," is the Divine Intelligence (analogous with Sophia), the first emanation from the Endless or Ein Sof.

Sefirot (*Heb.*, "emanations"). The ten emanations of Deity; the highest is formed by the concentration of the Ohr Ein Sof, or the Limitless Light, and each Sefirah produces by emanation another Sefirah. The names of the ten Sefirot are: 1. Keter — the Crown; 2. Chokmah — Wisdom; 3. Binah — Understanding; 4. Chesed — Mercy; 5. Gevurah — Power; 6. Tiferet — Beauty; 7. Netzach — Victory; 8. Hod — Splendour; 9. Yesod — Foundation; 10. Malkuth — the Kingdom.

The conception of Deity embodied in the ten Sefirot is an intensely sublime one. To the Kabbalist, each Sefirah is a picture of a group of exalted ideas, titles, and attributes, which the name but faintly represents. Each Sefirah is called either active or passive, although this attribution may lead to an error in understanding as "passive" does not mean a return to negative existence; the two words, "active" and "passive" express the relationship between individual Sefirot and not any absolute quality.

Seine. A river in France.

Self. A person has two selves: the higher and the lower, the impersonal and the personal. One is divine, the other semi-animal. A great distinction should be made between the two.

Self, Higher. The Supreme Divine Spirit overshadowing man; the crown of the upper spiritual triad in man — *atman*.

Sellin, Carl (1833–1910). A German Evangelical Lutheran theologian and spiritualist. Sellin was a member of the Theosophical Society in Germany, but left it shortly after joining and turned against Theosophy and Blavatsky. He brought the Hodgson Report to H.P.B. on New Year's Eve of 1886. Blavatsky wrote to A. P. Sinnett: "Last evening as we were at tea Professor Sellin made his appearance with the famous and long expected report of S.P.R. under his arm. I read it, accepting the whole as my karmic New Year's present — or perhaps as the *coup de grace* ['blow of mercy'] of 1885. . . . I am called in it 'publicly and in print' forger about 25 times, trickster, fraud, etc., and a Russian spy to boot."

Semitic. Refers to the peoples, cultures, and languages originating from the ancient Near East, including Hebrews, Arabs, and others.

Senzar. The language of the Sun based on symbolism and closely associated with Sound, Light, Colour, and Number. Currently Senzar is the secret sacerdotal language of the Great Teachers and their disciples used all over the world. It is taught in the secret schools of the East.

In the ancient past there was one body of knowledge and one universal language — Senzar. From the beginning of human evolution, these were transmitted from generation to generation. Yet during the time of Atlantis, when humanity fell into sin, this language, along with eternal knowledge, ceased to be available to posterity. All nations restricted themselves to their own national tongues and lost their connection with the Secret Wisdom, forgetting the one language. Humanity was no longer worthy of such knowledge. Instead of being universal, Senzar became limited to just a few. The biblical myth of the Tower of Babel and similar legends around the world symbolically testify to that enforced secrecy, narrating the story of when the Lord created several languages from the one original language so that sinners could no longer understand one another's speech. In mythology Senzar is often referred to as the language of the birds.

The tongues of all peoples through the ages have their origins in Senzar. The roots of many current eastern languages come from Sanskrit, which is based on Senzar. Many words of this most ancient language underlie not only Sanskrit but also Egyptian, Hebrew, Latin, and other languages of various known and yet-to-be discovered sacred texts. Thus, Senzar is similar to the roots that nourish a single Tree, and languages compose its crown, which is beautiful in its diversity.

The language of Senzar consists of many levels, having both spoken and written forms of speech which are significantly different from traditional understanding. It is also distinct from others in that it has no obsolete or ingrained forms of expression. Being rather succinct, it is able to most fully and concisely express any thought, including hugely sophisticated phenomena.

Its highest manifestations are closest to the Voice of the Silence and include thought-forms, the breathing of fires, the geometric expression of ray combinations, and so on, whereas its lowest manifestations resemble traditional writing systems, each with its own specific rules.

The writing system of Senzar combines seemingly incompatible elements. These include signs, syllables, and letters based on symbolism. A single symbol is capable of developing into an entire treatise, easily comprehended by an initiated disciple of any ethnic background. But the reader's level of consciousness is also important. Colour, light, number, and sound play a significant role in its alphabet from which words and sentences are composed. Each letter, possessing its own specific colour of the rainbow, shade of light, number, and mystic sound syllable, has its equivalent in the languages of all the peoples of the world and may be reproduced using different cryptographic methods with the aid of specialized calculation tables. Thus, a new cryptographic alphabet is created in a given tongue while numerological, geometrical, and astrological keys help the reader to precisely determine how to decode this secret writing system.

For example, the Zend language of the Avesta is one version of script in Senzar; the Angelic or Enochian language of John Dee, mysterious advisor to Queen Elizabeth I, is another, the script of the *Voynich Manuscript* being yet another.

Senzar has been discovered in inscriptions on stones and plants that do not lend themselves to deciphering. For example, on the territory of Kumbum Monastery in China grows the sacred Tree of Great Merit, also known as the Tree of Ten Thousand Images. Legend has it that the tree grew out of the hair of the great Buddhist reformer Tsongkhapa. In the past, according to witnesses, when the tree blossomed on each leaf there appeared a sacred letter or syllable of such astounding beauty and perfection that no other existing letter could surpass it. These mystic letters and syllables were written in Senzar, in their totality comprising the whole Teaching of Buddhism and the history of the world.

Seraphim of Sarov (1754/1759–1833). One of the most venerated Russian saints. He received suffering souls, comforting and healing them, sometimes receiving several thousand people a day.

Sevagram. A village in India where Mahatma Gandhi established his Ashram in 1936. Sevagram became a centre for Gandhi's social and political activities, promoting simplicity, non-violence, and self-sufficiency.

Seven steps in Knowledge or **seven factors of awakening.** Practices leading to enlightenment: 1) discerning what is true from what is false; 2) making efforts to practise what is true; 3) joy; 4) serenity; 5) mindfulness; 6) mystic concentration; 7) equanimity.

Sex. The union of masculine and feminine principles, both in its human (as man and woman) and Cosmic (as spirit and matter) aspects, with the aim of creating a new life through the Power of Love; the classification of living beings as male or female on the basis of their reproductive anatomy.

Sexual energy represents a powerful force that is the foundation of vitality and creativity. Humanity's abuse of this force has been so extreme that over many generations the abuse has resulted in its degeneration as well as many illnesses. *The Secret Doctrine* explains:

"Creative powers in man were the gift of Divine Wisdom, not the result of sin. This is clearly instanced in the paradoxical behaviour of Jehovah, who first *curses* Adam and Eve (or humanity) for the supposed crime committed and then *blesses* his 'chosen people' by saying, 'Be fruitful, and multiply, and replenish the earth' (Genesis 9:1). The curse was not brought on mankind by the Fourth Race, for the comparatively sinless Third Race, the still more gigantic Antediluvians, had perished in the same way; hence the Deluge was no punishment, but simply a result of a periodical and geological law. Nor was the curse of karma called down upon them for seeking *natural* union, as all the mindless animal-world does in its proper seasons; but, for abusing the creative power, for desecrating the divine gift, and wasting the life-essence for no purpose except bestial personal gratification. When understood, the third chapter of Genesis will be found to refer to the Adam and Eve of the closing Third and the commencing Fourth Races.

"In the beginning, conception was as easy for woman as it was for all animal creation. Nature had never intended that woman should bring forth her young ones 'in sorrow.' Since that period, however, during the evolution of the Fourth Race, there came enmity between its seed and the 'Serpent's' seed, the seed or product of karma and Divine Wisdom. For the seed of woman, or lust, *bruised the head* of the seed of *the fruit of wisdom and knowledge* by turning the holy mystery of procreation into animal gratification; hence the Law of Karma 'bruised the *heel*' of the Atlantean Race by gradually changing physiologically, morally, physically, and mentally, the whole nature of the Fourth Race of mankind, until, from being the healthy king of animal creation in the Third Race, man became in the Fifth, our Race, a helpless, scrofulous being, and has now become the wealthiest heir on the globe to constitutional and hereditary diseases, the most consciously and intelligently bestial of all animals.

"This is the real curse from the physiological standpoint, almost the only one touched upon in Kabbalistic esotericism. Viewed from this aspect, the curse is undeniable, for it is evident. The intellectual evolution, in its progress hand in hand with the physical, has certainly been a curse instead of a blessing — a gift quickened by the Lords of Wisdom, who have poured on the human *manas* the fresh dew of their own Spirit and Essence."

"During the previous Races, and at least at the beginning of the present one, those who indulged in marital relations during certain lunar phases that made those relations sterile were regarded as sorcerers and sinners."

"The question is often asked: Why should celibacy and chastity be a *sine qua non* condition of regular chelaship, or the development of psychic and occult powers? The answer is contained in the Commentary. When we learn that the third eye was once a physiological organ, and that later on, owing to the gradual disappearance of spirituality and increase of materiality, the spiritual nature being extinguished by the physical, it became an atrophied organ, as little understood now by physiologists as is the spleen — when we learn this, the connection becomes clear. During human life the greatest impediment in the way of spiritual development, and especially to the acquirement of yoga powers, is the activity of our physiological senses. Sexual action also being closely connected, by interaction, with the spinal cord and the grey matter of the brain, it is useless to give any longer explanation."

The pleasure inherent in sexual intercourse, both in the animal and human worlds, is a stimulus for the natural process of reproduction. When man became a conscious being, the gradually developed feeling of love became the driving force not only and not so much for physical intimacy, but for the individual's spiritual and creative growth.

Psychic energy, being the basis of life in all Kingdoms of Nature, increases with the growth of consciousness. For people of even average mental ability it is a powerful force, which they do not yet know how to guide in the right direction. It is the same for all purposes, and sometimes people expend it completely at the sexual level, leaving no strength for creativity or spiritual development. By using this supply of psychic energy wisely, they can channel it to meet all their needs. Physiological love is associated with the lower functions of the *kundalini* centre. It is this centre that initiates the movement of psychic energy in a person, opening higher centres of supreme consciousness without which there can be no path of spiritual ascent.

When uncontrolled expenditure of energy begins at the sexual level, a person is like a steam boiler with open valves — the energy does not rise to the higher centres, but instead vanishes into the air. Higher, spiritual phenomena cease and creativity freezes. From this it is clear that even with wonderful love in a legal marriage, sexual intimacy should not become routine, like daily nutrition.

With love of a sublime order and the utmost possible abstinence in sexual intimacy, development of the centres of higher consciousness does not stop; on the contrary, they are stimulated by a heart burning with love. All higher aspirations are kindled and an increase in creativity is observed.

The lower layers of the Astral World are the area of astral substance represented by animal desires and emotions associated with sexual reproduction. In these spheres, the energy of reproduction is connected to forms evoking erotic desire, and actions geared towards the intercourse between these forms of sexual energy.

Sexual satisfaction cannot be achieved without contact with this astral substance through one's brain centres. This is reached either through the astral body of the partner or an astral entity when there is no partner. In the latter case, hungry entities from the lower layers of the Subtle World are drawn to the person experiencing a state of sexual arousal. These entities of various degrees — from harmless and primitive elementals to strong disembodied perverts, rapists, and debauchees — like fish filling a pond, crowd the space around that person. If a person is consistently engaged in acts of sexual self-gratification, which sometimes begins in childhood, strong connections with these astral entities can be established. They feed on the sexual energy released; the entities follow it like hungry animals and become partial and sometimes complete possessors, demanding more and more.

Thus, the act of self-gratification is the evocation of erotic entities from the lower Astral Plane. Without their participation, there can be no sexual satisfaction. Self-gratification is now represented almost as a mandatory "medicinal remedy," but what happens around such a person on the invisible, astral plane is much more serious and dangerous even than the consequences for their physical organs that this causes. The person's entire sensory sphere starts and ends with the lower region of the Subtle World. Blavatsky explains:

"The Biblical sin of Onan. Involuntary and natural, or physiological is not held as sin, if one is *irresponsible*, though it is a *wall* against progress; but *mental* onanism is 1,000 times worse than the physical. You can hardly have control over your nerves — you *can* over your thoughts and imagination. *It is worse than the very (natural) act.*"

Further, in the recently published notebooks of Helena Roerich, we read the warning of Master M.:

"Onanism is an extremely harmful and dangerous habit, especially among boys. The consequences of onanism in most cases appear in old age, as swelling of the prostate and hence urinary retention. But still, this can be easily avoided if you stop the dangerous habit in time and explain to the boy the process and the danger of friction. Here a certain schedule and a new diet can moderate the ardour of youth. Sports and horse riding, and even simple walking can go a long way to help."

When there is normal physical intimacy between a man and a woman, Love serves as protection from the hungry flock mentioned above. High, strong Love envelops the whirlwind of energy they release with a kind of fiery blanket. The lovers' united energy passes into the higher regions of the Subtle World, attracting a highly spiritual being for incarnation — only a being of this kind can pass through the fiery cover.

On the other hand, the physical intimacy of people lacking love does not have this protective veil; not being united by love, their energies pass only to the lower layers of the Subtle World and attract low entities.

People who change partners like gloves often bring these debauched habits with them from depraved former lives. They involve new people in such relationships, tying new and yet more karmic knots, as no case of sexual intercourse is ever traceless. And during these intercourses, such people spew out their energy, polluting the Cosmos. Such energy does not have the properties of a building material, but it is used either by sorcerers for evil, or by disembodied entities, or extraterrestrial civilizations. And these individuals' karmic debts remain unpaid because they do not bear children.

The Cosmos is built economically — every pleasure has to be paid for. Payment from people who engage in sexual excess is taken in the Subtle World and in future lives (if they happen to be on Earth), when they will no longer be as healthy as they are in this one, both physically and mentally. Besides, everyone only has a certain amount of energy. If they waste it, they will lack it in the Subtle World where it is needed to rise higher than its lowest and darkest layers so as to avoid becoming stuck there.

Apart from the chaotic exchange of energies, each act of copulation for pleasure generates a certain entity that travels out into space. This can be anything from a light-weight entity, similar to a puff of smoke which quickly dissipates, to a very powerful and long-living being that will enslave other people forcing them to generate more of its kind. Sorcerers use these entities to fight the Forces of Light. Therefore, given that the evil forces have such an inexhaustible source of energy as the majority of unreasoning humanity, it is not surprising that after the Victory of Light in 1949, they were able to restore their strength quite quickly to begin the third phase of the fierce battle of Armageddon, now taking place in the Subtle World. For whereas people generate millions of such demonic entities *every hour*, the ranks of Light are not replenished to the same proportions. Hence, they fight in an unequal battle.

Orgies and debauchery have always been mandatory attributes of dark sects. Usually the participants in these scenes are not privy to the fact that their energies, released during these mass copulations, are exploited by knowledgeable sorcerers in the battle against the Forces of Light.

There is an element of mystery in physical intimacy that only two people are privy to. Outside spectators are inappropriate and inadmissible. They cannot connect with the true essence of what is happening, and "peeping," which Nature does not allow, ends badly for them.

The ancient legend of Artemis and Actaeon allegorically warns "peepers" — lovers of striptease, porn products, erotic films or books, and the like. The essence of the legend is that when the young hunter Actaeon saw the naked goddess Artemis bathing, the enraged goddess turned him into a stag, and his own hounds tore him to pieces.

The energies of erotic emotion generated by Love are drawn into the flow of cosmic magnetism and contribute towards the construction of the Universe.

But the energies arising from hungry lust and "peeping" remain in the space around the person producing them and attract lower astral entities — hounds in the legend cited above. A person who gives free rein to their animality turns into an animal internally, and a weak one, too — a stag. The person gradually becomes weaker than their creations, their base desires, and will be torn to pieces by them, defeated by the Dwellers on the Threshold, i.e., they will turn into matter that has lost the will to strive for self-improvement. Having wasted all their energy, their monad will have to start its journey from the very beginning, from the level of mineral on another planet.

When contemplating the sexual and erotic scenes, with which all media products, movies and books, are now oversaturated, in the majority of people, psychic energy begins to transform into sexual energy, hormones are released into the blood, and sexual arousal of varying degrees occurs. The energy that left the body due to this "hungry" excitement has already been thrown into space in the form of waste, whereas, it could have saved the individual in each case during the next impending viral epidemic or other disease, because the state of a person's immunity is connected to the amount of psychic energy in the body.

So it is that an erotic movie drains and throws away a sea of energy from these people, especially young men, who are the most active and excitable group within the viewing audience. At the same time, sexual arousal, unprotected by love, attracts from the Astral World lower entities which, in addition to lower elemental spirits (elementals), include disembodied lechers, sadists, rapists, and so on, as mentioned previously. When such media content is often watched in the house or books of a similar nature are read, then these entities will remain there to live invisibly, since only through contact with physically embodied people with the same habits can they, at least for a brief moment, experience this pleasure again. This is most dangerous when there are children in the house, because they become the victims of these invisible entities.

Substituting the concept of Love with physical intimacy is the greatest victory of darkness over human consciousness. If a person keeps the valve that releases psychic energy from their body constantly open, and, especially, if they start doing so in childhood, this person is an instrument in the hands of darkness, becoming a supplier of the energy it needs. High levels of inspiration, true creativity, and heroism are inaccessible to such a being. A child who has brought into life talents and accumulations of great abilities will not be able to actualize them if psychic energy at the sexual level is spent prematurely. As a rule, early onset of the sexual life shifts the focus of life to material existence.

Controlling the majority of the media, the brothers of the shadow call for the abandonment of all prohibitions: they try to involve the wider masses in the squandering of sexual energy as early as possible, to make it the goal of life. Then, after the death of the body, many of the disembodied individuals, who indulged in debauchery in their earthly life, become possessors, thereby destroying themselves definitively, because in the Subtle World, all uneradicated habits and feelings are intensified a thousandfold, and they simply have no other choice but to become vampires or leeches, sucking on the aura of people who are physically embodied and have the same inclinations.

By the same analogy, drinkers attract disembodied drinkers who, deprived of a body, can no longer enjoy this activity; drug addicts attract disembodied drug addicts, and so on, across all types of addiction.

In modern media products, woman is reduced to the level of an object of desire. She is most often presented as depraved, immoral, corrupt, and even able to kill more easily than a man.

To humiliate Woman and to corrupt her has always been a very important task for darkness. Man is, then, deprived of spiritually pacifying and uplifting leadership, and his strong energy can be directed towards bloody wars, destruction, and violence. Darkness wants to use all its tricks to convince man that woman is stupid, depraved, and corrupt, that she is not worthy of love and reverence, only of possession through violence. Drugs, cigarettes, and alcohol are used to intoxicate women. A man has a tougher nervous system and is more resistant to these poisons, but women, with a more sensitive and refined nervous system, are compromised very quickly. Narcologists know how difficult it is to treat women.

Over many centuries, darkness has achieved success in disrupting the Cosmic balance between the Feminine and Masculine Principles on Earth. But Nature stands guard over her Laws: whoever disturbs the balance of the Principles will suffer. A man who humiliates a woman by reducing her to a slave state will receive from her a son who is also a humiliated slave, because the energetical characteristics of the mother are inherited by the son, while those of the father are inherited by the daughter.

The sexual sphere is of particular interest to extraterrestrial civilizations, since it is the source of the birth of new life and the reproduction of humanity — a divine gift of which they are deprived.

One of these, whose planet perished, brought HIV/AIDS to Earth. Its representatives are located in the depths of the ocean and appear as UFOs, taking the form of glowing orange balls. Reports of their appearance can be found here and there in the news. They control the liquid gold that exists at the bottom of the ocean. If someone encroaches on their gold, they will attempt to destroy the world. But they are held back by the Forces of Light.

Their representatives can be born as human beings, but with very unusual abilities: they can enter any body that is not marked with a sign indicating that the person belongs to the Light, as well as fly and become invisible. It was through such a person, a woman, who lived in the Far East of Russia, that in the twentieth century representatives of this civilization passed on the formula for HIV/AIDS and said that, observing and respecting the Cosmic Laws of this Solar System, they would give humanity information on HIV/AIDS and how it could be cured. If humanity accepted this message, then they would leave; if humanity did not accept the information, then they would have the right to occupy the bodies of those who had contracted HIV/AIDS for the purposes of their own research and experiments. This woman sent a warning letter to the government of the USSR in Moscow, where naturally, it was considered nonsense. However, after some time, the epidemic spread suddenly to many countries around the world.

A person's physical health depends on the level of their consciousness, morality, and purity of thinking. Each earthly life either increases the accumulations of psychic energy, or destroys them quantitatively and reduces them qualitatively. A sharp decline in morality throughout the planet has led to a decrease in the quality and quantity of the psychic energy of large groups of people. Immorality is a violation of the Laws of Evolution.

According to reports, the main reason for the spread of the virus in Africa lies in multiple sexual partners and premarital and outside of marriage sexual activity. In a person with high psychic energy, the crystals of which circulate in the blood and are present in all secretions of the physical body, the virus that enters the body is immediately destroyed. In addition, such a person is protected from HIV/AIDS not only by the bactericidal fiery nature of their high energy, but also by their morality. The latter will not allow sexual intercourse without love or family betrayal, and a strong willpower (without it there cannot be high psychic energy) will keep them from getting drawn in to bad company and the enticements of drug dealers. Therefore, in addition to medical treatment of the consequences, the development of consciousness and morality is extremely important as a preventive measure against such epidemics.

An example covered in the press confirms the importance of psychic energy in the context of the plague of the twentieth century — HIV/AIDS. American doctors examining a large group of people infected and suffering from HIV/AIDS in Africa were perplexed: a woman who had sexual contact with many infected men for a number of years was completely healthy. This woman who could no longer be described as young was forced into prostitution due to poverty and hunger in order to feed her children. She explained to the doctors why she was still healthy: "I have always prayed and continue to pray. I believe that God will not allow me to get sick, for then my children will die of hunger." The lofty motive of a deed directs a person's thoughts into the Higher Worlds. It was not the desire for base pleasures or benefits that motivated this unfortunate woman's prayer, but love for her children. Therefore, each prayer returned as a stream of energy, protecting her from infection.

To protect people from falling into the abyss and destruction, all true religions and ethical teachings encouraged morality. It is for this reason that Jesus Christ sternly warns: "Ye have heard that it was said by them of old time: Thou shalt not commit adultery. But I say unto you that whosoever looketh on a woman to lust after her hath committed adultery with her already in his heart. And if thy right eye offend thee, pluck it out, and cast it from thee: for it is profitable for thee that one of thy members should perish, and not that thy whole body should be cast into hell. And if thy right hand offend thee, cut it off, and cast it from thee: for it is profitable for thee that one of thy members should perish, and not that thy whole body should be cast into hell" (Matthew 5:27–30).

In an Arhat sexual energy is transformed into higher creativity. A person can raise the vibration of the sexual centre by transmuting its substance with the help of the life force flowing through it, when it is subordinated to the higher centre of the Heart.

It is never too late to stop squandering energy at the sexual level. There are a number of saints who succeeded in overcoming their lower nature, now serving as role models for those who struggle. There is nothing impossible to the human will. The main thing is to decide whether to continue wasting this precious creative energy or to use it for the purposes of spiritual growth and development.

More about sex in its Cosmic aspect can be found in the book *The Song of Sano Tarot*, given by Master M. through Anna Fullwood. How to purify the body and soul is explained in *The Seven Laws of Spiritual Purity*, given by the disciple of Master M. through "Two Workers."

Shabda Brahma (*Sk.*, "Sound Absolute"). In Hindu philosophy, the concept of the "Word" or "Sound" as the Ultimate Reality or Divine Principle. It signifies that the universe and all creation originate from sound or vibration, and that Om is the primal sound or Shabda. Shabda Brahman is often equated with the eternal, cosmic sound that pervades all existence, and it is believed to be a manifestation of Brahman, in Vedanta philosophy, the supreme, formless reality.

Shaivas. Those who worship Shiva.

Shakespeare, William (1564–1616). An English playwright, poet, and actor, widely regarded as one of the greatest writers in the English language. His works include tragedies, comedies, and historical plays, such as *Hamlet* (1603), *Macbeth* (1623), and *Romeo and Juliet* (1597). William Q. Judge writes in *Echoes from the Orient* (1890): "The Adepts assert that Shakespeare was, unconsciously to himself, inspired by one of their own number."

Shakti (*Sk.*, "force"). Universal energy; the active female energy of the gods; in popular Hinduism, their wives and goddesses; in occultism, the crown of the Astral Light; force and the six forces of Nature synthesized; the female counterpart of the male Fohat. The six forces consist of:

1. *Para-shakti*, the Supreme Power which includes Light and Heat.
2. *Jnana-shakti*, the power of true Knowledge or Wisdom.
3. *Iccha-shakti*, the power of will, the force of desire. This willpower, while exercised in occult practices, generates the nerve-currents necessary to set certain muscles in motion and to paralyse certain others.
4. *Kriya-shakti*, the mysterious power of thought which enables it to produce external, perceptible, phenomenal results by its own inherent energy. The ancients held that any idea will manifest itself externally, if one's attention (and will) is deeply concentrated upon it; similarly, an intense volition will be followed by the desired result. This is the creative potency of the *siddhis* (powers) of the full yogis. This divine power is latent in the will of every man, and which, if not called to life, quickened and developed by yogi-training, remains dormant in 999,999 people out of a million, and atrophies.

The first and most important step in occultism is to learn how to adapt one's thoughts and ideas to one's plastic potency because, otherwise, one is creating things by which one may be generating bad karma. No one should go into occultism or even touch it before becoming perfectly acquainted with their own powers, and knowing how to commensurate these powers with their actions. And this a person can achieve only by deeply studying the philosophy of occultism before commencing the practical training. Otherwise, as sure as fate, he will fall into black magic.

The so-called "evil eye" simply means possessing enormous plastic power of imagination that is working involuntarily, and thus is turned unconsciously to negative uses. It is the great plastic power of thought, so great as to produce a current impregnated with the potentiality of every kind of misfortune and accident, which inoculates or attaches itself to any person who comes into contact with it. A *jettatore* (one with the evil eye) need not be imaginative necessarily, or have evil intentions or wishes. Such a person may simply be one who is naturally fond of witnessing or reading about sensational scenes, such as those involving murder, execution, accidents, etc. Such a person may not even be thinking of any of these things in the moment that their eye meets their future victim. But the currents have been produced and exist in that person's visual ray, ready to spring into activity the instant they find suitable soil, like a seed fallen by the way and ready to sprout at the first opportunity. That is, the "evil eye" is nothing but the direction of this invisible fluid, charged with malicious will and hatred, from one person to another, and sent out with the intention of causing harm. It may equally be employed for a good or evil purpose. In the case of the former, it is magic; in the case of the latter, sorcery.

The Secret Doctrine states that, during the Third Race, the "Sons of Will and Yoga" or the "Mind-born Sons" were created, not begotten, in a truly *immaculate* way through the power of *kriya-shakti*. They were the spiritual forefathers of all the subsequent and present Arhats, or Mahatmas, representing the "holy seed-grain" of the future Saviours of humanity. To give life to physical humanity, the first women were created by *kriya-shakti* before they were born naturally as an independent gender.

5. *Kundalini-shakti*, the power of life, the Universal Life Principle of which electricity and magnetism are manifestations. *Kundalini* means "the coiled-up" and is also called "the serpent power," because it is coiled like a serpent at the base of the spine. This power generates a certain light in those who sit for spiritual and clairvoyant development, being known only to those who practise concentration and yoga. When roused and purified by a trained yogi it leads to direct perception of Reality; but it can easily kill one who has not yet achieved absolute self-mastery being perfectly pure in mind and body.

6. *Mantrika-shakti*, the power or occult potency of mystic words, letters, numbers, speech, sounds, and music. Used in the chanting of sacred formulas or mantras, such as *Aum Mani Padme Hum*. Its crown is the Ineffable Name.

These six forces are the names of the Six Hierarchies of Dhyan Chohans, synthesized by their Primary, the seventh, who personify the Fifth Principle of Cosmic Nature, or the "Mother" in its mystical sense. Each Force has a *living conscious entity* at its head of which it is an emanation. Shakti is the female energy of a god in exoteric Hinduism and Lamaism. In the Tantrik and Dugpa schools, these energies become the female consorts of their deities and are often depicted in a highly degraded and sensual manner.

Shakya Thubpa (*Tib.*). The name of Buddha Shakyamuni.

Shambhala (*Sk.*, "place of peace"). The Stronghold of Light, the legendary kingdom hidden in the heart of the Himalayas. The Kingdom figures under different names in the myths and beliefs of various peoples of the world: Agartha, Belovodye, the City of Gods, the Garden of Eden, Mount Meru, the Pure Land, the White Island, and so on.

Shambhala is the Imperishable Sacred Land, the first and ever-present continent of the planet Earth, which never shared the fate of the others, for it is destined to continue from the beginning to the end of the Grand Cycle of Evolution. It is the cradle of the first human and contains the sacral Source of all religions, philosophies, sciences, and esoteric teachings. This mysterious place, which preserves Eternal Wisdom, lies at the intersection of the past, present, and future, as well as the physical, Subtle, and Fiery Worlds.

Shambhala was first mentioned in the Puranas as a birthplace of the Kalki Avatar, the Messiah, and the place from which He will appear. Information related to Shambhala filtered into the world at different times. Back in the tenth century, one of the monks of Kyivan Rus' stayed in the Ashram of the Great Brotherhood for several days, however, he was not allowed to talk about it, except upon his deathbed to tell his story "from mouth to ear." It was not until 1893, in fact, that this account was written down. In the twelfth and thirteenth centuries, Popes Alexander III and Innocent IV both attempted to establish contact with Prester John, the head of the Secret Spiritual Brotherhood in the heart of Asia, who had sent letters to a number of Christian sovereigns: Constantine the Great, Manuel I Komnenos, Frederick I Barbarossa, Louis VII of France, and others.

In the seventeenth century, the Portuguese Jesuit missionary, Estêvão Cacella, was the first to tell the Europeans of this mythical place, which he visited at the invitation of the Tibetans. In 1915, Albert Grünwedel published a German translation of the Guidebook to Shambhala, written by the famous Panchen Lama, Lobsang Palden Yeshe, in which the location of the legendary realm is indicated by a large number of symbols and complex geographical hints.

In the 1920s, Dr. Ossendowski described his conversations with Mongolian lamas, according to whom many people had visited the kingdom of Agartha. However, none among them revealed what they saw there, for they had taken a vow of silence. There is a legend about a hunter who accidentally enters the underground premises of Agartha through a cave. Upon his return, when he starts to describe what he has seen, the lamas immediately cut out his tongue in order to prevent any disclosure of the secret of secrets.

And in 1925, in many newspapers worldwide, there appeared an extensive article by the Mongolian explorer, Dr. Lao Chin, telling of his journey to the Valley of Shambhala. Although he was forbidden to write about the wondrous spiritual phenomena of the place, Dr. Lao Chin mentioned that the valley's inhabitants lived for many centuries despite looking middle-aged, and that they were characterized by clairvoyance, telepathy, and other higher abilities. Among other things, Dr. Chin witnessed them levitating, even becoming invisible to the naked eye.

Shambhala is the Ashram of the Great Brotherhood of the Teachers of Humanity, each of whom is a God, having become such for many nations, leaving the divine mark in human hearts as an equal among equals in the flesh. The work of the Mahatmas may be seen in three principal areas of research: improvement of the earthly plane, methods of communication with the Distant Worlds, and means of conveying the results of their study to humanity, the latter being undoubtedly the most challenging.

Earthly Shambhala may be thought of as a spaceport from which messengers are sent to the Distant Worlds and where ambassadors from the infinite Universe arrive. New ideas from other inhabited planets are tested in the laboratories of the Brotherhood; after being adapted to earthly conditions, they are conveyed to the world's scientists in the form of inspiration.

Here are made the most important decisions concerning the evolution of humanity and the planet. The Council of Shambhala convenes once in every hundred years (1924, 2024); the Council of the High Initiates takes place once every 60 years. This is a real World Government, which has little in common with earthly regimes, and yet has often contacted them through its messengers. Indeed, the history of all times and nations records testimonies to the Assistance of the Great Teachers, which has always been given secretly at turning points in the history of each country. However, while the people of the East often accepted the Great Teachers' advice, the West, as a rule, rejected it.

For example, in addition to the aforementioned information, it is known that warnings were received by representatives of the Habsburg dynasty and the Norwegian King Cnut the Great. Charles XII of Sweden was warned not to start his fatal campaign against Russia. The repeated warnings communicated to Louis XVI and Marie Antoinette of the impending danger to France and the French royal family are widely known. Napoleon was also warned not to go against Russia. A warning was given to Queen Victoria in 1851. And in 1926, the Mahatmas issued an austere warning to the government of the USSR, and the consequences of its rejection were indeed grave. Further, an unknown Tibetan lama passed a warning to Hitler through German zoologist Ernst Schäfer that he should not start a "great war." On the other hand, American Presidents George Washington and Abraham Lincoln heeded the advice of the White Brotherhood, which resulted in the powerful development of the United States. In the 1930s, however, when President Franklin Roosevelt was warned about the upcoming Second World War, unfortunately, his heart was not open enough to take on board all the advice he was given; if he had, today there would be a United States of *both* the Americas.

Several prominent individuals have visited Shambhala. As a rule, one or two candidates are admitted each "century" (which consists not of 100 years but of 60, in accordance with the Kalachakra calendar). For example, during their lifetimes, this Stronghold of Light was visited by: Gautama Buddha, Jesus Christ, Lao Tzu, Pythagoras, Plato, Apollonius of Tyana, Paracelsus, the Panchen Lama Palden Yeshe, Helena Blavatsky, Helena and Nicholas Roerich, and others, all of whom have played a significant role in the evolution of humanity. But not all the Great Spirits who had specific missions to fulfil visited the Brotherhood during their earthly life. Furthermore, anyone who visits the Abode of Light by the invitation that resonates deep within their heart takes a vow of silence, which may be broken only with the permission of the Great Lord of Shambhala. No uninvited guest will ever find the path to Shambhala.

To read Dr. Lao Chin's article about his journey to one of the Abodes of Shambhala, visit radiantbooks.co/bonus.

Shammars (*Tib.* "red hat"). See *Dugpas*.

Shan Mi Pai (*Ch.*, "school of virtue and esotericism"). See *Yogachara*.

Shangna (*Sk.*). A mysterious epithet given to a robe or vesture in a metaphorical sense. To put on the "Shangna robe" means to acquire Secret Wisdom and Initiation.

Shangnahexiu or **Shanavasa**. The great Arhat, regarded as one of the Indian patriarchs, the third of Shakyamuni Buddha's 23 or the fourth of his 24, successors. He was a wealthy man of Rajagriha, who decided to renounce the world and become a monk. Shanavasa was a disciple of Ananda, the favourite disciple of Gautama Buddha.

Shankaracharya. The great religious reformer of India and teacher of the Vedanta philosophy — the greatest of all such teachers, regarded by the Advaitists (non-dualists) as an incarnation of Shiva and a worker of miracles. He established many *mathams* (monasteries), and founded the most learned sect among Brahmins, called the Smartava. The legends about him are as numerous as his philosophical writings. At the age of 32 he went to Kashmir, and reaching Kedaranath in the Himalayas, entered a cave alone, whence he never returned. His followers claim that he did not die, but simply retired from the world.

Shantiniketan. A town in West Bengal, India, famous for Rabindranath Tagore's Ashram and the Visva-Bharati University founded by him. The university became a centre for education, culture, and the arts, promoting Tagore's vision of global unity and learning.

Shaolin. A renowned monastery in China, the birthplace of Chan Buddhism.

Sharira (*Sk.*, "body"). Envelope or body; also used as a synonym for *ringsel*.

Shelley, Percy Bysshe (1792–1822). A British poet and writer; the author of *Prometheus Unbound* (1820).

Shells. A Kabbalistic name for the phantoms of the dead, the "spirits" of the spiritualists that figure in physical phenomena; so named on account of their being simply illusive forms, empty of their higher principles.

Shenxiu (c.606–706). One of the most influential representatives of the Northern School of Chan Buddhism, known as the East Mountain School; in certain records, recognized as the sixth patriarch of Chan Buddhism, although other sources indicate Huineng as the sixth patriarch. Both were the disciples of Hongren, the fifth patriarch of the Chan School. Shenxiu spread Chan Buddhism in the north of China and emphasized "gradual awakening," teaching that enlightenment comes through progressive meditation and practice rather than "sudden" realization, as was taught by Huineng.

Shigatse. The second-largest city in Tibet, where Tashi Lhunpo Monastery, the seat of the Panchen Lama, is located.

Shila (*Pali*). Morality; perfect harmony in word and deed; one of the paramitas of perfection.

Shiva (*Sk.*, "auspicious one"). The third person of the Hindu Trinity (the Trimurti). A god of the first order, and in his character of Destroyer, he is higher than Vishnu, the Preserver, as he destroys only to regenerate on a higher plane. He is born as Rudra, the Kumara, and is the patron of all the yogis, being called, as such, Mahadeva (*Sk.*, "Great God").

In the current period of the Solar System, the Ray of Shiva — the First Ray of Will and Power — cannot be manifested in full measure, since it acquires a destructive aspect if there are not enough loving, pure hearts. In order to perceive this Ray, one must first assimilate the Ray of Vishnu — the Second Ray of Love-Wisdom. In the current Solar System the First Ray is manifest as the Seventh Ray — the Ray of Transfiguration whose Lord is Master Rakoczy, also known as Saint-Germain.

Shivananda, Swami (1887–1963). An influential Indian yogi and spiritual teacher; founder of the Divine Life Society. Shivananda promoted the practice of yoga and Vedanta, emphasizing selfless service, meditation, and the integration of body, mind, and soul.

Shivo'Ham So'Ham (*Sk.*, "I am Shiva, I am That"). A phase that signifies the realization of one's unity with the Divine Essence or universal consciousness represented by Shiva, affirming that the individual self is not separate from the ultimate reality.

Shrama (*Sk.*). Labour, exertion; hard study.

Shramanas. Buddhist priests, ascetics, and postulants for Nirvana; "they who have to place a restraint on their thoughts." The word *shaman* is a corruption of this primitive word.

Shravaka (*Sk.*, "one who causes to hear"). A preacher. In Buddhism it denotes a disciple or chela.

Shru (*Sk.*). To hear, listen, learn, study.

Shvapaka (*Sk.*). An outcast; a degraded class.

Sibelius, Jean (1865–1957). A Finnish composer and representative of the Golden Age of Finnish Art.

Siddhis (*Sk.*, "attributes of perfection"). Phenomenal powers acquired through holiness by yogis.

Sikkim. A state in India neighbouring Tibet.

Silliman, Benjamin, Jr. (1816–1885). A professor of chemistry at Yale University; the author of *Principles of Physics, or Natural Philosophy* (1866).

Sine qua non (*Lat.*). Something that is absolutely essential.

Sirius (*Gr.*, "glowing"). The brightest star, the dog-star, *Sothis* in Egyptian, the sacred star worshipped by the people of Egypt and reverenced by the occultists; by the former because its heliacal rising with the Sun was a sign of the beneficent inundation of the Nile, and by the latter because it is mysteriously associated with Thoth-Hermes, god of wisdom, and Mercury, in another form. Thus Sothis-Sirius had, and still has, a mystic and direct influence over the whole living Heaven, and is connected with almost every god and goddess. It was "Isis in the heaven" and called *Isis-Sothis*, for Isis was "in the constellation of the dog," as is declared on her monuments. "The soul of Osiris was believed to reside in a personage who walks with great steps in front of Sothis, sceptre in hand and a whip upon his shoulder" (*Egyptian Belief*).

Sirius is also Anuhis and is directly connected with the ring "Pass me not"; it is, moreover, identical with Mithra, the Persian Mystery god, and with Horus and even Hathor, called sometimes the goddess Sothis. Being connected to the Pyramid, Sirius was, therefore, connected with the Initiations which took place inside it. A temple to Sirius-Sothis once existed within the great temple of Dendera in Egypt. In Zoroastrianism, Sirius is especially revered, being called *Tishtrya*, "whom Ahura Mazda has established as a lord and overseer above all stars, in the same way as he has established Zarathustra above men." To sum up, Sirius is certainly found in connection with every religion of antiquity.

Since ancient times, 19 July has been a sacred date associated with the manifestation of the energies of Sirius. For example, the priests of ancient Egypt built the Great Pyramid of Giza in such a way that Sirius would always appear in its vertical corridor on 19 July, on the day of the Sun God Ra and the New Year, and illuminate the entire inner space of the pyramid, where Initiations would take place in the light of the star's rays.

The Egyptians believed that their Gods descended from Sirius, as they realized that Sirius plays a role of great importance in the development of civilization on Earth. Subsequently, it was closely associated with each of the ancient religions. For example, even in the Quran, verse 53:49 says that Allah, or God, is the Lord of Sirius. Similarly, Christianity has adopted much from ancient religions, having rightly identified the symbolism of the ancient Sun God with Christ.

Thousands of years have passed since those remote times, calendars have changed, and the phenomenon of precession has somewhat modified the location of celestial bodies in relation to Earth, and yet this date continues to play a significant role at the present developmental stage of humankind. Here it is the numerical code that is important.

The number 1 is the number of the Divine, and 9 is the number of Transfiguration. Together — 19 — they signify Divine Transfiguration. Added together these numbers give 10 — the number of the Human Kingdom. Here again, 1 is the Divine number and 0 symbolizes a New Round of Origination. And so, it would appear that 19 is the number of the New World.

July marks the peak of the Sun's manifestation of light in terms of the intensity of its fire and energetical impact. This explains why rituals associated with the ancient cult of the Sun were held in July.

Furthermore, according to ancient records, every six thousand years Sirius emits new currents carrying a renewed composition of energies that are directed toward Earth and the entire Solar System. These energies further the beginning of a new stage of development. Just as a human body renews its structure at the cellular level every seven years, so the Earth transfigures its energy structure every seven thousand years. Here the number six has great significance, since the seventh stage is, at the same time, the first at a higher level. Thus, the seventh millennium in which humanity is currently living is the last phase of the passing cycle and the first of the coming Golden Age.

For this reason, every year in modern times, 19 July is characterized with a special energy: all of humankind and the planet undergo a kind of Initiation in the rays of this mysterious star, which was worshiped by all the peoples of antiquity.

This day is a fortuitous time to visit energetically powerful places such as shrines and temples that attract a large number of people. After all, these were built in areas that are especially connected with the Cosmos in order to reinforce human prayers. Thanks to the phenomenon of global prayer, whether individual prayers are uttered in such places of power or simply wherever one happens to be, everyone can make an invaluable contribution to the cause of the triumph of Light on Earth.

In all the seven spheres of Earth there can be no more than one thousand representatives of Sirius because each bears the energy potential of 6 *argo* or more. A collective of more than this number would literally incinerate the planet.

Six glorious virtues. See *paramitas*.

Skanda (*Sk.*, "one who leaps"). Another name in Hinduism for Sanat Kumara.

So Ham or **Soham** (*Sk.*, "That is I"). A mystic syllable, being the reverse of *Hamsa*. Hamsa is equal to *A-ham-sa*, three words meaning "I am That"; while divided in still another way it will read *So-ham*, "That is I." In the word *Hamsa* is contained the doctrine of the identity of human essence with Divine Essence for those who understand the language of wisdom. In another context, Hamsa represents *evolution*, and Soham, *involution*.

Society for Psychical Research. A British organization, founded in 1882. In 1884, the S.P.R. issued an accusatory report against H. P. Blavatsky based on fabricated evidence. This substantially damaged Blavatsky's reputation and health. However, in 1986, the S.P.R. issued a press release headlined: "Madame Blavatsky, co-founder of the Theosophical Society, was unjustly condemned, new study concludes." Dr. Vernon Harrison, who re-examined the case, finished his report with the words: "I apologize to her that it has taken us one hundred years to demonstrate that she wrote truly."

Socrates (c.470–399 BCE). A Greek philosopher.

Sokpo Sherab Gyatso (d.1909). A Mongolian scholar, astrologer, monk, and tutor to the Eighth Panchen Lama. He founded Ghoom Monastery in 1850 and headed it until 1905. Later he went to Tibet and died in his province of birth. He is believed to have authored several books on Tibetan astrology, but these were lost from the library of Ghoom Monastery in later years.

Sherab Gyatso assisted his disciple, Lobzang Mingyur Dorje, in creating *Tibet-English Dictionary*, published in 1902 by Calcutta University. L. M. Dorje was very close to the Roerich family and collaborated with George de Roerich on numerous projects, being his teacher and friend. On one occasion Dorje brought an image of the Buddha to Helena Roerich saying that he did so at the command of the White Tara, who had appeared in his dream and ordered him to take it from his shrine and gift it to the lady who lived in Talai Pho Brang.

Solar System. A planetary system with a central star, the Sun. The present Solar System consists of 14 planets, although some of these are not yet visible or are in the process of formation.

The general scheme for the formation of any system is this: A comet partially cools and settles as a sun. Gradually it attracts around it planets that are as yet unattached to any centre, and over millions of years a Solar System is formed. The worn-out planet becomes a moon to a planet in another system.

Every planet is inhabited but they are at different levels of development. It is incorrect to assume that the farther a planet is from the Sun, the more primitive it is. Indeed, Uranus, Neptune, and Pluto are the most advanced planets of all; Venus is higher than Jupiter in its development; Mars and Mercury are currently undergoing a period of obscuration, or a subsiding of manifested life, but their new cycle of evolution will be at a higher level than the present one on Earth; Saturn is the lowest planet — there the process of creating conditions for life is just beginning.

According to esoteric tradition, Saturn was the firstborn son of Sirius and the twin brother of Uranus, being formed from the explosion of Sirius. Saturn became the central star, but was not inhabited because it lacked cosmic magnetism — essential for life and the proper development of the entire System — and was replaced by Uranus. Subsequently, the Sun appeared, first as a comet. Through tremendous force of magnetism it eventually became the central star, superseding Uranus.

Earth, Venus, Jupiter, and Mars are the carriers of humanity, but the physical phase of development occurs only on Earth.

Mercury is in the Fifth Round of Evolution. The development of life on the planet was peculiar and brief. There has been no conscious life on the planet for hundreds of millennia. Mercury is undergoing a process of obscuration which makes the situation on the planet very difficult; the elements are in a state of acute tension or struggle, making life here impossible at the current time. Mercury's new cycle, should one take place, will be more advanced than the current earthly cycle. The planet's proximity to the Sun will not condition its advanced development. Mercury's subtle spheres are exhausted, and those that inhabit them await a new planet to which they may move, since they were unable to adapt on Venus.

Venus is in the Seventh Round of Evolution and is inhabited by the Seventh Race. Those who dwell on it call the planet *Tula*. Venus was born during the Manvantara of Saturn, when Saturn was the central star of the system. Venus is more advanced than Jupiter in its evolution, as it has already completed the cycle in which its humanity was to achieve a certain level of perfection. No longer capable of giving its inhabitants anything new, they wait for a new planet to occupy. Nonetheless, the vibrations of Venus are so subtle, only the highest spirits from Earth could appear there, and at that, with no particular advantage to themselves. Evolution on Venus is different, marked by a high degree of spirituality but also by an intellectual development significantly inferior to that on Earth.

In its material form, life on Venus ended millions of years ago. It now exists in dense astral bodies, and therefore, the planet has a real kingdom of flight: people fly, birds fly, and even fish fly. Moreover, birds understand human speech. Instead of in newspapers, words are written in the air. The colours of birds and fish are characterized by amazing beauty and variety. There are no insects or predators on Venus at all. When the planet was in the previous Round, the Teachers transferred bees and ants to Earth for the edification of humanity. Legend has it that Isis brought wheat to Earth from Venus.

When in *The Mahatma Letters* it is said that the Buddha, having come to Earth, was a man of the Sixth Round, this means that before his coming to Earth, the Buddha resided on another planet, Venus, which was then in the Sixth Round of development; just as the previous Lord of Shambhala, known in his incarnation as Plato and Confucius, having come from Jupiter, then in the Fifth Round, can be called a man of the Fifth Round.

Despite the fact that humanity on Venus must undergo raging storms with which it has to fight, their whole life is quite calm compared to earthly existence. They know nothing of war, murder, or destruction. They experience neither envy nor jealousy, and they never take revenge with the cruelty that people on Earth do, for they know the karma of the avenger. People remember their previous incarnations and try their hardest to improve their karma.

On Venus, people live in densified astral bodies for up to 40 years before they disintegrate. To have a child, a man and a woman evoke the energy of space and, fixing their gaze, create a new being. At birth a baby will display the same stage of development as a seven-year-old child on Earth.

There is not the gap between the consciousness of the masses and high individuals that there is on Earth. The masses on Venus are so advanced in their development that no particular individual differs to any great extent.

A tree from Venus is now growing in Dokiood and drops of *prana* fall from the petals of its blossom.

When the New Planet appears in the Solar System, Mercury and Venus will become its moons, giving their entire lives to it, and then humanity on these planets will move to a new home.

Mars was inhabited during the previous Manvantara of Uranus, but has occupied a state of obscuration throughout the entire Manvantara of the Sun. The Martians left the physical planet Mars long ago and moved to other planets, but most are still present in the subtle spheres around Mars. This planet is beginning to come out of obscuration and will soon receive new life from the influence that the rays of new stars and planets will have upon it. On Mars, again, signs of life will appear but in exceedingly primitive form, as Mars lacks, still, the material necessary for the formation of bodies suitable to house spirits, such as spirits of earthly evolution. The formation of such bodies will take millions of years.

Civilization on Mars was destroyed by a catastrophe caused by the explosion of the planet referred to as Best Planet, Atlu (its full name cannot be given). Scientists have also named it Phaeton, after the son of the sun god Helios in Greek mythology, who with disastrous consequences loses control of his father's solar chariot and is eventually struck down by a bolt of Zeus' lightning.

Phaeton was a beautiful planet on which humanity had reached an exceptionally high level of development, higher than humanity's current level of development on Earth. Ancient Greek art was modelled on Lucifer's art on Phaeton, where, at that time, he was the creator of incredible harmony and a consummate sculptor of forms. However, like the history of Atlantis on Earth, Lucifer began his destructive activities on Phaeton which led to debauchery and the violation of Cosmic Laws reaching its apogee among the planet's population. Cosmic Justice was left with no other choice than to destroy Phaeton in order to preserve the other planets in the Solar System. Phaeton perished in a collision with a bolide, shattering into millions of asteroids that now form the belt located between Mars and Jupiter.

The explosion of Phaeton deprived Mars of all physical life and wiped out Martian civilization. Taking the blow upon itself, Mars protected and, consequently, saved Earth, a planet on which physical humanity was just beginning its existence in the form of primitive beings.

In the 1970s, photographs were taken on Mars of pyramids and a "face," which indicated that high forms of life had once existed there. Soon these photos in which the pyramids and the "face on Mars" could be clearly seen were suppressed. The explanation given was that a peculiar play of shadows had created an optical illusion, and, later, the photographs were replaced with newer ones that showed nothing of the kind. However, the interest of the US Central Intelligence Agency (CIA) in exploring Mars by means of the Stargate Project points to the fact that the first photographs were genuine. This secret US Army unit was established in 1977 to investigate anomalous phenomena. There is no doubt that the CIA worked with gifted individuals whose psychic abilities were real and verified.

The CIA document relating to Mars was declassified in 2017 and appeared online at the end of 2024. The psychic explorer was given exactly the same geographic coordinates as the area where the pyramids were spotted in the first photos released by NASA (the Cydonia region). The historical period was set to one million years BCE. When the explorer said, having observed this period, that there was a "geological problem," he was asked to go to the time before that period. The explorer saw the pyramids and the Martians, describing them in the following way: "They appear thin and tall, but they are very large . . . wearing some kind of strange clothes" (CIA, *Mars Exploration, May 22, 1984*). The experiment suggested that a human population died on Mars after intense storms ripped through the planet. The storms might have been blast waves from the destruction of Phaeton.

The population was warned of imminent disaster. Some managed to escape to Earth, others remained and died, moving into the Subtle Spheres of the planet, and still others were drawn into Mars' orbit. They needed to break through, but failed to move beyond the field of attraction; their souls left, yet their bodies remained in spaceships as satellites around Mars that have become enveloped in cosmic dust.

This is why *The Secret Doctrine* hints: "Mars has two satellites to which he has no right. . . . Phobos, the supposed 'inner' satellite, is no satellite at all."

In March 2010, after analysing data received in 2008 by the Mars Express mission, the European Space Agency (ESA) declared that Phobos was not natural. The ESA study abstract that appeared in the peer-reviewed *Geophysical Research Letters* revealed that Phobos was not what many generations of astrophysicists and astronomers had believed it to be: a captured asteroid.

"We conclude that the interior of Phobos likely contains large voids. When applied to various hypotheses bearing on the origin of Phobos, these results are inconsistent with the proposition that Phobos is a captured asteroid"

("Radio science result from 2008 Phobos Flyby now accepted for publication," *ESA Mars Express Blog*).

Later, the ESA official website published radio-tracking graphs, which were independently analysed. The findings strongly supported the idea that the graphs demonstrate what radar echoes would look like if they came back from inside a huge geometric hollow spaceship.

Of course, no bones can ever be found of those who originally came from Mars, because their bodily structures were more rarefied than our own physical bodies. At that time, while the habitat on Earth was different (distinct from that on Mars), it still maintained larger quantities of the fundamental materials found in the Red Planet. A Cosmic Experiment was undertaken with the aim of both surviving on Earth and at least partially preserving the evolutionary Martian branch which came to be established on Earth.

Firstly, the earthly atmosphere favoured the gradual densification of the rarefied tissues of the Martians.

Secondly, like the Sons of God who came from other Worlds and entered into relationships with women of Earth, the Martians also began to "join" the ranks of beings begotten by Earth. As a result of the merging of masculine and feminine principles, the Martians began to acquire flesh and blood; however, now a different "people" was formed, which later became known by the name of Maya. As concerns the first round of arrivals from Mars, it should be borne in mind that these Martians only remained "in pure form" for a certain period of time. Nonetheless, the Martian spirit was still partially preserved among the Mayan peoples.

Thirdly, it is impossible for the human mind to embrace the full scope of the Cosmic Experiment involving the two planets in which both the Guardians of Mars and the Masters of Earth's humanity played an active part. Nor can it be said in all confidence that a final full stop has been put to this cause.

Jupiter is approaching the Sixth Round of Evolution. It was begotten almost simultaneously with Venus during the Manvantara of Saturn, but it is older than Venus and Mars. Just like Venus, Jupiter can only accept very high-level spirits in a moral sense, for Jupiter is characterized by a high degree of morality overall.

The peculiarities of the evolution of Jupiter mean that this planet would not be able to provide Earth-dwellers with a greater degree of satisfaction and advancement. Intelligence and therefore imagination are little developed. To some extent knowledge of the spirit replaces what is lacking in intellect. For a great thinker life on Jupiter would be boring and monotonous. Its advantages — a wonderful climate and the constant atmosphere and beauty of springtime — might also prove tiresome.

Jupiter does not contain the number of elements necessary for the solidification of the planet or for the densification of the outer bodies of its inhabitants as these outer bodies are extremely subtle, similar to the mental bodies of Earth-dwellers. This state does not serve as an incentive for activity, since they do not experience need and exist in a state of constant bliss.

Mahatma Koot Hoomi explains: "The whole of our system is imperceptibly shifting its position in space. The relative distance between planets remaining ever the same, and being in no wise affected by the displacement of the whole system; and the distance between the latter and the stars and other suns being so incommensurable as to produce but little if any perceptible change for centuries and millenniums to come; no astronomer will perceive it *telescopically*, until Jupiter and some other planets, whose little luminous points hide now from our sight millions upon millions of stars (all but some five thousand or six thousand), will suddenly let us have a peep at a few of the *Raja-Suns* they are now hiding. There is such a king-star right behind Jupiter that no mortal physical eye has ever seen during this, our Round.

"Could it be so perceived it would appear, through the best telescope with a power of multiplying its diameter ten thousand times, still a small dimensionless point, thrown into the shadow by the brightness of any planet; nevertheless, this world is thousands of times larger than Jupiter. The violent disturbance of its atmosphere, and even its red spot that so intrigues science lately, are due 1) to that shifting and 2) to the influence of that Raja-Star. In its present position in space, imperceptibly small though it be, the metallic substances of which it is mainly composed are expanding and gradually transforming themselves into aeriform fluids — the state of our own earth and its six sister globes before the first Round — and becoming part of its atmosphere" (*The Mahatma Letters*).

The Beautiful Being mentioned in Elsa Barker's books, *Letters from a Living Dead Man* (1914) and *War Letters from the Living Dead Man* (1915), is from Jupiter.

Saturn is preparing to accept the majority of earthly humanity that has never been able to rise above animal instinct. Conditions on the planet are extremely difficult. Between Saturn and Earth there is a special connecting channel called the *Eighth Sphere*. In *The Mahatma Letters*, the Eighth Sphere is also called the "Dwelling of Mara" and the "Planet of Death." One may also come across instances in which the Moon was referred to by these same terms, and here it should be understood that this was the case because Mara (Satan) had his subtle-plane abode on the dark side of the Moon. Now Saturn is the Dwelling of Mara.

An outflow of human mass from Earth, which is unsuitable for further evolution, moves through the channel of the Eighth Sphere. If in past times only the most evil and hopelessly fallen entered the Eighth Sphere, now this also applies to all those on whose monads, over the course of numerous lifetimes, no light-bearing deeds have been imprinted. Their quaternaries will subsequently split into primary elements, which the elemental forces corresponding to them will absorb, and their triads will begin their evolution anew on Saturn, starting with minerals, in the complete darkness of the two-dimensional world. With time, five sixths of present humanity will move to Saturn through the Eighth Sphere. Subsequently, Saturn will have to leave the Solar System.

Of all the countries on Earth, not just on the physical plane, India represents the Entrance Gate of the Eighth Sphere for those destined for Saturn. This does not mean that all those incarnated there are doomed, quite the opposite: they have greater chances of remaining after the final test of life than those incarnated in other countries. If the Slavic lands represent the Heart of the planet, then India is the Liver, the functions of which are the formation and accumulation of energy essential to the body, and the cleansing of the blood of poisons and harmful substances. India is the striking Sword of Justice, which cuts the wheat from the chaff. Being a huge testing ground for billions of both incarnated and disembodied human souls, it provides them with their last chance. For some, the harsh conditions of India may seem like hell, but for others this country will become Paradise, because having tested the strength of their human spirits, it will rouse them to ascend to higher levels. This is why the lands of India have always seen the largest number of saints who have shown the one truly right Path. For example, the Spirit of Sathya Sai Baba was the permanent Teacher for the Third Race of humanity, and his last incarnation in India before moving to the Sun was intended to help people who were delayed on their spiritual path.

Uranus is an extinct sun that has undergone fiery transformation into a sacred planet. It was the sun of the Solar System many billions of years before the formation of the present Sun. Therefore, until it cools completely life on Uranus is closer to the Subtle Plane. Uranus is subject to the double attraction of the Sun and Sirius. The attraction of Sirius is the stronger, which explains why Uranus is gradually moving further away from the Solar System. This process will take many millions of years to complete. In the distant future Uranus will be covered with vegetation. No poisonous species will be admitted. Uranus will become the optimal planet for the highest representatives of humanity to inhabit, due to its high vibrations.

Neptune is a special sun, but not a planet, and like Uranus, it does not yet have any inhabitants aside from the High Spirits who watch over it. Neptune is younger than Uranus by a whole Manvantara, but it also originates from Sirius. Neptune is moving into a new system that is forming around the star that will appear in the future as a substitute for the current Sun.

Pluto is a large asteroid, or fragment, of the planet Phaeton, which perished in the previous Manvantara of Uranus.

The books of *Agni Yoga* talk about the battle between Uranus and Saturn. But more specifically, it is the radiation from these planets that takes part in the battle. After all, each celestial orb is a conglomerate of the special vibrations and radiations of everything that exists on it, and thus, each heavenly body represents a special individuality, strikingly different from any other. Therefore, among them one should find planets of completely differing degrees of intensity, properties, and qualities. When the rays of such diverse planets intersect due to the transitions and movements of the latter in space, it indeed appears to be a battle, as a result of which great perturbations occur throughout space, and especially on all those celestial bodies that are reached by these rays.

The planet Saturn is still in a very low state of development, while Uranus stands much higher than all the known planets in the Solar System in terms of the quality of its intensity. Neptune and Uranus already belong to the highest attractive force and do not depend so much on the Sun of the Solar System. Therefore, when the rays of Saturn intersect with the rays of Uranus, huge disharmony occurs, which is greatly reflected in the entire space affected by their rays. The rays of Uranus are much more powerful than those of Saturn, therefore, of course, the purification and raising of vibrations in the surrounding atmosphere has a serious impact on many people. The atmosphere of vice is now closer to Earth's inhabitants than the sublime purity of the rays of Uranus, which awaken and raise human consciousness to a new understanding of a more responsible life, directing them to carry out selfless heroic deeds for the sake of the common good.

Humanity represents the higher energy centres of each planet that it inhabits. From this it is clear that all who are living on a planet must strive to improve their spirit and to refine the qualities of their energies, so that the totality of the radiation of such a planet contributes to great harmony in space. Every second, worlds are destroyed and born in space. And the collapse of worlds occurs precisely on account of disharmony.

Planets are born under the supervision of Great Spirits, who often entrust the overseeing of their development and even their guidance to other Spirits that bear in the seed of their spirit energies that are identical in potential to the energies of a given planet and its progenitor.

The Lord of the populated world is a Spirit who has passed through countless existences over many aeons and even solar Manvantaras in different states and even in different worlds. Each inhabited world has its own Senior Leader as well as junior ones. The Senior Leader can move to a new planet and give it a new impulse before moving again to another planet, and so on. The Senior Leader is the long-suffering Hierarch of the Solar System, the Lord M.

The originators of worlds do not always stay there. They only serve to provide the initial impulse of conscious life on a planet and a certain degree of development. Then they move to other, higher worlds, which also need a new impulse for their further development. This can come only through contact with the consciousness of a human spirit that is in harmony with the aura of the planet or that already possesses the solar consciousness of the Supreme Hierarch.

Likewise, the Senior Leader is not always the progenitor of the planet. He only imparts His intense vibration and builds every ideal form and type. But the further development of subtle bodies into densified bodies occurs with the help of junior leaders who watch over their correct combination and development.

Subsequently, the development of the lower self on Earth or the awareness of one's separateness did not just bring forth confusion; freedom resulted in flawed combinations and gave birth to all the ugly forms and things, which were then swept away by catastrophes, or even self-destructed through unsuitable combinations. The Leaders selected the best and populated the planet again, and then, with the development of instinct, these beings gradually began to understand the vibrations or energies corresponding to them and gather into separate groups, and this is how the first castes were formed. Thus, castes were already established among the first people and animals.

Every spirit or monad is born under the rays of a certain celestial body, and therefore, the seed of his spirit contains in its potential all the identical energies inherent in this heavenly body, which remains his guiding star for the entire Manvantara. Thus, Lucifer had in his body all the features of the composition of Saturn, and the energies of the seed of his spirit are quite identical with the energies radiated by Earth. This gave him the Cosmic Right to become the ruler of the planet. However, he was never a Senior Leader, and his title "the Prince (not King) of this world" always reflected this.

The spirit of the Lord of the planet passes through *human form* (as indicated above, the higher centres of the planet are contained in the higher centres of the human being) as the primary teacher of how to master the matter inherent there. Lucifer knew the depths of Earth, and all its energies were subordinated to him. Therefore, along with other Sons of Light, who incarnated in various nations, he undoubtedly had to participate in the evolution of earthly humanity, its mental awakening and development.

Lucifer developed the might of densifying subtle bodies, thereby furthering the development of the intellect. But pride seized him. Lucifer fell because he wanted to limit the evolution of humanity, tying it only to Earth, to his principality. This desire arose from jealousy and envy of the Brothers who were at a higher spiritual level.

According to Eastern traditions, Lucifer's rebellion originated at the end of the Third Race. Then, in order to save humanity, the Great Lord, the Solar Hierarch of Uranus, who had come from Venus, took upon Himself responsibility for the planet, as well as the excruciating and selfless feat of awakening the spirit and shifting consciousnesses in the mass of beings Lucifer had condemned. Thus, having appeared on Earth, the Lord of Uranus opposed the darkness led by the Lord of Saturn. That is why during this Manvantara the Great Lord M. stands at the head both as a Manu and as the Teacher of Teachers. It is truly thanks to Him, the bearer and giver of Amrita, that the inhabitants of Earth joined the infinite existence. The Solar Hierarch constantly stands guard.

The radiations emanated by the planets are created by the mutual efforts of their inhabitants. But human free will is capable of creating hell out of paradise. So it is that Earth's aura, which once had a beautiful golden colour, turned into a slate-coloured sphere surrounded by clouds of grey-brown gas.

Armageddon is headed by Saturn on the side of the dark forces and by Uranus on the side of the Forces of Light. The main Battle ended with the defeat of Lucifer at the end of 1949. Saturn began to decompose and move away from the Solar System, but its lethal rays still remain and poison Earth's atmosphere. Of course, the rays of high Uranus and the invisible Star of the Mother of the World will cleanse Earth's atmosphere, but this will take time, which may also be filled with ominous events, especially in the West. Although the main cause has been eliminated, the centuries-old consequences of sowing malice and enmity cannot be eradicated or exhausted quickly and easily.

Of course, one cannot usually speak of a fight between the Logoi of the planets. But in this case, one could even go so far as to say that the Logoi of the planets Uranus and Earth fought among themselves, for it was the former lord of Earth who opposed every good influence that could have raised the vibrations of Earth creating an atmosphere that would have been intolerable for the fallen lord. That is why, when the Earth began to ascend to a higher stage of development, the Prince of this world had to retreat to the low planet Saturn, where its difficult conditions could bring about his redemption.

The example of Lucifer sufficiently demonstrates that individuality cannot be destroyed. *The Mahatma Letters* emphasize the eternal steady movement forward, which impels everything living to follow the same fundamental impulse, and therefore, every pause inevitably throws everything back. Likewise, even perfect earthly human beings, if they stop in their progress and do not come to their senses quickly enough, can, in their downward run, reach such a low state that all their higher centres will become silent. Their higher individuality will lose contact with the vehicles necessary for nourishment and those elements that compose the vortex of their auric environment, and, finally, become separated from their lower principles. Deprived of the power that holds them together, the lower principles of such soulless beings decompose and enter a period of recycling as cosmic waste. The separated higher individuality itself, after long cycles of time, will receive a new opportunity for incarnation on another planet, but it will have to build the vehicles, or bodies, required for incarnation starting from the lower kingdoms of Nature, until, finally, a human form is built in which it can again incarnate.

Therefore, if the majority of humanity wants to remain on Earth, it must be resurrected in spirit. The fiery energies referred to in all ancient teachings have already reached the planet. Lucifer feared these energies which is why he planned to explode the planet before its time. In due course, their intensity will become even higher, making existence impossible for those souls whose vibrations have not risen higher than those of animals.

During the Fourth Round, the visible Sun periodically renews the formula of its energy sound due to the strengthened influence of the Invisible Sun. That is, although the Sun itself remains, it changes completely at the energetic level. Therefore, in esoteric teachings it is said that there should be three Suns in total which manifest in the manner of the Trimurti of Brahma, Vishnu, and Shiva, and, accordingly, three Solar Systems, or rather, three periods of the Solar System.

The task of the First Solar System was Knowledge, the formation of the physical body, intellect, and mind; this was the Masculine System which covered the period from the First to the Fourth Races. It ended with green as its dominant colour, the colour of knowledge. Now, during the Fifth Race, the Second Solar System is being manifested. The Second System is Feminine and its task is to embody Love-Wisdom and the opening of the Heart. This is why all the Great Teachers worship and serve the Great Feminine Principle, the Mother of the World. Souls who were most advanced in the former System were the first to enter the Second Solar System. According to Cosmic Laws, evolution on a new stage always begins by repeating its forerunner, therefore, much knowledge has been imparted to humanity in the current System and the colour green is dominant in Nature. Two thousand years ago, the time came to start fulfilling the mission of Love-Wisdom and Christ was the first to bestow such an opportunity on Earth. The Third System will be Androgynous — the two Principles, Male and Female, Spirit and Soul, will reunite; its task will be to experience Divine Will and Power. This reunification is already begun in part and will manifest itself fully during the period of the Sixth and Seventh Races which will exist almost simultaneously. Only those who succeed in properly developing the heart and synthesizing Knowledge and Love in Divine Wisdom will move into the third period of the Solar System.

The change of the Sun during the time of Atlantis, symbolically marked as being the Sun of Uranus (since Uranus was the Sun in the previous Manvantara, although not in the current one), resulted in a powerful flood, a shift in Earth's magnetic poles, and a change in the tilt of Earth's axis. At the end of 1952, Master M. told Helena Roerich that the north magnetic pole would be located in Russia. In 2019, scientists noticed that the speed of its movement from Canada towards Russia had increased abruptly, namely by four times: from about 15 kilometres (9 miles) per year, as in the period 1990–2005, to 50–60 kilometres (31–36 miles) per year, suggesting that it would be likely to reach the coast of Siberia within the next decade. This process also indicates that the current Second Sun has begun its renewal at an energy level, and is gradually becoming the Third.

When creating the present Solar System, the number 7 was incorporated into its foundation as an energy code, hence the sevenfold manifestation of the world and the structure of man and the planets. The next Solar System will have a twelvefold energy code which would explain why the number 12 also plays a significant role in the current System.

Solomon. The Initiated king of Israel, during whose reign in the tenth century BCE the country experienced the greatest flourishing.

Soma. A female disciple of the Buddha. Prior to her conversion to Buddhism she gained access to the three Vedas and became a learned Brahmin.

In Sanskrit, Soma means the Moon and also the juice of the plant of the same name used in the temples for trance purposes; a sacred beverage. Soma, the Moon, is the symbol of Secret Wisdom. In the Upanishads the word is used to denote gross matter (with an association of moisture) capable of producing life under the action of heat.

Sophia (*Gr.*, "wisdom"). The female Logos of the Gnostics; Universal Mind; and the female Holy Ghost among others.

Sophic. Relating to wisdom or knowledge.

Soul. The *nephesh* of the Bible; the vital principle, or the breath of life, which every animal, down to the infusoria, shares with man. In the translated Bible the word stands indifferently for life, blood, and soul. "Let us not kill his *nephesh*," says the original text; "Let us not kill *him*," reads the Christian translation (Genesis 37:21), and so on.

Sovan (*Sin.*, "stream-enterer"). The first of the four Paths which lead to Nirvana in yoga practice.

Sovani. One who has entered upon the first Path.

Sparta. A powerful city-state in ancient Greece, famous for its militarism, bravery, discipline, and austere way of life.

Spirit. The lack of any mutual agreement between writers in the use of this word has resulted in dire confusion. It is commonly made synonymous with *soul*; and the lexicographers countenance the usage. In Theosophical teachings, the term *Spirit* is applied solely to that which *belongs directly to Universal Consciousness*, and which is its homogeneous and unadulterated emanation. Thus, the higher mind in man or his Ego (*manas*) is, when linked indissolubly with *buddhi*, a spirit; while the term *soul*, human or even animal (the lower *manas* acting in animals as instinct), is applied only to *kama-manas*, and qualified as the living soul. This is *nephesh,* in Hebrew, the "breath of life." Spirit is formless and *immaterial,* being, when individualized, of the highest spiritual substance — *Suddhasattva* (Sk., "pure essence"), a substance not subject to the qualities of matter; a luminiferous and (to humankind) invisible substance, the divine essence of which the bodies of the manifesting Gods and highest Dhyanis are formed. Suddhasattva is a conscious state of spiritual Ego-ship rather than any essence.

Therefore, the Theosophists reject the appellation "spirits" for those phantoms which appear in the phenomenal manifestations of the spiritualists and call them "shells," and various other names.

Spirit, in short, is no entity in the sense of having form; for, as Buddhist philosophy has it, where there is a form, there is cause for pain and suffering. But each *individual* spirit — this individuality lasting only throughout the Manvantaric life-cycle — may be described as a *centre of consciousness,* a self-sentient and self-conscious centre; a state, not a conditioned individual. This is why there is such a wealth of words in Sanskrit to express the different states of Being, beings, and entities, each appellation showing the philosophical difference, the plane to which such a *unit* belongs, and the degree of its spirituality or materiality. Unfortunately, these terms are almost untranslatable into the Western tongues.

Spiritualism. In philosophy, a state or condition of mind that contrasts materialism or a material conception of things. Theosophy is pure spiritualism in that its doctrine postulates that all that exists is animated or informed by Universal Soul or Spirit, and that not a single atom in our universe can exist outside of this omnipresent Principle.

As for the belief of the same name, that is, the belief in constant communication between the living and the dead, whether through the mediumistic powers of the individual or a so-called medium, it amounts to nothing more than the materialization of spirit and the degradation of human and divine souls. Those who believe in such communication dishonour the dead and perform constant acts of sacrilege. In days of old, this belief and practice was aptly termed *necromancy.*

The movement of spiritualism began with rappings and other psychic phenomena connected with the Fox sisters in America around the middle of the nineteenth century. In order to counteract the evils arising from indiscriminate communications with disembodied entities, human and subhuman, without any knowledge of their nature, H. P. Blavatsky was sent to America in 1873 by the Trans-Himalayan Initiates to put forward the esoteric teaching. She visited many of the materialization séances of the Eddy brothers in Vermont as well as others and demonstrated that she could control the manifestations by her own trained will. The phenomena which she herself produced, then and later, were merely illustrations for the same purpose but were used by her enemies as a basis for charges of fraud and imposture.

In 1879, after writing *Isis Unveiled* and incurring the bitter enmity of the spiritualists, Blavatsky went to India to promote the study of the ancient Aryan philosophy and establish a branch of the Esoteric School. Born with a highly developed psychic apparatus, her family records reveal that all kinds of phenomena occurred during her childhood, and she relates that it was only after "a terrible struggle and a supreme effort of will, with the help of initiated friends" (i.e., her Teachers in Tibet) that she obtained complete control of it. No one, therefore, could be better qualified than she through her own experience of both aspects to deal with the matter. In 1888, referring to *Isis Unveiled,* she said: "It was my duty to point to the dangerous phases of modern spiritualism, and to bring to bear upon that question all the assertions and testimony of the ancient world and its sages that I could find. . . . Occult philosophy rests on the accumulated psychic *facts of thousands of years.* Spiritualism is but thirty-five years old, and has not as yet produced one recognized non-mediumistic adept."

The methods most commonly used in spiritualistic séances are: 1) table rapping and tilting for the spelling out of messages; 2) automatic writing either directly through the hand or by means of a *planchette* — a form of which is commonly used in China for divination purposes; 3) speaking and writing while in trance; 4) materialization of forms and other physical phenomena in a darkened room, the medium being entranced and enclosed in a "cabinet."

According to occult philosophy, the entities which usually communicate by these means are denizens of Kama-loka and include: 1) the *kama-rupas* or "shells" of deceased persons; 2) elementals or soulless beings not yet human; 3) suicides and victims of sudden death who must spend the remainder of their appointed life-span as "earth-walkers" in Kama-loka.

The Initiates say that they decided to risk the danger of making some of the esoteric teachings more widely known because "the infamous Shammars ['red cap' sorcerers] were leading Europe's best minds into the most insane and fatal of superstitions — spiritualism" (*The Mahatma Letters*). Unfortunately, the enormous losses during the two world wars threw millions of the third class entities enumerated above into Kama-loka. A great many of these must have suffered the ill effects of being attracted to séances, either because of the desire of relatives to communicate with them, or their own wish to renew their physical life through a medium.

Spleen. Corresponds to the *linga-sharira,* and serves as its dwelling-place in which it lies curled. As the *linga-sharira* is the reservoir of life for the body, the medium and vehicle of *prana,* the spleen acts as the centre of *prana* in the body, from which the life is pumped out and circulated. It is consequently a very delicate organ, though the physical spleen is only the cover for the real spleen.

Sri or **Shri** (*Sk.*, "holy," "revered"). A title of respect and honour often used for deities, saints, and respected persons. Examples include Sri Krishna and Sri Ramakrishna.

Srimad Bhagavatam or **Bhagavata Purana** (*Sk.*, "beautiful ancient story of the Lord"). One of the eighteen great Puranas, a collection of symbolical and allegorical sacred writings of Hinduism.

Srotapatti (*Sk.*). "One who has entered the stream," i.e., the stream or path that leads to Nirvana, or figuratively, to the Nirvanic Ocean. The same as *Sovani*.

St. Petersburg. A major Russian city founded by Peter the Great in 1703; the capital of the Russian Empire until 1918.

Stanford University. A prestigious private research university located in Stanford, California, recognized globally for its academic strength, research output, and proximity to Silicon Valley which has fostered innovations and startups.

Steiner, Rudolf (1861–1925). An Austrian philosopher, writer, and social reformer, who founded Anthroposophy, a movement seeking to integrate science, art, and spirituality. He was head of the Theosophical Society in Germany from 1902 to 1913.

Stevenson, Ian, MD (1918–2007). A Canadian-American psychiatrist and professor at the University of Virginia School of Medicine, known for his pioneering research on reincarnation and cases of children who claimed to remember past lives. His work aimed to provide evidence of reincarnation through meticulous case studies. He authored a number of books, including *Where Reincarnation and Biology Intersect* (1997) and *Children Who Remember Previous Lives* (2000).

Stoic. A follower of the philosophical school of Stoicism in ancient Greece. Stoicism teaches that the path to happiness is through cultivating certain virtues, while accepting the things one cannot change.

Stonehenge. A prehistoric monument located in Wiltshire, England, consisting of a ring of huge standing stones. *The Secret Doctrine* mentions:

"There are records which show Egyptian priests — Initiates — journeying in a north-westerly direction, *by land*, via what became later the Straits of Gibraltar; turning North and travelling through the future Phoenician settlements of Southern Gaul; then still further North, until reaching Carnac (Morbihan) they turned to the West again and arrived, *still travelling by land*, on the north-western promontory of the New Continent. [Or on what are now the British Islands, which were not yet detached from the main continent in those days. 'The ancient inhabitant of Picardy could pass into Great Britain without crossing the Channel. The British Isles were united to Gaul by an isthmus which has since been submerged' (Nicolas Joly, *Man Before Metals*).]

"What was the object of their long journey? And how far back must we place the date of such visits? The archaic records show the Initiates of the second sub-race of the Aryan family moving from one land to the other for the purpose of supervising the building of *menhirs* and dolmens, of colossal zodiacs in stone, and places of sepulchre to serve as receptacles for the ashes of generations to come. When was it? The fact of their crossing from France to Great Britain *by land* may give an idea of the date when such a journey could have been performed on *terra firma*."

Straight-knowledge. The heart-based knowledge conveyed through intuition; knowledge accumulated over the course of many reincarnations and stored in the chalice, the heart chakra, in which memories relating to all a person's past lives are preserved. The degree of illumination directly depends on this accumulation.

Stygian. Very dark; relating to the River Styx in Greek mythology, the principal river of the underworld, which the souls of the dead must cross.

Substance. Theosophists use the word in a dual sense, qualifying substance as perceptible and imperceptible, and drawing a distinction between material, psychic, and spiritual substances, separating them into *ideal* (i.e., existing on higher planes) and real substance.

Subtle Plane or **Subtle World**. See *Worlds* and *Kama-loka*.

Suez Canal. A canal in north-east Egypt which joins the Mediterranean Sea with the Red Sea, providing a sea route between Europe and the Indian Ocean.

Sufism. The mystical branch of Islam that seeks a direct personal experience of God through practices like meditation, chanting, and devotion. Sufis aim to transcend the material world and unite with the Divine through love and self-discipline.

Suicide. The gravest crime a person can commit not only against the self but against others, since that person may then become an elementary that will vampirize them. The same applies to the practice of euthanasia that does not eliminate a person's pain or suffering but increases it manifold after they transit into the Subtle World.

According to the Kabbalistic theory, a person has a precise number of years, days, and hours to live upon earth, and when the Ego consciously and deliberately rids itself of the body before the hour marked, they must still live on as a disembodied suffering soul for not one minute less than the period allotted to that person by fate. The Ego, or the sentient individual soul, is unable to free itself from Earth's magnetic attraction and so must vegetate and suffer all the torments of the mythical hell within it. The soul becomes an elementary spirit; and when the hour of deliverance strikes, having learnt nothing and in its mental torture having lost any memory of the little it knew on earth, the soul is violently ejected out of the earth's atmosphere and carried adrift. In this state, it is prey to the blind current which forces it into some new reincarnation which the soul itself is unable to select as it otherwise might with the help of its good deeds.

The rule is that a person who dies a natural death will remain from "a few hours to several short years," within the earth's field of attraction, i.e., in Kama-loka. There are exceptions in the case of suicides and those who die a violent death in general. Hence, an Ego who was destined to live, say, 80 or 90 years, but who either committed suicide or was killed in some accident, let us suppose at the age of 20, would have to spend in Kama-loka not "a few years," but 60 or 70 years as an *elementary*, or rather an "earth-walker," since this person is, much to their own misfortune, not even a "shell."

After death, in the Subtle World, a person's feelings are intensified manifold, and a person who died prematurely will experience the last moments of their earthly life over and over again. They will seethe for a long time in the sufferings which led them to take such a step. For example, a person who has lost a close one or their beloved and in grief has decided to commit suicide will again and again experience the death of a loved one and the full depth of suffering, prepare for suicide, and go through with it. And this cycle is experienced a great number of times until the energy of the thoughts associated with this period of life is exhausted.

Each life is given to pay off karmic debts. The Lords of Karma, or Guardian Angels, reveal to souls before their new incarnations why this or that incarnation has been chosen for them, what reasons, sown in the past, led to it, and why they will incarnate in this or that nation and in this or that family. They are given a specific task that will pay off some part of the karmic debt, and the souls voluntarily and with full understanding agree to go through the life that the Lords of Karma see as the best in terms of the conditions in which debts can be paid off (not necessarily the easiest or the most comfortable). Depending on the souls' spiritual development, they may be offered various incarnations and be able to choose one of them for themselves.

"God will never give you more than you can handle." If a person believed that they were incapable of taking any more, this was an illusion and one that is often reinforced by dark forces, who benefit from suicides and premature deaths as a result of wars, terrorist attacks, and mass murders for their own gain.

If a person ends their life without achieving anything that the soul agreed to do or without managing to complete a set task, the debts multiply. It is the same as taking a loan from a bank for a very large sum and on the way back simply losing all the money. The bank will not write off the debt because it was not its fault that the person lost the money. Now, the person will be forced into even greater debt in order to pay off the huge old debt as well as the new one.

Thus, when the energy that holds the suicide in the lower layers is exhausted and the person is ready for the next incarnation (provided they have not become an elementary), then the conditions of their new earthly life will be even worse than in the previous life, even though it seemed to the person at that time, illusorily so, that things could not possibly be any worse.

Suicides are usually found in the layers closest to the earth (the Eighth Sphere) because the magnetic attraction of their energies to the earth has not yet been eliminated. Their etheric or lower astral body makes them especially attached to earthly sensations. Only in very high spirits does this lower shell dissolve during life. Having a clear consciousness helps in such a transformation. Of course, this sphere is very heavy, but if during life the spirit strove for the Light, even occasionally, then here too, if the spirit is able to gather and direct its will, it may find the rare influence of the Higher Forces and with their help be able to improve its position. For the most part though, suicides never think about the Higher Worlds, and therefore, they cannot understand what has happened to them. If consciousness during life was clouded, then, of course, this fogginess intensifies even more after separation from the physical body. Consciousness and its highest quality — psychic energy — must be very clear and active during earthly life for impressions or deposits of energy to become imprinted on the centres of the subtle body; otherwise, when changing bodies the human being remains in the Subtle World in a half-asleep state.

Psychic energy is essential during the transition or change from one state to another. Our psychic energy carries us to the sphere that corresponds to our accumulations, and the stronger the spirit's pre-death aspiration, the higher it can rise. And if the supply of psychic energy is insufficient for it to remain in the Higher Sphere to which it was carried by the last powerful impulse, it will still preserve forever the memory of the raptures of spirit experienced in the sphere corresponding to its spiritual achievements. That is why in ancient times people took such care to ensure that their last minutes on Earth were joyful, and directed their minds towards the sublime.

These unfortunate suicides halt all flow of psychic energy. The despair that pushes them to commit an act of such madness represents the complete outflow of psychic energy after which they remain in the power of the earth's magnetic field. And their anguish and suffering will continue until the time of their natural death. In exceptional cases, when consciousness has been only temporarily darkened by a grave chain of circumstances, these unfortunates, upon remembering the Light, can find the strength of will to turn to Higher Help and strive for redemption. Therefore, a sincere heartfelt prayer addressed to the Forces of Light to offer assistance to such unfortunate ones will not go unanswered, provided, of course, that these unfortunate ones strive to rise in spirit as well.

Of course, among suicides the lower entities can indulge in all sorts of excess. And vampirism is far from being a rare phenomenon. Uneliminated, untransmuted energies draw them by force towards earthly sensations. The separation of the monad represents loss of the memory of the personality, not of the individuality. But the final and total separation of the monad from a person's other principles is a terrible thing, the worst thing that could happen in fact, since it delays the evolution of the individuality for many, many millennia.

The elements or energies that constituted a personality that has lost the magnetic connection with its monad, after the so-called death of the personality on the physical plane, are finally decomposed and drawn into a whirlpool of elements or energies that represent cosmic waste that can fill the stones of neighbouring planets or other lower formations. Many millions of years will pass before the monad can again appear and create new subtle vehicles. A human being is a highly complex creation, a true microcosm, and the loss of one link in the structure will entail a millennia-long delay in their evolution.

Therefore, the only help that the relatives and friends of a suicide can render to that soul is to pray with all the might of their hearts to the Higher Powers, asking that they provide assistance to the unfortunate one, and then mentally and with all their heart to address this individual in prayer, prompting, or rather, commanding them to strive to find the strength in themselves to strive for the Light, so that they may receive support in passing through the trial that they have brought upon themselves. Sincere prayer is the energy that the suicide lacks, and if it reaches them, and if it works, their torment may be brought to an end after which they will fall asleep and remain sleeping until the time of their natural death.

Sukshma Vishayatvam (*Sk.*, "subtle perception," "ability to perceive the subtle"). In yoga philosophy, the capacity of the mind or consciousness to perceive or understand realities beyond the physical, gross level, especially through advanced states of meditation (*samadhi*).

Sumeru (*Sk.*, "excellent Meru"). See *Meru*.

Summum bonum (*Lat.*). The highest or ultimate good.

Sun. The central star of the Solar System. Here the Supreme Fiery Beings reside. The Sun revolves around the central star of another System, Sirius, as one of its sun-planets, despite its being located a considerable distance away. Without the Sun, there would be no consciousness.

The visible Sun is a reflection of the true Sun: this reflection, as an outward concrete thing, is a *kama-rupa*, and all the suns form the *kama-rupa* of the Cosmos. To its own system the Sun is *buddhi*, the reflection and vehicle of the true Sun, which is *atma*, and which is invisible on this plane. All the *fohatic* forces — electricity, etc. — exist within this reflection.

The matter of the Sun's revolution is a mystery, since here one must take into account multilevel aspects, such as the orbit of the physically visible body up to the trajectory of the Central Spiritual Sun. From the visible to the invisible level, the Sun comprises twelve bodies which follow certain "paths" that cannot be calculated by earthly astronomers. Earthly devices, like astronomers, mostly deal with physical or dense as well as more or less rarefied liquid and gel-like substances. However, the chemical composition of the gaseous structures of the Subtle and Fiery Planes of the Sun are very different and they pave their own paths, outlining circles of advancement through the depths of the Cosmos, which implies passing by or around certain constellations.

Each of the twelve solar bodies has its own orbit. For example, the physical Sun moves along its orbit towards the constellation of Hercules, bringing with it all the other planets with the exception of Uranus and Neptune. In contrast, the Central Spiritual Sun — which also conceals a fiery-white core comprised of the quintessence of all the star's twelve structures, like the rainbow that absorbs all colours — makes its own full orbit of the ellipse which takes at least a billion years to complete.

The Sun appeared in the System as a comet from the constellation of Lyra at a time when Uranus was the central star, during the previous Manvantara. The comet had a strong magnetism and began to attract and absorb other comets, small planets, and various celestial bodies. During the present Manvantara, after assimilating a great number of energies the Sun became the central star of the System.

Colour, Light, and Sound govern in the Cosmic Spheres, giving birth to a multitude of unknown worlds. And while Sirius, which sets the dominant of the White *Colour*, refracts its Ray through Solar *Light*, *Sound* is the attribute of the constellation of Lyra. Thus, a mysterious triad is formed which has a direct influence on the Evolution not only of Earth, but of the entire Solar System. It is no coincidence that in ancient legends the constellation of Lyra is associated with Orpheus, who placed his own instrument in the celestial sphere.

The Sun plays the role of the Heart within the Solar System, pulsating at intervals of eleven years. Hence, the Sun is the repository of the vital force that is essential to all beings and planets of the System. Through it, from the invisible and far more powerful Central Spiritual Sun, there passes a Cosmic Ray which contains all the elements and energies that are given to the planets by the Sun. Solar light is the reflection of Spiritual Light — the Light of the Central Spiritual Sun. Further, the Sun receives the waste energies of the planets, transmutes them, and sends them back into the System. Therefore, it can be understood that with its low-frequency thinking, humanity poisons not only its own planet but also the Sun, which processes waste energies at the cost of shortening its own life. The period of inhalation and exhalation of the Sun's vital energy ranges from four to five years.

Solar flares are intensified impulses which give off the necessary ingredients. If one of the planets is in need of additional life-giving energies, the Sun increases its activity. Any disturbance in the harmony and balance of energy on a particular planet affects the overall balance of the whole System. As a result, the Sun, along with other stars, must intensify the energy that it transmits exclusively towards that planet. Sunspots increase the chemical impact of ray energy, and this in turn affects the human nervous system. Sunspots and explosions on the Sun cause contractions in the Earth's core, and this gives rise to earthquakes and floods and may even alter the planet's axial tilt. Solar rays contain all the ingredients of the Solar System. They exert a powerful effect on all life, acting as regulator for the entire System. For example, studying the composition of solar rays can provide accurate information on the weather a month in advance.

High Spirits from other Systems enter and exit the Solar System through the Sun. So, in order for High Spirits from Sirius, for example, to be incarnated on Earth, they travel through the Constellation of Orion, pass through the Sun, then through Pluto and all the other planets to Venus, and from Venus to Earth. This is because the supreme fiery energies must adapt gradually to the conditions of the planet during the descent of the High Spirits. If they went directly from Sirius to Earth, Earth would simply be burnt to ashes by the powerful intensity of the Fires.

In connection with the Age of Fire — the Age of the Heart, accompanied by periods of maximum activity of Universal Fire — the Sun enters a phase of maximum activity as well, thereby exerting an impact on the higher human energy centres. High-frequency vibrations emerge from the fiery core of the Sun and are directed into human hearts, contributing to the transfiguration of every human being.

Currently, the rays of the morning Sun have most benefits. To receive these currents, one should stand for 24–27 minutes, with one's chalice (heart chakra) turned to face the Sun, and in the evening, one should stand with one's back to the sunset. One should not stay in the open Sun around noon, since at this time the Solar Logos transmits impulses at the level of the subtle bodies.

Due to the fact that the Sun is gaining power under the influence of the Spiritual Sun, it must have in its aura the presence of those who have power of influence on its fiery-white core. Therefore, many Masters, including Morya, have already moved to the Sun.

Sunyata or **Shunyata** (*Sk.*). Void, space, nothingness. The name of the objective universe in the sense of its unreality and illusiveness.

Sushupti (*Sk.*). The deep sleep state.

Sutra (*Sk.*, "thread"). A collection of aphorisms in Hinduism, Buddhism, or Jainism.

Sutta Nipata (*Pali*, "collection of discourses"). A Buddhist scripture.

Suzuki, D. T. (1870–1966). A Japanese philosopher and author of books on Buddhism.

Svapna (*Sk.*, "dream"). A trance or dreamy condition; clairvoyance.

Svasamvedana (*Sk.*, "reflection which analyses itself"). A synonym of *paramartha*.

Swami (*Sk.*, "master," "lord"). A Hindu title of respect for a spiritual teacher or monk, often used in the case of those who have renounced worldly life to pursue spiritual practices and teachings. Examples include Swami Vivekananda and Swami Shivananda.

Swastika (*Sk.*, "well-being"). An ancient solar symbol of auspiciousness and well-being in various cultures, including Hinduism, Buddhism, and Jainism. It is distinct from the negative connotations of the twentieth-century Western context.

In popular notions, the swastika is the Jaina cross, or the "four-footed" cross. In esoteric philosophy, it is the most mystic and ancient diagram — the originator of the fire by friction and the 49 fires. Its symbol was stamped on the Buddha's heart and, therefore, called the "Heart's Seal." It is laid on the chests of departed Initiates after death, and it is mentioned with the greatest respect in the Ramayana. Engraved on every rock, temple, and prehistoric building of India, as well as wherever Buddhists have left their landmarks, the swastika is also found in China, Tibet, Thailand, and among the ancient Germanic nations, where it is known as Thor's Hammer. In occultism, it is as sacred as the Pythagorean Tetraktys of which it is indeed the double symbol.

Swedenborg, Emmanuel (1688–1772). The great Swedish seer and mystic. Of all mystics, certainly it is he who has influenced Theosophy the most, yet he left a far more profound impress on official science. For while as an astronomer, mathematician, physiologist, naturalist, and philosopher he had no rival, in psychology and metaphysics he was behind his time. When 46 years of age, he became a Theosophist and a seer; but, although his life had been at all times blameless and respectable, he was never a true philanthropist or an ascetic. His clairvoyant powers, however, were remarkable and yet they did not go beyond this plane of matter. All that he says of subjective worlds and spiritual beings is evidently far more the outcome of his exuberant fancy than of spiritual insight. He left behind him numerous works which are, sadly, misinterpreted by his followers.

Symbolism. The pictorial expression of an idea or a thought. Primordial writing had at first no characters. Instead a symbol generally stood for a whole phrase or sentence. A symbol is thus a recorded parable, and a parable, a spoken symbol. The Chinese written language is nothing more than symbolical writing, each of its several thousand letters being a symbol.

T

Tagore, Rabindranath (1861–1941). An Indian poet, writer, philosopher, and Nobel laureate in literature. He is called *Gurudev* as a term of respect, and his works spanned poetry, music, and philosophy. He is the original composer of India's national anthem.

Talai Pho Brang (*Tib.*, "Dalai Lama's palace"). A house in Darjeeling, India, where His Holiness the Thirteenth Dalai Lama stayed from 1910 to 1913, being in exile to escape the Chinese invasion. For this reason, local Tibetans started to refer to it as the Dalai Lama's Palace. The Roerich family stayed here from 1924 to 1925 and again in 1928.

Tamasic (*Sk.*, "darkness"). In the context of the *gunas* (qualities of nature), the quality of darkness, ignorance, and inertia. A tamasic person is associated with laziness, confusion, negativity, and a lack of motivation, reflecting a state of disharmony and delusion.

Tamerlane (1336–1405). A Turco-Mongol conqueror who founded the Timurid Empire in Asia.

Tang dynasty. An imperial dynasty of China that ruled from 618 to 907.

Tanggu La (*Tib.*, "mountains that eagles cannot fly over"). A wide mountain pass in Tibet.

Tanha (*Pali*, "craving"). The thirst for life; the desire to live and clinging to life on this earth. This clinging is what causes rebirth or reincarnation.

Tantrika (*Sk.*, "relating to Tantra"). Ceremonies connected with the worship of the female power. As Shakti has a twofold nature, white and black, good and bad, the Shaktas are divided into two classes, the Dakshinacharis and Vamacharis, or the right-hand and the left-hand Shaktas, i.e., white and black magicians. The worship of the latter is most licentious and immoral.

Tantrikas. Those who worship the above.

Tantrism or **Tantra** (*Sk.*, "rule," "ritual"). As there are both magic (pure psychic science) and sorcery (its impure counterpart), so there are what are known as the "white" and "black" Tantras. One is of occultism in its noblest features, very clear and exceedingly valuable, and the other is a devil's chapbook of wicked instructions to the would-be wizard and sorcerer. Some of the ceremonies prescribed in the latter show to what depths of vile bestiality bad men and women are ready to plunge in the hope of feeding lust, hatred, cruelty, and other vile passions.

Tantras represent certain mystical and magical works, whose chief peculiarity is the worship of the female power personified in Shakti. Devi or Durga (Kali, Shiva's wife) is the special energy connected with sexual rites and magical powers — the worst form of black magic and sorcery. These Tantras originated in Hinduism and later spread into Tibetan Buddhism degrading it to the extent that in 1387 Tsongkhapa had to burn every book on sorcery on which he could lay his hands and left a whole library of his own works in their place. He established a reformed school of Tibetan Buddhism, the Gelug, that would adhere to the pure teachings of the Buddha.

Tao or **Dao** (*Ch.*, "path"). The fourth of the four Noble Truths in Chinese Buddhism: the path to liberation is the Noble Eightfold Path; the equivalent of *marga* in Sanskrit.

Tara (*Sk.*, "saviouress," "star"). The Mother of all Buddhas in Buddhism who embodies infinite wisdom and compassion. She manifests Herself through divine forms and hypostases. Twenty-one Taras are distinguished in Buddhism; the best known are White Tara, Green Tara, and Yellow Tara.

Taras represent the Sisters of the Great Brotherhood of Teachers, being named after the colour of their Rays that they use to help the world. See *Mother of the World*.

Taraka Raja Yoga (*Sk.*, "royal path that liberates"). One of the Brahminical yoga systems for the development of purely spiritual powers and knowledge which lead to Nirvana.

Tarot. A deck of 78 cards used for divination, spiritual insight, and meditation. The Tarot consists of two sections: the Major Arcana (22 cards representing archetypal themes) and the Minor Arcana (56 cards divided into four suits). It is often used in mysticism, esoteric traditions, and modern spiritual practices.

The real Tarot, in its complete symbology, can be found only in the Babylonian cylinders that are available to view or study in the British Museum and elsewhere. While these Chaldean antediluvian rhombs, or revolving cylinders, covered with sacred signs are available for public viewing, the secrets of these divining "wheels," or, as de Mirville calls them, "the rotating globes of Hecate," must remain untold for some time to come.

Tartary. A name for Central Asia. *Chinese Tartary* refers to the regions of Manchuria, Mongolia, and Xinjiang.

Tashi Lama. Another term for the Panchen Lama, deriving from the name of Tashi Lhunpo Monastery.

Tashi Lhunpo. The great centre of monasteries and colleges, a three-hour walk from Shigatse, the residence of the Tashi Lama. Formerly, it was home to the Esoteric School where Helena Blavatsky studied under the guidance of her Master. The monastery was founded in 1447 by Gedun Drub, a disciple of Tsongkhapa who was later recognized as the First Dalai Lama.

Tat (*Eg.*). An Egyptian symbol: an upright round standard tapering toward the summit, with four cross-pieces placed on the top. It was used as an amulet. The top part is a regular equilateral cross. This, on its phallic basis, represented the two principles of creation, the male and the female, and is related to Nature and the Cosmos. When the *tat* stood by itself, crowned with the *atf* (or *atef*), the triple crown of Horus — two feathers with the uraeus (cobra) in front — it represented the *septenary* man, the cross, or the two cross-pieces, standing for the lower quaternary, and the *atf* for the higher triad. As Dr. Birch well remarks: "The four horizontal bars ... represent the four foundations of all things, the *tat* being an emblem of stability."

Tat Tvam Asi (*Sk.*, "you are That"). One of the great sayings of the Upanishads expressing the idea of unity between the individual self and the ultimate reality.

Tathagata (*Sk.*, "one who is like the coming"). He who is, like his predecessors (the Buddhas) and successors, the coming future Buddha or World-Saviour. One of the titles of Gautama Buddha and the highest epithet, since the *first* and the *last* Buddhas were the direct immediate Avatars of the One Deity.

Tathagatagupta (*Sk.*). The secret or concealed Tathagata, or the "guardian" protecting Buddhas; used of the Nirmanakayas.

Tattvajnani (*Sk.*). The knower of *Tattva* (eternally existing "That") and *tattvas*, which are the different principles in Nature, in their occult meaning. Tattvas are also the abstract principles of existence or categories, physical and metaphysical; the subtle elements — five exoterically, seven in esoteric philosophy — which are correlative to the five and the seven senses on the physical plane; the last two senses are as yet latent in man.

Tau (*Heb.*). That which has now become the square Hebrew letter *tau* (*tav*), but which was, long before the invention of the Jewish alphabet, the Egyptian handled cross, the *crux ansata* of the Latins, and identical to the Egyptian *ankh*. This mark belonged exclusively, and still belongs, to the Adepts of every country. It was a symbol of salvation and consecration, and as such has been adopted as a Masonic symbol in the Royal Arch Degree. It is also called the astronomical cross and was used by the ancient Mexicans, as its presence on one of the palaces at Palenque shows, as well as by the Hindus, who placed the *tau* as a mark on the brows of their chelas.

Telekinesis (*Gr.*, "distant motion"). The ability to influence physical objects with the effort of thought or will.

Telepathy (*Gr.*, "distant perception"). The ability of the brain to transmit and receive thoughts, images, and feelings to and from another brain at a distance without the use of any known means of communication.

Teleportation (*Gr.-Lat.*, "remote carrying"). The ability to move from one place to another instantly.

Telugu. One of the Dravidian languages spoken in Southern India.

Templars. Members of the Temple of the People, founded by Francia La Due under Master Hilarion's guidance in Halcyon, California.

Temple of Azure Clouds or **Biyun Temple**. A Buddhist temple located in the Western Hills near Beijing, China.

Tendai (*Jap.*, "Tiantai"). The School of Mahayana Buddhism established in Japan, also known as the Tendai Lotus School.

Tennyson, Alfred (1809–1892). An English poet, Poet Laureate during the reign of Queen Victoria.

Teresa of Ávila (1515–1582). A Spanish saint, mystic, and reformer of the Carmelite order, known for her profound spiritual writings and experiences. Her works, such as *The Interior Castle* (1588) and *The Way of Perfection* (1566), explore stages of spiritual development and mystical union with God. She is one of the few women recognized as a Doctor of the Church.

Tesla, Nikola (1856–1943). A Serbian-American inventor and engineer known for his contributions to the development of alternating current (AC) electrical systems, radio, and wireless transmission technology. Tesla's ideas and inventions had a lasting impact on modern electrical engineering and electromagnetic theory.

Thangka (*Tib.*, "recorded message"). A traditional Tibetan Buddhist painting on cotton or silk, depicting Buddhist deities, influential lamas and their lives, mandalas, and other sacred subjects and images.

Thegpa Chenpoido (*Tib.*, "Mahayana Sutra"). The two-part Mahayana Sutra that contains invocations to 51 "Buddhas of Confession." Its translation into English and the Tibetan original were published by Emil Schlagintweit in *Buddhism in Tibet* (1863).

Theists. Those who believe in the existence of a god or gods who created and rule the world.

Theophany (*Gr.*). The actual appearance of a god to man; the visions of gods and of real immortal Spirits.

Theosophical Society. An organization founded on 17 November 1875 in New York City by H. P. Blavatsky and Colonel H. S. Olcott, helped by W. Q. Judge and several others. The Society's avowed object was at first the scientific investigation of psychic or so-called "spiritualistic" phenomena, after which its three chief objects were declared, namely: 1) Brotherhood of man, without distinction of race, colour, religion, or social position; 2) the serious study of the ancient world-religions for purposes of comparison and the selection therefrom of universal ethics; 3) the study and development of the latent divine powers in man.

Theosophist, The. A monthly journal, published by the Theosophical Society in India since 1879.

Theosophy (*Gr.*, "divine wisdom," "wisdom of the gods"). Wisdom Religion, the substratum and basis of all the world religions and philosophies, taught and practised by a few elect ever since man became a thinking being. In its practical bearing, Theosophy is purely divine ethics; the definitions cited in dictionaries are pure nonsense, based on religious prejudice and ignorance of the true spirit of the early Rosicrucians and medieval philosophers who called themselves Theosophists.

Theurgist. The first school of practical theurgy in the Christian period was founded by Iamblichus among certain Alexandrian Platonists. The priests, however, who were attached to the temples of Egypt, Assyria, Babylonia, and Greece, and whose business it was to evoke the gods during the celebration of the Mysteries, were known by this name or its equivalent in other tongues from the earliest archaic period. Spirits (but not those of the dead, the evocation of which was called *necromancy*) were made visible to the eyes of mortals. Thus, a theurgist had to be a hierophant and an expert in the esoteric learning of the Sanctuaries of all great countries. The Neoplatonists of the school of Iamblichus were called theurgists, for they performed the so-called "ceremonial magic" and evoked the *simulacra* or the images of the ancient heroes, "gods," and *daimonia* (divine, spiritual entities). In the rare cases that the presence of a *tangible* and *visible* "spirit" was required, the theurgist had to furnish the weird apparition with a portion of his own flesh and blood — he had to perform the *Theopoea*, or the "creation of gods," by a mysterious process well known to the old, and perhaps some of the modern, Tantrikas and initiated Brahmins of India. So reads the *Book of Evocations* of the pagodas. It shows the perfect identity of rites and ceremonial between the oldest Brahmanic theurgy and that of the Alexandrian Platonists.

The following is from *Isis Unveiled*: "'The Brahman Grihastha (the evocator) must be in a state of complete purity before he ventures to call forth the Pitris. After having prepared a lamp, some sandal-incense, etc., and having traced the magic circles taught him by the superior Guru, in order to keep away bad spirits, he ceases to breathe, and calls *the fire* (*kundalini*) to his help to disperse his body.' He pronounces a certain number of times the sacred word, and 'his soul (astral body) escapes from its prison, his body disappears, and the soul (image) of the evoked spirit descends into the *double* body and animates it.' Then 'his (the theurgist's) soul (astral) re-enters its body, whose subtle particles have again been aggregating (to the objective sense), after having formed from themselves an aerial body for the deva (god or spirit) he evoked.' And then, the operator propounds to the latter questions 'on the mysteries of Being and the transformation of the imperishable.' The popular prevailing idea is that the theurgists as well as the magicians worked wonders, such as evoking the souls or shadows of the heroes and gods, and other thaumaturgic works, by *supernatural powers*. But this never was the case. They did it simply by the liberation of their own astral body, which, taking the form of a god or hero, served as a *medium* or vehicle through which the special current preserving the ideas and knowledge of that hero or god could be reached and manifested."

Theurgy. A communication with, and means of bringing down to earth, planetary spirits and angels — the "gods of Light." Knowledge of the inner meaning of their hierarchies and purity of life alone can lead to the acquisition of the powers necessary for communion with them. To arrive at such an exalted goal, the aspirant must be totally worthy and unselfish.

Thomas of Kempis (1380–1471). A German-Dutch cleric, mystic, and author, best known for his work *The Imitation of Christ* (1418), a Christian devotional book emphasizing humility, piety, and the inner spiritual life.

Thought. Fire, or fiery energy, clothed by the will in material form of a certain level of firmness and durability, while striving to become realized. Thought-forms can be seen by powerful clairvoyants and can be recorded by scientific methods. The outer layer of any thought is invisibly linked to its creator. It becomes endowed by a person's will by means of a certain magnetic force.

Thought is the basis of everything that exists in the Universe. Thought is limited neither by time nor space; its power knows no bounds. Still, it is restricted by Cosmic Law. Therefore, every thought that has ever been generated, even thousands of years ago in previous lives, must sooner or later become manifest in action.

Since the nature of thought is subtle and fiery rather than physical — meaning that it is a higher energy that subordinates all lower energies to its power — it can shape the physical world surrounding a person. Thought produces an image which is consolidated and encased in the flesh of the Subtle World, and then embodied on Earth as a consequence, appearing in the corresponding form of matter. For thought to fulfil this purpose, the image must be sufficiently clear and distinct to endue it with the strength and shape required to overcome the limits of Time and to become manifest in the material world. Moreover, a person must work to create the necessary conditions. The magnetic power of thought attracts kindred and consonant elements from space on the principle of "like attracts like," growing like a snowball. Thus, a thought that has been sent out into space is still linked to its owner and periodically returns to this person for affirmation or negation, moving like a boomerang. A thought can revolve, like a comet, around the one who put the initial bundle of energy into creating it, and that energy determines the corresponding radius and orbit of revolution. If the person does not reject the thought and continues to make an effort to realize it, their will endows it with new force, and it again goes out into space, increasing the radius of its influence, and so on until the thought becomes a reality, having received sufficient energy both from its creator and the surrounding environment. On the other hand, if at any point the person begins to doubt the thought or no longer needs it, and they stop applying the effort required for its realization, then the thought loses force, gradually weakening, and eventually breaks down into primary elements, never revealing its potential. At the same time, creating a strong, clear thought and then forgetting about it completely does not equate to its destruction. The thought will again return to its producer and eventually come to realization, possibly many centuries later. Thoughts and dreams always come true but only when the environmental conditions and the composition of its elements favour their manifestation, and not necessarily at the time or in the way that people anticipate.

It is not difficult to imagine how huge conglomerates of the different thoughts generated by humankind hang over the heads of various individuals, like a giant storm or bank of luminous clouds. The thoughts that appear suddenly may gladden or upset them. A thought may push them to take their own life or to harm another being. Here it is for each to decide whether they will take an aggressive path and increase the destructive force, or respond with a prayer whose luminous power will bring albeit a tiny spark of light into the surrounding darkness, thereby helping the light-bearing conglomerates in space to grow.

Due to their energetic nature, thoughts are subject to the Supreme Laws discussed in all the sacred scriptures. The Supreme Laws are also energies that govern the Universe, but they are even higher in power, and therefore, all others submit to them. To change this is beyond the power of human beings.

Thus, dark thoughts are doomed to perdition by the power of Cosmic Laws, and since they are all connected to their creators, they pull these individuals along after them. In contrast, thoughts of light are eternal and can grow infinitely, giving spiritual ascent to their originators. Thoughts directed towards oneself soar close to that person, illuminating or darkening their consciousness, depending on their nature. It is scientifically proven that thoughts expressed in words affect water and plants, and therefore, it is not difficult to assume that they affect the human body and soul in precisely the same way. Evil and negative thoughts will destroy a person's vital force, serving as the cause of all kinds of disease. It should be borne in mind, however, that on the whole illnesses are categorized as *admitted* (due to ruinous actions and habits), *karmic* (as an unpaid debt from a past life), and *sacred* (as a result of a Fiery or planetary experiment). And vice versa: positive, optimistic, and joyful thoughts imbue the organism with the energies of life, increasing them in both the person and the space that surrounds them.

Thought creates a person's internal appearance, which to a certain extent is reflected in the physical body. We are the reflection of our thoughts, and eventually we become what and who we want to be. Consequently, thought is an instrument for the self-perfection (or involution) of human beings. Similarly, the collective thought of humanity powerfully affects the living conditions of the planet, making them better or worse depending on the common nature of thought.

It is generally accepted that thoughts are generated by the brain. Yet, in modern-day language, the brain can be likened to a physical computer that is only capable of perceiving thoughts that are in fact created on the invisible levels of human nature, both low and high, and projecting them into our physical senses of perception. An individual does not lose the ability to think if they lose the physical body. However, it is not only the brain that can perceive thought: so too can the heart. It is the heart that receives thoughts produced by our higher centres of consciousness, and only then does it transmit them to the brain for registration, often as flashes of intuition. The currents of thought passing through the heart are much more effective than those that pass through the brain and bypass the heart, because the heart imbues them with a special kind of energy that will help them overcome any obstacle. Thought can, therefore, be governed by two centres: the brain and the heart, each in its own way using particular types of energy of varying degrees of subtlety. Currents of thought sent by the heart are especially effective; the thoughts of the brain are much weaker and have a much smaller radius of action.

Thoughts can protect a person, certain places, and objects, as well as help another, uniting instantly with the object of aspiration. Their effect may last for a long or a short time, depending on the assigned period or volitional order. They may also have an accurately defined and strictly limited purpose. Everything depends on the strength of the heart energy, the fire that fuels the currents. The most powerful thoughts are those created by the Power of Love. Thoughts such as these are capable of creating entire worlds.

For example, the infamous "curse of the pharaohs" is a consequence of the fact that the objects belonging to the kings came long under the protection afforded by high priests with the help of thought. These objects of the past have a special energy and aura that have been in a state of harmony for considerable lengths of time. When scientists disturb the peace of the pharaohs' tombs, they do so without controlling their thoughts, and so their thoughts of profit or worldly fame, which represent low forms of energy, add dissonance, as though breaking a sacred protective net that was defending not only the mummified body of the pharaoh but his tomb, together with all the items placed inside. As a rule, in the case of a pharaoh, who would have passed certain degrees of Initiation, the protection is multilevel. In this matter, the focus should be on the invisible planes, because here, just as in Nature, the absolute heterogeneity of mental energies at play causes an invisible tornado which lifts up dangerous microscopic particles that are then inhaled by those who have disturbed the pharaoh's peace. The result can manifest in the form of a deadly disease.

Discipline of thought is the principal condition for progress. Because of the concept of *Time* in the material world, a certain period is required before the consequences of anything become apparent. But in the Higher Worlds, time no longer has this power, therefore, thoughts become a reality instantly, and people reap the fruits of the thoughts they produced during their lives on Earth. It is important now to learn how to control our thoughts so as to avoid creating additional problems for ourselves in the Subtle World.

The science of thought is the science of the future. Mastery of thought will lead to the mastery of many secrets of Nature and to the achievement of the might of spirit.

Three Great Perfections. The three *kayas* (Dharmakaya, Sambhogakaya, and Nirmanakaya), representing degrees of spiritual perfection, the most difficult being the third, or Nirmanakaya, that includes attainment of the first two.

Three methods of Prajna. Ways of gaining and developing wisdom by: 1) listening to or studying teachings from scriptures, books, teachers, or discussions; 2) reflection or contemplation on what has been learnt; 3) practical application of what has been learnt and direct spiritual experience of reality during mystical meditation.

Thus have I heard. A formula introduced by Ananda, the favourite disciple of the Buddha, that serves to confirm that the teachings are coming from the Buddha himself as a "seal of authenticity." It is usually found in the first introductory line of the Buddhist Sutras.

Tiantai (*Ch.*, "heavenly terrace"). A Buddhist temple, also known as the Guoqing Temple, on Mount Tiantai in China, where the Tiantai school of Mahayana Buddhism was founded in the sixth century by the Chinese teacher Zhiyi.

Tibetan Book of the Dead. The common name popularized by W. Y. Evans-Wentz for the Tibetan work known as the *Bardo Thodol* ("Liberation through hearing during the intermediate state"). The book contains a detailed description of the states (*bardo*) through which one's consciousness passes, from the process of dying to the moment of the next reincarnation in a new form. The four *bardos* are: life, dying and death, afterlife, and a new life. Special recommendations are provided for each stage.

Tiller, William A., PhD (1929–2022). A Canadian-born physicist, professor emeritus at Stanford University, and founder of the Tiller Foundation, he is known as the pioneer of psychoenergetic science and for his theoretical and experimental research into the physics of solidification for many materials, including water, metals, semiconductors, oxides, and polymers.

Tirthikas (*Sk.*, "heretical teachers"). An epithet applied by Buddhist ascetics to the Brahmins and certain yogis of India.

Tishtrya (*Av.*, "three stars"). The name of the star Sirius in Zoroastrianism; the God of Stars and Rain; the Lord of Sirius.

Titiksha (*Sk.*, "long-suffering, patience"). The ability to withstand pain, suffering, difficulties, and opposites (such as heat and cold, pleasure and pain) without distress, complaint, or deviation from one's path, but with patience, acceptance, and strength. It is personified in Titiksha, daughter of Daksha and wife of Dharma (divine law).

Tolstoy, Leo (1828–1910). A Russian writer, known especially for his works *War and Peace* (1869) and *Anna Karenina* (1878).

Toltecs. The third sub-race of the Atlanteans. It was during this period that Atlantis reached its greatest prosperity.

Tomas, Andrew (1906–2001). An Australian writer, traveller, and explorer, born in St. Petersburg, Russia. In the 1920s, his family moved to China, where he spent 21 years until Mao Zedong's revolution led to his moving to Australia whose citizen he became. He spent most of his life travelling extensively throughout the world, studying the profound philosophies of Taoists, Buddhists, and yogis of great spirituality.

In 1935, Tomas met Nicholas Roerich in Shanghai and from then onwards always considered him to be his Master. While doing research for his book *Shambhala: Oasis of Light* (1977), Tomas travelled to India three times, in 1956, 1966, and 1976, working his way from the South to the North and heading for the Himalayas, where he had a private meeting with His Holiness the Dalai Lama.

Receiving wide acclaim in Europe and America, Andrew Tomas' books, including *We Are Not the First* (1971) and *On the Shores of Endless Worlds* (1974), have been translated and published in more than 60 countries.

Tower of Chung (*Sen.*). The Central Tower of Shambhala. This multi-storey building is like a gigantic museum, which goes deep into the Earth and rises high up into the Subtle Spheres. All the works of art of all peoples that have ever existed on this planet are stored here. It is home to a large library of manuscripts and literary works created throughout the ages, including those that have been considered lost or destroyed.

The Tower of Chung also contains all the exhibits of the Mineral, Vegetable, and Animal Kingdoms, all the patterns of Life that have ever existed on Earth, including its subterranean and ethereal inhabitants. These are immersed in a centuries-old dormancy and stored in special niches which are filled with certain gaseous substances capable of preserving life at the cellular level.

It is in the Tower of Chung that the Great Lord of Shambhala tirelessly watches over the world.

Trai-Vidya (*Sk.*, "three kinds of knowledge," "three sciences"). Refers to the knowledge contained within the three of the four Vedas: the *Rig Veda*, the *Sama Veda*, and the *Yajur Veda*. The *Rig Veda* primarily contains hymns and prayers dedicated to various deities; the *Sama Veda* focuses on musical arrangements of Rig Vedic verses for rituals; and the *Yajur Veda* contains mantras used in sacrifices.

Triangle. The first geometrical figure and a symbol of the trinitarian mystery; a symbol of Deity everywhere. It represents the three great principles: spirit, force, and matter; of the active (male), passive (female), and the dual or correlative principle which partakes of both and binds the two together.

The equilateral triangle is a symbol of the creation of the Cosmos: the apex is the "Father"; the left side or line is the "Mother"; the right side represents the "Son," in every cosmogony perceived as being one with the apex, and so also "his Mother's Husband"; the base line is the universal plane of productive Nature, unifying on the phenomenal plane Father-Mother-Son, as these were unified in the apex in the supersensuous world. By mystic transmutation they became the quaternary, and the Triangle became the Tetraktys. All the triads of the gentiles were composed of the Father, the Mother, and the Son. By making it "Father, Son, and Holy Ghost," the Church changed the dogma only outwardly, as the Holy Ghost had always been feminine, and Jesus addresses the Holy Ghost as his "Mother" in every Gnostic Gospel.

The equilateral triangle is also the sign of high disciples, while three dots in the form of a triangle stand for a High Initiate or Master. The latter was used in the signatures of Masters M. and K.H. in their letters, as well as in that of Blavatsky in Esoteric Instructions. In *Chinese Buddhism* (1880), Joseph Edkins explains its origin: "At this time the kings of the Devas and Nagas urged Shakyamuni, but in vain, not to enter Nirvana at present. In reply, the World's Honoured One discoursed on the symbol 'I,' written with three dots (.*.), arranged as a triangle resting on its base. This he used as a symbol of the embodied form of Tathagata when released from the three methods of the Prajna."

Trinitarians. Followers of the doctrine of the Trinity in Christianity, which posits that God exists as three persons in one: the Father, the Son (Jesus Christ), and the Holy Spirit.

Trishna (*Sk*., "thirst," "craving"). In Buddhism, the desire for sensory pleasures, existence, or non-existence, seen as the cause of suffering and attachment in the cycle of rebirth.

Trulpe ku (*Tib*., "emanation body"). See *Nirmanakaya*.

Truth. A concept of the world surrounding man, based on the foundations, or Cosmic Laws. Secret knowledge is built on these laws, and is, therefore, an aspect of Truth which is eternal rather than transient through the ages.

Fragments of these foundations can be found in all the great religions and philosophies, but they are just that — fragments, for Truth in its entirety is beyond the grasp of human consciousness. Truth is accessible to High Spirits to a degree inconceivable to the human mind, and even then not completely, for Truth is boundless and continuously revealing its infinite essence to the Greatest Cognizants of Cosmic Life. Its foundations remain the same as at all times. They know neither separation nor contradiction having the inherent property of monolithic integrity.

All the Teachings of Light take into account the binary nature of human thinking, which is full of contradiction. People will either deny or accept the points contained in the Teachings. But when, through their messengers, the Great Teachers delve into concepts more deeply, blending two opposite principles into one, those who can make no room in their understanding for a single additional facet of the Truth instantly negate it, and quite violently. And this tendency is marked despite the fact that it is often in opposite and antagonistic phenomena that the different aspects of an issue or principle are perceived.

The Vedas, the Puranas, the Bhagavad Gita, the *Tao Te Ching*, the Avesta, the Bible, the Quran, *The Secret Doctrine, Agni Yoga, The Teaching of the Heart*, and many others, past and future, are all Teachings of Light, given to humanity from the One Source for thousands of years. Each contains precisely the knowledge which people of different nations needed to learn at the time, taking into consideration a multitude of evolutionary factors. No one teaching negates the verity of the previous Teachings, but extends and supplements them with new facets of the One Truth, urging people in their own unique way to purify their hearts and minds.

Consequently, the synthesis, or comparative study, of all religions, philosophies, and sciences — uniting into one the pearls of Cosmic Knowledge which have become fragmented and scattered — represents a path towards the comprehension of Infinite Truth.

Tsagiin Khurden (*Mon*.). See *Kalachakra*.

Tsepagme (*Tib*., "infinite life"). Amitabha in the Sambhogakaya vesture.

Tsi or **Chi** (*Ch*., "assembling of temptations"). The second of the four Noble Truths in Chinese Buddhism: the cause of suffering is desire; the equivalent of *samudaya* in Sanskrit.

Tsongkhapa (1357–1419). A famous Tibetan reformer of the fourteenth century, who introduced a purified Buddhism into his country. He was a great Adept, who being unable to witness any longer the desecration of Buddhist philosophy by the false priests, who made of it a marketable commodity, put a forcible stop thereto by a timely revolution and the exile of 40,000 sham monks and lamas from the country. He is regarded as an Avatar of Buddha, is the founder of the Gelugpa ("yellow caps") school, and of the mystic Brotherhood connected with its chiefs. The Tree of Ten Thousand Images (*Kumbum*) sprang, it is said, from the long hair of this ascetic, who, leaving it behind him, disappeared forever from the view of the profane.

Tukaram (1598/1608–1649/1650). A Marathi saint and poet from Maharashtra, India; a key figure in the Bhakti movement. Tukaram is renowned for his devotional songs emphasizing love and devotion to God (*abhangas*), dedicated to Lord Vithoba (a form of Vishnu).

Tulsidas (1532–1623). A Hindu poet-saint and author of the *Ramcharitmanas*, a retelling of the epic Ramayana in the Awadhi dialect.

Turiya (*Sk*., "fourth"). Almost a Nirvanic state in *samadhi*, which is itself a beatific state of the contemplative yoga beyond this plane. A condition of the higher triad, quite distinct (though still inseparable) from the conditions of *jagrat* (waking), *svapna* (dreaming), and *sushupti* (sleeping).

Turner, William (1775–1851). An English painter and watercolourist known for his expressive use of colour and light. His works, such as *The Fighting Temeraire* (1838) and *Rain, Steam and Speed* (1844), are celebrated for their innovation in depicting atmospheric effects.

Two Paths. 1) the Open Path, the Dhyana Path, the Path of Knowledge, or the Path of

Mind leading to enlightenment for one's own benefit and bliss; 2) the Secret Path, the Path of Renunciation, the Path of Love and Compassion, or the Path of the Heart leading to enlightenment for the sake and salvation of others.

Tyaga (*Sk.*, "renunciation," "sacrifice"). In Hindu philosophy, giving up material possessions, desires, or actions for the sake of spiritual growth and detachment from worldly concerns.

U

Uchen (*Tib.*, "with a head"). The classical Tibetan script style used for printing and formal documents.

Udumbara (*Sk.*, "auspicious flower from heaven"). A lotus of gigantic size, associated with the Buddha: the *Nila Udumbara* or "blue lotus," regarded as a supernatural omen whenever it blossoms, for it flowers but once every three thousand years. Its appearance heralds the forthcoming Advent of the King of the Golden Wheel, or the Messiah, in the world. It is said that one such flower burst forth before the birth of Gautama, and another, near a lake at the foot of the Himalayas in the fourteenth century, just before the birth of Tsongkhapa, etc. The same is said to be true of the Udumbara tree (*ficus glomerata*) because it flowers at intervals of centuries, as does a certain kind of cactus which blossoms only at extraordinary altitudes and only opens at midnight.

"Fruits and grain, unknown to Earth to that day, were brought by the 'Lords of Wisdom,' for the benefit of those they ruled from other Lokas [Spheres]."

So reads the Commentary on the *Book of Dzyan*, quoted by Helena Blavatsky in *The Secret Doctrine*. Thanks to this work it has been revealed to humanity that, for example, wheat "is not a product of the earth." Moreover, as ancient legend has it, the Gods brought from the higher planets not only wheat, but also bees, ants, and other species now inhabiting the Kingdoms of Nature.

In addition, the Sons of Light who came with a higher knowledge of agriculture offered Earth-dwellers other gifts in the form of modified varieties. For example, a certain number of Venusians incarnated in the Human Kingdom were engaged in a special type of activity — work with the life forms created by the planet Earth within the Vegetable Kingdom and the Animal Kingdom. Earthly plants were subjected to special experiments which were based on the knowledge that the Venusians brought with them and conducted using certain currents and vegetable spores of Venusian origin.

This is why some of the plant species that originated on the planet Earth do not have wild-growing counterparts — that is, equivalents that have the same form as people know them, and which are able to grow without the help of human hands. The same applies to many fodder crops and medicinal herbs. Aliens from other Worlds, mostly incarnated among the inhabitants of the Maya, Aztec, Toltec, and other peoples, created secret repositories of seeds that remain hidden until certain periods in time.

Just as there are sacred planets in the Solar System, some plants may belong to a sacred category, their mystery being revealed only to those who have reached a certain stage of Initiation. These include two flowers that have become known to the world under the names *Shin-dza* (*Sen.*) and *Udumbara* (*Sk.*). And while nothing can be said about the former, except that, being a symbol of the Initiates, it grows within Shambhala and is capable of releasing its roots from the soil in order to move to another location, it is possible, at least slightly, to lift the veil of secrecy that obscures the latter.

It can be said that the Sun, its fiery-white core in particular, was actively involved in the formation of the Udumbara flower before the Lord Buddha entered the conglomerate of the emerging Fires of the planet Venus.

Then, at the Subtle level, the Lord Buddha projected the Udumbara flower from Venus to Earth in the form of a Blue Lotus, which preserved fiery-white flames at its core. And this is why, in recent times, white hues have manifested themselves more actively in the microscopic Udumbara flowers that began appearing around the world at the end of the twentieth century. After all, the Lord of Love and Compassion is also the Master and Patron of the Age of Synthesis, whose dominant colour is White, at the same time including all seven colours of the divine rainbow.

So, the ancestral home of the Udumbara flower is Venus, and from here it was brought to Earth by the Lord Buddha millions of years ago. Of course, Venus is now in the Seventh Round of Evolution that no longer involves the development of its humankind or Nature in physical form. Therefore, while Venus was still in the Sixth Round, the Great Teachers brought certain species of plant, bird, and animal to Earth as gifts, as at this time, the Earth's Subtle Spheres were ready to accept them.

The Udumbara possesses the utmost degree of rarefaction, and the seed of the flower has a fiery nature. Periodically, at certain times associated with the Mystery of the manifestation of the Lord Buddha and His Rays, to life on Earth, the flower, so to speak, "incarnates itself at the dense level" in the most rarefied possible state. For the same reason, it may similarly disappear, leaving virtually no trace, after being "split" into the primary elements of fiery essence.

As mentioned above, legend has it that the Udumbara flower appeared in all its beauty just before the birth of Siddhartha Gautama. At another time, in the fourteenth century, it was seen near a lake at the foot of the Himalayas shortly before the birth of Tsongkhapa.

It should be noted that for individuals with developed spiritual sight who are able to see phenomena on the Subtle Plane, the Udumbara flower may be perceived as a fiery lotus of tremendous size, such as it is recorded in a number of legends. Such fieriness in the Subtle Spheres means "heavenliness," which has a bluish shade that is closer to white, if one is to describe it in earthly words, hence the appellation *Nila Udumbara*, or Blue Lotus.

However, it did not manifest itself at the physical level at the times mentioned above; in fact, people who saw it in those distant years perceived it with the eye of the heart. This is because the Udumbara flower is a dweller of Ethereal Spheres; it is extremely difficult for it to take root in any earthly soil, since the latter is insufficiently saturated with the ingredients of Fire — the main nourishing environment for this mysterious flower.

Over time, given the fact that very few people have seen the Udumbara flower with their own eyes, it has been more often regarded as a symbol illustrating the extreme rarity of the birth of Buddhas on Earth.

According to esoteric philosophy, the Messiah who is awaited under different names by all religions of the world is the bearer of the Three Rays of Maitreya, Buddha, and Christ. In the same way, the predictions of Nam Sa-go, the "Korean Nostradamus" of the sixteenth century, indicated that He would come into the world as the Buddha and would bear the Power of Three. Hence, the appearance of the Udumbara flower in present times is not unexpected.

Moreover, at the end of twentieth century, Earth entered an era of new development stimulated by Fire coming from the Cosmos. More precisely, the entire Solar System, while moving towards the Central Spiritual Sun located behind the constellation of Hercules, has entered a zone in which it comes under increased impact from currents emitted from the Central Spiritual Sun, and this is the cause of global warming. These supreme energy currents have begun to saturate all spheres of the planet with the ingredients of Fire. The process has enabled the heavenly Udumbara flower to acquire for the first time a physically visible and more stable form, albeit microscopic in size.

The first appearance in present times of this ethereal flower was noticed in July 1997 on the statue of the Buddha — the statue of the One with whom it is mystically linked — in Cheonggyesa Temple in the Gyeonggi Province of South Korea, and the event was broadly covered in the local media. Twenty-four flowers measuring 0.25 centimetres were found on the Buddha sculpture. It is worth noting that the number 24 is the number of Shambhala. In May 2005, Udumbaras were found on the statue of Maitreya Buddha in another temple located in the city of Gyeongju in South Korea. Since then, the flower has been seen in almost all the countries of the world, especially during the 2010s: in China, Malaysia, Australia, the USA, and Russia, to name a few. Many photographs of it can be found on the Internet.

Of course, when something unusual appears in the world, its appearance is immediately and vehemently denied. Fortunately, there were people who managed to photograph the tiny white flowers of Udumbara, even under a microscope, and any sane person can be convinced that it is indeed a flower and not "lacewing eggs" as certain sceptics would have people believe.

According to eyewitness reports, Udumbara blossoms in the most unexpected places: on stones, plants, windows, fences, steel pipes, doors, lampshades, and curtains, proving that it is not dependent upon the conditions traditionally required by any other flower. It is able to exist without water or earth, and at the same time, it does not wither for a long time, since, as indicated above, its "food" is the spatial Fire. And its stem is sufficiently sturdy as to straighten after being bent.

Udumbara justifies its Sanskrit name "flower from Heaven" as it suddenly appears and then disappears after filling the space it occupied with its unusual aroma.

Ume (*Tib.*, "headless"). A cursive style of the Tibetan alphabet used for everyday handwriting and shorthand.

University of Kassel. A university in Kassel, Germany, known for its diverse academic programmes, including strong faculties in the arts, social sciences, and engineering.

Upadhi (*Sk.*, "that which places its own attributes on something that is nearby"). Basis; the vehicle, carrier, or bearer of something less material than itself: as the human body is the *upadhi* of its spirit, ether the *upadhi* of light, etc.; a mould; a defining or limiting substance.

Upadhi also means "that through which a force acts." The word "vehicle" is sometimes used to convey the same idea. If "force" be regarded as acting, "matter" is the *upadhi* through which it acts. The lower *manas* is the *upadhi* through which the higher can work; the *linga-sharira* is the *upadhi* through which *prana* can work. The *sthula-sharira* is the *upadhi* for all the principles acting on the physical plane.

Upadya (*Sin.*). A spiritual preceptor or teacher; a shortened version of *upadhyaya*.

Upanishads (*Sk.*, "esoteric doctrine"). The third division of the Vedas. These deal with highly abstruse, metaphysical questions, such as the origin of the Universe; the nature and the essence of the Unmanifested Deity and the manifested gods; the connection, primal and ultimate, of spirit and matter; the universality of mind, and the nature of the human soul and Ego.

Upasaka (*Sk.*). Male chelas or rather devotees; *upasika* means female chelas. Those who without entering the priesthood vow to preserve the principal commandments.

Upasan (*Sk.*). A disciple or chela.

Uraeus (*Gr.*, "rearing cobra"). In Egyptian *urhek*, a serpent and a sacred symbol. Some see in it a cobra, while others say it is an asp. Cooper explains that "the asp is not a uraeus but a cerastes, or kind of viper, i.e., a two-horned viper. It is the royal serpent wearing the *pschent* . . . the *naya haje.*" The uraeus is "round the disc of Horus and forms the ornament of the cap of Osiris, besides overhanging the brows of other divinities" (*Egyptian Belief*). Occultism explains that the uraeus is the symbol of initiation and also of hidden wisdom, as the serpent always is. The gods were all patrons of the hierophants and their instructors.

Urga (*Mon.*, "palace"). The historical name for Ulaanbaatar, the capital of Mongolia. It was an important centre for trade, religion, and administration, particularly known for its Buddhist monasteries and as the seat of the Jebtsundamba Khutuktu.

V

Vach (*Sk.*, "speech"). The mystic personification of speech; the goddess of speech and the female Logos being one with Brahma who created her out of one-half of his body, which he divided into two portions; she is also one with Viraj (called the "female" Viraj) who was created in her by Brahma.

In one sense Vach is "speech" by which knowledge was taught to man; in another sense Vach is the "mystic, secret speech" which descends upon and enters into the primeval Rishis, as the "tongues of fire" are said to have "sat upon" the apostles. She is called "the female creator," the "mother of the Vedas," etc.

Esoterically, Vach is the subjective Creative Force which emanates from the Creative Deity (the subjective Universe, its "privation," or ideation) and becomes the manifested "world of speech," i.e., the concrete expression of ideation, hence the "Word" or Logos. Vach is "the male and female" Adam of the first chapter of the Bible's Genesis, and thus called "Vach-Viraj" by the sages. She is also "the celestial Sarasvati produced from the heavens," a "voice derived from speechless Brahma" (Mahabharata); the goddess of wisdom and eloquence. She also carries the name *Sata-rupa*, the goddess of a hundred forms.

Vairagi. One who practises *vairagya*, meaning detachment or renunciation. Vairagi is often used to refer to ascetics or spiritual practitioners who have renounced worldly pleasures and desires in pursuit of spiritual enlightenment.

Vairagya (*Sk.*, "dispassion," "detachment"). A state of being free from desire and attachment to worldly pleasures, considered essential for spiritual progress in Hindu and yogic traditions.

Vaisheshika (*Sk.*, "particularity"). One of the six Darshanas or schools of philosophy, founded by Kanada. It is called the *atomistic school*, as it teaches the existence of a universe of atoms of a transient character, an endless number of souls, and a fixed number of material principles by the correlation and interaction of which periodical cosmic evolutions take place without any directing Force, save a kind of mechanical law inherent in the atoms; a very materialistic school.

Vajra (*Sk.*, "diamond," "thunderbolt"). See *dorje*.

Vajradhara (*Sk.*, "diamond-holder"). The Supreme Buddha, the ultimate primordial; the Lord of all Mysteries.

Vajrapani (*Sk.*, "holder of a thunderbolt"). The Dhyani-Bodhisattva (as the spiritual reflex, or the son of the Dhyani-Buddhas, on earth) born directly from the subjective form of existence; a deity worshipped by the profane as a god, and by Initiates as a subjective Force, the real nature of which is known only to, and explained by, the highest Initiates of the Yogachara school.

Vajrasattva (*Sk.*, "diamond being"). The name of the Buddha of Supreme Intelligence, the sixth Dhyani-Buddha (there are but five in the popular Northern Buddhism) in the Yogachara school. The latter counts seven Dhyani-Buddhas and as many Bodhisattvas — the "mind-sons" of the Dhyani-Buddhas. Hence, the Orientalists refer to Vajrasattva as "a *fictitious* Bodhisattva." Vajrasattva is the Second Logos of Creation, from whom emanate the seven Dhyani-Buddhas.

Vajrayana (*Sk.*, "diamond vehicle"). The esoteric division of the Mahayana. Over the course of many centuries, the mixture of Buddhism with the Shaktism of Hindu Tantrika introduced much confusion which still hinders the right understanding of Vajrayana and its symbolism. As a result, practically everything that is publicly known about this complex practice is distorted and misinterpreted. The true Vajrayana in its pure form has never been available to the public.

Varkaris (*Mar.*, "pilgrims"). People who regularly undertake the pilgrimage to the temple of Lord Vithoba (a form of Vishnu) in the town of Pandharpur, Maharashtra state, India.

Vatican. The headquarters of the Roman Catholic Church and the residence of the Pope, located in Vatican City, an independent city-state enclaved within Rome, Italy. Blavatsky writes in *Isis Unveiled*:

"In what countries have 'divine miracles' flourished most, been most frequent and most stupendous? Catholic Spain and Pontifical Italy, beyond question. And which more than these two has had access to ancient literature? Spain was famous for her libraries; the Moors were celebrated for their profound learning in alchemy and other sciences.

"The Vatican is the storehouse of an immense number of ancient manuscripts. During the long interval of nearly 1,500 years they have been accumulating, from trial after trial, books and manuscripts confiscated from their sentenced victims, to their own profit. The Catholics may plead that the books were generally committed to the flames; that the treatises of famous sorcerers and enchanters perished with their accursed authors.

"But the Vatican, if it could speak, could tell a different story. It knows too well of the existence of certain closets and rooms, access to which is had but by the very few. It knows that the entrances to these secret hiding-places are so cleverly concealed from sight in the carved framework and under the profuse ornamentation of the library-walls, that there have even been Popes who lived and died within the precincts of the palace without ever suspecting their existence. But these Popes were neither Sylvester II, Benedict IX, John XX, nor the VIth and VIIth Gregory; nor yet the famous Borgia of toxicological memory. Neither were those who remained ignorant of the hidden lore friends of the sons of Loyola."

Vaticinia Nostradami (*Lat.*, "prophecies of Nostradamus"). A collection of cryptic prophetic watercolour illustrations attributed to Nostradamus, seen as a visual companion to his written prophecies. It was discovered in 1994 by Italian journalists in the Biblioteca Nazionale Centrale di Roma (Central National Library) in Rome, Italy.

Vaughan, Thomas (1621–1666). An English occultist, fire-philosopher, and great alchemist. His Rosicrucian name was Eugenius Philalethes.

Vedanta (*Sk.*, "end of the Vedas"). A mystic system of philosophy which has developed from the efforts made by multiple generations of sages to interpret the secret meaning of the Upanishads. In the Shad Darshanas (six schools or systems of demonstration), it is called *Uttara Mimamsa* and is attributed to the sage Vyasa, compiler of the Vedas, who is referred to as the founder of the Vedanta. The orthodox Hindus call Vedanta, a term meaning literally the "end of all (Vedic) knowledge" — *Brahma-jnana*, or pure and spiritual knowledge of Brahma. Even going by the late dates assigned by Orientalists to various Sanskrit schools and treatises, the Vedanta must be 3,400 years old, as Vyasa is said to have lived 1,400 years BCE. If, as Elphinstone has it in his *History of India* (1841), the Brahmanas are the Talmud of the Hindus, and the Vedas the Mosaic books, then the Vedanta may be correctly called the Kabbalah of India. But how vastly more grand! Shankaracharya, who was the popularizer of the Vedantic system and the founder of Advaita philosophy, is sometimes called the founder of the modern schools of the Vedanta.

Vedas (*Sk.*, "knowledge"). The most ancient and the most sacred scriptures in Sanskrit.

Vegetarianism. The practice of abstaining from the consumption of meat. Today, scientists and researchers around the world are finding more and more evidence in favour of renouncing meat and transitioning to a vegetarian lifestyle. They argue that not only does vegetarianism lead to benefits for health, it also has economic and ecological ramifications that can improve the state of the planet's natural environment.

Vegetarianism has existed since ancient times, and to the present day some religions have preserved periods of fasting that place temporary restrictions on eating meat. So, what is the main harm of eating meat?

Any spilt blood — man or animal — attracts a host of lower spirits who are drawn to any form of decay, thus cementing the near-Earth space with negativity. These lower spirits influence the human mind and body, bringing consequences in the form of illness. For this reason, meat of any kind, especially meat saturated with blood, can engender all sorts of disease. Moreover, the eating of meat strengthens the passional nature and the desire to acquire possessions, and, therefore, increases the difficulty of the struggle with the lower nature.

The "tradition" of eating dead bodies has been imposed on humanity by evil workers of black magic since the days of Atlantis, as this is one of the factors that deprives man of immortality and separates Earth from the Higher Spheres. A person who increases the burden on their karma through eating corpses displays a criminal attitude, not only towards the animal world and their own bodies — both physical and subtle — but also towards the planet and region of surrounding space.

In the eighteenth century, the famous German physician Franz Mesmer developed a theory of "animal magnetism," according to which every living being has a special magnetic energy that can be transferred to others. Helena Blavatsky confirmed this theory from the esoteric point of view and also added that animal meat, when it is eaten by humans, endows them with the characteristics of the animal to which it belonged.

From this point of view, the most negative effect on people is exerted by the meat of large, warm-blooded animals that stand very close to the Human Kingdom on the Ladder of Evolution; the effect is manifested to a lesser extent with the meat of birds and even less with fish which are closer to the Vegetable Kingdom. A danger of animal meat lies in the fact that it may contain a large amount of blood which bears within it the formula of the karmic interconnection of the entire Animal Kingdom. In consuming meat, humans introduce particles of these energies into their own cells. Furthermore, given the present state of the environment, most animals have malignant diseases which "migrate" into human bodies when people eat their meat. It is not surprising then that in 2015, after thorough research, the World Health Organization included meat products on its list of carcinogenic substances.

Later, a new facet of this matter was revealed in the *Agni Yoga* series by Helena Roerich. According to this Teaching, there is a poison called *imperil* which living beings secrete when experiencing negative emotions. This poison is deposited on the walls of nerve channels in the form of invisible crystals that spread throughout the body and also are emitted into space as an invisible, malodorous gas poisoning everything in its vicinity.

It is a well-known fact that animals sense when they are in danger or are about to be killed, regardless of the method. From fear — the strongest negative emotion — an enormous amount of *imperil* is emitted into their blood and poisons their tissues. And then, without the necessary processing to remove this poison, people go on to eat meat in which *imperil* has been crystallized. Of course, if the saying "we are what we eat," is true then this does not bode well for anyone in terms of health, physical or spiritual.

Moreover, emanations of *imperil* contained in products of decomposition (besides meat, alcohol and drugs) attract the lowest entities of the Subtle World for whom this is a kind of food. Like piranhas, they surround people who eat such foods and bite into their auras. If a person's aura is weak, then these entities will soon become real parasites that stimulate their victim to develop and establish bad habits and addictions as well as to constantly generate negative emotions, thoughts, and moods — everything that will supply them with abundant food in the form of emanations of *imperil*.

However, in mountainous and desert areas, where a good many people live, neither fruit trees or vegetables grow, nor is there fish or other seafood, and this makes it impossible to be vegetarian. However, the local people know special ways of cooking meat to clean it of *imperil* as far as is possible. For example, in Mongolia meat is dried in the Sun; the meat crystallizes the energy of the Sun and loses its malignant nature. And in many monasteries in Tibet monks know how to "neutralize" meat by soaking or cooking it with the use of certain herbs, some of which grow even under the snow.

Moreover, as we know from the works of Blavatsky and Roerich, many accepted disciples of the Himalayan Masters of Wisdom were Tibetans who were mainly meat-eaters for the reasons described above. And many great saints did not renounce meat. Vegetarianism is not, therefore, a determining factor for the path of spiritual growth. After all, a person may be a vegetarian, and yet be spiteful and poison everyone and everything around them with their venom, condemning those who do not follow the same lifestyle. Adhering to vegetarianism itself does not say much.

Furthermore, Christ said: "Not that which goeth into the mouth defileth a man; but that which cometh out of the mouth, this defileth a man" (Matthew 15:11). So the first priority must be to preserve the purity of one's thoughts, words, and actions, all of which in their negative manifestations have consequences in the form of deposits of *imperil* crystals in the body, even greater than the deposits caused by consuming the meat of animals.

At the same time, positive qualities such as *love*, *compassion*, and *joy* are also deposited in the form of invisible *ringsel* crystals, which become visible only after contact with fire. These crystallized positive energies can serve as an antidote that can neutralize both the poison of *imperil* and animal magnetism, and act to protect people from invisible vampires by turning their auras into fiery shields.

As their consciousness expands and grows, many people come to the thought of renouncing meat — not only out of respect for their own physical and spiritual health, but also out of compassion for animals. However, it is important to emphasize that renunciation should be gradual, so as to avoid doing harm and causing a shock to the body.

Nevertheless, there are people who have genuinely tried to become vegetarians but whose health simply has not allowed them to adapt to this new lifestyle. After all, each body acts as a small universe with its own laws. And one cannot deny that in meat there are indeed some elements, absent in other foods, that are essential for certain categories of people. In such cases, forcible renunciation would bring little benefit. In this case, one can only try to restrict one's intake of the meat of large animals, switching to poultry and fish. Decisions should be made on a strictly individual basis.

Venus. The Roman goddess of love, beauty, fertility, and victory; equivalent to the Greek Aphrodite, the Babylonian Ishtar, called "the eldest of heaven and earth," and the Indian Lakshmi, the wife of Vishnu, born of the churning of the ocean by the gods. For the planet Venus, see *Solar System*.

Via Fatale (*Lat.*). The Fatal Way.

Vibhuti Pada (*Sk.*, "chapter on mystical powers"). The third chapter of Patanjali's *Yoga Sutras* which deals with the supernatural powers or *siddhis* that can be acquired through intense meditation and yogic practices. It explores how these powers arise and the importance of transcending them for true spiritual progress.

Vibhutis (*Sk.*, "incarnation of power"). Supernatural powers or *siddhis* that arise from intense spiritual practice and meditation. These include abilities like clairvoyance, levitation, and other extraordinary phenomena.

Vidya (*Sk.*). Knowledge, occult science.

Vina. A kind of large guitar used in India and Tibet whose invention is attributed variously to Shiva, Narada, and others.

Viraga (*Sk.*). Dispassion, indifference to pleasure and pain; one of the paramitas of perfection.

Virya (*Sk.*). Energy, vigour; one of the paramitas of perfection.

Vishnu (*Sk.*, "all-pervasive"). The second person of the Hindu Trimurti (Trinity), composed of Brahma, Vishnu, and Shiva. In the *Rig Veda*, Vishnu is no high god but simply a manifestation of solar energy described as "striding through the seven regions of the Universe in *three* steps and enveloping all things with the dust of his beams." Whatever may be the six other occult significances of the statement, this is related to the same class of types as the seven and ten Sefirot, as the *seven* and *three* orifices of the perfect Adam Kadmon, as the seven principles and the higher triad in man, etc. Later on, this mystic type becomes a great God, the preserver and renovator, he "of a thousand names — Sahasranama."

Vishvakarman (*Sk.*, "all-creator"). In Hinduism the divine architect or craftsman.

Vivekachudamani (*Sk.*, "crest-jewel of discernment"). A philosophical treatise authored by Sri Adi Shankaracharya.

Vivekananda, Swami (1863–1902). An Indian Hindu monk and disciple of Ramakrishna. Vivekananda played a significant role in the introduction of Indian philosophies of Vedanta and yoga to the Western world, especially through his famous speech given at the 1893 Parliament of World Religions in Chicago.

Vogay (*Tam.*). A tree which rarely flowers, like the Udumbara. The Tamil proverb goes: "The Adept is as rare as the flower of the Vogay tree, which is most difficult to see."

Voice of the Silence. A single language consisting of all vibrations generated by the Cosmos. This is the Voice born by the beating of the great Cosmic Heart. Nevertheless, there is no silence in the Cosmos, for Silence is not silent. Some of these vibrations can be perceived by consciousness as sounds imbued with solemnity and beauty, as the harmony of supreme consonance, but these sounds are not like earthly sounds; this is Cosmic Music.

Every heart can speak this language. It does not require words, knows no distance, and pierces all obstacles. It is difficult to learn to hear the Voice of the Silence spoken by the heart overnight. This requires a special state of grace, which is accompanied by the outflow of fiery currents. In order to hear the Voice of the Silence, one must detach oneself from the hustle and bustle and chaotic train of thought. One who masters the speech of Silence will always be able to understand another, easily and without words.

The Voice of the Silence is the voice of the Higher Self, but it can also be the Voice of the Master, for these phenomena are almost inseparable. Can one really hear the Voice of the Teacher when the Self is half asleep? With true spiritual development (not the case of a medium), it is the Higher Self that perceives the Voice of the Teacher. Therefore, when we begin to hear the Voice of the Master, we can hear the voice of our Higher Self. But it should be remembered that no one can know the day or the hour that this might happen. Often people retreat at the very threshold of the achievement. When the student is ready, the Teacher will not delay in appearing. But neither we nor those around us can judge the degree of this readiness. The measure of the Master does not coincide with our earthly parameters.

Voodoos. The followers of Voodooism, a system of African sorcery or a sect of black magicians to which many in New Orleans are addicted. Voodooism flourishes, likewise, in Cuba and South America.

Voynich Manuscript. A mysterious manuscript held in Yale University's Beinecke Rare Book and Manuscript Library. It was named after Wilfrid Voynich, a Polish book dealer who purchased it from the Jesuits in 1912.

The manuscript is illustrated and handwritten in a language unknown to modern linguists but which is actually a variant of Senzar script. It contains information concerning the life activity of all seven Kingdoms of Nature: the Mineral Kingdom (corresponds to the physical body), the Vegetable Kingdom (*prana*), the Animal Kingdom (astral body), the Human Kingdom (animal soul), the Kingdom of Human Soul (*manas*), the Kingdom of Spiritual Soul (*buddhi*), and the Kingdom of Universal Spirit (*atma*).

Vril. An explosive substance of enormous destructive power featuring in Edward Bulwer-Lytton's novel, *The Coming Race* (1871). However, the Force itself is real. It is the terrible sidereal Force known to and named by the Atlanteans as *Mash-mak*. It is allegorized in the *Vishnu Purana*, in the Ramayana, and in other works. This vibratory Force, when aimed at an army, would reduce to ashes 100,000 men as easily as it would a dead rat.

Vyasa (*Sk.*, "one who expands or amplifies"). An interpreter, or rather a *revealer*, for that which he explains, interprets, and amplifies is a mystery to the profane. This term was applied in days of old to the highest Gurus in India. There were many Vyasas in Aryavarta; one was the compiler and arranger of the Vedas; another, the author of the Mahabharata — the twenty-eighth Vyasa or revealer in the order of succession — and the last of note was the author of Uttara Mimamsa, the sixth school or system of Indian philosophy. He was also the founder of the Vedanta system. The Orientalists put him as having lived around 1,400 BCE, but this date is certainly too recent. The Puranas mention only 28 Vyasas, who at various ages descended to Earth to promulgate Vedic truths, but there were certainly many more than this.

W

Wagner, Richard (1813–1883). A German composer, known for his operas.

Wallace, Alfred Russel (1823–1913). An English naturalist, explorer, geographer, anthropologist, biologist, and illustrator.

Ward, J. S. M. (1885–1949). An English author who wrote extensively on the subjects of Freemasonry and esotericism. While living in Myanmar, he deeply studied Chinese secret societies, as a result of which he co-authored with W. G. Stirling a definitive three-volume book on the subject, *The Hung Society, or the Society of Heaven and Earth* (1925).

Water. The first principle of things, according to Thales and other ancient philosophers. Of course this is not water on the material plane, but water in a figurative sense, the potential fluid contained in boundless space. The whole expanse of Heaven is called the "Waters of Space," the Celestial Ocean, etc. Akasha is the ethereal "waters of space," since it is in the bosom of "space" and on its seven planes that the "four orders of (lower) beings" and the three higher Orders of Spiritual Beings are born.

Primordial waters of space called "Father-Mother." This was symbolized in ancient Egypt by *Kneph*, the "unrevealed" god, who was represented as the serpent — the emblem of eternity — encircling a water-urn, with his head hovering over the waters which he incubates with his breath. "And the Spirit of God moved upon the face of the waters" (Genesis 1:2). The honey-dew, the food of the gods and of the *creative bees* on the Yggdrasil (the World Tree of Norse cosmogony), falls during the night upon the tree of life from the "divine waters, the birthplace of the gods." Alchemists claim that when pre-Adamic earth is reduced by the *alkahest* (the universal solvent) to its first substance, it is like clear water. The alkahest is "the one and the invisible, the water, the first principle, in the *second* transformation."

Holy water is one of the oldest rites practised in Egypt and, consequently, in Pagan Rome. It accompanied the rite of bread and wine. "Holy water was sprinkled by the Egyptian priest alike upon his gods' images and the faithful. It was both poured and sprinkled. A brush has been found, supposed to have been used for that purpose, as at this day" (*Egyptian Belief*). As regards the bread, "the cakes of Isis ... were placed upon the altar. Gliddon writes that they were 'identical in shape with the consecrated cake of the Roman and Eastern Churches.' Melville assures us 'the Egyptians marked this holy bread with St. Andrew's cross.' The *Presence* bread was broken before being distributed by the priests to the people, and was supposed to become the flesh and blood of the Deity. The miracle was wrought by the hand of the officiating priest, who blessed the food. ... Rouge tells us: 'The bread offerings bear the imprint of the fingers, the mark of consecration'" (*Egyptian Belief*).

Baptism and the Eucharist have their direct origin in pagan Egypt. There the "waters of purification" were used (the Mithraic font for baptism being borrowed by the Persians from the Egyptians) and so were bread and wine. "Wine in the Dionysiak cult, as in the Christian religion, represents that blood which in different senses is the life of the world" (Robert Brown, *The Great Dionysiak Myth*). Justin Martyr says: "In imitation of which the devil did the like in the Mysteries of Mithras, for you either know or may *know that they also take bread and a cup of water* in the sacrifices of those that are initiated and *pronounce certain words over it.*"

The Lotus and Water are among the oldest symbols in the world and in their origin are purely Aryan, though they became common property during the branching off of the Fifth Race. To give an example: letters, as well as numbers, were all mystic, whether in combination, or taken separately. The most sacred of all is the letter M. It is both feminine and masculine, or androgyne, and is made to symbolize Water in its origin, the Great Deep. It is a mystic letter in all languages, Eastern and Western, and stands as a glyph for the waves, thus /\/\/\. In the Aryan esotericism, as in the Semitic, this letter has always stood for the Waters. In Sanskrit, for instance, Makara, the tenth sign of the zodiac, means a crocodile, or rather an aquatic monster associated always with Water. The letter Ma is equivalent to, and corresponds with, the number 5, which is composed of a binary, the symbol of the two sexes separated, and of the ternary, the symbol of the third life, the progeny of the binary. This, again, is often symbolized by a pentagon, the latter being a sacred sign, a divine monogram. Maitreya is the secret name of the Fifth Buddha, and the Kalki Avatar of the Brahmins, the last Messiah who will come at the culmination of the Great Cycle. It is also the initial letter of the Greek Metis, or Divine Wisdom; of Mimra, the Word, or Logos; and of Mithras, the Mihr, the Monad Mystery. All these are born in, and from, the Great Deep, and are the Sons of Maya, the "Mother"; in Egypt, Moot; in Greece, Minerva, Divine Wisdom; of Mary, or Miriam, Myrrha, etc., the Mother of the Christian Logos; and of Maya, the Mother of Buddha. Madhava and Madhavi are the titles of the most important Gods and Goddesses of the Hindu Pantheon. Finally, mandala is, in Sanskrit, a "circle," or an orb, also the ten divisions of the *Rig Veda*. The most sacred names in India generally begin with this letter, from Mahat, the first manifested Intellect, and Mandara, the great mountain used by the Gods to churn the Ocean, down to Mandakini, the heavenly Ganga, or Ganges, Manu, etc.

Can this be called a coincidence? If so, what a strange one is it when we see even Moses, found in the water of the Nile, with the symbolical consonant in his name. And Pharaoh's daughter "called his name Moses; and she said, Because I drew him out of the water" (Exodus 2:10). Even to the seven daughters of the Midianite priest, who came to draw *water*, and whom Moses helped to *water* their flock; for which service the Midian gives Moses his daughter Zipporah, or Sippara, the *shining* wave, as wife (Exodus 2:16–21). All this has the same secret meaning, besides which, the Hebrew sacred name for God, beginning with the letter M, is Meborach, the "Holy" or the "Blessed," and the name for the Water of the Flood is Mbul. Mention of the "Three Maries" at the Crucifixion, and their connection with Mare, the Sea, or Water, closes this list of examples. This is why in Judaism and Christianity, the Messiah is always connected with water, baptism; and also with Pisces, the sign of the zodiac called Minam in Sanskrit, and even with the Matsya (Fish) Avatar, and the Lotus, the symbol of the womb, and with the water-lily, which has the same signification.

Water is deposited Light, being one with Fire in its essence. Water itself is neutral in nature, but reflects everything that surrounds it and serves as material for creating intermediate forms between the Fiery and earthly worlds.

Three basic states of water are known: liquid, solid, and gaseous. But further, as matter becomes subtler, water ascends to Light, and its projection penetrates all layers into the depths of the Waters of the Cosmos. This represents a special substance of Light, consisting of the crystallized currents of the Great Feminine Principle. The interchange of Cosmic Waters with earthly waters goes on continually: it passes from one sphere to another, and its mass sets a certain direction for the development of life. This interchange with the Cosmos causes the growth of ozone holes. All water masses in all their states on Earth must have a definite interrelation with each other.

Now Fire from the Cosmos is united with the water on Earth. Every drop of rain is imbued with sparks of Fire. Thus, low temperatures, together with abundant rains and snowfalls, have a beneficial effect on the acceptance of Fire by humanity, thereby facilitating a relatively painless cleansing of Earth and the acceptance of Baptism by Water and Celestial Fire. And here one's intracellular fluid reacts according to the accumulation of fiery property, which predetermines the throughput capacity of the cell itself, healing it and moving it onto the path of transformation, for only in the union of Fire and Water can an immortal being be born.

Western Paradise, **Western Heaven**, or **Sukhavati** (*Sk.*, "full of joy," "blissful"). A real place located in transcendental space. It is a locality in the mountains, or, to be more correct, one encircled in a desert among mountains. Hence, it is assigned as the residence of those students of Esoteric Wisdom — disciples of Buddha — who have attained the rank of Lohans and Anagamins (Adepts). It is called "Western" simply on account of geographical considerations; and "the great iron mountain girdle" that surrounds the Avichi, and the seven Lokas that encircle the "Western Paradise" are a precise representation of localities and things well-known to the Eastern student of occultism. See *Shambhala*.

In the Subtle World, there is the Stronghold of Light or the Abode of Forces of Light called *Dokiood*. High spirits try to avoid Devachan and strive to enter Dokiood where they are given the opportunity to continue their work under the Guidance of Great Teachers.

White Island. Another name for Shambhala as once it was an island amidst the ocean. See *Shambhala* for more.

Wilfred, Thomas (1889–1968). A Danish-American artist and inventor who pioneered art of light.

Will. In metaphysics and occult philosophy, will is that which governs the manifested universes in eternity. *Will* is the one and sole principle of abstract eternal *motion*, or its ensouling essence. "The will," says Jan Baptist van Helmont, "is the first of all powers.... The will is the property of all spiritual beings and displays itself in them the more actively, the more they are freed from matter." And Paracelsus teaches that "determined will is the beginning of all magical operations. It is because men do not perfectly imagine and believe the result, that the (occult) arts are so uncertain, while they might be perfectly certain."

Like everything else in the world, the will is *septenary* in its degrees of manifestation. Emanating from the one, eternal, abstract, and purely quiescent will (*atma* in *layam*, or zero-point), it becomes *buddhi* in its Alaya state, descends lower as Mahat (*manas*), and runs down the ladder of degrees until the divine Eros becomes, in its lower, animal manifestation, erotic desire. Will as an eternal principle is neither spirit nor substance but everlasting ideation. As expressed by Schopenhauer in his *Parerga and Paralipomena* (1851), "in sober reality there is neither *matter* nor *spirit*. The tendency to gravitation in a stone is as unexplainable as thought in the human brain.... If matter can — no one knows why — fall to the ground, then it can also — no one knows why — think.... As soon, even in mechanics, as we trespass beyond the purely mathematical, as soon as we reach the inscrutable adhesion, gravitation, and so on, we are faced by phenomena which are to our senses as mysterious as the will."

Winfrey, Oprah (b.1954). An American talk show host, television producer, author, media proprietor, and philanthropist, known for her influential *The Oprah Winfrey Show*, which popularized self-help, spiritual exploration, and personal growth. She has introduced millions of people to various spiritual teachings and philosophies that have changed the spiritual landscape of America and beyond for the better.

Wisdom. The "very essence of wisdom is contained in the Non-Being," say the Kabbalists; but they also apply the term to the Word, or Logos, the Demiurge, by which the universe was called into existence. "The one Wisdom is in the Sound," say the occultists; the Logos again being meant by Sound, which is the substratum of Akasha. Says the *Zohar*, the "Book of Splendour": "It is the Principle of all the Principles, the mysterious Wisdom, the crown of all that which there is of the Most High." And it is explained: "Above Keter is the Ayin, the No-Thing.... It is so named because we do not know, and it is impossible to know, *that which there is in that Principle*, because ... it is above Wisdom itself." This shows that the real Kabbalists agree with the occultists that the essence, or that which is in the principle of Wisdom, is still above that highest Wisdom.

Wisdom is Knowledge multiplied by Love. This is a necessary stage of evolution in the fulfilment of the chief mission of the present period of the Solar System. Since Love manifests itself solely in the heart, it is inevitable that the path to Wisdom should lie through the heart. Knowledge acquired throughout the ages but not imbued with the loving currents of the heart simply turns into information and eventually loses its significance.

The Masters of Wisdom are wise, not because they know everything, but because they have a compassionate love for the whole suffering world. Everyone knows that a drowning person must be rescued, but not everyone will throw themselves into deep water. Therefore, those who are heartless cannot enter the Era of the Heart and Wisdom, even if they do happen to be founts of knowledge.

Wisdom Religion. The one religion which underlies all now-existing creeds. There was a time, when there was on earth but one "lip," one religion, and one science, namely, the speech of the gods, the Wisdom Religion, and Truth. This was before the fair fields of the latter, overrun by nations of many languages, became overgrown with the weeds of intentional deception, and the national creeds invented by ambition, cruelty, and selfishness, broke the one sacred Truth into thousands of different fragments.

That "faith" which, being primordial, and revealed directly to humankind by their *progenitors* and informing Egos, required neither "grace," nor *blind* faith to believe, for it was *knowledge*. It is on this Wisdom Religion that Theosophy is based.

Witch (*Old Eng.*, "to know," "to divine"). At first called "wise women," until the day the Church took it unto itself to follow the law of Moses, which put every "witch" or enchantress to death.

Witch of Endor. In the Old Testament, a woman from Endor who at the request of King Saul, on the eve of the decisive battle, summoned the spirit of the late prophet Samuel to predict fate and offer advice.

Word. An outer layer of thought; its apparent physical form, regardless of whether it is expressed as sound or symbol. Word is inseparable from thought, which means that it is a carrier of Fire, either bright or dark. Every phrase ever uttered carries an energy component, which can be saturated with poisonous fumes or life-saving currents. Each word contains within itself either a constructive or a destructive power. The world was created by the Word. Therefore, the word is a powerful force, if used conscientiously.

Each letter, by virtue of its vibrational key, affects the human nervous system through its corresponding vibrations. Not only that, but it also awakens as yet unmanifest forces in space. Vowel sounds are fiery in nature, while consonants are perishable and earthly. Indeed, one can evoke healing energies from space through a particular combination of vowel sounds, whereas the low-frequency, hiss consonants are capable of causing rockslides, tornadoes, and other destructive phenomena, including earthquakes. Also, every word spoken represents fiery energy — transmitted, or radiated, by the body through the mouth. The affected nerves flare up like wires with fiery currents and cause an external flash in the form of fiery formations. Words fly through space like colourful balls of fire. Every letter creates fiery discharges. Even ordinary conversation can be imagined as an exchange of fires or coloured rays. Thought encased in words is cast into the surrounding sphere, and either remains there, influencing the environment long after the words are spoken and forgotten, or flies to its destination.

Words are the channels for the magnetic attraction from space of what their essence expresses. None of the energies, once put into action, disappear completely; each brings forth its own consequences, depending on its nature and especially its producer, for as the crystal of this energy remains in their aura, the energies are forever connected to their creator by a magnetic thread. They are the producer's spatial property and will not leave them until the magnetic force of the words is exhausted. The energies again return to their producer in order to be neutralized, in order that the balance, once disturbed, might be restored. Hence, one must be accountable for every word one utters. The dense conditions of the earthly plane often prevent the completion of this process, but after death, in the Subtle World, the process of neutralizing one's own created energies continues freely and unhindered until everything that one has generated on Earth — bad or good — is consumed entirely.

Since words are external symbols of the thoughts behind them, the repetition of any word calls into being the latent energy within it, and this affects a person and the space around them. Even the mental repetition of words which affirm high and positive qualities is beneficial. In this way, through words, we may bring ourselves and others into a harmonious or an inharmonious state. The power of verbal prayer, for example, has been known since ancient times.

The mystery of perfection in speech and text lies in the absolute harmony of form and content. The vibrational keys of words, their sound and tonality, and the colour of the thoughts concealed within them, should be in full consonance and harmony. Provided there is such an accord, spoken and written texts can be expressed in any rhythm and tonality. Words can be short and abrupt if the rhythm requires it, and sentences may feature peculiar constructions, since the power of influence resides not in the external form, but in the consonance between the words and the essence expressed therein. A properly and harmoniously constructed rhythm of speech or text has a tremendous invisible impact. This is why the creations of some writers and poets are considered great, and why some scriptures are held as sacred.

For the reasons cited above, all Teachings emphasize *discipline* in word and speech. After all, it is better to be silent than to experience the blows of spatial energy upon ourselves. Silence is golden: we do not squander our precious fiery energy in vain. Many people are sick because they waste their strength through their own talkativeness. Besides, great harm is done by idle chatter when one should really remain silent. For example, if one has made an important decision or special plans, one should not advertise this to anyone prematurely, since disembodied evil entities populating the near-Earth space may overhear it and do everything in their power to hinder these plans. It is easier to hide thoughts than words from subtle beings, for not all disembodied entities are capable of mind-reading.

Moreover, foul language is inadmissible, being the antipode of prayer. Everyone is familiar with the phrase "words can kill," and one must be aware that anyone who promotes death is killing themselves and their soul, first and foremost. Scientists have already discovered that "impure words" uttered in a loud or quiet voice (or even a whisper) have equally destructive effects on the living cells of our body. Therefore, instead of antipodal words, it is important to produce pure, light phrases that will assist and support both those who utter them and the surrounding space.

In the future, humanity will no longer send shockwaves into space through the sounds of its speech. Instead, communication will be mental or telepathic. Until then, we should be careful in our use of the great power of the word and employ it only for the good. It is worth attempting to follow the wise precept of Christ: "But let your communication be, Yea, yea; Nay, nay: for whatsoever is more than these cometh of evil" (Matthew 5:37).

Wordsworth, William (1770–1850). A major English Romantic poet, known for his nature-inspired poetry that emphasized emotion, imagination, and the beauty of the natural world. Notable works include *Lines Composed a Few Miles Above Tintern Abbey* (1798) and *The Prelude* (1850).

World Government. The Hierarchy of Light; the Government of Shambhala, also known as the Invisible Government and the Inner Government. It is opposed by a shadow government representing the forces of evil.

The World Government assembles in Shambhala and serves the ideals of the Common Good alone. Its decisions and activities are always aimed at helping, uniting, and saving whole peoples as well as the planet itself. And although this Government is otherworldly in nature, it has often offered its assistance to various national leaders, the acceptance of which has led to unprecedented prosperity, its rejection, to decline and even oblivion.

On this subject, Helena Roerich explained: "Perhaps, some are confused by the definition of the Hierarchy as the World Government, and a Secret one to boot? But what else is one to call the great invisible Care, Guidance, and Help received, without falling into ecclesiastical terminology?

"How would you name and explain the repeated and attested appearances of saints to their followers, after they have relinquished their earthly form, in order to warn them of danger or to give useful advice? ... One may cite innumerable manifestations of the Great Guidance of this light-bearing Host of the Hierarchy throughout all ages and all peoples. Therefore, rejoice in your heart, for, truly, the Hierarchy of Light represents the Fathers and Brothers of all humanity. Let your heart not be troubled by new names of the most ancient concepts. New definitions are more accessible to the younger generations" (7 May 1939).

Says Master M. in the book *Fiery World* (1933) of the *Agni Yoga* series: "You are absolutely right that the existence of the Invisible Government confuses many. But if there is an invisible, dark government, then how can there not be a Government of Light! Has the human mind become so darkened that it is easier for it to recognize anything that is dark than to think about the Light? Indeed, people understand and have heard on more than one occasion about the dark forces that are united worldwide, but the Government of Good and Light is deemed especially suspicious. People are not accustomed to uniting around the Good; they believe that the Good is simply a pretext for disunity. One can understand why then, the entire illness of the planet arises from the complete discord that exists between those who could unite in the Good. It is a great misfortune that even in the Temple, people's hearts are not transformed and made ready for mutual collaboration. So let us ponder every manifestation of amicability that is already a spark of cooperation."

Shambhala chooses the most worthy individuals for its mission to assist humanity. Of course, the most famous of these is the mysterious Count of Saint-Germain whose advice was heeded by the founding fathers of the United States, George Washington and Benjamin Franklin, and who in 1776 played a decisive role in the adoption of the Declaration of Independence of the United States.

It is well documented that Saint-Germain met with Louis XVI and Marie Antoinette, and advised them to initiate just reforms in France in order to prevent a future revolutionary explosion. They did not heed his warning, and the revolution resulted in a period of mass terror.

There is also evidence to suggest that Abraham Lincoln announced the Emancipation Proclamation in 1863 because he received a message from the Invisible Government in the most unusual and startling way.

In 1851, Mahatma Morya arrived in London as a member of a delegation from India to meet with Queen Victoria. The purpose of his visit was to warn the monarch that if Great Britain did not change its policy towards its vast colonies, in particular India, nothing would remain of it but an island. His warning went unheeded and different choices were made. The seed of the collapse of the Empire in the mid-twentieth century was sown almost 100 years prior to its actual demise, when the Queen rejected this Higher Assistance.

In 1926, the Ambassadors of Shambhala, Helena and Nicholas Roerich, arrived in Moscow to deliver a warning and advice offered by the Mahatmas to Joseph Stalin. But instead of receiving the Roerichs, the authorities ordered them to be arrested, and only a miracle prevented them from being imprisoned. Prime opportunities for building a just state on the territory of the USSR were missed, and instead there followed mass repression and the suppression of any manifestation of free will.

Likewise, President Herbert Hoover rejected the advice of the Lord of Shambhala, which, had he accepted it, could have aided him in preventing the 1929 stock market crash that resulted in grave economic crisis and the Great Depression.

However, one should also note a positive example of collaboration that took place in the twentieth century. In 1934, assistance from Shambhala was again offered to America through Helena Roerich who entered into correspondence with President Franklin D. Roosevelt. In accepting the guidance given through Helena Roerich, President Roosevelt was able to solve a number of problems facing the United States at the time, on account of which he became one of the greatest American presidents of all time.

For more see Helena Roerich, *The Divine Government* (New York: Radiant Books, 2023).

Worlds. The various states or planes of Cosmic matter. In the present Solar System, there exist Seven Worlds, each of which has seven sub-planes of varying degrees of density and purity.

In Hindu cosmology, there are three worlds: Svarga (Heaven), Bhumi (Earth), and Patala (hell). Esoterically, these are the Spiritual, Psychic (or Astral), and the Terrestrial spheres respectively.

The Buddhist division of the worlds is called *Trailokya*, or three regions (applied also to celestial beings) or seven planes or degrees, each broadly represented by one of the three chief characteristics, namely: *kama*, *rupa*, and *arupa*, or those of desire, form, and formlessness. All these are the worlds of post-mortem states.

The first, *Kamadhatu* or the world of desire, is composed of the Earth and the six inferior regions, the Earth being followed by *Kama-loka*. These taken together constitute the seven degrees of the material world of form and sensuous gratification. Kama-loka is the region of Mara, which medieval and modern Kabbalists call the "world of astral light" and the "world of shells." Kama-loka has, like every other region, seven divisions, the lowest of which begins on Earth or invisibly in its atmosphere; the six others ascend gradually, the highest being the abode of those who have died owing to accident, or suicide in a fit of temporary insanity, or who were otherwise victims of external forces. It is a place where all those who have died before the end of the term allotted to them, and whose higher principles do not, therefore, go at once into the devachanic state, sleep a dreamless sweet sleep of oblivion, at the termination of which they are either reborn immediately, or pass gradually into the devachanic state.

The second is *Rupadhatu* or "material form," also composed of seven localities. It is the celestial world of *form*, or what is called *Devachan*. Esoteric philosophy teaches that though for the Egos, for the time being, everything or everyone preserves its form (as in a dream), as Rupadhatu is a *purely mental region*, and a state, the Egos themselves have *no form* outside their own consciousness. Esotericism divides this "region" into seven Dhyanas, "regions," or states of contemplation, which are not localities but mental representations of them.

The third is *Arupadhatu* or "immaterial locality." However, this translation is not strictly correct as the term *dhatu*, in some of its special applications does not mean a "place" at all. For instance, Arupadhatu is a purely subjective world, a "state" rather than a place. Arupadhatu is also divided into seven Dhyanas, still more abstract and formless, for this "World" is without any form or desire whatsoever. It is the highest region of the post-mortem Trailokya, and as it is the abode of those who are almost ready for Nirvana, in fact, the very threshold of the Nirvanic state, it stands to reason that in Arupadhatu there can be neither form nor sensation, nor any feeling connected with the three-dimensional Universe.

The occultists and the Kabbalists both divide the Universe into superior and inferior worlds, worlds of Idea and worlds of Matter. "As above, so below," as Hermetic philosophy has it. The lower world is formed in accordance with its prototype, the higher world, and as the *Zohar* states, "everything in the lower is but an image (reflection) of the higher."

The Kabbalists recognize Four Worlds of Existence: Atziluth or the archetypal; Briyah or the creative, the first reflection of the highest; Yetzirah or the formative; and Assiah, the world of shells or *klipot* and the material Universe. The essence of Deity concentrated in the Sefirot is first manifested in the Atziluthic World, and their reflections are produced in succession in each of the four planes, with a gradual lessening of radiance and purity, until the material universe is reached. Some authors refer to these four planes as the Intellectual, the Moral, the Sensuous, and the Material Worlds.

According to esoteric philosophy, in the current Fourth Round of Evolution, Four Worlds are accessible to humanity and Earth:

1. *The physical world, the dense world*, or *the material world*. Earth itself on which physical humanity lives.

2. *The Subtle World, the Ethereal World*, or *the Astral World*. This is the world which everyone enters during sleep. It exists in spheres encircling Earth, and its dimensions are much larger than the earthly plane. It consists of many layers, from the lowest to the highest, to which each individual is drawn by consonance. All individuals assume an appearance corresponding to their inner essence, and reap what they have sown on Earth. Its matter is pliant and instantly becomes an expression of what the spirit is thinking and who that individual really is. Everything is created and moved by thought. Illumination occurs on account of the radiation of a person's subtle bodies, hence the lower spheres to which evil-minded people are drawn are dark. All earthly emotions and habits remain and assume a significantly intensified state. So if a person has not overcome their most primitive desires on Earth, here they will suffer from the absence of a physical body through which to satisfy them. The lower areas of the Subtle World are the closest to Earth. Therefore, those in this layer often use Earth-dwellers to satisfy their desires — hence the phenomena of possession. For good people, not bound by physical passions, the Subtle World provides limitless freedom of spirit; here they can fly, endlessly create, contemplate creativity in all areas of life, and study and explore anything they wish. Souls may remain in this world for thousands of years.

3. *The Mental World*, or *the World of Thoughts*. Consists of the product of the mental creativity of thinking beings: mental forms or thought-forms. Its layers are determined by the affinity of thought emanations that comprise

the content of the form. The line of attraction is determined by the attunement of one's consciousness. The process of attunement may take place subconsciously, but it can also take place by order of individual will. In this case, the will chooses the point of attunement and establishes the necessary control. Whereas on Earth people travel by car, train, etc., in the Mental World they travel in the vehicle of thought. Consciousness enters thought like a passenger enters a railway carriage, and the vehicle of thought carries it to the sphere chosen by the mind.

4. *The Fiery World, the Empyreal World*, or *the Spiritual World*. Matter belonging to this world is so subtle, perfect, and imbued with energy that it everywhere causes a fiery luminosity, hence its name. Here, neither time nor distance exists in the earthly sense; everything happens "here and now." The beauty of this world is magnificent. The flowers are especially striking and they are everywhere; they move and flutter, giving off marvellous fragrances and melodies. The elevated forms of matter and energy of which this world is comprised create an atmosphere of Joy and Love. However, not everyone is able to reach the Fiery World, because in order to do so they must have developed their immortal fiery body. This happens when the individual follows a spiritual path on Earth.

When the Worlds are listed, the Mental World is often omitted. It serves as the living link between the Subtle and Fiery Worlds, belonging more to the latter, as thought cannot exist without Fire. Hence, one might come across statements to the effect that there are Three Worlds accessible to humanity, and that the Fiery World is the World of Thought and vice versa.

The planet Earth exists in all these Worlds, and it is represented in each of them by its corresponding globe-sphere. All Four Worlds are combined concentrically one inside the other, forming the complex septenary body of the planet. Thus, Earth consists of dense physical matter, penetrated by spheres of subtle and fiery matter. All Seven Spheres of the planet in the Four Worlds are inhabited. Those who dwell in one World cannot see or sense the other Worlds, but they are continually moving from one World to another; dying in one, they are reborn in another, moving either upwards to the next higher planes or downwards once more to Earth. In this way, people pass through the Round of incarnations within the Planetary Chain.

Each of the consecutive bodies in which a person lives a conscious, full life, is restricted by the world and sphere to which it belongs, and is subject to its laws. All the Worlds have their boundaries and limitations, restricting people in some measure by the properties of matter. All ancient teachings prescribed certain norms of behaviour, diets, and so on, aimed at the purification or refinement of the matter of all human bodies. The crude astral body, weighed down by crude habits, cannot rise higher than the lower layers of the Astral World, which are in perfect correlation to the composition of the astral body. Having been released from the dense body, only individuals that have purified their subtle bodies from dense particles on Earth can succeed in soaring high. In the Subtle World each disembodied person undergoes a process of cleansing, and yet, for all that, they cannot ascend higher than the height they themselves have attained. The Law of Consonance is just and infallible.

The planet Earth has already passed the lowest point — greatest density — of its evolution, and so is now on a course of ascent. As a result, a convergence of the dense and Subtle Worlds is gradually taking place, and the planet is rising one step higher than before. Hence, the Subtle World is advancing on the dense world, expanding the spheres of its own influence, thanks to the addition of properties that rarefy the matter of Earth; the physical world, in turn, is harmoniously flowing into the layers of the Subtle Spheres. Similarly, the planet's Subtle World in its higher layers blends with the Mental World, and the Fiery World ascends into an even Higher World. Thus, in the Fifth Round, Five Worlds will be accessible to Earth and humanity, and the physical world will resemble the lowest layer of the Subtle World, that is, there will no longer be the sharp demarcation between the two that is evident at the present time.

Wu ming (*Ch.*). Ignorance, delusion, or nescience.

Wuliang Shou (*Ch.*, "immeasurable life"). See *Amitabha*.

X

Xizang (*Ch.*). Tibet.

Xuanzang (602–664). A Chinese Buddhist monk, scholar, and traveller who journeyed to India to study Buddhism and brought back with him numerous scriptures to China.

Xue Shan Bu (*Ch.*, "snow mountain school"). The Himalaya school.

Y

Yajna (*Sk.*). "Sacrifice," whose symbol or representation is now the constellation Mrigashira (deer-head), and also a form of Vishnu.

Yama (*Sk.*, "restraint"). In yoga, the ethical guidelines or moral restraints that are the first of Patanjali's eight limbs of yoga. These include non-violence, truthfulness, non-stealing, celibacy, and non-possessiveness.

Yana (*Sk.*, "vehicle"). A method of conduct or vehicle that will carry one to Nirvana.

Yantra (*Sk.*, "instrument of restraint"). A mystical, geometrical diagram used as a tool for meditation.

Yashodhara. The wife of Prince Siddhartha, who later became a Buddhist nun (Bhikkhuni) and attained the state of an Arhat.

Yeats, W. B. (1865–1939). An Irish poet, writer, playwright, and Nobel laureate, known for his lyrical poetry and involvement in the Irish Literary Revival. He joined the Theosophical Society in 1885.

Yekaterinoslav. The former name of Dnipro, a city in Ukraine. Located here is the house where Helena Blavatsky was born and spent her early years. It is now a museum dedicated to her memory.

Yoda. A fictional character in the *Star Wars* franchise, known as a wise, powerful Master with a distinct, unusual speech pattern.

Yoga (*Sk.*, "union"). 1) one of the six Darshanas or schools of India; a school of philosophy founded by Patanjali, though the real yoga doctrine, the one that is said to have helped to prepare the world for the preaching of Buddha, is attributed with good reason to the more ancient sage Yajnawalkya, the writer of the *Shatapatha Brahmana*, the *Yajur Veda*, the *Brihad Aranyaka*, and other famous works.
2) a spiritual practice leading to liberation and enlightenment as well as to the development of spiritual powers through the union or merger of the individual self with the Universal Self. Psycho-spiritual powers are obtained thereby, and induced ecstatic states lead to the clear and correct perception of eternal truths in both the visible and the invisible universe. One should beware of taking the exoteric works on yoga literally, for they all require a key.

The highest form of yoga is *Agni Yoga*, which is represented in the book series of the same name, given by Helena Roerich under the guidance of Master Morya.

Yogachara (*Sk.*, "yoga practice"). A mystic school that should not be confused with the Tantra, or Mahatantra school founded by Samantabhadra, for there are two Yogachara schools: one esoteric, the other popular. The doctrines of the latter were compiled and glossed by Asanga in the sixth century of the present era, and his mystic tantras and mantras, his formularies, litanies, spells, and mudra would certainly, if attempted without a Guru, serve the purposes of sorcery and black magic rather than real yoga.

Yoga-Vidya (*Sk.*). The science of yoga.

Yogi. A devotee, one who practises the yoga system. There are various grades and kinds of yogis. In India the term has now become a generic name used to designate every kind of ascetic.

Yu the Great. A legendary emperor of ancient China, traditionally credited with founding the Xia dynasty and controlling China's great floods. He is known for his wisdom, leadership, and hydraulic engineering efforts in taming the Yellow River. The emperor obtained his occult wisdom and his system of theocracy from Tibet, which, according to the oldest Chinese records, was the great seat of occult learning in the archaic ages, where dwelt the "Teachers of Light," the "Sons of Wisdom," and the "Brothers of the Sun." He was the first to unite in China ecclesiastical power with temporal authority, a system also used by the ancient Egyptians and the Chaldeans; that which existed in the Brahminical period in India and in Tibet, namely, that all the learning, power, temporal as well as secret wisdom was concentrated within the hierarchy of the priests and limited to their caste.

Yuga (*Sk.*, "age"). An epoch, or cycle of Evolution, in Hinduism. There are four Yugas, which follow each other in a series, namely: Krita (or Satya) Yuga, the Golden Age; Treta Yuga, Dwapara Yuga, and Kali Yuga. In addition, the ancients divided the life cycle into the Golden, Silver, Bronze, and Iron Ages, which correspond to the four Yugas. The Golden Age was an age of primeval purity, simplicity, and general happiness.

Esoterically, Kali Yuga ended in 1942. H.P.B. kept secret the actual period marking the end of Kali Yuga only using information which was available to all. Only in the late 1930s, once researchers themselves had understood that the gigantic figures indicated were simply symbols, and had widely informed the population of India of the fact, did the Masters confirm through Helena Roerich the accuracy of these calculations. And on 1 August 1943, the cosmic event occurred that was described in the *Vishnu Purana* as the sign of the beginning of Satya Yuga.

The four Yugas also correspond to Cosmic Seasons of the Solar System: Spring (Satya or Golden), Summer (Treta or Silver), Autumn (Dwapara or Bronze), and Winter (Kali or Iron). The global warming and temperature records broken every year on Earth as well as similar processes on Mars, Jupiter, and Pluto, testify to the fact that we are currently living in the very first phases of Cosmic Spring, although "winter colds" still make themselves felt.

See Ruth Marlaire, "A Gloomy Mars Warms Up," *NASA*; Irene Klotz, "Radar Images Reveal Mars is Coming Out of an Ice Age," *Reuters*; Philip Marcus, "Velocities and Temperatures of Jupiter's Great Red Spot and the New Red Oval and Their Implications for Global Climate Change," *Bulletin of the American Astronomical Society*; Robert Britt, "Global Warming on Pluto Puzzles Scientists," *Space*.

Z

Zanoni. A mystical novel by Edward Bulwer-Lytton, published in 1842. Zanoni is its main character.

Zen. See *Chan*.

Zend-Avesta (*Pahl.*). The general name for the sacred books of the Parsis, fire- or sun-worshippers. The term *Zend-Avesta* refers to the Avesta text together with its Pahlavi (Middle Persian) commentaries and translations, while *Avesta* specifically refers to the collection of Zoroastrian scriptures written in the Avestan language. Essentially, the *Zend-Avesta* is the Avesta text with its interpretations and explanations.

Very little is understood of the grand doctrines which are still to be found in the various fragments that comprise all that is left of this collection of religious works. The Avesta has two parts, now compiled together, the first portion containing the *Vendidad*, the *Visperad*, and the *Yasna*; and the second portion, called the *Khorda Avesta* (Small Avesta), being composed of short prayers called Gah, Nyayis, etc. *Zend* means "a commentary or explanation," and *Avesta* from the old Persian, "the law." As the translator of the *Vendidad* remarks: "what it is customary to call 'the Zend language,' ought to be named 'the Avesta language,' the Zend being no language at all, and if the word be used as the designation of one, it can be rightly applied only to the Pahlavi." But then, the Pahlavi itself is only the language into which certain original portions of the Avesta are translated. What name should be given to the old Avesta language, and particularly to the "special dialect, older than the general language of the Avesta," in which the five Gathas in the *Yasna* are written? To this day Orientalists are mute upon the subject. Why should Zend not be of the same family, if not identical to the *Zen-sar* (Senzar), meaning also the speech explaining the abstract symbol, or the mystery language used by Initiates?

Zhejiang. A province in Eastern China.

Zhoushan (*Ch.*, "boat mountain"). The largest archipelago of China comprising 1,390 islands. One of its islands, Mount Putuo, is associated with the Bodhisattva Guanshiyin.

Zohar (*Heb.*, "splendour"). A compendium of Kabbalistic Theosophy, which shares with the *Sefer Yetzirah* the reputation of being the oldest extant treatise on the Hebrew esoteric religious doctrines. While Moses de León was the first to produce the volume as a whole around 1280, yet a large part of some of its constituent tracts consists of traditional dogmas and illustrations, which have come down from the time of Shimon ben Yochai and the Second Temple. There are portions of the doctrines of the *Zohar* which bear the impress of Chaldean thought and civilization, to which the Jewish race had been exposed in the Babylonian captivity.

Zong-men (*Ch.*, "chief gate"). The esoteric school of Chinese Buddhism containing the tradition of the *heart* of Buddha. It was established by Bodhidharma who brought from the Western Heaven "the seal of truth" (true seal), and opened the fountain of contemplation in the East. He pointed directly to Buddha's heart and nature, sweeping away the parasitic and alien growth of book instruction.

Zoroaster. The Greek form of Zarathustra (*Zend*), the great law-giver, prophet, and founder of the religion variously called Mazdaism, Magism, Parseeism, Fire-worship, and Zoroastrianism. This was the last incarnation of Melchizedek that took place about six thousand years ago as the first, divine Zoroaster. He was given the revelation of Ahura Mazda, or the Creator, in the form of the holy scripture of the Avesta in the language of Zend, which is to a large degree similar to the language of Senzar.

Like Manu and Vyasa in India, Zarathustra is a generic name for great reformers and law-givers. The hierarchy began with the divine Zarathustra and ended with the great, but mortal man, bearing that title, and now lost to history. Only thirteen Zarathustra incarnations have been revealed to humanity, and each carried a sacred scripture which was lost over time, necessitating the manifestation of a new cycle of secret knowledge. The last Zoroaster was the founder of the Fire-temple of Azarakhsh in Iran, many ages before the historical era.

According to linguistic studies, the name Zoroaster translates as "the golden shining star" or "Golden Sirius." In Zoroastrianism, Sirius is especially revered and called *Tishtrya*, "whom Ahura Mazda has established as a lord and overseer above all stars, in the same way as he has established Zarathustra above men."

Zulu. A people in South Africa.

OTHER TITLES PUBLISHED BY RADIANT BOOKS

***The Land of the Gods* by H. P. Blavatsky.** Hidden in plain sight for 135 years, Blavatsky's story is a beautifully written account of an exceptional journey into Shambhala. Immersive and engaging, this profound book will provide you with a unique outlook on the deeper side of life, exposing our true nature, interior powers, and ultimate destiny. It explains grand, spiritual ideas more thoroughly and swiftly than any book you'll ever read.

***Revealing Cosmic Mysteries* by H. P. Blavatsky.** Lost for over a century, the full stenographic reports of meetings with Blavatsky in London have resurfaced recently. Immerse yourself in those very meetings at which Blavatsky revealed secret knowledge. The questions others posed may well have been your own, and her answers will unlock your deeper understanding of the Universe's profound secrets. You will be privy to Blavatsky's inspirational power, brilliant and penetrating mind, sharp wit and authentic wisdom.

***The Divine Government* by Helena Roerich.** A secret for many years, this book provides the first-ever evidence showing how the Divine Government, known as *Shambhala*, helped the United States during the Franklin D. Roosevelt presidency. It outlines profound principles for becoming a true leader who can guide any nation to prosperity by building just relations between the people and the state.

***The Temple of Mysteries* by Francia La Due.** Bridging spirituality and science, this classic work is a true gem of the world's esoteric legacy. The Master Hilarion, the Protector of America and Europe, transmitted it through Francia La Due, intending to assist humanity in resolving the challenges of modern civilization and guide us toward unity with the cosmic forces that shape our existence. *The Temple of Mysteries* will illuminate your path to self-realization and help you find answers to the most pressing questions that trouble your soul.

***From the Mountaintop* by Francia La Due.** Uplifting and poetic, this book invites you to rediscover your true essence and forge a future illuminated by the light of resonant wisdom. It is a collection of high vibrational messages of truth and beauty that imbue the very aura of humanity. Transcending time and space, these messages radiate the healing energies of faith, hope, and love. For those who aspire to embark on the Path toward Mystery, *From the Mountaintop* will serve as a celestial beacon in troubled times.

***The Mystery of Christ* by Thales of Argos.** Eye-opening and heart-touching, *The Mystery of Christ* brings a fresh perspective, an uncommon insight, and spiritual depth to the dramatic events which occurred two thousand years ago. As you read the profoundly stirring pages of this beautifully crafted narrative, you will comprehend the unequalled mission of Christ and the innermost secrets of Mary, culminating in an unexpected encounter with the new mystery of the Cosmos named Sophia.

The Living Waters of Joy by **Grace Lucia Kimball.** Through heartfelt revelations, this book will become your sanctuary — a spiritual oasis where your troubled soul can always find comfort, peace, and renewal, even in the most difficult of times. Like a healing balm, its eloquent prose flows as a gentle stream of living water, offering you a profound and uplifting experience of the Higher Presence.

The Song of Sano Tarot by **Anna Fullwood.** Unveiling the fundamentals of creation, this book relates the story of Seven Forces, or vibratory laws, that govern your life and the entire Universe. Each of us belongs to a particular vibration, and if you do not live in accordance with your natural force, you will reap negative consequences. From this viewpoint, the book offers insights and practical advice on how to determine your inherent force and transform your life, thereby guiding you toward inner balance and peace.

Becoming What You Are by **Two Workers.** Drawing on timeless spiritual wisdom, this book will take you on a journey toward self-realization and inner awakening. Its inspiring messages and practical advice will show you how to cultivate the qualities necessary for spiritual growth. It will help you align your actions with your highest potential and ultimately become what you are — a radiant and awakened being.

The Seven Laws of Spiritual Purity by **Two Workers.** Providing a profound and eye-opening perspective on achieving true spiritual purity, this thought-provoking and straightforward book draws practical advice from ancient wisdom to show you how to purify your mind, body, and soul. It is a passionate plea for a better world — a world in which humanity no longer has to accept and deal with the consequences of many sufferings but instead prevents their very causes.

The Kingdom of White Waters by **V.G.** For a thousand years, this secret story could be told only on the deathbed, for it revealed an inaccessible garden paradise hidden in the Himalayas — Shambhala, a place thousands of people searched for, but always failed to find. Each carrier of this secret story took a vow of silence that could be broken under only two conditions: when facing imminent death or in response to another's persistent requests for knowledge about the mythical Kingdom of White Waters.

www.ingramcontent.com/pod-product-compliance
Lightning Source LLC
Chambersburg PA
CBHW060545080526
44585CB00013B/450